TABLE OF CONTENTS

INTRODUCTION

MY INVOLVEMENT WITH PRESERVATION AND CONSER- VATION began with an interest in aesthetics dur- ing my college years. As I investigated the effects of restoration treatments on objects, I was led to a desul- tory but continuing study of techniques. In 1971, when Yale University Library decided to explore the utility of developing a preservation program for its collections, I was given the task of analyzing the needs of the library, then designing and implementing the program. Thus my research turned to paper as a medium and to the issues involved in the transfer of content from one medium to another when it was impractical to preserve an original object. Like many of the early researchers and practitio- ners in library and archival preservation, I moved from a background in literature, art, and philosophy to the emerging field of the preservation of library and archival materials.

This book has grown out of my practical experience as a preservation specialist and the recognition that dif- ferent libraries have different resources and problems. After twenty-odd years, I can look back and see that the approach that I took toward my work, based on sound museum principles, has worked successfully for libraries and archives. The issues and the managerial structures that we develop to deal with collection management and preservation are the same; only the objects are different.

This book will not tell librarians how to establish their preservation programs. As the bibliography for this book demonstrates, there are now many books that do so. Nor will this volume tell librarians and archivists how to repair their materials. That task is far better left to the professional conservator. Today I am more convinced than ever that librarians and archivists, unless they wish to change their professions, should not attempt the physical treatment of library and archival materials.

This book will examine various aspects of collection management and preservation and offer some practical guidelines. Its focus is preservation and access, for if materials are collected, then neglected, they will not be available for present and future generations. It discusses collection maintenance, ranging from good housekeeping practices to environmental controls. It examines problems with the variety of media found in libraries and archives, including books, prints, manuscripts, photographs, slides, microforms, sound recordings, videotape and film, magnetic and electronic media. Dealing with them is a challenge. The book is intended to provide practical advice and guiding principles to help librarians and archivists analyze their institutional operations and prepare programs to meet the particular needs of their institutions.

The production of this book would not have been possible without the support of my family and many friends and colleagues during the past fifteen years. People from far and wide have supplied me with clippings and references. Many colleagues have corresponded with me at length about the theory and practice of preservation. My home has been a way station for conservators and preservation professionals and they have welcomed me in theirs. This is a collaborative effort, but omissions are mine alone.

To those who had faith in my work and encouraged me to explore the complex issues of preservation, I owe special thanks: Harry P. Harrison, Thomas H. Mott, Rutherford D. Rogers, and David E. Sparks. My colleagues at Rutgers have been unfailing in their support. I am especially grateful to my supervisor, Dr. Robert E. Sewell, Associate Librarian for Collection Development and Management, for his continuing understanding and encouragement. The Alexander Library Circulation Department has provided continued assistance and support for my research for twenty years; my gratitude knows no depth. My former assistants, Catherine Weglarz and Lorraine Perrotta, are always there when I need them.

I acknowledge the help of the specialists who took the time to review sections of this book. Their encouragement as I progressed has been heartening, their technical guidance, criticisms, and suggestions well-taken. They include: Connie Brooks, Susan Dalton, Susan Duhl, George Farr, Gerald Gibson, Walter Henry, C. Lee Jones, Ellen McCrady, Albert Nigrin, Thomas A. Parker, Gary Saretzky, Barbara Sawka, Christine Sundt, and Eileen Usovicz. Anne Ames, Evelyn Frangakis, June Nogle, Mark Swartzburg, and Neha Weinstein have reviewed this manuscript and made many improvements. In addition to her editorial skills, honed at Cornell University, June Nogle served as research assistant, providing many helpful insights between trips to RLIN and photocopy.

Chapter 2 is based upon the work of Evelyn Frangakis, who has been instrumental in developing survey methodology, first at the Conservation Center for Art and Historic Artifacts in Philadelphia, later at the Conservation Consultancy, New York, and at present, with the Society of American Archivists Preservation Administration Training Program. We have employed this methodology successfully in our Preservation Management Institute offered annually through the Professional Development Program, School of Communication, Information and Library Studies, Rutgers University. We hope that the process will benefit other librarians and archivists.

As librarians, our goal is to collect, organize, preserve, and make available to all, the documents, no matter their format, of our culture. With our mission firmly in mind, we accomplish this task, no matter the media. As I complete the second edition of this volume, I rest assured that it is published on permanent and durable alkaline paper. It may, indeed, become accessible through an electronic format, although that medium will not be permanent. The technologies will change, but our mission remains the same. This book is for the librarians who work to preserve our documentary heritage.

Susan Garretson Swartzburg
New Brunswick, New Jersey
June 1994

PREFACE TO THE FIRST EDITION

ONLY A FEW YEARS AGO THE PRESERVATION of library materials was mainly the concern of a few rare book librarians and specialists in conservation. Books were rolling off presses faster than libraries could absorb them. Materials in all media were proliferating, and libraries were buying. Housing all this material led to a boom in library building expansion. Clearly the library field and education were experiencing unprecedented growth, and dollars were flowing from Washington. Then, early in the 1970s, the money started to flow less freely. Soon libraries no longer could afford to develop their collections on a cosmic scale and librarians were forced to take a hard look at the material already on their shelves. The realization came that while libraries were rapidly accumulating materials in the 1960s, the material in their collections was just as rapidly deteriorating—the newer materials as rapidly as the older ones.

Today preservation is recognized as a vitally necessary component of collection development and an area of librarianship that concerns all libraries. Indeed, at a recent gathering Nicolas Barker of the British Library observed that "the problem may occupy an increasing amount of money in keeping what is on the shelves together rather than acquiring more." (Lathem, E. C., ed. *American Libraries as Centers of Scholarship.* Hanover, NH: Dartmouth College Library, 1978, p. 40).

Almost all library schools are now offering courses on preservation, and several have developed specialty programs for librarians who are interested in working in this field.

Preservation concerns not only the conservation of a

book, or other object, in its original format but also, quite
literally, the preservation of the intellectual content of
library materials and the maintenance of the physical
plant where library materials are housed. Whether or not
librarians have items in their collections that require
special conservation, they are responsible for the general
preservation of all materials under their care.

Susan Garretson Swartzburg, the author of this mono-
graph, discusses the field of preservation in terms that the
general librarian can understand. Her handbook explains
in non-technical language why the materials in library
collections are decaying and what librarians can do to
retard this process. For the first time information that is
needed by the nonspecialist is pulled together in one
volume so that one can quickly find general answers and
sources of more specific information on a variety of
library preservation problems.

This book is therefore a welcome and timely contribution to librarianship and should serve in the years ahead
as a practical guide to a growing problem that will continue to plague librarians while requiring commitment
and resources to address and abate the problem.

> Thomas H. Mott, Jr.
> Dean, Graduate School of Library
>   and Information Studies
> Rutgers—The State University of
>   New Jersey

1. PRESERVATION IN THE LIBRARY: Historical & Philosophical Perspectives

Introduction

BOOKS, MILLIONS OF BOOKS, ARE FALLING APART. Over the past twenty-five years, librarians increasingly have become aware of the impermanence of their collections. We are all too conscious of the fragility of our books when we randomly flip through them in the stacks or examine them after they have circulated. In his research on paper, sponsored by the Council on Library Resources in the late 1950s, William Barrow discovered that many of the books published as he was conducting his research were made of such acidic paper that they were unlikely to survive the century (see *Bibliography* for the citations for his reports).

Every librarian faces a considerable range of library materials—books, documents, prints, maps, microforms, photographs, sound recordings, film, videotape, disks— that are in various states of deterioration. There are yellowed and embrittled newspapers, periodicals and books; volumes mildewed by storage in a damp spot, or sodden after being caught in a downpour with a patron; books with broken spines and missing pages. There are curled photographs, warped records, buckled slides, faded films and videos, molded microforms, garbled or peeling disks. A librarian needs to know what to do with each "sickly" object and, more important, what the various actions or treatments will cost. Unfortunately, we cannot afford to return every item to a usable condition, nor can we replace each one.

Librarians are well aware that not every book published

1

is worth keeping for posterity. Although it goes against
instinct, it has always been necessary to weed, or deaccess
from the collection those materials that are no longer
needed. A good many books in poor condition can be
withdrawn when the library has other copies, editions, or
the title is outside the scope of the collection. While we
have no "national library," such as the British Library or
the Bibliothèque Nationale, the Library of Congress, encouraged by United States copyright laws, has copies of
most books published in this country since the 1860s. The
Library recognizes its obligation to care for this national
collection which, as a collection of books published in the
United States or collected from other countries for the use
of its citizens, has its own intrinsic value.

A Sumerian tablet containing local laws, a papyrus
fragment of a play by Aristophanes, the magnificent illuminated manuscripts produced in the Middle Ages, the
Gutenberg Bible, William Blake's *Jerusalem,* the
Kelmscott Chaucer—these and similar special or unique
objects are treasured by their owners, who spare no
expense and make every attempt to preserve them as
closely as possible to their original condition. The physical treatment, or conservation, of such materials can cost
thousands of dollars, yet few will argue that their conservation is not worth the cost.

While few libraries possess a Gutenberg Bible or a
Kelmscott Chaucer, most libraries have their own treasures—their special objects that will require preservation
to maintain them as close to the original condition as
possible. These objects may well be rare books of considerable value, such as examples of eighteenth century
binding, first editions of Hawthorne's novels, a collection
of Civil War newspapers, or photographs of the region. If
a library cannot care for such material properly, it should
be sold, donated, or deposited at an institution that can do
so. A small public library may wish to keep and display a
rare collection of special bindings or first editions be-
queathed by a leading citizen, but such collections can be
used to far greater advantage in a setting where adequate
care is assured and where they are readily accessible to

researchers. This is not to suggest that every small community library promptly turn over valuable collections to large research institutions; rather, if a special collection requires care and servicing not easily affordable by the small institution, it should consider placing such items elsewhere. Fortunately for books and scholars alike, enlightened institutions are beginning to recognize the need to deposit special collections where they are offered both preservation and access.

Most libraries contain materials that are of intrinsic value to the library and to the community, but may not have great commercial value. Communities and institutions have an obligation to preserve the records of their culture and history. These records can consist of manuscript documents, newspapers, photographs, films, video, floppy discs, aural tapes of local interest, or collections of works by local authors and artists. The library, as a repository of culture, must care for these materials and see to their preservation. The bicentennial celebrations of the birth of our nation and the signing of the Constitution has created a resurgence of interest in the exploration and preservation of the documentary heritage of the United States.

A librarian is responsible for the *preservation* of the collections, ensuring that they are stored under the best possible conditions, determining which materials require special facilities or handling to prevent or retard deterioration, and deciding which materials merit conservation treatment. The physical treatment, or *conservation,* of damaged and deteriorated materials is undertaken by a *conservator,* a technically trained specialist who physically treats an object to conserve it as closely as possible to its original condition. The conservator explains what treatment is warranted to ensure physical stability, but will not determine what materials in a library's collection merit conservation. The conservator is precluded from monetarily or bibliographically appraising items by a professional code of ethics. It is the librarian's responsibility to determine which materials merit conservation treatment, and the extent of the treatment. Treatment options range from the stabilization of an item to full conservation treatment, which can mean significant intervention in an object's original integrity.

There is some confusion about the role of the librarian and the role of the conservator. A number of book and paper conservators have degrees in librarianship as well as professional training in conservation. Some have chosen to leave librarianship for conservation, quite a different, although related, profession. Conversely, some practicing conservators, after a number of years "at the bench," have attended library school for a Masters degree in librarianship, with the goal of a career as a preservation administrator. These librarians may supervise a library's repair workshop or conservation laboratory, but they no longer work at the bench. A busy preservation administrator does not have the time to make repairs or to treat objects and quickly loses the manual skills of the former profession. Skills are gained in collection management and grantsmanship.

The preservation administrator is the staff member who is responsible for establishing, implementing and overseeing policies and procedures for the preservation of library collections, including circulating and noncirculating materials in a variety of media. The preservation administrator is bibliographically sophisticated, understands the nature and role of the library, and possesses the managerial skills to oversee a systematic program for the management and preservation of the collections. In a small institution, the preservation administrator may have a variety of other responsibilities. In a large library system, the preservation administrator may supervise a staff, including technicians, conservators and scientists who work within a Preservation Department. The preservation administrator is responsible for the day-to-day operation of a department and for planning the long-range objectives of a collection management and preservation program in an institution. The preservation administrator is aware of the techniques and procedures followed by both the conservator and the materials scientist, but does not repair materials or undertake materials research.

Both the librarian and the conservator must be aware of the work of scientists in a number of fields and, upon occasion, work side by side with them to convey their needs in preserving library and archival materials. Librarians and conservators are not, however, scientists with laboratories full of test tubes and analytical equipment, but rather professionals who will make use of scientific knowledge to help them resolve the problems that they face in preserving and conserving library materials.

George Martin Cunha, Director Emeritus, Northeast Document Conservation Center, has defined the relationship between the librarian, the conservator, and the scientist in what he has termed the *tripartite* concept of preservation. This concept clarifies the role of the triumvirate of specialists working together to solve problems and preserve library collections. In his schema, Cunha places the librarian, or curator, whom he calls the administrator, at the apex of a triangle, for it is the librarian who is responsible for diagnosing the needs of the collections and advising the conservator and the scientist of what must be done. In his lectures, Cunha frequently shows a large sign stating, "The Buck Stops Here," at the apex. The "buck" does indeed stop with the administrator who, as custodian of the collections, is responsible for their ultimate fate.

History of Book Production

The earliest "books" were actually clay tablets inscribed with a stylus. They were used in Mesopotamia, the "cradle" of civilization. The Egyptians used strips of the papyrus plant crossed over one another and pressed together to make a sheet similar to paper. Palm leaves, bark, and similar materials have also been used as writing material. Many of these objects still exist and, as documents of our cultural heritage, require care and repair. Discussion of the care and preservation of such artifacts is beyond the scope of this book; they are considered museum objects and should receive treatment by skilled specialists when necessary.

THE TRIPARTITE CONCEPT OF CONSERVATION
Administration

Establish staff policies
Plan and provide funds for conservation program
Emergency plans
Support regional cooperative conservation
Advocate the teaching of conservation in schools and colleges
Provide learning opportunities for staff
Cooperate with scientists and professional conservators
Support professional groups

Professional Conservation
Provide advice and assistance in:
1. Environment control
2. On the site treatments of materials
Teaching for institution staffs
Training for technicians
Establish standards
Conduct surveys and inspections
Conduct seminars and workshops
Perform sophisticated repairs
Disaster assistance

Decision making based on *all* the considerations involved in addition to the conservation factors.

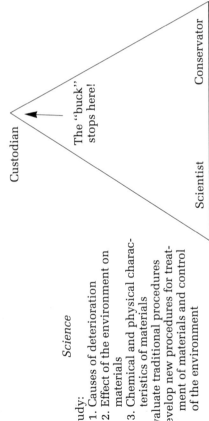

Custodian

The "buck" stops here!

Scientist   Conservator

Science

Study:
1. Causes of deterioration
2. Effect of the environment on materials
3. Chemical and physical characteristics of materials
Evaluate traditional procedures
Develop new procedures for treatment of materials and control of the environment

Credit: Henry Cioch

The most common writing materials in the western world prior to the introduction of paper were parchment and vellum, the skins of sheep or calves. Since both are extremely sturdy, significant numbers of early manuscripts have survived to the present. Prior to the fifth century, most books were produced in rolls. The codex format—manuscript sheets of vellum, parchment, or papyrus folded and placed between boards—was far more convenient for transportation and use and soon became the common format for the book. These early books were copied by monastic scribes for the clergy and royalty. With the emergence of a literate middle class in the thirteenth century, the production of books moved from the monastery to lay workshops where they were produced under the direction of master artisans.

The nobility demanded books of magnificence. By the early fifteenth century, however, the general public eagerly purchased block books, books printed from woodblocks containing moralistic pictures and messages. This "mass market" created the need for "mass production," which was met by the invention of movable type, first used by Johannes Gutenberg to produce his famous 42-line Bible, circa 1455–1456. Movable type and the expansion of papermaking facilities, coupled with the desire by the populace in the Renaissance period to acquire books, led to a healthy output: textbooks, tales, and religious tracts. Manuscript books, often richly illuminated, continued to be produced for wealthy patrons for nearly a century after the invention of printing. Incunabula, books printed before 1500, often had hand-illuminated pages; early publishers attempted to make printed books resemble manuscripts as closely as possible. The paper, hand-produced using procedures still followed today by the few remaining makers of fine paper, was made of rag fibers and is of excellent durability. When other materials were used in papermaking, the quality was likely to vary. Early books are often in far better condition than books that are the products of the past hundred years of publishing. During the eighteenth century, papermaking was mechanized, but paper was still composed chiefly of rags and its quality was satisfactory.

It was not until the 1860s, when groundwood pulp became the primary raw material for papermaking, that the quality of paper significantly declined. The higher the content of unprocessed wood pulp, the more rapidly paper deteriorates. Lignin, an acidic organic substance found in wood pulp, is a primary culprit; coupled with other impurities in groundwood pulp and the sizing on the paper to enable it to hold ink, it causes paper virtually to self-destruct so that eventually it crumbles at a touch. Examples can be found on every library shelf. If a copy of today's newspaper is left exposed to the light and air for a month, its deterioration is readily observed by its yellowed condition. The books that have been made of groundwood pulp paper in the past 130 years of book publishing are of particular concern to the custodians of library collections.

Fortunately, this acidic paper problem has an end. Paper manufacturers are now producing wood pulp paper that is free of lignin and other caustic ingredients that caused earlier wood pulp papers to disintegrate. More that 50 percent of the paper produced in the United States today has an alkaline reserve that buffers the paper and makes it more permanent. The "brittle book problem" refers to late nineteenth and twentieth century books. Our successors will face a variety of problems when preserving information stored on nonprint media, but paper should prove to be a relatively stable, permanent medium in the twenty-first century.

The Preservation Challenge

It is only in the past two decades that librarians, aside from a few prophetic specialists, have become aware of the gravity of the problems presented by the rapid deterioration of the materials in their care. Specialists from the late nineteenth century on were aware of the fragility of paper, but it was not until the 1950s that the enormous scope of the problem was recognized—that the bulk of our library materials would disintegrate, if not cared for, by the twenty-first century. A study commissioned by the Council on Library Resources in the late 1950s and conducted by William Barrow, conservator at the Virginia Historical Society, predicted that 90 percent of the books printed in the mid-twentieth century would be unusable by the year 2000 due to their physical deterioration.

Support for Barrow's research came from Verner Warren Clapp, the first director of the Council on Library Resources. He set the Council's agenda for the decades to come: basic research, technological development, and "methodological development and coordination of effort."(1) Clapp was described by his friend and colleague, Princeton University librarian William Dix, as "close to the center of almost every important development in scholarly librarianship for at least thirty years."(2) Clapp had recognized the problem of deteriorating books while serving in the early 1940s as the Librarian's general assistant at the Library of Congress. He became a member of the American Library Association's Committee on Permanent/Durable Paper in 1962, but was distressed with the uncooperative attitude of representatives from the paper industry. The committee never reached a consensus on the issue and dissolved in 1966.

The Association of Research Libraries (ARL), with strong encouragement from Clapp, established its Committee on Preservation of Research Materials in 1960. In 1966 Gordon Williams, director of the Center for Research Libraries in Chicago, undertook a study for the association. In his report, *The Preservation of Deteriorating Books,* Williams clearly articulated the magnitude of the problem. The Committee on Preservation then proposed the creation of a national central repository where librarians could send their valuable materials for storage under controlled environmental conditions. While this concept was sound in principle, the time was not ripe for a program requiring cooperation among competing institutions. Keyes D. Metcalf had discovered more than twenty years earlier, while attempting to establish a cooperative facility in the northeast, that competition between institutions could be a stumbling block.(3) The Williams report was followed by a second report in 1972, prepared by Warren J. Haas, who was then at Columbia University Library. Haas was instrumental in encouraging a dialogue between publishers, paper manufacturers, and librarians on the critical role of acid-free paper in the preservation of the documentary heritage. The council established and sponsored the Committee on Production Guidelines for Book Longevity in 1979. Its report, *Book Longevity,* was published in 1981 and its recommendations, with the guidelines promulgated by the National Historic Publications and Records Commission (NHPRC), formed the basis for the work of the American National Standards Institute (ANSI) Committee that drafted the *Standard for Permanence of Paper for Printed Library Materials* in 1984. This standard is currently being revised to include coated papers. The Haas report advocated the principle that all libraries should consider the preservation of their collections as an integral and important part of their general overall activities.

Haas became the president of the Council on Library Resources (CLR) in 1978. He played a leadership role in developing an awareness of preservation needs and spearheaded the implementation of preservation activities in the nation's leading academic and research libraries. The early role of the Council on Library Resources in the development of an awareness of the need for action to preserve library and archival materials is documented in Nancy Gwinn's article, "CLR and Preservation," which appeared in *College and Research Libraries* in 1981.(4) The council, under Clapp's leadership, served as a major provider of factual information on the problem of the deterioration of library and archival materials and broader preservation issues. Following Clapp's direction, Haas continued to involve the council in programs that supported basic research, technological development, and cooperative efforts to preserve library materials to ensure that they will be available for present and future generations.

In 1984 Haas brought together leaders from the academic and library communities to form the Committee on Preservation and Access (CPA) to address the problem of deteriorating books. Members recognized that the important consideration in preservation is *access;* books not preserved will not be available to future readers; access to the records of the past justifies preservation. With funding from the Exxon Education Foundation, the committee explored a variety of topics, including methods and technologies for the preservation of the human record. After a thorough review of current technology, microfilm was recommended as a surrogate medium for deteriorated books. The effect of the work of the committee on the efforts to save the deteriorating materials in the nation's libraries will be discussed throughout this book.

The New York Public Library conducted a survey of its research collection in 1963 and estimated that it would cost $12 million—at that time—merely to undertake minor repairs to make its collections usable for circulation. It was, however, the tragically dramatic catastrophe, the flooding of Florence, Italy, in 1966, that called the public's attention to the vulnerability of cultural property and to the work of conservators to preserve it. Several of the conservators who worked to salvage the badly water-damaged books from the Laurentian Library in Florence, including Carolyn Horton, Paul Banks, Peter Waters, and Don Etherington, subsequently returned or emigrated to the United States. They have been instrumental in establishing procedures for preservation, conservation, and disaster response, and in teaching about the care of library and archival materials. The damage caused by the flood had its impact; in 1968, the annual conference of the Graduate Library School at the University of Chicago focused on the problems faced by library administrators who are responsible for the preservation of their collections. The proceedings of this conference remain important professional reading.(5)

In 1971, George Martin Cunha, a graduate of the Massachusetts Institute of Technology and Conservator at the Boston Athenaeum, gave the first of his seminars on the preservation and conservation of library materials. Cunha was an engineer, bookbinder, and paper conservator, not a librarian. Upon his retirement from the U.S. Navy in the 1960s, he established a conservation laboratory at the Boston Athenaeum. In addition to the papers from this significant seminar, Cunha and his wife, Dorothy, also published their landmark guide for the librarian, *Conservation of Library Materials,* in 1971. It was followed, in 1972, by the publication of a comprehensive bibliography in a companion volume. The bibliography was updated in *Library and Archives Conservation: the 1980s and Beyond,* 2 volumes, published by Scarecrow Press in 1983. A third edition, prepared with the assistance of Robert E. Schnare and Susan G. Swartzburg, is in preparation.

New York Public Library, the Library of Congress, Harvard and Yale University libraries, and other major libraries had in-house binding and book repair facilities, but it was not until the late 1960s that library administrators recognized the need to establish preservation offices within the library. Preservation librarians were able to concentrate on a review of the physical condition of collections and develop priorities for dealing with the massive problem of deterioration in the stacks.

The Preservation Office at the Library of Congress was established in the late 1960s by Frazer Poole, friend and colleague of Verner Clapp. Poole had been involved in matters of book longevity and preservation as the director of the American Library Association's Library Technology Program. He brought Peter Waters, a British bookbinder and conservator who was a leader in the salvage and restoration effort in Florence, to the Library to become the director of its Conservation Division. Several of Waters's colleagues from England, including Christopher Clarkson and Don Etherington, both recognized for their significant contributions to the preservation and conservation fields, joined him at the Library and established the highest standards in conservation treatment procedures in the new division. John Williams, a chemist, was appointed to direct a four-man research unit. The need for a mass treatment for embrittled books was identified as a priority and led to the development, by scientist George

Kelly, of the diethyl zinc (DEZ) process for the deacidification of books. Poole introduced the "phased treatment" concept, whereby items are stabilized by cleaning and protective housing until they can be fully treated. Under the direction of his successor, Peter Sparks, a chemist and former director of the Winterthur graduate training program in conservation at the University of Delaware, the diethyl zinc method of deacidification has been tested and developed for commercial use. With encouragement from the Council on Library Resources, a National Preservation Program Office has been established at the Library of Congress to provide outreach and information to librarians throughout the country. The National Preservation Program Office also serves as a liaison with the International Federation of Library Associations and Institutions (IFLA) and other agencies to facilitate international cooperation in preservation.

In 1986, the Council on Library Resources Committee on Preservation and Access recommended the formation of an independent Commission on Preservation and Access (CPA) to ensure permanent funding and cooperative action. Patricia M. Battin, a seasoned library administrator, was named president of the Commission in April 1987. One of her primary tasks was "to set in motion a nationwide preservation effort designed to capture the contents of hundreds of thousands of 'brittle books' by microfilming or other means, and to make them permanently available to all who need them."(6) Working with the National Endowment for the Humanities and members of the United States Congress, the commission has been successful in launching a cooperative project to coordinate the microfilming of the nation's research collections. This massive preservation effort, managed by the NEH Division of Preservation and Access, is well under way.

One of the goals of the commission is to build and maintain effective communication with key organizations and to promote cooperative planning and programs among research institutions. Battin has brought together representatives from diverse communities who are con-

cerned with the preservation of the documentary record
in this country and, increasingly, abroad. She has met her
mandate "to foster, develop, and support systematic and
purposeful collaboration among libraries and allied organizations in order to ensure the preservation of the
published and documentary record in all formats; provide
enhanced public access to preserved materials through an
open distribution system."(7)

In the early 1970s, both Yale and Harvard University
libraries established preservation offices to oversee the
care and repair of books in their general collections.
Columbia University and a number of other research
libraries, following their lead, established similar offices
throughout the decade. The Yale University Library Preservation Department has served as a model for a number
of other institutions; its bibliographic procedures, developed to avoid duplication of effort, its reformatting programs, and its repair and conservation treatment units are
exemplary. Yale was among the first institutions to obtain
a grant from the National Endowment for the Humanities,
with matching funds from the Andrew W. Mellon Foundation, for an innovative program of internships that
trained twenty-four preservation administrators and book
conservators from 1979 to 1982. They assisted in a massive survey that documented the size and scope of the
deterioration problem at Yale. Many of these preservation
specialists and conservators have gone on to make a
substantial contribution to the field and today hold positions of leadership. The head of Yale's Preservation Department from 1972 to 1990, Gay Walker, advanced a
practical, common-sense approach to preservation
through her teaching and her publications.

New York Public Library had long been aware of the
deterioration of its collections and had undertaken a
number of efforts to halt it. It was not until 1972, however,
that a Conservation Division, similar in concept to the
model set by Poole at the Library of Congress, was established under the direction of John Baker. The division,
housed today in renovated quarters, includes units responsible for book repair and conservation. Baker super-

vised a complex preservation and conservation program that has achieved the preservation of a considerable body of the research materials in the New York Public Library, one of the world's great repositories. From the beginning, Baker recognized the necessity of permanent funding to ensure the preservation of the library's collections. The Lydenberg Society, named for Harry Lydenberg, the first librarian of the New York Public Library and a passionate preservationist, serves as the fund-raising arm for conservation among the library's friends.

The National Endowment for the Humanities (NEH) has been a catalyst for a number of the preservation activities that have developed in the past fifteen years. Historian Margaret Child, formerly of its Research Grants Division, recognized the need for the preservation of the documentary record. She encouraged projects, such as the Mellon internship program, that would achieve this mission. The Northeast Document Conservation Center (NEDCC), Andover, MA, the nation's first, and still the only, regional conservation center devoted exclusively to the preservation and treatment of library and archival materials, was able to strengthen its field services and its treatment facilities with leadership funding from NEH. Child, after a stint at the Smithsonian and as a consultant to the Committee on Preservation and Access, is currently a consultant for the field services that she was instrumental in founding at the Northeast Document Conservation Center, as well as for the Commission on Preservation and Access.

In December 1985, the National Endowment for the Humanities established a separate Office of Preservation to help address the preservation needs of the nation's libraries. Under the leadership of George Farr and with sharply increased funding from Congress, the Office began in 1989 to implement a multi-year preservation plan. Components of this plan included: an initiative to raise the rate of preservation microfilming in libraries and archives to a level that will preserve the intellectual content of three million brittle books and serials in twenty years; a program to locate, catalog, and microfilm United States newspapers on a state-by-state basis; and enhanced support for the preservation of special collections of unique materials in libraries and archives. The plan has the support and the encouragement of the Commission on Preservation and Access. Much has been done. Several states have already completed their newspaper projects while most others are well on their way; large collections of embrittled research materials have been microfilmed and are available for research. Microfilming of collections continues at a good pace. Rare and valuable items are being treated painstakingly by skilled conservators. The Division of Preservation and Access, under the direction of George Farr and his staff, has been responsible for the preservation of the intellectual content of much of America's printed heritage.

The Division of Preservation and Access also awards grants for preservation education and training on a regional and national level; the establishment of regional field services; research and demonstration projects that will serve as a model for other institutional initiatives; the creation of statewide preservation plans; and projects, such as the film *Slow Fires,* that will heighten public awareness of the preservation problem.

Congress appropriated additional funds for the Office of Preservation in 1990 to launch the National Heritage Preservation Program, which provides support to stabilize material culture collections. Awards are made for the housing and storage of objects, improved climate control, and the installation of new lighting, security, and fire prevention systems. Funds are available, as well, for programs to train conservators of material culture objects and institutional staff entrusted with the general care of such collections.

As of July 1991, the Office of Preservation was designated the Division of Preservation and Access and given responsibility for all collections-based activities previously funded in the Access category of the National Endowment's Research Division and for the "documentation" grants made from the Museums program in the Division of Public Programs. With this action, the Endowment has consolidated within a single division its support for projects and programs that will preserve and provide intellectual access to collections that are important for research, education, and public programming in the humanities. This indicates the strong federal support that the preservation of the nation's intellectual heritage will have during this decade and is a reflection upon the solid accomplishments of the Office of Preservation, working with librarians, archivists, and curators, since the mid-1980s.(8)

In 1980, preservation specialist Pamela W. Darling, then of Columbia University, was retained by the Association of Research Library's Office of Management Services (ARL/OMS) to conduct a survey of the preservation needs of ARL libraries and to develop a planning tool for preservation. Using the basic self-study methodology promulgated by ARL, Darling applied it to preservation management, tested it in several ARL libraries, and produced a major tool, *Preservation Planning Program: an Assisted Self-Study Manual for Libraries,* issued with a collection of readings for self-study teams. This manual was updated and revised in 1987 by Wesley Boomgaarden, preservation officer at Ohio State University, one of Darling's first students in the Preservation Administration Program at Columbia University. The self-study planning program continues to be a popular tool for planning and organizing preservation services among the nation's academic libraries. Its methodology, which can be adapted to a smaller scale, has much to offer every library. Although she has retired from the field, Darling's writings on preservation issues continue to have an impact on preservation initiatives today.

The Research Libraries Group (RLG) was founded in 1974 by Columbia, Yale, and Harvard Universities, and the New York Public Library, as an agency to address issues of cooperative collection management and development, enhanced resource sharing among institutions, the development of bibliographic control and technical resources to support information access, and preservation. Today RLG is a partnership of major American research libraries and institutions. The founding members of RLG were concerned with the problem of deteriorating library collections and recognized that the issue needed to be addressed cooperatively within the context of collection development and management, bibliographic control, and new information technologies. RLG's Preservation Committee, with representatives from its member libraries, planned and implemented a cooperative approach and assigned specific institutional responsibilities for preservation.

Preservation Committee members developed standards and procedures that have become the exemplar for the national preservation effort. By 1983 the RLG Cooperative Preservation Microfilming Project began, with funding from NEH and the Andrew W. Mellon Foundation; eight research libraries were able to film and catalog more than 30,000 embrittled volumes. By 1990 the Great Collections Microfilming Project was well underway. Today, over 175,000 volumes are being microfilmed annually, with the long-term goal of preserving the information contained in over three million volumes over a twenty year period. Keyes DeWitt Metcalf would be pleased with the initiatives of RLG to accomplish the task.

Undaunted by earlier difficulties in making the preservation of library materials a significant concern within the American Library Association, preservation librarians established a Preservation Committee, which evolved from the Binding Committee in the mid-1970s. The Preservation Committee functioned within the Resources and Technical Services Division (RTSD), which became the Association for Library Collections and Technical Services (ALCTS). By the end of the 1970s, a Preservation Discussion group and a Library/Binders Relations Subcommittee had been established. In 1980 these committees became the Preservation of Library Materials Section (PLMS) with nearly 14,000 members. PLMS provides a national forum for preservation administrators and librarians who are responsible for preservation activities in their institutions to discuss programs, policies, and procedures. PLMS developed a strong continuing education component, with programs and institutes on preservation management, commercial library binding, and other topics offered nationally. It works closely with other divisions of the American Library Association to develop policies and procedures for the preservation of collections.

The preservation of collections has always been a fundamental concern of archivists. In the early 1980s, the Society of American Archivists (SAA) appointed a preservation officer to design procedures and teach archivists basic preservation and conservation techniques for paper-based and photographic collections. This highly successful program resulted in the publication of two important books in the Society's Basic Manual series: *Archives & Manuscripts: Conservation, A Manual on Physical Care and Management* (1983, revised 1984) and *Archives & Manuscripts: Administration of Photographic Collections* (1984). Both were written by Mary Lynn Ritzenthaler, then Preservation Program Officer who directed the workshop series. A revised and updated edition of *Conservation,* now entitled *Preserving Archives and Manuscripts,* was published by the Society of American Archivists in 1994. It has become a standard text in the archival field. A Conservation Special Interest Group, now the Preservation Section, was formed within SAA in the early 1980s. The section's mission is the promotion of preservation as a fundamental concern for archivists. In the late 1980s the society completed a preservation needs assessment study to provide a foundation for the development of education and training programs in the 1990s. With funding from the National Endowment for the Humanities, the Society has undertaken a major initiative to train up to sixty archivists in preservation administration over a three year period. A series of courses, developed and led by Evelyn Frangakis, are being held in four regions of the United States through 1994. Increasingly, librarians and archivists are cooperating in preservation initiatives and activities on a national, regional, and state level.

By the late 1970s, librarians involved in preservation began to participate in the activities of the American Institute for the Conservation of Historic and Artistic

Works (AIC), the professional association for conservators. The dialogue between librarians and conservators has been invaluable. The Book and Paper Group, established within AIC in 1984, is one of the association's strongest divisions. Conservators are now participating on committees within the American Library Association and the Society of American Archivists, and working with state and regional associations to develop education and training programs.

In 1978, with support from the Andrew W. Mellon Foundation, the School of Library Service, Columbia University, held a month-long Preservation Institute for mid-level library managers, taught largely by Pamela Darling and Paul Banks, a distinguished book conservator, then President of AIC. The institute's goal was to teach the participants how to develop and implement a preservation program. One of the participants, Robert H. Patterson, now Vice President for Planning and Libraries at the University of Tulsa, Oklahoma, established *Conservation Administration News* (CAN), a quarterly publication to share news and views on preservation and conservation. *CAN* has become one of the foremost publications in the field of library and archival preservation with an international readership. Following the success of the institute, Columbia developed plans for two programs for advanced training to be offered at the School of Library Service. The Preservation Administration (PA) Program offered a sixth-year certificate; it has sent forth a cadre of highly trained library specialists who are making a significant contribution in the field. The Conservation Program, jointly administered with the Conservation Program at the Institute of Fine Arts, New York University, trained a corps of skilled book conservators to treat the nation's deteriorating collections.

In spite of the success of these innovative programs, Columbia's School of Library Service, the nation's first library school, did not survive the 1990s. The need for the graduates of its Preservation Administration and Conservation programs was demonstrated, but its students were too few in number to carry a foundering school. The

School of Library Service closed in 1992. The Preservation Administration and the Conservation Programs relocated to the University of Texas Graduate School of Library and Information Science, Austin, with funding for a two-year period from the National Endowment for the Humanities. Columbia's graduates undoubtedly will play a leadership role in the library field in the years to come, as will the future graduates of such programs at Texas and elsewhere.

There is no question about the need for further professional training in preservation for librarians and archivists. Today, preservation is included in the curriculum of all but a handful of North American library schools. Adjunct instructors, the specialists in the field, are being replaced by library educators, an acknowledgment of the acceptance of preservation in the basic curriculum. An innovative program for continuing education in preservation began in 1990 at the School of Communication, Information and Library Studies, Rutgers University. It offers a Certificate in Preservation to participants who have taken a series of courses one to three days in length. Similar programs are being developed at other library schools. Today every librarian needs to know something about collection management and preservation.

While most librarians will never face the magnitude of preservation problems found in the nation's leading research libraries, nor have the awesome responsibility of dealing with them, the leadership of the librarians who have developed and implemented the preservation programs in these institutions has benefitted most libraries. This book has been prepared for the general staff of a library that cannot afford to establish a special Preservation Department with highly trained staff. Librarians may use it as a guide and a model to draft instructions and procedures for their individual situations.

Notes

1. William Joseph Crowe, *Verner W. Clapp as Opinion Leader and Change Agent in the Preservation of Library Materials* (Bloomington: Indiana University, Ph.D. dissertation, 1986), 71.
2. In *Verner Warren Clapp, 1901–1971: A Memorial Tribute* (Washington, DC: Library of Congress, 1973), 6, and quoted by Crowe, 1.
3. Metcalf comments on library cooperation in his biography, *My Harvard Library Years* (Cambridge, MA: Harvard College Library, 1988); see especially chapter 6, "Cooperative Storage Problems," 56–71.
4. 42:2 (March), 104–126.
5. Press release from the Commission, April 17, 1987.
6. Commission on Preservation and Access. 1989 Fact Sheet.
7. Correspondence and discussion with George Farr, director, Division of Preservation and Access, August 1991.

Selected Readings

Belanger, Terry. "The Price of Preservation." *Times Literary Supplement,* Friday, November 18, 1977, 1ff.

Council on Library Resources. Committee on Preservation and Access. *Brittle Books.* Washington, DC: 1986.

Cunha, George M. and Dorothy G. *Conservation of Library Materials.* 2 vols. Metuchen, NJ: Scarecrow Press, 1971–1972.

Cunha, George M. and Dorothy G. *Library and Archives Conservation: 1980s and Beyond.* 2 vols. Metuchen, NJ: Scarecrow Press, 1983.

Darling, Pamela W. and Sherelyn Ogden. "From Problems Perceived to Programs in Practice: the Preservation of Library Resources in the U.S.A., 1956–1980." *Library Resources and Technical Services* 25:1 (January-March 1981): 9–29.

Higgenbotham, Barbra Buckner. *Our Past Preserved: A History of American Library Preservation, 1876–1910.* Boston, MA: G. K. Hall, 1990.

Merrill-Oldham, Jan and Merrily Smith, eds. *Library Preservation Program: Models, Priorities, Possibilities.* Chicago: American Library Association, 1985.

Paris, Jan. *Choosing and Working with a Conservator.* Atlanta, GA: Southeast Library Network, 1990.

II. THE PRESERVATION SURVEY:
Tool for Collection Management

Introduction

LIBRARIANS ARE THE STEWARDS OF COLLECTIONS for today and tomorrow. With stewardship comes the responsibility to practice preventive preservation—to ensure that the conditions under which a library's collections are housed retard, as much as possible, the deterioration of books and other materials. As David Vaisey, the Librarian of the Bodleian has stated, "It is simply not respectable for a librarian or an archivist to say that he or she is not involved in conservation and preservation. . . . The conservation part of our work, whether in libraries or in archives, has come to be accepted as an integral part of the service we provide to the owner or donor, to the archives, and to the researcher."(1)

Rare book specialist Terry Belanger addressed the question of institutional responsibility for collection care in a 1977 article, "The Price of Preservation," in the *Times Literary Supplement*. While Belanger speaks directly to institutions with special collections, his comments apply to every library. He states:

> Independent research libraries prosper because they have a clear understanding of their own purpose. . . . Libraries large and small should develop (or maintain) rare book and special collections only if they know why they are doing so, and only if they are willing to foot the bill. To the extent that [they] are properly housed, catalogued, serviced, exhibited, and maintained, they will enhance the reputation of their owners. University and college libraries which cannot

maintain such collections should give, lend or sell them to those who can and will.(2)

It is the responsibility of every institution that holds unique collections, regardless of its size and resources, to properly care for its collections for present and future researchers. By caring for materials in this lifetime, the custodians of collections ensure that the information in them is available for future researchers. *Access* for current and future users is a primary motive for preservation. Custodians of circulating collections also have a responsibility to maintain their materials, to ensure that they remain in the collection as long as possible. This is the least that the taxpayer, or the private donor, should expect. Librarians are collection managers, who ensure the collection, organization, preservation and access of collections on behalf of their public. Preservation is collection management.

The perfect storage facility for library and archival materials—and "perfect" is a relative term—would be an underground vault with a finely tuned and perfectly maintained environmental control system, with temperature and relative humidity controls, an air filtration system, and adequate air circulation. The vault would never be sullied by the presence of living creatures, including Homo Sapiens. The "perfect" facility is not designed to house materials that are meant for study and contemplation on a frequent basis. Although a national storage repository with controlled environment and access may be available to our successors in the twenty-first century, the librarian dealing with collections today needs to provide a facility that will retard the natural deterioration of materials that are meant to be used by a variety of people. In addition, librarians need to understand the physical nature of their materials and how to handle them to ensure their longevity. Librarians must be aware of current practices in preservation and conservation and eliminate practices and procedures that might prove harmful to the longevity of materials.

The first step toward a carefully considered collection

management and preservation program in a library is to undertake a preservation survey in order to inform administration and staff how well collections are managed and where needs exist. Surveys provide a wide variety of information about institutional goals and priorities; where an institution is at a given point in time; and information about collection condition and preservation needs. This chapter will deal with the general preservation survey, which assesses the way an institution houses and cares for its collections. The condition survey, in which a professional book or paper conservator comes as a consultant to examine the physical condition of one or more objects in a collection, or a discrete collection of materials, is a separate subject. Condition surveys are done after implementation of recommendations in a general preservation survey, to ensure that materials that undergo treatment by conservators will not return to poor conditions, which may have caused the problem in the first place.

The demand for guidance in preservation planning has been steadily increasing over the past decade. Preservation surveys, designed to assist and give direction to institutions that want to initiate preservation activities, are the first step in the preservation planning process. They serve to educate an institution about its specific needs. Increasingly, the preservation survey is a recognized tool for collection management and future planning; it assesses the condition of a collection as a whole and proposes solutions for both short and long term to improve conditions. The comprehensive preservation survey includes an assessment of the library building to evaluate its suitability as a repository for housing collections. Policies for collection management and maintenance and the storage of collections are reviewed. The survey takes into consideration the temperature, relative humidity, air quality, and light levels where collections are housed and evaluates housekeeping, exhibition, handling, lending, security, and emergency preparedness practices. In addition, each type of material within the collection is examined for condition, storage, and general preservation problems. The final survey report will include recommendations for the establishment of priorities for future actions to improve the conditions under which the library's materials are housed and used.

A preservation survey may be initiated in a variety of ways. The survey may be undertaken by the library staff. The Association of Research Libraries Office of Management Services (ARL/OMS) has developed a self-study methodology, and its resource and planning notebooks can be helpful for various types of institutions. The formal ARL/OMS self-study, conducted under the direction of a trained consultant from ARL, is a lengthy process, undertaken within an institution over a period of six months to a year. A significant number of staff are involved in task forces that study the organization, identify problems, and propose solutions. The cost to an institution can be substantial, yet the result is an educated staff committed to the maintenance and preservation of the library's collections. The Preservation Planning Program is available with or without ARL/OMS support, so that an institution can initiate a self-study to survey its collections and to develop recommendations under the leadership of a preservation specialist appointed from within or brought in as a consultant to the project.

The National Association of Government Archives and Records Administrators (NAGARA) has developed a three-part self-study instrument, consisting of a computer program using artificial intelligence technology, a printed manual about preservation planning strategies, and a collection of published and unpublished readings on preservation.(3) Aside from the computer component, it is similar in concept to the ARL/OMS approach. Although programmed queries and responses can be constricting, as there are so many variables when dealing with collections, the approach may serve as a model for institutions to adapt for their own internal use. As the computer plays an ever-increasing role in other library operations, its emergence in collection management and preservation decision-making is not unexpected. There will be increased use of this technology in library and archival management. Two computer-assisted self-study programs are now available for libraries, the Research Libraries Group (RLG) program and the California Preservation Program (CALIPR). These two instruments focus on a broad overview of collections. Their effectiveness has yet to be assessed.

As an alternative to an in-house survey, an institution may wish to bring in a consultant to undertake a general preservation survey. Such surveys were initiated by George Cunha at the Northeast Document Conservation Center (NEDCC) in Andover, MA. NEDCC was the first regional conservation center in North America dedicated to the preservation and treatment of library and archival materials and was the first to offer field services, including staff consultants for preservation and conservation surveys. Trained personnel visit an institution to survey the physical plant, environmental conditions, and the physical condition of collections, then provide a written evaluation. The report recommends measures, both short and long term, to preserve collections. It takes into consideration the organizational climate, organizational priorities, overall organizational needs, staffing, funding, and space. The report places preservation within the context in which it functions. Hence, the written report should provide a framework for a preservation plan. This framework will identify specific needs and priorities and will make recommendations for meeting them. The report is intended to be a flexible tool, to enable an institution to seize opportunities to address its specific preservation needs.

The National Endowment for the Humanities and several private foundations have provided funds so that regional centers, such as NEDCC, The Conservation Center for Art and Historic Artifacts (CCAHA) in Philadelphia, PA, and the Southeastern Library Network (SOLINET), Atlanta, GA, can provide consultants for surveys at a nominal cost to an institution. Several states, including New York and New Jersey, also provide funding for surveys and consultants to undertake them.

To date, there is no clear consensus of what precisely

the preservation survey should include and who is qualified to undertake it. Pioneers such as George Cunha and Paul Banks at the Newberry Library, Chicago, in the 1970s; Marilyn Kemp Weidner and Lois Olcott Price at CCAHA in the 1980s have trained a corps of skilled consultants who are developing clearer guidelines for preservation and conservation surveys in a variety of institutions. Preservation specialist and educator Evelyn Frangakis, formerly with CCAHA and the New York State Conservation Consultancy, has developed a series of points to review during the course of an on-site survey. She has built upon the work of Banks, Cunha, Weidner, and Price, and upon her own experience. Her work is incorporated into this chapter. The Association of Research Libraries has trained a number of librarians to direct the ARL/OMS self-surveys; these individuals are well-qualified to assist other institutions. Many of these people are available as consultants through a funded state or regional program. A capable consultant can provide a wealth of practical information during the survey and in the written report that will follow, including sources for supplies, education, and funding.

When selecting a consultant to survey the library or to assist staff in a self-survey project, inquire about his or her education and training in the field; since the field is so new, most consultants will not have been formally trained. Organizations such as the National Institute for Conservation (NIC) and the American Institute for the Conservation of Artistic and Historic Works (AIC), as well as the International Federation of Library Associations and Institutions (IFLA) and the International Council on Archives (ICA), are exploring ways to train consultants. Courses to teach preservation survey techniques are being developed at several library schools. When seeking a consultant to undertake a preservation survey, request a list of institutions that the consultant has surveyed and contact these institutions about their satisfaction with the survey. Different institutions require different kinds of surveys; for example, some survey reports are focused toward the specific requirements of grant applications. If possible, read a report that the consultant has prepared. Some surveys are lengthy and include considerable information to help implement improvements that are recommended in the report. Others are significantly shorter, with supplementary information on environment and other issues appended, as applicable to the institution.

A thorough on-site survey of an institution and its collections undertaken by a consultant will take at least one day; the preparation of a written report will take a minimum of two days. Preservation surveys are expensive, no matter how they are approached, but the survey should lead to actions that will result in sound collection management policies and procedures that will preserve collections for future access. In the long term, surveys are an extremely cost-effective management tool.

The preservation survey has five components: pre-survey planning, the on-site visit, the report, institutional actions, and the consultant's follow-up. Careful planning prior to the on-site survey will enable an institution to get the most from the consultant, and it will facilitate the consultant's task, as well, resulting in a more effective in-depth report. Information should be gathered together and reviewed by the library's staff and the consultant before the site survey. This information should include documentation for whatever policies and procedures currently exist for collection development and management. First and foremost are the mission statements for the institution and library. If such documents do not exist, this is a significant finding, for without them, planning for preservation is difficult, if not impossible. Prior to the actual survey, collection development policies should be reviewed and strengths and patterns of use in the circulating and special collections identified. Circulation, interlibrary lending, and exhibition policies and procedures should be examined, as well as technical service procedures for the receipt and processing of new materials. The commercial library binding contract and all other contracts for preservation and conservation services undertaken outside the library, such as preservation microfilming, should be carefully examined. The organization chart of the library should be scrutinized in the course of pre-survey planning. Who is responsible for which operations? Documentation about the building should be collected, including information about the building construction, floor plans, past problems, and the disaster plan, if the institution has one. Documentation about the institution's disaster and theft insurance should be reviewed. What security is provided, and how? Pre-survey review and planning will bring a number of issues to the foreground to be considered in depth during the site survey.

The first step of the on-site visit is a meeting with the senior administrative staff and members of the board of directors, if one exists. It is important to meet with administrators to discuss the purpose of the survey; their concerns, priorities, and goals for the survey; and their goals and priorities for the institution, so that preservation initiatives can work within that context. This provides an opportunity for the administrators and the consultant to express concerns, based upon their review of the documentation that has been collected and reviewed during the pre-survey process. The consultant will appeal to the administrators' enlightened self-interest; administration must "buy into" the process and become a part of it to make it work.

Next comes the walk-through of the physical plant, which will include the library's senior administrators and the engineer or person responsible for the physical maintenance of the building. The walk-through begins with a close look at the physical structure of the building: site, construction materials, roof, suitability as a repository for collections. Next the heating, ventilating, and air handling/conditioning (HVAC) systems should be examined, noting the HVAC system's functioning capacity, piping location, preventative maintenance, and malfunctions that have led to emergency situations. The consultant then focuses on the environment in the building, including temperature, relative humidity, incident, and ultraviolet (UV) light levels in collection-holding areas. Readings of temperature and relative humidity in different areas of the building can be taken with a motorized or sling psychrometer; light levels can be measured with a photographer's light meter, and ultraviolet light levels can be measured with a UV monitor. These readings often provide immediate justification for an environmental monitoring program. Although on-site readings represent conditions only at one point in time, they often indicate problem areas. Housekeeping and storage practices are examined. The condition, housing, size, and dates of each collection, along with books, documents, film, video, sound recordings, etc., are examined and described. Attention is paid to exhibition areas. Staff rooms where food is stored and eaten need careful scrutiny. Fire protection and security measures are reviewed.

A checklist can serve to focus a site visit and to enable the consultant, the administrators, and the engineer to get at a considerable body of critical information about a facility, its collections and institutional conditions. Fol-

Hygrometer

lowing is a checklist of points to consider during the walk-through of the library.

The Building

Type of building: new building, adapted to use; if the building is a historic structure, recommendations may be circumscribed.

What is its architectural style?

When was it built? Who were the architects/builders?

How long has the institution occupied this space? Is it a permanent home? Is it the only tenant, or is the building for multiple use? If so, who else occupies it?

What is it made of (construction materials)? What are the insulation materials? What is the condition of the walls? What is the condition of the foundation?

Have there been any renovations since its construction or occupation by the institution? If so, when?

What type of roof does it have; what are the roofing materials? Has the roof been changed or repaired; when and why? What is its condition? Is it regularly maintained?

How is drainage for the building achieved? (For example, gutters, downspouts, interior columns.) Check for and ask about problems with drainage resulting in damage to the facility and/or collections.

What is the inspection/maintenance cycle for the roof and drainageways? What are the procedures for such, and who performs the work?

Does the age of the building exempt, or modify it from current building codes?

Environment: Temperature and Relative Humidity

What type of heating, ventilating, and air conditioning (HVAC) system does the building have? If there is no one system, what components are in place and how is each achieved? Include this information for all collection-holding areas:
> heating
> ventilation/air circulation
> cooling

What type of filters are used for the heating, ventilation, and air-conditioning (HVAC) system? Do they filter particulate matter and gasses? What is the efficiency level of the filters? How often are they cleaned and/or replaced?

Is there adequate air circulation? Are windows used for air circulation or to otherwise manipulate the environment?

Do collections-holding areas have separate environmental control systems?

How old is the HVAC system (or systems)?

How often is the system maintained? What procedures are followed?

Are preventative maintenance measures employed?

Have there been problems with the system that have led to disaster situations?

Is the system on at all times? Is it designed to be on at all times? If not, what is its operation cycle?

What is the average temperature and relative humidity in the building and in collections-holding areas? What are the daily and seasonal fluctuations?

Is the building located in an area with considerable air pollution?

Is the institution located near a large body of water?

Does the institution use environmental monitoring devices? If so, what equipment and monitoring devices are used; how many? Are the units functioning properly? When were they last calibrated (how and by whom)?

Is there an environmental monitoring program in place? Are records kept? If so, the surveyor should examine and analyze them.

Environment: Light

What are the sources of light in areas where collections are stored or exhibited?

Take light level readings (overall/incident and ultraviolet) where collections are stored and exhibited; for each reading, note light source, time, and direction of exposure.

How long are collections exposed to light during the day?

Are lights in stack and storage areas turned off when not in use?

Are there other limitations to light exposure, such as draperies, blinds, illumination levels, timers, dimmers, etc.?

Are collections protected by ultraviolet (UV) filters on lights and/or windows? Which collections? Are the filters still effective? When were they installed or last replaced?

Housekeeping

What are the housekeeping/cleaning schedule and procedures for both the building and collections?

Is the building generally clean? Are the shelves/storage units clean? Are books and other materials clean?

Is trash emptied on a regular basis?

Is staff and/or the public permitted to eat and/or smoke in the facility? Are there designated locations for these activities? Is there evidence of food and drink consumption elsewhere in the building, e.g., in trash cans or study areas? Does the institution allow or sponsor special events where food and drink are consumed in the building?

Is there any sign of insect or vermin infestation, past or present?

Is there routine extermination performed in the building? If so, note frequency, company, and method, noting chemicals used, if applicable (or possible).

Is there evidence of mold anywhere? If so, what was its source? Have there ever been mold problems related to the HVAC system?

Storage and Handling

How are collection materials stored? For example, are folio books shelved separately; are manuscripts stored upright or flat? Are special collections separated?

Describe storage furnishings: adjustable or nonadjustable shelving, wooden or metal bookcases, file cabinets or drawers, sliding or stationary racks, map cases, etc. Note which is used for what collection/material.

Are materials, such as boxes, wrappers, and folders, that house collections made of chemically inert, alkaline, or lignin-free materials? If unsure, note name of manufacturer, address, item name, stock number, and check with the manufacturer; materials can also be tested if the consultant or the institution has access to a laboratory facility.

Is there adequate space for shelving and storage, or is there a space problem? Where could collections be housed? Where are stack/storage areas in relation to other parts of the building?

Who has access to the collections? Is there open access to all collections? How much use do the collections receive?

Are staff and users instructed in collection handling? If so, by whom? Are there written guidelines for handling for staff and the public?

What are the guidelines for duplication and photo-reproduction? Is photocopying done by staff or users? Who determines what can be safely copied? What type of equipment is used?

Disaster Preparedness

Is there a written disaster preparedness and recovery plan? Does it deal with safe evacuation of people, collections, or both? Does it deal with natural and man-made disasters, such as water, fire, bomb threats, vandalism? Does it include a building layout?

Is there a chain of command?

Is there a duplicate copy of the shelflist/inventory/register? Where is it kept?

Have the staff been instructed in emergency planning and recovery procedures? If so, how?

Note location(s) of water-bearing pipes. Are they above collections-holding areas? If so, are areas protected in any way?

Where are the custodian's closets and other locations of water-bearing pipes in relation to collections?

How far from the floor are collections stored?

Have there been past disasters, especially with regard, but not limited to overhead water-bearing pipes?

Fire Detection and Suppression

What type of fire detection system is in place? Is it connected to a central monitoring facility? If so, what is the name and location? What is the response procedure?

Does the institution have regular visits and/or inspections by the local fire department? What are the visits composed of, i.e., inspection, program on fire prevention, staff training?

Has the fire department been made aware of what collections are to be saved, of special procedures for special collections or formats?

Have fire hazards been identified? Are they visible?

What is the condition of the electrical wiring?

Where are the fire exits? Are they readily visible?

Are fire extinguishers available throughout collections-holding areas and the building in general? If so, note number and locations; type (e.g., Halon, multipurpose, electrical). Have staff been trained to use them? If so, by whom? When were they last inspected?

Is there a sprinkler system or any other type of fire suppression system in the building/collections-holding areas? Note the type (wet or dry pipe with delay mechanism, pre-action, etc.) and its location. When was it last tested, and by whom?

Security

What security system and/or procedures exist?

Is the security system monitored by a central monitoring facility? If so, what is its name and location? What is the action/response policy? How often is the system tested?

Are there security guards and/or a night watch shift?

Are there burglar/intrusion alarms? If so, where are they located? What is their periphery?

How many points of access are there to the building and to the collections-holding areas?

Who has keys to the building and/or collections-holding areas?

Does the building have windows? Are they locked? Can they be opened by anyone?

Do doors have alarms (contact units)? Note their locations.

The Collections

What is the general physical condition of the collections? Are they dirty (soiled, stained)? What is the level of wear and tear; the condition of paper, photographs, and other media?

Does collection material exhibit damage from light, poor handling, inadequate storage, insect infestation, water damage?

What are the policies and procedures for commercial library binding?

Are minor repairs made in-house? If so, what is done and
who does it? How is the material selected for treatment?

The consultant should meet with each curator or individual responsible for a collection to learn of their needs
and concerns. There should be a list of each type of
material contained in the collections with a note about
its physical condition, storage and housing conditions,
size, and the dates of their publication. Collection
strengths should be identified.

Exhibition

Is material exhibited from the collections? Is material
borrowed from other collections? How long, and under
what conditions?

Is material from the collections lent to other institutions?
If so, for how long, and under what conditions? Is there
a written loan policy?

Is the environment of the exhibition area monitored?

What is the source of lighting in the exhibition area:
natural, incandescent, fluorescent, or other?

Are exhibition cases lit internally or externally?

Are exhibits prepared by professionally trained staff?

What is the exhibition schedule?

How long do items remain on exhibit? How long has the
current exhibit been on view?

What are the packing and shipping practices? Who packs
and ships objects?

The on-site survey visit has both educational and obser-
vational components. It is an educational experience for

the participating staff and for the consultant, who learn from each experience. The site survey is a cooperative effort between the library's staff and the consultant, for everyone's input has an impact on the total picture. In the course of the site visit and walk-through of the building, the consultant, the administrators, the representative from physical plant, and the staff will discuss a number of collection management and preservation issues. This discussion lays the groundwork for the next part of the survey process, the report. In addition to collection condition, the survey report summarizes what the surveyor/consultant has observed concerning collection management and preservation practices within the institution. It notes what is being done and what could be done. A good survey report provides a framework for planning and implementation. Most funding agencies will not give money for the rehousing or treatment of materials until an institution has had a general preservation survey and can indicate that it can provide an appropriate environment for the collections covered in the grant request.

Every institution needs a carefully articulated mission statement that makes clear what its collections are, what is of informational, commercial, and/or intrinsic value, and what is highly used. If an institution lacks a mission statement and/or collection development policy, the preparation and approval of such a statement is a basic step toward the development of a long-term program to preserve collections. The preparation and implementation of such statements may often take several years. Yet an institution can begin to introduce sound collections care and preservation practices immediately. With the cooperation of physical plant personnel, many of the basic problems with the building and the library's environment can be easily remedied. Others will take a substantial financial investment. An awareness of what needs to be done is the first step. As George Cunha often remarks, "Preservation is good management."

Notes

1. "Archivists, Conservators, and Scientists: the Preservation of the Nation's Heritage," *Archives*, 18, no. 79 (April 1988), 133.
2. Terry Belanger, "The Price of Preservation," *Times Literary Supplement*, Friday, November 18, 1977, 1f.
3. The Project has been described by its director Bonnie Rose Curtain: "Is Conservation Ready for Artificial Intelligence?" *Abbey Newsletter*, 14:1 (February 1990), 1–2; "Archives Preservation: NAGARA GRASP Project Description." *Conservation Administration News*, No. 41 (April 1990), 3–5; "Preservation Planning for Archives: Development and Field Testing of the NAGARA GRASP." *American Archivist*, 53:2 (Spring 1990), 237–243.

Selected Readings

Applebaum, Barbara and Paul Himmelstein. "Planning for a Conservation Survey." *Museum News* 64:3 (February 1986): 5–14.

Association of Research Libraries. Office of Management Studies. *Preservation Planning Program; An Assisted Self-Study Manual for Libraries,* comp. Pamela W. Darling with Duane E. Webster; *Resource Notebook,* comp. Pamela W. Darling, rev. by Wesley L. Boomgaarden. Washington, DC: Association of Research Libraries, 1987.

Boomgaarden, Wesley L. "Preservation Planning for the Small Special Library." *Special Libraries* 76:3 (Summer 1985): 204–211.

Cunha, George, Howard P. Lowell and Robert E. Schnare. *Conservation Survey Manual.* Ballston Spa, NY: SMART, 1982.

Dillon, Phyllis. "Conservation Planning: Where Can You Find the Help You Need?" *History News* 42:4 (August 1987): 10–15.

Hutchins, Jane. "Conservation Surveys." *Technical Informa-*

tion (Virginia Association of Museums) (Winter/Spring 1987): 5–6.

Motylewski, Karen. *What an Institution Can Do To Survey Its Own Preservation Needs.* Andover, MA: Northeast Document Conservation Center, April 1991.

Reynolds, Anne L., Nancy C. Schrock, and Joanna Walsh. "Preservation: the Public Library Response." *Library Journal* 114:2 (February 15, 1989): 128–132.

III. COLLECTION MANAGEMENT:
The Care and Preservation of Library Materials

ONCE A LIBRARY HAS ARTICULATED A COLLECTION development policy and its collections have been surveyed, implementation of a sound collection management and preservation program can begin. Thorough housekeeping practices are at the core of sound collection management and serve as the basis for the development of preservation practices and procedures. The proper care and handling of library and archival materials will prolong their life.

Staff Training

The key to successful collection management and preservation is a training program in which all staff members are taught to respect the materials in their care. A staff training program can take on a variety of forms, including a brief discussion with all new staff members on the care of the collections; detailed instruction manuals; in-house training programs; and/or encouraging staff members to participate in continuing education opportunities at workshops and programs devoted to various aspects of preservation. Continuing education opportunities in preservation are increasingly common. They are sponsored by state or regional library agencies, as well as professional development programs at library schools. These workshops and courses range from the basic care of collections to specific topics, such as commercial library binding, preservation microfilming, disaster planning and recovery, and environmental controls. Both the American Library Association (ALA) and the Society of American Archivists (SAA) have developed a series of seminars on preservation-related topics.

While larger libraries now have in-house preservation officers or administrators, smaller institutions will usually delegate the responsibility for collection management and preservation to one staff member who has other responsibilities as well. Some libraries have a preservation committee, although shared responsibility often means little responsibility. No matter the size of the library, a good first step is to include collection management and preservation as a part of the orientation for all new staff. A number of excellent audiovisual materials: slides, tapes, and videos produced in the past few years can be used for staff training. Many are also appropriate for the education of the public in the care and preservation of library materials.

Operations manuals are useful; most libraries have them, and the preservation component can be incorporated easily into one. A collection management manual will include basic instructions on how to shelve books and other library materials; detailed instructions for commercial library binding; procedures for dealing with fragile and embrittled materials; and guidelines for reformatting, for example, preservation microfilming and photoreproduction, and for exhibition of materials. A number of libraries have prepared such manuals; it is helpful to study those of comparable institutions. The caveat is that manuals from other institutions should not be copied thoughtlessly. Each institution is different and needs to develop its own policies and procedures for collection management and preservation. Many problems have occurred because librarians did not take the time to analyze their own needs and attempted to implement the policies and procedures of other institutions that were not comparable. In-house training programs go hand-in-hand with procedure manuals.

Exhibitions are a dramatic way to raise the awareness of the library staff and the public of the need for preservation. A display case with mutilated books, brittle paper, and moldy photographs can be very effective. Preparing such an exhibition is a lesson in preservation in itself.

Housekeeping

Keeping the building clean is a primary element in the preservation and protection of library collections. Accumulations of dust and dirt hasten deterioration of materials due to their abrasive and chemical action. Pollutants in the air can cause a buildup of acid concentrations that are particularly harmful to paper. Insects and molds often find favorable conditions for breeding and feeding in dark, dank, and dirty corners. Libraries require periodic cleaning, not only of the floor and furniture, but also of the objects themselves: books, documents, recordings, films, and the shelves that contain them.

Housekeeping is a function of the maintenance staff. The responsibility of the custodial workers is to keep the library as dirt-free as possible while following safe procedures that will not harm the materials or themselves. Dusting and cleaning should be undertaken regularly, using great care. Some of the processes involved in cleaning the library and collections are particularly harmful to library materials. Rubbing, scrubbing, pulling, bending, wetting, drying, and the use of various cleansing agents can readily accelerate wear, cause breakage, lead to chemical damage, or augment other hazards. In a library, cleaning must be done as carefully as possible, rather than as quickly as possible. The librarian responsible for collection management and/or preservation should provide the maintenance staff with practical and technical advice, from the standpoint of preservation, on how the library should be cleaned. He or she must keep a careful watch over the effects of cleaning, informing the maintenance staff when methods appear to be harmful and helping to find new solutions.

The maintenance staff should consist of careful, responsible individuals who have been trained in cleaning procedures and are aware of the importance of their role in caring for the collections under their responsibility. Their manual skills should include gentleness and dexterity. Close cooperation and open communication between the maintenance and the library staffs is paramount.

In the *Manual for Museums* (Washington, DC: Government Printing Office, 1976), prepared for curators in the National Parks Service, Ralph Lewis suggests that the logical way to determine maintenance staff requirements and duties is to survey systematically the entire building and to record each household task. Properly done, the resultant list will be lengthy and detailed. To make the task more manageable, areas should be grouped according to the degree of cleaning required. Then comparable jobs in each area should be consolidated. Decide how each task should be done and estimate the amount of time that is necessary to accomplish it. Then multiply the staff-hours for each by the yearly requirements to derive the total number of hours required for proper housekeeping of the library. Housekeeping duties should be scheduled on a daily, weekly, monthly, and annual basis.

An ongoing program of cleaning and inspecting collections is the ideal. Both the Library of Congress and the New York Public Library have established mobile inspection and repair units that travel through the stacks, cleaning materials, making simple repairs, and identifying materials that need more specialized treatment. Few libraries can afford to implement such an operation, but if possible, it would probably save many thousands of dollars. The library would be practicing preventive preservation rather than undertaking costly conservation treatments to preserve materials that already show signs of serious deterioration, or being obliged to replace them. If an institution cannot implement a frequent and thorough schedule of housekeeping and maintenance, it can, at least, implement a program of collection management that will maximize available financial resources.

It cannot be emphasized too strongly that the library should be thoroughly cleaned as frequently as possible. When the books are removed from the shelves, they should be cleaned and inspected. Volumes requiring rebinding or repair should be set aside for review. Books can be vacuumed with small hand vacuum cleaners and compressed air guns (used under galvanized hoods), which are available at reasonable cost. Treated dust cloths, if used gently, can remove soil from bindings and fore-edges of books. Carolyn Horton's book, *Cleaning and Preserving Bindings and Related Materials* (Chicago: Library Technology Project, American Library Association, 1972), although no longer in print and somewhat dated, nevertheless provides clear instructions for organizing a library cleaning operation.

Handling Books in Poor Condition

Although it is not possible for most American libraries to establish procedures for cleaning and reviewing entire collections on an annual basis, it is possible for a library to adopt procedures that ensure that the most heavily used materials receive priority attention. One way to spot problems is to check materials that are returned to the circulation desk each day. Books with problems frequently lead to problem areas in the stacks.

All library staff members should be trained to recognize books in poor condition. These books will have loose or damaged bindings, torn or missing pages, brittle paper that is yellowed and breaks easily, a musty odor, or other signs of dampness and mildew. They should be set aside for careful examination by the preservation librarian.

A high percentage of books that have been returned to the circulation desk in poor condition simply will require rebinding, which is done by a reputable commercial library bindery at reasonable cost. Guidelines and specifications for commercial library binding are discussed in detail in Chapter 7. Administrators should remember that it costs considerably less to rebind a book than to withdraw it from the collection. While a well-staffed and well-financed institution may evaluate each title in poor condition to determine its relevance to the collection, this is impossible at most libraries. It is more practical to rebind and return a title to the shelves, deferring further preservation decisions on the assumption that selection of the volume for addition to the collection was at some point in time done with good reason.

Books with brittle paper, too fragile to tolerate commercial binding, can be identified by gently bending a corner of a page several times. This is known as the "double-fold test;" if the corner breaks after it is folded back and forth two times, the volume is probably too brittle to be rebound. The National Endowment for the Humanities recommends the double-fold test to define a brittle book. Most commercial library binders have a specific fold limit at which they consider a book too brittle to rebind. The *Guide to the Library Binding Institute Standard for Library Binding* (Chicago: American Library Association, 1990) also suggests the double-fold test. Every library should have procedures for dealing with books that are too battered or brittle to be commercially rebound. The first step is to search to see if other copies or editions are available in the library. A bibliographical statement for the title is prepared on a searching record form from information in the catalog. The form should include the following information:

1. Bibliographical description of the book in hand: author, title, place, publisher, date, pagination, note on illustrations, series statement, and any other significant bibliographical information useful in distinguishing the volume from others.
2. The call number of the book in hand.
3. Number of duplicate copies and other editions; their call numbers.

Next, duplicate copies and other editions in the stacks should be checked and their condition noted on the bibliographic search form. Condition reports need not be detailed; often a "good," "fair," or "poor" will suffice. Some libraries have established numerical codes to indicate condition on the report. Frequently, one will discover that there are sufficient copies or editions of a title available to allow the disposal of those in poor condition with no need for replacement. Other copies or editions that are in poor condition should be removed from the stacks and processed with the original fragile volume.

If a replacement copy is needed, a staff member should determine if a title is available commercially. In-print, reprint, and out-of-print catalogs may be searched, although consulting *Books in Print* is often sufficient, as it lists reprint as well as in-print titles. Larger libraries should have the appropriate international bibliographies for the searching of foreign titles. Replacement information is also recorded on the searching record form. This form is then reviewed by the subject specialist responsible for selection and disposition of materials. Often this review involves consultation with the preservation specialist. Many libraries have developed "decision trees" for their manuals, a graphic way to facilitate the decision-making process. The possibilities are outlined below.

1. Return the book to the stacks as is. This decision is made when the volume can tolerate several more circulations before it falls apart, and its paper is not too brittle for general use. This decision may also be appropriate for odd volumes in large sets when a replacement is not commercially available and the set is not heavily used. Such volumes should *never* be held together with an elastic band, as the band will cut into the brittle paper and binding; after a short time the rubber disintegrates and sticks to the binding. Books can be tied with a soft linen cord; special library cord is available from library supply houses.

2. A volume can be rebound. Some fragile books, with a little extra care, can be rebound successfully by a book conservator or a hand bookbinder at a commercial library bindery, although they cannot be oversewn.

3. A book can be placed in a protective enclosure, such as a box or an envelope of alkaline paper, also called a wrap-around, and returned to the shelf. This is useful for fragile materials, but it requires the skill of a dexterous staff member to measure and make the enclosures. A number of libraries are following this approach to preser-

vation. Book conservators have developed a wide variety of designs and have made available instructions for their construction.

4. Fragile books can be fitted to custom-made boxes constructed with acid-free materials. These boxes are not inexpensive, but their cost is far less than the cost of full conservation treatment. A box will preserve the physical integrity of a book and can provide a protective microenvironment for it. Some commercial library binders make custom boxes to order. Fit is important, otherwise further damage to a fragile book can occur. Ready-made boxes, although available, should be used with caution; they are usually not as satisfactory as a custom-made box. Fragile books that have been placed in boxes should not be returned to the stacks of a circulating collection as the continual movement of the materials on the shelf can be harmful and boxed books can be stolen easily.

In summary, books that simply need rebinding should be sent to the commercial library bindery; books that are too fragile to be commercially rebound or of less priority can be tied up and returned to the shelves for a short period of time while they await repairs; books in fragile condition can be placed in protective enclosures, or in custom-made boxes, and housed in a secure area.

5. A book can be repaired in-house, if a skilled conservation technician is available. While in-house repair units are popular, it is difficult to find adequately trained staff to work in them. Considerable damage can be caused by a well-intended assistant with little or no training attempting to repair a book or document. The costs of operating an in-house repair unit can be substantial; contracting such services to regional centers or even to commercial binderies with trained staff to undertake special repairs may well be more economical in the long run. Many in-house repair units established in the 1980s will probably be phased out in the 1990s as technicians are trained to staff regional centers and commercial binderies where most repairs can be done more cost-effectively. Nevertheless, some of the simple repairs that can be undertaken in-house are discussed later in this chapter.

6. A title can be replaced by another edition. This action is routine with titles in some demand when content is of value but the original edition is not essential. During the searching process, *Books in Print* and other appropriate bibliographies will have been checked and, if a title is available in print, it is noted in the search record (with LC and ISBN numbers when available, to facilitate ordering). Replacement copies are ordered; the originals can be held in a special area until the new editions arrive to replace them.

7. A title can be replaced with a facsimile or reprint edition. *Books in Print, Cumulative Book Index, Guide to Reprints,* foreign, and trade bibliographies will provide information on reprint editions. Acquiring a reprint edition is often the most satisfactory means of replacing a volume when its condition is beyond repair. Today alkaline paper is used by all reputable reprint houses. Although prices are frequently high, the convenience and quality of reprint editions make them desirable. Major scholarly works and heavily used titles are most likely to be reprinted. Preservation specialists often work closely with representatives from reprint publishers to identify embrittled materials that are of scholarly importance.

8. The replacement of a title with a microform edition (in microfilm or microfiche) is less convenient for the user, but it is a method that allows a research collection to maintain intellectual integrity. Microforms frequently are purchased for the replacement of serials or large sets. The microfilming of collections of books or papers for preservation is also a possibility, if the materials are unique or have not yet been filmed. Many important collections are in the process of being filmed. The Great Collections Microfilming Project is discussed in Chapter 1; preservation microfilming is discussed in detail in Chapter 12. The use, care, and storage of microforms requires special procedures and equipment, which will also be discussed. A library should be sure that a copy of the book to be reformatted is available in original format elsewhere before its copy is discarded.

9. Titles can be replaced with an exact duplicate of the

edition in hand. This is done easily when a title is still in print, but out-of-print searching usually is neither practical nor cost-effective. The condition of the replacement volume probably will be no better than the volume that is to be discarded. Paper quality tends to be identical within an edition. Out-of-print searching was undertaken at Yale University Library with a selected group of titles in 1971; the condition of the replacement volumes was unsatisfactory.

10. Library materials can be replaced by photoreproduction. This is a satisfactory solution for the replacement of titles in demand, but it is not a satisfactory solution for long-term preservation. If a title is scarce, it should also be microfilmed. Photocopies should be made on alkaline paper even if it is assumed that a reprint edition will be available in the future. Using a finely tuned photocopier and trained staff, Yale University Library's Preservation Office has photocopied books in poor condition for a number of years. Several companies will produce facsimile reproductions of brittle books upon request at a reasonable price. The quality of these reproductions is usually excellent. Reformatting by photoreproduction may prove a viable solution for valued materials in heavily used collections; the option is certainly worth exploring. Although significant scholarly texts may be microfilmed for preservation, books in hardcover are the preferred format for scholarly use.

Photocopying of missing pages should not be attempted if the photocopiers or the quality of the paper is poor, except on an emergency basis. Such copies may not last more than a few months. Replacing missing pages and sections of books by photoreproduction is a practical preservation practice if an institution has photocopying machines dedicated for the purpose and uses alkaline paper. The replacement pages may be tipped in or bound with the original text block. It is possible to request replacement pages on alkaline paper from many libraries through interlibrary loan; alkaline paper must be specified.

Experiments using digital imaging as a reformatting medium are underway. The technology offers considerable potential for access, but it is not in itself a preservation medium. Materials should be microfilmed according to stringent specifications for preservation; digitized copies can be produced easily from the microfilm for access.

Making Repairs

Librarians and library assistants are not conservators, so when approaching the topic of repairs of library materials it is wise to keep in mind what should *not* be done. The conservator's guideline, the principle of reversibility, mandates that one should not undertake a treatment that cannot be undone. This should be kept in mind when attempting even the simplest repair. Commercial library binders, recognizing the libraries' need for simple repairs at a reasonable cost, are beginning to establish repair units at their binderies. This is an option that should certainly be explored and can result in real cost-savings for an institution. The bindery will already have on hand the equipment and space necessary for a book repair unit. The significant capital outlay required to establish even a basic unit within a library is usually prohibitive. The binder usually can repair and return a volume within a short period of time. The commercial library bindery, long familiar with librarians' needs, is an appropriate place for basic book repair.

With the support of the Library Binding Institute (LBI), a professional association of commercial library binders, a program to train conservation technicians for the library binding industry was established in 1986 at the North Bennet Street School in Boston, MA. Most of its graduates have opted for the full two years of bench training, and many have become book or collections conservators. It is hoped that some of the graduates of the program will opt to join binderies and supervise repair workshops.

Simple repairs can be done in-house if a staff member can be trained by a conservator in proper procedures and selection of materials. Unfortunately, it is easier to receive such training in some parts of the country than others, but as regional centers develop, excellent training for conservation technicians may be available within a reasonable distance of most institutions.

The most common problem to be found at the book return is the volume with broken spine, loose hinges, and/or loose pages. If the book is not brittle, with acidic yellowed and deteriorated paper, the simplest and most cost-effective action is to send it to the library binder if the volume is to be retained in the collection. A trained technician can recase a volume and tip in pages in an in-house repair unit so that the volume will survive for a few more years. Recasing, if done correctly, is not a simple task, so the bibliographic value of the volume should justify the expense.

Torn pages are another common problem discovered at the book return. Such books should *never* be repaired with pressure-sensitive adhesive tape. While several library suppliers advertise "archival" adhesive tapes that are safe for repair, none have proved satisfactory. Some libraries will tape a volume together if it needs to survive another few months on reserve before it is discarded. This is a poor practice because it suggests to the public that adhesive tape on torn books is safe; it is not.

Torn pages can be mended with Japanese tissue paper and paste, but this takes time and skill; no staff member should attempt this repair without training. A heat-set tissue, which is adhered to the page with a heated tacking iron, is also used for repairs, but it is not as durable a repair as one made using the traditional method. While heat-set tissue and a tacking iron are easier for an amateur to use, conservators find this technique awkward and usually make repairs employing the traditional method more quickly, achieving a repair that is virtually invisible. Heat-set tissue will make a better repair on highly calendared modern papers with little or no texture, as it sets better.

Torn pages can also be replaced with photocopies, but the copies must be made on alkaline paper. Tipping in replacement pages, or loose pages, is a simple procedure that can be done in-house if a staff member has had some training and practice.

Books that are returned badly marked with pencil often

can be cleaned using an architect's soft rubber eraser. The marks should be rubbed carefully and gently with the grain of the paper; overzealous erasing can wear a hole through a page. Books annotated in ink, alas, cannot be cleaned in the library. While some inks can be removed by a conservator using chemical solvents, ballpoint inks and most Magic Marker inks are a permanent reminder of a reader's abuse.

In-house repairs are feasible, if they are done with great care in an appropriate space. During training, prospective technicians should practice first on materials that are of minor value. The work should be reviewed regularly by a conservator. It is essential that a technician understand the reason for treatment decisions and anticipate what potentially can go wrong even when doing the simplest procedure. Conservators have seen many books with holes in their pages and/or loss of text caused by heavy-handed cleaning. The use of inappropriate adhesives and glues make subsequent conservation treatments more difficult and complex. Polyester encapsulated items placed in contact with the sealing adhesive tape are all too common a sight. A number of books and videos are available on the repair of library and archival materials, but in the main, staff members should not attempt most repairs. Leave the job to the professional conservator or trained conservation technician.

Shelving Books

As books spend most of their lives on shelves, shelf conditions have a direct effect upon their life expectancy. Usually shelving is done by custodial, student, or clerical personnel. It is imperative that each shelver, as well as all staff members, be aware of the proper methods of shelving books. The following guidelines for the shelving of books and other library materials are recommended:

1. Shelves should never be crowded. A shelf is considered too full when a book will not slide back into its place with a gentle push. A packed shelf can crack the spines of books. Further damage can result when a person attempts

to remove a volume, pulling it from the top of the spine, at the headband, to loosen it. If the reader encounters a volume wedged tightly on the shelf, the desired volume should be eased out by pushing in the volumes on either side of it, then carefully grasping the center of the spine and removing it.

2. Most books should be shelved vertically. When a book is askew on a shelf, stresses are placed on the spine leading to premature cracking or tearing, then covers become loose and corners break. Books shelved haphazardly can easily fall off the shelf. Books that are shelved with the fore-edge placed on the bottom will soon fall out of their cases; *gravity always wins*. Shelves should be adjusted to the proper height for the books they house. Oversized folio volumes should be housed separately. Ideally, elephant folios should be stored flat, one to a shelf that is adjusted to be slightly larger than the volume. If folio volumes are to be stacked, a poor idea, the largest should be placed on the bottom and the smallest on the top. More than three volumes should never be stacked together. If a reader needs the volume on the bottom, he or she will have to remove those above it with care.

3. Sturdy library bookends should be used to support the books on a shelf and should be the appropriate size to support the books firmly. Short bookends cannot support tall books. Bookends with a wide profile provide the best support. If bookends are not sufficiently sturdy, they will soon bend, which can easily lead to torn covers and pages. Sharp bookend edges can cut both people and books. If they must be used, the corners should be filed down. Better yet, they can be covered with buckram, the fabric used for the binding of most library books. Non-skid bookends should always be used. If they are not immediately available, a thin sheet or strip of rubber or other nonskid material can be cemented to the bottom to prevent slippage.

4. Very thin volumes should be housed on slotted shelves, which allow the insertion of fixed dividers at intervals along the shelf. Shelving with brackets that attach to the underside to separate materials below are

effective. Regular bookends, with a single flat upright piece also can be used, spaced intermittently along the shelf to provide support and stability.

5. There should be some space left behind the books on the shelves to allow the air to circulate freely. Insufficient air circulation will encourage the growth of mildew in warm, damp weather. The shelves should be wide enough for the books to stand free, about one inch from the front, with spines in an even line parallel to the front of the shelf. This will simplify shelf reading and reduce the possibility of small volumes being pushed to the back of the shelf; it also equalizes the pressure on the shelved books and reduces the mental fatigue of the shelf reader. If shelves are kept tidy, the users will tend to leave them that way.

To ensure proper stack maintenance, one staff member should have specific responsibility for a given area of stacks. The stack attendant is responsible for the daily shelving, daily tidying up of the area, and for shelf reading. He or she should also be responsible for keeping the shelves clean and removing books for review when they appear to be in poor condition. The stack attendants should be encouraged to suggest shifts of materials, rearrangement of shelves, requests for more bookends, or other needs. The stack attendants are in the front line of a library's preservation program. Their assistance in maintaining the collection should be solicited and their contribution to a sound preservation program should be acknowledged.

The Packing of Books for Shipment

Many libraries use padded bags for shipping books. This is a relatively inexpensive method of transport encouraged by the postal authorities; books packaged in this manner can be easily processed by automatic sorting equipment. Experience has shown, however, that this is not the most reliable and safe way to send books. Too frequently, and especially when there is only one book in a bag, the corners of the book can get bent and battered through rough handling at the post office or in transit.

When books of moderate value are to be shipped, such as interlibrary loan materials, it is best to secure each book in tightly wrapped kraft paper or plastic bubble wrap. If there is more than one book to a shipment, the books should be laid in two short stacks, spine to spine. Then a protective layer of corrugated cardboard is placed on the top and bottom of the book or books with supporting pieces placed around the edges, reducing the possibility of damage to the materials during shipment. A sensible precaution against water damage is to place a wrapping of polyethylene-lined paper around the package, sealing the seams. The parcel is finally covered with another layer of kraft paper wrapping and sealed with pressure-sensitive filament-reinforced tape. The package should present a flat appearance, as flat parcels travel better and are less frequently damaged.

Rare and/or fragile items should not circulate on interlibrary loan. If they are being lent for exhibition, they should be hand delivered by a courier. A more secure method is recommended for wrapping such materials. First, the book is wrapped in glassine, a plasticlike slick paper that prevents abrasion. Next it is wrapped in a cellulose packing material that provides both cushioning and insulation. The package is then wrapped in polyethylene-lined kraft paper and all seams are sealed with pressure-sensitive tape. Layers of corrugated cardboard are then placed on the top and bottom of the book, and supporting pieces are placed around the edges. The package is then wrapped in kraft wrapping paper. This method is fully described by Paul Banks in his essay, "Preservation of Library Materials," in the *Encyclopedia of Library and Information Science*, volume 23, 198–199.

Books to be moved from one building to another can be packed in sturdy cartons or crates. They should be placed upright in one layer, as they will be damaged more easily if placed in different directions, especially when the books are placed on top of one another. Care in planning and engineering when moving collections can eliminate many of the hazards.

Selected Reading

Association of Research Libraries. Office of Management Studies. *Preservation Guidelines in ARL Libraries.* Washington, DC: September 1987. (SPEC Kit 137).

Atkinson, Ross W. "Selection for Preservation: A Materialistic Approach." *Library Resources and Technical Services* 30:4 (October–December 1986): 341–353.

Boomgaarden, Wesley L. "Preservation Planning for the Small Library." *Special Libraries* 76:3 (Summer 1985): 204–211.

Clark, Lenore, ed. *Guide to Review of Library Collections: Preservation, Storage, and Withdrawal.* Chicago: American Library Association, 1991. (Collection Management and Development Guides, 5).

Dean, John. "Conservation Officers: The Administrative Role." *Wilson Library Bulletin* 57:2 (October 1982): 128–132.

Hazen, Don C. "Collection Development, Collection Management, and Preservation." *Library Resources and Technical Services* 26:1 (January–March 1982): 3–11.

Larsen, A. Dean and Randy Silverman. "Preservation." *Library Technical Services: Operations and Management,* 2nd ed., ed. Irene P. Godden. New York: Academic Press, 1991, 205–269.

Lewis, Ralph H. *Manual for Museums.* Washington, DC: National Park Service, 1976.

Waters, Peter. "Phased Preservation: A Philosophical Concept and Practical Approach to Preservation." *Special Libraries* 81:1 (Winter 1990): 35–43.

IV. ENEMIES OF BOOKS
Introduction

" " **A** LIBRARY IS A CONCENTRATION OF FOODSTUFFS, including starches, cellulose, and proteins which form a banquet for insects, rodents, and mold;" states Thomas A. Parker, an entomologist who specializes in pest control in libraries and museums.(1) Consequently, library materials are often attacked and damaged by these pests. Throughout history, librarians have attempted to eliminate the presence of pests and microorganisms in libraries through a variety of approaches, some more effective than others. Today it is recognized that the most effective pest control can be achieved through a sound integrated pest management program, known as IPM. IPM "minimizes, and in some instances may actually eliminate, the use of chemicals, in their place emphasizing cultural, mechanical, and biological controls."(2) It is a decision-making approach to pest control that considers the whole ecosystem when determining methods to suppress insect, rodent, and/or mold infestation. IPM has four basic components:

1. regular monitoring of pest activity and the environment;
2. determination of the tolerance level for a given pest population;
3. selection and application of control methods, emphasizing the least toxic treatments;
4. evaluation of treatments through continued monitoring.(3)

The IPM approach to pest control in libraries is important because of an increasing awareness of the hazards of chemical pest control measures. Chemical measures can have serious and harmful side effects on the people who work in libraries, those who use library materials, and on the materials themselves. Library personnel have legitimate concerns about exposure to pesticides, especially because pesticides are retained for a considerable length of time in materials that have been exposed to them. Books can be stained, altered, or even destroyed by contact with pesticides. The fogs that traditionally have been used to disinfect libraries are usually oil-based; during application, small droplets of the oil/insecticide mixture are dispensed into the air and eventually settle on materials in the area.(4)

The "least chemical approach" strategy depends first and foremost upon good housekeeping practices and environmental control strategies. The goal is to prevent pests from entering the library. Unfortunately, librarians have little control over the conditions in the homes of their patrons, nor of where materials may reside while in transit. The library building can, however, be secured against pest invasion, and the staff can regularly monitor the collections to prevent potential infestations. Regular cleaning of a facility will remove a number of the food sources that appeal to pests. Environmental control will also make the collection less susceptible to mold and fungal infestation, because both generally prefer moist, warm conditions.

An important measure that a library can take to control pest infestation is to learn to identify pests that are common to libraries and the traces of their presence. Some academic institutions have entomologists on their faculty who can be called upon to identify insects found in libraries and advise on their domestic habits. Some of the more common pests are described on the following pages.

Insects

We have all heard about bookworms, tiny creatures who live among and omnivorously devour books. But until we encounter our first larvae or insect in a book-in-hand, we are not really convinced that they exist. Bookworms and

other insect species do exist and thrive on books. Insects
are not as great a problem in the temperate climate of
North America or Northern Europe as in the tropics, but
they exist in sufficient numbers to cause serious damage
to library and archival collections. A librarian will probably encounter a variety of species in the course of a career.
In a charming and informative little book (if the appalling
drawings are disregarded), *Facts About Bookworms* (London, 1898), the Reverend Father J.F.X. O'Connor, then
Librarian of Georgetown University, describes his first
encounter with a bookworm:

> On a summer's day in the venerable Georgetown
> Library where it seemed that the old tomes had kept
> within them the odor of ages past, as I beheld in my
> hand an open folio bound in leather, a little ridge of
> dust along the inner edge of the binding attracted my
> attention. On closer examination I found small holes
> near the edge of the dust heap. Taking a pen-knife I
> raised the paper on the inside of the cover. What
> behold! there before me lay a little brown insect. It was
> covered with bristles and looked for all the world like
> a tiny hedge hog, curling himself in his spikes to insure
> protection.(5)

Beetles and other devourers of books have existed and
damaged libraries since antiquity. Aristotle noted in chapter 32, Book V, of his *Historia Animalium* that "in books
also other animals like those found in cloth, resembling
tailless scorpions, but very small" can be found, believed
to be a species of book scorpion, *Chelifer Cancroides*.
Pliny and several medieval authors have made note of
small creatures that they have found in books, but it was
not until the end of the seventeenth century that scholars
and naturalists began to examine more closely the creatures found in their books, and to identify and describe
them. At the beginning of the nineteenth century, the
Royal Society of Goettingen investigated the problem to
determine what kinds of insects were destructive to books
and documents, what materials in books they feed upon,
and what the best methods of controlling them might be.

Their recommendations are summarized in Mathias Koops' *Historical Account of the Substances Which Have Been Used to Describe Events and to Convey Ideas, from the Earliest Date to the Invention of Paper* (2nd ed., London 1801). Koops' recommendations include: (1) the abolition of the use of wood and woolen cloth for binding books; (2) that bookbinders use glue mixed with alum in place of paste; and (3) that books be aired and dusted frequently. The third recommendation fits into current IPM practice.

Oils and varnishes were the earliest preservatives used to protect against insect and fungal infestation of books and documents. These early methods often caused nearly as much damage to the materials that were treated as the insects themselves. By the beginning of the twentieth century, European librarians and scholars turned serious attention to methods for preventing insect infestation in libraries. Until recently, however, there were few books devoted to the topic of insect enemies of books. The classic study by C. Houlbert, *Les Insects Enemies des Livres* (Insect Enemies of Books, Paris, 1903), won an award from the International Congress of Librarians, for whom the study was done. In the past two decades there has been considerable research into techniques for curtailing the very serious damage that insects can cause to collections within a short period of time. Today a number of books and pamphlets are available to assist in the identification of pests and in determining how best to eliminate them. Several are cited at the end of this chapter and in the bibliography. Following is a brief description of the insects that are commonly found in the temperate zone of North American libraries.

Cockroaches

There are more than 3,500 known species of cockroaches in the world.[6] The German cockroach (*blatta germanica*) is the most common roach in North America. It is typically 1/2 inch long, pale brown in color, and has two dark longitudinal stripes on the thorax. The German cockroach is often found in cooking areas and other warm, moist areas. Another common species is the American cockroach (*periplaneta americana*). It is large, 1 $^1/_2$ inches or more in size, with long reddish-brown wings and a sleek thorax marked with a diffused central dark blotch. The American cockroach is often found in basements, bathrooms, and around pipes and plumbing fixtures. The oriental cockroach (*blatta orientalis*) is about an inch long, dark brown or black in color, with wings shorter than its body. The female is nearly wingless. The oriental cockroach is also often found in cool, damp areas, such as basements and around pipes. The brown-banded cockroach (*supella supellectilium*) has more recently appeared in North America. It is normally under a half-inch in length and darkish in color, the male being more slender and lighter colored than the female. It has a light horizontal band on the thorax. The brown-banded cockroach is often found in warm, dry areas, such as closets and drawers.

The cockroach is a creature of darkness, a survivor from prehistoric times. Cockroaches are suspected of spreading disease. Their bodies are equipped to invade any nook and cranny. Cockroaches are most active at night, and water is more essential to their survival than food. Binding glues and cellulose are attractive food sources. American cockroaches often stain library materials with a brown liquid as they feed on books. Because cockroaches reproduce at a constantly high rate, immediate action is called for when they are spotted to prevent damage if an area becomes infested.

Cockroach infestation is prevented by scrupulous cleanliness, which is why it is important that patrons not be permitted to eat and drink in the library and staff eating is restricted to an area well removed from the stacks. Roaches, however, can invade when they are hidden away in a book returned by a patron living in an infested house, so the library staff should be constantly on guard against these insect pests.

In order to avoid infestation from neighboring areas, pipelines should be tightly sealed to prevent insects entering through floor and basement walls and all cracks should be filled. Floor drains should be covered with insect screening to prevent ingress from municipal sewer systems. Good housekeeping coupled with a keen eye should prevent major infestations of cockroaches even in metropolitan areas.

Cockroach control is usually a job for a professional pest control operator. One or two treatments will usually eliminate the problem of cockroach infestation. However, as chemical means of extermination can be harmful, it is wise to discuss the plan of action and possible effects on people and materials with pest control personnel before treatment of a building.

Silverfish (Lepisma saccharina)

This primitive insect is also known as fish-moth, silver moth, sugar-fish, bristle tail, sugar louse, or slicker. This small, white-gray, glistening, carrot-shaped insect will grow up to a half inch long and scurry rapidly when exposed to light. Silverfish feed on vegetable and dead insect matter and are particularly fond of library materials: bookbindings, papers, cards, and boxes. They especially like bindings and sized paper, or any area where there is glue. Silverfish also like the corrugated cardboard boxes indigenous to libraries and tend to nest and breed in them.

Silverfish are very rarely found in dry, light, well-ventilated areas. Ordinary good housekeeping procedures should keep their numbers down in libraries. If they appear numerous or if any indication of their damage is found in books, a pest control expert should be called to deal with the problem.

Book Lice (Psocids, Troctes divinatoria)

These minute insects are also known as dust lice, bark lice, or deathwatches. A person with keen eyesight may perceive a book louse, scarcely more than a millimeter in size, scurrying across a page. It is a pale, almost colorless, wingless soft-bodied insect with a well-developed head and chewing mouth parts. The diet of the book louse consists of animal and vegetable matter, most often the microorganisms that develop on library and archival materials when they are stored in damp and musty conditions. They will also eat starches used to size books and photographs.

Book lice are not considered a significant enough problem to adopt special measures for their control. If they are found in old books, a thorough airing, drying, and cleaning of the room where they have been found is all that is necessary. Dry heat at 140 degrees Fahrenheit for three or four hours will destroy them should they appear to be a problem in the library.

Moths

There are several species of moths that are responsible for damage in North America. While most people are aware of their preference for fabrics, especially woolens, they will also eat leather and certain bindings. Adult moths lay their eggs on the object upon which their larvae will feed. The larvae are small, from 1/16th of an inch when first born to a third of an inch when full grown, and they are of whitish color. It is unlikely that moths will infest a library if cleanliness and proper ventilation prevail.

Bookworms

The infamous bookworm is actually the larva of certain species of beetle. Eggs are laid on the edges of books and the larvae, when they hatch, burrow into the books proper, eating their way through the leaves, leaving little tunnels. The most infamous is the drugstore beetle (*Sidodrepa panicea*), which is addicted to books as well as drugs and is the species that invaded the Huntington Library in the early 1930s.(7) It is cylindrical in form and about a tenth of an inch in length. The larvae are white, cylindrical, and curved, with dark mouth parts. These grubs can penetrate a book and munch through it to emerge as a beetle after about fifteen days.

The white-marked spider beetle (*Ptinus fur*) was first observed by Linnaeus, who noted that it was injurious to libraries. The larvae resemble those of the drugstore beetle, and their cycle and dietary habits are very similar.

The larder beetle (*Dermestes lardarius*) appears to be the culprit that Father O'Connor found in great number in the older books in the Georgetown Library. Normally it feeds on animal matter, such as ham and cheese, found in larders, as well as horsehair, skins, and dried beeswax. It will eat leather bindings when nothing more appetizing is available. Larder beetles are dark brown, with a yellowish band across their wing covers, and they are about a third of an inch in size. Their larvae become full-grown after about a month and a half.

Termites (reticulitermes flavipes or "Reticulitermes"— Southern Termite)

Workers are white, occasionally with a dark head, and are 4.5 to 7 mm in size. Soldiers are white or brown with enlarged heads, usually brown, 4.5 to 8 mm in size. The winged forms have a black or dark brown body, with grayish or smoky wings, and are 8 to 12 mm in size.

These insects, which are sometimes called white ants, although they are neither white nor ants, are creatures of wood-boring or subterranean habits, creatures of darkness that have inhabited the earth for millions of years. They build their nests in the ground or in logs and extend them to building timber that may be in contact with the ground. They live in colonies that are highly organized into caste systems. Their primary foodstuff is cellulose and includes grass, humus, dried plants, timber, woodwork, other termites, books, files, photographs, prints, and catalog cards. Their damage to books is secondary to their damage to woodwork, and they attack books and paper only after they have eaten through the wood in contact with them. Their presence can be detected by tunnels, fine dust, and droppings, the presence of dead winged termites or their wings near infested wood, and/or when large numbers of winged termites are swarming. Dogs are now trained to detect termites.

Termite-proofing is the only method that provides a permanent barrier against reinfestation. A professional pest control expert should be called to advise on termite-proofing and on eliminating existing populations of termites in a building and in soil near the infested area. Killing adult winged termites when they are found may cut down the reproductive cycle, but it is only a part of the real cure, which requires the attention of the professional pest control expert.

Mold and Mildew

Molds are numerous and subsist on organic matter. They are actively responsible for the decomposition of cellulose, which is the basis of most paper. Molds stain paper with a variety of colored spots. Their deleterious effect was recognized shortly after paper was introduced into the western world. In 1221, Frederick II of the Holy Roman Empire decreed that all acts recorded on cotton paper were invalid and had to be transcribed onto parchment within two years because paper was susceptible to such damage. Mold spores are everywhere, but they thrive and germinate in a moist, warm atmosphere where there is poor ventilation. Parker notes that "when the relative humidity of a library exceeds 75 percent and remains in this range for a period of time, serious mold problems will result on library materials. Even if temperatures are low, the effects of high humidity will stimulate spores to germinate en masse."(8) Molds and mildew are the two common forms of fungi that are found in North America.

It is best to house library and archival materials in air-conditioned, well-ventilated quarters, but if this is impossible, ventilation is possible by installing fans. Books that have been packed too tightly on the shelves are especially prone to fungal attack. Mildew can be eliminated if the temperature is kept below 70 degrees Fahrenheit and the relative humidity (RH) below 60 percent, with the free circulation of air. Controlling the environment of the library is the best and safest way to curtail or avoid mold and mildew problems.

When mildew or mold first appear on book covers, the infected areas will be white in color and the book itself will have a musty odor. Small lots of books can be decontaminated by moving them promptly into a well-ventilated dry area. Active mold spores can be brushed off with a small sable-tipped brush or vacuumed with a brush attachment and a wet/dry vacuum containing diluted germicide in water. The covers and endpapers of a book should always be examined carefully, for these are the places where mildew first appears. Covers can be gently wiped off with a lightly dampened cloth. Books should be left to dry in fresh or well-circulated air for two or three days.

During the 1970s a number of libraries installed vacuum-sealed fumigators in which books and documents could be treated for mold and insect infestation using ethylene oxide gas, a powerful fumigant. Early in the 1980s conservators learned that this treatment was hazardous for the people responsible for it and that there was a strong possibility that a residue of the chemicals left on treated materials could be hazardous to future users. Such fumigation chambers are no longer used.

Entomologist Thomas Parker notes: "Attempts to control mold on library materials by using various chemicals . . . are usually ineffective. As soon as these chemicals have volatilized from the surface, the object is vulnerable to new mold spores landing on the surface."(9) Over the years, conservators have used a variety of chemicals to destroy mold, but they are increasingly aware of their harm and their ineffectiveness. Thymol chambers are still used by some conservators and in some libraries. Thymol, however, has proved to be a carcinogenic chemical, and, once the thymol is volatilized from the object, that object is no longer protected from a new invasion of mold spores. Prevention of the problem is its solution.

The annoying rust-brown measlelike spots that are

frequently found on paper in older books and prints are known as foxing. Foxing is evidence that fungi have been at work but are no longer active. Foxing can also be a result of the chemical action between iron impurities in the paper and the organic acids released by the paper. Foxing is especially evident in books manufactured in the eighteenth and nineteenth centuries, when paper was made by machines that produced particularly thin fibers. Foxing stains can be removed only by bleaching, a hazardous operation that can easily damage a book or print. Bleaching is not recommended for most library materials; it is a treatment that should be undertaken only by an experienced conservator. In short, foxing is an unpleasantness best ignored.

Freezing Infested Materials

In the late 1970s the Beinecke Rare Books and Manuscript Library at Yale University experienced an infestation of bookworms. An astute library assistant noticed dead beetles and sawdust on a shelf in the stack area. Inspection revealed a species of deathwatch beetle, common in the Mediterranean area where the infested books had come from, although the species was a new one, unique to Yale. When the insects were first detected, advice was sought from Professor Charles L. Remington, curator of entomology at Yale's Peabody Museum of Natural History, who recommended a deep-freezing technique to kill the insects and their larvae. Starting with 167 infested volumes, moving through the entire floor, and finally throughout all the floors in the Beinecke Library, books were packed in individual polyethylene bags, then placed in a blast-freezer chamber constructed for the purpose in the basement of the library. The books remained in a chamber at a temperature of −20 degrees Fahrenheit for 72 hours. The books that were infested and the entire Beinecke collection has been carefully monitored since that time for further signs of infestation. None has been found. The treatment was effective.

If traditional fumigation procedures had been followed,

the building would have been vacated and sealed for treatment, a method now known to be harmful to people and to books. The deep-freezing technique was controversial when it was introduced to solve Yale's problem, but the technology has been explored in the past decade and appears to offer a safe and reliable solution to insect infestation in library and archival collections.

Infested materials are treated by freezing them rapidly (blast freezing), at below zero Fahrenheit, thawing them, then refreezing them. The first freezing cycle will kill at least 90 percent of the larvae; the second freezing cycle is to ensure that all potentially damaging insect stages have been killed. Scientist Mary-Lou Florian continues to work on this technique at the Canadian Conservation Institute. Freezing is a safe "mass treatment" for infested materials, one that is also applied to the salvage of water-damaged materials. A prototype freezer, developed by Richard Smith of Wei T'o, Inc., was in use at Columbia's School of Library Service for the Conservation Program. It is hoped that the technology will be available to libraries at a reasonable cost within a few years. Treatment centers, offered through a regional conservation center, or even the commercial library binder, may prove a solution to the problem of infestation. Some research library administrators are interested in the freezers to treat incoming materials from areas of the world known to be heavily infested with harmful pests. Yale University Library uses its freezer for the purpose.

Rodents

It is said that the rodent population is more numerous than the human population in the world's major cities. Because they are so rarely seen, it is difficult to realize that rodents are so abundant. Their attack on books and paper poses difficult problems for preservation. Rodents destroy books and paper to make their nests and can make an unpleasant, smelly mess. Yash Pal Kathpalia, who undertook considerable research on the preservation and conservation of library materials throughout the world, claimed that rodent damage may have affected as much as 20 percent of the total world's books.(9) Once rodents have settled into a building, they are difficult to dislodge. Infestation can be controlled if the exterior of a building is sealed as tightly as possible. George Cunha has written:

> The best protection against rodents is to deny them access by sound building construction, tight screens, and by plugging all holes in foundation walls, particularly around water and sewer pipes and gas mains. It is vitally important to eliminate conditions encouraging procreation of rats and mice. Dark, damp basements, pools of water, accumulations of waste and debris, and spilled food particles in eating areas all attract these pests.(10)

Fortunately, newer library buildings, due to care in construction, are not as vulnerable as older buildings. When evidence of rodents is found in a building, however, the first act is to inspect the building to determine and eliminate the source of access. A house mouse can enter through a hole as small as a dime.(11) Once infestation is discovered, mechanical traps are a useful devise for eliminating rodents. Toxic baiting programs should not be used, as the rodents will die in the walls, floor and ceilings of the building, causing an unpleasant odor and providing food for other harmful pests. It is important to inspect the building thoroughly on a regular basis to identify infested areas. Traps should be placed at spots where fecal droppings are discovered. Parker recommends that droppings be removed two or three weeks after a trapping program has begun to determine its success. He also recommends that trapping programs be initiated in late summer and fall when mice tend to invade buildings.

People

The best way to protect library and archival materials from biological infestation is to store them in temperature-controlled sealed vaults with uncontaminated air, well away from pests and people. People, by their careless handling of library materials and the bacteria and mold spores that they carry, are the creatures most injurious to books. But books and other library materials are for people, so libraries must rely upon a few rules to instill in their patrons some feeling of respect for the physical objects that they will handle.

Librarians themselves, as Randolph Adams observes in his famous article, "Librarians as Enemies of Books", are often guilty of treating their collections too casually. Who among us has not reviewed a few choice acquisitions over morning coffee or lunch, or nibbled a few sweets at the desk during the day? Perhaps it is unrealistic to expect that the staff and the public will give up all bad habits, but one should munch with care!

Food and drink should be prohibited in the library; coffee, ice cream, chocolate, and the like can cause considerable damage to books as well as attract pests. A number of libraries have initiated food campaigns to make the public aware of the problems that food can cause in a library building. Exhibitions, posters, and newspaper articles have drawn attention to the problem. Every member of the staff should be mindful of the problem and be trained to deal tactfully but firmly with patrons who are eating and drinking in the library.

Manuscripts and rare books require more protection than a general circulating collection. Pens should not be permitted for use by patrons working with these collections, for ink can cause considerable damage. Patrons should wash their hands before handling rare materials. Lessing J. Rosenwald, the great collector of rare books and incunabula, generously allowed qualified researchers to work with his materials and provided a special soap in a washroom for the purpose in his private library. A number of repositories, chiefly European, where the spirit of egalitarianism is less strong than in North America, provide trained attendants, or the curator, to turn the pages of rare books and manuscripts for readers. Thus, requesting our patrons to clean their hands before handling materials and to use pencils instead of pens does not seem unreasonable.

Summary

In the past decade, librarians, archivists, scientists, and conservators have made great strides in developing techniques and technologies for the preservation of collections. It is possible that by the end of the century regional centers will have specialists on their staff who can deal with the biological problems facing institutions that house cultural property. But the best prevention remains, and will remain, a controlled environment, good housekeeping procedures, and, more formally, an integrated pest management program. Many problems can be avoided by a library staff that cares for its collections, a staff with an awareness of the hazards to which its collections are subject, and one that constantly monitors the collections to identify small problems before they become big ones. The procedures for preventing damage are far simpler than those required for correcting damage.

Notes

1. Thomas Parker, "Integrated Pest Management for Libraries," *Preservation of Library Materials,* ed. Merrily Smith, vol 2 (Munich, New York: Saur, 1987), 103.
2. Michael Trinkley, president, Chicora Foundation, quoted in *Solinews* 16:4 (Spring 1990): 9.
3. *Ibid.*
4. Parker 105.
5. J.F.X. O'Connor, *Facts About Bookworms* (London: Suckling, 1898), 15–16.
6. William Olkowski, Helga Olkowski, and Sheila Daar. "IPM for the German Cockroach," *The IPM Practitioner* 6:3, 7.
7. Thomas M. Iiambs, "Preservation of Rare Books and Manuscripts in the Huntington Library," *Library Quarterly* 2:4 (1932): 375–386.
8. *Conservation of Library Materials* (Paris: Unesco, 1983), 64.
9. Parker 116.
10. George Martin and Dorothy G. Cunha, *Conservation of Library Materials,* vol. 1 (Metuchen, NJ: Scarecrow, 1972), 14.
11. Note from Sandra Nyberg, Field Service Officer, SOLINET, July 1990.

Selected Reading

Nyberg, Sandra. *The Invasion of the Giant Spore.* Atlanta, GA: Southeastern Library Network, November 1987. (SOLINET Preservation Program Leaflet, 5).

Parker, Thomas A. "Integrated Pest Management for Libraries." *Preservation of Library Materials,* vol. 2, ed. Merrily Smith. Munich, New York: Saur, 1987, 103–123.

Price, Lois Olcott. *Mold.* Philadelphia, PA: Conservation Center for Art and Historic Artifacts, 1994. 6 leaf pamphlet. (CCAHA Technical Series, 1).

Story, Keith O. *Approaches to Pest Management in Museums.* Washington, DC: Smithsonian Institution, Conservation Analytical Laboratory, 1985.

Zycherman, Lynda A. and John Richard Schrock, eds. *A Guide to Museum Pest Control.* Washington, DC: Foundation of the American Institute for Conservation/Association of Systematics Collections, 1988.

V. ENVIRONMENT AND PRESERVATION

A number of environmental factors contribute to the deterioration of books and other library materials. These include temperature, relative humidity, air pollution, dirt, and light. Each is related to the other and, when conditions in the library are poor, they can work together to cause serious damage within a short period of time. When these factors are controlled, the natural decay of library materials can be greatly retarded.

Temperature, Humidity, and Air Pollution

The temperature and relative humidity in a library building must be considered together, for they work together to preserve or destroy library and archival materials. This section will discuss some basic facts about the relationship between temperature and relative humidity and between relative humidity and absolute humidity. *Relative humidity* (RH) is the amount of the weight of the water vapor in a given volume of moist air. It is expressed as a percentage of the weight that would be contained in a small volume of saturated air at the same dry bulb temperature. Dry bulb temperature is determined by an accurate thermometer without the influence of evaporating water.

Absolute humidity is the actual weight of water vapor in a unit of moist air and is expressed in grams per cubic centimeter. As the temperature changes in a room, the absolute humidity often remains constant, but the relative humidity can fluctuate drastically. When considering the effect of temperature on library and archival materials, it is generally accepted that for every 21 degrees Fahrenheit (8 degrees Celsius) increase in temperature, the rate of the chemical action that destroys paper and bindings is doubled.(1)

Hygroscopic materials, materials that absorb and retain moisture, such as paper, will give up, adsorb, moisture when the relative humidity decreases and will absorb, take in, moisture when relative humidity increases. The approximate relationship between relative humidity and the water content of paper can be expressed thus: At 100 percent RH, moisture content in paper is about 30 percent; at 60 percent RH, moisture content in paper is about 7–8 percent; at 30 percent RH, moisture content in paper is about 5–6 percent. Fluctuations of temperature and relative humidity are most damaging to paper-based materials, especially when they occur over a short period of time. These rapid changes stress and break down the paper fibers. Fluctuations of temperature and relative humidity will cause more damage than constantly high readings. A low temperature, in and of itself, does little damage to books, but a high temperature coupled with low relative humidity will dry out paper, adhesives, and leather bindings. A high temperature coupled with a high relative humidity (more than 70 percent) encourages the growth of mold and fungi and will, in addition, accelerate the general decomposition of paper. The moisture in the air in immediate contact with an object can often vary considerably from that of the room in which the object is housed. Therefore it is essential to see that humidity and temperature are controlled together in a library building. Most library and archival materials will survive best in cool temperatures, zero degrees Fahrenheit or less. As people cannot work in such an environment, the temperature can safely range in the mid to upper sixties as long as it remains nearly constant. Relative humidity should be maintained at between 35 and 50 percent. Once the RH is more than 60 percent, the possibility of microbiological infestation arises. The rate of the decomposition of paper will also increase.

As people grow familiar with the need to conserve natural resources, it is possible for libraries to lower the temperature somewhat in the winter and allow it to rise slightly in the summer. However, temperature in the building must not exceed 70 degrees Fahrenheit. The relative humidity should be in the 35–40 percent range in the winter; higher RH levels can cause damage to the fabric of the building. The relative humidity will rise in the summer months, but it should never exceed 60 percent. Collections can be slowly acclimated to changes in temperature and relative humidity during the seasonal changes within a four- to six-week time period.

In addition to fluctuating temperature and relative humidity, many collections are vulnerable to the effects of air pollution and smog. In industrial areas, sulphur dioxide is released into the air; automobiles release tons of raw gasoline and nitrous oxide daily; heating by-products release numerous chemical compounds. All of these pollute the atmosphere in which we live. In addition, nature can compound the matter by creating an air inversion, keeping those pollutants in a tight circle around and above us. Air pollutants can weaken nylon hosiery, cause headaches and watery eyes, and even cause fatalities. Therefore it is not surprising that air pollution damages library materials. It is only within the past two decades that the Western world has made a serious attempt to grapple with the hazards of air pollution. We do not yet know the extent that it has affected humankind and the objects of our cultural heritage. In the temperate industrialized climate of North America, the chemicals in polluted air can compound the damage inflicted upon library and archival materials caused by fluctuations in temperature and relative humidity. An informal examination of several books, published in the late nineteenth and early twentieth centuries, held in the New York Public Library and the Royal Library in The Hague, Netherlands, dramatically demonstrated the effect of a poor environment on library materials. The books held at the Royal Library, although made of poor materials, were in relatively good condition. The air of The Hague is not unduly polluted and its climate is somewhat cool and moist. New York

City is highly polluted and located in a region of wildly fluctuating extremes of temperature and humidity between and within seasons.

The most reasonable solution to curtail the slow decay of library materials is to install an air-conditioning and air-filtration system, referred to as the heating, ventilating, and air-conditioning (HVAC) system. An environmental control system, when designed and operated in the interest of library materials, and in accordance with the tolerance of the building envelope, provides the fullest and most effective control against damage caused by fluctuating temperature and relative humidity and air pollution. The decision to install an environmental control system in older buildings is a serious one because of its feasibility. An air-conditioning system can be very damaging to older structures that were not designed for them. If an HVAC system can be installed, the cost may be considerable. It is advisable to have an environmental consultant survey the building to determine what can be done to curtail fluctuations in temperature and relative humidity and to control air pollution. Often methods can be implemented that will work successfully and not cause damage to the building envelope. Too many librarians with collections in older buildings have learned the hard way about the damage that a new, ill-considered HVAC system can cause.

It is important to be sure that the environmental control system that is installed in new buildings is suitable for the building. The construction of a building and the site are important factors in the installation of a system. A high-technology system, finely tuned, is extremely complicated to maintain and few institutions have the expertise necessary to do so. Such systems, out of control, have caused serious damage to library and museum collections. There are now a number of consultants available to assist in the planning and installation of environmental control systems for libraries, archives, and museums, and they are well worth their fee.

A sensible, low-cost approach to environmental control is the use of humidifiers and dehumidifiers to raise or lower the relative humidity in an area as necessary. Local air-conditioning units can be used to cool air in the summer. Fans can be used to keep air circulating. Double-glazed windows and/or thermal drapes can be installed. The library should keep a hygrothermograph in operation, or at least a recording hygrometer, to measure relative humidity on a regular basis. This equipment can be used to check conditions around the library, so action can be taken if the humidity becomes either too high or too low.

Light

The radiant energy of light absorbed by the molecules in an object can damage it. Nearly all library materials are susceptible to light damage. Much of the light energy entering a room is converted into heat, but even the minute fraction of light absorbed by library materials is responsible for the acceleration of natural deterioration.

RH Indicator Card
Credit: Light Impressions Corporation

RH Hygrometer
Credit: Light Impressions Corporation

The most damaging of the light wavelength ranges is ultraviolet. This is the shorter range of the spectrum. But all light is harmful. Objects exposed to direct sunlight are particularly threatened; observe how frequently curtains must be replaced. Sunlight is rich in visible and ultraviolet light. The poorer grades of paper, made of wood pulp, will disintegrate in a short period of time when exposed to direct light. This is illustrated graphically when a page of the daily newspaper is left by a window for a few days. This damage is caused by photolysis, the rupture by light rays of the bonds in the paper molecules. This starts a chain reaction that causes a loss of strength and discoloration in paper. It is aggravated by the synergistic effect of air pollutants, high temperature, and the impurities within paper itself.

Damage from light, especially ultraviolet rays, can be prevented by allowing as little light as possible to enter areas where library and archival materials are stored. Patrons and staff should be urged to "conserve" by turning out lights in stack areas when they have finished working in them. There are lighting systems for libraries and archives that will turn off automatically when people leave the area. On/off systems and/or timers can be installed easily in the stack area. Incandescent lighting is usually less harmful in ultraviolet light than fluorescent lighting, although it generates more heat. Yet, fluorescent lighting, high in ultraviolet content, is usually installed in libraries because it generates less heat and is more economical to operate. Special filters, treated plastic sleeves, can be purchased to cover fluorescent lighting tubes. They curtail the harmful ultraviolet rays; they can be more effective in preventing damage to the materials than incandescent lighting. These sleeves will be effective for several years, but they should be checked periodically to ensure that they are offering the necessary protection. Readings taken with a photographer's light meter on a regular basis will document visible light levels; a Crawford UV meter will measure ultraviolet light levels.

Halogen lighting systems are now available on the market. They have fewer ultraviolet light rays than fluorescent lighting and are more efficient to operate, but their initial cost to install remains high. Nonetheless, we are on the threshold of more effective, efficient, and protective lighting systems that may be available for libraries, archives and museums during the 1990s. Research into light and its effect on cultural objects, as well as people, continues at a rapid pace. It is probable that much will be published on the subject of lighting in cultural institutions during the decade.

From the days when natural light was the primary source of illumination, libraries have been designed with windowed areas. Large windows are common in library buildings constructed from the late 1940s to the early 1970s, and they continue to be designed and built by architects and librarians who are unaware of the harmful effect of light and heat on library material, and on the people who must work near windows. Such buildings have proved difficult to maintain; readers protest when excessive light and heat enter a room, but the materials that are exposed quietly disintegrate. Whenever possible, windowed areas should be curtained to prevent the harmful ultraviolet rays from penetrating a room. It is possible to purchase ultraviolet shielding sheets to place over windows for protection, a costly, yet often necessary measure. Unfortunately, these sheets break down in a relatively short period of time, admitting unwanted light and becoming unsightly in appearance. Large ultraviolet filtering shades are also available for library windows and can be effective. Many libraries and museums have used whitewash on skylights and other windowed areas to provide their collections with some protection. Expanses of windows do not belong in library buildings; they are harmful to the collections and to the users.

Design and Renovation of Buildings

Many librarians have to make the best of buildings that were constructed without consideration for the maintenance and protection of collections or the comfort of users. Librarians who are fortunate enough to receive funds for a new building or the renovation of an older structure need to be aware of the environmental factors that play a key role in the preservation of collections and the comfort of patrons and staff. The late Keyes D. Metcalf, distinguished librarian of Harvard University, planned innumerable library buildings in a career that spanned over fourscore and ten years. He wrote prolifically on library planning and design.(2) His 1965 text, *Planning Academic and Research Library Buildings* (McGraw-Hill), has been revised and expanded by David C. Weber and Philip Leighton of Stanford University (American Library Association, 1986). The revised edition takes a more theoretical approach than the classic 1965 edition, but much of the best material in Metcalf's original text is retained. Metcalf's chapters on lighting and heating, ventilating, and air-conditioning (HVAC) systems in the 1965 volume remain timely and accurate. The 1986 edition makes the care and preservation of library materials a primary consideration in the planning of a building. Metcalf, 1965 and 1986 editions, should be read with care by *every* librarian who is planning a new building, an addition, or a renovation. Metcalf clearly recognized the need for library buildings that would preserve collections as well as promote access, and he did not see a dichotomy between the two goals.

There are four points that should be considered when planning for library construction:

1. Library construction should be such that it prevents infestation from rodents and insects.
2. Air-conditioning equipment, humidifiers, and filtering systems should be installed in new buildings to inhibit atmospheric damage to library materials.
3. The building should be designed so that minimal light, incandescent or halogen, is installed in areas where library materials are housed.
4. Construction should minimize the hazards of fire and water damage.

Once a librarian has communicated these needs to the

architect, the architect, as a specialist, should incorporate them in the design. But the librarian, in addition to memorizing Metcalf, should be familiar with the technical literature on library buildings and environment. Several organizations produce materials that are of considerable assistance when planning the construction of a library building. Both the International and the American Institutes for the Conservation of Historic and Artistic Works (IIC and AIC) are concerned with the development of standards for the construction of museums, libraries, and archives that will ensure the protection and preservation of their collections. The National Fire Protection Association (NFPA) is also concerned with the protection of library and archival collections; several of its publications, updated frequently, are essential reading when planning library construction. In addition, no program of construction should be undertaken before carefully studying relevant documents from the National Institute of Standards and Technology (NIST), formerly the National Bureau of Standards (NBS), the American National Standards Institute (ANSI), and Building Officials and Code Administrators International, Inc. (BOCA).

There are a variety of library building consultants available. The Library Administration and Management Association (LAMA) of the American Library Association (ALA) periodically issues a list of consultants from its membership. The list, however, does not endorse anyone, nor is it selective in any substantial way. The consultant may or may not be a professional librarian. Keyes Metcalf suggested that a consultant should have had experience with at least three previous buildings. By checking a consultant's previous projects, an administrator can make a reasoned choice.

A consultant should be involved in the planning process from its inception, when his or her advice will have the greatest impact. Metcalf has observed, "The mission of the consultant is to call to the attention of librarians and architects the problems they have to face, and to suggest different solutions to these problems rather than to tell them what to do." (3)

Exhibition

Libraries are under increasing pressure to exhibit their materials as a part of an institution's mission of education and outreach to the public. The exhibition of library materials dates back to the eighteenth century. John Cotton Dana, the distinguished American librarian and director of the Newark (NJ) Public Library and Museum, observed in 1909 that exhibition was a proper part of the library's work in the community.(4) Dana then, and librarians today, consider exhibition a part of "access", a catchword for the 1990s. Exhibitions are an effective means of making the public aware of library resources and can attract funding. New library buildings usually include exhibition space. Exhibitions, however, even when mounted for a brief period of time, can cause measurable damage to library and archival materials. This section will discuss how librarians can strive to balance the needs of preservation and access when planning for the exhibition of materials.

Temperature, relative humidity, air pollution, light, insects, and people are the "enemies" of library and archival materials. When planning an exhibition, the objective is to reduce, as much as possible, the physical damage that each can cause to the objects on display. This calls for careful planning, beginning with the exhibition space. Most libraries have to make do with space already allotted for exhibition and with antiquated cases. Other institutions are fortunate to be able to design or renovate new areas for exhibition, benefitting from the advice of one of the many knowledgeable consultants available today.

First assess the space allotted for exhibition and determine what is good and what is bad. The first priority is to curtail light, as it can cause rapid damage to library and archival materials. Skylights and windows can be sealed off or draped. The ambient light level in the room can be lowered; exhibitions can be viewed in a relatively low level of light. When the exhibition is closed, the room should be darkened. A light meter should be used to determine the amount of light striking the materials on display. These should be taken in natural and artificial light. Steps can be taken to control the environment of the exhibition area to ensure that temperature and relative humidity remain as constant as possible. Food and drink should not be permitted in the exhibition area, even at openings.

The exhibition cases should be carefully examined. Felt, the traditional material for the lining of cases, should be removed, as it attracts insects. A neutrally colored linen is an excellent lining for exhibition cases. Cases provide a microenvironment for the objects contained in them. Lighting in cases generates heat as well as the ultraviolet rays that are especially damaging to paper-based materials. There are a variety of approaches to the problem of lighting in cases, from shielding the bulbs with UV filters to placing mini-fans in cases to cause some ventilation. If possible, the light source for an object on display should be outside, not inside, the case. Silica gel can be used to help control fluctuations in relative humidity. There is a considerable body of literature on the use of silica gel to stabilize the environment surrounding materials on exhibition; several articles are cited in the bibliography at the end of this volume. Temperature and relative humidity levels in exhibition cases should be monitored on a regular basis. There are a variety of hygrometers available that can be placed unobtrusively in a case. A simple, inexpensive, and effective way to measure relative humidity is by placing an RH indicator card in each case. The change in color is obvious, and immediately signals a problem. These cards should be replaced every few months. A sophisticated public expects to see a monitored exhibition case; collections have been lost to institutions that did not bother to do so.

Materials considered for exhibition must have their physical condition assessed. Some materials simply are

RH Indicator Card
Credit: Light Impressions Corporation

too fragile for exhibition; their display today will prevent access in the future. Rare and fragile documents, such as the Declaration of Independence, are exhibited for long periods of time; however the measures taken to protect them are formidable, as is the cost. If there is a question about an object's ability to physically tolerate exhibition, a conservator should be consulted. The New York Public Library has a full-time conservator on its exhibitions staff; he participates in the decision process when items are reviewed for possible exhibition and prepares materials for display.

Once materials are selected for exhibition, special care should be taken in their display. Whenever possible, objects should be displayed flat. Upright exhibition cases have problems with the effect of gravity. Paper-based materials expand and contract as temperature and relative humidity fluctuate, so they cannot be nailed or strapped down. Pushpins have no place in an exhibition case; the "little hands" that are used to mark relevant passages in books and manuscripts on display are harmful. Documents, maps, and broadsides can be hinged to alkaline paper mats. Each book on display must be cradled, reducing stress on its spine and text block; stress on a volume can cause immediate damage. At one institution, a small Book of Hours, strapped into a holder for display, broke in half within twenty-four hours. Conservator Christopher Clarkson, when at the Library of Congress, developed custom-made Lucite cradles to support the Lessing W. Rosenwald collection, which was on display at the library in the early 1970s. Today a variety of adjustable Lucite cradles are available for purchase at reasonable cost. Cradles can also be made by a technician out of cardboard covered with fabric to fit each book. Instructions for the making of custom book cradles are readily available.

Paper-based materials, books, documents, maps, photographs, and works of art on paper should never be displayed longer than a month to six weeks. When books are exhibited, it is best to turn pages frequently to prevent too much exposure on any one page. When the great illuminated manuscripts of Ireland were lent for exhibition at several North American museums in 1977–1978, special cases were designed and constructed to display these priceless treasures. Atmospheric controls were built into each case. The pages of the manuscripts were turned every few days, even though they were exposed to minimal light. These cases set new standards for design. A similar principle was used for the exhibition of the Magna Charta in the United States in 1986. As the original Declaration of Independence and Constitution must be on display at the National Archives at all times, several million dollars were spent to design cases that protect these treasures from the environment.

Photographs are particularly sensitive to exhibition conditions. When displaying them, keep light levels as low as possible. Ultraviolet glazing, known as UV3, is recommended to protect photographic images from ultraviolet light, although it may distort the color and the image to some degree. Unless the photographic image has some intrinsic value that demands its display, it is wisest and safest to use copies, so identified, for exhibition. Even copies, however, should be protected.

Traveling exhibitions are a delight to the beholder and a bane to the librarian or archivist responsible for organizing them. No matter how carefully they are planned, it is impossible to anticipate all the hazards that the objects will encounter on their rounds. Facsimiles should be used in traveling exhibitions whenever possible; they can be nearly as effective as original documents. Adequate packaging of materials that are to travel is essential. Packaging should be simple, so it can be repeatedly disassembled and reassembled easily. Whenever possible, a curator or, better yet, a conservator should travel with an object to ensure its safety and should remain for its installation. The Rare Books and Manuscript Section, American Library Association, has recently developed *Guidelines for Borrowing Special Collections Materials for Exhibition*.(5) Despite any previous agreements, if a curator discovers that its institution's property is not exhibited properly, the objects should be removed from display.

After an object has been on exhibition, it should rest. For some reason, when they are returned to a quiet, dark, environmentally sound environment, library materials, like people, recover from the trauma of travel and exhibition. Thus, it is important to keep records on when, and for how long, materials have been on display. Ideally, items should not be put on display more than once every ten years.

Common sense and a knowledge of the physical nature of library and archival materials can help to curtail the harmful effects of exhibitions. There are a number of excellent guides to exhibition that are cited at the end of this chapter and in the bibliography at the end of the book.

Notes

1. Discussions with Ellen McCrady and information in her *Abbey Newsletter.*
2. Metcalf began helping in the Oberlin College Library, which his brother-in-law directed, as a child. He remained an active library consultant until his mid-90s. See his autobiographical books, *Random Recollections of an Anachronism.* New York: Readex Books, 1980, and *My Harvard Library Years.* Cambridge, MA: Harvard College Library, 1988.
3. Keyes Metcalf, "The Role of the Building Consultant," *College and Research Libraries* 40:3 (July 1969), 365.
4. Discussion with William Dane, Newark Public Library.
5. Published in *College & Research Libraries News* 51:5 (May 1990), 430–434.

Selected Readings

Applebaum, Barbara. *Guide to Environmental Protection of Collections.* Madison, CT: Sound View Press, 1991.

Casterline, Gail Farr. *Exhibitions.* Chicago: Society of American Archivists, 1980.

Lull, William P. *Conservation Environment Guidelines for Libraries and Archives.* Albany, NY: New York State Program for the Preservation of Library Research Materials, Division of Library Development, New York State Library [1991].

Metcalf, Keyes D. *Planning Academic and Research Library Buildings,* 2nd ed. by Philip Leighton and David C. Weber. Chicago: American Library Association, 1987.

Ogden, Sherelyn, ed. "The Environment." *Preservation of Library & Archival Materials.* Andover, MA: Northeast Document Conservation Center, 1992. Unpaged section.

Stolow, Nathan. *Conservation and Exhibitions: Packing, Transport, Storage and Environmental Conditions.* London: Butterworths, 1987.

Thomson, Garry. *The Museum Environment,* 2nd ed. London: Butterworths, 1986.

VI. EMERGENCY PLANNING AND LIBRARY SECURITY

Disaster Planning

The world discovered, following the disastrous flood of 1966 in Florence, Italy, that no cultural property is invincible against the onslaught of the elements: earth, air, fire, and water. A disaster can strike suddenly, be it mud slide, earthquake, tornado, hurricane, flood, or fire. While all can destroy library and archival collections, it is the water, which usually accompanies a disaster, that causes the greatest damage. Immediate action is required to prevent irreparable damage to materials, but it is difficult to take action to rescue library and archival materials in a general emergency situation. However, if an institution has planned for emergencies and for disaster situations, the salvage of materials can be undertaken more readily.

While the Western world still mourns the loss of such great treasures as the Cimabue crucifix, which was destroyed by the floodwater of the Arno in Florence, Italy in 1966, there is no question that the library community benefitted in the long run from the experience gained after this disaster. World attention was caught as volunteers rushed to Florence to assist in the salvage of its treasures. The best book and paper conservators in Europe and North America supervised volunteers and assisted with the salvage and repair of the books from the Laurentian Library. Out of necessity, these conservators learned a great deal about the physical nature of library and archival materials. Since 1966, they have developed a number of new techniques that have greatly enhanced our ability to salvage library and archival materials following a disaster.

The best protection against disaster, be it natural or man-made, is prevention. This involves adequate library construction, a well-trained staff, and good housekeeping procedures—those measures discussed in earlier chapters. The building structure itself can offer considerable protection against disaster. Unfortunately, too many library buildings do not offer the necessary protection for the collections. Most librarians will have to deal with flawed structures when planning for emergencies.

The first and most important step in planning for disaster is the development of a disaster plan, carefully thought out and adopted before disaster strikes, and ready to be put into action. Disaster planning and recovery specialist Sally Buchanan has observed: "First, such a written document acknowledges that disasters are possible, and that there is a commitment on the part of the organization to accept responsibility in a sensible and logical way. Second, preparation and a written plan eliminate panic, assure proper decisions, reduce the damage to collections, and limit the cost of recovery. Third, a plan consolidates ideas and provides step-by-step instructions which are clear and easy to follow for anyone who is called upon to use them."(1)

Unfortunately, most institutions do not prepare disaster plans until they have already been touched by disaster. Although most library managers are well aware of the need for a disaster plan, they face more immediate needs, and disaster planning is postponed. Simply put, most people do not believe that they will be involved in a disaster—consider how many people continue to occupy expensive homes on the San Andreas fault in California.

Librarians learned, following the Corning, NY, flood of 1972, that prepared professionals, working with staff and volunteers, were able to do a great deal to save their valuable collections. The Corning Museum and Library had a collection of about 6,000 volumes on the history of glass. The cabinets in which they were stored collapsed. Yet both the librarian and the assistant librarian knew exactly where the rare books and other important materials were located. As soon as they took care of the immediate needs of their families, they rushed to the library, darkened and filled with muck, and went directly to the area where their treasures were scattered. These librarians personally packed books in boxes and took them out in station wagons to freezers in the farm communities in neighboring areas that were not flooded. Plans had been made, priorities established, and the staff was familiar with the options available under the circumstances.

On the other hand, there was no disaster plan for the Temple University Law Library. Following a devastating fire in 1972, all library materials were salvaged and sent to be freeze-dried. Even with the new technological developments in vacuum and freeze-drying, restoration of materials can be significantly more expensive than replacement. Much of the general material in this library could have been replaced at significantly less cost than it took to restore it. As was the case following the flood in Florence, the techniques developed in the wake of this disaster have greatly contributed to our understanding about the salvage of library materials. Officials at Temple University and their insurers, however, rightfully may inquire if this contribution to librarianship need have been done on such a massive scale and at their expense.

It is wise for the librarian to appoint a disaster planning team, with representatives from the different units of the library. The senior library administrator who bears the responsibility for the facility may wish to chair the committee, or may delegate the task to the library's Safety Officer, Preservation Officer, or another responsible individual. In larger libraries, the responsibility for disaster prevention is delegated to the staff member who is also responsible for insurance coverage, monitoring the maintenance of fire protection equipment and services, overseeing the maintenance of the physical plant, and initiating public relations regarding safety and security for library materials and the people in the library.

The preservation survey, detailed in Chapter 2, is the starting point for the preparation of a disaster plan. A thorough review of the building will indicate potential problems and hazards. The *Fire Safety Inspection Form for Libraries,* issued by the National Fire Protection Association (NFPA), used in conjunction with the building survey, is a useful tool for disaster planning. It focuses on potential hazard areas such as the heating plant, the electrical system, concealed spaces, lighting, and fire protection equipment. Heating and electrical systems are major sources of fires. These should be properly installed according to code and checked frequently. Electrical circuitry should not be overloaded, an all too common problem in libraries as they attempt to automate services in older buildings. The survey will bring problem areas to light, and many can be easily remedied. It helps the disaster planning team determine the extent to which flooding, fire, and other emergencies can be prevented and predict the extent to which library property may be damaged when disasters occur. When these factors are analyzed, the organization for a plan for disaster response will emerge.

The establishment of a sound fire prevention program, as recommended by the National Fire Protection Association, is a good beginning project for the disaster planning team. Such a program is based upon good housekeeping practices, proper maintenance of equipment, and the prohibition of smoking and the use of open flame devices in the library. Even under the best of circumstances, however, there is the possibility of fire, which must be contained and controlled. Fire may occur from a variety of different causes including spontaneous ignition, vandalism, carelessness, electrical failure, as well as natural disasters. It is imperative that clearly marked exits are available and that they are not impeded by security measures. This will take careful planning, for increasingly libraries are faced with the problem of theft, but it can be achieved satisfactorily by a review of existing standards and common sense.

A good in-house program for fire prevention should include the following practices, all of which are a part of good housekeeping procedures:

1. Safe containers should be provided for the collection of wastepaper, packing materials, and other refuse.

Wastepaper and rubbish should be removed from the premises at regular intervals.

2. Paint rags and custodian's oily cloths should be disposed of as soon as their immediate use is over as they are subject to spontaneous ignition.
3. When exhibits made of combustible materials cannot be avoided, they should be located in an area that will localize the hazard if they ignite. Portable extinguishers should be located nearby.
4. Holiday decorations should always be of fire retardant materials. They should be placed well away from sources of ignition, such as light fixtures.
5. Frequent inspections should be made by the safety officer to detect unsafe conditions and to impress upon the staff the importance of immaculate housekeeping in the library. Recycled paper must be picked up regularly.
6. Smoking should be prohibited in the library, as smoke is harmful to library materials and people. However, a designated smoking room, located well away from library materials, may be made available to staff and patrons. It should contain ashtrays suitable for the safe disposal of smoking materials. From a preservation perspective, it is fortunate for library collections that smoking increasingly is banned in public buildings.
7. Heating and air-conditioning equipment should be maintained, inspected, and tested in accordance with recognized safe practices. Heaters and ductwork should be kept free of combustible deposits. The use of portable heaters or other small electrical appliances should not be permitted.

When the library is in order, the disaster planning team can turn its attention to the preparation of the disaster plan. The first rule in planning for disaster is to prepare for all conceivable situations. The librarian and planning team should take advantage of technical consultants and legal counsel when preparing the plan to ensure that it meets all requirements for the protection of staff, patrons, and property. Many, if not most, insurance companies are aware of the special needs of libraries, archives, and museums and can provide assistance in disaster planning and prevention.

A disaster plan has six important objectives:

1. to lessen the potential for loss by anticipating the possibilities and appropriately reducing them whenever possible;
2. to ensure that the library staff has received adequate orientation and training in emergency and disaster response and that this training is updated on a continuing basis;
3. to ensure frequent inspection by appropriate agencies such as fire and building code teams, to prevent changed conditions from having a deleterious effect upon the safety of the building;
4. to ensure appropriate action by all agencies, public and private, in dealing with a disaster situation;
5. to reestablish normal functions promptly and efficiently after a disaster;
6. to lessen the chances of recurrence by taking advantage of experience gained.

The librarian and/or the designated disaster planning officer should prepare and post an evacuation plan for the library, appoint wardens for floors and sections of the building, conduct fire drills and provide fire instruction for all new employees, and establish lines of communication for reporting emergencies. Clear and precise procedures should be established for sounding the fire alarm, calling the fire department, evacuating the building, and accounting for all persons within the building. The librarian, or delegated individual responsible for the building at the time of an emergency, is responsible for the initiation of special actions as needed. This individual should cooperate with both police and fire departments. The library administrator is responsible for the preparation of a full report on damage and loss, the initiation of salvage activities, and the restoration of library functions.

The primary record of the holdings of a library can be

found in its catalog, be it the traditional card catalog or an automated record. If this record is destroyed, the job of assessing loss is nearly insurmountable. As more libraries are putting their catalogs on-line, with the data on holdings stored outside the library, the ability to assess loss has become far easier. Card catalogs should be microfilmed; the film should be updated on a regular schedule. The microfilm copy of the card catalog should be stored off-site, preferably in another geographic location to minimize loss in the event of a major regional disaster.

The librarian and staff should review all collections and determine which will be given priority attention in a disaster. Early printed books, for example, are far more difficult to replace than the collected works of modern authors. Archival records that are unique to the region are usually of major significance. Materials that are to be salvaged should be clearly identified on the floor plans that accompany a written disaster plan. Estimates of the cost of each collection should be prepared, as they are an aid at the moment of a disaster and serve as a guide to the establishment of priorities for action in the weeks to follow. A general knowledge of the value of each collection will aid considerably in determining what is to be restored, replaced, or discarded. Most important, for insurance purposes it is a necessity.

Every library should have a detailed written contingency plan for the moment when disaster strikes. The librarian and the disaster planning team should develop and practice disaster recovery procedures with the assistance of local and regional agencies. It is important to involve the local fire and police departments in the development of the plan. They need to know the priorities of the library; for example, where special collections are housed. At institutions with risk management personnel, they will also play an important role in the development of the library's disaster plan, for it will be a part of an overall institutional plan. In a catastrophic situation, the salvage of human life will take priority over the materials in libraries, archives, and museums, but if the agencies involved in rescue and salvage are aware of the library's needs, much can be done to curtail the damaging effect of fire, flood, or other catastrophe. The essential elements of a written disaster plan are outlined below.

1. Floor plans of the building with locations of all collections clearly marked. The more valuable collections should be identified and some estimate of the value of these collections should be appended. The floor plans should also indicate the location of fire exits, extinguishers, salvage kits, and other emergency equipment.
2. The home and office telephone numbers of key library personnel, staff members who have been trained in disaster recovery techniques, and staff members who have volunteered to be a part of a disaster recovery team.
3. Telephone numbers of local, state, and regional agencies that will assist in disaster recovery. The telephone number of the National Preservation Program Office at the Library of Congress.
4. Telephone numbers of area conservators and other specialists who have agreed to assist in disaster salvage and recovery.
5. The names and telephone numbers of suppliers of milk crates, fans, generators, tables, plastic wrapping and bags, unprinted newsprint, freezer space, refrigerated trucks, and other materials and services that might be needed in a salvage operation.
6. Detailed salvage and recovery instructions to be followed by library personnel in case of an emergency or in a disaster situation.

All library staff should be familiar with the disaster plan and copies should be readily available for staff review at any time. The master copies, however, should remain off-site, with the librarian or an appropriate officer who can be available on the scene at once. At academic institutions, copies are also kept with campus police and fire departments and with the risk management officer for the institution. A disaster plan within a burning building is of no use.

Water damage can devastate paper-based library and archival collections; traditionally, librarians have gone to considerable lengths to protect collections from water. Still, the disastrous fires at the Los Angeles Public Library and at the Academy of Sciences Library, St. Petersburg, Russia, have reminded librarians of the destruction to collections that is caused by fire. While books do not burn easily, the library contains many highly flammable materials, including carpeting, furnishings, and draperies. These materials can smolder for a period of time, then flare up, quickly reaching the flash point of spontaneous combustion. At this point, books burn quickly. Sprinkler systems can serve as a great deterrent to fire damage. Careful consideration should be paid to their installation.

Until a few years ago, most librarians and archivists struggled with risk management personnel and insurers over the installation of sprinkler systems for the protection of collections. Most sprinkler systems contained water within them and, where there is water, there can be leaking. While wet-pipe sprinkler systems are still available, most libraries, archives, and museums opt for dry-pipe systems. There are a wide variety of sprinkler systems available; in 1990 the National Fire Protection Association published a book that describes them.(2) The sprinkler systems of the 1990s offer real protection against the threat of fire. A few dampened books are far easier to restore than a badly burned, and soaked, collection. Insurers quite reasonably encourage, if not insist, that they be installed in libraries. Sprinklers are a sound disaster prevention measure.

For several decades, rare book repositories, archives, and computer rooms have relied on Halon systems, containing Freon, to smother fires. Computers cannot tolerate water, and librarians want to protect rare and valuable objects from water damage, if possible. Halon was the answer. Halon is a clear, odorless gas that can make a person who is exposed to it over a period of time feel ill, but it is not permanently harmful to people. Only a small concentration is needed to extinguish most fires. Halon is expensive to install and expensive to replace. Halon systems can go off accidentally. The gas explodes from its canisters with considerable force and has been known to destroy loose documents. The major problem with Halon systems is that they contain Freon and are not considered to be environmentally safe. Halon systems have, however, served well as protective systems, and it appears that there is a sufficient market for them to make it worthwhile to develop an environmentally safe formula for their continued use. There is a need for a gaseous extinguishing system that is reasonably safe for people.

Disaster Recovery

The greatest threat to library and archival materials in most disaster situations is water. Even if books are badly burned, they will also be soaked from the gallons of water pumped onto them to stop their burning. Disaster recovery procedures for library and archival materials rightly focus on recovery from water damage.

When the library has been struck by water damage from fire or flood, weather is the critical factor in determining the immediate course of action. It is important to stabilize water-damaged materials as quickly as possible. If the weather is hot and humid, salvage must be initiated with a minimum of delay to prevent or control mold growth. If the weather is cold, more time can be taken to plan salvage operations and explore the efficacy of various drying procedures. It sometimes may be a week or more before areas affected by fire, flood, or other natural disasters can be approached, but if certain areas are identified as being of great value and particularly vulnerable to destruction, the fire marshal may be able to facilitate means of access.

Conservator Peter Waters, chief of the Conservation Division at the Library of Congress, the man who helped direct the salvage operations in Florence in 1966, tells librarians that it is imperative to seek the advice and help of trained conservators with experience in salvaging water-damaged materials as soon as possible. His pamphlet,

Procedures for Salvage of Water-Damaged Library Materials (2nd edition, 1979), is being revised by the Library's National Preservation Program Office, with updated information about sources of supplies. The Metropolitan Reference and Research Library Agency (METRO) in New York City has also prepared a guide to disaster planning and salvage, *Hell and High Water,* that contains a lengthy resource list that is of use to everyone. A number of states and regions in the country have prepared disaster plans and resource lists that have proved effective in emergency situations.

The Library of Congress National Preservation Program Office (NPPO) is a source of technical advice and can be contacted in case of emergency. In the northeast, libraries have recourse to the services of the Northeast Document Conservation Center (NEDCC) in Andover, MA. NEDCC has specialized in assisting libraries in the recovery of water-damaged materials for more than eighteen years and can provide immediate technical assistance if needed. Other regional conservation centers, while not specializing in books or paper-based materials, nevertheless can provide knowledgeable conservators to assist in recovery. A number of states and regions have organized disaster recovery services and *D*isaster *R*ecovery *A*ssistance *T*eams (DRAT) that can respond quickly to an institution's emergency needs. South Carolina's libraries, museums, and archives had just completed a project for statewide disaster assessment and training of personnel for salvage when Hurricane Hugo struck in the fall of 1989. The trained personnel sprang into action, salvaging much material that might otherwise have been lost due to delays in organization of recovery efforts. Although Florida libraries had been involved in statewide disaster planning, lines of communication had not been clearly established. When Hurricane Andrew struck in 1992, valuable time was lost because librarians, in the crisis, did not know how to implement the plan.

There are a number of techniques for drying water-damaged materials. Several firms that specialize in dehumidification to maintain dry cargo holds for the shipping industry have turned their attention to the needs of libraries, archives, and museums. These companies have equipment that can lower the humidity level in a flooded area, drying it rapidly. The results of dehumidification treatment are impressive. If the process can begin quickly, paper-based materials can be stabilized, then returned to good condition with little further attention.

The accepted method of stabilizing water-soaked materials, including paper, leather, fabric, and film, is by freezing and storing them at low temperatures (minus 20 degrees Fahrenheit). This procedure provides for time to plan and coordinate drying operations. Interlocking plastic milk crates make excellent containers for packing wet materials. Boxes that are used for the housing and storage of archival records also work well for the freezing and recovery process. A box has been designed for the process, but it is expensive. However, institutions may want to purchase several to have on hand in case of emergency.

If possible, staff members should be trained in salvage techniques before disaster strikes, so that they will be available to supervise volunteers who retrieve damaged materials and pack them for freezing. Workers should not attempt to force waterlogged books back into shape as this can cause further damage; books can be frozen as they are to stabilize them. Although there are techniques for cleaning materials that are covered with mud and debris, untrained workers should not attempt to do so.

Books should be packed spine down, in a single layer, in plastic crates or cardboard boxes. If there is time, books can be wrapped individually in *unprinted* newsprint paper, freezer paper, or, even better, Remay, a spunbonded polyester web, before being boxed. Documents should be packed in their folders or in stacks; no attempt should be made to separate them. Boxes should be numbered and their contents identified, in pencil or waterproof ink. A record of the boxes should be kept separately and in duplicate with other documentation about the materials.

Photographic materials present unique problems because of their emulsions. Photographs may be rinsed very gently in cold, clean, distilled water, and air-dried, if possible. If a collection of photographs must be frozen to stabilize it, the freezing should be done quickly, as large ice crystals can scratch the emulsion. Libraries with collections of slides and magnetic media should seek assistance from specialists in appropriate salvage operations.

The traditional method for drying wet paper-based materials is air-drying. This technique is appropriate and effective when materials are dampened, not soaked, or when only a small collection of materials are wet. Air-drying can take place in any space with good air circulation and low humidity. It may be possible to undertake the operation working with a company specializing in dehumidification; this has been effective in a number of recovery operations. Books are interleaved carefully with absorbent paper and placed upright. If materials are only slightly dampened, they can be fanned open and do not need interleaving. If books are soaked, they will need to drain and dry somewhat before the interleaving process can begin. Sheets of absorbent paper should be placed every few pages in a book, but not so close together as to distort its shape. The sheets need to be replaced frequently as the books dry. When books are almost dry, they may be pressed. At this stage, most can be returned to the shelves without further treatment. However, they should be watched closely for signs of mold growth.

Documents should be placed flat on non-glossy, uncoated waxed paper or on unprinted newsprint, which can be obtained from a local newspaper publisher. Hair dryers, on cool settings, can be effective to dry documents, if done with care. When the documents are almost dry, they can be pressed, then returned to new files. If possible, collections of documents should be kept in order during air-drying; this necessity requires careful supervision of volunteers. Not all documents are worth the effort of saving in original format. Photocopying machines can be rented for the recovery process. Wet documents can be copied and discarded. This proved to be a very effective method of disaster recovery for the records salvaged when the Salisbury, CT, town hall and archives burned in the early 1980s. The town records administrator oversaw the copying of informationally important documents, while volunteers, under the supervision of a preservation specialist and the state records administrator, air-dried the more valuable documents. Air-drying requires appropriate space and personnel; it is not an effective approach when major water damage has occurred. Large quantities of wet materials must be frozen as quickly as possible to stabilize them, then recovered at a later date. Collections can be removed piecemeal from the freezer and air-dried, but under most circumstances, that will not be the most cost-efficient and effective way to deal with the damaged materials.

The dehumidification of the space where water-damaged library materials are housed has proved to be an effective method of drying collections that are not thoroughly soaked. Enormous dehumidifiers are brought to the site to lower the relative humidity to the desired level. The dry, circulating air evaporates the moisture in the area. Collections dry in good condition.

There are three acceptable techniques that are used to dry collections of books and documents after freezing: freeze-drying, vacuum drying, and vacuum freeze-drying. Robert DeCandido clearly explains the techniques in his article, "Out of the Question: From the Ridiculous to the Sublimated," *Conservation Administration News,* No. 32 (January 1988), pages 21–22.

DeCandido explains: "To dry out a book it is necessary to convert the water in the paper to water vapor, a gas, and then remove the gas." This is accomplished by evaporation or by sublimation. Materials will dry quickly when they are placed in a very cold freezer. The freezer draws out and condenses water from the air. DeCandido observes that the drying process works on the same principle as frost-free freezers. Vacuum drying is accomplished when books and documents are placed in a vacuum chamber with the temperature raised and the pressure lowered. The point to which a book must be heated depends upon the degree of the vacuum that has been created. This process of drying is not really satisfactory for library materials, as the heat can damage the books.

Photographs and other film-based media should never be vacuum-dried. They may stick together and the emulsion can separate from the base support.

Vacuum freeze-drying is accomplished when a book is frozen, then placed in a vacuum chamber and the pressure is reduced. The books never thaw as they dry. The ice crystals in the books and documents will begin to sublimate without converting to liquid form. Mild heat is introduced to speed the process to completion. This process causes less distortion of the treated materials than the others. Sally Buchanan notes that coated papers respond well to vacuum freeze-drying as long as they are frozen before they started to adhere badly.(3) The process pulls dirt and silt to the surface of the book more effectively than vacuum drying. Buchanan also notes that magnetic tapes have been vacuum freeze-dried without loss of information.(4)

DeCandido concludes, "Unfortunately, none of these processes is without its drawbacks and limitations, and the roles which each might play and the needs they may fulfill are still unclear."(5) These techniques have each worked very effectively to dry some materials and have not worked very well in treating others. The degree of success seems to depend on the physical nature of the materials and on the extent of the damage. At this time, it is necessary to seek advice from conservators who have had experience with these techniques to help make the decision as to which technique, or techniques, will be used to dry large collections of water-damaged materials.

None of these drying techniques restores materials. Buchanan reminds us that "once materials are dry, the work of sorting, cleaning, repairing, binding, restoring, housing, and reshelving begins." She continues, "This rehabilitation phase should be planned carefully to reduce costs and produce the most efficient result possible."(6) While the damaged materials are safely stabilized in freezers, there is time to plan for further recovery. Estimates for the cost of recovery are necessary, including the cost of labor and materials for work to be done in-house, and for the treatment of more valuable materials by a conservator. Much of the material simply will need to be rebound by the commercial library binder, but this is an additional expense. At least some of the material can be replaced in hard copy or in microform. Replacement copies will need to be recataloged, another additional cost. Finally, the materials will have to be reshelved. An institution's insurance may cover all or part of the costs for salvage or rehabilitation. The scope of insurance coverage should be clearly understood before disaster, not afterward.

The salvage of fire-damaged collections is especially difficult. In addition to the damage from water, there is always serious damage from soot and smoke. Leather and vellum bindings can shrink and distort badly. Photographic emulsions can shrivel. Most damaging to the collections is the particulate matter that is contained in the smoke and soot, much of which will be impossible to remove. The heat will affect all books in the area, hastening their embrittlement, even if they were not scorched. There are firms that specialize in the recovery of fire-damaged materials and conservators who have considerable experience in doing so, but Buchanan, after reviewing the possibilities for salvage and recovery, states, "Careful consideration should be given to replacing collections exposed to fire rather than rehabilitating them. Not only is the cost of recovery high, but once burned or exposed to extremely high temperatures, books and manuscripts [and photographs] will never be the same, nor are they restorable to their pre-fire state."(7)

Security

With the recent and well-publicized increase in the number of thefts of library materials, librarians and archivists have been forced to review measures for the security of their collections. The rise in the cost of library materials and the inconvenience to patrons and staff when they are missing or damaged have made security a priority for most librarians. Theft is even more of a concern for the curators of special collections, as the materials that are lost or damaged are often irreplaceable.

In his book, *Design for Security,* Richard J. Healy writes, "Physical security controls are an essential factor in protecting modern facilities."(8) While to a certain extent a neat, tidy, and efficiently run library discourages vandalism, or malicious damage, even theft, it is essential that security be maintained in the library at all hours. The library staff should undertake a careful assessment of security needs when evaluating the physical plant. The police and fire departments, as well as representatives from the library's insurance company and security firms can be of considerable assistance in developing appropriate security measures.

Vandalism, malicious damage, and increasingly the problem of the homeless are further considerations for security. The library should have adequate exterior lighting and suitable fencing. The interior of the building can be modified to inhibit vandalism and/or theft. Homeless people are a serious problem in many libraries. While it can be a heartrending decision to displace them from the library, homeless people can be a serious threat to the security of the building. They can stop up plumbing, causing serious water damage, and cause small fires. In addition to monitoring their entry and exit, physical changes can be made in the building that will make it more difficult for people to disappear into remote corners. These considerations are an important element in an assessment to make a building safe and secure.

Uniformed guards and theft alarm systems may be warranted in some situations. Library security systems, such as Tattle-Tape, are effective as deterrents, but can easily be made ineffective by a person determined to have a book. Libraries should have book inspectors to examine the bags of every patron and staff member as he or she exits the building. The book inspectors need to have the support of the senior library staff, for their job can on occasion be difficult. The Association of College and Research Libraries' (ACRL) "Guidelines for the Security of Rare Book, Manuscript, and Other Special Collections," approved in 1990, advises: "Staff should know their legal and procedural responsibilities for security and know their own and the readers' legal rights in handling possible problems."(9) Security measures are for everyone, including senior staff. They set the example for the staff and public. The good administrator has his or her briefcase checked when leaving the library; the poor administrator goes out the back door. Both are observed. Thorough security and safety procedures for closing the library should be established to ensure that all unauthorized persons have vacated the building and that all doors and windows are secure. Photocopiers, computers, and other appliances should be turned off. Waste receptacles and other potential fire hazards should be checked nightly before the building is closed. A written checklist of closing procedures should be prepared and posted; the task should be delegated to specific individuals who are accountable for their daily performance.

The Rare Book and Manuscript Section (RBMS) of the American Library Association, working in close cooperation with the Society of American Archivists (SAA) and the Antiquarian Booksellers Association of America (ABAA), has formed a Security Committee to study means of dealing with theft and premeditated damage to library and archival materials. The Committee has developed guidelines and model legislation to help curtail theft and to provide for collection security as well as the "Guidelines for the Security of Rare Book, Manuscript, and other Special Collections" cited above. These are useful documents for all libraries; circulating collections are even more vulnerable to theft than special, noncirculating collections.

A written security policy is an important part of the library's disaster plan. The ACRL's "Guidelines" states: "The policy should include a standard operating procedure on dealing with a theft: determining the circumstances of the theft, reporting the theft to the proper authorities within an organization, and to the local and (where appropriate) national legal authorities. The Security Policy should be kept up-to-date with current names and telephone numbers of institutional and law enforcement contacts."(10) The Rare Book and Manuscript Section's "Guidelines Regarding Thefts in Libraries," approved in 1988, provides detailed instructions that serve as a model for most libraries to develop with appropriate legal authorities. Cooperation with local law enforcement agencies in preparing policies and guidelines for the handling of theft is important.

Several lessons have been learned by librarians and archivists who have had to cope with theft in recent years. First, if a thief wants a book badly enough he will probably get it, as the Stephen Blumberg thefts have made clear.(11) The problem patron can often be the untrustworthy patron. One notorious thief, foul-smelling and obnoxious to the staff, managed to steal a considerable number of documents from several repositories before he was caught. The staff avoided him because he was unkempt and unpleasant. Other thieves have gained the staff's confidence over years of "research." In one sad case, the thief was given access to the rare book vault; in others, the "scholars" removed numerous valuable documents from the files they were "consulting." Often thefts are not discovered until the materials are offered for sale. Saddest of all is internal theft. Difficult as it is, staff members must be screened. The ACRL's "Guidelines for the Security of Rare Book, Manuscript, and Other Special Collections" states: "The staff should be chosen carefully. Background checks and bonding of staff members may be considered through regular institutional channels. Careful personnel management is an ongoing necessity; a weak point in any security system is the disgruntled staff who may seek revenge through the theft, destruction, or willful mishandling of collections."(12)

It is important to maintain good working relationships with community representatives regarding matters of safety and security in the library. The police and fire departments can provide invaluable service to the library on a continuing basis, not only at the time of an emergency. These agencies should be thoroughly familiar with the needs and operating procedures of the library. When a library is well-organized and its staff is prepared for any emergency, should disaster strike, loss and much of the trauma can be reduced considerably.

Notes

1. Sally A. Buchanan, *Disaster Planning: Preparedness and Recovery for Libraries and Archives* (Paris: Unesco, 1988), 7.
2. John L. Bryan, *Automatic Sprinkler and Stand Pipe Systems.* 2nd ed. (Boston: National Fire Protection Association), 1990.
3. Buchanan 86.
4. *Ibid.*
5. DeCandido 22.
6. Buchanan 96.
7. Buchanan 86.
8. Healy 2.
9. *College and Research Libraries News* 51:3 (March 1990): 241.
10. *College and Research Libraries News.* 51:3 (March 1990): 241.
11. J. Stephen Huntsberry, "The Legacy Thief: The Hunt for Stephen Blumberg," *Art Documentation* 10:4 (Winter 1991): 181–183.
12. *College and Research Libraries News.* 51:3 (March 1990): 241.

Selected References

Allen, Susan M. "Theft in Libraries or Archives." *College and Research Libraries News* 51:10 (November. 1990): 939–943.

Eulenberg, Julia Niebuhr. *Handbook for the Recovery of Water Damaged Business Records.* Prairie Village, KS: ARMA International, 1986.

Fortson, Judith. *Disaster Planning and Recovery: A How-To-Do-It Manual for Librarians and Archivists.* New York: Neal-Schuman, 1992.

Hendriks, Klaus B. and Brian Lesser. "Disaster Preparedness and Recovery: Photographic Materials." *American Archivist* 46:1 (Winter 1983): 52–68.

Morris, John and Irving D. Nicols. *Managing the Library Fire Risk.* 2nd ed. Berkeley: University of California, 1979.

National Fire Protection Association. *Protection of Libraries and Library Collections.* Boston, MA: NFPA, 1992. (NFPA Publ. 910)

O'Connell, Mildred. "Disaster Planning: Writing and Implementing Plans for Collections-Holding Institutions." *Technology & Conservation* 8:2 (Summer 1983): 18–24.

Waters, Peter. *Salvage of Water-Damaged Library Materials,* 2nd ed. Washington, DC: Library of Congress, 1978.

VII. BOOKBINDING

History

COVERS, OR BINDINGS, FOR WRITTEN MATERIAL were used prior to the development of the book in the codex format, a collection of sheets superimposed upon one another, folded across the middle, then secured by stitching so that the sheets fall into pages. The book as we know it today began to gain favor over the traditional scroll, or roll, by the first century A.D., for it was a far more convenient format for use. By the fourth century, the codex format became the predominant form for the book. Its pages inspired both scribe and illuminator, and the rectangular boards protecting the leaves invited ornament. Early bindings were often made of precious metals embellished with jewels, ivories, or paintings. Masterpieces of the binder's art were created throughout the Middle Ages and the Renaissance. The tradition continues today as hand binders create works of art for the contemporary collector who can afford luxuriously produced books and bindings.

In her introduction to *The History of Bookbinding, 525–1950,* a catalog of an exhibition at the Walters Gallery (Baltimore, MD: 1957), Dorothy Miner reminds us that the real history of decorative bookbindings is the history of the working of leather.(1) The earliest leather bindings were produced by the middle of the fifth century in North Africa. Coptic craftsmen also executed the first European and Near Eastern book covers. The use of leather in Europe depended upon the availability of hides. The hides of oxen, asses, calves, sheep, pigs, horses, stags, does, goats, seals, and a variety of other animals were used

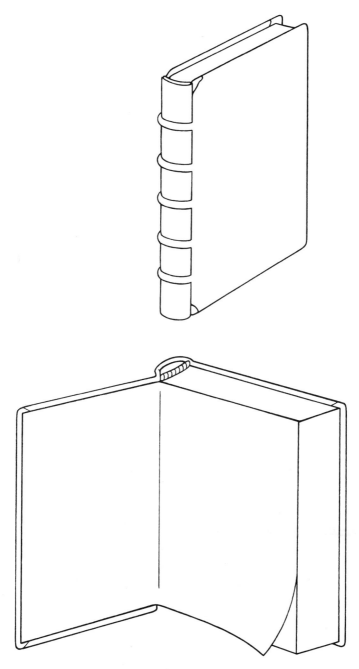

Book Structure

for binding books in the Middle Ages. The finest leather came from Morocco, where it was prepared from goatskin; "morocco" remains a term applied to luxurious bindings today, although it can refer to a variety of covering materials. Leather bindings became popular in Western Europe in the twelfth century, concurrent with the rise of universities and a more secular interest in books. The nobility and the new wealthy class of merchants began to acquire books for personal use. These owners were also fond of bindings of the finest textiles—silk brocade, embroidery, and rich velvets—which were further adorned with gold and silver fittings.

Gold tooling, a technique for the decoration of leather by means of heated metal stamps or tools, first appeared in the Mediterranean Islamic world in the fourteenth century, and by the sixteenth century the technique was introduced into Western Europe through Spain and Italy. The introduction of gold-tooled leather bindings revolutionized the art of bookbinding, for Renaissance craftsmen responded to this medium and created magnificent designs of great intricacy. Because earlier textile bindings were especially fragile, most medieval manuscripts that we see today are in fine leather bindings of the sixteenth century, or later, when these superb bindings replaced the worn original ones. Books for general use were bound more simply. Each monastery developed its own technique; many of them were highly satisfactory, combining practicality and ease of use. The commonplace printed books of the Renaissance were bound in a soft doeskin and frequently had extra flaps of leather to protect the edges of the book and to serve as a clutch.

Today, distinguished book conservators, such as Christopher Clarkson, Anthony Cains, Nicholas Pickwoad, and Guy Petherbridge, are carefully analyzing book structures of the medieval and early Renaissance periods and adopting many practical techniques that can be used for the conservation of modern books. Their research is of considerable importance and will have a real influence on the preservation and conservation of library materials, both old and new, in the decades to come. It serves as a reminder to librarians of the importance of preserving the evidence found in the physical construction of old books.

From the earliest days of printing until the beginning of the nineteenth century, books were published unbound. Anton Koberger of Nuremberg (circa 1435–1513), one of the great early publishers, sent his books to the retailer in flat sheets for easy packing. The retailer would bind the volumes or, more frequently, the wealthy customer would commission his own binding from his special binder. Splendid bindings were executed for connoisseurs such as Jean Grolier de Servières (1479–1565), the great Renaissance collector. The French binders were especially adept at decorative gold tooling on leather, and many of the greatest designs are French. The tradition of decorative binding remains strong in France today; books are often published in paper wrappers with the intention that the owner will have the volumes bound.

As the reading public expanded, more and more books were bound to the order of the bookseller. These bookseller's bindings may be called the first trade bindings, but they were not publisher's bindings. The development of the cloth binding over boards, with which we are familiar today, began early in the nineteenth century; its history is a part of the history of the industrial revolution. A series of technological developments led to the production of whole editions ready-bound in permanent covers. The ever-expanding middle class demanded manufactured articles, including books. The first cloth bindings were originally created as an improvement on the temporary paperboard coverings, but they soon became an accepted substitute for leather bindings. The first publisher's cloth bindings made their appearance in the late 1820s, and by 1850 publishers had assumed the responsibility for the binding of trade editions in England and North America.

Until the end of the eighteenth century, books were truly bound; that is, the text block was sewn onto the boards that were to cover it. A bound book, well executed, is durable and easy to read. Today, machine-bound books are cased-in. The cover, or case, for a cased-in book is made separately and the sewn (or glued) text block is attached to it. Although it is generally assumed that a bound book is stronger than a cased-in book, that may not necessarily be so. The cords decay and the volume will eventually break at the joint. If the materials and execution of a cased-in binding are sound, the book will have a strong structure, although it, too, will eventually break at the joint, the weakest part of the book structure.

The basic procedures for the binding of books were established by 1870. Since that time, changes in bookbinding technique have been due to changes in taste or to economic factors. It is only within the past decade that the research undertaken by the new breed of professional book conservators is making its impact on a profession that has been tradition-bound, developing, as it has, from a craft tradition. This research will have a favorable impact on library collections, ensuring that books are bound well at reasonable cost.

Library Binding

Early in the century it became apparent to librarians that books subjected to repeated use in circulating library collections required special, sturdy bindings. The pioneer of library binding was Cedric Chivers (1853–1929) of Bath, England, who purchased printed sheets from publishers and bound them with sturdy material and construction for heavy use in libraries. He established plants in Britain and the United States. The American Library Association (ALA) established a Bookbinding Committee in 1905. British librarians had similar committees and produced a *Manual on Library Bookbinding,* written by Henry T. Coutts and George A. Stephen (London: Libraco, 1911). The ALA produced a booklet of suggestions for library binding in 1915 and the first set of specifications for library binding was issued in 1923. A machine for oversewing was perfected in 1920. This machine led to the development of a separate library binding industry, for it reduced the cost of binding and led to the mechanization of many library binding procedures.

Library binding differs from edition or designer book-

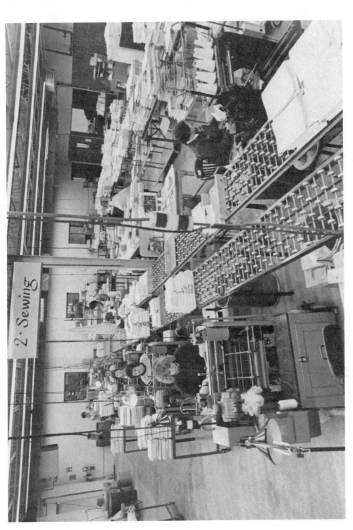

Commercial Library Binding
Credit: Library Binding Institute

binding, for it is intended for materials that are expected to circulate from a lending library. It is expected (perhaps unrealistically) that a library book should circulate approximately thirty times before it will require rebinding. The American Library Association, in conjunction with the Book Manufacturer's Institute, issued standards for library binding in 1934. In 1935 the Library Binders Section withdrew from the Book Manufacturer's Institute to form its own separate organization, the Library Binding Institute (LBI), which is today the professional association for commercial library binders. It has worked closely with the American Library Association to develop guidelines for commercial library binding and standards that will enable a book to work well and withstand approximately one hundred circulations.

A sound, protective structure for the text block is the primary concern. Books that receive commercial library bindings may, in a sense, be considered disposable. They are not intended to be permanent additions to a library's collection and will be in sorry condition after their hundred-odd readings. Books of permanent value—a collection of first editions of contemporary authors, for example—should be kept in their original bindings, housed in rare book and special collections, and restricted from general circulation. Much of the value of such books depends upon their being in their *original state,* which includes the publisher's binding and dust jacket. Collectors and bibliographers will consider a book in a library binding distinctly inferior because it is not in its original published state. Rebound books are of little value to bibliographers, scholars of the book, who need to examine materials in their original format. The housing and preservation of such special materials are discussed later in this chapter.

The ALA Library Technology Project investigated library binding quality in the 1960s and established qualitative procedures for evaluating standards. The three most important factors in a library binding are: 1) workmanship, evidenced by the appearance of the book; 2) "openability" (an unfortunate, but descriptive word), evidenced by the ability of a bound volume to be opened easily and to lie open unaided; 3) durability, evidenced by the durability of the binding. A standard is the lowest common denominator below which a binding should not fall; many libraries require bindings that exceed the standard. Working closely with the Preservation of Library Materials Section (PLMS) within ALA, the Library Binding Institute has formulated industry standards for library binding. Its publication, *Standards for Library Binding,* eighth edition, issued in 1986, serves as a guideline for libraries and belongs in every library. In 1990, the American Library Association published a *Guide to the Library Binding Institute Standard for Library Binding* to facilitate understanding and use of this standard. The Library Binding Institute participates in the work of the Library-Binder Relations Committee, within PLMS, to ensure that librarians understand and can implement the standards. The librarians on the committee communicate professional concerns for durability and for preservation. The eighth edition of the *Standards* reflects the concern for preservation and acknowledges that there are a variety of appropriate sewing structures that can be employed in rebinding a book, depending upon its use in the library. It is the responsibility of every library to develop its own specifications for the rebinding of its collections and to see that the commercial library binder meets them. The LBI *Standards* provides a base upon which an institution can develop standards and specifications to meet its needs.

During the past decade, library binders have developed a variety of techniques and technologies for the binding of books. Some of these are successful; some are not. The use of adhesives, rather than a sewn-in binding was, and is, a problem, if the application of the adhesive is done incorrectly. Yet, an adhesive binding can be the most successful style for a variety of materials, providing a flexible, sturdy, and inexpensive covering that meets the standards of workmanship, "openability," and durability.

Oversewing is the most common technique used for the rebinding of books today. The LBI *Standards* define oversewing as "a method of sewing thin sections (i.e., piles) of leaves, one to another in succession, to create a semi-flexible text block," (page 3). This operation is done by a machine using multiple needles and threads that pass through the binding margin of each section, forming stitches that link it to adjacent sections. In order to oversew a book, the spine of the volume must be trimmed to free the sheets for the machine stitching. The *Standard* specifies that no more than 1/8 inch of the spine shall be removed, but this can present a problem when the text of a volume is printed close to the inner margin. If the text is too close to the inner margin, the volume cannot be oversewn. A committee is working through the National Information Standards Organization (NISO) to develop a standard requiring that publishers leave sufficient space in that all-important inner margin. Larger volumes are often oversewn by hand. While oversewing is frowned upon by some preservation purists, done correctly and appropriately, it can provide a sturdy, even flexible binding for certain books; it is the appropriate option for many materials in the general library collection.

Sewing through the fold is usually the binding method of choice when a book is in signatures. The LBI *Standards* define sewing through the fold as "a method of attaching separate signatures, one to another in succession, to create a text block," (page 4). This may be done by hand, using one needle and thread, or it can be done by machine, using multiple needles and threads.

The eighth edition of the LBI *Standards* allows for flexibility in choice of materials and style of binding. The selection of a binding style appropriate for the materials in a collection is the responsibility of the librarian, not the library binder. What is appropriate for one collection may be quite inappropriate for another. Books that need to be rebound should be evaluated for the use that they will receive in a collection. Commercial library binding consumes a substantial proportion of a library's budget, and the books in a library's collection are a tangible asset that are meant to be preserved as long as possible. Librarians need to educate themselves about the latest binding technology to determine what methods of binding are appropriate for the books in their collections. The Library Binding Institute and the American Library Association sponsor workshops and produce publications and visual aids on commercial library binding. These are helpful for an understanding of library binding processes and in formulating standards and specifications to meet institutional needs. There is little excuse for a professional librarian who has the responsibility for an institution's binding program to be unfamiliar with the options that can meet the needs of the collections.

Every librarian, not only the staff members involved with commercial library binding, should visit a bindery to understand how it works and the costs involved. Commercial library binding remains a small, labor-intensive industry, operating on a relatively small margin of profit. As much as possible, books are bound on an assembly line. Every operation that pulls a volume out of the stream will cost more. For example, the decision not to trim a book before rebinding means that it must be removed from the assembly line so it is not automatically guillotined. It is much easier for the binder to trim books to uniform sizes before they go through the binding process. The more preservation options such as "no trim" policies become the norm, the less they will cost.

While many books purchased for libraries will have library bindings, trade editions with trade, or publisher's, bindings are also purchased or received as gifts and are added to library collections. Many of these books can tolerate only five to ten readings before it will be necessary to send them out for rebinding. Some trade editions receive what is known as perfect binding that is, in reality, far from perfect. The pages are attached and encased using a flimsy adhesive material; when the pages fall out of their cover, they are especially difficult to rebind. Perfect bindings are anathema to authors, but because librarians rarely receive materials with such bindings, the profession did not, until recently, complain about them as vociferously as the members of PEN and the Author's League. Today, librarians are beginning to work with authors and publishers to ensure that books are produced properly at reasonable cost. The American Library Association is involved in the development of standards for book production that will produce a well-made book encased in a sound binding, with the all-important inner margin that allows for easy rebinding.

It is cheaper to rebind a volume than to replace it. At some point, however, a volume will be "read to death" and should be discarded. Replacement volumes, new editions of the work, can be purchased if the book belongs in the library's permanent collection. If a replacement copy is not available, a book can be photocopied onto alkaline paper, then bound for the stacks. This preservation option is discussed elsewhere; it is an option increasingly common in libraries and one in which the binder can be of real assistance.

Pamphlet Binding

For years, the bindings that were available commercially for pamphlets were extremely acidic. It is startling to see the damage they have caused to the material inside them in even as short a period of time as twenty years. The metal staples used for attachment have caused as much harm as the acid boards, staining and weakening the paper; too often they were carelessly placed over the text. Fortunately, binders and suppliers became aware of this problem, and by the early 1980s most reputable suppliers of library materials were providing permanent/durable pamphlet binding covers for their customers. Conservators and binders also have developed a wide variety of pamphlet bindings to accommodate the variety of materials found in library collections.

Pamphlet binding can be done efficiently in-house by a library assistant or technician under the supervision of a professional book conservator. Librarians should become familiar with the variety of pamphlet binding structures that are available to ensure the best possible housing for their collections. Increasingly, commercial library binders are offering pamphlet binding service at reasonable cost. The binder can provide pamphlet binding structures that meet the needs of special materials. In most cases, it is more practical for a library to have its pamphlet binding done by a commercial library binder on the simple principle that the greater the volume, the lower the cost.

In the past, both librarians and collectors tended to bind collections of pamphlets on a given subject together to make a fairly large volume. While this may have presented a relatively easy method of bibliographic control, this method of saving pamphlets actually hastened their decay. Pamphlets published on highly acidic paper eat away at their neighbors; pamphlets of various sizes, bound together, pull and strain against the binding, come loose, and tear. Slowly, libraries are disassembling these collections and rehousing each pamphlet in an appropriate pamphlet binding. Some collections are also microfilmed for preservation and access. Although the process of disassembling and reassembling these collections is costly, librarians are finding materials of considerable value in the process, which are thus made more accessible to scholars. The preferred methods of the preceding generation for preservation and access have proven unsatisfactory. Today's remedies, with their respect for the object itself as well as its content, enhance collections today and for the future. Pamphlets that are worth keeping are worth preserving.

Rare and Unusual Bindings

When library books are to be preserved in their original bindings, these bindings deserve special protection and care as objects of intrinsic value. Poor environmental conditions, especially air pollution, accelerate the deterioration process inherent in leather. Ensuring that special collections are housed in a proper environment is the essential first step in preserving them.

For years, the oiling of leather bindings for their preservation, to prevent cracking and visible decay, was an accepted practice in libraries. However, conservators have discovered that all too often oiling has done more harm than good to books. The oiling of leather bindings, especially on books bound in the nineteenth century, should never be done by anyone but a specialist. Leathers have been, and are today, tanned by a variety of processes, few of which are understood. Too often the materials that were used in the tanning process react badly with the emollients used in oiling, causing damage not only to the binding itself, but also to the interior of a text and to its neighbors. There is no question that oiling bindings will enhance, for the short term, the physical appearance of a library of beautifully bound leather books. Oiling, if it is to be done, must be undertaken under the supervision of a conservator who has considerable experience in working with leather. To date, there is no evidence that oiling prolongs the life of a leather binding; at best, it does no harm to some leathers. It is not a recommended practice.

Some bindings are not really leather, but a composite of paper-based materials put together to resemble a fine leather bookbinding. The production of such bindings was common in the nineteenth century. Attempting to oil such bindings will create a mess.

Vellum and parchment bindings are hygroscopic and respond badly to changes in humidity. If they cannot be stored in an air-conditioned area, they should be kept in specially constructed cases that keep the covers under a constant pressure to prevent expansion and contraction. Vellum can be cleaned by washing, but this is a task for a skilled conservator. Surface dirt can be removed in-house by a trained technician.

Books in their original wrappers and those with elaborate decorative bindings should be housed in protective boxes that are specially constructed to prevent damage and to prevent the bindings from causing damage to other books. A conservation technician can undertake a boxing and wrapping program in-house if there is sufficient material to merit the expense. A number of commercial library binders are also offering this service. A program to train technicians to undertake boxing and repairs in commercial library binderies was established at the North Bennet Street School, Boston. There are a wide variety of boxes and wrappers that can be constructed to house and preserve books; the key factor is to select the appropriate structure for the volume. Ready-made boxes usually will not fit the books properly and thus are of limited value for preservation. Measurements of the dimensions of the book must be exact. If wrappers and boxes are to be made by the commercial library binder, it is important that the librarian carefully reviews the needs of the collections with the technician who will be supervising the job. The librarian should inspect the product when it is returned from the binder to ensure that it is satisfactory.

Interest in art, or designer binding was revived at the turn of the century, inspired by William Morris, the Arts and Crafts Movement in England, and the Roycrafters in America. A similar revival is under way today and outstanding examples of the bookbinder's art are being created in Europe and America. These contemporary designer bindings frequently are made of new and unusual materials and can be unusual in shape. They require special boxing for storage. These materials can create special preservation problems.

All books that are to be preserved indefinitely in their original format will require the skill of the professional book conservator. The conservator can preserve the original binding or, if it is beyond repair, create a new binding that will duplicate the original or be in the style of the original. Such treatment is costly, ranging upward from $100 per volume. Thus it is appropriate only for material that is to remain permanently in the library's collection.

Notes

1. Miner, vii.

Selected readings

Dean, John. "The Role of the Bookbinder in Preservation." *Wilson Library Bulletin* 56:3 (November 1981): 182–186.

DeCandido, Robert. "Out of the Question: How Are Binding Specifications Developed?" *Conservation Administration News,* No. 27 (October 1990): 9, 17.

Jacobson, Bruce F. "Librarians and Binders: Toward a Cultural Understanding." *The New Library Scene* 4:5 (October 1985): 1, 13.

Library Binding Institute. *Standard for Library Binding,* ed. Paul A. Parisi and Jan Merrill-Oldham. 8th ed. Rochester, NY: 1986.

Merrill-Oldham, Jan. "Binding for Research Libraries." *The New Library Scene* 3:4 (August 1984): 1, 4–6.

Montori, Carla. "Managing the Library's Commercial Library Binding Program." *Technical Services Quarterly* 5:3 (1988): 21–25.

Parisi, Paul A. and Jan Merrill-Oldham. *Guide to the Library Binding Institute Standard for Library Binding.* Chicago: American Library Association, 1990.

VIII. PAPER: Problems and Solutions

Introduction

MODERN MACHINE-MADE PAPERS ARE MADE OF macerated fibers, principally of wood. These fibers are ground into a pulp and various chemicals are added, determining the basic chemical composition of the paper stock. The pulp mixture is placed on a papermaking machine called a Fourdrinier; this mechanical marvel, which is as long as a city block, forms the paper, which emerges in long sheets. Much of the paper manufactured today is neither permanent nor intended to be permanent. Unfortunately, much of the written record of the past 150 years has been produced on impermanent papers. Librarians and archivists have inherited a legacy of decaying books and documents to preserve for future generations.

History of Papermaking

According to tradition, paper was invented in China by the courtier T'sai Lun, circa A.D. 105. During the past decade, archaeologists have found several paperlike fragments dating to earlier centuries. Certainly T'sai Lun brought the development of papermaking to fruition. One of the earliest fragments of Chinese paper dates to A.D. 109. The technique of papermaking spread to Korea by the end of the second century A.D., and thence to Japan. The *Chronicles of Japan* report that papermaking was introduced in A.D. 610. Concurrently the knowledge of papermaking spread west with the silk trade, and by the end of the eighth century paper was being made in Samarkand

129

and Baghdad. By the middle of the eleventh century, paper was a popular commodity in the Arab world. The Moors introduced papermaking into Spain; the first paper mills in the western world were established by 1150. The craft spread to Italy; the Fabriano mill, which continues to produce handmade paper of the finest quality today, was established by the late thirteenth century. Paper mills began to appear in Northern Europe in the next century. The first paper mill in England was established in Hertfordshire by John Tate before 1495, and his paper was used to produce Wynken de Worde's *Golden Legend* and an edition of Chaucer in 1498.

In the Americas, the Mayan and the Aztec Indians were producing a paperlike substance by beating the bark of fig and mulberry trees long before the Spanish introduced European methods, circa 1580. Papermaking was not introduced into the North American colonies until a century later when William Rittenhouse, an immigrant from Germany, established his mill in 1690 on the Wissahickon Creek near Philadelphia. Within twenty years, other paper mills sprang up in the Philadelphia area, and papermaking quickly spread to other colonies.

The technique of papermaking changed very little from its inception until the late seventeenth century. Originally the Chinese beat the wet pulp by hand in a stone mortar to separate the fibers. The pulp was later pounded with mallets; the Arabs invented a manpowered triphammer for this purpose. Various fermentation processes were used to prepare the pulp. Easier methods of production soon were developed in Europe. Pulp was prepared in a water-powered stamping mill; it was pounded in wooden or stone troughs by rows of wooden hammers that rose and fell by means of a series of cams on an axle.(1) Then, as today, the macerated pulp, or slurry, is poured into a mold, originally a rigid, rectangular form with thin bamboo strips. The European papermakers developed a rigid hardwood frame containing a series of parallel wooden ribs crossed with closely spaced brass wires that leave impressions, called "laid lines," on the paper. Widely spaced fine wires, perpendicular to the laid lines, are called "chain lines." These form a wire screen that is dipped into the slurry. A wooden frame, the deckle, fits over the mold to prevent the slurry from escaping. This method is still used today for handmade paper.

When the sheet of paper has formed on the mold, it is removed and carefully laid on a felt cloth. After a sufficient number of wet sheets have accumulated in a stack, it is placed in a press. In earlier times, workers at the mill were summoned to turn the long lever on the press that squeezed out excess water and reduced the height of a post of papers from about two feet to six inches. At this point the "layman" removes the felts. The sheets then receive a series of small pressings until the desired smoothness is achieved. Sheets are then hung on a line to dry, four or five sheets together to prevent wrinkling. Finally the paper is "sized," treated with a solution to make the sheets of paper, which are porous webs of fibers, suitable to receive the ink of the scribe or printer. Various substances have been used for sizing through the ages, from gypsum to animal gelatin. By 1850 rosin size had come into use. Unfortunately, it produces a chemical action that hastens the decomposition of even the finest rag papers.

After the stamping machine, the next invention to make papermaking easier was the Samson, an adaptation of a ship's windlass. It could be turned by four to six men to press the paper, and produced a paper of a more compact texture. A glazing hammer, a mallet run by waterpower, pounded the sheet and gave it a smoother and more uniform appearance than had been achieved by the hand method. The Clanedal roll, invented by the Dutch, replaced the glazing hammer as a finisher. In this process, dry sheets of paper were fed between two large wooden cylinders to produce a superior, calendered finish.

The "hollander," or beater, which mechanically macerated the fibers to make paper, was invented in the Netherlands by 1680 and is still in use today. It evolved from other machines designed to facilitate the making of paper and was very simply constructed. A cylinder with thirty or more blades, set in an oblong tub, ground the rag materials against a bedplate. The revolving motion of the roller kept the pulp circulating constantly in the tub, passing it under the blades until the desired degree of shredding was obtained.(2) When driven by waterpower, the hollander beater could be used with stampers to provide mechanization using far less power. Furthermore, it sped up the raw pulp fermentation process and saved much material previously lost through the deterioration of the rags during fermentation. The "hollander" beater chopped fibers into short pieces rather than spreading the long rag fibers as did the stampers. Thus began the decline of quality in paper. While certainly sturdier than modern papers, eighteenth century paper is not always as sturdy as earlier papers.

The industrial age, leading to the block-long Fourdrinier, has brought about vast changes in the papermaking process. Unfortunately, with the increase in ease and economy of production there has been a concurrent decrease in quality. Papers in the West were originally made of rag fibers that were almost entirely pure, without materials in their composition that would lead to deterioration. Often rag fibers were difficult to obtain and manufacturers continually looked for adequate substitute materials, some of which were quite bizarre. At the same time, bleaching techniques increasingly utilized chemicals; after 1800 these chemical bleaches left an acid residue, another factor in the deterioration of modern paper.

The first papermaking machine, the prototype of the Fourdrinier, was invented in 1798. Within the next decade it was successfully adapted to mechanized papermaking, and it revolutionized the industry. Basically, it transformed the wet macerated fibers into a thin web of dry paper. This process was accomplished upon a long wire screen traveling continuously over rollers. The fibers flowed onto the screen in water, and the water was then removed by suction. The moist web of matted fiber was then transferred to a felt roll, which carried the thin web of paper through the press rolls to remove excess water. By this time, the paper was strong enough to go over steam-heated cylinders for drying. The Fourdrinier mechanically imitated all of the operations that had been performed by people in traditional hand papermaking. By the middle of the nineteenth century, wood pulp became an effective and economical material for papermaking. Inexpensively produced paper enabled printed matter to be disseminated widely and helped bring the printed word to an increasingly literate public. Only later were its problems recognized. Alum rosin sizing caused paper to deteriorate quickly and groundwood fibers produced an inherently weak paper that deteriorated with age and exposure to ultraviolet light. By the turn of the century, librarians in England and the United States began to recognize that wood pulp paper was impermanent and identified the acids used during the manufacturing process as a primary cause.

Paper: The Late Twentieth Century

In the late 1930s, William J. Barrow of the Virginia Historical Society in Richmond began the search for a permanent and durable paper. He had developed a successful laminating process and a method for deacidification, the removal of acid from paper, which is necessary before paper can be laminated. In 1957, at the suggestion of its prescient director, Verner W. Clapp, the Council on Library Resources gave Barrow the funds to begin his study of book papers. His research indicated that 97 percent of the nonfiction books published between 1900 and 1939 would deteriorate to the point of being useless by the end of the century.(3) Barrow then developed specifications for a permanent/durable paper that, when tested by artificial aging, shows a useful life of 200 years.(4)

Librarians, and the reading public, need not settle for books that are printed on acid paper, books that are here today and gone to dust tomorrow. Today, papers produced with a pH reading of 7.0 or higher, with an alkaline reserve, can be manufactured more cheaply and efficiently than paper with a high acid content. While it is expensive for the paper manufacturers to convert their equipment, they are obliged to do so as rapidly as possible because the old production method does not meet the standards for pollution control that have been set by the Environmental Protection Agency in the United States, and in most Western European countries. In 1979 the Council on Library Resources, with funding from the Andrew W.

Mellon Foundation, which continues to support national and international preservation and conservation initiatives, formed a Committee on Production Guidelines for Book Longevity with representatives from the library, archival, publishing, and manufacturing communities. Its goals were to increase knowledge about the longevity of books and other library materials and to encourage improvements in their physical properties.(5) The committee's primary concern was the preservation of books in the future. Its investigations resulted in the publication of reports on book paper and binding, published originally in the May 29, 1981 and the July 2, 1982 issues of *Publishers Weekly,* and reprinted for distribution by the council in 1982.

The committee recognized that it would be absurd to suggest that all paper production be "permanent." However, it offered guidelines for the production of permanent/durable papers suitable for library and archival materials of permanent value. These guidelines were incorporated into the American National Standard for Information Sciences, "Permanence of Paper for Printed Library Materials," ANSI (American National Standards Institute) Z39.48.1984. The standard, the minimum requirement for uncoated permanent paper, requires a minimum pH of 7.5, a minimum cross-direction folding endurance of 30 double folds at 1 kg. tension for 30 to 60 pound paper, a tear resistance meeting ANSI/TAPPI (Technical Association of the Pulp and Paper Industry) standard T414 om-82, a minimum alkaline reserve equivalent to two percent calcium carbonate based upon the oven dry weight of the paper, and paper stock that includes no groundwood or unbleached pulp. The standard defines "permanent" as "paper that should last at least several hundred years without significant deterioration under normal library use and storage conditions."(6) With only slight revision, it promises to become the international standard for the production of permanent and durable paper.

The committee suggested that books that meet the guidelines for permanence and durability so indicate below the copyright line. To that end the infinity sign has been adopted to indicate compliance with the standard, usually accompanied by the statement, "The paper used in this publication meets the minimum requirements of the American National Standard for Information Sciences—Permanence of Paper for Printed Library Materials, ANSI Z39.48–1984."

The standard has been adopted by the majority of publishers of scholarly works today, as well as an increasing number of trade publishers. The library community has worked hard to encourage publishers to use permanent/durable papers, which become easier to obtain each year as mills convert. *Library Journal* and other publications for the library profession use the infinity symbol in book reviews to indicate those books printed on alkaline paper that meet the standard.

The standard Z39.48–1984 is currently being revised, for it has become clear that an alkaline reserve over pH 7.5 offers even greater protection for permanent papers. Further, groundwood can be used for paper production if the offending ingredient, lignin, is removed in the production process. Thus, today the preferred term for permanent papers is "alkaline," or "lignin-free," rather than Barrow's term, "permanent/durable," for these terms are more accurate. The standard will also cover coated papers to ensure that books published on coated paper, such as expensive art books, are also permanent. The revised standard will incorporate the results of recent research on paper permanence and will also address the issue of recycled papers.

As librarians and archivists laud William Barrow and Verner Clapp as early soldiers in the battle against self-destructing books and records, today another advocate of permanent paper, Ellen McCrady, has gained international recognition and respect. McCrady, with a missionary's zeal and energy, has taken on the cause of permanent paper for permanent records. In addition to her distinguished publication, *Abbey Newsletter,* McCrady began publishing the *Alkaline Paper Advocate* in 1988 "to provide a forum for producers and consumers, who now find communication difficult because of the complexity of the marketplace." McCrady is president of Abbey Publications, Inc., a nonprofit organization that serves as an advocate for the production of permanent and durable library and archival materials to ensure their preservation. She has facilitated communication between librarians, archivists, publishers, and paper manufacturers throughout the world. McCrady is a preservationist who acts, not reacts. She plays a leading roll in the efforts to ensure that papers for permanence are produced in the future.

The issue of the 1990s is "preservation" of paper and of the earth. While librarians and archivists seek legislation to ensure that permanent records are published on permanent paper, the preservationists of the earth are promoting legislation to have official records published on recycled paper, to preserve our forests. Recycled paper can be alkaline. One problem is that once printed paper has been recycled several times, the inks tend to make the paper produced more acidic. Librarians, archivists, and legislators need to address this problem, not ignore it, and to work with paper manufacturers to resolve it. Too little is known at present about the nature and constitution of printing inks, but those concerned about the preservation of the written word are going to have to learn about them. Scientists need to determine what inks are best for use on paper that is to be recycled, if we are to "preserve" in every sense of the word. Cooperation will lead to preservation.

Paper is still made by hand, but its production is costly and few papermills produce it. In the past decade there has been revived interest in hand papermaking as a small craft business for the art and fine press market. Many private press printers, artists, and hobbyists produce their own paper. Handmade paper is as good as the ingredients used to make it. If it is made with fine linen rags and no chemicals are used, it can be beautiful, permanent, and durable. If it is made with wood pulp and/or chemicals, it will deteriorate as rapidly as machine-made wood pulp paper.

Conservation

While librarians and archivists are working with publishers and the paper manufacturers to ensure that alkaline paper is used for book and paper production in the future, they must still cope with the vast majority of materials in their collections that have been published in the past 150 years and are rapidly deteriorating. Fortunately, many deteriorating books in library collections can be discarded. Replacement copies in new, reprinted, or microtext editions are available for much of the material that is needed in libraries. Reformatting options are discussed elsewhere in this volume. Yet, there remains a small body of materials in the library—books, documents, original prints, maps, even local newspapers—of special value to an institution. This material, if it is to be preserved in its original format, requires the skills of a professional conservator. A skilled conservator can save almost anything—at a cost. The treatment undertaken by a conservator is accomplished methodically by hand; there are few mechanical devices to aid in the delicate task of repair. A conservator is a highly trained and skilled professional who has studied intensively the techniques of repairing and conserving objects. It takes knowledge, experience, and demonstrated skill to become a Fellow of the International Institute for the Conservation of Historic and Artistic Works (IIC) and/or the American Institute for the Conservation of Historic and Artistic Works (AIC).

A conservator will estimate the cost of a conservation treatment and will work closely with curators of collections to establish priorities within budget limitations. In most instances treatments undertaken by conservators are reversible. It is possible to make some immediately needed repairs on an object to stabilize it, then store it in a controlled environment until funds for more extensive, and expensive, treatment become available. This has come to be known as "phased" conservation, an approach to preservation originally developed at the Library of Congress.

A conservator, or a trained conservation technician working under the supervision of a conservator, can clean paper, repair tears, remove destructive backings, mat and frame materials for exhibition, encapsulate materials in polyester, and construct a wide variety of envelopes, wrappers, and boxes for the storage of paper-based materials. A conservator also can help an institution achieve optimal environmental controls for the housing of special materials. There is little point in treating materials if, after treatment, they are to be returned to the environment that abetted deterioration in the first place. Along with phased conservation, conservators have introduced the concept of object containerization for library, archival, and museum collections. Containers can provide a microenvironment for materials that must be stored for periods of time under less than optimum conditions. Boxes and wrappers for library and archival materials can be produced in an in-house workshop, although the cost of equipping and staffing such workshops is relatively high, even if student or volunteer labor is used. The simplest workshop, to be at all efficient, requires an outlay of at least $15,000 to $20,000 for basic equipment, exclusive of staff and supplies. Increasingly, commercial library binders are offering the boxing of materials and basic paper repair as services that can be done more efficiently and cost-effectively in a commercial bindery setting, as was discussed in Chapter 7.

A number of libraries with extensive special collections of paper-based materials have established conservation laboratories staffed with one or more conservators and conservation technicians. It is more practical, however, for smaller institutions to contract for the services of a conservator when necessary and to send materials in need of treatment to the conservator's laboratory. Increasingly,

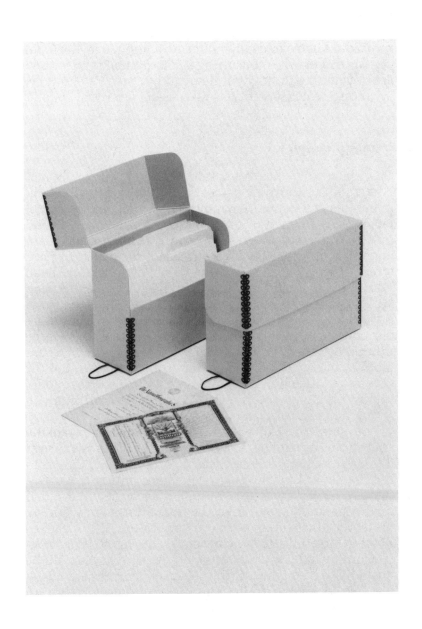

Archival Boxes. Credit: Light Impressions Corporation

funds are being provided through public and private agencies to pay for the preservation and conservation of individual items and collections of significance. Regional centers can provide consulting and treatment services and are developing throughout the country; their role in preservation and conservation is discussed in the final chapter of this book.

Deacidification

To restate what has been said before, most books and documents published since the 1860s are printed on paper that is deteriorating rapidly due to a combination of factors. The paper is made of processed groundwood pulp, which soon becomes acidic. These acidic, frequently embrittled books are housed, for the most part, where they are exposed to the damaging effects of heat, humidity, air pollution, and light, each and all of which synergistically hasten their deterioration. The expense of preserving every book published since 1860 is formidable. Much of this material can be reformatted to preserve informational content. Rare and unique books and documents can be deacidified by hand, then treated, but for several decades librarians and archivists have been longing for a mass treatment that can deacidify, even strengthen paper-based materials.

The deacidification of paper involves the removal of the acids from the paper, for the acids are the primary cause of its deterioration. This is usually accomplished by washing the paper by hand in an aqueous solution to remove the impurities. Then an alkaline buffering agent is added to the paper to neutralize the remaining acids and to protect against future acidic deterioration. The deacidification and alkalization of paper by hand is a time-consuming and costly process. Some materials cannot be deacidified through washing because their inks are unstable. Because of the limitations and cost of deacidification by washing and buffering paper, librarians and archivists have been eager to find a method for nonaqueous deacidification that can be used in a "mass treatment" procedure.

A number of techniques have been developed for the mass deacidification of paper. Some of these techniques are still new and have not been fully tested and evaluated. Some may strengthen the paper, which is a goal for treatment of the embrittled specimens that are the legacy of the past 150 years. Each process has strengths and weaknesses. As of this writing, several processes are available for use in libraries on a commercial basis. It is of critical importance that librarians and archivists carefully analyze the needs of their collections and select an appropriate deacidification treatment, if this is a chosen method of treatment for a collection. While much has been written about these processes and there have been many claims about their effectiveness, sound, factual data about what they are and how they work is not readily available at this time. Librarians and archivists who hope to make use of one or more of these processes need an independent review of the strengths and weaknesses of each; more will be said concerning this need at the conclusion of this section.

The Research Section of the Library of Congress Preservation Division and the now defunct W. J. Barrow Research Laboratory were instrumental in the development of a morpholine vapor deacidification process whereby one hundred books could be treated at a time. The basic process consisted of the impregnation of the text block with morpholine gas under moderately elevated temperatures in a vacuum chamber. The gas is forced into the book paper, causing a reaction that neutralizes the acidic components that are destroying the paper. This process was not successful, however. It was only mildly effective as a deacidifying agent and did not introduce a buffering chemical into the treated pages. Moreover, it had an unpleasant odor.

Under the direction of George Kelly, the Library of Congress developed a mass treatment using the chemical compound diethyl zinc (DEZ) in the 1970s. The diethyl zinc gas, when bled into a vacuum chamber, permeates the books and papers selected for treatment and neutralizes the acids in the paper. Large quantities of materials can be treated in the vacuum chamber with relatively little preselection of books. In the trial runs, however, a rainbow effect was observed on some book covers. While the distribution of the diethyl zinc gas was somewhat uneven, all materials were impregnated to some degree. The discoloration problem was solved by a change in the design of the racks that held the books and in the chamber itself. Unfortunately, diethyl zinc is a hazardous material that is spontaneously flammable in the open air. It must be used with great care by trained professionals. During its trial runs at the Goddard Space Center, Fort Detrick, MD, there were several accidents caused by procedural problems, equipment malfunctions, and faulty design of the diethyl zinc delivery system. Because of the engineering and safety concerns, Congress, which had supplied funding for the development of the system, requested an independent review of the DEZ and other potential processes by the Office of Technology Assessment (OTA). The OTA analysis concluded that there was insufficient data available on the other processes to be able to assess their effectiveness. The OTA also concluded that the Library of Congress had not evaluated sufficiently other potential processes, nor had it sufficiently developed strategies to efficiently and effectively treat its collections. The report concludes: "As the costs and capabilities of alternative processes become better defined, it may be appropriate to do a more careful analysis of the costs and benefits of pre-selection."(7) The issue of preselection is, indeed, an important factor in the choice of a mass deacidification process for the treatment of collections.

While the Library of Congress continued to maintain that the DEZ process offered the best potential for the successful treatment of its collections, it abandoned the concept of a government-owned and operated facility, and agreed to contract its work to a firm with expertise to handle the engineering and safety complexities. The DEZ process was licensed to the Netherlands-based company, Akzo Chemicals, Inc., which undertook further tests to ensure its safety and effectiveness. In February 1990, a select group of preservation professionals met at the

Library of Congress to review the Library's Request for Proposals (RFP) for mass deacidification of its collections. After a careful review of three processes, DEZ, Lithco, and Wei T'o, which resulted in the publication of four volumes of data on these systems, it was concluded that none entirely met the Library's requirements. Several research libraries contracted with Akzo, however, and are continuing the testing and review of this mass deacidification treatment for books and documents to determine its cost and effectiveness as a preservation tool. The DEZ process may prove to be an appropriate process for the deacidification of books and papers. It is not at all clear that it will prove to be the most effective and efficient process to treat all acidic library and archival materials. Because of its limitation and the lack of a large enough market, Akzo closed its treatment facility in Texas in December 1993.

The Wei T'o Nonaqueous Book Deacidification System was developed by chemical engineer Richard D. Smith in the late 1960s while he was a doctoral candidate at the University of Chicago's Library School. It is "a liquefied gas process designed to dissolve, transport, and deposit chemicals into book pages to neutralize any acids present in the paper, and to deposit buffering chemicals that will neutralize any acids that may subsequently contaminate the paper."(8) During its development, Smith has used a variety of chemicals for its deacidifying agent. The system has been in operation at the Public Archives of Canada since 1981, and some cost data has been made available. The system does require some preselection; approximately three percent of the books selected for deacidification cannot be treated because of solvent problems with inks and colors.(9) There is considerable interest in the Wei T'o system in Europe. A potential problem for the Wei T'o process at this time is its use of Freon in its formulation.

Wei T'o also has developed a spray deacidification system that is in use in several institutions. However, this is not a mass deacidification system. Susan Batton, former Head of Treatments, Princeton University Library, where the Wei T'o spray system is installed, notes that it is "a large scale manual spray deacidification system having merits separate from any (other) developments in mass technology."(10) George Cunha, who has reviewed the deacidification systems currently developed, observes, "What makes it important is its efficiency and the remarkable effectiveness of the ventilation system which moves an enormous amount of Wei T'o-laden air away from the treatment booths into the open air," making it possible for treatment booths to be located in a conservation unit in an institution.(11) The Wei T'o spray system is, however, an aqueous treatment that requires preselection and testing. It is an expensive and labor-intensive process. The system is used effectively to treat newspapers at the British Library's Newspaper Library in Colindale and the Bibliothèque Nationale's newspaper preservation facility in Provins, France.

The Austrian National Library has also developed a mass treatment for newsprint that is embrittled, but not yet physically damaged. It is based upon an aqueous immersion treatment, followed by freezing and freeze-drying, that deacidifies and strengthens paper. At present, further studies are under way to improve the engineering of the process and to enlarge its capacity.

The British Library is exploring graft copolymerization techniques for the strengthening of embrittled paper. The process is based upon the introduction of short chained monomers in liquid form, without the use of solvents, within a closed container. The monomers are converted to long chained polymers via exposure to low-intensity gamma rays; the polymers are formed within the cellulose fibers, on and between the fiber surfaces, which increase fold endurance between five and ten times.(11) This process is still under development; its significance is that it is a mass process that deals with paper strengthening, rather than a deacidification process, which leaves paper in the same condition as it was before treatment. Paper strengthening is really the key to a mass treatment process for embrittled paper-based materials.

In 1981 the Koppers Company, in Pennsylvania, began to explore the possibility of developing a mass deacidification treatment for libraries that would be simple, safe, and economical. A process was developed to the testing stage, then the project was terminated, probably because the company realized that the potential income from the process was not sufficient to merit production. Its engineer, Richard Spatz, acquired the patent and has established a company, Preservation Technologies, Inc., to develop the Bookkeeper process. The beauty of this process is in its chemical simplicity. The Bookkeeper process is currently being tested for its effectiveness by the Library of Congress. One problem with the process is that some of the chemicals used in the solvents are harmful to the ozone layer of the earth. If this problem can be resolved, the Bookkeeper process holds promise as a treatment that can be installed and operated efficiently in an institution or a regional treatment facility.

In 1988, Information Conservation, Inc., a commercial library binding company headquartered in Greensboro, NC, announced its association with Book Preservation Associates (BPA), in Carteret, NJ, to offer a low-cost mass deacidification process for libraries. Deacidification is accomplished using ammonia and ethylene oxide at a treatment facility. The process results in the creation of amines that neutralize the acid in paper and act as a buffering agent. The process does raise the pH level in a text block after treatment and appears to strengthen the paper. Paper is somewhat darkened following treatment. Ethylene oxide is a powerful fumigant and destroys microorganisms in books during treatment; yet, the use of ethylene oxide raises safety concerns that will need to be addressed before this process can be effectively marketed. Although some preliminary testing has shown the treatment to be less than satisfactory, the BPA process has the potential to be an effective and efficient method of deacidifying books. If it indeed works, it should require little preselection; however, little has been heard of this process since 1991.

In 1988, the Lithco Corporation of America (Lithco), Gastonia, NC, a subsidiary of FMC Corporation's Chemical Products Group, developed processes using organometallic compounds that are proving to be effective in deacidifying and strengthening paper.(13) The Lithco process has three steps: preconditioning (drying), impregnation with active ingredients, and solvent removal.(14) Its prototype facility in North Carolina opened in June 1990. While little is known to date about the precise nature of this process, the fact that it can strengthen as well as deacidify materials has significant implications for libraries and archives. Cunha has noted that the Lithco process has the potential to "make it possible for mildly brittle books to be returned to circulation."(15)

Deacidification has been a catchword in libraries and archives for at least a decade as institutions have recognized the problem of deteriorating and embrittled collections. It is heartening that so much research and development is now under way. A solution to the problem of the acids slowly destroying the paper-based materials created in the past 150 years, one that will enable institutions to keep original material rather than surrogate copies, is greatly desired. There are several serious considerations for "mass treatments" that are only now being addressed.

First, any treatment to deacidify and/or strengthen books and paper is, to some extent, irreversible. The treatment will change the physical nature of the paper to some degree. This fact should be kept in mind when debating the merits of a treated original versus the merits of a surrogate copy, with the original preserved in its original condition in a controlled environment.

Second, as George Cunha reminds us, "One bothersome fact is that the effectiveness of each system has been determined in-house, so to speak, by its vendor—even when the vendor has used independent laboratories for the tests."(16) Librarians and archivists owe George Cunha a debt of gratitude for his efforts to evaluate, with limited information, the processes available in his two *Library Technology Reports.* These reports forced open discussion among and between producers, librarians, and archivists. The vendors themselves have acknowledged the need for thorough, unbiased testing. Robert Wedinger, a developer of the Lithco process, has proposed an "Evaluation Strategy: Paper Preservation Systems," which was circulated to producers and preservation specialists in the spring of 1990. In the document, Wedinger provides a model for the testing and evaluation of deacidification and paper-strengthening processes. His document has served as a focus for discussion, as the author intended, for further testing and evaluation of the processes.

In 1990, Peter Sparks, a physical chemist and former Director for Preservation at the Library of Congress, prepared a report, "Technical Considerations in Choosing Mass Deacidification Processes," for the Commission on Preservation and Access. This report outlines the evaluation procedures that should be undertaken by institutions that are considering the use of one or more mass treatment techniques. Sparks's report was prepared "to give those institutions which have decided to investigate mass deacidification as a preservation alternative an understanding of the technical and other related factors they need to consider, as well as the rationale for considering them" (Page 1). In the fall of 1991 a number of institutions working with the Association of Research Libraries explored the potential of several mass deacidification treatments following the evaluative procedures outlined in the Sparks report. Several research libraries then contracted with Akzo Chemicals, Inc., to have collections treated using the DEZ process.

The rationale for considering mass deacidification treatments brings us to the third and final point. "Deacidification of already brittle books is an exercise in futility," George Cunha states in his 1989 evaluation of the processes. He continues, "Now, it could very well be that those systems that deacidify only, no matter how well they do it, will soon be obsolete, as a system (or systems) that deacidifies and strengthens paper simultaneously becomes practical."(17)

In order to evaluate the mass deacidification and/or strengthening systems that will soon be available, librarians and archivists must determine which materials they want treated, and for what purpose. Are original materials to be deacidified and/or strengthened for preservation and access, or will surrogate copies suffice in most institutions? Libraries are attempting to address the brittle paper problem collectively through coordinated efforts to microfilm endangered collections of books and documents. In many cases, original materials have not been saved, usually because librarians believed they were beyond saving without drastic, and costly, intervention, but too often original materials have been lost through carelessness. Many curators and scholars are unhappy that librarians have opted to discard some original material without full discussion of the importance of the original books as primary research materials for the scholarly community. Deacidification and strengthening processes offer the hope of preservation of materials as closely as possible to their original nature. But scholars, librarians, and archivists have not really addressed the question of just what materials they wish to have preserved in original format, why they wish them saved, for what purpose. There has been little collaborative effort between scholars and librarians to establish guidelines for the preservation of materials in original format. This is the major preservation issue of the 1990s. It is a question that needs to be addressed in every institution before any treatment action is considered, and it is one, ultimately, that the scholarly community as a whole needs to address.

There is a legacy of 150 years of acidic paper in the nation's library and archival collections, but by the end of the decade books and important documents should be produced on alkaline paper that promises permanence and durability for centuries to come. We return to the question of what of our documentary heritage we want preserved, and in what format. We cannot save every book and document that has been produced since the 1860s, but we can determine, in concert with scholars, which materials will be saved and who will be responsible for them, in whatever appropriate format.

In its summary of the DEZ and other deacidification processes, the Office of Technology Assessment report concludes, "It may also be worthwhile to determine ways to encourage the use of acid-free paper. The more books that are printed on acid-free paper, the fewer that would require deacidification. To accurately compare and optimize strategies, more information would be needed to be collected on trends in acid-free paper production, the make up of existing and future Library of Congress collections and the range of benefits from deacidification to be expected for the variety of books and papers in the collection."(18) This is now being done, thanks, in part, to the efforts of Ellen McCrady, and signals the end of "the dark age" of our documentary heritage.

Encapsulation

Even if paper has been deacidified, it will still be very fragile unless it has been strengthened in the treatment process. The technique of encapsulation, placing a sheet of paper between two sheets of polyester to protect it, was developed at the Library of Congress in the early 1970s to preserve such materials. The deacidified sheet is encased in sheets of polyester. It is relatively easy to attach the polyester and there are a number of techniques for sealing it. The simplest approach is to score the polyester sheet to make a folder that will hold the object. While static electricity will tend to keep the object in place, it can slide, thus this technique is not recommended for collections of great value.

The more typical approach is to seal the polyester package with an acetate double-sided adhesive tape that easily can be removed. The adhesive can cause serious damage to paper when it comes into contact with it, however. The instructions for polyester encapsulation stress the need to place the tape at least 1/4 inch away from the item being encapsulated. Unsupervised workers, unaware of the reason for this instruction, have too often been careless and placed the tape closer to the document. While the static electricity holds the encapsulated item in place reasonably well, over time there is slippage. Archivists and librarians are discovering documents that have slipped and are stuck to the adhesive tape, or adhesive in the tape that has oozed and crept onto a document. There is some concern about the continued use of this technique. The use of double-sided adhesive tape to secure encapsulated items of great value is not recommended.

In 1978, conservator William Minter of Chicago developed an ultrasonic welder for encapsulation. It does the job quickly, safely, and allows for a flexibility that was lacking before. For example, the Conservation Center for Art and Historic Artifacts in Philadelphia treated a collection of early Coptic documents belonging to Dropsie College, Philadelphia, PA. The fragments of parchment and papyrus had not been identified by scholars. Using the welder to encapsulate a series of fragments, the conservators were able to construct volumes in post bindings. These fragments can be studied, identified, and moved easily, as necessary.

Although the early ultrasonic welders were individually produced and cost approximately $14,000 each, they were a godsend to conservators. This equipment is now being manufactured by a company in Great Britain, but the cost is still significantly beyond what most libraries can pay unless they have extensive collections that require preservation through encapsulation. Most regional conservation centers and a number of conservation facilities now offer encapsulation at reasonable cost using the ultrasonic welder. For example, one regional library binder with a conservation laboratory will lease the use of the ultrasonic welder by the hour to conservators or technicians from institutions in the area. Clients can come to the bindery to use it under the supervision of the conservator. The applications of the ultrasonic welder have yet to be fully explored by the library and archival communities.

Lamination

Lamination, the reinforcement of a sheet of paper on both sides with a thin, transparent textile or plastic fiber, has been a method used for the strengthening of paper since early in the century. However, the restorers who used lamination techniques were unaware that a primary cause of weakness in the paper was due to its acidic content, and paper was not deacidified before it was laminated. While the early lamination techniques ostensibly are reversible, in reality, the treatment of these objects today is a difficult and time-consuming process. It is made more difficult by the significant physical deterioration of the sheet that was laminated, and the deterioration of the material used for lamination, such as silk. Hence, the technique has received poor press and a bad name in conservation.

Lamination as a preservation technique, however, has its place. The lamination technique developed by William Barrow and, until recently, done by his company in Richmond, VA, uses a cellulose acetate film on a sheet of paper that has been deacidified. The material is applied with heat and pressure, done so quickly that it causes little damage to an object. Lamination by this method may be an appropriate technique for the preservation of maps and other documents in some situations.

Another laminate process is the parylene process for strengthening materials. This process actually "plasticizes" an object. It is commonly used to preserve specimens in natural history museums. The Union Carbide Corporation is exploring the effectiveness of the parylene process to treat severely embrittled or damaged library and archival materials. The parylene process violates a cardinal rule of conservation, that any treatment be reversible and noninvasive. With a variety of rare and unique objects, conservation can be accomplished only by an invasive treatment, however. In short, if a very fragile or damaged, unique document is not "plasticized" to preserve it as closely as possible to its original format, the world may not have the document at all. Once it is treated, it is sturdy and is accessible. The mass treatments that "deacidify" materials also cause a chemical change in the paper that is not reversible.

Lamination is a technique that can be used for preservation under certain circumstances. As with any treatment for conservation, its applications require careful curatorial evaluation. Librarians and conservators are rethinking the concept of reversibility in the treatment of valued documentary materials. This is the time to evaluate thoroughly the procedures that can be used for the preservation and conservation of materials, such as lamination, and to make decisions about their use in the context of the collection and its use. One library's solution will not be another's.

Leaf Casting

A technical development that has greatly facilitated the work of the paper conservator is the invention of the leaf casting machine. This machine is a modern refinement of the hand papermaking technique of putting a wire screen under a slurry of fibers and then lifting out the wet paper on the screen. In leaf casting, paper fibers bond together on the screen to form a sheet. The repair of holes or tears in paper documents can then be made by placing the damaged leaf on the screen and forming a new leaf around holes, missing corners, worn edges, and other damaged areas. This technique will not deposit particles on the undamaged portion of a document and obscure its text. It takes about three minutes to make this repair, and it is superior to the hand repairs of even the most skilled conservator. A leaf caster can repair several sheets of paper at a time. Today, many are computer-driven to measure the precise composition and amount of slurry needed to repair a damaged item. While these machines are expensive, they cut repair time considerably and thus have become an integral part of the conservator's laboratory.

Conclusion

This chapter explains some of the reasons for the deterioration of books and paper, a problem rooted in the paper manufacturing processes dating back to the mid-nineteenth century. For the past fifteen years, librarians have been announcing the demise of their collections, consumed by acid. Technology marches on, however, and the paper manufacturing industry with it. For at least a decade, it has been less expensive for the manufacturer to produce an alkaline paper that is both permanent and durable. The problem has been the cost and effort involved in the conversion of a papermill to produce alkaline paper. But the paper manufacturers have no choice, and the public increasingly is demanding that the documents of its cultural heritage be printed on permanent and durable alkaline paper. Although library materials make up only a small percentage of a publisher's market, librarians are an effective lobby for the manufacture of permanent and durable books and are increasingly vocal. Efforts today will curtail serious preservation problems for future generations.

Notes

1. For a detailed description of hand papermaking process, see Dard Hunter, *Papermaking: The History and Technique of an Ancient Craft.* New York: Dover, 1978.
2. Hunter 162ff.
3. Barrow, William J. *Deterioration of Book Stock, Causes, and Remedies: Two Studies on the Permanence of Book Paper* (Richmond, VA: Virginia State Library, 1959): 15.
4. Barrow, W. J., Research Laboratory Inc. "Barrow Laboratory Research: Specifications for Permanent/Durable Book Papers." *American Archivist* 38:3 (July, 1975): 405–415.
5. *Book Longevity,* Reports of the Committee on Production Guidelines for Book Longevity. Washington, DC: Council on Library Resources (1982): 5.
6. Foreword to the American National Standard for Information Science-Permanence of Paper for Printed Materials, ANSI Z39.48–1984.
7. *Book Preservation Technologies: Summary,* Washington, DC: U.S. Congress, Office of Technology Assessment (May 1988): 13.
8. George M. Cunha. "Mass Deacidification for Libraries," *Library Technology Reports* 23 (May–June 1987): 410.
9. George M. Cunha. "Mass Deacidification for Libraries: 1989 Update." *Library Technology Reports* 25:1 (January–February 1989): 27.
10. Quoted in "Mass Deacidification for Libraries: 1989 Update," 29.
11. *Ibid.*
12. Clements, D.W.G. "Graft Copolymerisation Techniques for Strengthening Deteriorated Paper: British Library Developments," *Proceedings,* TAPPI Paper Preservation Symposium, Washington, DC (October 19–21, 1988): 155–156.
13. "Mass Deacidification for Libraries, 1989 Update," 56.
14. Robert S. Wedinger. "Lithco Develops Deacidification/Strengthening Process," *Abbey Newsletter* 13:7 (November 1989): 126.
15. "Mass Deacidification for Libraries, 1989 Update," 57.
16. *Ibid.,* 62.
17. *Ibid.,* 63.
18. *Book Preservation Technologies: Summary,* 13.

Selected Readings

Alkaline Paper Advocate, ed. Ellen McCrady. Vol. 1, 1988 and succeeding issues, written by the profession's leading advocate of alkaline, permanent and durable papers for library and archival materials.

Buchberg, Karl. "Paper: Manuscripts, Documents, Printed Sheets, and Works of Art." *Conservation in the Library,* ed. Susan G. Swartzburg, 31–54. Westport, CT: Greenwood Press, 1983.

Clapp, Anne F. *Curatorial Care of Works of Art on Paper: Basic Procedures for Paper Preservation.* New York: Nick Lyons, 1987.

Clapp, Verner W. "The Story of Permanent/Durable Book Paper, 1115–1970." *Scholarly Publishing* 2 (1971): 107–124, 229–245, 353–367; reprinted in *Restaurator,* Supplement 3, 1972.

Cloonan, Michèle Valerie. "Mass Deacidification in the 1990s." *Rare Book and Manuscript Librarianship* 5:2 (1990): 95–103.

Cunha, George Martin. "Mass Deacidification for Libraries." *Library Technology Reports,* 23:3 (May–June 1987), 361–472; "Mass Deacidification for Libraries: 1989 Update." *Library Technology Reports* 25:1 (January–February 1989): 5–81.

Luner, Philip, ed. *Paper Preservation: Current Issues and Recent Developments.* Atlanta, GA: TAPPI Press, 1990.

Paris, Jan. *Choosing and Working With a Conservator.* Atlanta, GA: Southeast Library Network, 1990.

S. D. Warren Company. *Paper Permanence: Preserving the Written Word.* Boston: S.D. Warren Company, 1981, 1983.

Sparks, Peter G., ed. *A Roundtable on Mass Deacidification,* report of a meeting held September 12–13 in Andover, MA, sponsored by the Association of Research Libraries and the Northeast Document Conservation Center. Washington, DC: Association of Research Libraries, 1992.

IX. SPECIAL MATERIALS IN THE LIBRARY

Introduction

MOST LIBRARIES CONTAIN A WIDE VARIETY OF OBJECTS. This chapter will discuss the housing and care of archival records, ephemera, newspapers, maps, fine prints, paintings, and other materials that require special attention and can pose problems in storage and access.

Both the Society of American Archivists (SAA) and the American Association for State and Local History (AASLH) have extensive publishing programs, providing print and video information on the care and preservation of special collections of materials. The Society of American Archivists publication *Preserving Archives and Manuscripts* by Mary Lynn Ritzenthaler (1994), is an invaluable source of information for any institution with collections of manuscripts, autographs, ephemera, and other paper-based materials. Workshops on the care and preservation of maps, prints, and archival materials sponsored by professional organizations and library schools are increasingly common.

Archival Records and Ephemera

Many, if not most, libraries have collections of archival records and ephemera that are of special interest to the community and may be rare or unique. Institutions with such materials have a responsibility to ensure their care and preservation for present and future generations. If an

DIAGRAM OF MAT

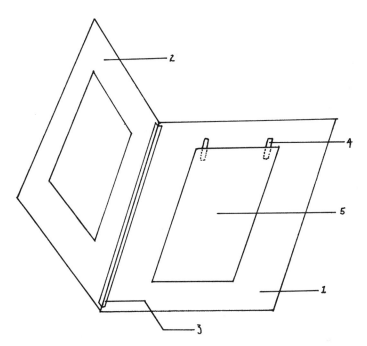

1. Back of Mat
2. Window Mat
3. Gummed White Cloth Tape
4. Hinge
5. Work of Art

Diagram of a mat. Credit: Karl Buchberg

institution cannot provide adequate housing, preservation, and access, it should place its special collections "on deposit" or give them to an institution that can ensure that the materials will be preserved and made accessible to researchers, present and future. Alternatively, the materials can be deaccessioned and sold, to provide funds to meet the identified needs of a library.

Archival collections contain personal papers and institutional records, numerous individual paper-based items, many of which are unique. These materials should be stored under "archival" conditions, with strict environmental controls and appropriate housing, including safe and easy retrieval and adequate work areas. They should be protected from fire and theft. Details on housing, safety, and security for collections are explored elsewhere in this volume.

Archival materials should be arranged and cataloged so that they are accessible to scholars without unnecessary handling of irrelevant material. Increasingly, photocopies of documents are used in lieu of original copies for research purposes; rare and fragile items are often photographed. Copies can be handled, reproduced, and otherwise manipulated by researchers, while the original materials are preserved for use only when it is critical to consult them; for example, to examine a watermark for accuracy in dating material.

Today, many important archival collections are microfilmed for preservation and access. New imaging technologies, already on the horizon, should improve access to materials, no matter how removed the researcher is from the institution where the original materials are held. Collections, organized and reproduced on compact discs, can be sent around the world while the original materials will remain safe in their protected environment. For the past decade, considerable funding has been available from federal agencies, such as the National Endowment for the Humanities (NEH) and the National Historic Publications and Records Commission (NHPRC) for the arrangement and microfilming of archival collections, thus making collections accessible to researchers wherever their physical location. A number of states also grant funds for preservation microfilming of rare and unique collections.

The Northeast Document Conservation Center (NEDCC), in Andover, MA, was the first regional center established for the preservation of library and archival materials; NEDCC was a pioneer in preservation microfilming. The Council on Library Resources, recognizing the need for imaging technology for preservation, obtained funding to establish the Mid-Atlantic, Preservation Service now Preservation Resources, Inc., a nonprofit regional microfilming center in Bethlehem, PA. It microfilms collections of books, newspapers, and archival materials following stringent specifications for preservation. A number of commercial vendors have entered the field of preservation microfilming. Some have been in the microfilming business for a number of years, filming collections of materials for sale to libraries and archives; they have considerable experience, and follow the guidelines for preservation microfilming that have been established by the Library of Congress and the Research Libraries Group (RLG). The guidelines for the microfilming of archival collections are discussed in chapter 12; these should be followed carefully when any project is undertaken to ensure the intellectual integrity and permanence of the material that is filmed.

Ephemera are those transient everyday items of paper that are produced specifically to use and to throw away. Yet this written or printed miscellany provides basic documentation about how we live. One of the earliest extant papyrus documents is a fragment of a laundry list. Most ephemeral material is printed on poor quality paper. It receives incredible abuse in unspeakable environmental conditions, yet some ephemera survives and becomes a part of an archival collection. The ephemera of 1776 became the treasures of 1976 in the United States. Indeed, the Bicentennial Celebration of the birthday of the nation significantly increased the public's interest in ephemeral materials and its desire to preserve them.

Libraries have developed extensive collections of political broadsides, shopping bags, invitations, menus, and the like, which are used by a variety of scholars and in exhibitions. Ephemera present special problems of preservation and access that may be complex and require ingenious solutions, yet most institutions that have dealt with their collections of ephemera report that their effort has enhanced the institution's archives.

The best approach to the preservation of paper-based materials is to ensure that archival collections are properly housed in alkaline archival boxes. A variety of boxes, folders, and envelopes have been designed to hold collections of manuscripts and ephemeral materials of every shape and size. They are available from suppliers of archival materials (see appendix).

Fragile and/or heavily used flat materials can be encapsulated in polyester or placed in polyester folders, which are appropriate for storage and exhibition. Polyester material used for encapsulation is inert and offers protection from ultraviolet light. There is some question about encapsulating material that has not been deacidified, for there is increasing evidence that destructive acids are "trapped" in the polyester enclosure and hasten decay. On the other hand, a polyester enclosure will protect fragile items from some of the harmful effects of the environment. The housing of fragile archival collections calls for careful planning and consultation with a conservator or preservation specialist to ensure the best possible environment.

Librarians should not attempt to make repairs on archival materials. Repair and treatment, when necessary, should be done by a conservator or by a trained conservation technician under the supervision of a conservator. While many repairs, such as mending and cleaning paper, appear straightforward, they can actually cause serious damage when attempted by untrained staff. If a mending program is to be started in a library, it calls for considerable thought and planning, consultation with a conservator, and adequate staff training and supervision.

Collectors will collect almost anything, and libraries

frequently find themselves custodians of this material. Too often it is stashed away in corners awaiting the day when the librarian has the time and the staff to deal with it. If collections of archival materials and ephemera are to be kept in the library and are to enhance its collections, they should be preserved. The primary task in organizing an archival collection for preservation and access is re-housing the material and controlling the environment where the collection is kept.

Newspapers

"A newspaper is a serial publication which is designed to be a primary source of written information on current events connected with public affairs, either local, national and/or international in scope;"(1) it is printed, appears at regular and frequent intervals, and concentrates on current events. The evolution of the newspaper is closely related to the development of print, which enabled people to communicate news and views far more widely than was possible in manuscript form. Because of this, newspapers have been, and still are, controversial. The newspaper is not a passive entity; it is at the center of activity, yet it is also ephemeral in that it is purchased, read, and disposed of usually within the course of a day. Newspapers record events with unique immediacy and impact and preserve cultural attitudes and biases within their historical context.(2) Historians turn to newspapers to see how events were interpreted at the time that they occurred. With an increased interest in social history, newspapers as a resource are appreciated more than ever.

Until the middle of the nineteenth century, most newspapers were printed on durable rag paper; those that have survived the ravages of man can survive for generations to come. By the 1860s, the use of untreated wood pulp for the production of newspapers was common. Newsprint is especially sensitive to heat, humidity, air pollutants, and light. Ironically, it was at the end of the nineteenth century that librarians and archivists recognized the research value of newspapers and began to collect and preserve them. Libraries, historical societies, and archive repositories often hold considerable runs of newspaper files, crumbling and barely usable. By the 1930s the U.S. government recognized the problem of rapidly deteriorating newspapers and realized that it would be an impossible task to attempt to preserve every newspaper in its original format. Microphotography was chosen as the solution to the problem of preservation and access. By 1942, the Library of Congress Photoduplication Service oversaw a full-fledged newspaper preservation program, which eventually became self-supporting. Other preservation microfilming initiatives were undertaken by major research libraries. By 1978, there were over 70,000 U.S. and foreign newspapers known to be preserved in microform(3), but this represented only about a quarter of the estimated 250,000 newspapers published in the United States alone. The remainder were slowly decaying in the nation's libraries, archives, and historical societies. Obviously a massive national effort was needed to preserve these newspapers.

In the early 1970s the Organization of American Historians received a two-year grant from the National Endowment for the Humanities to determine what it would take to organize a national program to preserve the nation's newspapers. The survey demonstrated that the most logical way to proceed was to work on a state-by-state basis. It was recognized from the beginning that libraries would play an important role in an undertaking of such magnitude. The development of the Machine Readable Cataloging (MARC) format in the later 1960s and the establishment of the Ohio College, later the Online Computer Library Center (OCLC) in the early 1970s provided the technical facility for the development of a national newspaper data base. The CONSER (Cooperative Online Serials) Program, begun in 1976, provided the necessary bibliographic standards, quality control, and coordination for the project. The *Specifications for the Microfilming of Newspapers in the Library of Congress* (1972) established the standard for microfilming.

The United States Newspaper Program (USNP) was formally established in 1982. This program is "a coordinated effort to identify, to preserve, and to make available to researchers a significant portion of the newspapers published in the country since the seventeenth century."(4) In the fall of 1982, the National Endowment for the Humanities awarded six grants to national repositories of newspapers; by May 1983, sixteen planning grants were awarded, and full cataloging grants were awarded to Montana and the Virgin Islands. Today the USNP, through the NEH Division of Preservation and Access, funds statewide projects to survey newspaper repositories and to assess the status of bibliographic control and preservation of collections.

The preservation of a state's newspapers is a shared effort between the public and the private sector, with funding for preservation microfilming provided jointly by the National Endowment for the Humanities, state libraries and historical societies, and services in kind from the institutions participating in the project. While the National Endowment will ensure that newspapers in danger of imminent destruction will be filmed, and thus preserved, newspapers that are, at present, stable may not be filmed at this time. Priority must be given to newspaper files that are in greatest physical jeopardy.

Not every United States newspaper will be preserved in its original format. While every newspaper could be physically stabilized using a variety of conservation techniques, the nation lacks the time and the resources to do so. Mass deacidification and strengthening technologies may provide a solution in the future, but microfilming, to provide preservation and ready access, will continue for the present.

Institutions that participate in their state's newspaper project are contributors to the national effort to preserve the nation's documentary heritage. A master negative, a printing master, and service copies are made for every newspaper filmed. The master negatives and printing masters should be housed under secure, environmentally

controlled conditions. Most institutions opt to have them
stored in a state-approved repository for microfilm masters. Service copies can be obtained upon request.

Many institutions opt to have the original newspapers
returned after they have been microfilmed, with the hope
that they can be conserved in the future. Many newspapers, however, are extremely brittle and cannot survive
the microfilming process; the preservation of their contents, through microfilm, is better than nothing. If newspapers are to be preserved in their original format, they
must be kept in a controlled environment to slow their
inevitable decay. Archival quality boxes are available for
newspaper storage. The acidic kraft paper traditionally
used to wrap newspaper files has caused more damage
than protection from the environment. Bound newspaper
files are usually in somewhat better condition than unbound files. Whenever possible, they are not disbound for
filming if the original newspapers are to be preserved.
These large and heavy volumes are awkward and difficult
to use, however, and they do not allow for ready access.
They should be stored flat, preferably one to a shelf, as
recommended for the storage of folio volumes.

Mass treatment technologies may eventually enable
librarians to preserve many newspapers that have survived in their original format, but the national effort to
identify, catalog, and film endangered materials cannot
wait for a cost-effective solution to the newspaper problem while these technologies are developing. Microfilm,
as will be discussed in Chapter 12, is an effective preservation medium, cost-effectively permitting preservation
and access for materials that would not otherwise survive.
The U.S. Newspaper Program is a laudable national preservation effort that demonstrates how librarians and
scholars can work together to preserve the nation's documentary heritage.

The United States is by no means the only nation to
recognize the need to preserve its newspapers. In 1980,
the International Federation of Library Associations and
Institutions (IFLA) Section on Serial Publications established a Working Group on Newspapers to consider all

matters relating to newspapers in libraries. It is currently surveying preservation policies of newspaper collections worldwide. As Great Britain, Germany, and France began to address the problems of preservation and access for their own newspaper collections, it became clear that their libraries often held the most complete files of newspapers published in their former colonies. Libraries in the United States not only have newspapers representing almost every ethnic group, but also have extensive files of newspapers from the native lands of these peoples. IFLA's Working Group on Newspapers is actively promoting and supporting initiatives for the preservation of the world's newspapers for future generations. International cooperation is needed to preserve the world's newspaper heritage, and libraries in the United States will play an active role in the years to come.

Fine Prints

A print is defined as anything that is printed: posters, postage stamps, bank notes, magazine advertisements, and so on. This section will deal with prints that are, of themselves, works of art: fine prints.

Many techniques have been used to produce prints. The oldest is the *relief* technique, because the design is produced by creating a three-dimensional printing plate such as a woodcut or wood engraving. *Intaglio* is the opposite of relief; its design is incised below the surface of a metal plate with an engraving tool and acid. This process produces an engraving or etching. The *planographic* method is based upon the antipathy of oil and water. An image is created on a lithographic stone or metal plate with a greasy medium and the stone is dampened. Oil-based ink will then be repelled by the dampened areas but will stick to the greased areas to make the print. Thus a *lithographic* print is created. Other popular techniques are *stenciling* and *silk screen printing.* Only a limited number of good prints can be made by any of these processes, hence the value of prints.

The earliest prints were woodcuts, first produced at the

end of the fourteenth century. This was an inexpensive method of preparing playing cards, introduced in the West by the Crusaders, holy pictures, and simple picture books for the populace. Soon the print became an art form in its own right. Some prints have survived in pristine condition, but many more have been lost or badly damaged by neglect and poor treatment.

Occasionally, but not frequently, the print itself has been made on acid-free paper. Contemporary printmakers and the papermakers who make the paper for them, increasingly are aware of the need for rag paper in the production of a fine print. If the print itself is on acid paper, it can be treated by a conservator to retard further deterioration. This process is a painstaking one, involving the removal of the acids and other contaminants and introducing buffering agents. Treatment requires the skill of an experienced conservator.

A print, a work of art on paper, must be handled with care and carefully stored if it is to be preserved. Damaged prints require the service of a skilled paper conservator, and the cost of treatment can be dear. Remedies by untrained hands too frequently result in the total loss of a valuable but fragile work of art. Thus, preventive care is the best preservation technique.

Prints should be stored in alkaline buffered folders or in 100 percent rag mats. Framed prints should be removed from the frame and examined carefully before they enter a collection. Frequently, framed prints are backed with acidic paperboard, or, worse yet, old newspaper or wood. If old mats are of historic interest or aesthetic value (for example, containing the signature of the artist), they should be preserved with the print and specially protected by acid-free materials. If mats are made of 100 percent rag paper, in good condition, show no sign of age, discoloration, or foxing, they can be reused, but the backboard should be replaced with new 100 percent rag board and a one-ply rag barrier sheet should be inserted between the old mat frame and the print. While colored 100 percent rag mats can be used, they may not be as free of impurities as white mats. Their color can fade and they might also discolor the print, if exposed to moisture. The traditional mat is the best safeguard against damage. Conservator Christa Gaehde explains, "A mat consists of a supporting board and a covering frame of a varying width, whose window—or aperture—displays the print."(5) The support and the covering frame, or "window mat," are hinged together, which allows for the opening of the mat to examine the print. The hinges, too, must be free of acid content. Hinges should be made from Japanese paper. Paste that is totally free of contaminants and preservatives must be used to affix the print; most conservators make their own wheat starch paste. Most prints require only two hinges. A print should have its hinges at the top regardless of format. Prints with no margins, either because of design or because they have been trimmed, must "float" in the window of a mat. If they are to be framed or exhibited, they can be hinged on the top and the bottom near the corner.

For convenience of storage and framing, mats can be made in standard sizes, which will accommodate most prints and allow for better storage. It is essential that the person who does the matting and framing of materials for the library understands the need to do this correctly using the appropriate materials; there is no margin for compromise. In recent years the Professional Picture Framers Association has gone to considerable effort to ensure that its members and the public understand "conservation" framing and use appropriate materials.

Until recently, prints were commonly attached by gluing them to the backboard of the mat or by using gummed adhesive tape along the margins of the print. Both of these techniques cause permanent damage to the print and lower its value. The removal of adhesives is a difficult and time-consuming process. Unfortunately, the physical damage produced by adhesives causes unsightly stains that are usually permanent.

The best, safest, and most convenient way to store matted prints is in acid-free boxes that are sturdy and airtight. Solander boxes, originally designed for the protection of botanical specimens, have been adapted for the protection of prints and rare or fragile books. These boxes come in assorted sizes or can be custom-made to suit any collection. Boxes can hold several prints but should not be filled too tightly. They can be placed on wide shelves, housing prints alphabetically or in any system desired. Boxes offer real protection against the pollutants in the environment and create a microenvironment, limiting exposure to changes in the environment outside.

Storage drawers suitable for housing print collections are available commercially or can be custom-made. Wooden cabinets produce gasses that can be harmful to paper-based objects. This phenomonon is known as "offgassing." Wooden shelves and storage cabinets must be specially treated to ensure that this problem has been eliminated. Baked enamel cabinets have also been known to emit gasses, but the problem, one of quality control, has been remedied; today baked enamel cabinets are recommended for print storage. Even though boxes made of alkaline board offer excellent protection, print collections should be housed in a safe, environmentally controlled atmosphere.

Once prints are suitably arranged and matted, they will be safer for storage and use. Prints should be covered with an interleaving cover paper, which must be removed from the face of the print before it can be viewed. Transparent polyester covers are not recommended. They can cause problems if there is too much moisture in the atmosphere and encourage the growth of mold on the face of a print. In addition, they cause static electricity, which can cause damage to the image. The face of a print should never be touched. Moisture, dirt, and oils from the hands will transfer to the paper and cause permanent damage and staining. Most curators request that patrons wash their hands before examining prints. Inexpensive white cotton gloves can also be worn when working with prints. Needless to say, researchers should never have pens in the print room.

Prints should not be exposed to light for an extended

period of time. As discussed in Chapter 5, prints can be exhibited for a month or two, then placed back in their boxes to rest for a period of time before they are exhibited again. It is possible to shield prints with Plexiglas specially treated to curtail exposure to ultraviolet light, the rays at the harmful end of the light spectrum. Plexiglas attracts dirt to its surface, however, and some viewers complain that the Plexiglas distorts the image. The Conservation Center for Art and Historic Artifacts, Philadelphia, produces a sealed package with a UV-filtering Plexiglas on the front, the matted artwork and alkaline corrugated board and Mylar on the reverse. The edges of the package are lined with an alkaline paper and taped, thus producing a microclimate. This is an excellent protective technique for fragile prints, especially if they are to be exhibited.

Prints that are stored in frames should be monitored on a regular basis to see if there is any sign of condensation or other damage apparent to the eye. They should be removed from their frames for a thorough examination at least once every decade. Prints that are kept in areas with no environmental controls or where there is likely to be a good deal of fluctuation in temperature and humidity (typical of the climate in most of the United States) should be examined frequently for evidence of moisture or mold, which can be visible in a matter of hours. Dust should never be allowed to accumulate on framed prints and in storage areas.

Maps

Clara LeGear, for many years the map librarian at the Library of Congress, observed that because maps have presented librarians with problems, they have too frequently been set aside as fugitive material. Yet, "if properly handled, maps are easy to use. When they are kept flat with adequate facilities for spreading them out, they can be consulted readily."(6) Maintaining a map collection can be costly and time-consuming, but maps are primary source materials that are an integral part of every library collection. The majority of maps are prints produced by the same techniques outlined in the previous section, and they are subject to the same consideration and care.

Most maps can be stored, as prints, in archival, acid-free boxes or in cabinets, but their variation in size tends to prevent the easy adaptation of a system for storage and access. Map librarian Mary Larsgaard notes:

> Any librarian deciding on filing equipment should realize . . . that the choice of filing equipment will depend on: type of maps to be stored; place of storage; amount of available wall and floor space; desired degree of user access to maps; the collection's present size and future possible expansion; the relative costs of the various types of equipment; the availability of equipment; and the frequency of use of the collection.(7)

The selection of adequate equipment for the storage of maps is essential. A map librarian needs to review carefully the needs of a collection and the space available to house it, and should consider the use that the collection will receive before purchasing and installing systems for storage. Many libraries use horizontal metal filing cases with shallow drawers. The drawers of these cases should not exceed the height of 2 $1/2$ inches, a 44-inch width, or a 30-inch depth, or there will be problems with the removal of materials from the drawers. Individual maps should be placed in alkaline paper or polyester folders. The advantage of polyester folders is that the user can see through them; the disadvantage is the weight and volume of the polyester in a system of storage cases.

Large maps provide problems and challenges for the map curator. Large maps are sometimes encapsulated and hung. This is a technique that is increasingly popular for the display of heavily used large maps that are mounted on canvas and rolled into metal containers, to be pulled down like a window shade when they are consulted. Often these maps receive extensive conservation treatment first and are rebacked on linen before encapsulation.

They can be rolled around the outside of an acid-free cardboard tube that is at least six inches in diameter. There are a number of ways of suspending them to allow both preservation and access. While rolling materials is the least desirable storage format because it is difficult to manage and potentially harmful, there is no other feasible method for collections of large maps. A conservator or preservation specialist can provide assistance in designing a system for the storage of large maps.

Frequently maps are placed in the pockets of gazetteers, travel books, and directories. If they are to be kept in a book, a new envelope should be made of alkaline paper; there are a variety of styles that can be adapted for this purpose. It may be advisable, for security and preservation, to remove maps from their pocket and house them separately, stored flat. The Library of Congress unfolds such material, encapsulates it, and houses it in a separate folder. Folded maps with text attached to their covers are normally removed from the covers and stored flat. The cover can be placed in an alkaline envelope and placed in the folder holding the map, so they can be used together easily. Over the years, map librarians, working with conservators, have developed a variety of techniques for the housing of map collections, and the novice map librarian should become familiar with the literature of the field.

Maps are frequently found in deteriorated condition due to poor storage conditions and heavy use. Like all prints, they should be treated and repaired by a conservator. Once a valuable map has been cleaned and repaired, it can also be hinged into a 100 percent rag board mat to retard its deterioration and to facilitate its use. Polyester encapsulation, which is an inexpensive and reversible process, is often the most practical way to prepare fragile maps for use. Rare maps, to be kept in a permanent collection, should not be laminated, a technique frequently used in the past by libraries where maps are in heavy use. Lamination techniques can be very damaging. Lamination can be an appropriate technique for the protection of maps that are heavily used for a short period of time and are not unique or of permanent value. The decision of how to prepare maps, especially fragile maps, for preservation and access ultimately must be based on the needs of the collection. Planning should be done in consultation with a conservator.

Atlases are usually housed with map collections. As most are oversized, the same practices outlined for the storage of folio volumes in Chapter 3 should be followed. Atlases that are oversized should be stored flat; only one should be placed on a shelf to prevent warping. Atlases are frequently consulted and thus can deteriorate over a relatively short period of time. A number of institutions have begun the practice of disassembling their heavily consulted atlases, repairing the pages, encapsulating them, and placing them in post bindings. This method of housing is expensive and requires considerably more space for storage, but it is by far the best way to provide access yet protect valuable and heavily used atlases.

Globes and relief models, often found in map collections, are especially difficult to protect. They are particularly susceptible to dust, environmental changes, and careless handling. They should be covered when not in use or, if on display, when the collection is closed. They can also be housed in alkaline boxes with interior supports; these are available from a number of library and archival suppliers, or can be custom-made. Recently a new product, the Poly-case, has come on the market. These are polyester exhibition cases, easily assembled and disassembled and moved. They can be purchased in a variety of sizes and can be ordered custom-made. They offer excellent protection for three-dimensional globes and models on display.

Map collections are frequently consulted; thus filing and storage systems should be developed that can best meet the needs of the collection. The system selected should enable users to get at the materials they require with relative ease, involving a minimum amount of handling of unwanted material. There is a considerable body of literature on the subject of the bibliographic control of map collections, but for the protection of the collection it is essential that each library develop a system that best meets its own mode of use rather than to follow blindly another institution's set of guidelines.

A map room should contain work areas large enough to accommodate large maps that patrons are studying, for the best storage facilities will mean little if the user has to roll or fold large maps to properly work with them in cramped quarters. Some libraries have installed movable tables that can be placed together to hold larger items for consultation.

A map collection contains fragile works on paper and merits special care and consideration. While rare and unique maps are usually housed in special collections and consulted only under monitored conditions, most map collections are established and organized for unrestricted use. A common sense approach to map librarianship allows for preservation and access.

Paintings

Paintings are often found in library collections. They may be pictures of local sights or personages or works by local artists. All too frequently they are neglected due to the suspicion that if they were really good, they would be in museums. While these works may not always be important for aesthetic reasons, they are artifacts that document the cultural heritage and deserve care and conservation. If they are to be kept, they should be preserved and displayed properly. While a comprehensive discussion about the care and conservation of paintings is beyond the scope of this book, this section will discuss briefly the basics of their display and preservation.

Paintings may be done on any surface, but most are on wood panels or on canvas. Both of these materials respond to changes in their environment, as does paper, and they require the same environmental controls to prevent irreparable damage from fluctuations in temperature and humidity, dirt, air pollution, excessive light, fungi and molds, insects and vermin. Paintings also need to be protected from people who handle or store them carelessly.

Paintings should be examined periodically for signs of damage and age. At present, the Institute of Museum Services (IMS), a governmental agency, offers grants to enable institutions to bring in a professional conservator to examine collections and to make recommendations for storage and display. Libraries with collections of prints and paintings are eligible for such surveys. If deterioration is obvious, a reputable conservator of paintings should be contacted. The American Institute for the Conservation of Artistic and Historic Works (AIC), the professional organization for conservators, has a Conservation Services Referral System that provides inquirers with a computer-generated list of conservators, grouped by geographic location, specialization, and type of services offered. The conservators on the list are members of AIC and have received satisfactory recommendations from at least five institutions. It is the responsibility of a library to contact these institutions to discuss the nature of the treatment to be undertaken by the conservators under consideration and to find the right individual for consultation and possible treatment. Fellows of AIC are listed in its annual *Directory,* which has an index arranged by specialty. Potential clients can also consult with area museums; many have professional conservators on the staff. In addition to undertaking a conservation survey of the library, a conservator can also examine individual paintings and make a full report on the extent of the damage and estimate the cost of treatment. Such documentation can be presented to the trustees of the library, local benefactors, or funding agencies to obtain the necessary funds for conservation.

Institutions with paintings in their collections should have a copy of Caroline K. Keck's clearly written and informative publication, *A Handbook on the Care of Paintings for Historical Agencies and Small Museums,* for this handbook directly addresses the problems that are encountered in libraries.

Notes

1. Robert Harriman. *Newspaper Cataloguing Manual* (Washington, DC: Library of Congress, 1984): 2.
2. T. F. Mills. "Preserving Yesterday's News for Today's Historian," *Journal of Library History,* 16:3 (Summer 1981), 464.
3. *Ibid.* 472.
4. Jeffrey Field. "The U.S. Newspaper Program," *Conservation Administration News,* no. 25 (April 1986): 5.
5. Carl Zigrosser and Christa M. Gaehde. *A Guide to the Collecting and Care of Original Prints* (New York: Crown, 1965): 101.
6. Le Gear, Clare. *Maps, Their Care, Repair and Preservation in Libraries* (Washington, DC: Library of Congress, 1956): 2.
7. Larsgaard, Mary Lynette. *Map Librarianship,* 2nd ed. (Littleton, CO: Libraries Unlimited, 1987): 165.

Selected Reading

Clapp, Anne F. *Curatorial Care of Works of Art on Paper.* New York: Nick Lyons, 1987.

Ehrenberg, Ralph E. *Archives & Manuscripts: Maps and Architectural Drawings.* Chicago: Society of American Archivists, 1982. (Basic Manual Series)

Ellis, Margaret Holben. *The Care of Prints and Drawings.* Nashville, TN: American Association for State and Local History, 1987.

Keck, Carolyn K. *A Handbook on the Care of Paintings for Historical Agencies and Small Museums.* Nashville, TN: American Association for State and Local History, 1965.

Larsgaard, Mary Lynette. *Map Librarianship,* 2nd ed. Littleton, CO: Libraries Unlimited, 1987.

Pederson, Ann, ed. *Keeping Archives.* Sydney: Australian Society of Archives, Inc., 1987.

Ritzenthaler, Mary Lynn. Chicago: Society of American Archivists, 1994.

Swartzburg, Susan G. "Preserving Newspapers: National and International Cooperative Efforts." *Preservation and Conservation of Nonprint Media,* ed. Kathryn L. and William T. Henderson, 73–89. Urbana-Champaign, IL: University of Illinois Graduate School of Library and Information Science, 1991.

X. PHOTOGRAPHIC MATERIALS:
Care and Preservation

Introduction

THE PHOTOGRAPH HAS BEEN DESCRIBED as "a chemically fixed image, holding a lens-produced pattern of light, an aggregate of space, and a finite amount of time."(1) The term *photography* means literally "to write with light," and today the typical photographic processes produce an image in a sensitive layer by reactions initiated by exposure to light. The modern photographic image has two forms, the negative and the positive photographic print. The positive print is the image made from the negative, the final part of the negative-positive picture-making process.

Photographs can be considered works of art on paper, but because of their additional chemical components, they are even more fragile and subject to physical and environmental hazards than other paper-based materials. Photography has been with us for 150 years, yet it is only within the past twenty years that there has been serious interest in this medium, both as an art form and, more to the point for the library, as another format for recording and containing information.

The earliest photographic images were daguerreotypes, which appeared in 1839. The image of the daguerreotype was made directly upon a sheet of highly polished silver-plated copper, covered with a sheet of protective glass, then encased in a shallow plush box. The ambrotype is another photographic technique, in which a nearly transparent thin glass negative was made into a positive image by putting a dull black surface beneath the negative. The

177

image was then covered by glass. The tintype, or ferrotype, which was a fairly common technique well into the twentieth century, produced a direct positive image on a sensitized iron base. These images are not made from negatives and are thus considered originals, for they cannot be reproduced unless the original is rephotographed and prints are made from the negative.

The earliest photographs made from negatives and printed on paper were called calotypes, or talbotypes, after the inventor of the technique, William Henry Fox Talbot, who developed the process about 1840. Although the process is the ancestor of the negative/positive processes of modern photography, these images are extremely rare. By the 1850s the wet-collodion glass negative was introduced, permitting the production of multiple paper positive prints. This technique replaced the earlier single-image processes. If a negative is made on a piece of glass, it is called a "glass negative," but if it is made on cellulose nitrate or plastic film, it is a "film negative." In the nineteenth century, prints were usually the same size as their plates, or negatives, as enlarging equipment had not come into wide use.

Albumen paper was introduced in 1850 and was common from 1860 into the twentieth century. Millions of prints were produced using this process. Thin sheets of paper were coated with egg white mixed with sodium chloride, then sensitized by an application of silver nitrate. Prints were made by placing the negative and the albumen paper in physical contact in a glass-covered frame, then exposing the frame to light to achieve the print. Firing, toning, and washing then followed. These photographs often were mounted on cardboard backings for protection and ease in handling. Most common are the wallet-sized "Cartes-de-visite" from this period. When they begin to deteriorate, they fade around the edges, show yellowing in the highlights, and their tone changes to a dull brown-yellow. Albumen prints, stored under reasonable conditions, are in remarkably good condition today.

Collodion, or gelatin emulsion papers, known as printing-out papers (POP), were introduced in the 1880s. The paper base is thicker and more opaque than albumen papers and has a high gloss. Collodion chloride paper, which also became popular in the early 1890s, had a surface coated with collodion emulsion that supported the light-sensitive silver chloride. Collodion prints tend to be brittle, with a surface of tiny cracks. A popular collodion trade paper was Aristotype; mounted prints marked "Aristotype Print" on the verso of the face are relatively common.

Gelatino-chloride paper, still available today, has been made since 1891. It has a gelatin emulsion and a high gloss. Developing-out paper (DOP) was introduced about 1880, and by 1900 it had superseded the printing-out papers, as it is faster and more versatile. The basic types of developing-out papers are bromide paper, chloride paper, and chloride-bromide paper.

Stereographic views were enormously popular from about 1858 to 1920 and sets of scenes, with or without their stereoscopic viewer, are likely to find a home in libraries, museums, and historical societies. A stereograph is a pair of photographic prints mounted adjacent to one another on a three-and-a-half by seven-inch card. The early cards are flat; cards manufactured later are sometimes slightly curved along the vertical axis, from top to bottom. Sterographic prints almost always contain valuable handwritten or printed information about the images that should be preserved. They deteriorate in the usual way of photographs, but because they were handled so much for viewing, they may be badly damaged by dirt and abrasions. Stereographs can be cleaned and repaired, but this work must be done by a skilled photographic technician.

Many old photographs have been exposed to environmental and physical hazards for years, which has unbalanced their already unstable chemical composition, hence they are in extremely fragile condition. These images require great care in handling. Physical treatment must be undertaken by a skilled photographic conservator. Because of their physical and chemical fragility, these artifacts are more subject to inadvertent damage by amateur hands than other works of art on paper, including books.

Photographs have until recently been the stepchildren of the library and the historical society, stored in boxes in basements, attics, or remote corners of a building. It is only in the last two decades that guidelines for the housing and care of photographic collections have emerged, as photographic images have become valued for what they can tell us about ourselves and our society in times past. Today, institutions large and small receive considerable funding from national, regional, and state sources for the organization and preservation of collections. Newly discovered and recovered images have enhanced scholarship in a variety of ways.

Preservation of Photographs

Because of their complex chemical composition, the physical nature of photographic images is more complicated than that of paper and ink. It has only been since the 1960s that the specialty of photographic conservation has emerged. The Photographic Materials Group, a section of the American Institute for the Conservation of Artistic and Historic Works, usually meets twice a year and annually publishes papers on photographic conservation. The Image Permanence Institute, located at Rochester Institute of Technology (RIT), Rochester, NY, was established in 1988 to investigate the causes of instability in filmed images. Workshops on the care and preservation of photographic materials are sponsored by Rochester Institute of Technology, the Getty Conservation Institute, and a number of organizations on a regular basis.

The common problems that the curator of a photographic collection will encounter are chemical deterioration and contamination; tears, abrasions, scuffs, fingerprints; dirt; marks with pointed or pressurized objects such as pens, pencils, stamps, or paper clips; broken glass plates; bent prints; cracked emulsions; scratched and soiled negatives; and photographs mounted on highly acidic, brittle paper or board. Damage to delicate images is caused by intrinsic and extrinsic factors. One of the more troublesome elements in many photographic collections are photographic negatives. Eastman Kodak began to produce cellulose nitrate-base film in 1889. It was used for roll film until the latter 1930s, when safety-base film was introduced, eventually replacing it. Until the mid-1930s, most photographic film was made of nitrate stock, which was discovered to be an extremely unstable and unsafe material. Under optimum storage, a cool, dark place, a nitrate negative will remain relatively stable. But over time it will shrink and shrivel, become tacky, soft or brittle, and the image will fade and discolor to a yellow-brown color. Finally, it will emit gaseous fumes with the odor of nitric acid (much like caramel) and will bubble and foam until only a fine powder is left. Nitrate-base film is highly combustible; if it is stored in a warm area, it can ignite spontaneously. Nitrate fires are difficult to control. The storage of nitrate-base film is illegal in many communities. Nitrate negatives need to be identified, removed from the collection, and sent to a safe storage place where they can be dealt with, as they are already deteriorating.

As many negatives in a collection are at least fifty years old, they will probably show some visible sign of deterioration that can aid in a positive identification of their composition. In their book, *Collection, Use and Care of Historical Photographs,* Weinstein and Booth recommend a "float test" that can be performed on suspect film. While it is risky, it is a procedure that some librarians and archivists follow to identify suspect material.

Snip off about ¼" corner of the film in question, place it in a small bottle of trichloroethylene, available from a chemical supplier. Shake the bottle to make sure the film clip is completely immersed. If the sample sinks, it is nitrate-base film. Care should be taken to be sure the test sample should not be accidentally wet with water before testing, as nitrate film wet with water will not sink.(2)

If the film is not too badly deteriorated, new copy negatives can be made. Old envelopes that contained nitrate-base negatives should never be reused as they will contaminate any material stored in them. Information on these envelopes should be recorded before their disposal and placed with the new copy negatives. While certain archival repositories may wish to store nitrate-base negatives for as long as possible, this requires special cold storage facilities, which is not possible or appropriate for most institutions.

Early safety film has a cellulose acetate or diacetate base with an adhesive layer of cellulose nitrate. As the film ages, the base shrinks, causing the gelatin emulsion to separate as the cellulose nitrate adhesive deteriorates. The film wrinkles, bubbles, and will turn yellowish in color as it shrivels. It can be mistaken for cellulose nitrate film, but the deterioration and the smell of acidic acid (citrus) are different. Many safety films are marked "safety" on the negative. While the deterioration of safety film is not a safety hazard, the damage that it causes to the image is as serious; copying is the best means of replacement. Most film manufactured today has a polyester base that is strong, stable, and has greater resistance to degradation when exposed to extremes of temperature and humidity. Cellulose acetate and polyester film bases have excellent keeping properties when stored under controlled environmental conditions.(3)

There are considerable variations in the quality of film that has been and is being produced for photography. Henry Wilhelm, an independent researcher of Grinnell, IA, has documented the problems of most of the films used for photographic reproduction. Wilhelm's concern is the instability of the color image. He began his research into the causes of color fading and deterioration in 1974. He demonstrated that most color films, which are extremely susceptible to the hazards of heat, humidity, and light, will fade even in the dark in storage. Wilhelm's book, *The Permanence and Care of Color Photographs: Prints, Negatives, Slides and Motion Pictures* (1993) is the distillation of his research on the causes of the impermanence of most color films. Wilhelm's mission is "to make color-image stability a more visible factor—even a competitive feature—in the photographic industry . . . to provide photographers—both amateur and professional—with reliable comparative data so that they can choose the most stable materials that fit their other photographic criteria."(4) Henry Wilhelm has done much to make the library and archival communities aware of the impermanence of color materials and the problems that institutions face when attempting to preserve photographic images and to provide access to them. He is concerned especially with unique images that are quietly deteriorating, even in storage; one of his goals is "to convince museums, archives, and all other holders of large photographic color collections that they must install refrigerated, humidity-controlled storage rooms" to house collections of original images.(5)

The enemies of photographs are high temperature and relative humidity, rapid fluctuations of both, air pollution, light, and improper handling. Because the photograph is already chemically and physically fragile, these enemies become even more dangerous. Heat and high relative humidity speed up the chemical processes that cause the deterioration of paper. Photographs are hygroscopic and thus are especially susceptible to atmospheric changes. Air pollution contaminates the atmosphere with noxious gases, particularly sulphur dioxide, which can be absorbed in paper and film. In addition, it combines with oxygen and the moisture on the photographic paper to form sulfuric acid, which will attack the photographic image itself as well as the paper with the resultant disintegration of both paper and image. Light causes paper to deteriorate; in addition, it can hasten the deterioration caused by the chemicals that form the photographic image. Photographs also attract insects and microorganisms that will attack the ingredients in the image as well as the paper. Photographic collections should be housed with as great, if not greater, care as print, manuscript, and rare book collections. In recent years conservators have worked closely with archival suppliers to develop a variety of storage envelopes and containers to house photographic collections.

People are often the greatest enemies of photographs. Because photographs readily can be made without great skill, people have tended not to take them as seriously as objects created by an "artist." Photographs, like prints, should never be touched on their surface. The photographic image should always be protected. Study collections of original images can be housed in polyester enclosures or in acid-free mats. Pens should not be allowed in the study room, for ink, if it accidentally should come in contact with a photograph, can cause very serious damage. Researchers should be required to use inexpensive white cotton gloves when examining unsleeved images.

Many photographic archives maintain a study collection in addition to original photographic images. These can range in level of sophistication from electrostatic copies of the original photographs to full-color reproductions on an optical disk, as is done at the Library of Congress. The use of optical digital technology to provide access to photographic materials is an approach that ensures the protection and preservation of the original images. The potential for high-quality reproductions in these new media promises visual access to collections anywhere in the world.

Another increasingly popular, although expensive, alternative for historically valuable collections is to have photographic copies made of the original images for study and use, thus preserving the originals. This also enables an institution to undertake the conservation of valued originals without curtailing access.

The copying of photographs to produce images for study and use is a common practice in archival collections, but it is important that the copies are made by a professional photographer who understands that he or she is dealing with rare and fragile archival materials. Copying negative and positive images is a difficult process; a variety of techniques can be used. Klaus Hendriks writes, "It is a discipline which requires familiarity with photographic technology, such as sensitometry, and photographic processing control."(6) The copying should be faithful to the original image, insofar as that is possible, although this can be challenging when the original negative is severely damaged. In spite of the difficulties involved, copies of original photographic images are useful in archival collections and can be used for exhibition in many instances. Done well, copying deteriorating or damaged images is an excellent preservation technique. There has been some question about the enhancement of images in copying; this is not an accepted conservation practice for archival materials. The image should be as close as possible to the original image, even if the original is damaged.

A general maintenance program for a photographic collection can be developed with the assistance of an experienced conservator. Photographs are difficult to repair or restore. Well-intentioned people attempting to repair a photograph can cause irreparable damage. An inexperienced technician can destroy a photograph in the course of a complex conservation treatment. Even in the hands of the most skilled conservator, treatment results can be uneven and photographs are lost. The Society of American Archivists (SAA) has published an invaluable volume, *Archives & Manuscripts: Administration of Photographic Collections,* by Mary Lynn Ritzenthaler, Gerald J. Munoff, and Margery S. Long (1984), based on a series of workshops that the society offered for archivists in the early 1980s. It is an essential reference for libraries with collections of photographs. Because of increasing interest in photographs, there is finally a growing body of literature on the nature and care of photographic collections to guide the curator.

Photographs on Exhibition

A photographic image is worth a thousand words and photographs are dramatic additions to exhibitions. While original photographs may be required for certain types of exhibitions, copies should be used whenever possible. If original photographs are displayed, they should never be placed where they are exposed to direct sunlight or ultraviolet light. They should be carefully matted and framed, as with any work of art on paper. Plexiglas that filters out the ultraviolet rays of light is often recommended for photographs that are to be placed on exhibition; however, Plexiglas is controversial for use with photographs because it is an acrylic plastic that can release peroxide that can harm silver images. The use of Plexiglas also poses aesthetic concerns because it tends to cast a yellowish tinge on the image, distorting it slightly, and it attracts dust. Ultraviolet light filters can be placed over the windows in areas where photographs are displayed. Care should be taken to control the amount and intensity of incandescent lighting used near the photographs. No matter what protective measures are taken, original photographs should not be displayed for more than six or eight weeks, or else serious, and visible, damage will occur in the image. As conservators are learning more about early photographic techniques and the chemicals that were used, they are preparing specific guidelines for the storage and display of photographic collections. Information on the care and display of photographic images is available from most regional centers and from the Visual Resources Association, cited in the appendix.

Slide Collections

Slides are another form of photographic image that are a heavily used part of a library collection. Consultants Nancy Carlson Schrock and Christine Sundt note, "The term *slide* indicates a photographic format rather than a single photographic process. The base must be transparent, either glass or film stock, so that the image, either black-and-white or color, can be viewed when projected."(7) Slide collections require special handling and care. Slides are frequently used in presentations before large groups of people, yet because of their fragile, even temporary, nature, each handling, each showing, causes a fraction of irreparable damage.

The stereographs that became popular in the Victorian household after the Civil War might be called the precursor of the modern color slide. These rectangular cardboard mounts were intended for three-dimentional viewing in a special stereographic viewer. With this viewer, our grandparents could observe the Victorian world from the comfort of the parlor. At this time, also, the first lantern slides became available. These are glass transparencies that, like modern slides today, are meant for viewing by projection. Early lantern slides were photographically processed on the glass itself. The development of flexible film led in the late 1880s to rolled cellulose-base film as we know it today.

Color film was introduced in the mid-1930s, but color materials have, until now, been considered fugitive. As Henry Wilhelm's research clearly has demonstrated, color films are not permanent and will fade. Today many slide transparencies are in color. Even if they are stored under the best conditions, their color will fade in a relatively short period of time. Wilhelm's definitive book on color film, when it is published, promises to be essential reading for curators of slide collections.

The knowledgeable slide curator is aware that a slide collection, by its very nature, is in a continuous state of destruction. The gelatin emulsion is made of chemical compounds that may be unstable and the color dyes are fugitive and subject to fading. The slides are placed in a cardboard mount that may be acidic or a plastic one that at least appears to be relatively stable. Slides in collections are often covered in glass to keep them flat in the projector and prevent distortion. They are usually bound with an adhesive material that may cause damage by itself and can cause further damage if the slide overheats in the projector. Lenses are available that will compensate for the curvature of cardboard-mounted slides when they are projected, but there is no magic from the manufacturers of film to prevent insidious deterioration.

Slides, especially color slides, are extremely susceptible to the hazards of heat, light, and moisture. Experiments have shown that the single greatest harm to the slide occurs at the moment of projection when the image is suddenly exposed to intense heat and light. The heat and light produced by the lamp used to illuminate the projection cause a fraction of deterioration with each exposure.

Damage may already be inherent in a slide before it has been mounted. Bubbling slides indicate trouble to come if the residual moisture is not removed before it turns to mildew. The bubbling may also be caused by an overheating projector and, if this is the case, the slide will be irreparably damaged. The rainbow effect that occasionally occurs when a slide is projected is known as Newton's Rings and is caused when two shiny surfaces come together; the phenomenon is not necessarily a cause for alarm.

Always use the correct wattage bulb in a projector and never use a bulb that has a higher wattage than recommended with the equipment. It is essential that the projector be functioning properly before operation and it is advisable to warm up a projector prior to use. Newer projectors that have magazines or carousels for holding the slides not only aid the lecturer but also help protect the slide, for the slide is gradually warmed up while in the magazine awaiting its turn for projection. After slides are projected for a period of thirty seconds, continued exposure to heat and light occasionally can cause damage; the effect is cumulative. Slides that are used frequently in teaching situations, such as art history courses, will be projected for varying lengths of time and should be considered disposable materials that will have to be replaced at some point.

Libraries with older slides and equipment should undertake a careful review of the equipment. In the long run, it will prove far cheaper to discard outmoded equipment that will damage slides and to invest in good equipment that will cause the least harm to the slides. The *Guide to Equipment for Slide Maintenance and Viewing,* published and frequently updated by the Visual Resources Association, is an indispensable addition to the professional bookshelf in a library with a collection of slides.

Most slide collections consist of secondary images, purchased from commercial sources or made directly from books, postcards, or other sources. While they should last as long as possible, they are not, of themselves, of value. Slide curator and art historian Christine Sundt, the founder of the Visual Resources Association, explains, "Duplicate slides are reproductions from an original positive or negative image. They are derivative images which are at least twice removed from the original object or scene."(8) The value of an original image "is measured by the rarity of the representation—a site that no longer exists or that has been permanently altered; an event that cannot be recreated; a reproduction of an art work that is otherwise unavailable for public viewing. . . . An original slide is valuable to a collection when it faithfully reproduces the original work or site without undue distortion caused by shadows, contrast, lighting, angle, depth-of-field, distance from object, and it is free from distracting elements in the surrounding area."(9) Original slides should be treated as archival objects. They require careful storage and preservation and should be used with great care for general research purposes. A photographic conservator should be consulted to assist in the planning for the housing of original slide collections; they do not belong in a circulating or heavily used research collection.

Information on the care and maintenance of slide collections is appearing more frequently in library literature. As with other nonprint material, a library should develop a storage and retrieval system for slides that meets the needs of its clientele and prevents undue handling. Sundt suggests the plastic storage page, "an inexpensive and easy-to-handle means for grouping twenty 2-inch by 2-inch slides in a standard loose-leaf sheet format. The slide pages fit neatly into a notebook or file folder."(10) It is important that the slide pages are made of inert and/or acid-free materials, obtained from a dependable supplier of archival quality materials. Pages made of polyvinylchloride (PVC), commonly found for the housing of photographs in albums and for slides, will cause an adverse reaction to film. Slides can also be stored in inert plastic frames that fit into filing cabinets. Slide sets that are frequently used are sometimes stored in their carousel trays, but they attract dust if they are not properly covered. The boxes that come with carousels are acidic and are not appropriate for the storing of slides.

Sundt writes, "The best kind of container for storing slides is one made of either metal with a baked enamel finish or high-impact plastic."(11) There has been some concern about off-gassing from some baked-enamel storage cabinets, but the problem has been resolved with a change in the paints used to color the cabinets. Wooden slide trays are not appropriate, as the wood will hasten the deterioration of cellulose-base materials, as has been discussed. *Slide Libraries: A Guide for Academic Institutions, Museums, and Special Collections,* by Betty Jo Irvine (1979), provides considerable information about the arrangement and housing of slide collections. Even slides in circulating collections should be kept in an environmentally controlled area.

To facilitate easy access, slides should be clearly marked so they can be located and assembled for showing in the correct position. Immediately after a slide is mounted, or upon receipt of the mounted slide, place a circular dot or thumb mark on the lower left-hand corner on the front, as it is viewed in the normal upright position. When the slide is placed in the slide holder in an upside-down position, the dot appears on the upper right-hand corner, facing the projector lamp. It is a good idea to draw a diagonal line across the tops of slides when sets are housed in trays or drawers, so one can see at a glance if a slide is misfiled upside down or out of order.

Although slides are fragile, proper handling can greatly extend their useful life span. During the past decade a considerable amount of helpful information has been published on the storage and housing of slide collections. The Visual Resources Association, for slide and picture curators, publishes the journal *Visual Resources* and the *Visual Resources Association Bulletin.* Christine Sundt has done much to publicize Wilhelm's work on film among librarians and archivists. In addition, she has done considerable research into the problems of housing and storage of slides. Her columns in the *International Bulletin for Photographic Documentation of the Visual Arts,* which began in the late 1970s, and her other published writings have provided a wealth of technical information for librarians who are responsible for the care and management of slide collections. New films and new technologies will bring significant changes in preservation and access for slide curators in the decade to come, but with a knowledge of the media involved in the reproduction of the visual image, the opportunities for the librarian are limitless.

Notes

1. Robert A. Weinstein and Larry Booth, *Collection, Use and Care of Historic Photographs* (Nashville, TN: American Association for State and Local History, 1977): 4.
2. *Ibid.* 191.
3. Klaus Hendriks, *The Preservation and Restoration of Photographic Materials in Archives and Libraries: A RAMP Study With Guidelines* (Paris: Unesco, 1984): 79.
4. Bob Schwalberg with Henry Wilhelm and Carol Brower, "Going, Going, Gone!" *Popular Photography* 97:6 (June 1990): 60.
5. *Ibid.*
6. *Conservation of Photographs,* (Rochester, NY: Eastman Kodak, 1985). 41.
7. Nancy Carlson Schrock and Christine Sundt, "Slides," *Conservation in the Library,* ed. Susan G. Swartzburg (Westport, CT: Greenwood Press, 1983), 105.
8. Christine Sundt, *Conservation Practices for Slide and Photograph Collections* (Ann Arbor, MI: Visual Resources Association, 1989), 1–2.
9. *Ibid.* 2.
10. *Ibid.* 37.
11. *Ibid.* 39.

Selected Readings

Albright, Gary. "Photographs." *Conservation in the Library,* ed. Susan G. Swartzburg, 78–102. Westport, CT: Greenwood Press, 1983.

Hendriks, Klaus B. "The Preservation, Storage, and Handling of Black-and-White Photographic Records." *Conserving and Preserving Materials in Nonbook Formats,* 91–104. Urbana-Champaign, IL: University of Illinois Graduate School of Library and Information Science, 1991.

Keefe, Lawrence E., Jr. and Dennis Inch. *The Life of a Photograph: Archival Processing, Matting, Framing, and Storage,* 2nd ed. Boston, London: Focal Press, 1991.

Rempel, Siegfried. *The Care of Photographs.* New York, NY: Nick Lyons, 1987.

Ritzenthaler, Mary Lynn, Gerald J. Munoff, and Margery S. Long. *Archives & Manuscripts: Administration of Photographic Collections.* Chicago: Society of American Archivists, 1984. (Basic Manual Series)

Schrock, Nancy C. and Christine Sundt. "Slides." *Conservation in the Library,* ed. Susan G. Swartzburg, 103–128. Westport, CT: Greenwood Press, 1983.

Sundt, Christine L. *Conservation Practices for Slide and Photograph Collections.* Ann Arbor, MI: Visual Resource Association, 1989. (VRA Special Bulletin, No. 3)

Wilhelm, Henry. "Color Photographs and Color Motion Pictures in the Library: For Preservation or Destruction?" *Conserving and Preserving Materials in Nonbook Formats,* 105–111.Urbana-Champaign, IL: University of Illinois Graduate School of Library and Information Science, 1991.

Wilhelm, Henry, with Carol Brower. *The Permanence and Care of Color Photographs: Traditional and Digital Color Prints, Color Negatives, Slides and Motion Pictures.* Grinnell, IA: Preservation Publishing Co., 1993.

XI. IMAGE AND SOUND: The Care and Preservation of Motion Pictures, Sound Recordings, and Videotape

Introduction

MOTION PICTURE FILMS, AUDIO, AND VIDEO CASSETTES are among the most popular materials in a circulating library's collection. Today's library patron is visually and verbally literate. Film, video, and recorded sound are informational and entertainment media, but because of their unstable and impermanent nature, they present considerable problems in preservation and access. Because they were, and are, perceived as entertainment media, most librarians have not considered their long-term value as documentation of our society. In most libraries, the archival value of film and sound is not a consideration, but every film librarian should be aware of the intellectual as well as the entertainment value of these media. And the user is entitled to have as good a reproduction as possible, whether for study or for entertainment.

Motion Picture Film

Motion picture film is one of the most fragile materials to be found in libraries and archive repositories. Film historians Eileen Bowser and John Kuiper observe: "It is an astounding fact that mankind, with a thousand-year-old tradition of archives, failed to comprehend immediately upon the invention of the motion picture camera, the significance of preserving motion pictures the way that

194

written documents, books, music scores and paintings are kept. Because of this failure, even the richest and most developed countries in the world have enormous gaps in the continuity of collections of motion pictures and film documents."(1)

At present, it is estimated that fewer than 15 percent of the motion picture films made in the 1920s have survived to some degree intact; the rest have been lost or destroyed, or they have deteriorated beyond repair. Those that have survived are rapidly deteriorating. In the late 1970s, filmmaker Martin Scorsese and a number of his colleagues, who had received academic film training before becoming professional filmmakers, expressed their concern over the continuing loss of their work and that of their predecessors. Their public outcry over this loss has aroused the American public at large, and there is more support for efforts to save the nation's film heritage for future generations.

A concern for the preservation of motion picture films dates back to the 1930s, when the Museum of Modern Art began to collect and preserve films as works of art. The Museum was a founding member of the International Federation of Film Archives (FIAF), founded in 1938, which continues to sponsor important research into the preservation and conservation of film. Susan Dalton of the National Center for Film and Video Preservation has traced the history of the nation's efforts to preserve motion picture film for future generations. She writes: "The National Archives and the International Museum of Photography at George Eastman House soon joined in the preservation effort. The Library of Congress, which received films as copyright deposits until about 1912, began to acquire films for the motion picture division in the mid-1940s and established a preservation program in 1958. Although the efforts of these archives were considerable, much of early cinema had already been lost."

Dalton continues: "In 1967, the American Film Institute began a nationwide effort to locate and acquire nitrate films for preservation. To assist in this effort, the National Endowment for the Arts established the AFI/NEA Film

Preservation Program to fund the conversion of nitrate film to safety stock. Over the next twenty years, many thousands of early films were saved through the combined efforts of the major archives."(2)

It soon became evident that video is even more impermanent than film. In 1984, the National Center for Film and Video Preservation was created by the American Film Institute and the National Endowment for the Arts to serve as "an instrument of national coordination" for efforts to preserve the moving image. To that end, the center designed and implemented a National Moving Image Database (NAMID) that eventually will provide data on film and television holdings in archives, studios, and networks.

The first motion picture film was shown to the public in 1895. Until the early 1950s, most 35 millimeter films were made of cellulose nitrate negative stock, which is an extremely unstable material. Film historian and curator Eileen Bowser has noted that although the hazards of nitrate film as a highly flammable material were recognized early on in a series of disastrous fires, it was used for motion picture film until about 1951.(3) Most 8 and 16 millimeter film is not nitrate-based, but even the films produced on safety film are deteriorating because of the vulnerability of the cellulose base.

Older, nitrate-based films should be removed from the library's collection. As was discussed in the previous chapter, the disposal of nitrate film should be done carefully. Film specialists strongly recommend, however, that before nitrate film, even if there appears to be a copy, is destroyed, the film librarian should check with one of the major film archives, or the National Center for Film and Video Preservation, to be sure that it is not the last surviving copy or the survivor in the best physical condition. Old containers that contained nitrate-base film should be destroyed.

Although the majority of motion pictures were produced in black and white until the 1950s, color film was available from the earliest days of the medium. At first, color was applied by hand to each frame of film. There were many color film processes, but the Technicolor process was the predominant one between 1934 and 1953. The Technicolor process produced a more permanent color image, but it is also more expensive to produce. The Chinese set up Technicolor laboratories in Beijing in the late 1970s and China remains the one place where Technicolor film is still being produced. Motion picture films made from the 1950s on had the dye layers built into the film stock, but, as Henry Wilhelm's research and the viewer's eye make clear, the colors are fugitive. The colors that are seen today in motion pictures that are only a few years old are a ghost of the original image.

Colorizing of faded film is a possibility for preservation. Films that were originally made in black and white are now colorized with relative ease, using computer-imaging technology. However, colorizing is not an acceptable archival practice. Martin Scorsese and his colleagues have protested vigorously against the colorizing of black and white films never intended for color. A color-enhanced film must be viewed and judged as a new film. The aesthetic and ethical questions raised by the color-enhancement of faded color films still need to be addressed by film historians and archivists.

While aware of the serious problems that the medium of film presents for archivists, the librarian who runs an active film center is concerned with keeping films in working order for circulation for as long as possible. Preservation is a relatively short-term matter, not an issue of permanence. Yet, if motion picture film is housed in a good environment and used carefully, it should have a relatively long life in a circulating collection.

Film is a medium that is extremely sensitive to its environment. The temperature where film is stored should not exceed 70 degrees Fahrenheit, nor should the relative humidity exceed 60 percent, or serious deterioration can occur in a relatively short period of time. Film attracts mold under conditions of high humidity. Placing archival film in cold storage has proved effective in retarding its deterioration, but it is inappropriate to attempt to store circulating film under such conditions. Film should also be protected from light. Films should be stored flat. If shelved upright, the weight of the film resting on edge will result in warping and buckling over time. However, if films must be shelved upright, they should be well-supported, like books. Motion picture film should be wound on a core of inert material and kept in a sturdy metal or plastic container that provides proper support and protection. Films are especially susceptible to air pollutants, dust, dirt, and fingerprints, which can damage their surface. It is possible to coat projection prints with a treatment that offers some protection from scratches and moisture, but this should never be done to original prints that are potentially archival.

Libraries with circulating collections of motion picture films need to have staff trained to make simple repairs, such as mending tears in the perforation and splicing broken film together. Adhesive tape should never be used for repairs on film; it can cause the projector to jam and otherwise damage the film. Ultrasonic splicers are available and do their job quickly and efficiently; investment in one for a circulating film collection is well worth the cost. Film can be sent to a dependable film laboratory for cleaning. Light cleaning can be done in-house while running the film through the rewinding equipment. Unfortunately, there are still too few training programs for film technicians who work in libraries. Most technicians learn from books and from experience.

The film librarian should establish a good working relationship with suppliers to ensure that the library gets good quality projection prints. Once the print is received, it should be inspected. Defective prints should be returned.

Libraries with circulating motion picture film collections should have appropriate equipment for inspection and repairs and adequate space for these operations. Circulated film should be inspected after every use at the time that it is returned to the library. Films should not be returned to the shelf until it has been determined that they have suffered no damage during circulation. Inexpensive white cotton gloves should always be worn when handling or inspecting film.

Film is easily damaged if it is not projected correctly. The library's equipment should receive regular, scheduled maintenance, following the manufacturer's recommended procedures. Projectors should be cleaned after every use and their bulbs should be checked to ensure that they are producing the proper illumination; what appears to be poor film quality may in reality be a dimmed projector lamp. Staff members who operate the equipment should be instructed to do it properly.

Guidelines for the care and projection of films can be sent out in the package when films are circulated. This does not guarantee the safety of the material, but it will encourage most borrowers to handle the film with care. If film is carefully cared for in the library, it will provide both pleasure and education for many people for a long period of time.

Sound recording

In the history of communication, the invention of sound recordings can be considered comparable to the invention of the printing press. It permitted people to preserve oral material so that it could be heard in aural form again and again, just as the printing press had enabled people to preserve handwritten or oral material in a written form available to those who could read. The sound recording has become as important an information medium as the written word. Collections of sound recordings are a heavily used part of a library collection, yet less is known about the care and preservation of sound recordings than of printed materials. Recorded materials appear in a variety of media and formats, all of which are unstable and impermanent.

Thomas A. Edison developed the phonograph in 1877. His invention used the energy in sound to cause a stylus to carve a grooved pattern into a cylindrical surface. When a needle is placed in the groove, it reproduces the sound. The system developed to play back the sound was mechanical. The recordings were made of a variety of materials. These early sound recordings are valued objects today, collected and protected in sound archives and museums. Edison saw the relationship of sound to image and linked them mechanically, as did a number of other pioneers. However, it was not until the late 1920s that it was possible to incorporate a sound track with a film track, revolutionizing the film industry.

By the 1920s sound recordings were produced on 78 rpm disks. Early phonograph records were made of wax, metal cylinders, and shellac, a compound of a variety of ingredients. These recordings are now collector's items, to be found in private collections and in sound archives. They do not belong in a library's circulating collection. Long-playing, "unbreakable" 33 ⅓ rpm recordings were introduced by 1950 and, with these qualities, rapidly superseded the earlier 78s. These recordings are made of a light plastic material, usually a polyvinyl chloride acetate copolymer, known as PVC, to which are added lubricants, extenders, stabilizers, and dyes. Such recordings were predicted to have a life of 25 years before intrinsic deterioration would destroy their fidelity. While most recordings will wear out from use long before that time, a number of these disks have survived in surprisingly good condition. As this recording medium is being superseded by the compact disk and tape cassette, it, too, is becoming a collector's item. These recordings are still being produced and exist in circulating collections, but as they are being replaced by new sound technologies, those that have survived the hazards of general circulation also will achieve the status of treasured artifacts.

When establishing policies and procedures for the use of sound recordings, it is important to determine whether the material is kept for archival purposes or for general circulation to the public. Because of the diverse physical nature of early cylinders and disks, the requirements for their preservation in "archival" conditions is not fully understood. Researchers are working to determine the best conditions for their preservation. The Association of Recorded Sound Collections (ARSC) Associated Audio Archives (AAA) Committee, with funding from the National Endowment for the Humanities, undertook a major study in 1986 to identify the problems of preservation and access for sound recordings. Its report, *Audio Preservation, A Planning Study* (1988), is a document of 860 pages. The report serves as a working tool, for it brings together current knowledge of the physical nature of audio recordings and their preservation, and identifies an agenda for further research into the nature of the recording media and methods of preservation and access.

At present, the works of distinguished artists and performances are being rerecorded using techniques that can restore much of the recording's fidelity. As with brittle books, much effort has been devoted to the reformatting, or rerecording, of this material to retain as much as possible the quality of the earlier recordings. This is a highly technical, complex field. Yet, because of the impermanence of recorded sound, it is only through rerecording that the general public can have access to a rich aural heritage.

This section addresses the problems that libraries face when dealing with sound recordings, in an ever-increasing range of formats, that are to be circulated to the public. Both *High Fidelity* and *Stereo Review* magazines provide accurate and up-to-date information about new products and technologies. They enable a librarian who is not a specialist in sound recordings to keep up with the rapid developments in audio technology. A good rapport with the local audio equipment dealer is also recommended. The Association of Recorded Sound Collections (ARSC), with its membership of archivists responsible for special and unique collections, has published a journal since 1968 that provides considerable information on the care, handling, and preservation of sound recordings, as well as informative articles on recorded sound and discographies.

Most collections of sound recordings circulate in-house or to a user's home. Thus the recording will become significantly impaired after a certain number of circulations and will have to be discarded. The library should request that care be taken when playing disks or tapes on home equipment; helpful brochures on the correct handling of the material can be prepared for the user to take when borrowing a recording. Unfortunately, home equipment cannot be monitored. People who take immaculate care of recordings and tapes may then play them on poor or average equipment that will alter the recording so that distortion will be obvious when it is played by a user on high-quality equipment.

If recordings are used only within the library, high-quality playback equipment can be purchased that will extend their life significantly. As is true of all library materials, a clean, well-ventilated environment will extend considerably the life of sound recordings and playback equipment. Disks and tapes are especially sensitive to the effects of heat, humidity, particulate matter, and light. As with books, audio materials should be housed in an area with a constant temperature of 68 degrees Fahrenheit plus or minus five degrees, and a relative humidity of 40 to 55 percent, with a fluctuation of plus or minus five percent. Sound recordings, especially tapes, are very sensitive to rapid fluctuations of temperature and relative humidity. It is important that disks and tapes be kept in a clean environment. Air pollutants and dirt can quickly destroy them. Smoking should never be permitted where recordings are kept, for the pollutants in cigarette smoke are especially harmful. Tapes and disks should be kept away from heat sources; direct exposure to heat will distort and destroy them. Exposure to direct sunlight will destroy a sound recording in an exceedingly brief period of time.

Disks should be stored on metal shelves in an upright position, not too tightly packed, but close enough together so that each record is upright. Like books, sound recordings that are askew on the shelves will warp. This warping will cause deterioration and sound distortion and can make a disk or tape unplayable. Partitions placed every four to six inches along the shelf will help hold disks in an upright position. Wooden shelves are not recommended, for the acids in the wood may react adversely with the properties within a disk or tape and accelerate deterioration. Metal shelves, coated with baked enamel, are recommended for library materials, including sound recordings. If a new storage area is to be created, research on appropriate shelving will ensure that even an impermanent collection survives as long as possible.

When phonograph records are received, they should be removed from the sleeves that contain them within their envelopes and placed in protective sleeves or envelopes that can be obtained from suppliers of archival materials. The plastic wrappers that surround the envelope and disk should be discarded; they are not inert and can damage the recording. Few envelopes are made of acid-free board. Bags of inert plastic will offer the disks a great deal of protection and they can be purchased from suppliers of archival materials. These bags are worth purchasing, even for circulating collections.

The most common extrinsic factor in LP disk deterioration is the dirty or worn stylus. The outstanding qualities of the diamond needle, although costly to purchase, make it the most practical for use in collections of disks. The diamond needle must be replaced after 1,000 hours of use if damage to the recording is to be prevented. The stylus can be cleaned with an inexpensive stylus cleaning brush moistened with ethyl alcohol and gently brushed back and forth against the stylus. It is the static attraction of the PVC phonograph recording that attracts dust, and a grimy disk will soon wear out from scuffing, scratching, and gritting. A number of safe anti-static products are available to help protect the recording.

A number of products have been recommended for cleaning LP disks, the most common being mild soap and water applied with a soft cloth. Liquid washes are not recommended because water and the chemicals in commercial washes do not interact well with polyvinyl chloride. Disks should be cleaned after each use by using a clean, soft cloth and wiping them very gently in a circular motion around the grooves. Although even a soft dry wipe can be abrasive, it seems to be one of the better methods for cleaning disks in general collections.

By the mid-1980s compact disks with digitally encoded sound entered the commercial market; increasingly, they are purchased and circulated by libraries. A benefit of digitally recorded sound is its fidelity; it is a more acoustically accurate medium than the grooved disk. Compact disks, played back by a laser rather than a stylus, were supposed to be impervious to the hazards that threatened earlier disks, including playback, improper handling, and dirt. Originally the disks were advertised to be "permanent." While compact disks do offer considerable protection from risks of rough handling and playback, they have had their problems. Digital recording is a complex matter and many of the early disks were defective. The loss of even a few bytes of sound can be dramatic. Quality control has improved considerably, but there are no standards for digital recording technology, which itself is in an evolutionary phase.

A further problem with compact disk recordings that has recently been recognized is that they are not as intrinsically stable as they once claimed to be. This should not be surprising, because, like earlier disks, compact disks are made up of a variety of materials, some of which have proved to be susceptible to a variety of environmental conditions, including high temperature and/or relative humidity, rapid fluctuations in temperature and relative humidity, and contaminants in the air. The resultant loss of information encoded on the disks can make some unplayable in a relatively short period of time. A disease, called "laser rot," was first noticed by videodisc owners as early as 1983, when the images on the disks became "snowy," due to a loss of digital data. For a clear discussion of the problem, see the report, "Where's the Rot?" prepared by Rebecca Day, *Stereo Review,* April 1989. In addition, the inks on the labels of the disks have reacted adversely with the materials within the disks and caused loss of information. Adhesives used to attach these labels are also suspect. These problems also occur with CD-ROM disks, which will be discussed in the following section.

Day cautions, "Keep in mind that the manufacturers' longevity claims are based on the disks' being handled under proper conditions." To prolong the life of a compact disk, she offers a number of sound suggestions:

1. Don't leave oily finger deposits on compact disks. Handle them on the outer edges only, holding them between the thumb and fingers.
2. Don't bend a disk when removing it from its box.
3. Be sure that the blank side is dust-free before placing the disk in the player. Remove dust with a soft, lint-free cloth, wiping the disk in a radial direction, from the center to the outer edge. Do not use solvents that might damage the label or the protective coating on the disk.
4. Do not use markers or gummed stickers to label compact disks. They could eat through the protective coating and destroy the disk.(4)

Day concludes, "Right now, there's no definitive way to predict the life span of a CD."(5) Like the phonodisks that preceded them, these sound recordings, if stored properly and used with care should last for a long time. At this time, "long time" is a relative term. Compact disks are considered to be a transitional medium, not a medium of record. Over time, as the technology for the recording of sound evolves and changes, compact disks will become increasingly scarce. In time, those that survive will become a part of the aural heritage, stored in archival repositories and rerecorded for the listening pleasure of future generations. The librarian who manages a circulating collection of sound recordings should know the risks and budget for the replacement of damaged items. The librarian with a sense of history and technology will be able to identify recordings that are now scarce and see that they are "archived." Sound collection management principles are appropriate for all media.

Optical Disk Technology

The videodisk, a technology for storing images or machine-readable information on disks, was introduced in the early 1980s. It was originally intended to be a home entertainment medium. The information/image digitally encoded on a disk is read with a laser scanner and displayed on a conventional display monitor. Its storage capacity, from its beginning, was significantly beyond any other medium. Its potential as an information medium is enormous. Optical/videodisk technology is in its infancy and, as yet, there are no standards for production and playback. It is a technology that, increasingly, is in use in the library. It offers incredible possibilities for the preservation of the content of print, visual, and aural materials, and the potential to send this information anywhere in the world where there is playback equipment.

The CD-ROM (Compact Disk—Read Only Memory) has invaded the library, often replacing paper-based information tools. CD-ROM data bases are an invaluable addition to a library's information resources, but they involve a considerable investment in money and require considerable care and handling. Unfortunately, because of a lack of standardization, nearly every CD-ROM data base is different; many come with their own specially designed playback equipment. Although CD-ROMs are a visual, not an aural medium, these disks are subject to the same hazards as the compact disk sound recordings, discussed in the previous section. The problems with quality control in production of the disks, in the physical composition of the disk, and in handling are the same. Quality control remains the most serious concern, for a library makes a significant investment when it replaces printed information sources with these recorded sources and too often the defects in the system are not recognized for some time.

CD-ROMs should be kept and used in an environmentally controlled area. The problems that high temperature and relative humidity can cause with the disks are discussed above. Laser rot attacks optical disks as well as compact disk sound recordings. Air pollutants and contaminants can seriously harm the disks and cause loss of data. Under no circumstances should smoking be permitted in areas where CD-ROM equipment is housed. Thorough cleaning procedures are necessary for the area; cleaning should be planned as a special responsibility, separate from general housekeeping procedures. Static electricity, a problem in North American libraries, especially in the winter months, can also damage CD-ROMs and cause the loss of information. Static inhibitors should be placed under all terminals.

The rules for the care and handling of CD-ROM disks remain the same as those for compact disk sound recordings. If possible, the disks should be installed permanently in their playback equipment to protect them from abusive handling by the public. If a library invests in CD-ROM technology, it should provide a technician on the staff to serve as a troubleshooter for the service. Considerable damage can occur when a patron or a hapless library assistant (or, worse, a librarian) attempts to "fix" a malfunctioning CD-ROM player.

Magnetic Recordings

Tape recordings are made on a thin plastic ribbon, which is magnetized; thus they are subject to the same hazards as film. Like film, aural tapes require storage in a controlled environment where the temperature and relative humidity do not fluctuate. Archival materials are stored in much cooler temperatures than those found in circulating collections, for cold storage with a controlled relative humidity has proven to be the best way to preserve them.

Reel-to-reel tapes became a popular medium for sound recordings in the mid 1950s because of their generally higher quality of sound reproduction and the higher quality of tape equipment. This medium continues to offer the best sound reproduction. However, reel-to-reel tape is not as easy to handle as a tape enclosed in a cassette. It is therefore subject to more hazards from the environment and from handling. Reel-to-reel tape recordings are uncommon in circulating library collections today.

If a library has a collection of reel-to-reel tapes, they should be kept in an environmentally controlled area, placed in appropriate protective containers (available from several suppliers of archival materials). Tapes should be shelved so that the reel is in an upright position. Stacking tapes that are laid flat is never recommended, as the containers on the bottom of the pile can be damaged and cause distortion on the tape.

Ironically, reel-to-reel tapes are subject to some of the same neglect as early motion pictures. As a popular medium for recording rather than an archival medium, reel-to-reel tapes were used and discarded, especially when replaced by the more practical tape cassette, discussed below. Yet reel-to-reel sound recordings contain considerable information about ourselves and our society. Efforts are under way to collect and preserve this material. If original reel-to-reel recordings are found in collections, they should not be discarded until the Motion Picture, Broadcasting and Recorded Sound Division of the Library of Congress, or another sound archive is notified.

The tape cassette recording is especially popular today because each cassette is a contained unit, resistant to mishandling and simple to use, although its sound quality is inferior to that of reel-to-reel tape. As the users of circulating sound collections do not demand the finest quality of reproduction, the tape cassette is a convenient way to circulate sound recordings from a non-archival collection. A major problem with cassette tape recordings is the nonalignment of the tape within the cassette. Cassettes should be checked after each use to be sure that the tape is aligned properly or soon distortion will be detected. If the tape cassette recording is played on poor equipment that is badly adjusted, it will suffer misalignment and other damage that can destroy it.

It is important to house tape cassette recordings in an environmentally controlled area if they are to be preserved for any time at all. If possible, magnetic tapes should be kept in an environment with a cool temperature and a somewhat lower relative humidity than for paper-based materials. Once they are circulated, the library has no control over the conditions under which they are used. Archival boxes can be purchased to house cassettes and provide a better microenvironment for them. A variety of archival packaging is now available for the housing of tape recordings. The manager of a collection needs to carefully evaluate the use that a collection receives, then determine how best to house it.

Videotapes are among the most popular materials in the library. Videotape is an electromagnetic medium that dates back to the early 1950s, one that revolutionized television production because videotape filming and editing could be done with relative ease, giving a real immediacy to news coverage. By the late 1970s, videotape became a popular medium for home entertainment. Because videotape was relatively inexpensive, easy to operate, and could serve as a recording medium as well as a playback medium, the videodisk, originally marketed as an entertainment medium, could not compete for a place in the home market.

Videotapes come in their own cases and are easily inserted into playback equipment, thus there is slight chance that the tape will be damaged in handling. As a magnetic medium, however, videotape is extremely susceptible to damage from high temperature and relative humidity, rapid fluctuations in temperature and relative humidity, air pollutants, and dirt. Videotapes in circulating collections should be stored in the same environmental conditions as other audiovisual materials. The recommended temperature for the housing of videotape in circulating collections is 65 to 68 degrees Fahrenheit plus or minus two degrees. The relative humidity should range from 35 to 45 percent; it should be slightly lower than for collections of paper-based materials if at all possible. High levels of heat and humidity cause deterioration that can resemble the damage caused by dirty heads on the playback equipment. As with any information medium, dust and air contaminants should be kept at a minimum. Equipment in the library should be cleaned after every use. Magnetic tape is sensitive to magnetic or electric fields and should be protected from them.

Videotape is not an archival medium. Its circulating life is brief. Brochures on the proper use of videotape can circulate with the tapes. They should remind the user to keep the cassette in a cool place when it is not in use, to keep cassettes away from possible sources of electromagnetic fields (such as color television sets and microwave ovens), to clean the heads on equipment before playing the cassette, and to report any difficulties in viewing the tape to the library when it is returned.

Every videocassette should be inspected by a staff member when it is returned to ensure that there are no problems with it. Most libraries with video collections have trained technicians who can inspect and repair videotapes that have come loose or broken in their cassettes. Lint-free cotton gloves should be used by people handling the videotape. Not all videotapes come in convenient cassette format. If tapes on reels are to be circulated, they should be packaged in cassettes for convenience in storage and circulation.

Video is an increasingly popular entertainment and creative medium and is used to document a variety of events for which a permanent record is desired. This material is an exciting part of the nation's cultural heritage, yet it is nearly impossible to preserve original videotape. At present, considerable research is under way to determine how best to preserve usable videotape. The best solution at present is to retape original materials on a regular schedule, every two or three years, using the most recent popular technology. This is expensive, but it is the only way to preserve unique videotapes at this time.

Computer Technology

In 1983 Susan B. and Allan E. White observed:

> The last quarter of the twentieth century has produced a quantum increase in the reliance on computers for the storage and retrieval of information, much of which formerly was not available at all or was stored in traditional paper format, that is, in books, on cards, or on sheets of paper in manila folders.(6)

The library has entered an electronic age in which information increasingly is stored and retrieved by electronic impulse. The computer facilitates a variety of operations, from basic recordkeeping chores to sophisticated information and communication systems. The computer is revolutionizing the library. This section is not the forum to discuss the effect that the computer has, and will have, on library services, nor the role that librarians will play in the information age. It can only address some of the complex issues of preservation and access to computerized information. Librarians are embracing the computer wholeheartedly, for it can organize materials and provide access to information with speed and efficiency unimaginable a century ago. The computer, however, cannot *select* the information to be stored and manipulated, nor can it *preserve* it. The computer is a very useful tool, but at this time it has no intelligence. Therefore, it must be used intelligently.

The world is in the infancy of the computer age, an age where interactive technologies will provide extraordinary access to information. There are breakthroughs in technologies every month that make older technologies obsolete. Whatever systems that librarians install are already obsolete when patrons and staff begin to work with them. The skilled information specialist must anticipate the technological developments on the horizon and plan systems for information storage, manipulation, retrieval, and transmission that can evolve with no loss of information as they are upgraded.

Librarians and archivists know a great deal about the storage and preservation of paper-based materials and very little about the storage and preservation of nonprint media, such as film, video, and sound recordings. Considerable research is under way to determine how information in these media can be preserved before it vanishes as if it never existed. Librarians and archivists know even less about the preservation and retrieval of information in an electronic format. Much of this information has been lost over the past two decades because no one thought to save it as the new computer technologies evolved. Some information got lost because librarians, and others, could not save it. Much information has also been saved indiscriminately. Computer files filled with unorganized information are almost useless; the critical information in them has been lost in the detritus.

The first task of the librarian is to determine what information is suitable for computerization and how that information is to be organized for retrieval. That is the "proactive" stance recommended by information specialists today.(7) Many operations that have been computerized in the library in the past did not lend themselves to computerization and have resulted in great expense, inefficiency, and loss of service to the public. In 1975 Ellsworth Mason commented, "Extremely bad library functions are still maintained because they are computerized."(8) Too many of these systems exist in the 1990s, and many more have been developed. Until librarians determine what information and what procedures for information retrieval the computer can manage effectively, much energy will be spent unnecessarily and much important and necessary information will be lost. Bluntly put, "Garbage in—garbage out."

Backup systems and files are essential for computer operations. All information stored on a computerized data base is impermanent; it can disappear at any time. Computer equipment is exquisitely sensitive to the environment. Excessive dryness, dampness, or too high a temperature can ruin equipment and cause loss of data. Static electricity, which occurs under low-humidity conditions, is a serious problem in computer rooms and where public access computer terminals are located. Uncontrolled variations in the line voltage can cause loss of information. Surge protectors are necessary to protect computers from power surges and/or brownouts. Managers should be sure that the power service to which computers and terminals are connected is capable of supplying the required power. A power line is necessary for the operation of the machinery, but it can also be a source of problems. It is necessary to make sure that the computer is not overloading the service; this is a very real and serious problem in many libraries. In a number of cases when a computer failed to operate it has been because the computer was not plugged in, or external cables were loose. When problems do occur, the facilities officer or electrician should be notified as quickly as possible.

A more important concern, in the long run, is that as computer technology changes, playback becomes difficult if not impossible. It is extremely difficult today to retrieve data from punched cards that were produced in computer centers in the 1960s. Information that took up several reels of magnetic tape to store a decade ago can now be stored on tiny disks. The hard disks in computers have replaced the miles of magnetic computer tapes from the past two decades that are now in storage. Computer technology is developing at a rapid rate. Even microcomputers have an astonishing capacity to store information. In an age of information overkill, there is insufficient discrimination between information that is needed and that which is not. The computer cannot discriminate and the costs of people doing so, and reformatting information into new systems, is high.

The advent of the information age and the adaptation of computer technology to library uses gives librarians the opportunity to reexamine how they can best collect, organize, preserve, and make available information to document and advance our culture. The computer cannot preserve information, but librarians can.

Conclusion

This chapter makes clear that librarians do not have definitive guidelines for the care and preservation of nonprint materials. Yet, good housekeeping practices, common sense, and caution when handling these fragile objects should prolong their useful life in the library. A little knowledge about new technologies can help librarians preserve the information in them. Each medium has its magazines and technical journals, but a careful reading of the business pages in such papers as *The Wall Street Journal* and *The New York Times* will keep the astute librarian abreast of new developments in information and communications technology.

Increasingly, librarians and archivists are becoming involved in the development of standards for the new media and new technologies, serving on National Information Standards Organization (NISO) Z39 committees to formulate standards that then move forward to the American National Standards Institute (ANSI), and thence to the International Standards Organization (ISO). This is a slow process, and by the time an international standard is established for a communication medium, the technology usually has moved on. The setting of standards is a learning experience for information professionals and vendors, for the process enables the information specialist to communicate needs to the vendor.

Although most librarians will not preside over archival collections of rare and unique nonprint materials, they should be familiar with the problems that such curators face in their efforts to preserve these documents of our cultural heritage and to make them available. Librarians have demonstrated how they can cooperate to preserve the nation's newspapers, and the profession can cooperate with archivists and others to preserve the nonprint heritage. Researchers like Henry Wilhelm, who has done so much to address the problems with color film; James Reilly, at the Image Permanence Institute at Rochester (NY) Institute of Technology; and those in archives around the country, and the world, deserve the library profession's appreciation and support for their work. Librarians and archivists, information professionals, past, present, and future, will manage the new information technologies as successfully as they have done in the past and will preserve the intellectual heritage for future generations.

Notes

1. *A Handbook for Film Archives,* (Brussels: Federation Internationale des Archives du Film, 1980), 3.
2. Susan Dalton, "Moving Images: Conservation and Preservation," *Conserving and Preserving Materials in Nonbook Formats* (Urbana-Champaign, IL: University of Illinois Graduate School of Library and Information Science, 1991), 62.
3. "Motion Picture Film," *Conservation in the Library* (Westport, CT: Greenwood Press, 1983), 139.
4. Rebecca Day, "Where's the Rot? A Special Report on CD Longevity," *Stereo Review,* 54:4 (April 1989): 23–24.
5. *Ibid.* 24.
6. "The Computer: When Tomorrow Becomes Yesterday," *Conservation in the Library* (Westport, CT: Greenwood Press, 1983), 205.
7. For the roles that the archivist and librarian might play in the future, see Bruce I. Ambacher, "Managing Machine-Readable Archives," *Managing Archives and Archival Institutions,* 121–133. Chicago: University of Chicago Press, 1988. Peter S. Graham, "Electronic Information and Research Library Technical Services," *College and Research Libraries,* 51:3 (May 1990): 241–250.
8. "Balbus; or the Future of Library Buildings," *Farewell to Alexandria,* ed. Daniel Gore (Westport, CT: Greenwood Press, 1975): 32.

Selected Reading

Bowser, Eileen. "Motion Picture Film." *Conservation in the Library,"* ed. Susan G. Swartzburg. Westport, CT: Greenwood Press, 1983.

Bowser, Eileen and John Kuiper, eds. *A Handbook for Film Archives.* New York: Garland Press, 1991.

Henderson, Kathryn Luther and William T., eds. *Conserving and Preserving Materials in Nonbook Formats.* Urbana-Champaign, IL: University of Illinois Graduate School of Library and Information Science, 1991. (Allerton Park Institute, 30). See especially "Preservation and Conservation of Sound Recordings," by Gerald D. Gibson; "Preservation of Computer-Based and Computer-Generated Records," by Gordon B. Neavill; and "Moving Images: Conservation and Preservation," by Susan Dalton.

Pickett, A. G. and M. M. Lemcoe. *Preservation and Storage of Sound Recordings.* Washington, DC: Library of Congress, 1959; reprint ed. Silver Spring, MD: Association of Recorded Sound Collections, 1992.

Sargent, Ralph N. *Preserving the Moving Image.* Washington, DC: Corporation for Public Broadcasting, 1974.
An important publication, now, alas, out of print.

Smolian, Steven. "Preservation, Deterioration and Restoration of Recording Tape. *ARSC Journal,* 19:2–3 (1987; issued January 1989): 37–53.

Ward, Alan. *A Manual of Sound Archive Administration.* Aldershot, Hants.: Gower, 1990.

White, Susan B. and Allan E. "The Computer: When Tomorrow Becomes Yesterday." *Conservation in the Library,* 205–219. Westport, CT: Greenwood Press, 1983.

XII. REFORMATTING FOR PRESERVATION: Microform and Facsimile

Introduction

THE REPRODUCTION OF LIBRARY AND ARCHIVAL MATERI-
ALS in paper format is an important method of
preserving information that would otherwise disintegrate and be lost, materials already deteriorated and in
fragile condition. This chapter will discuss how surrogate
copies, microforms and facsimiles are used as a format for
the preservation and access of information.

The history of the photographic reproduction of written
documents parallels the history of photography. Microfilm dates back to the Franco-Prussian War in 1871 when
photographically reproduced messages in a microformat
were transmitted by carrier pigeon. By the turn of the
century, forward-looking librarians sensed that photographic reproduction could solve preservation problems
in libraries, for, increasingly, they were aware of the
impermanence of paper and books, especially those published after 1870. In 1944, the distinguished librarian
Fremont Rider, in his book, *The Scholar and the Future of
the Research Library,* suggested that microforms might
also be a method of solving space problems in libraries.
He suggested that serials and infrequently used sets that
were needed chiefly by researchers might be filmed and
stored far more economically than housing the originals
in the stacks of the library.(1) Microphotography came
into its adolescence in the second World War when, once
again, the rapid reproduction and transmission of material became a necessity. The microfilmers who served the

nation during the war became the pioneers in a new industry, micropublishing.

Microforms

While the Library of Congress, the British Library, and several major research institutions and agencies are exploring optical disk technology and how it might be applied to the problem of preservation and access of library and archival materials, it is clear that optical technology, currently in its infancy, is not an appropriate medium for the preservation of information at this time. The current technology has not proved its permanence, nor has there been an attempt, in the midst of a rapidly developing technology, to define the guidelines for playback and transfer of data. Until these problems are resolved, optical digital information media must be considered impermanent. Information stored in these media cannot be retrieved easily in the decades to come. It needs to be transferred to a new medium as the old becomes obsolete. To grasp the problem for scholarship, imagine a scholar in the twenty-first century, working away in a warehouse in Maryland that the Smithsonian Institution has constructed to house the vast number of optical readers that developed in the final quarter of the twentieth century. The report *Preservation of Historical Records,* by the Committee on Preservation of Historical Records, National Materials Advisory Board, and the Commission on Engineering and Technical Systems, National Research Council, evaluated the technologies that might be employed for the preservation of the paper records in the National Archives. Its conclusion was that *at the present time* microfilming technology is the least expensive and most effective technology for the preservation and access of documentary records.(2)

During the same period that the committee's report was being prepared, the Council on Library Resources (CLR), with funding from the Exxon Education Foundation, was examining technologies for the preservation of brittle books and other materials that were published on acidic papers from the 1860s to the present. While the Council's Committee on Preservation and Access initially was enamored with the new technologies for image storage and retrieval, its members, too, determined that microfilming technology is the most practical, cost-effective, and permanent method for the preservation and access of library and archival materials at this time. Microfilm is relatively inexpensive to produce, and it has proved its permanence and durability as well as its relative ease of use. Microfilm can be easily converted to another technology if that is desirable.

With further funding from Exxon, a group of research libraries established the first nonprofit regional center exclusively for preservation microfilming, the Mid-Atlantic, now Preservation Resources, Inc., located in Bethlehem, PA. In the fall of 1990 Preservation Resources officially became a part of the Online Computer Library Center (OCLC), a nonprofit membership organization that operates an international bibliographic computer network used by more than 11,000 libraries in the United States and abroad. Its name was changed to Preservation Resources to reflect its broader scope. Its founder and first president, C. Lee Jones, formerly with the Council on Library Resources, had a firm grasp of the technical and managerial complexities in establishing and operating a nonprofit technical service for the library and archival communities. The link of the center to OCLC has resulted in expanded and more efficient service to libraries. The link of a preservation microfilming center to a major bibliographic utility is significant, as utilities such as OCLC enable institutions to work together to address preservation concerns.

The National Endowment for the Humanities and other funding agencies, public and private, continue to support the preservation microfilming activities at the Northeast Document Conservation Center (NEDCC), located in Andover, MA, the first regional center established for the conservation of library and archival materials. While it, too, can handle routine microfilming projects, it is able to deal with more fragile and difficult projects that would slow production at Preservation Resources. Microfilming for preservation is most important in the areas of serials, newspapers, archival documents, and scholarly monographs. These are not the materials that the reader will want to read comfortably in bed, but rather scholarly or technical materials that need to be scanned or studied for research purposes. This material is most easily and inexpensively reproduced in microform. Microform is the generic term for a format, usually on a film base, that contains microimages. A microimage is an image (normally a page) of information too small to read without magnification. A microform may be microfilm, microfiche, microprint, or other kinds of micropublication.

Microfilm consists of a film, a clear pliant base, coated with a photosensitive emulsion. When the photosensitive material in the emulsion consists of silver halides, the film is a "silver film," recommended for archival preservation. The widths most often used in libraries are 16 millimeter (mm), 35 millimeter, 70 millimeter, and 105 millimeter. Standard microfiche are made on 105 mm film with 60 to 98 frames on each card. Fiche cards are usually 105 x 148 mm, nominally 4 x 6 inches in size, upon which microimages are arranged in seven rows and fourteen columns for a maximum of 98 pages per fiche. This is the format adopted by most micropublishers today, although other sizes have been available.

Microforms can preserve a large amount of material in a small amount of space, and the medium lends itself to retrieval systems designed for researchers. There is a considerable body of literature on the storage and retrieval of information in microtext format. It cannot be emphasized too strongly that the system adopted should meet the needs of the library it serves, not fit specifications for a system developed for another institution. Such a system should utilize the special advantages of microforms in the areas of space savings, the capability of being reproduced easily, durability, file integrity, and automatic retrieval.

Many of the journals published in the past 120 years are

in poor condition today. Research libraries have a responsibility to preserve scholarly and scientific journals of the day as documents of our cultural and intellectual history. The reproduction of these journals is a large part of the contemporary micropublication industry. Reproduced volumes can be purchased in book form, but microform editions have proved to be the most satisfactory method for maintenance and preservation. These publications are not likely to be browsed, but rather they are consulted for specific information. Journals on microfilm lend themselves to computerized access systems that can provide the user with greater flexibility than can be provided by the codex format. Microform reading areas are an integral part of the research, academic, and special library, and have become more common in the modern public library. Once a researcher becomes accustomed to handling research material in this different format, he or she can appreciate the world the microform brings to the fingertips.

Smaller libraries normally do not serve the demanding researcher who wants, as rapidly as possible, yesterday's information today, but they are the repository for archival materials, newspapers, town records, and other special materials that should be made available to the community as well as the scholarly researcher. It is precisely this material that the community has the responsibility to preserve. A number of states now have grant programs administered through the State Library, Historical Society, or Historical Commission that have been developed to preserve this unique material through microfilm and appropriate storage and access.

While there are commercial microfilmers, such as University Microfilms, Research Publications, and Chadwyck-Healey, that are willing to take on the task of microfilming library and archival collections that are commercially viable, a number of microfilming companies are now approaching libraries and archives promising "preservation" services. With the considerable publicity about the "brittle book" program, encouraged by the Commission on Preservation and Access, and the U.S.

Newspaper Program, they, no doubt, envision the profits to be made from the efforts to preserve the nation's documentary heritage. In addition, several commercial library binding companies that already provide an array of services to their customers are expanding to include preservation microfilming among them. While competition to meet library needs is more than a little welcome, librarians will need to ensure that the quality of the work meets the standards necessary to assure permanence, durability, and accuracy.

In 1988 the American Library Association published an important manual, *Preservation Microfilming,* edited by Nancy E. Gwinn. It includes chapters on every aspect of preservation microfilming written by such experts as Sherry Byrne (University of Chicago) and Carolyn Harris (then Head of Preservation at Columbia University Library), who were involved with major preservation microfilming projects for a number of years. Like any publication on a timely and technical topic, it is already in need of modest revision, but its practical advice and recommendations can help avoid hours of work and costly errors when planning a preservation microfilming program for a library's collections.

It is critical that preservation microfilming be done correctly the first time around; there is rarely a second chance. The keys to a successful preservation microfilming program are bibliographic control and preparation prior to filming. Both of these aspects must be addressed before materials are sent to be filmed, and they are usually the most costly part of a preservation microfilming project. To begin, it is important to be sure that the material has not previously been filmed; if it has, it is essential to be sure that previous filming is adequate. All film must be carefully inspected.

The physical preparation of materials for filming should, if at all possible, be done in-house. It is necessary to have trained professional staff to supervise the collation of the material to be filmed and the creation of the targets. To be specific, the supervisor of the project should have a degree in librarianship or the equivalent, bibliographical experience, and, if possible, previous microfilming experience. At the beginning, professional staff must decide a number of bibliographical matters. Title changes, editions, and other such information need to be recorded on the microfilm and in the appropriate bibliographic data bases.

Every journal, newspaper, book, or document file that is to be microfilmed should be examined and collated, page by page. It is important to have an accurate record of missing and badly damaged pages or other problems that could confuse a reader. The contents of each reel of film need to be programmed prior to filming so that the filmers know beforehand what issues are to appear on a given reel. Targets that include primary bibliographic information need to be prepared. A target is a document, or chart, that contains identification information, coding, or test charts. It is an aid to technical and bibliographic control that is photographed on the film preceding or following the document. The preparation of targets can be accomplished with the help of a computer. Quality control is essential and should be a major concern of the microfilmer. However, it is ultimately the responsibility of the library. Each reel of microfilm must be inspected for image quality and bibliographical accuracy when it is returned from the microfilmer. Microfilmed materials should not be disposed of until inspection is completed, no matter how substantial the file. The New York Public Library had to hold one large newspaper file for five months before filming and inspection were completed.

A number of standards to ensure quality in microfilm reproduction have been established in the past decade. Standards protect the consumer by spelling out procedures. The Association for Information and Image Management (AIIM), formerly the National Micrographics Association, was founded in the early 1950s with a goal of establishing some standardization among micrographics publishers. Its Standards Committee served as a catalyst for the viewpoints of the Department of Defense, the Library of Congress (where microfilming began), the Society of American Archivists, the American Library Association, the American National Standards Institute (ANSI) and the International Standards Organization (ISO). The standards that have evolved were developed by experts in the field and their purpose is to aid and protect the consumer. Gwinn observes: "Microfilms have been subjected to more stringent standards, to a much more thorough analysis of their stability and image quality, than any other recording medium in history. Today's microform standards serve to protect the consumer, to educate the user, and to guide both the manufacturer of microfilm materials and the library, archives, or commercial producer of microforms."(3) AIIM standards for preservation microfilming can now be purchased as a package and are well worth the cost.

The Research Libraries Group (RLG), which developed and manages a large-scale preservation microfilming program among its member libraries, has developed its own set of standards and specifications. A committee to develop standards and specifications for preservation microfilming began its work in 1980. The *RLG Preservation Manual,* with extensive information on preservation microfilming, was issued in 1983 and revised in 1984. The RLG manual has again been completely revised by the members who participate in the RLG preservation microfilming project, for the librarians involved have gained a great deal of experience in overseeing projects for the microfilming of brittle books and archival collections. The *RLG Preservation Microfilming Handbook,* edited by Nancy E. Elkington, was published in 1992. It is a comprehensive guide to preservation microfilming on a large scale. The RLG project has led to many improvements in techniques and technology for preservation microfilming.

Because micropublishing is an industry still in its infancy and standards are always a compromise based upon existing technical capabilities, microfilming standards need to be reviewed regularly for suitability and modified as necessary. Every American National Standards Institute (ANSI) standard is reviewed every five years. The work of preparing standards and making compromises between diverse groups with diverse interests is long and somewhat tedious. Frequently, it appears that the technology of micrographics is ahead of the thinking of the group of producers and users as a whole. Thus, if a preservation microfilming job is to be undertaken, it is wise for the administrator to review existing standards and current literature on micrographics and other reproductive technologies in the light of the institution's specific needs. Then specifications can be selected, or modified, that will serve both the needs of an institution and meet the standards acceptable to the scholarly community at large.

Every preservation microfilming program will generate a master negative, the film used in the camera. This is called the "first generation" film, and it is the archival copy of the material that has been filmed. The former Archivist of the United States, James B. Rhoads, described in 1975 how the National Archives and Records Administration (NARA) defined the term "archival" for its purposes; that definition can serve the library community well. Rhoades wrote:

> Essentially the term "archival" is synonymous with "permanent" and the two are frequently used interchangeably. To us they have the same meaning: that is, forever. To say that we are going to keep forever everything that is now classified as archival, or permanent, is a rather positive statement and one which none of us can guarantee, yet it does express our intention in relation to records which have been appraised as being of permanent value, or archival.(4)

Gwinn observes, "Film used for preservation should be the sharpest available. . . . Preservation microfilming of source documents should employ only the slowest, highest resolution films available."(5) The accepted film for preservation microfilming is a silver-gelatin film on a polyester base. Silver is recognized as a stable metal, and the image on the silver film is metallic silver. Silver-gelatin film has been in use for many years and subjected to stringent testing. It is considered capable of producing an archival image. It is recommended that the master negative be stored in a safe place. Most institutions opt to contract for storage through an intermediary service, which is offered by the Research Libraries Group or through state and regional services.

In addition to the master negative, a copy negative, also called the printing master, should be produced on a silver-gelatin film, to be stored and used only to produce "service" copies of the microfilm, copies produced for use. Preservation Resources stores printing masters and can supply service copies to its clients upon request. Microforms in libraries are purchased for use. Silver-gelatin, or "archival" microfilm is not a good film for general use in a library. It is easily scratched, subject to fungal and oxidative attack (the gelatin base), and the image will deteriorate if the film has not been processed correctly. Silver-gelatin film is especially sensitive to environmental changes and does not keep well in a general library collection. There are two film stocks available that serve far better as the medium for service copies in the library, diazo and vesicular. Diazo and vesicular microfilm can be purchased at significantly less cost than silver-gelatin film and is far more suitable for everyday use. Standards for the production of diazo and vesicular film ensure suitable and dependable microfilm that will satisfy the needs of the library collection.

Diazo film is a slow print film, sensitized by a coating of diazonium salts, which, when exposed to light, form an image. The image can be either positive or negative, depending upon the polarity of the film from which it is printed. The color of the image is determined by the composition of the diazonium compound and the couplers used in the process. For a number of years, there has been a concern about the use of diazo film because of the possible fading of the dyes and staining of the clear portion of the film. Yet, if the film is kept under "archival" conditions, that is, stored away from light and humidity, it shows little change. Service copies in the library setting are not expected to last. Most service copies will wear out from use before significant deterioration from the environment can take place. Diazo film is sturdy and durable and serves well in a library setting. It can take a fair amount of abuse.

Vesicular film is also an extremely sturdy and durable film. Its image consists of small bubbles, called vesicles, within a plastic layer, that contain the latent image. The latent image becomes visible and permanent by heating the plastic layer and then allowing it to cool. At this time, however, it is not clear how permanent vesicular film might be. It has not been sufficiently tested and there is a concern that, over time, the vesicles will collapse if subjected to prolonged heat. Another problem with vesicular film produced in the past is that it can emit fumes that can cause damage to materials around it; this problem is now solved, but older reels of vesicular film in the library can cause a serious problem. Today diazo and vesicular films are suitable and appropriate for general library use; silver-gelatin, or "archival" film, is not.

Color microfilm cannot be considered a stable medium for archival microfilming at this time, although the research done by Henry Wilhelm and others indicates that there are several films that appear to offer the color stability necessary for the preservation microfilming. The problems with color film have been discussed in Chapter 9. Further research is under way at the Image Permanence Institute, affiliated with Rochester Institute of Technology. Preservation Resources is also investigating the permanence and durability of new color films and color microfilming technologies that are coming on the market. Some libraries are already doing preservation microfilming projects using these films, and the library world awaits the evaluation of their success.

Microform collections in the library, even if they are not archival, need proper storage, care, and preservation. Microforms are a photographic material composed of unstable chemical compounds that are particularly susceptible to hazards in the environment and from everyday use. Once a paper-based photocopy is bound and placed in the stacks, it is afforded the same care that other books on the shelf receive. But the microform copy requires different preservation procedures.

Proper storage and handling are the keys to the preservation of a working microform collection. The best storage conditions are in an air-conditioned area maintained at a constant temperature of 65 to 68 degrees Fahrenheit, with 40 to 60 percent relative humidity. Silver-gelatin film is susceptible to microbial, fungal, and oxidative attack because of its gelatin emulsion. Microforms should be stored in a dry area, above ground, and placed in cabinets or boxes that do not have open vents or holes. Shelving should be made of a noncombustible material, such as baked enamel with a nonplasticized lacquer. The storage area should allow the free circulation of air-conditioned air. If microforms are stored in airtight tins, they should be inspected and exposed to the air every six months. Older vesicular film should be stored separately, in plastic containers made of polyethylene, away from the rest of the microform collection. In fact, it is recommended that generically different types of film not be stored within the same housing.

Reels and containers for microforms should be made of a noncorroding material that has no "off-gassing." Rolls of films should be stored in closed containers for protection from dirt and to provide a comfortable microenvironment for the film. The film should be secured by acid-free paper bands, never rubber bands, which can damage the film in a relatively short period of time. Adhesive tapes should, of course, never be used on microfilm. Many commercially prepared microforms come prepackaged and indexed; not all prepackaged microforms are packaged correctly, however. Microforms should be inspected when they arrive, not only to be sure that they are not defective, but also to ensure that they are housed correctly when they enter the collection. Rubber bands should be removed from the film; paper bands, which can be purchased from archival suppliers, should be used to secure the microfilm roll.

While a number of vendors advertise that they supply microfilm reels in archival boxes, this is, too often, not the case. It is possible to test each package, to be sure that it is not acidic, but at this time most institutions find it safer and more cost-effective to purchase their own archival-quality boxes for the storage of microfilm and to place all new films in these boxes. Several committees within the American Library Association are working hard to convince microtext vendors to supply products that meet all standards for storage and use, but it is not the norm in the trade at present.

Microfiche should be stored in neutral, lignin-free envelopes that are available from archival suppliers; fiche should be placed in these envelopes upon receipt. The seam of the envelope should not rest on the image area of a microfiche. Microfiche should not be crammed into cabinets, for overcrowding will make retrieval difficult and can cause damage to the materials. As with microfilm, generic film bases should be stored separately.

Storage and retrieval systems for microform collections should be devised for efficiency of retrieval and the protection of materials to prevent undue handling of other film. A number of excellent books are available on the care and storage of microform collections. A visit to the exhibits of microform vendors and the suppliers of archival-quality supplies at ALA, SAA, regional, and state professional conferences is the best way to learn about equipment and supplies in a rapidly changing field.

Playback Equipment

Microforms cannot be retrieved from a shelf or cabinet and used in the same manner as a book. It is necessary to insert the microform into a compatible reading device to be able to consult it. A microform reader is a viewing or projection device used to magnify the microimage to readable size. Microform readers of today have come a long way from the heavy and cumbersome machines of the past; nevertheless, they do present an obstacle between the material and the user. Most are easy to use; their image quality is good and does not strain the eyes. Operating instructions should be placed in a visible area on or near each machine, but patrons who are using the equipment for the first time usually require additional assistance. Readers trying to cope with unfamiliar equipment without assistance can cause serious damage to both the microform readers and the microforms themselves. At a major university, a frustrated professor, working in an unattractive room with outdated equipment, scratched the lens of a reader-printer in a fit of pique, causing permanent damage. While such behavior is unpardonable, the conditions under which he was working hardly demonstrated that the library cared about the microform or the user. Who among us has not had the urge to smash a machine when it is not working properly and there is no one available to help us? Microtext readers are machines and they require that a technician be available to assist the patron. People can cause a great deal of damage to microforms and equipment, but if a conscientious staff properly cares for its collections, human damage may be kept to a minimum.

Microform reading rooms should be pleasant, welcoming places, just as the rest of the library should be, to encourage readers to come and to work comfortably. Before a microform reading room is equipped, a study should be made to determine how it will be used. Today there is ample information in the library literature on the planning and equipping of the microform reading room. A trip to a library conference will overwhelm the librarian with a plethora of new equipment. Because of the rapid developments in microform technology, there have been many improvements in equipment in the past few years. The librarian should be aware of new equipment and how to evaluate it. Basically, one should check for image quality and brightness; ease in loading and film advance; viewing angle; image rotation; screen size, tint, and material; focus magnification; construction; lamp, cooling, and electrical systems; service and warranty offered; and, finally, cost. *Microform Review* and *Micrographics Newsletter* provide up-to-date reviews of equipment in addition to reviews of new micropublications.

When microform equipment is purchased, the manufacturer should supply a manual for each piece of equipment and should train staff members to use each properly.

It is advisable to review the service contract that the manufacturer offers. It may be worthwhile to pay the additional cost, for the manufacturer will have a service section that can provide better care for its equipment than most library handypersons. Staff members should be trained to check microforms for condition, not only when they are new, but after each use, to replace damaged film, and to spot potential problems, such as damaged equipment, immediately.

As is true of all media to be found in the library, cleanliness is the most important aspect of the maintenance of the microtext reader. Particulate matter, dirt and dust, is the enemy of film and equipment. Lenses, film holding devices, and optical mirrors can be cleaned with a sable or camel hair brush. Equipment should be covered or stored in a closed container when not in use and kept free of oils, especially oils from fingerprints. Rear-projection viewers have plastic or glass screens that can be washed with a mild ammonia and water solution, but care should be taken when using ammonia solutions near diazo film. Front-projection viewers have opaque screens that can be washed with mild soapy water.

When a lamp burns out, it should be removed only after it has cooled. The glass of quartz halogen lamps should not be touched with bare hands. The protective covering around the lamp should be left on when it is inserted into the socket, for if the glass is touched it will probably shorten the life of the lamp.

Microforms may appear to be more difficult to care for properly than library books because the librarian must deal not only with the microform itself but also with the equipment needed to use it. Yet, librarians and their assistants increasingly are adept at handling multimedia materials, and library schools are providing more basic training, although "hands-on" training is minimal. Slowly (too slowly), programs to train library technicians are developing in community colleges; these trained technicians should be welcomed with open arms by librarians, for their skills are invaluable in caring for and protecting microform and other nonprint collections.

Photographic Reproduction

In many libraries, it may be appropriate to provide a photocopy of a book or an article for use in the circulating collection in addition to, or in lieu of, a preservation microform. Scholarly books are far more easily consulted and read in hard copy than in microformat. While the effort to save the contents of a legacy of embrittled books through microfilming is both necessary and heroic, access to this material is difficult for the researcher who needs to use the material. The surrogate copy, or photocopy, bound, cataloged, and housed in the circulating collection, meets the need for ease of access to preserved materials.

Photocopiers were in use in the 1930s; in the late 1940s the Xerographic method, an electrostatic copying process, was developed. This process enabled the publisher, or copyist, to reproduce by photographic means material in the codex, or book format. Other direct copying techniques were perfected, and by the early 1960s copying machines were a commonplace fixture in many libraries. With these machines, which were simple to operate, one could reproduce pages or whole texts of volumes at a relatively small cost and in a fraction of the time that it took to copy such material by hand. Exit the age of hand copying and enter the age of paper proliferation and copyright complications yet to be resolved. The photographic reproductions, in which the image is made electrostatically on paper, are only as permanent as the paper upon which they are made and in some cases may only last a few months.

Electrostatic copies are the most popular form of photographic reproduction for preservation purposes in most libraries today. However, with the rapid development of reprographic technology there has been a corresponding lessening of the quality of the equipment. The library market is a very small part of the photocopying market; while a large library may produce over 10,000 copies a month, a large corporation may require 100,000 to half a million copies a month, produced on high-speed, technically sophisticated machines receiving regular attention. Libraries cannot afford such equipment and the support staff to maintain it. If a copying machine is not functioning correctly and is not hot enough to set the toner and the image, the image can rub off. The face-up machines that dominate the market today make it difficult to photocopy bound library materials, especially volumes that are tightly sewn with text close to the spine. Brittle books may break under even the slightest pressure. Several companies are developing photocopiers that can copy embrittled books. As these machines enter the market, they should be evaluated carefully for in-house reformatting projects.

The Physical Quality of Library Materials Committee, Preservation of Library Materials Section (PLMS), American Library Association, issued "Guidelines for Photocopying for Preservation Replacement" in 1990. These guidelines cover the type of paper to be used, the contrast setting, the minimum border to be left for binding or for tipping-in, and the bibliographic note that everything in the text should be copied, excepting some graffiti, marginalia, or stray marks. It is recommended that copies then be bound following accepted standards for commercial library binding.

Several commercial vendors make use of reprographic processes to reproduce out-of-print copies of scholarly books. Copies are printed on alkaline paper and some companies will provide sturdy bindings for a nominal extra charge. For many, if not most, libraries this is a cost-effective alternative to establishing a preservation photocopying unit in-house. The copies produced by these vendors are of excellent quality and they are certainly more "user-friendly" than filmed copies. The application of laser technologies in printing is already making the reproductive process attractive to the library market.

Conclusion

When considering a preservation reformatting program, it must be remembered that the products that are produced are surrogate copies for the original materials. There is an increasing concern among a number of scholars and librarians that in the process of filming large collections of embrittled materials insufficient attention has been paid to the originals. The response, and a serious response it is, is that we cannot save everything. The legacy of 150 years of acidic and rapidly deteriorating materials in our libraries and archives is too great. We need to move quickly, using the best technology (microfilm) available, to capture the information in this material before it is lost.

The cost of preserving even one example of every printed item issued in the United States is astronomical. In the case of the nation's heritage of newspapers, large numbers of badly deteriorated runs cannot, practically speaking, be saved. Considerable effort has been made to gather intact copies together to be filmed; this preparation is often time-consuming and costly. Further conservation treatment is cost-prohibitive. American librarians are criticized for this decision, for most European countries preserve at least one copy of every newspaper published. The United States of America, founded by dissenters, advocates of the free press attracted to the medium of print for a variety of reasons, produced vast quantities of newspapers surpassing the published output in most, if not all, other nations. The small state of New Jersey published more newspapers in its 350-year history than the total number of newspapers published in France. Deciding what is to be preserved, and how, is not an easy decision.

Yet embrittled books have intrinsic value. Every book, even those "mass produced" since 1860, is a separate entity, different from every other book. Bibliographers and scholars of the book would like to see every book preserved but realize that this is impossible. What the scholars seek is some assurance that at least one copy of an edition of a book is preserved, somehow, in its original form. This does not mean that libraries are expected to undertake extensive conservation treatment, to make the book usable. Rather, scholars hope that librarians will ensure that at least one copy of an edition be placed in storage, boxed, in its own microenvironment, as an object of our culture and as an item that can be examined physically to tell the researcher in the future something about its text and production. It is now clear that a number of research libraries engaged in large-scale preservation microfilming projects of scholarly texts did not take the responsibility to preserve the original texts. Thus librarians must be careful, when deaccessioning brittle books that have been microfilmed, to be sure that they are not disposing of the last extant physical copy.

As the 1990s begin, the efforts to microfilm the world's documentary heritage continue. With the blessing of Congress and funding from the National Endowment for the Humanities, scholars in a number of academic disciplines are taking a hard look at the problem of preservation and recognizing the impermanence of the tools of their trade. Academics are beginning to work closely with librarians to determine priorities for preservation in surrogate format, and to make it clear that a national reformatting initiative must ensure the preservation of at least one original copy. Librarians have the responsibility to ensure such preservation through cooperative efforts.

Notes

1. New York: Haddon House, 1944.
2. Washington, D.C.: National Academy Press, 1986.
3. Nancy E. Gwinn, *Preservation Microfilming* (Chicago: American Library Association, 1987), 114.
4. Letter from Peter Z. Adelstein, *Journal of Micrographics,* 9 (March 1976), 193–194.
5. Gwinn 119.

Selected Reading

Association for Library Collections and Technical Services. *Preservation Microfilming: Planning and Production.* Chicago: American Library Association, 1989. Papers from the RTSD Preservation Microfilming Institute, New Haven, CT, April 21–23, 1988.

Calmes, Alan. "Microfilm as a Preservation Medium." *Journal of Imaging Technology* 10 (August 1984): 140–142.

Child, Margaret. "The Future of Cooperative Preservation Microfilming." *Library Resources and Technical Services* 29:1 (January–March 1985): 94–101.

Dodson, Suzanne Cates. "Microfilm Types: There Really is a Choice." *Library Resources and Technical Services* 30:1 (January–March 1986): 84–90.

Elkington, Nancy E., ed. *RLG Preservation Microfilming Handbook.* Mountain View, CA: Research Libraries Group, Inc., 1992.

Frieder, Richard. "The Microfiche Revolution in Libraries." *Microform Review* 16:3 (Summer 1987): 214–216.

Gwinn, Nancy E., ed. *Preservation Microfilming: A Guide for Librarians and Archivists.* Chicago: American Library Association, 1987.

Stewart, Robert W. "Does This Project Deserve the Erasmus Prize?" *Conservation Administration News* No. 54 (July 1993): 4–5, 33–37.

XIII. THE PRESERVATION OF OUR CULTURAL HERITAGE: The 1990s and Beyond

THERE IS MUCH THAT LIBRARIANS CAN DO TO PRESERVE THE MATERIALS for which they hold responsibility and to make them accessible to the public. The enormity of the problem of preserving most of the materials that are decaying in our collections is staggering and beyond the scope of any one library in the country today. The research of William Barrow has demonstrated that many of the books that have been written in the past one hundred years will not survive another hundred years unless drastic action is taken. Much of the material in our libraries need not survive en masse, for, like the paperback thriller that is read for pleasure and then discarded, only a few copies need to survive to document the literary taste of the period. A Hemingway first edition—of which there are many—needs to be preserved by some libraries to document in its original state the work of this influential twentieth century author. But the average reader can and ought to read Hemingway in a handy and disposable paperback edition. A delight and appreciation of Hemingway does not require that one hold a copy of the first edition, first printing, in hand.

The library has the responsibility to provide a healthy climate for its materials so that they can be used for as long as possible before they disintegrate. Readers may well wear out a copy by repeated use long before the physical decay inherent in the book occurs. Only a small part of the library collection is "permanent." These are the documents that in themselves are our cultural property and require special care.

Northeast Document Conservation Center
Credit: Northeast Document Conservation Center

Even the larger museums and libraries in the United States cannot provide the special treatment necessary to preserve many of their objects indefinitely. The National Conservation Advisory Council (now the National Institute for Conservation) issued a preliminary report, *Conservation of Cultural Property in the United States,* in 1976. Several sections dealt directly with the problems that libraries face in preserving the documentary heritage. The report recommended that a national program to preserve the national heritage be undertaken. It was somewhat tempered by the fact that there was, and is, a shortage of trained conservators in the United States. Nonetheless, the government has recognized the problem and has been generous in its support of preservation and conservation during the past decade. Examples of governmental support to libraries and archives for preservation and access are the U.S. Newspaper Program and the brittle books microfilming initiatives.

Librarians are familiar with the concept of cooperation—interlibrary loans have been a standard part of library service for decades. Resource sharing has become a catchword of the 1990s. In principle, the Library of Congress serves as the national locus for preservation activities in the nation. To that end, the National Preservation Program Office (NPPO), a program in the Preservation Department, expanded its services in 1984, under the joint direction of Merrily Smith and Carolyn Clark Morrow, to provide "information, educational support, and coordination among cooperating institutions engaged in preservation activities around the country."(1) Prior to that time, the Library's Preservation Office staff, under the leadership of Frazer G. Poole, willingly made themselves available to all who sought their assistance. While the Library of Congress will continue to serve as a focal point in the national effort to preserve the documentary heritage, it is clear that infrastructures among libraries and other cultural institutions on a regional and state level need to be developed during the 1990s and beyond.

During the 1970s, librarians who were facing preservation problems at their institutions and developing programs to address them began to coordinate their efforts with members of other professional groups, such as the Society of American Archivists (SAA) and the American Institute for Conservation of Historic and Artistic Works (AIC). A planning conference for a National Preservation Program was held at the Library of Congress in 1976. Participants included conservators, archivists, and representatives from academic institutions, the publishing industry, and major foundations, as well as librarians. The preservation problems faced by libraries were thoroughly discussed. It became clear that cooperative approaches to preservation activities were necessary. The proceedings of the conference were published in 1980.

An important cooperative solution to meet the preservation needs of the country rests in the establishment of regional centers for conservation treatments and for preservation services. The New England State Librarians, the "advance guard," cooperatively established the New England (now Northeast) Document Conservation Center (NEDCC) in 1973, governed by the New England Library Board (NELB)—including the State Librarians from Maine, New Hampshire, Vermont, Massachusetts, Connecticut, and Rhode Island. The center became known as "Northeast" rather than "New England" when the New York and New Jersey State Libraries became associate members several years later, although NEDCC serves states and institutions throughout the country. The NELB Interstate Library Compact, Article 1, stated:

> Because the desire for the services provided by libraries transcends governmental boundaries and can most effectively be satisfied by giving such services to communities and people regardless of jurisdictional lines, it is the policy of the states party to this compact to cooperate and share their responsibilities: to authorize cooperation and sharing with respect to those types of library facilities and services which can be more economically or efficiently developed and maintained on a cooperative basis, and to authorize cooperation and sharing among localities, states, and others in providing joint or cooperative library services in areas where

the distribution of population or of existing and potential library resources make the provision of library service on an interstate basis the most effective way of providing adequate and efficient service.

The purpose of NEDCC is to administer and supervise a conservation laboratory with the necessary facilities and staff to conserve, preserve, and maintain at a reasonable cost the physical condition of books, prints, maps, broadsides, manuscripts, photographs, and similar documentary materials of historic, archival, or cultural interest.

NEDCC includes a facility that provides archival quality preservation microfilming service for libraries, archives, records repositories, and other institutions. The need for such a service became obvious once the center was functioning and could concern itself directly with the needs of its area and strive to meet them. Today its preservation microfilming service is an important part of the national effort to preserve deteriorating collections. The expertise and the involvement of the center's staff have done much to develop the standards and guidelines for preservation microfilming that exist today. *Preservation Microfilming: A Guide for Librarians and Archivists,* edited by Nancy E. Gwinn, (American Library Association, 1987) was produced with the cooperation and participation of the center.

One of the most important components of NEDCC is its field services, yet these services are not self-supporting. They are funded through grants. The founding director of the center, George Cunha, was committed to the need for collections surveys, and trained a number of today's leading preservation specialists and consultants. As discussed in the first chapter, the National Endowment for the Humanities (NEH) and the Andrew W. Mellon Foundation recognized Cunha's efforts at outreach in the late 1970s. They provided funding to hire a field services officer, Mildred O'Connell, who conducted preservation surveys of institutions in the member states at a nominal cost. These surveys, and the methodology for them, which evolved from Cunha's concept and training, are now the cornerstone of preservation planning and programs. They are an integral part of the field services offered by every regional center and program today. The preservation survey is a requirement for most preservation and conservation grants. The federal government, through NEH, and private foundations have been generous in their support of field services. Public money has been spent wisely and well. In the long run, however, field services at the regional centers require endowed funds to insure their continuation and expansion. The challenge for the 1990s is to let the public know about the accomplishments of the regional centers to preserve the nation's cultural heritage and to build the endowed funds that will enable these services to continue and grow.

The Northeast Document Conservation Center has served as the prototype of the regional center designed to serve library and archival needs. The challenges of establishing its services and the lessons learned as the center grew were to be shared with other cooperative agencies. Ann Russell, director of NEDCC, received funding to bring the directors of fledgling state and regional services together in Andover, MA, in 1986 to discuss and share mutual concerns. These directors continue to meet annually to discuss concerns and problems and to establish goals and objectives for the future. They have initiated a program to identify, reprint, and distribute through their programs important publications that are among the "gray literature" of preservation.

The educational role that regional centers have played and will continue to play is of major significance. Their programs have reached a large number of librarians, archivists, and other people who are eager to learn how they can preserve documentary collections. The staff of the regional centers participate in national, regional, and state workshops and programs. They teach in library schools and in continuing education programs sponsored by library schools. There is an ongoing need to educate librarians and the public at large about the services and programs provided by the regional centers, including their costs and their benefits. The role that the regional center staff plays in education and training will increase as the decade progresses, but this will require increased staff and funding. Education does not pay for itself. Funding and marketing are important elements of a state or regional center's operations.

The education of librarians and archivists in preservation theory and practice is of critical importance. Most North American library schools now include courses on the preservation of library and archival materials in their curriculum. Several library schools are developing innovative continuing education programs for librarians, archivists, and other specialists in the field. Library educators now recognize that information management means making information in all format available *in good condition* to users and that any medium containing information is also an object subject to deterioration. As collection management and preservation become an integral part of library education, faculty members are needed to teach the courses. Few of the graduates of doctoral programs in librarianship have a background in preservation. During the 1990s, institutes will be held to teach the teachers, for the Commission on Preservation and Access has recognized the problem. The preservation specialists in the field, who until now have been the faculty for courses in library schools, and the staff of the regional centers will play an important role in the training of library educators in preservation.

The preservation specialists in the field as well as the staff from the regional centers are playing an increasingly important role as instructors in the continuing education programs in library schools. The need today is to teach practicing librarians, archivists, and their staffs specific skills to address specific preservation problems in their institutions. One- to three-day courses, addressing specific topics such as preservation survey methodology, commercial library binding, preservation microfilming, and environmental management, can be taught effectively within the context of a continuing education program at a library school, using experts in the field as faculty. The School of Communication, Information and Library Studies (SCILS) at Rutgers University was the first library school to offer a certificate program in preservation through its Professional Development Program. Participants earn the certificate after taking a requisite number of short courses including the three-day Preservation Management Institute, offered each year, or the three-credit preservation course in the M.L.S. curriculum. This program can serve as a model for other library schools. The advantage of such programs, within the context of the university, is the stringent control of content and quality. Credits are offered for continuing education courses, leading to an advanced certificate, ensuring quality. Another advantage is the continuing role of these programs. The expert does not fly in, talk, then depart, never to be seen again. The faculty for continuing education programs at most library schools are experts who live and work in the region and offer their courses on a regular basis. These continuing education programs will enable libraries and archive repositories to have staff trained in preservation at reasonable cost to meet the specific needs of the institution over a period of time. New staff can be trained as necessary. These short courses will reach beyond the general collection management and preservation courses that are offered within the M.L.S. curriculum.

There is a continuing demand for more professional conservators and conservation technicians. The Conservation Program at Columbia University successfully trained a group of book conservators who are assuming a leading role in the field of book and paper conservation. The Conservation Program is now located at the University of Texas, Austin. The North Bennet Street School, located in Boston, MA, was established by representatives from the library binding industry to train conservators and technicians for the industry. A number of the graduates of this program, superbly trained by Mark Esser, have become collections conservators in libraries. Too few of them have gone to work for the commercial library binders at this point. However, as the need for quality treatment of library materials continues to grow, more commercial library binders will establish conservation laboratories to undertake specialized treatments for their customers. Contracting for such service through the library binder is, in reality, the most cost-effective approach to conservation for most libraries.

Funding for research in preservation and conservation to ensure the preservation of the world's documentary heritage is another area of critical importance in the 1990s; it is a need that reaches across national boundaries. The funding from the Council on Library Resources for the ground-breaking research by William Barrow was the beginning of an effort to apply scientific investigation to the problems of preserving library materials. Thanks to Barrow and successive researchers, librarians now know a great deal about the problem of acidic paper and the causes of deterioration of books in the library and papers in the archive. Technologies for the mass treatment of deteriorated and deteriorating books and documents are evolving as this book goes to press. Still, there is much to be done. Researchers such as Henry Wilhelm, in Grinnell, IA; James Reilly at the Image Permanence Institute, Rochester Institute of Technology, Rochester, NY; the staff of the Getty Conservation Institute and Preservation Resources; and other photographic conservators and materials scientists are engaged in research and development to improve the quality of film and to ensure image stability. Research is under way in North America and in Europe determine how to preserve and when to reformat magnetic and electronic media.

Materials scientists who can analyze the physical nature of the variety of media to be found in library and archival collections and develop techniques for their preservation are still too few and far between. The Smithsonian Institution offers an innovative program in conservation science through Johns Hopkins University. Universities throughout the country, and the world, need to be encouraged, and funded, to develop conservation science programs and to undertake the research necessary to identify the causes of deterioration and to develop cures. The National Endowment for the Humanities, recognizing this need, is developing a program to support further training for materials scientists and their research. The support of research and development in conservation and preservation should, however, be a shared responsibility of government and industry. Innovative approaches to education and training, research and development are an important component in an agenda for preservation in the 1990s.

Another area of concern for librarians and archivists is the need for standards for the production and the preservation of the documentary heritage. The United States, through the National Information Standards Organization, committee Z39 (NISO-Z39), is developing standards for book production, paper, and for the wide variety of information media available today. NISO-Z39 works with the American National Standards Institute (ANSI) to create standards for the United States and cooperates internationally through the International Standards Organization (ISO) to develop and promulgate standards for information media on a worldwide basis. It is important that librarians and archivists become more involved in the process of the creation of standards, for they profoundly affect our daily work. Standards, especially those for electronic media, will have a strong bearing on issues of preservation and access in the future. If librarians, the professionals responsible for organization, preservation, and access to information, do not play a leadership role in the development, use, and preservation of electronic data, it will not survive.

American librarians now understand the need for cooperation in the effort to preserve the nation's documentary heritage, but the need extends beyond the nation. The establishment of the European Community should lessen communications barriers between its member nations. The Eastern European countries, long isolated from the technological mainstream, will become a part of that community. The world truly is becoming a global village. Communications technology in all of our libraries will allow librarians to share information on the broadest scale. Bibliographic data bases and networks will reach across borders.

Librarians in the United States have been innovators, establishing models for cooperative programs in collection development, information management, and in preservation. The Conspectus approach to cooperative collection development, management, and preservation initiatives is a tool used by librarians in the Research Libraries Group. It was "developed as a simple system to describe library resources and policies in terms of a hierarchical subject classification,"(3) and it provides a methodology for collection evaluation that can be used anywhere in the world. Information technology enables a librarian in California to find out if a title is in the British Library, the condition of the book, and whether that library has reformatted or physically treated it. While each nation holds the primary responsibility for preserving its documentary heritage, all nations share in the responsibility to ensure that the task is done.

The Eighteenth Century Short Title Catalogue (ESTC), now on-line, demonstrates how widely eighteenth century books and pamphlets, printed in English, have spread around the globe. Newspaper librarians in the United States, an immigrant nation, have discovered how many newspapers from other nations around the world have found their way into America's repositories and realized that these copies may not have survived in their native lands. Cooperation is necessary and possible as we approach the millennium. On a grand scale, the United Nations provides a framework for cooperation, but within librarianship the goals and objectives of cooperative international efforts to preserve the documentary heritage need to be defined and articulated.

The International Federation of Library Associations and Institutions (IFLA) is the organization that provides the means for cooperation among librarians from around the world. Like any organization with a diverse membership and the requisite bureaucracy, IFLA programs move ahead slowly. Yet, IFLA provides the forum where concerned librarians from many countries can come together and talk about issues. Friendships are forged across boundaries and modern technology facilitates communication. Friendship, communication, and innovation lead to cooperative action that will result in significant preservation initiatives in the 1990s and beyond.

International cooperative activities are already under way. The IFLA Working Group on Newspapers meets annually to develop an international approach to preservation and access using a variety of technologies. The Conservation Section developed and promulgates its *Principles of Conservation and Restoration in Libraries* (1979 and 1987), a working document for every library, in every country. The Preservation and Conservation (PAC) Core Programme was established in 1986; its focal point is at the Bibliothèque Nationale in Paris, with regional centers in Sablé, France; Leipzig, Germany; Caracas, Venezuela; Canberra, Australia; and Tokyo, Japan. The PAC Core Programme encourages the development of print and nonprint resource materials on the preservation of library and archival materials in all formats and is developing a model core curriculum for preservation and conservation education.

When this book was first written, well over a decade ago, I hoped that it would foster regional and national cooperation to preserve the nation's documentary heritage. The programs and projects that have evolved in the 1980s are astonishing in their scope and in their accomplishment. They demonstrate that diverse people in diverse places can get together and work together to address problems and effect solutions. Developments in information and communications technology make cooperation a necessity today, not a possibility. Cooperation on a global scale can be accomplished in the 1990s. Education and training, research and development, standards, and priorities for preservation and conservation, bibliographic control, and access to information are issues of international concern and shall be addressed. Every library will participate in the effort to preserve the documentary heritage and to make it available to present and future generations.

Notes

1. U.S. Library of Congress, Preservation Office, *A National Preservation Program* (Washington, DC), 1980.
2. "National Preservation Program Office Expands," *LC Information Bulletin*, 43:45 (November 5, 1984): 365.
3. Crispin Jewitt. "Conspectus: A Means to Library Cooperation," *Library Conservation News*, No. 22 (January 1992): 4.

Suggested Reading

Hazen, Dan C. "Preservation in Poverty and Plenty: Policy Issues for the 1990s." *Journal of Academic Librarianship* 15:6 (January 1990): 344–351.

Schmude, Karl G. "The Politics and Management of Preservation Planning." *IFLA Journal* 16:3 (1990): 332–335.

Swartzburg, Susan Garretson. "Preservation of the Cultural Patrimony." *Art Libraries Journal* 15:1 (1990): 18–21.

Vaisey, David. "Archivists, Conservators, and Scientists: the Preservation of the Nation's Heritage." *Archives* 18:79 (April 1988): 131–143.

Vitiello, Giuseppi. "European Register of Microform Film Masters (Eromm)." *International Preservation News* No. 4 (August 1990): 3–4.

Walch, Victoria Irons. "Checklist of Standards Applicable to the Preservation of Archives and Manuscripts." *American Archivist* 53:2 (Spring 1990): 324–337.

Welsh, William J. "International Cooperation in Preservation of Library Materials." *Collection Management* 9:2–3 (Spring–Summer 1987): 119–131.

Glossary

This is a glossary of terms from a variety of specialties that can be used in the context of preservation and conservation of library and archival materials. The definitions have been compiled over the past two decades from a wide range of sources. The glossary has been edited, with the assistance of experts in several fields, for the use of librarians involved in preservation, not for specialists in the respective fields that are covered. The language of preservation is broadly encompassing and evolving even as this edition of the glossary is prepared. It is hoped that this glossary will not only be helpful to people in the field, but will also lead to reflection, discussion, and some debate about how preservation specialists, librarians, archivists, conservators, and those in related fields use language to communicate.

ABRASION: A rubbed or scuffed area on paper or bindings.

ABSOLUTE HUMIDITY: The amount of water vapor in any unit volume of air.

ABSORBENCY: The property in paper that permits a sheet to take in the liquids it contacts.

ACCELERATED AGING: A test that subjects material in a laboratory setting to extreme conditions for short periods of time to simulate the effects of natural aging over longer periods.

ACETATE FILM (Acetate Base Film, Safety Film): Film that has a base of cellulose acetate, diacetate, or triacetate rather than the highly flammable and unstable cellulose nitrate or the highly stable polyester. It tends to be a brittle format.

ACID: Noun: A chemical substance that has a pH below 7. A pH below 5.5 is considered significantly acidic in paper because it hastens its deterioration. Adjective: Having a pH below 7.

ACID-FREE: See ALKALINE PAPER.

ACID MIGRATION (Acid Transfer): The transfer of acid, usually in gaseous form, from acidic material, such as groundwood paper, to a less acidic material when the two are stored adjacent to one another. Acid transfer will usually cause paper to become stained and weakened.

ACID-NEUTRALIZING PAPER: See BUFFERED PAPER.

ADAPTATION: Adjustment to environmental conditions, i.e., the principle by which the retina becomes accustomed to more or less light than it was exposed to during an immediately preceding period.

ADHESIVE: A substance capable of holding materials together by a surface attachment. It includes such materials as glue, mucilage, and paste.

ADHESIVE BINDING: A binding technique in which single leaves are held together using an adhesive, usually polyvinyl acetate (PVA), rather than a sewn attachment.

AGING: Changes in the characteristics of materials over time.

AIR-CONDITIONING: The process by which the temperature, humidity, movement, and quality of air in buildings are mechanically controlled and maintained to secure health and comfort, and to provide the proper environment for the materials housed within. See also HVAC.

AIR FILTER: An assembly of dust-, gas-, or air-absorbing materials fitted into a ducted system to clean the air passing through it. This can be part of an air-conditioning system.

ALKALI (Base): A substance having a pH above 7. It has the quality of neutralizing acid.

ALKALINE: Having a pH above 7, which is neutral.

ALKALINE PAPER (Permanent/Durable Paper): Paper having a buffer or reserve of alkaline substance, usually of from 10 to 20 percent precipitated calcium or magnesium carbonate. These papers may also be referred to as acid-free papers, although this literally may not be so. See also BUFFERED PAPER.

ALKALIZATION: The process to add a buffer to paper after it has been washed to remove accumulated acids; the second step in the DEACIDIFICATION process.

ALL-RAG PAPER: Paper made of 100 percent rag or cotton material. "Rag Content" paper is made with a smaller percentage of rag or cotton fiber.

ALUM: Aluminum sulfate, an acid salt often used with rosin to size paper, giving it water-resistant properties.

ALUM-TAWED SKIN: Skin (usually pigskin) treated with alum and salt instead of tanning agents. These skins are usually found on volumes bound from the twelfth century to the Renaissance and have demonstrated considerable durability and permanence.

AMBIENT LIGHT: The surrounding light; general room illumination or light level. See also VISIBLE LIGHT.

AMINES: Alkaline compounds, derivatives of ammonia, in which one or more of the hydrogen H+ atoms have been replaced by hydrocarbon radicals.

AMPLIFIER: A device used to increase or reinforce the strength of an electronic signal.

ANTIQUE FINISH: On paper, a natural rough finish similar to early handmade paper.

APERTURE CARD: A card with a rectangular hole or holes specifically designed for the insertion of a frame of microfilm.

ARCHIVABILITY: The length of time that data stored on a medium, such as magnetic tape, will remain stable without deterioration.

ARCHIVAL QUALITY: (1) The ability of a material to resist

deterioration. (2) Of microfilm, the degree to which a processed print or film will retain its characteristics during a specified period of use and storage.

ARCHIVES: (1) An organized body of noncurrent records made or received in connection with the activities of its affairs by a government agency, an institution, organization, or other corporate body; or the personal papers of a family or individual, which are preserved because of their continuing value. (2) The agency or department responsible for selecting, organizing, preserving, and making available such materials. (3) Noun: The repository itself.

ART PAPER: A high-gloss coated paper.

ARTIFICIAL PAPER: Chemically coated material made to resemble leather and used for the binding of books.

AUDIORECORDING: The generic term for the recording of sound in disk, cylinder, roll, wire, magnetic tape, or digital format.

AUTOGRAPH: A person's handwriting, usually including a signature, but not to be used as a synonym for signature.

BACKBONE: See SPINE.

BACKGROUND: The area of a drawing, print, photograph, or microform frame other than the principal subject or text, including blank areas.

BACKING: (1) The process of sewing and shaping the spine of a sewn text block, resulting in the formation of shoulders. Backing follows the rounding operation and precedes CASING-IN. (2) A method of reinforcing a work on paper by applying a sheet of paper to the reverse side with an adhesive.

BANDS: (1) The cords or tapes onto which the sections of a book are sewn. (2) The ridges found horizontally across the spine of some leather-bound books.

BARRIER SHEETS: Pieces of well-sized alkaline paper used as

barriers to prevent the migration of acid or oil from one material to another.

BARROW LAMINATION: A process of document repair and restoration named after William J. Barrow (1904–1967) that involves deacidification, the use of tissue to increase the strength of the original document, and thermoplastic lamination.

BASE (Carrier): (1) The material, such as cellulose triacetate, polyester, paper, glass, or metal, upon which a light-sensitive emulsion or other material may be coated. (2) See ALKALI.

BASE EXPOSURE: In microfilming, the exposure required to record a typical black-and-white document of average quality. Variations in exposure for atypical documents are expressed in percentage or time intervals greater or less than the base exposure.

BASE PLUS FOG: See DMIN.

BEATER: In papermaking, a large mixing tub in which paper pulp is prepared. The fibers of the pulp are mechanically processed while additional ingredients, fillers, dyes, and resins are mixed in.

BIBLE PAPER: See INDIA PAPER.

BIBLIOCLAST: A destroyer of books.

BIBLIOGRAPHIC TARGET: See TARGET.

"BIND AS IS": An instruction to the binder to bind material in the order or in the condition in which it is submitted, regardless of any apparent imperfections.

BIND IN: To fasten securely into the binding; usually referring to supplementary material.

BINDER: A substance to help the basic materials of a recording compound, disk or tape, to adhere together. In magnetic tape, it is also used to keep the magnetic particles on the coating separate from one another.

BINDER'S BOARD: A heavy-grade, usually of single-ply solid paper, board used for book covers. It is usually made from mixed paper stock and low-grade rags.

BINDING: (1) In book manufacturing, the process of assembling the finished book; the concept of securing the leaves of sections of a text so as to keep them in proper order and protect them. (2) The structural materials, such as thread and glue, that hold a book together, and the attachment of a cover that may be made of any number of materials. See also ADHESIVE BINDING, CASE BINDING, CONSERVATION BINDING, PAMPHLET BINDING, PERFECT BINDING, POST BINDING, SPIRAL BINDING. (3) The style in which a book is bound and decorated.

BINDING SLIP: The sheet of instructions sent to the bindery with each volume specifying the binding requirements for that particular volume. Today binding instructions are often in a computerized data base for ease and accuracy.

BIT: The smallest division of memory. A bit is an electrical charge that is either On (represented by 1) or Off (represented by 0).

BLANKET ROLLER: In offset printing, a roller covered with a sheet of rubber that receives an ink image from a master copy and transmits it to the paper.

BLEACHING: (1) Chlorine or similar chemical solutions used to whiten paper fibers in the manufacturing process. (2) A cosmetic process, using chlorine or similar solutions, or the radiant energy of sunlight, to lighten paper and reduce discoloration. This process will weaken cellulose fibers.

BLEED: In binding, when the volume is trimmed so that the text or illustrations are cut into.

BLEEDING: (1) The seepage of ink; it can be caused by too much oil in the ink, too much pressure when printing, or both. (2) The loss of color from paper as a result of contact with oil or water.

BLEED-THROUGH: A defect in photomechanical reproduction in which an image printed on one side of a paper, or other material, can be detected on the opposite side. See also PRINT-THROUGH.

BLEMISH (Oxidation-Reduction, Redox Blemish): In film, a defect caused by the oxidation of silver grains and/or other factors. Often called "measles," they are microscopic red, orange, or yellow spots no smaller than a single grain of silver. In microfilm, it may be caused by peroxide contamination from cardboard boxes or other environmentally transmitted oxidants.

BOARDS: (1) The wood, paperboard, or other base used to protect the sides of a bound book. (2) Original boards, backed with paper, in which many books were temporarily encased for distribution prior to the 1830s, when EDITION BINDING came into use.

BOLT: An uncut fold of paper at the head, fore-edge, and/or tail of a signature in a book. It must be cut before a page can be read; see UNOPENED.

BOND PAPER: A strong and durable paper with good absorbing and erasing qualities. It originally referred to paper used for legal documents, stock certificates, and government bonds.

BOOK BLOCK: See TEXT BLOCK.

BOOK BOX: A box that provides a protective microenvironment for a volume and substantially reduces physical damage.

BOOK JACKET (Book Wrapper, Dust Cover, Dust Jacket, Dust Wrapper): A detachable protective paper cover for a book that folds around the binding with the ends tucked in between the cover boards and the free endpaper.

BOOK PAPER: A term used to indicate a class of papers used for the printing of books.

BOOKPLATE (Ex Libris): A book owner's identification label that usually is printed, has a distinctive design, and is usually pasted to the inside front cover of a book.

BOOKWORM: A term used to refer to insects, moths, or beetles whose larvae destroy books by feeding on their bindings and pages.

BOSSES: Brass or other metal knobs fastened upon the covers of books for ornament or for the protection of the covering material.

BREAK: A parting of adjacent sections of a book due to the loosening of the sewing.

BREAKING COPY: A book, especially a color plate book, that is so imperfect that it seems fit only for breaking up so that plates and pages of typographical or artistic interest can be sold separately.

BRIGHTNESS: In paper, the property that is measured by the amount of light reflected from a sheet.

BRISTOL: A paperboard that is hard, strong, and rugged and has a smooth surface suitable for writing. Index cards are an example.

BRITTLE: Fragile, easily broken. Paper and film become brittle as a result of deterioration, which is accelerated by exposure to heat, moisture, and light.

BUBBLE: Commonly used defect term for disk recordings, most often caused by faulty pressing.

BUCKLING: A warping and twisting in several directions. (1) In books, it occurs when books are improperly shelved. (2) In recording, deformation of the circular form of a roll of magnetic tape, caused, generally, by a combination of adverse storage conditions or improper winding tension. Such deformation has a seriously detrimental effect on the quality of sound during playback.

BUCKRAM: A filled binding cloth with a heavy weave cotton base. In the United States, it is made to the specifications of the National Information Standards Organization (NISO). It is especially sturdy.

BUFFER: A material that resists changes in pH; commonly

refers to an alkaline substance, usually calcium carbonate or magnesium carbonate, incorporated into paper to act as a buffer against atmospheric pollution. See ALKALINE PAPER.

BUFFERED PAPER: A type of paper that contains an alkaline buffer/neutralizer intended to absorb any acidity that may appear in the environment of a book, document, print, or drawing.

BULK: (1) The degree of a paper's thickness relative to its weight. A sheet with high bulk lacks compactness. (2) The thickness of a book between its covers.

BUMP: In disk recording, a defect caused by a raised surface on a portion of the playing surface of a disk, causing sonic distortion or groove jumping by the stylus.

BYTE: The amount of memory required to store a single character, such as a letter. One byte is made up of 8 BITs.

CALCIUM CARBONATE ($CaCO_3$): One of the most stable, common, and widely used deacidifying materials.

CALIBRATE: To determine, check, or correct the gradation of an instrument scale.

CALL NUMBER (Class Mark): A combination of numbers assigned to a library book to indicate its place on the shelf relative to other books.

CALLIGRAPHY: From the Greek, meaning beautiful writing; penmanship. A calligrapher is a trained scribe. Calligraphic types are designed in close sympathy with the spirit of good handwriting.

CANCELS: Any part of the book substituted for what was originally printed. It may be of any size, from a tiny scrap of paper bearing one or two letters pasted over the original sheet, to several sheets replacing the original ones. The most common cancel is the single leaf inserted in place of the original leaf. For a full discussion of cancels and their significance, see John Carter, *The ABC for Book Collectors,* 6th edition. (New Castle, DE: Oak Knoll Books, 1992).

CANTON FLANNEL: A soft cotton fabric with a nap on one side used as a spine lining material in library bindings.

CAPSTAN: A motor-driven rod that moves magnetic tape at a constant speed past the recording and playback heads.

CARBON BLACK: An inert filler used to protect the basic resin in a record compound from the action of light by absorbing radiant energy; an antistatic element in magnetic tape.

CARBON DIOXIDE (CO_2): A colorless, odorless, electrically nonconductive inert gas that is a suitable medium for extinguishing fires. Related to combustion of fuel, the predominant product of the combustion process.

CARRIER BASE: See BASE.

CARTRIDGE: (1) A plastic enclosure around a roll of microfilm that provides protection and ease in handling. (2) An enclosed container for magnetic film, similar to a cassette.

CASE: The cover of a book, printed, stamped, and made the proper size to be attached to a book.

CASE BINDING: The process of preparing the cover separately from the text, then attaching it to the text. See CASING-IN.

CASING-IN: Attaching the book to its cover.

CASSETTE: (1) In tape recording, a standard container with two spools that hold magnetic recording tape. (2) In microfilm, a double-core container enclosing processed roll microfilm designed to be inserted into readers, reader-printers, or other retrieval devices, usually for automatic threading. (3) In phototypesetting, a portable container for light-sensitive materials. The cassette usually attaches directly to the typesetting machine either to feed or receive material.

CATALYST: Substance that increases the rate of chemical reaction without being materially altered in the process.

CATCHWORD: A word printed on the foot of one page indicating the first word of the page following. It was used as a guide to collating, but its practice has become archaic in modern printing.

CELLULOSE ACETATE: A synthetic polymer compound used as a base in the manufacturing of coatings and films. It is an unstable material.

CELLULOSE FIBER: The primary component of paper. It is obtained by separating the non-fibrous elements from wood, woody plants, cotton, and other sources.

CELLULOSE NITRATE: A transparent plastic that was once used almost universally as a film base. Because of its flammability, it has been replaced by other plastic film bases, e.g., polyester.

CELLULOSE TRIACETATE (Safety Film): A film base for photographic materials; often referred to as "safety film" and so marked. It is also used as an enclosure for photographic materials but it is not stable. See also CELLULOSE ACETATE.

CHAIN LINES: The widely spaced lines, about one inch apart, that run parallel to the GRAIN on LAID PAPER. They result from the chain wires that hold the laid wires together on the papermaking frame.

CHANNEL: A single path for recording or reproducing sound.

CHEMICAL PULP: Paper pulp made by cooking wood with strong acids or alkalis. Most pulp today is made by the kraft (sulfate) process.

CHEMILUMINESCENCE: Luminescence due to a chemical reaction usually at low temperature, often too faint to see with the naked eye.

CHIPBOARD: A paperboard manufactured to a low density from mixed wastepapers or low-grade pulp; it is neither permanent nor durable.

CLASP: A catch for holding together the two covers of a book.

CLEANING: The removal of non-original materials from an object that were either accidentally deposited, such as dirt, or applied purposely.

CLIMATIZATION: See AIR-CONDITIONING.

CLOTH: The most common material used for the binding of books published in the English-speaking countries since the second quarter of the nineteenth century.

COATED PAPER: Paper with the surface coated with adhesive and mineral pigments.

COATING: (1) The outer layer of a laminated disk or cylinder in which the grooves are cut. (2) The layer of finely divided magnetic material, bonded in plastic and polished to allow smooth flow over tape heads, that carries the magnetically recorded signal in tape.

COCKLING: A pucker, bulge, or ripple in paper caused by uneven tension or distribution of moisture during its manufacture or by atmospheric changes during its use.

COLLATION: The bibliographical description of the physical composition of a book. Verb: to collate; to examine a book or periodical volume leaf by leaf, and by signature, or section, to verify its full content and arrangement.

COLLECTED EDITION: The reissue of the works of an author in a uniform style and edition.

COLLOTYPE: A photomechanical method for reproducing photographic images.

COLOPHON: (1) An emblematic design; a trade emblem or device of a printer or publisher. (2) Historically, it is the final page of a book or manuscript, giving the facts about its production.

COLOR-PLATE BOOKS: Books with plates in color, whether printed or hand colored on an engraved or lithographed base.

COM: (1) *C*omputer *O*utput *M*icrofilm: microfilm containing data processed by a recorder from computer-generated electrical signals. (2) *C*omputer *O*utput *M*icrofilmer: a recorder that converts data from a computer into human language and records it on microfilm. (3) Computer Output Microfilming: a method of converting data from a computer into human language contained on microfilm.

COMBUSTION: A chemical reaction that releases heat and light.

COMFORT ZONE: That range of temperature, or other environmental condition, in which people are comfortable.

COMPACT DISK (CD): A fast rotating, variable speed aluminized disk with a very fine spiral pattern of extremely small "pits" in its surface that are detected by a laser beam to reproduce sound.

COMPATIBILITY: The ability to transport physically one form of media to another and read or otherwise use the information directly.

CONDENSATION: A condition that causes moisture to appear on a surface when its temperature falls below the dew point of the ambient air.

CONJUGATE LEAVES: The leaves in a section, formed from a single sheet, that belong to one another.

CONSERVATION: Physical and chemical treatment of materials to retard their further deterioration, including the RESTORATION of rare and valuable objects; see also PRESERVATION.

CONSERVATION BINDING: A binding designed and constructed with conservation priorities governing all aspects of the work. The structure is intended to support and protect a text when used. It should not cause any damage to the original leaves and the finished binding should be sympathetic to the original.

CONSERVATION TECHNICIAN: A person trained to execute treatments or to repair library and archival materials under the supervision of a CONSERVATOR.

CONSERVATOR: A specialist who has undertaken advanced

training in the repair and restoration of materials, such as books, documents, and photographs.

CONSPECTUS: A framework to increase options for cooperative collection planning and management based upon a set of standard codes for representing collection intensities, strength of existing collections, and characteristics of materials collected.

CONTACT PAPER: Sensitized paper used for making prints by the contact method.

CONTACT PRINTING (Contact Copying): A method of printing in which the unexposed stock is held in direct contact with the master or intermediate print bearing the image to be copied.

CONTAINER: A generic term for boxes, cans, cartridges, magazines, cassettes, or other structures designed to hold materials such as books, documents, films, or other objects.

CONTAINERIZATION: The placing of an object, or objects, in containers to provide a microenvironment for protection and preservation.

CONTRAST: Differences in the tonal values of a photochemically reproduced image. Where the degree of difference is slight, contrast is said to be low. Where the degree of difference is marked, contrast is said to be high.

COPY NEGATIVE: A negative made by photographing a print or copying a negative for the purpose of reproduction, enlargement, or preservation.

COPY PRINT: A print made from a copy negative.

COPYFLO: The trademark of the Xerox Corporation for a line of Xerographic printing devices and materials designed to print a paper copy from a microfilm copy of a book or collection of documents.

COPYRIGHT: The right guaranteed by a government to the authors of works to control their reproduction so they will be guaranteed a return that will compensate for their effort.

COPYRIGHT PAGE: The back of the title page, on the left-hand side of an open book. It supplies the information on copyright and where to seek permission to reproduce all or part of the work.

CORDS: See BANDS.

CORE: The basic support or central layer of material in a laminated disk or cylinder.

COVER, COVERS: The outer covering of a volume, no matter what material is used. The upper cover is the front and the lower cover is the back of the binding.

COVERS BOUND IN: The original covers included within a later binding. Often the cloth or paper covers of a rare edition are preserved when the volume is rebound.

CRACK: A fissure through a sound recording, visible on both sides; will cause noticeable distortion or faulty tracking on playback.

CRACKLE: The distorted sound created due to a buildup of electrostatic charge on the surface of a sound recording, or detritus permanently embedded in the grooves of a disk or on the surface of a tape.

CRADLE: A structure, often of board, that supports a book on exhibition. In microfilming, a mechanical device for supporting and leveling a book at a precise plane to facilitate image capture.

CRASH: See SUPER.

CROP: To trim to fit into a specified space. The margins of a book or print are cut down by the binder's knife, often resulting in damage; see also BLEED.

CURL: The tendency of paper or film to roll up.

CUT: To trim the edges of a book. To cut is not as serious as to crop a book. The term "uncut" is not to be confused with "unopened."

DAMP STAINED: Paper that has been exposed to dampness and is slightly and uniformly browned.

DARK FADING: A general term to describe the color fading and staining that occurs in photographic images when light is not present. The rates of fading are principally the result of unstable dyes, but are influenced by environmental contaminants, temperature and, to a lesser extent, humidity.

DATA BASE: A collection of digitally stored records. The total data elements, including printed text and pictures, constituting a file, collection, library, etc., or a given segment thereof.

DEACCESSION (Weed): To remove materials lacking continuing or permanent value from library collections; euphemism for "sell" or "discard."

DEACIDIFICATION: A process that neutralizes the acidic components in paper and usually provides an alkaline buffer to counteract acidic buildup in the future.

DECKLE: (1) The frame that forms the border of a hand paper mold. (2) The rubber apron that confines the flowing pulp on the screen of a paper machine.

DECKLE EDGE: The untrimmed feathered edge of a sheet of handmade paper, created by the pulp that flowed over the frame at the time of drying. These edges are often left untrimmed in fine books.

DEFINITION: Overall sharpness of an image produced by lens and film. The impression of clarity of detail perceived when viewing a photographic image.

DEGAUSSER (Bulk Eraser): An instrument used to demagnetize recording heads and other metallic surfaces of magnetic recordings or reproducing equipment. See DEMAGNETIZATION.

DEHUMIDIFICATION: The process of abstracting moisture from air.

DEHUMIDIFIER: An electronic device used to remove excess moisture from the air. See also HUMIDIFIER.

DE-INKED PAPER STOCK: Recycled stock from which previously imprinted ink has been removed through a combination of mechanical and chemical processes. It is possible, although at present not usual, for recycled paper to have an alkaline pH.

DEMAGNETIZATION: (1) The erasure of magnetic tapes by neutralizing the oxide particles in the tape coating, achieved through a high frequency current passing through an erase head over which the tape passes, or through the use of a bulk eraser. (2) The neutralizing of the heads and other parts of a tape recorder that come into contact with the tape to prevent magnetic buildup, which can erase or demagnetize the tape.

DENSE: Relatively opaque; generally applied to film images or areas that are darker than normal.

DENSITOMETER: A device used to measure the optical density of an image or support material by measuring the amount of incident light that is reflected or transmitted.

DENSITY: (1) The light-absorbing quality of a photographic image. In film, the degree of opacity; in paper prints, the degree of blackness. (2) In sound recordings, the number of bits of a single linear track measured per unit of length of the recording medium.

DETERIORATION: The chemical and physical destruction of material in the environment in which it has been placed. The aging process is more rapid in poorly made, chemically unstable material, and is accelerated by high and fluctuating temperature and relative humidity, light, exposure to polluted air, pests, mold, and use.

DEVELOP: To subject to the action of chemical agents for the purpose of bringing to view an invisible or latent image produced by the action of light on a sensitized surface.

DEVELOPER: A chemical substance in dry, liquid, or gaseous form used to make visible a latent image.

DEW POINT: The temperature to which a given parcel of air must be cooled at constant pressure and constant water-vapor content in order for saturation to occur. When this temperature is below zero degrees centigrade, it is sometimes called frost point.

DIAPOSITIVE: See LANTERN SLIDE.

DIAZO (Diazotype, Diazotypy, White Printing): A generic term for films employing light-sensitive diazonium salts for the production of the film image. The image is a dye and thus subject to fading and discoloration, although long-life (100 years) diazo film is now available.

DIGITAL OPTICAL RECORDING (DOR): A recording made through the digital recording process onto a disk that has the digital data stored on its surface as a series of tiny pits that can be detected by a focused laser beam for playback purposes. It is capable of storing both audio and visual materials. See also DIGITAL RECORDING.

DIGITAL RECORDING: A sound recording made by a process whereby the source sound and/or image is transformed into continuously variable voltages. Reproduction involves tracing or "reading" the stored pattern and converting it to a recorded format for playback.

DIRECT IMAGE FILM: A film that will retain the same POLARITY as the previous GENERATION or the original material.

DIRECT POSITIVE PROCESS (DOP): A photographic process that produces a positive image (or a negative image if the material is used to copy a negative) without a reversal step or negative intermediate.

DISASTER: Any event causing loss or suffering on a scale sufficient to warrant an extraordinary response from outside the affected area or community.

DISASTER MANUAL: A written plan prepared by an organization for dealing with emergencies or disaster.

DISASTER PREPAREDNESS: Action designed to minimize loss of life or damage and to organize and facilitate timely and effective rescue, relief, and rehabilitation.

DISASTER PREVENTION: Measures designed to prevent natural phenomena from causing or resulting in disaster or other related emergency situations.

DISBIND: Removing bound material from its covers for rebinding or preservation.

DISK (Diskette): A magnetic-coated storage device that is flat and round and stores information by having its magnetic charges changed.

DISTORTION: In audio and video recording, (1) an undesired change in the wave form; (2) poor quality reproduction caused by change in the wave form of the original signal.

DISTRIBUTION COPY: See SERVICE COPY.

DMAX: Maximum density. In microfilming, background density.

DMIN: Minimum density. In microfilming, this is the density of the clear areas of processed film; also known as Base Plus Fog.

DOCTORED (Sophisticated): An object that has been repaired, restored, or rebuilt; used in the pejorative sense.

DOCUMENT: A written, typed, or printed paper.

DOG-EARED: Books with leaves turned down or broken at the corners, or broken corners on the covers.

DRAWING: An original representation done by pencil, pen, or crayon in which form predominates over considerations of color.

DROPOUT: Partial loss of an audio or video signal, caused by dirt or other foreign material on the tape, faulty head-to-tape alignment, or a lack of magnetic coating on a portion of the tape.

DRY CLEANING: See SURFACE CLEANING.

DRY MOUNTING: A bonding process that uses heat and a fusing tissue to seal or mount materials.

DRY POINT: A method of intaglio printing on metal plates incised with a sharp needle, producing fine lines without acid.

DRY SILVER PROCESS: Thermatically processed silver film; a trade name of the 3M Company for a process in which a latent image is formed on a silver-sensitized material by the action of light and developed by means of heat.

DUPLICATE NEGATIVE: An exact replica of a negative made via an optical system or contact printing using direct duplicating negative film or the interpositive method.

DURABILITY: The degree to which a paper retains its original qualities and strength under continual usage.

EDGE FLAKE: The peeling or flaking of the coating material from the vertical edge of a disk or cylinder. It causes no damage to the aural or visual content, but signals that the coating layer is in danger of deterioration.

EDITION BINDING (Publisher's Binding): The binding of an edition or a number of copies of the same book in identical style, usually mass-produced in relatively large quantities.

EDITION DE LUXE: A sumptuous book; a book produced to be admired for its appearance rather than to be read. Such publications were especially popular in the Victorian period.

ELECTRONIC IMAGING: A representation of a page of a document as an array of dots.

ELECTRONIC PUBLISHING: The use of electronically generated material, usually displayable on a cathode ray tube, in the publication processes; includes creation, editing, layout, printing plate manufacture.

ELECTROPHOTOGRAPHY: An electrostatic copying process. A generic term used to refer to the photographic processes in which electrical energy is used to sensitize certain materials to the action of light or to form a visible image. See also XEROGRAPHY.

ELECTROSTATIC: An electric charge potential on a photoconductive surface used in electrophotographic reproduction, such as XEROGRAPHY.

EMULSION: In photography, one or more coatings of gelatin or other material on a film, paper, or other support base, the layers being sensitive to electromagnetic radiation, usually silver halides, that create a latent image upon exposure. When developed, a visible image appears.

ENCAPSULATION: Enclosure of a document between two sheets of polyester film sealed with pressure-sensitive tape, sewn, or by ultrasonic welding. The two layers support the sheet and allow it to be handled and seen from both sides. Encapsulation is reversible.

ENCLOSURE: Any material not a part of a book that has been inserted into it.

ENDPAPER (End Leaf, End Sheet): The paper placed at the beginning and the end of a book, one half being pasted to the inside of the cover.

END BAND: See HEADBAND.

ENERGY SURVEY: Inspection of an energy-using system with the intent to identify wasteful practices, excessive heat loss, or fluctuations of temperature and relative humidity.

ENLARGEMENT: An enlarged print. The term usually refers to a paper-based print with an image that has been optically magnified from an original, smaller negative.

ENLARGER-PRINTER: A machine that projects an enlarged image, such as microfilm, and develops and prints the image on a suitable material.

ENVIRONMENT: Physical surroundings; the conditions that affect the organisms and materials in a space.

ENVIRONMENT-RESISTANT: A general term indicating the capability of a device or system to operate under extremes of temperature, humidity, vibration, sound, and dust.

EPHEMERA: Transient everyday items that are manufactured specifically for use and disposal.

ESPARTO: A North African grass used as a papermaking fiber

to produce a soft fibered sheet; can be archival.

ESTER: A class of compounds resulting from the combination of an alcohol and an acid.

ETCHING: (1) Print made from a plate into which the design has been etched by acid. (2) The process of producing such a plate.

EVAPORATION: The conversion of liquid into vapor by heating.

EX LIBRIS: See BOOKPLATE.

EXAMINATION: The preliminary procedure taken to determine the original structure and materials comprising an artifact and the extent of its deterioration, alteration, and loss.

EXCERPT: See EXTRACT.

EXPOSURE: (1) The act of exposing a sensitive photographic material to a light source. (2) A section of film containing an individual image. (3) The duration of time that a sensitive surface is exposed to a light source.

EXTENDED: A leaf that has been renewed or remargined and reattached to the inner margin of a book.

EXTRA BINDING (Fine Binding): Traditional term for the binding of books by hand in accordance with the traditional techniques of the craft, using the finest materials and the highest standards of quality and workmanship. See also CONSERVATION BINDING.

EXTRA-ILLUSTRATED (Grangerized): Volumes that have had added to them engraved portraits, prints, autographed letters, documents, etc., usually cut from other sources.

EXTRACT (Offprint, Excerpt): Papers, articles, stories, etc., reprinted separately from periodicals and scholarly journals and listed individually.

FACSIMILE: (1) An exact copy or representation of an original document. See also FAX, TELEFACSIMILE.

FADING: Loss of density in an image.

FAX: A term used in reference to certain types of electronic systems used for transmitting graphic images over long distances and at great speed. The images produced are impermanent. See TELEFACSIMILE.

FEEDBACK: A squeaking sound from a loudspeaker, produced by reentry of the amplified sound into the microphone.

FERROTYPE: Glazing, or the unwanted appearance of shiny patches on the gelatin surface of a photograph. Caused by contact with a smooth surface, particularly plastic enclosures or glass, under conditions of high relative humidity.

FIBER COVER: A stiff but slightly flexible cover board used to bind large pamphlet material.

FIBRILLAE: Threadlike elements that make up cellulose fiber. They are partially separated from the fiber wall by the action of the beater roll in papermaking.

FIDELITY: A subjective term used to describe the degree of faithfulness with which recorded and reproduced sound copies the original.

FILLING: The treatment of paper or fabric with a chemical compound to fill the interstices and/or coat the fibers to give it body, color, or other physical or chemical properties.

FILM: A transparent flexible plastic material, usually of cellulose acetate or polyester, on which a light-sensitive emulsion is coated, or on which an image can be formed by various transfer processes. See also MOTION PICTURE FILM.

FILTER: A layer of more or less transparent material used to modify the quality or quantity of radiation (ULTRAVIOLET rays) emitted from light sources.

FINE BINDING: A unique, one-of-a-kind binding intended to be considered a work of art.

FINE PAPERS: (1) Paper intended to be printed or written upon.

(2) In private press printing, the finest quality of papers, usually handmade.

FINISH: The general appearance and feel of paper, the composite result of its visual and tactile properties, including smoothness, gloss, softness.

FINISHING: A bookbinder's term for the decoration of the binding after a book has been put into its cover. In hand binding, it includes the polishing of the leather and the addition of ornamentation and lettering.

FIRE ALARM SYSTEM: An electrically operated system consisting of manual stations that will activate audible and/or visual alarm signals, or both, throughout a building.

FIRST EDITION: (1) The first appearance of a work, independently, between two covers. (2) The whole number of copies first printed from the same type and issued at the same time.

FIXER: See HYPO.

FLAG: A marker placed to protrude from the leaves of a book to show its shelf position or to indicate that special attention should be given to the book or the page marked.

FLAKING: The loss of bonding or adhesion between the base and coating of laminated disks or magnetic tape, resulting in pieces of the coating breaking loose from the base.

FLAMMABLE: Igniting easily and burning rapidly.

FLATBED CAMERA: See PLANETARY CAMERA.

FLEXIBLE GLUE: An adhesive made of a mixture of glue and some material like glycerin to keep it from becoming dry and brittle.

FLEXIBLE SEWING: A style of sewing on raised supports meant to allow a book to open flat.

FLOPPY DISK: A small, flexible disk carrying a magnetic medium in which digital data is stored for later retrieval and use. See also DISK.

FLUORESCENCE: The emission of visible light from a substance, such as a phosphor, as the result of, and during, the absorption of radiation of shorter wavelengths.

FLYLEAF: (1) A blank leaf at the beginning or end of a book; the leaf of the endpaper that is not pasted down. (2) Bibliographically, a binder's blank, additional to and following the free front paper.

FOCUS: (1) Verb: To adjust the relative positions of the lens and film to obtain the sharpest possible image. (2) Noun: The plane in which rays of light reflected from a subject converge to form an image of the subject after passing through a lens.

FOG: Also called base fog, it occurs in processed film. It may be caused by (1) the action of stray light during exposure (see DMIN); (2) improperly compounded processing solutions; (3) improperly stored or outdated photographic materials.

FOLDED: Usually of leaflets, unsewn, unstitched; by implication, as issued.

FOLIO: (1) A volume made up of sheets of paper folded once; the largest size. (2) A leaf numbered on the recto; the numeral itself in a book or manuscript in which the leaves are numbered.

FOOTCANDLE (Meter-candle): A term for the measurement of light; the illumination produced when the light from a point source of one candle falls on a source one foot, or meter, away from the candle. See also LUX.

FORE-EDGE: The front edge of the leaves of a book; the edge opposite the folds of a SECTION.

FORMAT: (1) The physical makeup of a book including size, pagination, binding, margins, typography. (2) In bibliographical context, it is used to indicate the size of a volume in terms of the number of times that the original printed sheet has been folded to form its constituent leaves.

FOURDRINIER: A wire mesh table over which the paper pulp moves to form a sheet of paper; the name of the wet end of the type of paper machine invented by Louis Robert and financed by the Fourdrinier brothers early in the nineteenth century.

Today it is usually applied to an entire papermaking machine, including the dry end.

FOXING: Spots of various sizes and intensity, usually brownish in color, that disfigure paper. They are caused by varying combinations of fungi, paper impurities, and dampness.

FRAME: (1) To enclose a picture in a protective arrangement of wood and glass. (2) A decorative design around a picture. (3) In photography, the area of film exposed to light in a camera during one exposure. (4) A single area in a grid pattern.

FREE SHEET (Wood Free): Paper made from purified wood pulp containing no groundwood or unbleached pulp.

FREEZE-DRYING: A method of freezing wet archival and library materials, then evaporating the ice in the material directly into steam by SUBLIMATION. The process takes place at very low temperature. See also VACUUM FREEZE-DRYING.

FROST POINT: See DEW POINT.

FUGITIVE COLORS: Dyes, pigments, or inks that are not permanent. They deteriorate when stored, but fading and changes in color are often accelerated when they are exposed to light. The term is also used to refer to colors and inks soluble in water.

FULL BINDING: The binding of a book completely in one material; traditionally the term is used to refer to leather bindings.

FUMIGATION: Killing or deactivating mold or insects by exposure to poisonous fumes or vapor, usually done in a vacuum or other airtight chamber.

GATHERING: See SECTION.

GELATIN: (1) A colloidal protein used as a medium to hold silver halide crystals in suspension in photographic emulsions; as a protective layer over emulsions; or as a carrier for dyes in filters or color films. (2) A material used to size paper.

GENERATION: A term used for the printing of copies from

copies; the measure of remoteness of a particular copy from the original material. For example, in microfilm, a negative of the original material is called the first generation, and it is one generation away from the original. Copies made from the negative are second-generation negative or positive images.

GLAIRE: A mixture of beaten egg whites that is used to hold gold leaf when stamping book covers and in edge gilding.

GLASSINE: A glazed, highly beaten, semitransparent paper not easily penetrated by air, used to make envelopes and sleeves for storing photographs, stamps, and other paper materials. Glassine papers are usually acidic and hygroscopic. Some are now produced that are alkaline and can be used to house collections.

GLITCHES: In video, a form of low-frequency interference appearing as a narrow horizontal bar moving through a picture.

GLUE: An adhesive whose principle constituent is protein from animal sources. See ADHESIVE, FLEXIBLE GLUE.

GRAIN: (1) The direction in which most of the fibers lie in a sheet of machine-made paper. (2) In photography, the clusters of light-sensitive silver halides in a negative that are changed into black metallic silver when developed.

GRANGERIZED: See EXTRA-ILLUSTRATED.

GRAPHICS: Presentation of data in visual form.

GRAVURE: A photomechanical reproduction process in which the image elements are recessed below the surface of an otherwise flat or cylindrical printing plate; often used for photographic books and frontispieces.

GREENHOUSE EFFECT: The air temperature under a glass or transparent cover increases when subjected to heat radiation. This is caused by the absorption of radiation by the surfaces under the glass and by the ready absorption of radiation in the long wave, or infrared length.

GROUND NOISE: Random variations, associated with reproduction systems, that limit the fidelity of sound reproduction.

GROUNDWOOD PAPERS: A generic term applied to papers made with a substantial proportion of wood pulp with chemical additives. These papers are normally used for low-cost printing purposes.

GUARD: A strip of paper, muslin, or other thin material used to attach or reinforce leaves or inserts in books and to permit free handling.

GUILLOTINE: A machine used for cutting paper. Most books are trimmed by guillotine.

GUTTER (Back Margin): The two inner margins of facing pages in a book.

HALF BINDING: A bookbinding with leather spine and outer corners and cloth or paper sides. The leather of the back usually extends about a quarter or a third of the distance of the front cover.

HALFTONE: A printed illustration in which tonal gradation is simulated by a pattern of small dots that may vary in size.

HALIDE: Any compound of chlorine, iodine, bromide, astatine, or fluoride and another element. The compounds are called halogens; the silver salts of these halogens are the light-sensitive materials used in silver-halide emulsions.

HALOGEN: See HALIDE.

HALONS: Halogenated fire-extinguishing agents; hydrocarbons in which one or more hydrogen atoms have been replaced by halogen atoms, thus changing a flammable substance into one that extinguishes fire.

HARD DISK: A storage device permanently encased in a computer's cabinet.

HARDCOPY: An enlarged reproduction from a microform, or from computerized data, usually printed on paper.

HARDWARE: The electrical and mechanical equipment used in telecommunications and computer systems. Any mechanical or electrical device capable of changing the state of itself or some object; the equipment involved in the production, storage, distribution, or reception of electrical signals.

HEAD (Recording Head, Reproducing Head, Erasing Head): The part of a tape or video recorder that applies or detects a magnetic field.

HEADBAND (End band): A small ornamental band of cloth or worked threads sewn or glued to the back of the head and tail of a volume. Today it is decorative; in the past it was a part of the sewn structure of a bound book, adding strength to the structure.

HEADER (Heading): The area at the top of a microtext for eye-legible information, bibliographical information, or other relevant material.

HEADS OUT: A tape recording rewound so that the beginning of the recorded content is ready for immediate replay. See also TAILS OUT.

HINGES: (1) The inside junctions of the sides of a binding with the SPINE. (2) Paper or muslin GUARDS that permit the free turning of an insert, leaf, or mat.

HISS: An undesirable wide spectrum noise heard when a recorded tape is played back, caused by various factors, including taping at too low a speed or poor quality tape.

HOLOGRAM: The photographic record of the interference pattern formed at the photographic plate when two sets of coherent (laser) light waves interfere. One of these acts as a reference wave, and the other is the (coherent) light reflected from the scene to be recorded.

HOLOGRAPHY: A photographic recording and viewing process that allows the reconstruction of three-dimensional images of diffuse objects.

HUMIDIFIER: A device used to add moisture to dry air. It should be used in conjunction with a humidity-measuring mechanism. See also DEHUMIDIFIER.

HUMIDITY: Absolute humidity is the amount of water vapor in any unit volume of air. Relative humidity (RH), usually meant when the term "humidity" alone is used, is the percent of moisture relative to the maximum level that air at any given temperature can retain without precipitation.

HVAC: The abbreviation for *h*eating, *v*entilating, and *a*ir *c*onditioning systems. The purpose of the HVAC system is to add or remove heat (energy), add or remove moisture, filter or clean air, and distribute conditioned air evenly through designated spaces. See also AIR-CONDITIONING.

HYDRATION: In paper, when the chemical components in paper are combined with moisture and the paper expands.

HYDROLYSIS: The decomposition of organic compounds, such as paper, by the removal or interaction of water. The presence of acid or alkali ions catalyzes the process.

HYGROMETER: An instrument used to measure the relative humidity in the atmosphere at a given point of time. See also PSYCHROMETER.

HYGROSCOPIC: Material, such as paper, that picks up and emits moisture that is in the air.

HYGROTHERMOGRAPH: An instrument used to measure temperature and relative humidity over a period of time, such as a week or a month.

HYPO (Fixer, Fixing Bath): Originally an abbreviation for sodium hyposulfite, but now used to refer to sodium thiosulfate, the chemical agent used in fixing baths to remove unexposed silver halides from silver emulsion film. It is also more generally used to refer to a fixer solution that may also contain certain acids and/or hardening agents.

ILLUMINANCE: The strength of light; illumination value or level.

IMAGE: A representation of perception or thought, or an object. In photography, the representation of an object or information sources produced by light rays. In contemporary usage, synonymous with photographic print, e.g., "I have a number of images by Edward Weston in my collection."

IMAGING: The process of reproducing images.

IMPRINT: (1) The name of a publisher, normally with the place and date of issue, usually placed at the bottom of the title page; (2) the name of the owner of a book stamped on its binding; (3) the name of the printer on any printed matter; (4) the name and address of a bookshop on a circulated list.

INCANDESCENT LIGHT: Produced by a light bulb with a filament in a vacuum, which glows at a white heat. Common bulbs are the tungsten and quartz lamps.

INDIA PAPER (Bible Paper, Oxford India Paper): A strong, lightweight opaque book paper used where low bulk is important, as in Bibles and encyclopedias; see also RICE PAPER.

INERT: Chemically stable.

INFRARED: Invisible rays of radiant heat that are just beyond the red end of the spectrum.

INHERENT VICE: A defect or cause of loss arising out of the material itself, such as the acid content in paper, which will eventually destroy the paper.

INK EROSION: Damage that occurs when iron gall ink, which is acidic, attacks the paper in the center of the pen stroke where it is concentrated and destroys the paper under the ink.

INSERT (Inset): An extra page or set of pages inserted into a book; in bibliographical terms, a folded section of paper placed within another, completing a sequence of pagination. An illustration, map, or other document produced separately from the body of a book, but bound into it.

INTAGLIO PRINTING: A technique in which the areas to be printed are cut into a plate, so that when the plate is inked and then wiped, the depressed areas will retain the ink.

INTERLEAF: To alternate blank pages with the printed leaves of a book; a technique used for the drying of wet volumes.

INTERMEDIATE COPY: A duplicate microform specifically prepared for producing further copies.

INTERPOSITIVE: A positive image on film made from a negative by contact printing or through an optical system.

INTRINSIC VALUE: Inherent value; the worth of an object dependent upon some unique factor, such as age, PROVENANCE, monetary value, or the circumstances surrounding its creation.

JACKET: (1) A transparent plastic carried with single or multiple pockets to hold microforms in flat strips. (2) A container, usually made of cardboard, to hold phonograph records. See also BOOK JACKET.

JAPANESE TISSUE: A highly absorbent, strong, quality paper made from plant fibers and used in the repair of paper in conservation.

JOB BINDERY: A bindery that specializes in binding or repairing small lots of books.

JOINTS: (1) The groove forming the outside junctions of the side of a binding adjacent to the spine of a book. (2) Reinforcements applied to the end linings or end sections of a book to strengthen the binding.

JORDAN: A pulp-refining machine that macerates wood pulp and other fibers between a conical plug revolving in a matching conical shell.

KELVIN SCALE: The absolute scale of temperature. Kelvin degrees are used to indicate the color temperature of light sources.

KRAFT PAPER: A tough, strong paper made entirely from wood pulp. See also SULFATE.

LACUNAE: A missing part, or parts, of a document or book.

LAID LINES (Wire Mark, Wire Lines): The close-set lines in laid paper, made by the wire mesh in the bottom of the frame. The lines are distinguishable parallel wires crossed at right angles by other wires set at a wider interval, which are called CHAIN LINES.

LAID PAPER: Paper showing the wire lines of the hand paper-maker's mold, or watermarked by devices on the dandy roll used in the process of machine manufacture.

LAMINATION: The fusing of sheets of thermoplastic cellulose acetate or polyethylene film to the sides of paper by means of heat and pressure. This process is only partly reversible because solvents cannot remove all of the film from the pores of the paper. See also SILKING.

LANTERN SLIDE (Diapositive): A mounted transparency, frequently on a glass plate or bound in glass, that is placed in a still projector for the projection of an enlarged image onto a screen. It is usually shortened to "slide."

LASER: *L*ight *A*mplification by *S*timulated *E*mission of *R*adiation. A device that transmits an extremely narrow beam of electromagnetic energy.

LATENT IMAGE: An invisible image contained on film or paper, which can be made visible by chemical development.

LATERAL REVERSAL: An image that has been reversed from left to right, as in a mirror image. A camera negative is normally reversed and is reoriented correctly in the printing process. Direct positive processes, notably daguerreotypes, ambrotypes, and tintypes, usually are laterally reversed unless taken using a mirror.

LEADER: Film or magnetic tape without image or sound at the beginning of a roll that is used for the threading of the film or tape into a camera, projector, or processing machine. See also TRAILER.

LEAF: The basic bibliographical unit of a book; a sheet of paper containing two pages.

LEAFLET: Leaves of paper, or sheets folded into leaves, unstitched, and containing printed matter.

LETTERPRESS: The original Western printing technique, dominant until the middle of the twentieth century.

LIBRARY BINDING: (1) Binding done by commercial library binders according to set specifications. (2) The process used in producing such a binding.

LIGHT: See VISIBLE LIGHT.

LIGHT BOX: A device for inspecting film and transparencies that employs a back-illuminated translucent surface; it is also used as an aid in paper repair.

LIGHT-SENSITIVE: Inks, dyes, and other materials that undergo physical changes when exposed to light. The commonly used photographic light-sensitive materials in films and papers are the silver halides, diazo dyes, biochromated gelatin, and the photoconductive materials used in Xerography. With most photographic materials, the changes are not apparent until the material is developed.

LIGHT STAIN: Discoloration on paper caused by overexposure to any light source, particularly light energy sources with substantial ultraviolet energy.

LIGNIN: An acidic organic substance found in wood pulp. It is removed in the chemical pulping process, but is not removed in the manufacture of low-grade papers made of groundwood pulp, such as newsprint.

LIMP BINDING: A binding, usually of leather, that has no rigid covers and that permits rolling and bending.

LIMP VELLUM: A binding style traditionally used to cover

inexpensive or educational texts, but one that has proved to be both flexible and durable; a style of considerable interest to book conservators. See also VELLUM.

LINING: (1) Various layers of cloth, paper, or leather that are pasted down on the SPINE of a text block after it has been sewn and backed to allow a book to open more easily. The operation is usually referred to as "lining-up." See also BACKING. (2) In paintings conservation, adding or placing a piece of material inside another to give it strength and protection.

LITHOGRAPH (Planographic Printing): Printing from smooth, porous stone. The image carrier is ink receptive and water-repellent in the printing areas, thus the inked area transfers to the paper.

LOOSE: A term used when the covers of a book are loose or nearly detached.

LUMEN: See FOOTCANDLE.

LUX: A unit of illumination. Illumination on the surface of a sphere or radius of one meter when a point source of one candle is at the enter of the sphere; see also FOOTCANDLE.

MACHINE-MADE PAPER: Paper made by machine rather than by hand; it may be of any quality depending upon the materials used in its manufacture.

MAGNESIUM BICARBONATE: A bicarbonate used in the de-acidifying of books.

MAGNETIC DISK: A form of computer storage in which data is encoded in magnetic oxide that coats a plastic or metal disk. The data is recorded and played back, or read, by magnetic heads that traverse the rotating disk under programmed control.

MAGNETIC TAPE: A ribbon of paper, acetate, metal, or plastic, coated or impregnated with magnetic material, capable of storing information in the form of magnetically polarized areas.

MARBLING: Coloring sheets of paper or the edges of books by

touching the paper or book edges to the patterns of color floating on specially prepared liquid base.

MARGIN: (1) The area beyond the printed matter in a drawing, fine print, printed book, or document. (2) In microfilm and fiche, the nonimage area outside the margins of the document, but without the frame.

MASS STORAGE: A device that can hold large amounts of information cheaply and provide automated access on demand.

MASS TREATMENT: A production scale process to stabilize and/or strengthen library and archival materials.

MASTER COPY: An original document, film, sound recording, or a copy of a document, film, or sound recording from which copies can be made; usually the first generation copy.

MASTER NEGATIVE FILM: The first generation microform copy of a document, from which subsequent copies can be made as intermediate or distribution copies.

MAT: A sandwich of two pieces of board hinged together. The bottom piece supports the print and the top piece contains the opening, or window, through which the print may be seen.

MECHANICALS: Mechanical systems including heating, ventilating and cooling systems, boilers, or any application that uses gas, liquid, or solid fuel.

MENDING: The act of repairing damaged pages and sections of a book; less than full conservation treatment.

METHYL CELLULOSE: An adhesive, or size, made from cellulose that has been chemically treated to provide a neutral and stable material.

METER-CANDLE: See FOOTCANDLE.

MICROCOMPUTER: (1) A small computer; (2) a set of microchips that can perform all the functions of a digital stored program computer.

MICROCOPY: A small copy of an image obtained by photography in a size too small to be read without a device for magnification.

MICROFACSIMILE: The transmission and/or reception of microimages via facsimile transmission.

MICROFICHE: A series of microimages on a flat sheet of film, usually arranged in a grid pattern. The most common size produced today is the 105mm x 148mm, and the format is 60 to 98 pages of information per fiche.

MICROFILM: A transparent flexible film used for the photographic reproduction of documents. Photographic reproductions on this film can be viewed with a reading device or enlarged to make readable prints.

MICROFORM: The generic name for any film format that contains microimages.

MICROGRAPHICS: (1) In the use of microimage recording, retrieval, and reproduction techniques in an information system. (2) The industry that reduces visual text information to a micrographic medium.

MICRO-OPAQUE: A sheet of opaque material bearing one or more microimages.

MICROPHOTOGRAPHY: The photographic recording of information with a substantial reduction in size.

MICROPRINT: Microimages on opaque paper, produced by printing, as distinct from microimages produced on photographic material.

MICROPUBLISHING: The publication of new or previously published information in multiple-copy microform for sale or distribution.

MICROREPRODUCTION: (1) Copy rendered in sizes too small to be read without magnification and that is produced photographically on transparent or opaque paper; (2) the process of making microimages.

MILDEW: A thin, whitish, furry coating or discoloration produced by fungi on organic material stored in damp environments.

MOISTURE CONTENT: The percent of moisture found in finished paper. The amount varies according to atmospheric conditions because paper is HYGROSCOPIC.

MOTION PICTURE FILM: A transparent film, with or without a soundtrack, bearing a series of images that create the illusion of movement when projected in rapid succession.

MOTTLE: A defect in photographic prints that have been underdeveloped, in which the density is not uniform and gives the print a mottled effect.

MOUNTED: (1) Of printed matter or illustrations pasted down or lightly attached to a leaf or mat. (2) Of damaged leaves that have been laid down upon or backed with paper.

MUDDY: Lack of definition or clarity in a recording, playback system, or sound reinforcement system; may be caused by many factors.

MULL: See SUPER.

MUSEUM BOARD: Originally 100 percent rag fiberboard used for matting printed works for framing. It now includes alkaline paperboard manufactured from highly refined wood pulp.

MYLAR: Du Pont trade name for a clear, flexible, inert polyester plastic sheet used for ENCAPSULATION, to cover prints, or as a base for magnetic tape.

NEGATIVE: A photographic image in which the tonal values are reversed from the original subject. Black areas of the original scene are white on the negative and vice versa. See also POSITIVE.

NEWSPRINT: A generic term used to describe paper of a type generally used in the publication of newspapers. It is usually of a high groundwood content.

NEWTON RINGS: A pattern of rings of distorted shapes that are produced when two surfaces are separated by a small distance and illuminated; an occurrence in slide projection.

NICK: A defect in a sound recording causing some sonic distortion.

OFFPRINT: See EXTRACT.

OFFSET: The accidental transfer of ink from a printed page or illustration to another page.

OFFSET PRINTING: A method for printing a large number of impressions, in which the image is transferred from one roller, or plate, to another and then printed on paper.

OPACIMETER: A testing instrument used to determine the degree of a paper's OPACITY.

OPACITY: The quality of non-transparency, which is especially important on thin papers used for the printing of books.

OPAQUE SCREEN: A microform reader screen of opaque material on which an image is produced by reflected light.

OPTICAL DISK: See DIGITAL OPTICAL RECORDING.

OVEREXPOSURE: See UNDEREXPOSURE.

OVERSEWING: Sewing by hand or machine through the edge of each SECTION of a book in consecutive order, utilizing perforated holes through which the needle passes. This is the principle means of securing the leaves of books in commercial library binding.

OXFORD PAPER: See INDIA PAPER.

OXIDATION: The reaction of a substance with oxygen; chemical changes that weaken paper as a result of the reaction of paper pulp and other papermaking substances with oxygen. (2) On microfilm, oxidation can cause microscopic blemishes; see BLEMISH.

OZONE (O_3): Produced as a secondary reaction product

through the combined synergy of sunlight, oxygen, oxides of nitrogen, and hydrocarbons.

PAGINATION: (1) The sequence of figures with which the pages of a book are numbered. (2) The arrangement of pages or microimages of pages on a microform.

PAMPHLET BINDING: A wire-stitched or saddle-stitched binding for pamphlets and periodicals.

PAPER: A thin tissue of fibrous material that is suspended in water and then matted into sheets by dipping screens into the water suspension and lifting the fibers out. The fibers bond together to form a sheet of paper.

PAPER LOSS: Absence, in any degree, of an area of original paper.

PARCHMENT: The inner portion of the split skin of a sheep, which is not tanned but cleaned of adhering flesh, hair, fat, and muscle, and preserved by soaking in a lime solution, then scraped and polished.

PEELING: Separation of the coating layer of a laminated disk from its base or core. See also FLAKING.

PERFECT BINDING: A method of holding pages of a book together with glue, using no stitching or sewing. The spines of the books are shaved off, leaving a rough surface to which adhesive is applied.

PERMANENCE: Lasting or intending to last indefinitely without significant change.

PERMANENT/DURABLE PAPER: See ALKALINE PAPER.

pH VALUE: *P*otential of *h*ydrogen. The numerical expression used by chemists to describe hydrogen ion concentration. A measurement, or numerical expression, that tells if paper is acidic or alkaline. Seven is neutral; each point is a tenfold increase. Material below seven is acidic; above it is alkaline.

PHASE BOXING: The placement of fragile books in protective

wrappers until full conservation treatment can be undertaken. See also BOOK BOX.

PHASE CONSERVATION: Planned sequential stages in conservation treatment when the entire prescribed treatment cannot be completed. The goal is to stabilize an object.

PHASE PRESERVATION: A long-term program for stabilizing a collection in successive stages when more extensive conservation treatment is not immediately available or appropriate.

PHONOGRAPH: A machine that can reproduce sounds from indented, incised, or engraved cylinder or disk records.

PHONOTAPE: See AUDIO RECORDING.

PHOTOCOMPOSITION: Typesetting by exposure on a sensitive material from a negative of type characters or other symbols.

PHOTOCOPY: (1) Noun: A reproduction produced by placing a document in an electrostatic copying machine. (2) Verb: To apply electrostatic processes for the reproduction of an object.

PHOTOCOPY PAPER: Paper used in electrostatic copiers. It is made to perform well in any of a number of photocopy machines. Alkaline paper, for permanence, is available for use in photocopiers.

PHOTODEGRADATION: The destruction of material by light, or ULTRAVIOLET energy. It is irreversible.

PHOTODUPLICATION: See REPROGRAPHY.

PHOTOGRAPHY: Literally, to write with light; the science, engineering, art, and craft of producing relatively permanent images by the action of light (and similar electromagnetic radiation) on sensitive materials. In a narrow sense, the use of a camera to make images by the action of radiation and sensitive films or papers.

PHOTOREPRODUCTION: See REPROGRAPHY.

PICKUP: Device that translates the mechanical motion of a

stylus riding a record groove into electrical impulses in a playback system.

PIT: (1) Term used to describe the depressions in the surface of a laser disk that contain the digitally encoded program material to be "read" by the tracking laser beam in PLAYBACK. (2) Commonly used term to describe a defect in sound recordings.

PLANETARY CAMERA (Flatbed or Step Camera): A type of microfilming camera in which the document being photographed and the film remain in a stationary position during the exposure. The document is on a flat surface at the time of filming. See also ROTARY CAMERA.

PLANOGRAPHIC PRINTING. See LITHOGRAPHY.

PLASTIC BINDING: See SPIRAL BINDING.

PLATE: (1) Illustrations prepared separately and inserted into a book when bound; see also COLOR PLATE. (2) A master surface from which printing is done. (3) A photographic negative made on a glass plate.

PLAYBACK: The reproduction of a sound recording on a sound system to hear its contents.

PLY: A single layer; the term is used when several sheets of material are bonded together, such as in paper or polyester film used for encapsulation.

POINT SYSTEM: Of type, a numerical system for the measurement and description of type. A point is equal to $1/72$ of an inch.

POLARITY: A word used to indicate the change or retention of the dark to light relationship of an image.

POLYESTER: A polymer built up from ESTER. A flexible, transparent, inert plastic sheeting; used (1) as a base for film and magnetic tape because of its transparency, chemical stability, and relative nonflammability; (2) to make protective sleeves and envelopes; (3) for ENCAPSULATION. See also MYLAR.

POLYETHELENE: A chemically inert translucent thermoplastic that has a low melting point.

POLYVINYL ACETATE (PVA): A strong adhesive emulsion, frequently used in bookbinding.

POROSITY: The structure and density of a material. Of paper, the minute openings in the fiber through which air and light might pass.

PORTFOLIO: (1) A case for holding loose papers, consisting of two covers joined together at the back and usually tied in the front and the ends. (2) A group of prints or drawings issued by an artist.

POSITIVE: A photographic image on paper, film, or glass in the same polarity as the original subject in all details.

POST BINDING: A structure that holds usually large and heavy pages together by metal posts in holes drilled through the book next to the binding edge. This structure is useful for binding polyester encapsulated sheets into a book.

POST PROCESSING: Additional steps after normal photographic processing to enhance permanence, such as toning.

PREBOUND: A term applied to new books bound in a library binding prior to, or at the time of sale.

PRESERVATION: The maintenance of objects as closely as possible to their original condition through proper collection maintenance, repair, and physical treatment. See also CONSERVATION.

PRESSING: In sound recording, the production process whereby a machine flattens, compresses, and squeezes the vinyl and shapes the grooves or pits.

PRINT THROUGH: The unwanted transfer of a magnetic field (and the sound signal) from one layer to another within a roll of tape. It is caused by the magnetic instability of magnetic oxide on tape.

PROCESSING: Developing, fixing, washing, and drying exposed photographic film to make the latent image visible. See also POST PROCESSING.

PROCESSOR: (1) A machine, or person, that performs various operations necessary to process photographic material. 2) An individual who prepares an archival or manuscript collection for storage and use.

PROGRAMMING: In microfilming, a prefilming task performed after collation to determine the maximum page capacity per reel for multireel titles.

PROJECTION: (1) The display of an image through optical means onto a sensitized surface or viewing screen, usually magnified in size; (2) an image that is visible after it has been optically projected through space onto a surface.

PROTECTIVE ENCLOSURE: Any form of container for a book or document that is designed to provide physical stabilization and minimize hazards from the environment and handling.

PROVENANCE: (1) The history of the ownership and transmission of an object, such as a book or manuscript. (2) In archival practice, the originating entity that created or accumulated records, or the source of personal papers.

PSYCHROMETER: An instrument for determining relative humidity in which wet and dry-bulb temperature readings are compared with a chart that shows relative humidity. See also HYGROMETER.

PUBLISHER'S BINDING: See EDITION BINDING.

PUBLISHER'S REINFORCED BINDING: A term used by publishers to identify those of their bindings that are purported to be strengthened for use in libraries.

PULP: The preliminary raw material of ground up fibers from which paper is made.

QUALITY INDEX: In microfilming, the relationship between the size of the printed text and the resolution pattern resolved in a microimage; used to predetermine legibility in the resulting image and subsequent generations of film.

QUARTER BOUND: A book with leather spine and sides covered entirely with cloth or paper.

QUIRE: (1) A standard parcel of paper, a printer's quire being 24 sheets. (2) See SECTION.

RADIANT HEAT: Shortwave infrared energy that passes as a ray or beam through air with little absorption or dispersion.

RAG CONTENT: A term that indicates the presence of cotton or linen rag fibers in a sheet of paper. The content can vary from 25 to 100 percent.

RAISED BANDS: Ridges, from the horizontal cords upon which sections of a book are sewn, that appear on the spine of books when these cords have not been embedded in the paper. See also BANDS.

READER: A projection device for viewing an enlarged microimage with the unaided eye.

READER-PRINTER: A machine that combines the functions of a reader and an enlarger-printer.

REAM: A standard parcel of paper, formerly 20 QUIRES, or 480 sheets, now usually 500 sheets.

RE-BACKED: A term used when the binding of a book has been given a new back, or SPINE.

REBINDING: The rehabilitation of a worn volume including putting on a new cover.

RECASED: A text block that has been replaced in its cover after it has loosened or come free.

REDOX BLEMISH: See BLEMISH.

REDUCTION: (1) A measure of the number of times a given linear dimension of an object is reduced when photographed, expressed as 16X, 24X, etc. (2) Decreasing the optical density of a photographic image using chemical or other means.

REDUCTION RATIO: The relationship between the dimensions of a microimage and the corresponding dimensions of the original master. It is expressed 16:1, 20:1, etc., or 16X, 20X, etc.

REEL: A metal or plastic flanged holder on which processed roll film or magnetic tape is wound, designed to be inserted into retrieval devices. See also SPOOL.

REFORMAT: To change the medium in which information is recorded, e.g., from paper to microfilm, from microfilm to electronic image.

REINFORCE: To strengthen the structure of a weakened volume, usually by adding material.

REJOINT: A repair made when the joints of a book have deteriorated badly.

RELATIVE HUMIDITY: The ratio of the quantity of water vapor present in the air to the quantity that would saturate that air at any given temperature. See also HUMIDITY.

RELIEF PRINTING: A generic term for printing from surfaces that are raised so that ink is deposited only on the image that is to be transferred to paper.

REPAIR: Partial rehabilitation of a worn volume.

REPRODUCTION: The act of copying or duplicating a document. See also REFORMAT.

REPROGRAPHY (Photoreproduction, Photoduplication): The science, technology, and practice of document reproduction. A term used to refer to the processes and methods, using light, heat, or electrical radiation, employed for copying and duplicating documents and photographs.

RESET: (1) To reset type for a new leaf or edition of a book. (2) RECASED. (3) Of leaves that have been stuck back into a book with paste after they have come loose. See TIPPED IN.

RESEWING: Removing old sewing, sewing anew.

RESOLUTION: The ability of optical systems and photographically reproduced materials to render visible the fine detail of an object; a measure of the sharpness and clarity of an image. It is often expressed in lines per millimeter (mm).

RESTORATION: Treatment procedures that attempt to return an object as closely as possible to its original condition, incorporating original materials as much as possible. See CONSERVATION, the preferred term for preservation.

RETENTIVITY: Measure of a tape's ability to retain magnetization after the force field has been removed. It serves as an indication of the tape's sensitivity at high frequencies.

REVERSIBLE: Easily and safely disassembled to correct an error in conservation treatment or to replace worn components. A tenet of conservation is that processes in treatment be reversible.

RICE PAPER: A misnomer for paper made from the pith of a small tree found in the Far East. It is often, erroneously, called INDIA PAPER.

ROLL MICROFILM: A length of microfilm on a reel, spool, or core.

ROSIN: The additive most commonly used for the sizing of paper.

ROTARY CAMERA (Flow or Continuous Camera): A microfilming camera that photographs documents while they are being moved by a transport mechanism. The document transport mechanism is connected to a film transport mechanism and the film also moves along during exposure so that there is no relative movement between the film and the image of the document. See also PLANETARY CAMERA.

ROUNDING: In binding, shaping the sewn, glued spine of a book into a slightly rounded shape.

SADDLE-STITCHING (Side Stitching): Stitching together double leaves inserted one within the other, with thread or wire passing through the bulk of the volume at the fold line.

SADDLE WARP: Warpage that occurs when a phonodisk is removed from the press because the paper grain of both labels on a sound recording is not running in the same direction. The natural curl of the paper places unequal stress on the disk's center surfaces.

SAFETY FILM: A comparatively nonflammable film base composed mainly of cellulose esters, e.g., cellulose triacetate or polyester.

SAWING IN: Making grooves in the back of an unbound book with a saw to receive the bands for binding.

SCHOLARLY REPRINT PUBLISHER: One who assumes the responsibility for the selection, production, and sale of new copies of scholarly works that were available at an earlier date from another publisher or institution.

SCRAPE: Visible, and serious, marring of the surface of a recording, causing sonic distortion in PLAYBACK.

SCRATCH: Commonly used term to describe a visible marring on the surface of a sound recording, causing distortion when the stylus runs over it in PLAYBACK; see also SCRAPE.

SECTION (Gathering, Quire): A term applied to each unit of folded leaves comprising a book. The group of leaves formed after the printed sheet has been folded to the size of the book and before it is combined in proper order with another section for binding.

SELF ERASURE: The process by which a piece of magnetized tape tends to demagnetize itself by virtue of the opposing fields created within it by its own magnetization. It can be avoided by storing tapes in a stable environment, using high quality tapes, and avoiding the use of excessive equalization boost at high frequencies.

SEPARATE: See OFFPRINT.

SERIOGRAPHY: See SILK-SCREEN PRINTING.

SERVICE COPY (Distribution Copy): A microform copy that is

distributed for use, usually a third generation copy; a sound recording designated for playback for listeners.

SEWED: A pamphlet stitched without covers.

SEWING: In bookbinding, the fastening of SECTIONS together, one at a time, by means of a needle and thread, until the whole book is fastened together.

SHAKEN: A term used to describe a book that is LOOSE in its case, but with the case intact.

SHAVED: A term used when the binder has trimmed off the whole margin of a leaf and touched ink, but has not cut off more than the outer edge of any printed letters. See also CROP.

SHEET: A printer's unit; the full size of the paper when printed, forming a SECTION of a book when folded.

SHELF LIFE: The period of time before deterioration renders material unusable.

SIGNATURE: (1) A folded, printed sheet ready for sewing. (2) A letter or number placed at the bottom of the first page of each signature of folded SECTION to serve as a guide for the binder.

SILICA GEL: Highly absorbent granules of silicone and oxygen; used as a dehumidifier in exhibition cases. It turns from blue to pink as it absorbs moisture from the air and can be regenerated by conditioning.

SILK-SCREEN PRINTING: A stencil technique of printing.

SILKING: The repair of fragile papers by reinforcing them on one or both sides with a thin translucent textile or paper. See also LAMINATION.

SILVER HALIDE: A compound of silver and a member of the halogen family. Film coated with an emulsion containing this compound is said to be of "archival quality," as contrasted with images made with dyes, like diazo or chromogenic color materials.

SIZE: A glutinous or viscous wash used in the preparation of many papers that imparts water-resistant qualities to the paper.

SLEEVE: The inner protective envelope for a disk within a cardboard or paper slipcase. Archival quality sleeves are available for sound recordings.

SLIDE: See LANTERN SLIDE, TRANSPARENCY.

SLIDE MOUNTER: A device for converting positive transparent images into mounts for projection.

SLIPCASE: Box designed to protect a book, covering it so that only its spine is exposed.

SLURRY: The suspension of fibers and water from which paper is made.

SMYTHE SEWING: Sewing a book through the folds using a Smythe sewing machine.

SOFT COPY: An enlarged copy that appears on the screen of a microform reader or a computer terminal.

SOFTWARE: (1) Textual or illustrative material that is viewed with special equipment. (2) Programming instructions that direct a computer. See also HARDWARE.

SOLANDER CASE: A box with a hinged top, shaped like a thick book, that can house prints, pamphlets, and documents. This term can also refer to a closed book box with a removable top into which a book is placed for extra protection. See BOOK BOX.

SOUND RECORDING: An artifact that has been constructed and used for the specific purpose of storing a representation of energy for the further purpose of reproduction in the audio portion of the spectrum. The activity of using an audiotape recorder and related audio equipment to record sound on an audiotape, magnetic film, or optical disk.

SOUND TRACK: A narrow band, usually along the margin of a sound film, that carries the SOUND RECORDING.

SPECIFICATION: A formal, detailed description of materials or services, usually associated with bids, purchase orders, and contracts.

SPECTROPHOTOMETER: An instrument capable of measuring amounts of light energy transmitted or reflected from a sample, in narrow frequency bands throughout the visual and ultraviolet spectrum.

SPINE (Back, Backbone, Backstrip): (1) The part of a book that is visible when it stands closed on the shelf. (2) The bound edge of a text block before the cover is attached.

SPIRAL BINDING (Plastic Binding): A type of binding in which the single leaves and the separate front and back covers are fastened by means of a specially cut piece of plastic with prongs that pass through slots near the binding edge and are curled back within the plastic cylinder.

SPLICE: A joint made when attaching two pieces of paper, film, or magnetic tape together so they will function as a single piece when passing through a camera, processing machine, projector, or other apparatus.

SPOOL: A flanged holder on which unprocessed roll film is wound, designed to be fitted into cameras and processors; see also REEL.

SPRINKLER SYSTEM: An integrated system of underground and overhead piping designed in accordance with fire protection engineering standards to suppress fire in a building.

STAB SEWING (Side Sewing, Side Stitching): A form of sewing, or stitching, in which the thread, wire, or other material passes through the entire body of the book from front to back.

STABILITY: The degree to which materials change in reaction to light, heat, atmospheric pollution, or other chemical reactors.

STABILIZERS: Substances added to the basic compounds of a disk or tape recording to prevent deterioration or the loss of the desired physical properties.

STANDARD: The result of a particular standardization effort, approved by a recognized authority. It may take the form of a document containing a set of conditions to be fulfilled or a fundamental unit or physical constant.

STATIC: The distortion created in disk or tape PLAYBACK when the recording has a buildup of electrostatic charge.

STEP-AND-REPEAT CAMERA: See PLANETARY CAMERA.

STEREOGRAPH: A pair of photographic prints mounted adjacent to each other on a 3 ¹/₂ by 7 inch card, which gives a three-dimensional, or stereographic, image when used with the proper viewer.

STEREOPHONIC: A multiple channel sound system in which each channel carries a unique version of the total original performance. When the channels are played simultaneously, they re-create the breadth and depth of the original performance. At least two channels are required for stereo operation.

STEREOTYPE: The method or process of printing in which a solid plate of type metal, cast from a papier-mâché or plaster mold taken from the surface of a form of type, is used in lieu of the form itself for printing.

STITCHING: As distinguished from SEWING in BOOKBINDING, the fastening together of leaves with thread and wire, each stitch of which passes through the entire volume. See also STAB SEWING.

STOCK: Paper pulp that has been beaten and refined, treated with sizing, color and fillers, and which, after dilution, is ready to be formed into paper.

STRIP FILM: A length of film too short to be wound on a reel, generally housed in a small can or inserted in a jacket or other type of holder.

STUB: (1) The part of an original leaf that is left after most of it has been cut away from its conjugate leaf. (2) A narrow strip of paper or linen sewn between sections of a book for the purpose of attaching plates, maps, etc.

STYLUS (Needle): The cutting stylus or needle used in making a recording and the playback needle that engages a groove of a recording and transmits the waves for transmission to sound.

SUBLIMATION: Converting frozen materials to the vapor phase by application of heat without going through the liquid phase.

SULFATE: An alkaline process of cooking pulp for paper; see KRAFT PAPER.

SULFITE: (1) An acid process of cooking pulp for paper; (2) pulp cooked by this process.

SUPER (Crash, Mull): Coarse open-weave, starched cotton goods used in edition binding for reinforcing the spine.

SURFACE CLEANING: Cleaning of an object without immersion in a solution.

SURFACE NOISE: In sound recording, the noise component in the electric output of a pickup due to irregularities in the contact surface of the grooves.

SWELLING: (1) The thickness added to the spine of a book by the accumulation of sewing threads and other material that may have been bound into the text. (2) In microfilm, the increased thickness of films as they acclimate to humidity levels in excess of 50 percent.

TAILBAND: See HEADBAND.

TAILS OUT: A tape recording that is stored after recording or PLAYBACK without being rewound; i.e., with the tail end of the tape outermost on the reel. Tails out storage is preferable because the tape "pack" tends to be smoother, hence safer, than if the tape had been rewound; see HEADS OUT.

TARGET: A sign or note photographed on the subject frame preceding or following the document being microfilmed to provide the user with bibliographic or corrective information, or technically precise images, measures, and shades to measure resolution and camera performance.

TELEFACSIMILE: The process or result of the process by which fixed graphic images are scanned, transmitted electronically, and reproduced. An image-oriented electronic technology that is used to transmit and reconstitute full pages of text or images over a telecommunications medium. See FAX.

TEMPERATURE: The state of a substance that determines the direction of heat flow to or from that substance; the degree of hotness or coldness of an object.

TENSILE STRENGTH: The ability of a sheet of paper to withstand tension.

TERMINAL: Any device capable of sending and/or receiving information over a communications channel.

TEXT BLOCK: The body of a book made up of leaves or signatures, excluding any papers added by the binder.

THERMOPLASTIC: The general basic synthetic or partially synthetic ingredient in most contemporary disk recordings; it will soften repeatedly when heated and harden when cooled.

THREE-QUARTER BINDING: Binding in which the leather back extends well over the sides, and with leather corners. The leather of the back and the leather of the corners almost meet. See also HALF BINDING, QUARTER BOUND.

TICK: Break or distortion in sound recording caused by a flaw in the surface of a disk.

TIDE LINES: The boundaries of a water stain to which the dissolved impurities in the liquid, or within the medium itself, have been carried and dried.

TIE: In binding, narrow strips of leather, linen, or other material attached to the covers of a book to be tied across its front edges to prevent curling of the bindings.

TIPPING IN: To lightly attach a leaf onto a sheet or printed book with paste. Colored prints are often "tipped in" expensive art books.

TISSUE PAPER: Any thin, lightweight, nearly transparent paper, often tipped in to cover the face of illustration in a book to prevent OFFSET of the ink of an engraved or etched illustration onto the text page opposite it. Some are acidic and have stained the adjacent page.

TITLE PAGE: A page on the right-hand side of the beginning of a book that gives the bibliographic information about the work.

TONER: (1) In reprography, the material employed to define a latent electrostatic image. (2) In photography, a compound used to impart a color to a developed black-and-white silver image.

TRACK: The path on magnetic tape on which the signal is recorded.

TRAILER: The film without images at the end of a roll to permit proper handling of the film. See also LEADER.

TRANSLUCENT SCREEN: A sheet of treated glass or plastic on which a visible image is formed in microform readers. The image is projected onto the back of the screen and viewed from the front.

TRANSPARENCY (Slide): An image on film or glass, usually positive, intended to be viewed by means of light passing through the image and base using a viewer or projector. See also LANTERN SLIDE.

TREATMENT: Intervention to stabilize an object. Any direct activity that lengthens the useful life of an object, or its intellectual or artistic content. See also MASS TREATMENT.

TRIMMED: The edges of a book are said to be trimmed when only the edges of the larger leaves have been cut, thus the edges are roughly leveled rather than smooth.

ULTRAFICHE: Microfiche containing images with a reduction ratio of 90X or more.

ULTRAVIOLET (UV): Pertaining to the electromagnetic energy, invisible light, immediately beyond the blue end of the visible spectrum.

ULTRAVIOLET (UV) FILTERS: Plastic sleeves that fit over

fluorescent light tubes to absorb the damaging ultraviolet rays. They are available in standard sizes and are easy to install, but must be replaced periodically as their useful life is exhausted.

ULTRAVIOLET (UV) MONITOR: A device that measures non-visible ultraviolet radiation from natural and artificial light sources. A reading of about 75 LUX requires that light sources be filtered.

UNCUT (Untrimmed): The edges of a book that have not been TRIMMED in any way.

UNDEREXPOSURE: Insufficient exposure of sensitized material due to insufficient illumination, too short an exposure time, or too small a lens aperture, resulting in a low-contrast image lacking detail in areas that were darker in the original scene. Opposite of overexposure, which results in loss of detail in brighter areas.

UNOPENED: A book with folded edges that have not been sliced open, so that its component sections are still intact at the top and fore-edges.

UNPRESSED: A book that has not been to the binder's press, so that the original crisp texture of the paper is preserved.

UNTRIMMED: See UNCUT.

VACUUM FREEZE-DRYING (Lyophilization): A process in a chamber that transforms water into vapor, which can be piped or condensed from the chamber; see also FREEZE-DRYING.

VELLUM: The skin of a calf, usually not more than six weeks old, cleaned of adhering flesh hair, fat, and muscle, and preserved by soaking in a lime solution, then carefully dried, stretched, scraped, and polished; used for writing or printing upon, or as a binding material.

VERMIN: Any of various small destructive or troublesome animals, as flies, lice, rats, etc.

VESICULAR FILM: A generic term for film that has light-sensitive diazonium salts suspended in a plastic layer. Upon exposure, it creates strains within the layer in the form of a latent image. The strains are released and the latent image made visible by heating the plastic layer. The images are formed by vesicles (bubbles) that harden and become stable when cooled. A pressure-sensitive film capable of having images crushed out of existence.

VIDEO: (1) The bandwidth and spectrum position on the signal resulting from television scanning; (2) the picture portion in a television signal.

VIDEOCASSETTE (Videotape Cassette): A video recording on magnetic tape enclosed in a plastic container or CASSETTE.

VIDEODISK: A flat, circular disk upon which both audio and visual information can be stored for PLAYBACK by means of a LASER.

VIDEO RECORDING: A recording designed for television playback.

VIDEOTAPE: Magnetic tape for the recording and playback of television and audio signals.

VIDEOTEXT: Information delivery by wire or microwave, through telephone lines or coaxial cable; a system that integrates various technologies in a variety of ways.

VISCOSITY: The internal resistance offered by a fluid to any change of its shape or to the relative motion or flow of its parts.

VISIBLE LIGHT: Nonionizing, or radiant, energy capable of producing a visual sensation; the portion of the electromagnetic spectrum from about 380mm to 700mm in wavelength. See AMBIENT LIGHT.

WASHING: (1) Of paper, using a bath of distilled or deionized water to remove stains and other blemishes. Treated thus, the paper will require a new SIZE bath. (2) In photography, washing prints and films with water to remove residual processing chemicals; such chemicals may cause image deterioration if they remain on the film or photograph, or may help preserve the image.

WATER STAIN: Discoloration of paper caused by direct contact with fluids or excessive humidity.

WATERMARK: The mark made within a sheet of paper by a raised design on the screen of a paper mold, which serves as the mark of the papermaker. It may be seen by holding the paper up to the light.

WEED: See DEACCESSION.

WINDOW: The opening in a MAT through which a print is viewed.

WIRE MARK: See LAID LINES.

WOOD: A heterogeneous material that is the raw material for making chemical and mechanical pulps used in the manufacture of paper and other products.

WOOD-FREE: See FREE SHEET.

WOOD PULP: Prepared for papermaking from trees of various kinds. The process of manufacture includes two distinct classes: (1) mechanical wood pulp or groundwood from which newsprint is made; (2) chemical pulp produced by various methods.

WORMHOLE: The hole, or holes, made by the larvae of certain insects in the text block, boards, and leather in bookbindings.

WOVE PAPER: Paper with an even, granulated texture, usually made on a continuous close-meshed wire belt. Wove paper does not have wire marks.

XEROGRAPHY: A proprietary term for a process developed by the Xerox Corporation for the formation of a latent electrostatic image by action of light on a photoconducting insulating surface. The latent image may be made visible by a number of methods. See ELECTROPHOTOGRAPHY.

XYLOGRAPHY: Printing from blocks of wood, especially of an early or primitive kind.

Appendix A ORGANIZATIONS

ABBEY PUBLICATIONS, INC.
7105 Geneva Drive
Austin, TX 78723
512/929–3992
Ellen McCrady, President

Mission. Abbey Publications is a nonprofit corporation formed
in 1986 to foster and support the efforts of Ellen McCrady to
publish *Abbey Newsletter* (begun in 1975) and *Alkaline Paper
Advocate* (begun in 1988), and to disseminate news and
information on preservation and conservation to the library and
archival communities.
Publications. *Abbey Newsletter* and *Alkaline Paper Advocate;*
occasional publications on preservation and conservation
issues.

AMERICAN ASSOCIATION FOR STATE AND LOCAL
HISTORY (AASLH)
172 Second Avenue, Suite 102
Nashville, TN 37204
615/255–2971

Mission. A nonprofit educational organization, founded in
1940, dedicated to advancing knowledge, understanding, and
appreciation of local history in the United States and Canada. It
has an extensive publishing program, confers prizes and awards
in recognition of outstanding achievement in the field, and
carries on a broad educational program and other activities
designed to help members work more effectively in
organizations concerned with local history.
Publications. *History News,* Technical Series of reports, books,
and audiovisual materials.

AMERICAN ASSOCIATION OF MUSEUMS (AAM)
P.O. Box 33399
Washington, DC 20053
202/338–5300

Mission. The American Association of Museums was founded
in 1916, and its membership now consists of more than 4,000
individual members and 1,300 institutions. Its purpose, as a
nonprofit service organization, is to promote museums as major
cultural resources. It represents the interests of the museum
profession on a national level.
Publications. Museum News, a journal established in 1917;
Aviso, a newsletter for its membership; books and pamphlets
dealing with the care and preservation of museum objects.

AMERICAN CHEMICAL SOCIETY (ACS)
1155 16th Street, N.W., Rm. 716
Washington, DC 20036
800/424–6747

Mission. Founded in 1876, the professional organization of
chemists and chemical engineers; addresses scientific and
educational concerns of its membership.
Publications. On-line data bases: *Chemical Abstracts* and
Chemical Journal Online, which offer full text of 18 journals
and other journals in its specialties.

AMERICAN FILM INSTITUTE
J.F. Kennedy Center for the Performing Arts
Washington, DC 20566

Mission. A national nongovernmental corporation founded in
1967, dedicated to preserving and developing the nation's
artistic and cultural resources in film and video; to catalog and
preserve America's film heritage; and to promote American film
and filmmakers.
Publications. American Film (monthly); guides to college film
courses; and catalogs of motion pictures of the United States.

AMERICAN INSTITUTE FOR CONSERVATION OF HISTORIC
AND ARTISTIC WORKS (AIC)
1717 K Street, N.W., Suite 301
Washington, DC 20006
202/452–9545

Mission. The American Institute for Conservation, formerly an affiliate of the International Institute for Conservation of Historic and Artistic Works (IIC), became an independent, nonprofit professional organization in 1973. Its purpose is to set and uphold standards of professional conduct and to coordinate and advance knowledge and practice in the maintenance and preservation of cultural property. Its membership includes professional conservators, conservation scientists and educators, conservation administrators, museum curators, librarians, and others interested in the field of conservation. *Publications.* Semiannual *Journal of the American Institute for Conservation* and a bimonthly newsletter for its membership.

AIC BOOK AND PAPER GROUP (BPG)
American Institute for Conservation
1717 K Street, N.W., Suite 301
Washington, DC 20006

Mission. Established in 1982 to encourage and facilitate the exchange of ideas and information about the conservation of books and works on paper; to promote paper conservation and the development of sound treatment practices; to promote the publication of scholarly articles on book and paper conservation; to foster closer relationships with related organizations; and to disseminate responsible information about the conservation of books and works on paper. *Publications. Book and Paper Annual,* a compilation of papers presented at conferences or contributed by its members, and *Paper Preservation Catalogue,* an inventory of current treatment practices, updated on a regular basis.

AIC PHOTOGRAPHIC MATERIALS GROUP (PMG)
American Institute for Conservation
1717 K Street, N.W., Suite 301
Washington, DC 20006

Mission. Established in 1979 to encourage and facilitate the exchange of ideas and information about photographic conservation; to promote and disseminate responsible information on the care of photographs and photographic conservation; to encourage and promote the development of sound conservation practices; to promote the publication of scholarly articles on photographic conservation and related topics; to develop closer ties with other related disciplines.

Membership is open to all members of the American Institute
for Conservation, but is intended for those whose major field of
interest is the conservation of photographs.
Publications. Topics in Photographic Preservation; an annual
collection of occasional papers.

AMERICAN LIBRARY ASSOCIATION (ALA)
50 East Huron Street
Chicago, IL 60611
800–545-2433

Mission. Established in 1876, the American Library Association
is the professional association for the library profession. Its
divisions, sections, round tables, and discussion groups are
formed and operate to meet the needs of the profession. Its
Preservation of Library Materials Section (PLMS), of the
Association for Library Collections and Technical Services
(ALCTS), was formed in 1980 to meet the specific needs of
librarians involved with the preservation of library materials.
PLMS has more than 1,400 members and sponsors workshops
and publications on all aspects of preservation. The Rare Books
and Manuscripts Section (RBMS), of the Association of College
and Research Libraries (ACRL), also has several committees
specifically concerned with preservation and conservation.
Publications. American Libraries, published eleven times a
year for the membership, carries news about preservation and
conservation. Division and Section journals, including *Rare
Books and Manuscripts Librarianship, College and Research
Libraries, College and Research Libraries News,* and *Library
Resources and Technical Services* frequently contain
substantive articles on preservation issues.

AMERICAN NATIONAL STANDARDS INSTITUTE (ANSI)
1430 Broadway
New York, NY 10018
212/354–3300

Mission. The American National Standards Institute is the
coordinating organization for the United States' federated
national standards system. It was established in 1918 as the
American Engineering Standards Committee, created by the
U.S. Chamber of Commerce to oversee the establishment of
voluntary standards to facilitate mass production in
manufacturing. After undergoing several changes, its present

name was adopted in 1969 and the ANSI prefix took effect on all of the organization's existing and new standards. Its function is to coordinate the voluntary development of national standards, establish a consensus on standards, and to provide effective representation of U.S. interests in international standardization. Trade, technical, professional, consumer, and labor organizations submit standards developed under their own procedures to ANSI, and those that meet national consensus receive the ANSI prefix.

Publications. ANSI Reporter, free to members and available by subscription. The Z-39 series, issued by the National Information Standards Organization (NISO), covers standards for library work, documentation, and publishing practices. The ANSI PH and MS series include standards relating to photoreproduction.

AMERICAN SOCIETY FOR TESTING AND MATERIALS
(ASTM)
1916 Race Street
Philadelphia, PA 19103
215/299–5400

Mission. Established in 1898, ASTM is the largest standards-developing organization in the United States.
Publications. ASTM *Standards* (annual); *Standardization News* (monthly); technical journals.

AMERICAN SOCIETY OF HEATING, REFRIGERATING AND
AIR-CONDITIONING ENGINEERS, INC. (ASHRAE)
1791 Tullie Circle, N.E.
Atlanta, GA 30329
404/636–8400

Mission. Established in 1894, the technical society of heating, ventilating, refrigeration, and air-conditioning engineers sponsors research programs with universities, research laboratories, and government agencies.
Publications. ASHRAE Transactions (semiannual); *ASHRAE Journal* (monthly); a monthly newsletter; annual handbook.

AMIGOS Bibliographic Council, Inc.
12200 Park Central Drive, Suite 500
Dallas, TX 75251
800/843–8482

Mission. The bibliographic utility for the Southwest, AMIGOS
has a strong preservation outreach program offering continuing
workshops and training.
Publication: Que Pasa?.

ASSOCIATION FOR INFORMATION AND IMAGE
MANAGEMENT (AIIM)
1100 Wayne Avenue
Silver Spring, MD 20910
301/587–8202

Mission. The Association for Information and Image
Management, formerly the National Microfilm Association
(NMA), which had its beginnings in 1943, is the trade
organization for the micrographics industry. It sponsors
conferences, expositions, meetings, and seminars and has been
instrumental in developing industry standards
Publications. AIIM's publications program plays a major role in
the continuing flow of information on new technology. It
publishes the *Journal of Micrographics,* which is issued six
times a year, and a newsletter for its membership,
Micrographics Today. Proceedings of its annual conference are
published in hard copy and microfiche editions. *Guide to
Micrographic Equipment,* an illustrated directory, is published
every three years. The *Buyer's Guide* is an annual listing of
products and services offered by AIIM trade members. Its
"Consumer Series Pamphlets" and "Reference Series"
publications have many titles of interest to librarians.

ASSOCIATION OF AMERICAN PUBLISHERS (AAP)
220 East 23rd Street
New York, NY 10010
212/689–8920

Mission. A trade association, established in 1970, representing
publishers of books, educational materials, globes, tests, and
software.
Publications. AAP Monthly Report; other informational
material for the trade.

ASSOCIATION OF CANADIAN ARCHIVISTS (ACA)
P.O. Box 2596, Station D
Ottawa, ON K1P 5W6, Canada
613/830–9663

Mission. Founded in 1975 to promote standards through exchange and dissemination of information.
Publications. Archivaria, a semiannual journal; *ACA Bulletin* (monthly); membership directories.

ASSOCIATION OF MOVING IMAGE ARCHIVISTS (AMIA)
National Center for Film and Video Preservation
The American Film Institute
P.O. Box 27999
2021 North Western Avenue
Los Angeles, CA 90027
213/856–7637

Mission. A professional organization, founded in 1992, to provide a means for cooperation among individuals concerned with the collection, preservation, exhibition, and use of moving image materials. Its objectives are to exchange information, promote archival activities and professional standards, facilitate research, and encourage public awareness of film and video preservation.
Publications. AMIA Newsletter (quarterly).

ASSOCIATION OF RECORDED SOUND COLLECTIONS (ARSC)
P.O. Box 10162
Silver Spring, MD 20904

Mission. Founded in 1966, ARSC is a nonprofit organization to foster the development of discographic information in all fields and periods of recording and in all sound media. It works to encourage the preservation of historical recordings; to promote the exchange and dissemination of research and information about the care and preservation of sound recordings; and to foster an increased awareness of the importance of recorded sound in our cultural heritage. Its grants program is designed to encourage and support scholarship and publication in any field of sound recording or audio preservation.
Publications. ARSC Journal (3/year); *ARSC Bulletin* (annual); *ARSC Newsletter* (quarterly); *Membership Directory,* (annual).

ASSOCIATION OF RECORDS MANAGERS AND ADMINISTRATORS (ARMA)
4200 Somerset Drive, Suite 215
Prairie Village, KS 66208–5287
913/341–3808

Mission. Established as an affiliate of ARMA International, the professional association for people working in records and information management. Offers networking and educational opportunities.
Publications. Technical publications created to help records managers improve procedures and meet the challenges of a rapidly changing profession.

ASSOCIATION OF RESEARCH LIBRARIES
21 Dupont Circle, N.W., Suite 800
Washington, DC 20036
202/232–2466

Mission. Established in 1932 to identify and solve problems fundamental to large research libraries so they can effectively serve the needs of students, faculty, and the research community; to ensure that the information needed by the research community will be available now and in the future. Its Preservation Committee has been instrumental in establishing the preservation agenda in United States libraries.
Publications. CPA Newsletter; statistical and other information; reports on preservation and collection management. The Office of Management Services (OMS) publishes SPEC Kits, a number of which provide information on policies and procedures for preservation management. OMS also developed a *Survey Program* and *Manual* that is a valuable tool for all types of libraries.

BIO-INTEGRAL RESOURCE CENTER (BIRC)
P.O. Box 7414
Berkeley, CA 94707
415/524–2567

Mission. A nonprofit center, formed in 1978, to provide practical information on least-toxic methods for managing pests.
Publications Common Sense Pest Control (quarterly); *The IPM Practitioner,* newsletter; and pamphlets on pest control management.

BRITISH LIBRARY NATIONAL PRESERVATION OFFICE
Great Russell Street
London WC1B 3DG
England, United Kingdom
071/636–1544

Mission. Created in 1984 to promote an awareness of preservation and conservation throughout the United Kingdom; to provide information and referral services on preservation issues; and to encourage cooperative initiatives.
Publications. *Library Conservation News* (quarterly); occasional publications and seminar papers; videos.

CAB INTERNATIONAL MYCOLOGICAL INSTITUTE (CMI)
Ferry Lane
Kew, Surrey TW9 3AF
England, United Kingdom
081/332–1171

Mission. Founded in 1920 as one of four scientific institutes of CAB International, focusing on the identification of fungi, biological attack by organisms, and the use of fungi in environmental monitoring.
Publications. *Biodeterioration,* the proceedings of the International Biodeterioration Symposiums; *Culture, Collection & Industrial Services Newsletter* (2–3 annually); *Biodeterioration Abstracts* (quarterly), and other scientific journals.

CANADIAN BOOKBINDERS AND BOOK ARTISTS GUILD (CBBAG)
Suite 220, Chalmers Building
35 McCaul Street
Toronto, Ontario
M5T 1V7, Canada
416/581–1071

Mission. Founded in 1983 to further the interest of Canadian bookbinders. Sponsors workshops and exhibitions.
Publications. *CBBAG Newsletter* (quarterly); list of supplies and suppliers, updated frequently; bibliographies and exhibition catalogs.

CANADIAN CONSERVATION INSTITUTE
1030 Innes Road
Ottawa, ON K1A 0M8, Canada
613/998–3721

Mission. Established to provide treatment, consultation, survey, and training services to publicly owned museums and art

galleries across Canada. Its Research Services Division is the
scientific arm of the Institute.
Publications. *CCI News* (quarterly); technical publications.

CANADIAN INSTITUTE FOR HISTORICAL
MICROREPRODUCTIONS
P.O. Box 2428
Station D/C.P., Terminal D
Ottawa, ON K1P 5WS, Canada

Mission. Founded in 1978 as an independent, nonprofit
organization to improve access to printed Canadiana already in
the country; to make Canadiana not in Canada available to
researchers; to make rare and scarce Canadiana more widely
available; to bring together fragmented collections of
Canadiana; and to ensure the preservation of Canadiana in
Canada and elsewhere.
Publications. *Canada: The Printed Record; A Bibliographic
Register with Indexes.* The Institute makes its cataloging
available in the CAN-MARC format.

CANADIAN LIBRARY ASSOCIATION (CLA)
200 Elgin Street, Suite 602
Ottawa, ON K2P 1L5, Canada
613/232–9625

Mission. A professional organization for individuals and
institutions dedicated to the development and maintenance of
standards in library and information science; promotes the
exchange of information.
Publications. *Feliciter,* a monthly newsletter; professional
monographs.

CENTER FOR SAFETY IN THE ARTS
5 Beekman Street
New York, NY 10038
212/227–6220

Mission. Established in 1977, seeks to gather and disseminate
information about health hazards encountered by artists,
craftspeople, teachers, and others working with art materials;
provides on-site assessment of the health and safety features of
facilities used by artists, craftspeople, and students; responds to
inquiries concerning art-related hazards. Operates the Art
Hazards Information Center, a project engaged in research and

education on health hazards of chemicals found in arts and crafts materials; provides written and telephone reference service; offers lectures and workshops. Operates a small reference library.
Publications. *Art Hazards News* (10/year); newsletter; Art Hazards Information Center *Newsletter* (13/year); articles and data sheets on hazards and precautions.

COMMISSION ON PRESERVATION AND ACCESS
1400 16th Street, N.W., Suite 740
Washington, DC 20036-2217
202/939-3400

Mission. Created as a nonprofit corporation on July 1, 1988, based on the recommendation of the Committee on Preservation and Access, sponsored by the Council on Library Resources. The main goal of the commission is to foster, develop, and support systematic and purposeful collaboration in order to ensure the preservation of the written record in all formats and to provide equitable access to that information. It serves as a central, catalytic agency to address the entire range of problems related to the preservation and access of our documentary heritage.
Publications. In addition to a newsletter reporting on national preservation program activities and the commission's work, the commission also regularly publishes background papers and reports.

CONSERVATION CENTER FOR ART AND HISTORIC ARTIFACTS (CCAHA)
264 South 23rd Street
Philadelphia, PA 19102
215/545-0613

Mission. Founded in 1977 as a regional conservation center serving nonprofit cultural, educational, and research institutions as well as private individuals and organizations. It specializes in the treatment of art and artifacts on paper, rare books, photographs, and library and archival materials. CCAHA offers consultation services; emergency assistance; educational programs; and offers apprenticeships, internships, and fellowships in conservation.
Publications. Occasional *Newsletter;* brochures.

Appendix A

COUNCIL ON LIBRARY RESOURCES, INC. (CLR)
1400 16th Street, N.W., Suite 510
Washington, DC 20036–2217
202/483–7474

Mission. Established in 1955 with a grant from the Ford
Foundation to support research and development of techniques
and mechanisms that will help solve the acute problems of
libraries. Among its early concerns was the systematic
investigation into the causes of paper deterioration. The
investigations of the council led to the establishment of the
Commission on Preservation and Access in 1988.
Publications. A newsletter (irregular); annual report; occasional
publications and proceedings.

DESIGNER BOOKBINDERS
6 Queen Square
London WC1N 3AR
England, United Kingdom

Mission. Founded in 1955 as the Guild of Contemporary
Bookbinders; reorganized under its present name in 1968. It is
devoted to the preservation and improvement of the design and
craft of fine bookbinding; arranges exhibitions, sponsors an
annual competition, and organizes classes and seminars on
aspects of design and craftsmanship of fine binding, restoration,
and conservation.
Publications. The New Bookbinder, an annual journal;
members' *Newsletter;* directories of supplies and suppliers.

EASTMAN KODAK COMPANY
343 State Street
Rochester, NY 14650
716/325–2000

Mission. The Eastman Kodak Company, founded by George
Eastman in 1880, is an international corporation engaged in the
manufacture and sale of photographic and optical materials,
apparatus, and equipment. Its research and development staff
play an important role in the development of photography as a
medium for preservation and in the preservation of
photographic materials.
Publications. Eastman Kodak publishes a significant list of
books on photography and the care of photographs as well as

pamphlets on all aspects of photography. Their publication lists, information, and pamphlets can be obtained from their Consumer Markets Division, Photo Information.

EPHEMERA SOCIETY (EPHSOC)
12 Fitzroy Square
London W1P 5HQ
England, United Kingdom
071/387–7723

Mission. Established in 1975 as an international body concerned with the preservation, study, and presentation of printed and handwritten ephemera. There are societies in Australia, Canada, and the United States, brought together in the International Ephemera Council, based in London.
Publications. The *Ephemerist* (quarterly); books on printed ephemera.

FIRE PROTECTION ASSOCIATION
Aldermary House
Queen Street
London EC4N 1TJ
England, United Kingdom
071/248–5222

Mission. A central advisory organization, financed by insurance companies and Lloyds, providing technical and general advice on all aspects of fire protection.
Publications. The Association publishes extensively and its list of publications, *Fire Booklist,* is available upon request. It also publishes two journals, *Fire Prevention* and *Fire Prevention Science and Technology.*

GETTY CONSERVATION INSTITUTE (GCI)
4503 Glencoe Avenue
Marina del Rey, CA 90292–6537
213/822–2299

Mission. The Getty Conservation Institute, an operating program of the J. Paul Getty Trust, was created in 1982 to enhance the quality of conservation practice in the world today. Through a combination of in-house activities and collaborative ventures with other organizations, the institute plays a catalytic role that contributes substantially to the conservation of the cultural heritage. Its Scientific Research Program conducts basic and applied research activities to benefit the entire conservation field. The Training Program sponsors practical and theoretical training activities and professional seminars. The Documentation Program facilitates the exchange of information. Special projects and publications are undertaken as needed by the field.

Publications. Conservation, the GCI Newsletter; *Art and Archaeology Technical Abstracts;* occasional technical reports.

GUILD OF BOOK WORKERS
521 Fifth Avenue
New York, NY 10175

Mission. The Guild is a national, nonprofit organization founded in 1960 to foster the practice of book arts: binding, calligraphy, illumination, and paper decorating, and to establish and maintain a feeling of kinship and mutual interest among book workers. It provides information and an exchange of ideas to its members and to the public through its publications and by sponsoring seminars, lectures, and exhibitions.

Publications. Opportunities for Study in Hand Bookbinding and Calligraphy, updated frequently. The Guild of Book Workers *Journal* (3/year), available to institutions on a subscription basis; *Newsletter* (6/year); occasional exhibition catalogs, supply directories, and membership directories.

IMAGE PERMANENCE INSTITUTE (IPI)
Rochester Institute of Technology
70 Lomb Memorial Drive
Rochester, NY 14623-5604
716/475-5199

Mission. Founded in 1985 as a nonprofit academic institute whose main purpose is research in the stability and preservation of imaging materials. Its principle sponsor is the Society for Imaging Science and Technology (SIST). Its board includes photographic manufacturers, museums, federal agencies, archival suppliers, and micropublishers.

Publications. Its staff publishes technical reports and articles in conservation, imaging, and micrographics journals, but does not currently have a newsletter.

INSTITUTE OF PAPER CONSERVATION (IPC)
Leigh Lodge
Leigh, Worcester WR6 5LB
England, United Kingdom

Mission. Established in December 1977 as a specialist
organization concerned with the conservation of paper and
related materials. Its purpose is to increase professional
awareness of the contemporary conservation situation by
coordinating the exchange of information and facilitating
contacts between its members, both nationally and
internationally. It is administered by an executive committee of
practicing conservators elected from the membership together
with technical, scientific, and curatorial advisors.
Publications. *The Paper Conservator,* the journal of the Institute
(annual); a newsletter, *Paper Conservation News* (3/year).

INSTITUTE OF PAPER SCIENCE AND TECHNOLOGY (IPST)
Georgia Institute of Technology
575 14th Street, N.W.
Atlanta, GA 30318
404/853–9500

Mission. Originally Institute of Paper Chemistry, IPST was
founded in 1929 as a tax-exempt educational institution whose
members are companies with paper, paperboard, or pulp
production in the United States. The purpose of this Institute is
to serve the industry in education, research, and information. It
is a center for graduate education in the physical sciences with
programs leading to the M.S. and Ph.D. degrees. The research
program undertakes projects funded by the membership and
contracts research for individual companies, groups, and
organizations. The institute is the technical and scientific
repository for the paper industry.
Publications. *Abstract Bulletin,* the organ for the dissemination
of current information throughout the industry; annotated
bibliographies relating to the technical aspects of the paper
industry.

INTERNATIONAL ASSOCIATION FOR CONSERVATION OF
BOOKS, PAPER AND ARCHIVAL MATERIALS (IADA)/
International Arbeitsgemeinschaft der Archiv-, Bibliotheks-,
und Graphik Restoratoren
Wehrdaerstrasse 135
D-3550 Marburg, Germany

Mission. Established in 1957 to address the professional concerns of those working in the field of document conservation. It organizes courses and exchanges.
Publications. Maltechnic Restauro (quarterly), in English and German; the proceedings of its meetings.

INTERNATIONAL ASSOCIATION OF MUSEUM FACILITY ADMINISTRATORS
(IAMFA)
P.O. Box 1505
Washington, DC 20013–1505
202/842–6158

Mission. An international organization, established in 1990, to serve the needs of museum facility administrators in their efforts to reach and set standards of excellence and quality in planning, development, design, construction, operation, and maintenance of world-class museum facilities in all countries around the world. IAMFA meets annually to conduct seminars and meetings on topics of concern to its membership.
Publications. Papyrus, the IAMFA newsletter.

INTERNATIONAL ASSOCIATION OF SOUND ARCHIVES
(IASA)
Media Library
Open University Library
Milton Keynes
Bucks. MK7 6AA
England, United Kingdom

Mission. Founded in 1969, an association of organizations and individuals with an interest in sound archives and institutions that preserve sound recordings. It seeks to facilitate international cooperation among members representing all recorded sound archives and maintains several working groups.
Publications. Phonographic Bulletin (3/year); *Directory* of its membership; technical manuals.

INTERNATIONAL CENTRE FOR THE STUDY OF THE PRESERVATION AND THE RESTORATION OF CULTURAL PROPERTY (ICCROM)
13 via di San Michele
1–00153 Rome, Italy

Mission. Founded in 1959, ICCROM promotes the preservation, restoration, and preventive conservation of cultural property,

including library and archival materials. It collects, examines, and disseminates documentation concerning the scientific and technical problems of preserving cultural property and conducts courses for conservators in a variety of fields.
Publications. Annual newsletter, library acquisitions lists and subject indexes, proceedings of its conferences and seminars, and *The International Index on Training in Conservation of Cultural Property,* issued every few years.

INTERNATIONAL COUNCIL OF ARCHIVES (ICA)
60 rue des Francs-Bourgois
F-75003 Paris, France

Mission. Established in 1948 under the auspices of UNESCO as a federation of national and international archival associations, central archival administrations, archival institutions, and individuals in 121 countries to encourage the preservation of archives and to advance their administration. It has an active Preservation Committee.
Publications. ARCHIVUM (annual); *ICA Bulletin* (semiannual); annual directory.

INTERNATIONAL COUNCIL OF MUSEUMS (ICOM)
Maison de l'Unesco
1 rue Miollis
75732 Paris Cedex 15, France

Mission. A professional organization founded in 1946 dedicated to the improvement and advancement of the world's museums. Its committees coordinate a vast international effort aimed at continuing improvement of museums in their scientific, educational and conservation roles. ICOM acts as a nongovernmental professional adviser to UNESCO, providing services and technical assistance. Its Conservation Committee holds triennial conferences; Working Groups on library and archival preservation.
Publications. Conference proceedings, periodicals, and monographs on museum-related subjects.

INTERNATIONAL FEDERATION OF DOCUMENTATION (FID)
P.O. Box 90402
2509 LK The Hague, Netherlands

Mission. Established to promote, through international cooperation, studies and research as well as the organization and practice of information science in all fields. FID provides a world forum for the exchange of ideas and experiences and the opportunity for interested organizations and individuals to coordinate their efforts.

Publications. R & D Projects in Documentation (bimonthly); *International Forum on Information and Documentation* (quarterly); *FID News Bulletin* (monthly).

INTERNATIONAL FEDERATION OF FILM ARCHIVES (FIAF)
70 rue de Coudenberg
B-1000 Brussels, Belgium

Mission. Founded in 1938, a federation of national, regional, and local film libraries and museums. It seeks to preserve the artistic and historic heritage of the cinema.
Publications. Books on the preservation of film and on the management of film archives.

INTERNATIONAL FEDERATION OF LIBRARY
ASSOCIATIONS AND INSTITUTIONS (IFLA)
CONSERVATION SECTION
CORE PROGRAMME ON PRESERVATION AND
CONSERVATION (PAC)
Secretariat
Bibliothèque Nationale Paris
2 Rue Vivienne
75084 Paris Cedex 02, France

Mission. IFLA is concerned with promoting librarianship around the world and assisting countries in learning how to deal with their problems. Although IFLA had an active Conservation Section for many years, the importance of conservation was recognized in 1986 when a Core Programme on Preservation and Conservation was launched. Its Secretariat is located at the Bibliothèque Nationale, Paris, with regional centers in Australia, France, Germany, Japan, and Venezuela. The PAC Programme and Conservation Section work closely together to promote preservation awareness around the world, to help in education and training, and to serve as a source of information and advice.
Publications. The Core Programme publishes a newsletter, *International Preservation News,* and has issued a number of publications through IFLA, including the document, *Principles of Conservation* (1986). Proceedings of conferences are published through K. G. Saur, IFLA's publisher.

INTERNATIONAL FEDERATION OF TELEVISION ARCHIVES
(IFTA)
Centro Documentation RTVE
Aportado 150.135
E-28080 Madrid, Spain

Mission. An organization of archive directors and television
organizations responsible for the preservation and management
of documents broadcast on television. Founded in 1977, its
aims are to promote the improvement and compatibility of
documentation relative to audiovisual materials and to
document exchanges; to preserve collections; to study
conservation techniques and materials; to study all questions
relating to television archives and evaluate the best use of their
holdings. It has a Preservation Commission.
Publications. Newsletter.

INTERNATIONAL INSTITUTE FOR CONSERVATION OF
HISTORIC AND ARTISTIC WORKS (IIC)
6 Buckingham Street
London WC2N 6BA
England, United Kingdom

Mission. An organization of professional conservators and
those concerned with the structure, composition, deterioration,
and conservation of objects, founded in 1950; concerned with
the whole field of inanimate objects considered worthy of
preservation, whether in museums and libraries, or exposed
externally. Members are able to keep abreast of technical
advances through publications, congresses, and participation in
regional groups.
Publications. Studies in Conservation, the journal of the IIC,
(quarterly), available by subscription; *IIC Newsletter*
(quarterly); proceedings from its congresses; monographs in
cooperation with commercial publishers.

INTERNATIONAL INSTITUTE FOR CONSERVATION OF
HISTORIC AND ARTISTIC WORKS—CANADIAN GROUP
(IIC-CG)
P.O. Box 9195
Ottawa, ON K1G 3T9, Canada

Mission. Established in the 1970s and incorporated in 1989 for the dissemination of knowledge concerning the conservation of Canada's cultural property. Its membership is open to all individuals and institutions with interest in the conservation of cultural property.

Publications. Journal of the International Institute for Conservation—Canadian Group (JIIC-CG) (annual); *IIC-CG Bulletin* (quarterly); conference proceedings; *Code of Ethics and Guidance for Practice for Those Involved in the Conservation of Cultural Property,* in association with the Canadian Association of Professional Conservators.

INTERNATIONAL MUSEUM OF PHOTOGRAPHY AT GEORGE EASTMAN HOUSE (IMP/GEH)
900 East Avenue
Rochester, NY 14607
716/271–3361

History. The International Museum of Photography was established in 1949 to present to the public information and artifacts on the history and aesthetics of photography, the development of the motion picture, and the development of the camera. The museum makes extensive loans and sponsors traveling exhibitions.

Publications. Image, a quarterly journal covering all aspects of photography, available by subscription, or can be purchased separately. The Museum also publishes monographs on photographers and photography.

INTERNATIONAL ORGANIZATION FOR STANDARDIZATION (ISO)
Case postale 56
CH-1211 Geneva 20, Switzerland

Mission. A specialized international agency that coordinates the work of national standards bodies from throughout the world; The American National Standards Institute (ANSI) is the United States representative. ISO conducts its work through technical committees that focus on specific technologies, materials, or methods.

Publications. Composite handbooks that provide texts of standards on specific topics; i.e., *Handbook 23: Paper, Board and Pulps* (1984).

INTERNATIONAL SOCIETY FOR OPTICAL ENGINEERING
(SPIE)
P.O. Box 10, 1000 20th Street
Bellingham, WA 98227–0010
206/676–3290

Mission. A technical society established in 1955, dedicated to
advancing engineering and scientific applications of optical,
electro-optical, and photoelectronic instrumentation systems
and technology.
Publications. Optical Engineering (monthly); *Optical
Engineering Reports* (monthly); proceedings of conferences.

LEAGUE OF EUROPEAN RESEARCH LIBRARIES/LIGUE DES
BIBLIOTHEQUES EUROPEENNES DE RECHERCHE (LIBER)
c/o Hans-Albrecht Koch
Staats-u. Universitetsbibliothek
Bibliothekstrasse, Postfach 330160
D-2800 Bremen 33, Germany

Mission. Established in 1971 under the auspices of the Council
of Europe, its membership includes European universities,
national and special libraries from 25 countries. Its mission is to
foster ties between libraries and collaboration between national
and university libraries. It seeks ways to improve library service
through expert consulting and surveys.
Publications. LIBER Bulletin (3/year); *LIBER News Sheet;* a
directory of library bibliographic networks in Europe.

LEATHER CONSERVATION CENTRE
34 Guildhall Road
Northampton NN1 1EW
England, United Kingdom

Mission. A nonprofit organization established in 1978 to
provide research, practical conservation, information, and
training in leather conservation. It undertakes research into
leather deterioration; develops conservation techniques to treat
specific problems; evaluates materials used in conservation.
Publications. Several important studies on leathers and their
conservation.

LIBRARY BINDING INSTITUTE (LBI)
7401 Metro Blvd., Suite 325
Edina, MN 55439
612/835–4707

Mission. Established in 1935, it is the national association of library binders. It serves as the source of information and assistance to binders and librarians on problems relating to the preservation of library materials. It sponsors workshops with the American Library Association and regional organizations on commercial library binding.

Publications. The New Library Scene (bimonthly); *Standard for Library Binding,* revised periodically.

LIBRARY BINDING INSTITUTE BOOK TESTING
LABORATORY
Graphic Arts Research Center
Rochester Institute of Technology
One Lomb Memorial Drive
Rochester, NY 14623
716/475–2698

Mission. A nonprofit laboratory established for the purpose of studying the physical characteristics of books, principally library volumes. It is owned and administered by the Graphic Arts Research Center, Rochester Institute of Technology, and has several functions: to investigate the physical characteristics of books, problems of wear, longevity, etc.; to evaluate new materials and methods available from commercial suppliers; to sponsor workshops for binders, publishers, and librarians; to serve as a resource center for materials relating to binding.

LIBRARY OF CONGRESS
Preservation Directorate
110 First Street, S.E.
Washington, DC 20540
202/707–5213
202/707–1840 (National Preservation Program Office)

Mission. The Library of Congress Preservation Office began developing its present organization in 1967 and now consists of six offices, including Binding, Collections Maintenance, Preservation Microfilming, Research and Testing, Conservation, and the National Preservation Program Office. The Preservation Directorate is responsible for directing and coordinating activities throughout the library relating to the preservation, protection, maintenance, and conservation of all library materials. In addition, it is responsible for review and coordination of programs for the protection of the Library's collections and for development of plans for a national preservation program, centered at the Library of Congress, to include determination of policies, management needs, and technical requirements. The National Preservation Program Office (NPPO) provides brief responses to inquiries on technical and management matters related to preservation. *Publications.* Occasional publications on preservation and conservation. The National Preservation Program Office occasionally publishes *National Preservation News.* The *LC Information Bulletin* frequently carries news and information about the Preservation Directorate and its activities.

NATIONAL ARCHIVES AND RECORDS ADMINISTRATION (NARA)
Washington, DC 20408

Mission. A governmental agency established to identify and make available federal government documents of historic value; to administrate a network of regional storage centers and archives. Its Preservation Policy and Service division is responsible for conserving textual and nontextual records in the archives, including video, sound recordings, motion pictures, still photographs; conducts research and testing for materials purchased by and used in the archives. The Advisory Committee on Preservation advises the Archivist of the United States on preservation technology and research relating to the preservation and access to the records of the United States. *Publications.* Technical reports; bibliographies.

NATIONAL ASSOCIATION OF GOVERNMENT ARCHIVISTS AND RECORDS ADMINISTRATORS (NAGARA)
New York State Archives, Rm. 10A75
Cultural Education Center
Albany, NY 12230
518/473–8037

Mission. NAGARA is a national organization of local, state, and federal records administrators and others interested in improved administration of government records. It is an adjunct member of the Council of State Governments. The association has been active in preservation concerns since 1984 when it conducted a nationwide study of preservation needs in the 50 state archives. NAGARA has developed and field-tested an archives preservation survey process (GRASP) that features use of artificial intelligence and a software package that helps an archival institution plan its preservation survey.

Publications. Preservation Needs in State Archives, 1986; reprinted 1988; *We Are Losing Our Past* (brochure); NAGARA GRASP *Guide and Resources for Archival Strategic Preservation Planning,* Dec. 1990.

NATIONAL CENTER FOR FILM AND VIDEO PRESERVATION
P.O. Box 27999
2021 North Western Avenue
Los Angeles, CA 90027
213/856–7636

John F. Kennedy Center for the Performing Arts
Washington, DC 20566
202/828–4070

Mission. Created by the American Film Institute in 1984, the Center works with film studios, television networks, and independent producers and collectors to preserve the nation's film and television heritage. It serves as the central office for establishing and implementing American moving image preservation policies on a national scale.
Publications. AFI Catalog of Feature Films, a documentation project providing comprehensive information on American films by decade; *Moving Image Materials: Genre Terms.*

NATIONAL CENTRE FOR INFORMATION MEDIA AND TECHNOLOGY (CIMTECH)
University of Hertfordshire
College Lane
Hatfield, Herts. AL10 9AB
England, United Kingdom
072/72–79691

Mission. CIMTECH was established in 1967 as the National Reprographic Centre for Documentation (NRCd). It is the national information and advisory center for impartial information about newer technologies and methods for originating, distributing, storing, and retrieving information. It serves more than 900 subscribing organizations from information service organizations and industry.
Publications. Information Media & Technology, a bi-monthly journal, and special reports.

NATIONAL COMMISSION ON LIBRARIES AND
INFORMATION SCIENCE (NCLIS)
1111 18th Street, N.W., Suite 310
Washington, DC 20036
202/254–3100

Mission. Established in 1971, NCLIS was created by an act of
Congress to work with federal, state, and local governments and
agencies, libraries, citizens' organizations, and the private
sector to improve library and information services for all
citizens.
Publications. Annual reports and commissioned studies on
library and information science issues.

NATIONAL ENDOWMENT FOR THE HUMANITIES (NEH)
Division of Preservation and Access
1100 Pennsylvania Avenue
Washington, DC 20506
202/786–0438

Mission. A separate Office of Preservation was established in
1985 to help address the needs of the nation's libraries and
archives. It was designated the Division of Preservation and
Access in 1991 to provide support for projects that will preserve
and provide intellectual access to collections that are important
for research, education, and public programming in the
humanities.
Publications. NEH Overview; guidelines for grants.

NATIONAL FIRE PROTECTION ASSOCIATION (NFPA)
Batterymarch Park
Quincy, MA 02269
617/482–8755 or 800/344–3555

Mission. Founded in 1896, today it is a nonprofit, voluntary
membership organization and an independent source of
information on all phases of fire prevention, fire protection, and
fire fighting; administers an extensive consensus system for
developing standards and publishes the National Fire Codes; and
conducts a national public education program on fire safety.
Publications. The NFPA publishes four journals: *Fire Command,
Fire Technology, Fire News,* and *Fire Journal;* the latter two are
available to members only. Various sections of the NFPA have
their own newsletters. Its list of publications is extensive; it
issues an annual catalogue of publications.

NATIONAL HISTORIC PUBLICATIONS AND RECORDS
COMMISSION (NHPRC)
National Archives Building
Washington, DC 20408
202/724–1083

History. The commission encourages collecting and making
available for use records that further an understanding and
appreciation of American history. Its mission is to further the
editing and publishing of the papers of outstanding Americans
and other documents important for the study of American
history. The commission operates primarily through its
Historical Documents and Historical Records Programs.
Publications. Information about its programs and guidelines for
application, plus a newsletter, *Annotation.*

NATIONAL INFORMATION STANDARDS ORGANIZATION
(NISO)—Z39
National Institute of Standards and Technology
Administration 101, Room E-106
Gaithersburg, MD 20899
301/975–2814

Mission. NISO was established in 1939 by the American
Standards Association (precursor to the American National
Standards Institute), and took its present name in 1984. It is a
nonprofit association, supported by its membership: libraries,
information services, publishers, and abstracting and indexing
services. It develops technical standards used in a wide range of
information services and products.
Publications. Information Standards Quarterly; NISO standards.

NATIONAL INSTITUTE FOR CONSERVATION (NIC)
The Papermill, Suite 403
3299 K Street, N.W.
Washington, DC 20007
202/625–1495

Mission. The National Institute for Conservation, formerly the
National Conservation Advisory Council, grew out of a
conference held in 1973 to review needs in training for the
conservation of cultural property. Funds to establish an
advisory council were provided by the National Museum Act,
and the council held its first meeting in November 1973. The
purpose of the organization is to identify and to offer

recommendations for the solution of conservation problems. It serves as a national forum for cooperation and planning among institutions and programs concerned with the conservation of cultural property in museums, historic properties, libraries, archives, and related institutions in the United States.
Publications. NIC has issued a number of documents and reports from its committees, which are available from its headquarters.

NATIONAL INSTITUTE OF STANDARDS AND
TECHNOLOGY (NIST)
Gaithersburg, MD 20899
301/975–2000

Mission. The National Bureau of Standards (NBS) was established by Act of Congress in 1901. Its name was changed in 1988 to reflect the bureau's increased scope. It provides the basis for the nation's measurement standards. Its goal is to strengthen and advance the nation's science and technology and facilitate their effective application for public benefit. Among its concerns are energy conservation, fire prevention, and consumer product safety.
Publications. NIST Standards and reports are available from the National Technical Information Service (NTIS), U.S. Department of Commerce, Springfield, VA 22161.

NORTHEAST DOCUMENT CONSERVATION CENTER
(NEDCC)
100 Brickstone Square
Andover, MA 01810
508/470–1010

Mission. Under the aegis of the New England Library Board, the center began operation as the New England Document Conservation Center in 1973. In 1981, New York and New Jersey became associate members of the center, which changed its name to reflect its expanded region. Today NEDCC serves libraries, archives, museums, and historical societies throughout the east. Its nonprofit conservation laboratory is equipped and staffed to treat documentary materials of historical, archival, or artistic value. NEDCC also offers field services, including surveys of institutional needs, seminars, and workshops; it assists in the salvage and recovery of materials in the event of disaster.
Publications. NEDCC Newsletter for its members and clients.

PRESERVATION RESOURCES, INC.
9 South Commerce Way
Bethlehem, PA 18017
215/758–8700

Mission. Established in 1981 with support from the Council on Library Resources and the Exxon Foundation, Preservation Resources, Inc. is a nonprofit organization dedicated to preserving endangered library and archival materials via preservation microfilming. Today Preservation Resources, Inc. operates under the direction of the OCLC (Online Computer Library Center, Inc.), in a facility specifically designed for preservation microfilming.

PROFESSIONAL PICTURE FRAMERS ASSOCIATION (PPFA)
P.O. Box 7655, 4305 Sarellen Road
Richmond, VA 23231
804/226–0430

Mission. Established in 1971 for individuals, firms, or corporations engaged in picture framing and fine arts businesses, to provide guidance and service in developing quality craftsmanship in the arts of picture framing. Researches and disseminates information concerning technical and service problems.
Publications. Artframe Today (8/year); directory.

RESEARCH LIBRARIES GROUP, INC.
1200 Villa Street
Mountain View, CA 94041
415/962–9951

Mission. Founded in 1974, RLG is a nonprofit corporation owned and operated by the nation's leading research libraries and institutions; it also serves programmatic members who participate in one or more of its programs to support collections. RLG is dedicated to improving the management of information resources necessary for the advancement of scholarship. Its Preservation Program has been instrumental in defining and developing guidelines for preservation microfilming and coordinating a major preservation microfilming effort to preserve research collections.
Publications. RLIN Register of Microform Masters, updated periodically; *RGL Handbook on Preservation Microfilming,* 1991; newsletter; miscellaneous publications.

ROYAL PHOTOGRAPHIC SOCIETY
The Octagon
Milsom Street
Bath, Avon BA1 1DN
England, United Kingdom

Mission. A learned society, founded in 1853 to promote
photography in all its aspects by sponsoring conferences and
exhibitions, by presenting the interests of photographers
whenever possible, and by its publications.
Publications. The Photographic Journal (monthly);
Photographic Abstracts; Journal of Photographic Science,
devoted to scientific and technical matters; monographs on
photography and the care of photographic materials.

SMITHSONIAN INSTITUTION
Conservation Analytical Laboratory
Museum Support Center D-2002
Washington, DC 20560
301/238–3700

Mission. Conducts technical and scientific research on museum
objects and related materials aimed at better preservation of
collections and a fuller understanding of their historical
context. Its training program offers educational opportunities
for students in conservation, materials science, archaeology, or
art history. It also sponsors an annual series of short training
courses for library and museum personnel.
Publications. Approaches to Pest Management in Museums
(1985).

SOCIETY FOR IMAGING SCIENCE AND TECHNOLOGY
(SIST)
7003 Kilworth Lane
Springfield, VA 22151
703/642–9090

Mission. Established in 1947 for individuals who apply
photography to science, engineering, and industry.
Publications. Journal of Imaging Science (bimonthly); *Journal
of Imaging Technology* (bimonthly); *Handbook of Photographic
Science and Engineering.*

SOCIETY OF AMERICAN ARCHIVISTS (SAA)
600 South Federal Street, Suite 504
Chicago, IL 60605
312/922–0140

History. Founded in 1936, a professional association of individuals and institutions interested in the preservation and use of archives, manuscripts, and current records, as well as machine-readable records, sound recordings, pictures, films, and maps. The society, with an international membership, serves the archival profession through its publications program, annual meetings, continuing education workshops and seminars, and information referral.
Publications. American Archivist (quarterly); *SAA Newsletter* (6/year). Its Sections also issue newsletters. SAA has a vigorous publications program designed to meet the needs of the profession.

SOCIETY OF LEATHER TECHNOLOGISTS AND CHEMISTS, LTD. (SLTC)
1 Edges Court
Moulton, Northampton NN3 1UJ
England, United Kingdom

Mission. Established in 1897 to hold meetings and publish journals on all aspects of leather science and technology.
Publications. Journal (6/year); *Official Methods of Testing and Analysis for Leather.*

SOCIETY OF MOTION PICTURE AND TELEVISION ENGINEERS (SMPTE)
595 West Hartsdale Avenue
White Plains, NY 10607
914/761–1100

Mission. Established in 1916; a professional society of engineers and technicians in motion pictures, television, and allied arts and sciences; develops standards for motion pictures, television, and optical and magnetic recording, and sponsors ANSI standards.
Publications. SMPTE Journal (monthly); newsletter; lists of technical terms; bibliographies, annual directory.

SOUTHEAST REGIONAL LIBRARY NETWORK (SOLINET)
PRESERVATION PROGRAM
1438 West Peachtree Street, N.W.
Suite 200
Atlanta, GA 30309-2955
404/892–0943, 800/999–8558

Mission. SOLINET was established in 1973 as a regional
nonprofit agency to coordinate resource-sharing activities
among libraries. Its Preservation Program was created in 1985 to
promote preservation awareness among its members; to inform,
educate, and train staff members; to promote and assist in the
development of local preservation programs; to encourage
support of cooperative preservation projects; and to participate
on regional and national levels.
Publications. The Preservation Program regularly publishes
pamphlets and brochures on preservation topics.

TECHNICAL ASSOCIATION OF THE PULP AND PAPER
INDUSTRY (TAPPI)
Technology Park, P.O. Box 105113
Atlanta, GA 30092
404/446–1400

Mission. Established in 1915 to stimulate interest in the science
of pulp and papermaking; to provide means for the interchange
of ideas among members; and to encourage original
investigation in the pulp and paper industry. Its fundamental
purpose today is to collect and disseminate technical
information for the industry.
Publications. TAPPI Journal (monthly); *TAPPI Testing
Methods,* 2 vols.; monographic works of a technical nature.

TECHNOLOGY ORGANIZATION, INC.
One Emerson Place
Boston, MA 02114
617/227–8581

History. Founded in the late 1970s by Susan Schur to provide
information and hold seminars on technical aspects of
conservation and preservation.
Publications. Technology and Conservation (irregular).

UNDERWRITERS LABORATORIES (UL)
333 Pfingsten Road
Northbrook, IL 60062
708/272–8800

Mission. Established in 1894, a nonprofit organization that
evaluates the safety of a wide variety of products; establishes
and operates product safety certification programs. Includes
departments of fire protection and heating, air-conditioning
and refrigeration.
Publications. Catalog of Standards for Safety (semiannual);
product directories.

UNITED NATIONS EDUCATIONAL, SCIENTIFIC AND
CULTURAL ORGANIZATION (UNESCO)
Maison de l'Unesco
7 Place du Fontenoy
75007 Paris, France

History. Established in 1946 "to contribute to the peace and
security in the world by promoting collaboration among
nations." Its projects and programs are intended to generate
self-reliance in developing countries. One of its priorities is to
protect and preserve mankind's cultural heritage and to instill
in member nations a sense of cultural and historic identity. It
conducts programs to study and preserve cultural monuments
of archaeological and artistic importance.
Publications. Museum, a quarterly publication; reference
books, bibliographies, and a series of RAMP studies, several of
which deal with the preservation and conservation of library
and archival materials.

UNIVERSITY OF MANCHESTER INSTITUTE OF SCIENCE
AND TECHNOLOGY (UMIST)
P.O. Box 88
Sackville Street
Manchester M60 1QD
England, United Kingdom
061/236–3311

Mission. The Paper Science Research Group in the Department
of Paper Science was set up in 1984. It carries out research
on various aspects of paper conservation and the degradation

and permanence of paper. Provides technical advice on a cost basis.
Publications. Papers and articles.

VISUAL RESOURCES ASSOCIATION
Christine Hilker, Treasurer
School of Architecture
209 Vol Walker
University of Arkansas
Fayetteville, AR 72701

Mission. Established in 1982 to provide a continuing forum for communication and to further research and education in the field of visual documentation.
Publications. Visual Resources: An International Journal of Documentation; VRA Bulletin; monographs and special bulletins on various aspects of visual resources administration and image retrieval.

Appendix B:

Selective List of Periodical Publications

Not all of the publications listed below have been written for librarians or archivists, but each frequently contains information that is of considerable interest to professionals who are responsible for planning and overseeing a preservation program in a library or archive.

The Abbey Newsletter
Ellen McCrady, Editor
Abbey Publications, Inc.
7105 Geneva Drive
Austin, TX 78723

1, 1975; 5–6/year.
A general newsletter edited by a librarian, binder, and preservation specialist.

Alkaline Paper Advocate
Ellen McCrady, Editor
Abbey Publications, Inc.
7185 Geneva Drive
Austin, TX 78723

1, 1988; 6/year.
A newsletter for paper manufacturers and advocates of permanent and durable alkaline paper.

American Institute for Conservation of Historic and Artistic Works. *Journal.*
American Institute for Conservation
1717 K Street, N.W., Suite 301
Washington, DC 20006

1, 1960; semiannual.
Publishes research in all areas of conservation, with frequent articles on paper and photographic materials.

ARSC Journal
Association of Recorded Sound Collections
P.O. Box 10162
Silver Spring, MD 20904

1, 1968; semiannual.
Papers on all aspects of recorded sound, including
preservation.

Art and Archaeology Technical Abstracts (AATA)
Getty Conservation Institute
4503B Glencoe Avenue
Marina del Rey, CA 90292–6537

1, 1955; semiannual.
A comprehensive, analytical bibliography of the literature on
conservation technology, including bibliographies on special
subjects. Originally sponsored by the International Institute for
Conservation of Artistic and Historic Works and known as *IIC
Abstracts,* these abstracts are now available through the
Conservation Information Network, an on-line data base, as
well as in the hardcopy edition.

BiN: Bibliography Newsletter
Walrus Press
32 Trimountain Avenue, P.O. Box 280
South Range, MI 49963

1, 1973; irregular.
News of the rare book world with information on the
preservation of rare books.

Book and Paper Annual
American Institute for Conservation
1400 16th Street, N.W., Suite 340
Washington, DC 20036

1, 1984; annual.
Papers from the Book and Paper Group meeting and other
contributions from members to share information.

CBBAG Newsletter
Canadian Bookbinders & Book Artists Guild
Suite 220, Chalmers Bldg.
35 McCaul Street
Toronto, ON M5T 1V7, Canada

1, 1984; quarterly.
News and papers on bookbinding and book conservation.

Halios
Canadian Conservation Institute.
1030 Innes Road
Ottawa, K1A 0M8, Canada

1, 1989; irregular.
News about conservation activity in Canada and at the CCI.

Conservation, formerly *Getty Conservation Institute Newsletter*
The Getty Conservation Institute
4503 Glencoe Avenue
Marina del Rey, CA 90292–6537

1, 1985; 3/year.
Information about and reports on the research and educational
programs of the Getty Conservation Institute.

Conservation Administration News (CAN)
Preservation and Conservation Studies
School of Library and Information Science
EDB 564
University of Texas at Austin
Austin, TX 78712

1, 1979; quarterly.
A current awareness publication for librarians, archivists,
conservators and others concerned with the preservation of the
documentary heritage.

Disaster Recovery Journal
P.O. Box 510110
St. Louis, MO 63151

1, 1987; quarterly.
Covers all aspects of disaster recovery, with emphasis on
computer operations.

Focus on Security
The Triad Company
P.O. Box 9930
Moscow, ID 80203

1, 1993; quarterly
Focus on library, archive, and museum security.

Guild of Book Workers *Journal*
521 Fifth Avenue
New York, NY 10175

1, 1962; semiannual.
Practical and scholarly articles about bookbinding and binding materials.

High Fidelity
High Fidelity and Musical America
One Sound Avenue
Marion, OH 43302

1, 1951; monthly.
Articles on current topics, including equipment reports.

History News
American Association for State and Local History
172 Second Avenue, Suite 102
Nashville, TN 37204

1, 1940; bimonthly.
A magazine for historical agency and museum professionals.

Inform
Association of Information and Image Management
1100 Wayne Avenue, Suite 1602
Silver Spring, MD 20910

1, 1967; monthly.
A magazine of information and imaging technologies; has had several title changes to reflect changes in the micrographics industry.

Information Media & Technology
Cimtech
University of Hertfordshire
College Lane
Hatfield, Herts. AL10 9AB
England, United Kingdom.

1, 1967; quarterly.
News, feature articles and equipment reviews and evaluations in the micrographics field; formerly *NRCd Bulletin*.

Information Standards Quarterly (ISQ)
National Information Standards Organization—Z39
Administration 101, Room E106
Gaithersburg, MD 20899

1, 1989; quarterly.
News on standards that relate to library materials.

International Conservation News
IFLA/PAC Secretariat
Bibliothèque Nationale Paris
2 Rue Vivienne
75084 Paris Cedex 02, France

1, 1987; irregular.
Information on preservation and conservation activities around
the world.

Journal of Micrographics
Association for Information and Image Management
8728 Colesville Road
Silver Spring, MD 20910

1, 1969; quarterly.
Focuses on all aspects of micrographics and the micrographics
industry. Formerly the National Microfilm Association *Journal*,
it is the official organ of AIIM.

Library and Archival Security
Haworth Press, Inc.
75 Griswold Street
Binghamton, NY 13904

1, 1975; quarterly.
Shorter articles and topical issues on all aspects of security and
the preservation of library and archival collections.

Library Conservation News (LCN)
National Preservation Office
The British Library
Great Russell Street
London WC1 3DG
England, United Kingdom

1, 1988; quarterly.
News of current activities in the United Kingdom and
elsewhere in the world.

Microform Review
Microform Review, Inc.
P.O. Box 405, Saugatuck Station
Westport, CT 06880

1, 1972; bimonthly.
Current news and information about microforms, the
management of microform collections, and reformatting
programs.

Micrographics Equipment Review
Microform Review, Inc.
P.O. Box 405, Saugatuck Station
Westport, CT 06880

1, 1976; quarterly.
Evaluations of microform equipment.

Museum
Unipub, Inc.
Box 433, Murray Hill Station
New York, NY 10016

1, 1948; quarterly.
Formerly *Mouseion;* a Unesco publication that deals with
topical problems in museology.

Museum News
American Association of Museums
P.O. Box 33399
Washington, DC 20007

1, 1924; bimonthly.
Frequently contains useful material on preservation and
conservation. In the early 1970s it ran a column, "On
Conservation," with brief essays by leading conservators; they
remain timely reading.

New Bookbinder; Journal of Designer Bookbinders
Designer Bookbinders
6 Queen Square
London WC1N 3AR
England, United Kingdom

1, 1981; annual.
Focuses on progressive, technical aspects of modern fine
binding, historical developments and conservation techniques.

The New Library Scene
Library Binding Institute
7401 Metro Blvd., Suite 325
Edina, MN 55439

1, 1982; bimonthly.
Library binding and conservation topics.

The Paper Conservator
Institute of Paper Conservation
Leigh Lodge
Leigh, Worcester WR6 5LB
England, United Kingdom

1, 1976; annual.
Dissemination and exchange of ideas and information relating
to the conservation of works of art on paper.

Restaurator; International Journal for the Preservation of
Library and Archival Materials
Munksgaard International Publishers, Ltd.
35 Nørre Sogaard
DK-1370 Copenhagen K, Denmark

1, 1969; quarterly.
International in scope, includes technical and scholarly papers
on topics in preservation and conservation.

Studies in Conservation
International Institute for Conservation
6 Buckingham Street
London WC2N 6BA
England, United Kingdom

1, 1952; semiannual.
Technical papers on all aspects of conservation.

TAPPI Journal
Technical Association of the Pulp and Paper Industry
One Dunwoody Park
Atlanta, GA 30338

1, 1949; monthly.
Technical journal for the paper industry.

Technology and Conservation
One Emerson Place
Boston, MA 0214

1, 1976; irregular.
Articles and information on conservation technology.

Video Librarian
P.O. Box 2725
Bremerton, WA 98310

1, 1986; 11 issues a year.
Practical articles on video, maintenance and repair.

Visual Resources; International Journal of Documentation
Gordon & Breach Science Publications
240 Eighth Avenue
New York, NY 10011

1, 1980; quarterly.
Devoted to the visual arts.

BIBLIOGRAPHY

Chapter 1

Abelson, Philip H. "Brittle Books and Journals," *Science* 238:4827 (30 October 1987), 595.
Editorial on the causes and scope of the brittle book problem.

Abt, Jeffrey. "Objectifying the Book: The Impact of Science on Books and Manuscripts," *Library Trends* 36:1 (Summer 1987), 23–38.
Summarizes "the history of scientific investigations into the makeup and care" of library and archival materials. Abt concludes that "science has exceeded the ability of institutions or individuals to utilize it."

America's Museums: The Belmont Report. Washington, DC: American Association of Museums, 1969. 81p.
Report by a Special Committee of the American Association of Museums to the Federal Council on the Arts and the Humanities. Discusses the preservation needs of museums and libraries.

Association of Research Libraries. Office of Management Studies. *Brittle Books Program.* Washington, DC: Association of Research Libraries, March 1989. 121p. (SPEC Kit, 152)
Policies and guidelines for dealing with publications that are so deteriorated that they must be reformatted for preservation. Includes documents for planning, work flow, procedures and forms, guidelines for microfilming and photocopying, and record keeping.

Association of Research Libraries. Office of Management Studies. *Planning for the Preservation of Library Materials.* Washington, DC: Association of Research Libraries, July-August 1980. (SPEC Kit 66)

Documents on initial planning, program and policy statements, with historical perspectives, including a history of the preservation program at Yale University Library.

Association of Research Libraries. Office of Management Studies. *Preservation Guidelines in ARL Libraries.* Washington, DC: Association of Research Libraries, September 1987. 110p. (SPEC Kit, 137)

Preservation guidelines, policies, and procedures issued by selected ARL libraries since 1981. Bibliography.

Association of Research Libraries. Office of Management Studies. *Preservation Planning Program: An Assisted Self-Study Manual for Libraries,* expanded edition by Pamela W. Darling and Duane E. Webster. Washington, DC: Association of Research Libraries, 1987. 117p.

A guide for libraries undertaking a formal study of preservation needs.

Baker, John P. "Preservation Programs of the New York Public Library," *Microform Review* 10:1 (Winter 1981), 25–28; 11:1 (Winter 1982), 22–30.

A history of preservation efforts, many of which have led to national programs.

Baker, John P. and Marguerite C. Soroka. *Library Conservation; Preservation in Perspective.* Stroudsburg, PA: Hutchinson and Ross, 1978. 459p.

A selection of readings on preservation.

Banks, Paul N. "Education for Conservators," *Library Journal* 104:9 (May 1, 1979), 1013–1017.

A preliminary statement and proposal for the training of preservation administrators, books and paper conservators, and conservation technicians.

Banks, Paul N. Education in Library Conservation," *Library Trends* 30:2 (Fall 1981), 189–201.

Barclay, Bob. "CCI: The First Twenty Years," *CCI Newsletter,* No. 10 (September 1992), 1–4. French/English.

A history of the accomplishments and the activities of the Canadian Conservation Institute.

Barrow, William J. *Deterioration of Book Stock, Causes and Remedies; Two Studies on the Permanence of Book Paper*, ed. Randolph W. Church. Richmond, VA: Virginia State Library, 1959. 70p. (Virginia State Library Publication, 10)
Results of the study of twentieth century book papers funded by the Council on Library Resources.

Barrow, W.J., Laboratory, Inc. "Barrow Laboratory Research: Specifications for Permanent/Durable Book Papers," *American Archivist* 38:3 (July 1975), 405–416.
Summary of the report of the research project to develop specifications for uncoated permanent/durable paper.

Belanger, Terry. "The Price of Preservation," *Times Literary Supplement*, Friday, November 18, 1977, 1ff.
An excellent overview of the preservation problem.

Bello, Susan E. *Cooperative Preservation Efforts of Academic Libraries*. Urbana, IL: University of Illinois Graduate School of Library and Information Science, October 1986. 52p. (Occasional Paper, 174)
Describes national efforts for preservation programs by the Association of Research Libraries, Library of Congress, and the Research Libraries Group from 1954 to 1985.

Brahm, Walter. "Conservation as I Remember It: An Undocumented Hindsight," *Preservation Issues* (Ohio State Library), No. 11 (March 1993), 2p.
Recollections by an early advocate for library preservation programs and a founder of the Northeast Document Conservation Center.

Brahm, Walter. "Regional Approach to Conservation: The New England Document Conservation Center," *American Archivist* 40:4 (October 1977), 421–427.
Early history of the Northeast Document Conservation Center; a statement for regional centers for the treatment of library materials.

Brichford, Maynard J. "A Brief History of the Physical Protec-

tion of Archives," *Conservation Administration News,* No. 31
(October 1987), 10, 21.
   A brief sketch of the policies and procedures adopted over
the centuries that define modern archival practice.

Brown, A. Gilson. "The American Institute for Conservation of
Historic and Artistic Works," *Conservation Administration
News,* No. 28 (January 1987), 8.
   A description of the goals, objectives, and services of the
professional organization for conservators.

Buck, Richard. "On Conservation: Conservation Defined," *Museum News* 52 (September 1973), 15–16.
   Definition of the conservation profession.

Byrne, Sherry and Barbara Van Deventer. "Preserving the Nation's Intellectual Heritage: A Synthesis," *College and Research Libraries News* 53:5 (May 1992), 313–315.
   Briefly discusses factors that have led to a national strategy
for preservation: the brittle books program, the creation and
role of the Commission on Preservation and Access, increased awareness of the factors that cause deterioration, and
the trend toward comprehensive collection management programs.

Calmes, Alan R. and Norbert Baer. "National Archives Advisory Committee on Preservation: Science Advice to the Archivist of the United States," *Restaurator* 10:1 (1989), 16–31.
   A survey of the activities of the committee in its first
decade.

Cannon Brooks, Peter. "The Art Curator and the Conservator,"
Museum Journal 75:4 (March 1976), 161–162.
   A cogent statement on the training of curators and conservators to enable them to work together to preserve materials.

Clareson, Thomas F. R., Norman Howden, Kenneth Lavender,
and Lisa C. Roberts. *AMIGOS Preservation Service Preservation Needs Assessment Survey Analysis: Final Report.* Dallas,
TX: AMIGOS Bibliographic Council, 1992. 80p.; 11p. survey.
   A discussion of the needs-assessment survey: applicability,
clarity, and results.

Cloonan, Michèle Valerie and Patricia C. Norcott. "Evolution of

Preservation Librarianship as Reflected in Job Descriptions from 1975 through 1985," *College and Research Libraries* 50:6 (November 1989), 646–656.

Examines the job descriptions for preservation librarians placed in major professional publications. The report reflects the considerable variation in perception of their duties.

Cloonan, Michèle Valerie. "Preservation Education in American Library Schools: Recounting the Ways," *Journal of Education for Library and Information Science* 31:3 (Winter 1991), 187–203.

Summaries of the presentations on library education programs presented at the 1989 program of the Preservation Education Special Interest Group, Association for Library and Information Science Education.

Conservation Administration, ed. Robert C. Morrison, Jr., George M. Cunha, and Norman P. Tucker. North Andover, MA: New England Document Conservation Center, 1975. 351p.

Transcript of the Seminar on the Theoretical Aspects of the Conservation of Library and Archival Materials and the Establishment of Conservation Programs, October 1973.

"Conservation/Preservation," *The Bookmark* (New York State Library) 45:3 (Spring 1987), 138–193. Entire issue.

Describes national preservation initiatives, several state programs, and the New York state program.

"The Conservator-Restorer: A Definition of the Profession," *ICOM News* 39:1 (1986), 5–7.

Document for the museum and conservation professions prepared by the Committee for Conservation, Working Group for Training in Conservation, International Council of Museums.

Conway, Paul. "Practical Preservation Practice in a Nationwide Context," *American Archivist* 53:2 (Spring 1990), 204–222.

Discusses the results of his survey of preservation practices.

Council on Library Resources. Committee on Preservation and Access. *Brittle Books.* Washington, DC: Council on Library Resources, 1986. 31p.

Report focuses on the problem and the need for cooperation for its solution.

Crowe, William J. "Verner Clapp and Preservation of Library
Materials, the Years at the Council on Library Resources,"
*Academic Librarianship: Past, Present and Future: A Fest-
schrift in Honor of David Kaser,* ed. John Richardson, Jr. and
Jinnie Y. Davis. Englewood, CO: Libraries Unlimited, 1989,
43–66.

History of Clapp's efforts to arouse concern for preservation
and to deal with the problems of brittle paper and poorly
bound books.

Cunha, George Martin. "Current Trends in Preservation Research," *American Archivist* 53:2 (Spring 1990), 192–202.

An overview of current research in preservation and conservation, including climate control, mold and pest control,
disaster prevention and recovery, mass deacidification, and
paper strengthening.

Cunha, George M., Frazer G. Poole, Clyde C. Walton. "The
Conservation and Preservation of Historical Records," *American Archivist* 40:3 (July 1977), 321–324.

Discusses the viability of regional and national conservation centers and education programs.

Cunha, George M. and Dorothy G. *Conservation of Library
Materials: A Manual and Bibliography on the Care, Repair,
and Restoration of Library Materials,* 2nd ed., 2 vols. Metuchen, NJ: Scarecrow Press, 1971–1972.

Vol. 1 covers historical background, preventive care, repair
and restoration, disaster planning. Vol. 2: bibliography.

Cunha, George M. and Dorothy G. *Library and Archives Conservation: The 1980s and Beyond.* 2 vols. Metuchen, NJ: Scarecrow Press, 1983.

Vol. 1 updates the history of library conservation efforts
and identifies current trends and needs. Vol. 2 continues
Cunha's comprehensive bibliography.

Darling, Pamela W. "Expanding Preservation Resources: The
Corps of Practitioners and the Core of Knowledge," *Conserving and Preserving Library Materials,* ed. Kathryn L. and

William T. Henderson. Urbana-Champaign, IL: University of Illinois Graduate School of Library and Information Science, 1983, 19–36.
Describes projects and programs to develop informed librarians.

Darling, Pamela W. and Sherelyn Ogden. "From Problems Perceived to Programs in Practice: The Preservation of Library Resources in the U.S.A., 1956–1980," *Library Resources and Technical Services* 25:1 (January–March 1981), 9–29.
A review of the growth of preservation planning in the library profession.

Darling, Pamela W. "Preservation Epilogue: Signs of Hope," *Library Journal* 104:15 (September 1, 1979), 1627.
Problems, developments, and the future of preservation activities.

Dean, John. "Conservation Officers: The Administrative Role," *Wilson Library Bulletin* 57:2 (October 1982), 128–132.
Emphasizes the need for preservation planning and describes the role of the conservation officer as an administrator with wide responsibilities.

Desmarais, Ellen. "Conservation at the National Archives of Canada," *CBBAG Newsletter* (Canadian Bookbinders and Book Artists Guild) 10:1–2 (Spring, Summer 1992), 3–8, 3–6.
Describes the development of preservation programs, the organization of the Conservation Branch, and its book preservation and conservation program, from selection for treatment, options, and a description of techniques for full treatment.

Farr, George F., Jr. "NEH's Program for the Preservation of Brittle Books," *Advances in Preservation and Access,* vol. 1. Westport, CT: Meckler, 1992, 49–60.
Description of the Brittle Books Microfilming programs, how each works, and what has been accomplished.

Field, Jeffrey. "The Goals and Priorities of the NEH Office of Preservation," *Conservation Administration News,* No. 25 (April 1986), 4–5, 23–24.

Describes the program's philosophy, principles, and funding. Discusses the need for more cooperative efforts and education in preservation.

Field, Jeffrey. "The NEH Office of Preservation, 1986–1988," *Microform Review* 17:4 (October 1988), 187–189.
A survey of the preservation initiatives supported by NEH, including the U.S. Newspaper Program, basic conservation research, and grants for the preservation of special collections.

Friedman, Hannah B. "Preservation of Library Materials, the State of the Art," *Special Libraries* 59:8 (October 1968), 608–613.
Defines preservation and describes preservation efforts at New York Public Library; emphasizes the need for further research and the training of librarians in library schools.

Geh, Hans-Peter. "Conservation/Preservation: An International Approach," *Library Resources and Technical Services* 30:1 (January–March 1986), 31–35.
Describes the new Conservation Section of the International Federation of Library Associations and Institutions and the need for an international focal point for research, conservation centers, and international agreements for storage and transfer of materials and information.

Gracy, David B. II. "Between Muffins and Mercury . . . The Elusive Definition of Preservation," *New Library Scene* 9:6 (December 1990), 1, 5–7.
Describes what "preservation" includes and the difficulty that the library profession has in defining it.

Grant, Julius. *Books and Documents; Dating, Permanence, and Preservation.* London: Grafton, 1937.
A study of the dating of books and manuscripts, causes of deterioration, and their preservation.

Gwinn, Nancy E. "CLR and Preservation," *College and Research Libraries* 42:2 (March 1981), 104–126.
History of the Council on Library Resources' contribution to advances in the field of preservation. Bibliography of publications resulting from or related to CLR-supported programs, 1956–1980.

Gwinn, Nancy E. "A National Coordinated Preservation Program: Its Time Has Come," *Proceedings,* Association of College and Research Libraries Third National Conference, Seattle, WA, 1984, 259–262.
   Author suggests that the ability to add preservation data to bibliographic data bases, increased commitment of research libraries to preservation, and support from funding organizations are optimum conditions for a cooperative plan for the preservation of the nation's documentary heritage.

Gwinn, Nancy E. "Preservation Planning at RLG," *Conservation Administration News,* No. 10 (July 1982), 5–6.
   A review of the activities of the Preservation of Library Materials Committee, Research Libraries Group.

Gwinn, Nancy E. "The Rise and Fall and Rise of Cooperative Projects," *Library Resources and Technical Services* 29:1 (January–March 1985), 80–86.
   Historical overview of cooperative preservation microfilming projects.

Haas, Warren J. *Preparation of Detailed Specifications for a National System for the Preservation of Library Materials, Final Report.* Washington, DC: Association of Research Libraries, 1972. 30p.
   Identifies specific steps that might be taken collectively to resolve the problem of deteriorating materials; report prepared for the U.S. Office of Education, Bureau of Libraries and Educational Technology.

Hammer, John H. "On the Political Aspects of Book Preservation in the U.S.," *Advances in Preservation and Access,* vol. 1. Westport, CT: Meckler, 1992, 22–40.
   Summary of the efforts by the scholarly and library communities to obtain funding for the "brittle books" program.

Harris, Carolyn, Carol Mandel and Robert Wolven. "A Cost Model for Preservation: The Columbia University Libraries' Approach," *Library Resources and Technical Services* 35:1 (January 1991), 33–54.
   A model for identifying the processes in preservation and their associated costs.

Harrop, Dorothy A. "Pioneers of Conservation: Roger Powell

and Sydney Cockerell, *Book Collector* 35:2 (Summer 1986), 179–190.

A tribute to the bookbinders who were responsible for defining book conservation "as a serious and exacting scientific discipline" and training leading book conservators.

Harvard University Library. Task Force on Collection Preservation Priorities. *Preserving Harvard's Retrospective Collections.* Cambridge, MA: Harvard University Libraries, April 1, 1991. 74p.

Coverage of factors relating to preservation priorities at one of the nation's leading research libraries.

Hedley, George. "Finding a Structure of Collaboration," *CCI Newsletter* (Canadian Conservation Institute), (Autumn/ Winter 1990), 8–9. French/English.

Emphasizes the need for collaboration between conservator and scientist.

Henderson, Cathy. "Curator or Conservator: Who Decides on What Treatment?" *Rare Books and Manuscripts Librarianship* 2:2 (Fall 1987), 103–107.

Describes the concerns of the American Library Association Rare Books and Manuscripts Section's Committee on Curatorial Issues Raised by Conservation.

Henderson, James W. and Robert G. Krupp. "The Librarian as Conservator," *Library Quarterly* 40:1 (January 1970), 176–192.

Provides historical background and describes the organization of a preservation program. Bibliography.

Henderson, James W. *Memorandum on Conservation of the Collection.* New York: New York Public Library, 1970.

Describes the organization and measures taken to protect the Research Library's collections.

Henderson, Kathryn Luther and William T., eds. *Conserving and Preserving Library Materials.* Urbana-Champaign, IL: University of Illinois Graduate School of Library and Information Science, 1983. 207p.

Papers from the Allerton Park Institute, 1981, to assess the state of preservation and to set objectives for the 1980s.

Higgenbotham, Barbra Buckner. *Our Past Preserved: A History of American Library Preservation, 1876–1910.* Boston, MA: G. K. Hall, 1990. 346p.
A history of librarians' efforts to preserve library collections.

Howell, Alan G. "Paper Conservation: New Directions." *Preserving the Word.* London: Library Association, 1987, 63–69.
A bibliographic overview of what a conservator believes a librarian should read on preservation and conservation.

International Federation of Library Associations and Institutions. Section on Conservation. "Principles of Conservation and Restoration in Libraries," *IFLA Journal* 5:4 (1979), 292–300.
Basic principles for preservation and conservation of library collections prepared by the IFLA Section on Conservation.

Jolliffe, John. "International Cooperation in Preservation," *Collection Management* 9:2/3 (Spring/Summer 1987), 113–118.
Describes the tension that can arise between preservation and conservation and how the curator and conservator can cooperate to preserve materials for future generations and to arrest deterioration.

Jones, C. Lee. "The Mid-Atlantic Preservation Service (MAPS): New Options for Preservation Microfilming," *Microform Review* 18:3 (Summer 1989), 142–144.
Describes MAPS and its services.

Kaplan, Hilary A. and Brenda S. Banks. "Archival Preservation: The Teaming of the Crew," *American Archivist* 53:2 (Spring 1990), 266–273.
Reviews the current state of archival preservation activities; existing and potential educational opportunities; the role of personnel; and the differences between library and archival preservation.

Keck, Caroline K. "The Position of the Conservator in the Last Quarter of the Twentieth Century," *Journal of the American Institute for Conservation* 18:1 (Autumn 1978), 3–7.
Traces the development of the profession of conservator; a

personal statement from a leading practitioner on how it should develop in the future.

Langwell, W. H. *The Conservation of Books and Documents.* London: Pitman, 1957.
A basic manual by a pioneer in library preservation.

Larsen, A. Dean and Randy S. Silverman. "Preservation," *Library Technical Services,* 2nd ed., ed. Irene P. Godden. New York: Academic Press, 1991, 205–269.
Overview of preservation management and issues of the 1990s. Bibliography.

Library Association (United Kingdom). *Preserving the Word.* London: 1987. 147p.
A collection of papers describing programs in place and efforts that are needed in the United Kingdom, originally presented at the Library Association Conference, Harrogate, 1986.

Library of Congress. Preservation Office. *A National Preservation Program; Proceedings of the Planning Conference.* Washington, DC: 1980. 125p.
A review of preservation developments in the nation and a call for more coordinated efforts in the future.

Lowell, Howard P. "Preservation Needs in State Archives," *Conservation Administration News,* No. 24 (January 1986), 5, 23.
Summary of the findings of a two-year study undertaken for the National Association of Government Archives and Records Administrators (NAGARA).

Lydenberg, Harry Miller and John Archer. *The Care and Repair of Books.* New York: Bowker, 1932, 1945.
An early text by the director and the conservator at New York Public Library.

McAusland, Jane. "A Short History of the Institute of Paper Conservation: The First Ten Years." *Paper Conservation News,* No. 39 (September 1986), 4–5.
A history of the professional organization for paper conservators.

McClung, Patricia A. "Conservation Action: RLG's Preservation Program," *Advances in Preservation and Access,* vol. 1. Westport, CT: Meckler, 1992, 61–70.
Summary of the Research Library Group's preservation program.

McCrady, Ellen. "History of the Abbey Publications," *Library Resources and Technical Services* 35:1 (January 1991), 104–108.
McCrady describes how her publication, *Abbey Newsletter,* developed into an advocacy publication and led to a full-time publication and research program by McCrady.

Merrill-Oldham, Jan. "Preservation in Research Libraries: A New Approach to Caretaking," *The New Library Scene* 5:6 (December 1986), 1, 5–6.
Defines preservation librarianship, its scope, and responsibilities.

Merrill-Oldham, Jan, Carolyn Clark Morrow, and Mark Roosa. *Preservation Program Models: A Study Project and Report.* Washington, DC: Association of Research Libraries, 1991. 54p.
A report prepared to assist the administrators of research libraries in the shaping of programs to preserve the nation's research collections.

Merrill-Oldham, Jan and Merrily Smith, eds. *Library Preservation Programs: Models, Priorities, Possibilities.* Chicago: American Library Association, 1985. 117p.
Covers the history of the development of local preservation programs, assessment of needs and priorities, and sources of fiscal support. Papers from a conference for library administrators, with emphasis on organization and planning.

Morrow, Carolyn Clark. *The Preservation Challenge: A Guide to Conserving Library Materials.* White Plains, NY: Knowledge Industries, 1983. 231p.
Discusses the causes of deterioration and options for preservation. Case studies of activities in several institutions.

Mosher, Paul H. "Book Production Quality: A Librarian's View, or the Self-Destructing Library," *Library Resources and Technical Services* 28:1 (January–March 1984), 15–19.

Discusses the importance of book production guidelines for publishers to ensure permanent/durable books in library collections.

National Archives and Records Administration. *Intrinsic Value in Archival Materials.* Washington, DC: National Archives and Records Administration, 1982. 6p. (Staff Information Paper, 21)
   NARA defines the term and discusses characteristics: physical form, aesthetic quality, unique features, age, value for exhibition, questionable-need authorization, public interest, legal significance, significance for policy.

National Conservation Advisory Council. *Conservation of Cultural Property in the United States: A Statement.* Washington, DC: National Conservation Advisory Council, 1976. 42p.
   A statement of national needs in conservation: training personnel, educating users of conservation services, developing scientific support, developing national standards.

National Conservation Advisory Council. *Conservation Treatment Facilities in the United States.* Washington, DC: National Conservation Advisory Council, December 1980. 44p.
   A report on the types of facilities and their services.

National Conservation Advisory Council. *Dialogue on the Issue of a National Institute for Conservation.* Washington, DC: National Conservation Advisory Council, May 6, 1980. 9p.
   Paper giving historical background and a list of concerns, prepared for the 1980 American Institute for Conservation Annual Conference.

National Conservation Advisory Council. *Discussion Paper on a National Institute for Conservation of Cultural Property.* Washington, DC: National Conservation Advisory Council, 1978.
   A proposed structure for the institute and an outline of the scope of its activities.

National Conservation Advisory Council. *Proposal for a National Institute for the Conservation of Cultural Property.* Washington, DC: National Conservation Advisory Council, 1982. 54p.
   The proposal covers background, need, and structure of the

institute, including divisions for information services, educational services, and scientific research and development.

National Conservation Advisory Council. *Report of the Study
Committee on Education and Training.* Washington, DC:
National Conservation Advisory Council, 1979. 64p.
   Traces the history of the development of conservation
training in the United States and examines the need for
expanded opportunities, curriculum, and standards.

National Conservation Advisory Council. *Report of the Study
Committee on Libraries and Archives: National Needs in
Libraries and Archives Conservation.* Washington, DC: Na-
tional Conservation Advisory Council, November 1978. 56p.
   A review of problems and needs, with proposals for action,
and endorsement of the concept of a National Institute for
Conservation.

National Conservation Advisory Council. *Report of the Study
Committee on Scientific Support.* Washington, DC: National
Conservation Advisory Council, 1979. 75p.
   Addresses the need for scientific support in conservation;
recommends funding for scientists and conservators.

National Conservation Advisory Council. Regional Centers
Study Committee. *Report.* Washington, DC: National Conservation Advisory Board, March 1976. 25p.
   A survey of existing conservation facilities and a recommendation for the establishment of regional centers.

Ogden, Sherelyn. "The Impact of the Florence Flood on Library
Conservation in the United States of America," *Restaurator*
3:1/2 (1979), 1–36.
   An evaluation of the impact of the flood on the development of preservation and conservation activities through a
study of the literature. Bibliography.

Ogden, Sherelyn. "A Regional Perpective on Preservation: the
NEDCC Experience," *Libraries and Culture* 27:1 (Winter
1992), 49–58.
   History of the Northeast Document Conservation Center.

O'Toole, James M. "On the Idea of Permanence," *American
Archivist* 52:1 (Winter 1989), 10–25.

A provocative essay that explores the concept of permanence, noting its shift from an emphasis on intellectual content to original material.

Paris, Jan. *Choosing and Working With a Conservator.* Atlanta, GA: Southeast Library Network, 1990. 24p.
Explores the issues surrounding the selection of a conservator; the nature of conservation; the role of the conservator; how to find and deal with one. Information resource list; selective bibliography.

Pederson, Ann, ed. *Keeping Archives.* Sydney: Australian Society of Archives, 1987. 374p.
Introductory manual for archivists with emphasis on collection management and preservation; see especially Ch. 8: "Conservation," by Michael Piggott.

Perry, Alan F. "The Role of Federal Agencies in Cooperative Conservation," *Conservation Administration News,* No. 28 (January 1987), 6, 22.
Describes the role that the National Endowment for the Humanities, the National Historic Publications and Records Commission, the National Archives and Records Administration, and the Smithsonian Institution play in assisting nonfederal agencies in funding.

Pilette, Roberta and Carolyn Harris. "It Takes Two to Tango: A Conservator's View of Curator/Conservator Relations," *Rare Books and Manuscripts Librarianship* 4:2 (Fall 1989), 103–111.
Discusses the information necessary for an intelligent conservation decision and how it can be obtained.

Plenderleith, Harold J. and A. E. C. Werner. *The Conservation of Antiquities and Works of Art: Treatment, Repair, and Restoration.* 2nd ed. London: Oxford University Press, 1971.
Long regarded as a standard text in the field of conservation.

Poole, Frazer G. "Some Aspects of the Conservation Problem in Archives," *American Archivist* 40:2 (April 1977), 163–171.
A summary of the preservation problem and statement of the need for action on a national basis.

Ratcliffe, F. W. "Preservation: A Decade of Progress," *Library Review* 36 (Winter 1987), 228–236.
Report on preservation activities in British libraries and archives.

Ratcliffe, F.W. *Preservation Policies and Conservation in British Libraries.* London: The British Library, 1984. 131p. (Library and Information Research Report, 25)
Report of the Cambridge University Library Conservation Project to determine preservation practices and policies in British libraries and to identify training facilities. Notes the need for a national initiative in addition to local efforts to preserve the nation's documentary heritage.

Ringrose, Jayne. "Making Things Available: The Curator and the Reader," *Book Collector* 39:1 (Spring 1990), 55–73.
Discussion of the issue of preservation and access from a manuscript librarian's perspective. "Readers (and all the rest of us) are required to treat the books with care and tenderness and so to use them that they will survive in good condition for future generations."

Ritzenthaler, Mary Lynn. *Archives & Manuscripts: Conservation; A Manual on Physical Care and Management.* Rev. ed. Chicago: Society of American Archivists, 1983. 151p. (Basic Manual Series)
An essential guide for administrators and preservation personnel. Bibliography.

Ritzenthaler, Mary Lynn. *Preserving Archives and Manuscripts.* Chicago: Society of American Archivists, 1994. 225 p.
Revised edition of the above.

Roy, Gillian. "The Camberwell Paper Conservation Degrees," *Library Conservation News,* No. 36 (July 1992), 2–3.
Description of the structure, goals, and objectives of the Camberwell courses in conservation.

Russell, Ann. "Northeast Document Conservation Center: A Case Study in Cooperative Conservation," *American Archivist* 45:1 (Winter 1982), 45–52.
The history of the center, its services, and the future for conservation centers.

Russell, Ann, Karen Motylewski, Gay Tracy. "Northeast Document Conservation Center: A Leader in Preservation," *Library Resources and Technical Services* 32:1 (January 1988), 43–47.
History and mission of the center with a description of its services.

Russell, Joyce R., ed. *Preservation of Library Materials.* New York: Special Libraries Association, 1980. 96p.
An overview of preservation issues; proceedings of a seminar held at Rutgers University, July 1979.

Schur, Susan E. "Conservation Profile: The Preservation Office of the Library of Congress," *Technology & Conservation* 7:2 (Summer 1982), 26–33, 46, 49.
History of preservation efforts at the library and a description of the responsibilities of the Preservation Office.

Shaffer, Norman J. "Library of Congress Pilot Preservation Project," *College and Research Libraries* 30: (January 1969), 5–11.
Describes the library's first attempt to determine the scope of the brittle book problem and to deal with it.

Shelley, Karen Lee. "The Future of Conservation in Research Libraries," *Journal of Academic Librarianship* 1:6 (January 1976), 15–18.
Describes the need for a preservation/conservation librarian in research libraries and the scope of the job, with discussion of the programs at the Library of Congress, Harvard, and Yale libraries.

Slate, Jane. "Caring for the Nation's Wealth: A National Study Assesses Collections Management, Maintenance and Conservation," *Museum News* 64:2 (October 1985), 39–45.
Summary of a study that highlighted current conditions of collections of cultural property, with an overview of resources available for collections care.

Smith, Merrily, ed. *Preservation of Library Materials.* 2 vols. New York: Saur, 1987.
Papers from an international conference in Vienna, 1986, that examine approaches to preservation from the technical and theoretical perspective.

Stam, David. "International Programs in Preservation," *Preserving the Word*. London: Library Association, 1987, 10–16.
An outline of some of the factors and considerations that influence the development of international cooperative efforts in preservation.

Steckman, Elizabeth. "Preservation Program Thrives in New Jersey," *Conservation Administration News*, No. 48 (January 1992), 1–2,24.
A report on the Maintenance and Preservation of Library Collections grant program, administered by the New Jersey State Library.

Stevens, Norman D. "The Role of Networks in the Preservation of Library Materials," *Journal of Academic Librarianship* 7:3 (July 1981), 171–172.
Urges that networks cooperatively approach preservation problems and decisions by recording preservation data in an agreed-upon system, and by designating institutions that can house rare and unique materials in an appropriate environment.

Sullivan, John and Jennifer Johnson. "The Preservation Directorate: Saving the Library's Legacy," *New Library Scene* 10:5 (October 1991), 1,5,10.
Describes the current operations of the preservation directorate at the Library of Congress. Reprinted from *LC Information Bulletin*, July 1, 1991.

Swartzburg, Susan G. "Preserving Newspapers: National and International Cooperative Efforts," *Conserving and Preserving Materials in Nonbook Formats*, ed. Kathryn Luther and William T. Henderson. Urbana-Champaign, IL: University of Illinois Graduate School of Library and Information Science, 1991, 73–89.
Describes the history and activities of the U.S. Newspaper Project.

Swartzburg, Susan Garretson. "Preservation of the Cultural Patrimony," *Art Libraries Journal* 15:1 (1990), 18–21.
A brief history of efforts to preserve the cultural heritage; discussion of the problems preservationists face in determining what is to be saved for future generations.

Swartzell, Ann. "Preservation." *RTSD Newsletter* 11:1 (1986), 6–7.
Discussion of the different approaches to preservation administration and reporting structures in preservation departments, programs, and policies.

Swartzell, Ann. "Preservation Efforts of the ARL Office of Management Studies," *RTSD Newsletter* 10:4 (1985), 40–42.
Describes the OMS studies and SPEC (Systems and Procedure Exchange Center) kits available on preservation topics.

Sylvestre, Guy. "A National Preservation Program for Library Materials in Canada," *Libri* 31:3 (September 1981), 185–192.
An outline of Canada's needs, including a national preservation policy and a preservation awareness program.

U.S. Congress. House of Representatives. Subcommittee on Post-Secondary Education. *Oversight Hearing on the Problem of 'Brittle Books' in Our Nation's Libraries.* Washington, DC: Government Printing Office, 1987. 144p. (100th Congress, 1st Session, Washington, DC, March 3, 1987, Serial no. 100–1)
Testimony on the need for support of preservation of library collections.

Vaisey, D. G. "The Archivist as Conservator," *Journal of the Society of Archivists* 6:2 (October 1978), 67–75.
Asks that archivists accept responsibility for the preservation of collections, be knowledgeable, and understand the role of the conservator.

Walch, Victoria Irons. "Checklist of Standards Applicable to the Preservation of Archives and Manuscripts," *American Archivist* 53:2 (Spring 1990), 324–338.

Walker, Gay. "Preservation Efforts in Larger U.S. Academic Libraries," *College and Research Libraries* 36:1 (January 1975), 39–44.
Results of a survey of larger libraries, with recommendations for establishing a preservation unit.

Weiss, Dudley A. "LBI at 50 . . . Achievements and Principles," *The New Library Scene,* 4:2 (April 1985), 11–14.
A history of the Library Binding Institute and a look to the future of the commercial library binding industry.

Weiss, Dudley A. "Upon Looking Back," *Library Scene* 10:3 (September 1981), 24–27.
A reflection upon his career as director of the Library Binding Institute for thirty years, and on the interest in preservation that developed among librarians during that time.

Welsh, William J. "The Library of Congress: A More-Than-Equal Partner," *Library Resources and Technical Services* 29:1 (January–March 1985), 87–93.
Discussion of the Library's contribution and role in cooperative preservation microfilming efforts.

Williams, Edwin E. "The Book-Preservation Problem as Seen at Harvard," *Harvard Library Bulletin* 29:4 (October 1981), 420–444.
History of preservation initiatives at Harvard.

Williams, Gordon. *The Preservation of Deteriorating Books: An Examination of the Problem with Recommendations for a Solution.* Washington, DC: Association of Research Libraries, September 1964.
Report with recommendations prepared for the Committee on the Preservation of Research Library Materials. Abridged in *Library Journal* 91 (January 15, 1966), 189–194.

Wilson, Alex. "For This and Future Generations: Managing the Conflict Between Conservation and Use," *Library Review* 31 (Autumn 1982), 163–172.
Observes that librarians are no longer knowledgeable about the production of books, nor about their preservation; a call to action.

Winger, Howard W. and Richard D. Smith, eds. *Deterioration and Preservation of Library Materials.* Chicago: University of Chicago Press, 1970. 200p.
Papers on all aspects of preservation, given at the 34th Annual Conference, Graduate Library School, University of Chicago, August 1969. An important collection.

Winterble, Peter G. "In Pursuit of Preservation," *Influencing Change in Research Librarianship; A Festschrift for Warren J. Haas.* Washington, DC: Council on Library Resources, 1988, 53–58.

Traces Haas's efforts to meet the need for preservation through collaborative efforts, beginning with the compilation of his report for the Association of Research Libraries in 1970 up to his effort to establish the Commission on Preservation and Access in 1988.

Wright, Sandra. "Conservation Program Planning at the National Archives of Canada," *American Archivist* 53:2 (Spring 1991), 314–322.
　　Describes the development and implementation of the NAC conservation policy, which integrates conservation with all archival functions.

Chapter 2

Applebaum, Barbara and Paul Himmelstein. "Planning for a Conservation Survey," *Museum News* 64:3 (February 1986), 5–14.
　　A clearly written article about the nature of conservation surveys and how to organize them; how to work with the conservator, what the conservator expects of the curator, follow-up.

Association of Research Libraries. Office of Management Studies. *Preservation Planning Program; An Assisted Self-Study Manual for Libraries,* expanded ed. Washington, DC: Association of Research Libraries, 1987. 117p.
　　A guide for librarians undertaking a formal study of preservation needs. Covers preparation for the study, its framework, examination of environment and the physical condition of collections, organization, disaster control, resources.

Bond, Randall, Mary DeCarlo, Elizabeth Henes, Eileen Snyder. "Preservation Study of the Syracuse University Libraries," *College and Research Libraries* 48:2 (March 1987), 132–147.
　　Report of a survey and the methodology for assessing the condition of non-rare materials in a circulating collection.

The Conservation Assessment: A Tool for Planning, Implementing and Fundraising. Marina del Rey, CA: Getty Conservation Institute/National Institute for Conservation, 1990. 50p. *Bibliography, 45p.*

Addresses basic conservation needs within a museum, provides methods for gathering, interpreting, and reporting information essential for collections care policies and practices. Includes a client contract form, pre-visit questionnaire; collections assessment guidelines and checklist; architectural assessment guidelines.

Cunha, George M., Howard P. Lowell, Robert E. Schnare. *Conservation Survey Manual.* Balston Spa, NY: SMART, 1982.

General manual, based upon the Northeast Document Conservation Center's approach. Includes "What an Institution Can Do to Survey Its Conservation Needs," a basic checklist by George M. Cunha.

Curtin, Bonnie Rose. "Archives Preservation: NAGARA GRASP Project Description," *Conservation Administration News,* No. 41 (April 1990), 3–5.

Description of a computer-driven self-study program developed by Curtain for the National Association of Government Archives and Records Administrators (NAGARA).

Curtin, Bonnie Rose. "Is Conservation Ready for Artificial Intelligence?" *Abbey Newsletter* 14:1 (February 1990), 1–2.

Brief description of the computer-driven self-study program developed by Curtin for the National Association of Government Archives and Records Administrators (NAGARA).

Curtin, Bonnie Rose. "Preservation Planning for Archives: Development and Field Testing of the NAGARA GRASP," *American Archivist* 53:2 (Spring 1990), 236–243.

Development, design, and field testing of the GRASP computer-driven self-study program are described.

Densky, Lois. "CAPES: The New Jersey Experience," *Conservation Administration News* No. 47 (October 1991), 4–5.

Describes the Caucus Archival Project Evaluation Service, started in 1988 by the New Jersey Caucus of the Mid-Atlantic Regional Archives Conference with funding from the New Jersey Historical Commission. Specialists evaluate collections for organization, preservation, and access and educate institutions about collection management.

Dillon, Phyllis. "Conservation Planning: Where Can You Find the Help You Need," *History News* 42:4 (August 1987), 10–15.
Information on locating specialists and undertaking a conservation survey for planning. Describes the survey process and suggests sources of funding.

Fortson-Jones, Judith. "Practicality Peaks for This Conservation Survey Method," *The New Library Scene* 1:2 (November–December 1982), 1,4,8,14.
Provides methodology, and a worksheet, for a survey of the physical condition of the State Archives Division, Nebraska State Historical Society.

Gertz, Janet, Charlotte B. Brown, Jane Beebe, Daria D'Arienzo, Floyd Mernett, and Lynn Robinson. "Preservation Analysis and the Brittle Book Problem in College Libraries: the Identification of Research-Level Collections and their Implications," *College and Research Libraries* 54:3 (May 1993), 227–239.
Using Atkinson's methodology, examines the extent of the brittle book problem in college libraries.

Horton, Carolyn. *Cleaning and Preserving Bindings and Related Materials,* 2nd rev. ed. Chicago: Library Technology Project, American Library Association, 1969. 87p.
Describes the organization and management of a systematic survey of stack conditions.

Hutchins, Jane. "Conservation Surveys," *Technical Information* (Virginia Association of Museums) (Winter/Spring 1987), 5–6.
Discusses general and collection surveys, noting that the conservation survey is an important part of an institution's long-range plan for collections care.

Keene, Suzanne. "Audits of Care: A Framework for Collections Condition Surveys," *Storage.* London: United Kingdom Institute for Conservation, 1991. 6–16.
Describes the methodology developed by the Museum of London for assessing the condition of museum collections.

National Association for Government Archives and Records Administrators (NAGARA). *Guide and Resources for Archival Strategic Preservation Planning (GRASP),* 2 vols. Albany, NY: NAGARA, 1990.

A computer-assisted self-study tool based on an expert system, a manual offering specific preservation strategies, and a resource guide and bibliography of more than 600 citations.

Pollack, Michael. "Surveying the Collections," *Library Conservation News*, No. 21 (October 1988), 4–7. Tables.
Report on the survey of a collection of the British Library's monographs and periodicals to determine binding condition and the fold strength of paper. The survey method is described and the implications of the survey are discussed.

Reed-Scott, Jutta. *Manual for the North American Inventory of Research Library Collections,* rev. ed. Washington, DC: Association of Research Libraries, 1988. 98p.
Guide for libraries undertaking conspectus-based collection assessments; provides a methodology and procedures.

Reynolds, Anne L., Nancy C. Schrock, and Joanna Walsh. "Preservation: The Public Library Response," *Library Journal* 114:2 (February 15, 1989), 128–132.
Describes the collections survey undertaken by the Wellesley (MA) Public Library and how the results are used to obtain funding for conservation treatments and a continuing collection maintenance program.

Rutledge, John and Willy Owen. "Changes in the Quality of Paper in French Books, 1860–1914: A Study of Selected Holdings of the Wilson Library, University of North Carolina," *Library Resources and Technical Services* 27:2 (April-June 1983), 177–187.
The results of a study to determine the condition of French books in the library's collection.

"Shaping a Conservation Plan Through General Surveys," *American Institute for Conservation Newsletter* 113:2 (March 1988), 1–2.
Describes the Institute for Museum Services (IMS) funded surveys and the need to undertake them to assess condition of collections and set priorities.

Shenton, Helen. "A Conservation Strategy for Books at the Victoria and Albert Museum," *Institute of Paper Conservation Conference Papers, Manchester 1992.* Leigh, Worcs.: Institute of Paper Conservation, 1992, 133–140.

Outlines the procedure for a conservation survey of the collection to assess needs and develop preservation and conservation strategies.

Smith, Merrily A. and Karen Garlick. "Surveying Library Collections: A Suggested Approach With Case Study," *Technical Services Quarterly* 5:2 (1987), 3–18.
Describes the components of a successful survey: planning, execution, analysis, and implementation.

Torres, Amparo E. de, ed. *Collections Care: A Selected Bibliography.* Washington, DC: National Institute for Conservation, 1990. 119 p.
Topical bibliography.

Walker, Gay. "Advanced Preservation Planning at Yale," *Microform Review* 18:1 (Winter 1989), 20–28.
Planning for the long term using the Association of Research Libraries Office of Management Studies preservation self-study methodology. Subject strengths were identified, using the Research Libraries Group Conspectus as a tool, and strategies for system-wide preservation activities were developed.

Walker, Gay, Jane Greenfield, John Fox, Jeffrey S. Simonoff. "The Yale Survey: A Large-Scale Study of Book Deterioration in the Yale University Library," *College and Research Libraries* 46:2 (March 1985), 111–132.
Describes the methodology of the survey to determine the physical condition of books in the Yale University Library.

Webster, Duane. "Self-Assessment as an Improvement Strategy: Background on the ARL Preservation Planning Program," *Bookmark* (New York State Library) 45:3 (Spring 1987), 191–193.
Describes the ARL/OMS program.

Wiederkehr, Robert R. V. *The Design and Analysis of a Sample Survey of the Condition of Books in the Library of Congress.* Rockville, MD: King Research, Inc., March 1984. 23p. and appendices.
Describes a sample survey of more than 1,000 volumes with characteristics of each observed and recorded. Statistics

analyzed to determine the percent of books in the collection that would benefit from deacidification.

Willard, Louis Charles. "An Analysis of Paper Stability and Circulation Patterns of the Monographic Collection of Speer Library, Princeton Theological Seminary," *Essays on Theological Librarianship Presented to Calvin Henry Schmitt.* Philadelphia: American Theological Library Association, 1980, 163–173.
Summary and review of the results of a survey of the condition of books in the general collection, 1976. The methodology of the survey is clearly detailed.

Chapter 3

Adams, Randolph G. "Librarians as Enemies of Books," *Library Quarterly* 7 (1937), 317–331.
An eloquent statement against the trend of library managers to neglect their responsibility for the care and preservation of their collections.

Amodeo, Anthony J. "A Debt Unpaid: The Bibliographic Instruction Librarian and Library Conservation," *College and Research Libraries News* 49:9 (October 1988), 601–603.
Advocates the teaching of the care and handling of books within the context of the bibliographic instruction program.

Amodeo, Anthony J. "Special Collections Desk Duty: Preventing Damage," *College and Research Libraries News* 44:6 (June 1983), 177, 180–182.
Instructions for the handling of rare books by attendants and users.

Applebaum, Barbara. "Criteria for Treatment: Reversibility," *Journal of the American Institute for Conservation* 26:2 (Fall 1987), 65–73.
Principle examined by clarifying its definitions and examining the variables that make treatment possible.

Association of Research Libraries. Office of Management Studies. *Brittle Books Program.* Washington, DC: Association of Research Libraries, March 1989. 121p. (SPEC Kit, 152).

Policies and guidelines for dealing with publications that are so deteriorated that they must be reformatted to avoid loss. Covers planning, policies and procedures, management.

Association of Research Libraries. Office of Management Studies. *Preservation Guidelines in ARL Libraries.* Washington, DC: Association of Research Libraries, September 1987, 110p. (SPEC Kit, 137)

Guidelines, policies, and procedures issued by ARL libraries since 1981.

Atkinson, Ross W. "Selection for Preservation: A Materialistic Approach," *Library Resources and Technical Services* 30:4 (October–December 1986), 341–353.

An articulate discussion of the decision-making process for preservation actions.

Bagnall, Roger S. and Carolyn L. Harris. "Involving Scholars in Preservation Decisions: The Case of the Classicists," *Journal of Academic Librarianship* 43:3 (July 1987), 140–146.

Describes the project to preserve the most important works in classical studies published between 1850 and 1918, and the education of scholars about preservation.

Baker, John. "Typical Costs in Conservation Planning for the Small Library," *Library Security Newsletter* 1:6 (November–December 1975), 1,3–5.

Discussion of the methods for preserving library materials, costs and benefits.

Banks, Joyce M., ed. *Guidelines for Preventive Conservation,* rev. ed. Ottawa: National Library of Canada, 1987. 45p. English/French.

Covers the principles of preservation, storage, and handling, conservation awareness, disaster planning. Bibliography. Appendix includes the Preservation Policy of the Library Services of the National Museums of Canada.

Banks, Paul N. "Preservation of Library Materials," *Encyclopedia of Library and Information Science,* vol. 23. New York: Marcel Dekker, 1978, 180–222.

An overview of preservation, including causes of deterioration, methods of preservation and conservation; collection management. Bibliography. Reprinted by the Newberry Library, Chicago, 1978.

Bansa, Helmut. "The Conservation of Modern Books," *IFLA Journal* 9:2 (1983), 102–113.
Defines conservation as the responsibility of library management. Recommends that librarians encourage the production of permanent/durable books.

Barker, Nicolas. "Conservation and Preservation: A Problem of Library Management, A British Library View," *Libri* 31:3 (September 1981), 193–197.
Statement of the library administrator's role and responsibility.

Baumann, Roland M., ed. *A Manual of Archival Techniques.* 2nd ed. Harrisburg, PA: Pennsylvania Historical and Museum Commission, 1982. 134p.
Covers archival management, including preservation and conservation. Bibliography.

Blades, William. *The Enemies of Books,* rev. and enl. London: Eliot Stock, 1886. 196p.
Classic, still relevant book on the care and preservation of library materials. Abridged in *AB Bookmans Yearbook,* pt. 1 (1971), 3–22.

Bloomfield, B. C. "The Librarian as Custodian; or, A Policeman's Lot," *Journal of Documentation* 40:2 (June 1984), 144–151.
Addresses the issue of what librarians should preserve for the future; discusses collection management and staff training.

Boomgaarden, Wesley L. "Preservation Planning for the Small Special Library," *Special Libraries* 76:3 (Summer 1985), 204–211.
Covers the nature of materials, environmental conditions, and collection handling and treatment.

Brown, Charlotte B. and Janet E. Gertz. "Selection for Preservation: Applications for College Libraries," *Building on the First Century.* Chicago: Association for College and Research Libraries, 1989, 288–294.

A study testing the applicability of Ross Atkinson's typology for preservation selection.

Campbell, Barbara. "Rare Government Documents: Identification and Protection," *Conservation Administration News,* No. 42 (July 1990), 10–11.
Discusses the need to identify rare government documents and to protect and preserve them.

Cave, Roderick. "The Care and Restoration of Rare Books," *Rare Book Librarianship.* London: Clive Bingley; Hamden, CT: Linnet Books, 1976, 83–93.
What curators should and should not do to preserve their collections.

Chapman, Patricia. *Guidelines on Preservation and Conservation Policies in the Archives and Libraries Heritage.* Paris: UNESCO, 1990. 40p. (RAMP Study, PG1–90/WS/7)

Child, Margaret S. "Further Thoughts on 'Selection for Preservation: A Materialistic Approach,' " *Library Resources and Technical Services* 30:4 (October–December 1986), 354–362.
Amplification on the Atkinson paper, with a strategy for preservation by reformatting research collections.

Child, Margaret S. "Selection for Preservation," *Advances in Preservation and Access,* vol. 1. Westport, CT: Meckler, 1992, 147–158.
Discussion of criteria for selection of materials for preservation; cost of quantifying the decision-making process.

Clark, Lenore, ed. *Guide to Review of Library Collections: Preservation, Storage, and Withdrawal.* Chicago: American Library Association, 1991. 41p. (Collection Management and Development Guides, 5)
Guidelines for collection management and preservation based on a review of current practices.

Cluff, E. Dale. "The Role and Responsibility of the Library in Preservation and Conservation," *Conserving and Preserving Library Materials,* ed. Kathryn L. and William T. Henderson. Urbana-Champaign: University of Illinois Graduate School of Library and Information Service, 1983. 181–196.
Defines the scope of preservation activities in a library.

Columbia University Libraries. *The Preservation of Library Materials: A CUL Handbook.* New York: Columbia University Libraries, updated frequently.
Policies and procedures for the library system.

Commission on Preservation and Access. Task Forces on Archival Selection. *The Preservation of Archival Materials: Report.* Washington, DC: Commission on Preservation and Access, April 1993. 7p.
Addresses the need to integrate preservation of records into archival management.

Conway, Paul. "Preserving History is Future: Developing a Nationwide Strategy for Archival Preservation," *Advances in Preservation and Access,* vol. 1. Westport, CT: Meckler, 1992, 244–260.
Describes a nationwide preservation strategy based upon the model of the Society of American Archivists.

Cunha, George Martin. "Housekeeping," *Seminar on Library and Archive Conservation.* Boston: Boston Athenaeum, 1971, 121–129.
Basic information on collections care.

Darling, Pamela W. " 'Collection Officer' or 'Collector': The Preservation Side of the 'Development' Responsibility," *Collection Development in Libraries: A Treatise,* ed. Robert D. Stueart and George B. Miller. Greenwich, CT: JAI Publications, 1980, 281–288. (Foundation in Library and Information Science, 10)
Outlines the problems in the production and the housing of books, emphasizing the need for collection maintenance.

Dean, John. "Conservation Officers: The Administrative Role," *Wilson Library Bulletin* 57:2 (October 1982), 128–132.
Describes the role of the conservation officer as an administrator with wide responsibilities.

Dean, John. "Growth Control in the Research Library," *Steady-State Zero Growth and the Academic Library,* ed. Colin Steele. London: Clive Bingley; Hamden, CT: Linnet Books, 1978, 83–108.
Discusses the need for proper storage and the deaccessioning of materials when appropriate, with a note on preservation.

De Candido, Robert. "Out Of the Question," *Conservation Administration News,* No. 53 (April 1993), 32–33.
Reflective essay on the challenge of collection management and selection for preservation.

De Candido, Robert and GraceAnne A. "Micro-Preservation: Conserving the Small Library," *Library Resources and Technical Services* 29:2 (April–June 1985), 151–160.
Outlines procedures for the preservation of resources in the smaller library.

De Somogyi, Aileen. "Access Versus Preservation," *Canadian Library Journal* 31:5 (October 1974), 414–419.
Discusses the problems that arise in open stack collections and advocates some control.

Dowler, Lawrence. "Deaccessioning Collections: A New Perspective on a Continuing Controversy," *Archival Choices,* ed. Nancy E. Peace. Lexington, MA: Lexington Books, 1984, 117–132.
Discussion of the emotional issues surrounding the decision to deaccess materials.

Enright, Brian, Lotte Hellinga, and Beryl Leigh. *Selection for Survival: A Review of Acquisition and Retention Policies.* London: The British Library, 1989. 104p.
The report of a management team that reviewed the British Library's acquisition and retention policies; presents a "life cycle model" for library materials.

Garlick, Karen. "Planning an Effective Holdings Maintenance Program," *American Archivist* 52:3 (Spring 1990), 256–264.
The steps that can be taken to improve the storage environment for archival collections.

Harris, Carolyn, Carol Mandel, and Robert Wolven. "A Cost Model for Preservation: The Columbia University Libraries' Approach," *Library Resources and Technical Services* 35:1 (January 1991), 33–54.
A comprehensive model for identifying the processes involved in preservation and their associated costs; provides a methodology for determining unit costs.

Harvey, Ross. *Preservation in Australian and New Zealand*

Libraries: Principles, Strategies and Practices for Librarians. Wagga Wagga, NSW: Centre for Information Studies, Charles Sturt University, 1990. 373p. (Topics in Australasian Library and Information Studies, 3)
    A general text on preservation.

Hazen, Dan C. "Collection Development, Collection Management and Preservation," *Library Resources and Technical Services* 26:1 (January–March 1982), 3–11.
    The management perspective; an attempt to define who should be responsible for the preservation of the collections.

Hazen, Dan C. "Preservation in Poverty and Plenty: Policy Issues for the 1990s," *Journal of Academic Librarianship* 15:6 (January 1990), 344–351.
    Examines some underlying assumptions in current activities and whether they effectively meet needs. Suggests a national collection and considers its international implications.

Henderson, Cathy. "Curator or Conservator: Who Decides on What Treatment?" *Rare Books and Manuscripts Librarianship* 2:2 (Fall 1987), 103–107.
    Considers the need to examine relationships with conservators and to educate them about curators' needs.

Holland, Michael E. "Material Selection for Library Conservation," *Library and Archival Security* 6:1 (Spring 1984), 7–21.
    Describes the conservation selection strategies reported in the literature. Author advocates comprehensive resource management and a sound collection policy.

Horton, Carolyn. *Cleaning and Preserving Bindings and Related Materials,* 2nd rev. ed. Chicago: Library Technology Program, American Library Association, 1969. 87p.
    Describes the management of a systematic survey of stack conditions and a program of care for collections.

Hubbard, William J. *Stack Management: A Practical Guide to Shelving and Maintaining Library Collections.* Chicago: American Library Association, 1981. 102p.
    A basic manual, including a chapter on "Care of Books," which covers the shelving and handling of materials, basic repair, and staff training.

Jones, Norvell M. M. and Mary Lynn Ritzenthaler. "Implementing an Archival Preservation Program," *Managing Archives and Archival Institutions*. Chicago: University of Chicago Press, 1989, 185–206.
Basic, programmatic approach to preservation for archival collections. Covers causes of deterioration, elements of a preservation program, implementation, management, and conservation. Bibliography.

Kellar, Scott. "Collections Conservation: An Emerging Perspective," *Conservation Administration News,* No. 43 (October 1990), 8–9.
Explores the emerging role of the collections conservator in libraries and the collections approach to preservation and treatment.

Krasnow, Lawrence L. "Legal Aspects of Conservation: Basic Considerations of Control and Negligence," *Technology & Conservation* 7:1 (Spring 1982), 38–40.
Advice on contractual agreements for service between client and conservator.

Larsen, A. Dean and Randy S. Silverman. "Preservation," *Library Technical Services* 2nd ed., ed. Irene P. Godden. New York: Academic Press, 1991, 205–269.
An overview of preservation management and issues of the 1990s, with citations from the literature.

[McCrady, Ellen]. "Selection for Preservation," *Abbey Newsletter* 6:4 supplement (August 1982), 4p.
Summary of editor's thoughts at a period in time when there was considerable debate among preservation librarians.

MacDonald, Eric. "Creating a Preservation Department from Existing Staff Resources: The UC Irvine Experience," *Conservation Administration News,* No. 55 (October 1993), 6–7, 34–35.
Examines personnel considerations with emphasis on the need for "planning, communication, and support from all levels, especially at the top administrative level."

Magrill, Rose Mary and Constance Rinehart. "Selection for Preservation: A Service Study," *Library Resources and Technical Services* 24:1 (Winter 1980), 44–57.

Authors devised a simple rating scale for evaluating the condition of books and applied it to a sample collection in Western European literature.

Merrill-Oldham, Jan. *Conservation and Preservation of Library Materials: A Program for the University of Connecticut Libraries.* Storrs, CT: University of Connecticut Libraries, 1984. Detailed, comprehensive analysis of the preservation needs in a medium-sized research library.

Merrill-Oldham, Jan, Carolyn Clark Morrow, and Mark Roosa. *Preservation Program Models: A Study Project and Report.* Washington, DC: Association for Research Libraries, 1991. 54p. Provides an outline of components for a preservation program; emphasis on research collections that need to be preserved in the national interest, but a useful document for all libraries.

Milevski, Robert J. and Linda Nainis. "Implementing a Book Repair and Treatment Program," *Library Resources and Technical Services* 31:2 (April–June 1987), 159–176. A workable design for an in-house repair unit. Personnel requirements, cost of equipment and supplies are discussed.

National Archives and Records Administration. *Intrinsic Value in Archival Materials.* Washington, DC: National Archives and Records Administration, 1982. 6p. (Staff Information Reprint, 21) Defines "intrinsic value" and discusses characteristics: physical form, aesthetic quality, unique features, age, value for exhibition, public and legal significance.

Oakland Library Consortium. *Preserving Library Resources: A Guide for Staff.* Pittsburgh, PA: Oakland Library Consortium, 1990. 24p. A brief, basic handbook for library personnel.

Paris, Jan. *Choosing and Working With a Conservator.* Atlanta, GA: Southeast Library Network, 1990. 24p. Explains the issues surrounding the selection and use of a conservator.

Patterson, Robert H. "Organizing for Conservation," *Library*

Journal 104:10 (May 15, 1979), 1116–1119. (LJ Series on Preservation, 2)
  A model for librarians planning a broad-based program with administrative support.

Piggott, Michael. "Conservation," *Keeping Archives*, ed. Ann Pederson. Sydney: Australian Society of Archives, 1987, 219–252.
  An overview of preservation concerns, emphasizing the importance of preservation and its relationship to other archival functions.

Pilette, Roberta and Carolyn Harris. "It Takes Two to Tango: A Conservator's View of Curator/Conservator Relations," *Rare Books and Manuscripts Librarianship* 4:2 (Fall 1989), 103–111.
  Discusses the information that is necessary for an intelligent conservation decision and how it can be obtained.

Reed-Scott, Jutta. "Implementation and Evaluation of a Weeding Program," *Collection Management* 7:2 (Summer 1985), 47–58.
  Describes how libraries can undertake successful weeding programs.

Reeve, Phyllis. "Binding: From Basement to Boardroom," *Technical Services Quarterly* 1:1/2 (Fall/Winter 1983), 203–205.
  Emphasizes the importance of book repair and binding in the library of the future.

Sandwith, Hermione and Sheila Stainton, comp. *The National Trust Manual of Housekeeping*. London: National Trust/Penguin, 1985. 273p.
  Focus on preventive preservation, with emphasis on environmental controls.

Schofer, Ralph E. *Cost Comparison of Selected Alternatives for Preserving Historic Pension Files*. Washington, DC: National Archives and Records Administration, June 1986. 52p. (NBSIR 86–3335)
  A cost-benefit study of the microfilming of records; concluded that the least expensive method for the preservation

and access of original paper documents was hand retrieval of materials housed in environmentally sound conditions.

Smith, Richard D. "Guidelines for Preservation," *Special Libraries* 59:5 (May-June 1968), 346–352.
Outlines the causes of paper deterioration and recommends the preparation of a written preservation policy. Outlines the preliminary findings of Smith's research to develop the Wei T'o process for deacidification.

Streit, Samuel A. "Research Library Deaccessioning: Practical Considerations," *Wilson Library Bulletin* 56:9 (May 1982), 658–662.
A reasoned discussion of the issues: ethical, legal, intellectual, bibliographical, historic, artistic, and financial.

Streit, Samuel A. "Transfer of Materials From General Stacks to Special Collections," *Collection Management* 7:2 (Summer 1985), 33–46.
Describes the collection development policy, clearly stating areas of responsibility and workable criteria for selection of materials to be transferred to storage.

Stueart, Robert D. "Weeding of Library Materials; Politics and Policies," *Collection Management* 7:2 (Summer 1985), 47–58.
An overview of the weeding process and the factors supporting the development of a weeding (collection maintenance) program.

Swartzell, Ann. "Preservation," *RTSD Newsletter* 10:7 (1985), 88–90.
A description of cleaning projects and programs in libraries.

Swartzell, Ann. "Preservation: Book Repair," *RTSD Newsletter* 10:2 (1985), 12–14.
A review of manuals on preservation and book repair; sound guidelines on how to review and select them.

Tomer, Christinger. "Identification, Evaluation, and Selection of Books for Preservation," *Collection Management* 3:1 (Spring 1979), 45–54.

A statistical model, developed by the author, that demonstrates that the publication date of a title is a reasonably reliable indication of condition.

Tomer, Christinger. "Selecting Library Materials for Preservation," *Library and Archival Security* 7:1 (Spring 1985), 1–6.
Use as a factor for the selection of materials for preservation.

Waters, Peter. "Phased Preservation: A Philosophical Concept and Practical Approach to Preservation," *Special Libraries* 81:1 (Winter 1990), 35–43.
Discusses the evolution of the concept of phased preservation as an extension of collection maintenance and an alternative to conservation. Describes projects at the Library of Congress and the Academy of Sciences Library, St. Petersburg, Russia.

Watson, Duane A. "The Divine Library Function: Preservation," *School Library Journal* 33:3 (November 1986), 41–45.
Basic article on collection management and preservation for school librarians.

Wessel, Carl J. "Deterioration of Library Materials," *Encyclopedia of Library and Information Science,* vol. 7. New York: Marcel Dekker, 1972, 69–120.
A survey of the factors that cause deterioration; bibliography.

Westbrook, Lynn. "Developing an In-House Preservation Program: A Survey of Experts," *Library and Archival Security* 7:3/4 (Fall/Winter 1985), 1–21.
A summary of current thinking at the time, based upon the author's survey of preservation librarians.

Williams, Lisa B. "Selecting Rare Books for Physical Conservation: Guidelines for Decision Making," *College and Research Libraries* 46:2 (March 1985), 153–159.
Discusses the need for educated decision-making and the criteria used at the University of Chicago.

Winkle, Becky. "Preservation on a Shoestring," *American Libraries* 16:11 (December 1985), 778–779.
Examples of what libraries can accomplish with limited funds.

Repair Manuals

Greenfield, Jane. *Books: Their Care and Repair.* New York: H. W. Wilson Co., 1983. 204p.

Kyle, Hedi. *Library Materials Preservation Manual; Practical Methods for Preserving Books, Pamphlets, and Other Printed Materials,* with Nelly Balloffet, Judith Reed, and Virginia Wisniewski-Klett. Bronxville, NY: Nicholas T. Smith, 1983.

Lewis, A. W. *Basic Book Binding.* New York: Dover, 1957. 144p.

Milevski, Robert J. "Book Repair Manual," *Illinois Libraries* 67:8 (October 1985), 648–684.

Morrow, Carolyn Clark and Carol Dyal. *Conservation Treatment Procedures: A Manual of Step-by-Step Procedures for the Maintenance and Repair of Library Materials.* 2nd ed. Littleton, CO: Libraries Unlimited, 1986. 225p.

Mustardo, Peter J. "Protective Enclosures for the Care of Books," *AB Bookman's Weekly* 83:25 (June 19, 1989), 2730–2733.

Chapter 4

Baas, Valerie. "Know Your Enemies," *History News* 35:7 (July 1980), 40–41.
Briefly describes the habits of several pests that plague libraries, archives, and museums.

Bio-Integral Resource Center. *Least Toxic Pest Management: Cockroaches.* Berkeley, CA: Bio-Integral Resource Center, n.d. [11p.]
A collection of articles on the biology and control of cockroaches.

Burke, John. "Current Research Into the Control of Biodeterioration Through the Use of Thermol or Suffocant Conditions," *AIC News* (American Institute for Conservation) 18:2 (March 1993), 1–4.
Summary of recent research on pest control methods that are safe and effective. References.

Butcher-Younghans, Sherry and Gretchen E. Anderson. "A Holistic Approach to Museum Pest Management," *History News* 45:3 (May–June 1990); 8p. (Technical Leaflet 171).

Discusses the problems with traditional chemical pest control methods and describes freezing technology in the context of a museum's pest control program.

Chamberlain, William R. "A New Approach to Treating Fungus in Small Libraries," *Biodeterioration Research 1,* ed. Gerald C. Llewellyn and Charles E. O'Rear. New York: Plenum, 1988, 323–327; updated in *Abbey Newsletter,* 15:7 (November 1991), 109–111.

Outlines basic steps for treating infested areas; discusses problems in need of basic research.

Daniel, Vinod, Gordon Hanlon and Shin Maekawa. "Eradication of Insect Pests in Museums Using Nitrogen," *WAAC Newsletter* (Western Association for Art Conservation) 15:3 (September 1993), 15–19.

Briefly describes some of the results of testing underway at the Getty Conservation Institute and the J. Paul Getty Museum.

Davis, Mary. "Preservation Using Pesticides: Some Words of Caution," *Wilson Library Bulletin* 59:6 (February 1985), 386–388, 431.

Discussion of the harm caused to humans by pesticides and fumigants. Recommends good housekeeping procedures to curtail infestation in the library. Describes freezing and other basic pest control technologies.

Edelson, Zelda. "Peabody Notebook: Beinecke Library vs. the Deathwatch Beetle: Charles Remington Describes Deep Freezing," *Discovery* 13:1 (1978), 45–46.

A note describing the infestation and treatment of the Beinecke Library, Yale. Illustrated.

"Examining Insect Infestation," *CCI Notes* (Canadian Conservation Institute) 3:1 (April 1986), 3p.

Practical pamphlet on prevention and treatment.

Florian, Mary-Lou. "The Freezing Process—Effects on Insects and Artifact Materials," *Leather Conservation News* 3:1 (Fall 1986), 1–13, 17.

A review of the literature and recommended procedures for freezing insect-infested artifacts.

Florian, Mary-Lou. "Integrated System Approach to Insect Pest Control: An Alternative to Fumigation," *Conservation in Archives; Proceedings of an International Symposium,* Ottawa, May 10–12, 1988. Paris: International Council on Archives, 1989, 253–262.
Demonstrates an approach to insect pest control that does not use fumigation. Emphasis on prevention of infestation through monitoring and environmental controls. Guidelines for implementing a program.

Frankie, G. W. and C. S. Koehler, ed. *Urban Etymology: Interdisciplinary Perspectives.* New York: Praeger, 1983. 493p.
Basic text on contemporary issues in urban entomology and integrated pest management.

Haines, John H. and Stuart A. Koehler. "An Evaluation of Ortho-phenyl Phenol as a Fungicidal Fumigant for Archives and Libraries," *Journal of the American Institute for Conservation* 25:1 (Spring 1986), 49–55.
Report of a text demonstrating that neither O-phenyl phenyl (OPP) nor thymol are totally effective in preventing fungal spores from germinating.

Harmon, James D. and Christopher Coleman. "Pest Management and Disaster Preparedness," *Conservation Administration News,* No. 52 (January 1993), 6–7.
Discusses current pest control techniques and the Integrated Pest Management (IPM) approach; describes the implementation of an IPM program at the University of California-Los Angeles Libraries.

Hicken, Norman. *Bookworms: The Insect Pests of Books.* London: Sheppard Press, 1985. 176p. Illus.
Describes insects and the damage they cause in libraries.

Iiams, Thomas M. "Preservation of Rare Books and Manuscripts in the Huntington Library," *Library Quarterly* 2:4 (October 1932), 375–386.
Decribes bookworm infestation at the Huntington Library and the treatment developed; an early, still timely article on infestation.

Kowalik, Romuald. "Microbiodeterioration of Library Materials," *Restaurator* 4:2, 3–4 (1982), 135–219; 6:1–2 (1984), 61–115.
Describes the causes of microbiodeterioration of library materials, the characteristics of microorganisms, methods of testing, and problems of toxicity. Recommends standardization of safe methods for the treatment of collections.

Lasker, Reuben. "Silverfish, a Paper-Eating Insect," *Scientific Monthly* 84:3 (March 1957), 123–127.
Describes the eating habits and mechanism of silverfish.

McCall, Nancy. "Ionizing Radiation as an Experiment: A Case Study," *Conservation Administration News,* No. 23 (October 1985), 1–2, 20–21.
Report of a technique used to treat an archival collection badly infested by insects, rodents, animal droppings, and fungi. While the treatment was effective in the sterilization of the material, its long-term effect on paper is unknown.

Mallis, Arnold. *Handbook of Pest Control.* 6th ed. Cleveland, OH: Franzak and Foster, 1982. 1,101p.
Information on pest biology and integrated pest management for control. Describes the life cycles and habits of common pests.

Nesheim, Kenneth. "The Yale Non-Toxic Method of Eradication Book-Eating Insects by Deep Freezing," *Restaurator* 6:3–4 (1984), 147–164.
Presents the rationale for the freezing treatment of the Beinecke Library collection and describes the program in its first two years of operation.

Nyberg, Sandra. *The Invasion of the Giant Spore.* Atlanta, GA: Southeast Library Network, November 1987. 19p.
Outlines the causes of mold, mildew, and fungi, and treatments. Chemical treatments are described, but the maintenance of a clean environment is considered the critical factor.

Olkowski, William and Helga. *Contracting for Pest Control Services; Cockroaches, Mice, Rats and Flies in Public and Private Buildings: A Consumer's Guide.* Berkeley, CA: Bio-Integral Resource Center, n.d. 39p.
Describes the tasks required of a professional exterminator,

safe methods of control, and the role of the building occupant in reducing the problem.

Olkowski, William and Helga. "Pests that Damage Paper: Silverfish, Firebrats and Booklice," *Common Sense Pest Control* 3:1 (Winter 1981), 1–5.
Describes the insects, their habitat, and the damage they can cause. Methods of control are described.

Olkowski, William and Helga and Sheila Daar. "IPM for the German Cockroach," *IPM Practitioner* 6:3 (Summer 1990), 7–10.
Describes the biology of the cockroach, how to establish a monitoring program, methods of changing the environment to inhibit roaches, and uses of insecticides.

Olkowski, William and Helga and Sheila Daar. *Integrated Pest Management for the German Cockroach.* Berkeley, CA: Bio-Integral Resource Center, 1984. 22p. (BIRC Technical Review)
Describes the biology and habitat of the cockroach and methods of roach control. Bibliography.

Olkowski, William and Helga and Sheila Daar. "What Is IPM?" *Common Sense Pest Control* 4:3 (Summer 1988), 9–16.
Describes integrated pest management (IPM), a combination of strategies to eliminate pests.

Parker, Thomas A. "Integrated Pest Management for Libraries," *Preservation of Library Materials,* ed. Merrily Smith, vol. 2. Munich, New York: K. G. Saur, 1987. 103–123. (IFLA Publication 41)
A review of the common pests found in libraries and archives; discussion of the advantages and disadvantages of fumigation. Recommends a common-sense approach to pest control.

Parker, Thomas A. *A Study on Integrated Pest Management for Libraries and Archives.* Paris: UNESCO, 199p. (RAMP Study).
Examines major pests affecting library/archival collections, the damage they cause, techniques for pest prevention and control; the development of an integrated pest management program.

Pelz, Perri and Monona Rossol. *Safe Pest Control Procedures for Museum Collections.* New York: Center for Occupational Hazards, 1983. 8p.
Information about fumigants used in museums and discussion of the problems.

Pinniger, David. *Insect Pests in Museums.* London: Institute of Architecture Publications, 1989. 45p.
Describes common pests and treatments. Provides practical advice on the detection, prevention, and control of insects. Describes safe and effective use of insecticides.

Raynes, Patricia. "Insects and their Control in the Library," *Conservation Administration News,* No. 27 (October 1986), 4, 24–25.
Decribes measures taken through the centuries to protect collections from damage by insects, with discussion of current methods of pest control and the problem of fumigation.

Smith, Richard D. "Fumigation Quandary: More Overkill or Common Sense?" *Paper Conservator* 10 (1986), 46–47.
Consideration of several options for pest control that are not harmful to humans.

Smith, Richard D. "The Use of Redesigned and Mechanically Modified Commercial Freezers to Dry Water-Wetted Books and Exterminate Insects," *Restaurator* 6:3–4 (1984), 165–190.
Describes the modification and use of a supermarket freezer to dry water-damaged books and exterminate insects.

Steckman, Elizabeth. "The Giant Spore vs. the New Jersey State Library," *New Jersey Libraries* 26:3 (Summer 1993), 19–21.
Case study of treatment of an outbreak of mold in the collections.

Story, Keith O. *Approaches to Pest Management in Museums.* Washington, DC: Conservation Analytical Laboratory, Smithsonian Institution, 1985. 165p.
Describes insects and the damage they can cause; reviews methods of pest control. Bibliography.

Strassberg, Richard. "The Use of Fumigants in Archival Repositories," *American Archivist* 41:1 (January 1978), 25–36.
An overview essay with a focus on the safety problems caused by fumigants.

Strong, Thomas J. K. and John E. Dawson. *Controlling Museum Fungal Problems.* Ottawa, ON: Canadian Conservation Institute, 1991. 8 p. Eng./Fr. (CCI Technical Bulletin, 12)
Describes causes of fungal attack and methods of control. Bibliography.

Strong, Thomas J. K. and John E. Dawson. *Controlling Vertebrate Pests in Museums.* Ottawa, ON: Canadian Conservation Institute, 1991. (CCI Technical Bulletin, 13)
Describes damage that rodents and other vertebrates can cause in a museum and methods, mostly nonchemical, to control them.

Weinstein, Frances Ruth. "A Psocid by Any Other Name . . . (Is Still a Pest)," *Library and Archival Security* 6:1 (Spring 1984), 57–63.
Identifies several insects that commonly infest libraries and describes preventive measures.

Weiss, Harry B. and Ralph H. Carruthers. *Insect Enemies of Books.* New York: New York Public Library, 1937. 63p.
History covering 2,200 years; bibliography.

Wood, Mary Lee. *Prevention and Treatment of Mold in Library Collections With an Emphasis on Tropical Climates.* Paris: UNESCO, 1988. 81p. (RAMP Study)
Information on preservation and basic treatments for mold, with emphasis on prevention of infestation. Bibliography.

Zycherman, Lynda A. and John Richard Schrock, ed. *A Guide to Museum Pest Control.* Washington, DC: Foundation of the American Institute for Conservation and the Association of Systematics Collections, 1988. 205p.
Covers policy, law and liability, pests and pest identification, treatment. Extensive bibliography compiled by Karen Preslock.

Chapter 5

Applebaum, Barbara. *Guide to Environmental Protection of Collections.* Madison, CT: Sound View Press, 1991. 270p.
Basic manual on physical care of collections. Describes the physical nature of objects in collections and how they react to

their environment. It covers collection management and preservation; how to assess the needs of materials. The role that the conservator plays in collection management is emphasized.

Association of Higher Education Facilities Officers. *Preservation of Library and Archival Materials.* Alexandria, VA: Association of Higher Education Facilities Officers, 1991. 66p.

Papers from a seminar cosponsored by the Commission on Preservation and Access. Librarians, conservators, and facilities engineers consider the physical maintenance of library buildings to provide and maintain an environment for the preservation of materials.

Ayers, J. Marx et al. "Energy Conservation and Climate Control in Museums: A Cost Simulation Under Various Outdoor Climates," *International Journal of Museum Management and Curatorship* 8 (1989), 299–312.

A study of a modern structure, using computer simulations, to determine method and cost.

Baer, Norbert S. and Paul N. Banks. "Indoor Air Pollution: Effects on Cultural and Historic Materials," *International Journal of Museum Management and Curatorship* 4:1 (March 1985), 9–20.

Discussion of pollutants, their causes, including emissions from building materials, which are introduced by heating and air-conditioning systems, and their effect. Extensive bibliography.

Banks, Paul N. "Environmental Conditions for Storage of Paper-Based Records," *Conservation in Archives.* Paris: International Council on Archives, 1989, 77–88.

Discusses the environmental factors that affect the longevity of records: temperature, relative humidity, air pollutants, and light. Notes the lack of research to document their effect and the difficulty this presents in creating standards for the storage of paper-based materials,

Banks, Paul N. "Environmental Standards for Storage of Books and Manuscripts," *Library Journal* 99:3 (February 1, 1974), 339–343.

Describes the standards established for the Newberry Library.

Berns, Roy S. and Franc Grum. "Exhibiting Artwork: Consider the Illuminating Source," *Color Research and Application* 12:2 (April 1987), 63–72.
Describes steps to be taken for proper illumination of works of art; notes that fluorescent lighting, when properly filtered, will emit lower levels of ultraviolet radiation than incandescent light.

Bradshear, James Gregory and Mary Lynn Ritzenthaler. "Archival Exhibits," *Managing Archives and Archival Institutions.* Chicago: University of Chicago Press, 1989, 228–240.
Addresses policy, concepts, and technical issues, including the preservation problems that must be faced in an exhibition program.

Brill, Thomas B. *Light: Its Interaction with Art and Antiquities.* New York: Plenum, 1980. 287p.
Discusses the nature of light and its effect upon materials. A basic text that presumes that the reader has a modest background in general and organic chemistry. Bibliography.

Crews, Patricia Fox. "A Comparison of Selected UV Filtering Materials for the Reduction of Fading," *Journal of the American Institute for Conservation* 28:2 (Fall 1989), 117–125.
Results of tests that demonstrate which UV filtering materials are appropriate.

Dahlø, Rolf. "Cold Storage," *Library Conservation News,* No. 37 (October 1992), 1–3.
Describes the preservation strategy of the National Library of Norway to house paper-based library and archival collections in cold storage to retard deterioration.

Daniels, V. "Air Pollution and the Archivist," *Society of American Archivists Journal* 6:3 (April 1979), 154–156.
Discusses the pollutants that are the most troublesome to archivists and some solutions, such as protective wrappers.

Dubin, Fred. "Mechanical Systems and Libraries," *Library Trends* 36:2 (Fall 1987), 351–360.

Practical discussion of environmental factors and mechanical design for libraries from the preservation perspective.

Dunlap, Ellen S. and Kathleen Reed. "Borrowing of Special Collections Material for Exhibition: A Draft," *Rare Books and Manuscript Librarianship* 2:1 (Spring 1987), 27–37.
Draft guidelines for loans, with a sample loan agreement form. The guidelines reflect a concern for the physical protection of materials loaned for exhibition.

Environmental Specifications for the Storage of Library and Archival Materials. Atlanta, GA: Southeast Library Network, 1985. 5p.
Clearly written, informative pamphlet that covers temperature, relative humidity, air pollution, and light. Adapted from a document prepared by the Midwest Cooperative Conservation Program.

Gardner, James B. "Indoor Air: Problems and Solutions," *Construction Specifier* 40:3 (March 1987), 100–114.
Reviews the causes and the effects of the air pollution problem, legislative initiatives, and implications, with recommendations.

Guichen, Gael de. "How To Make a Rotten Showcase," *Museum* 146 (1985), 64–67. Illus.
Eleven timely tips.

Gwinn, Nancy E. "Politics and Practical Realities: Environmental Issues for the Library Administrator," *Advances in Preservation and Access,* vol. 1. Westport, CT: Meckler, 1992, 135–146.
Overview of environmental requirements for housing of library and archival materials; discussion of standards.

Lafontaine, Raymond H. and Patricia A. Wood. *Fluorescent Lamps.* Ottawa, ON: Canadian Conservation Institute, 1982. 11p. Eng./Fr. (CCI Technical Bulletin, 7)
A review of visual characteristics of fluorescent lighting.

Lee, S. B., J. Bogaard and R. L. Feller. "Darkening of Paper Following Exposure to Visible and Near-Visible Ultraviolet Radiation," *Journal of the American Institute for Conservation* 28:1 (Spring 1989), 1–18. Graphs.

A series of experiments demonstrate that the darkening of paper is chiefly influenced by the lignin content and the pH of the paper.

Lewis, Ralph H. *Manual for Museums.* Washington, DC: National Park Service, 1976. 412p.
Describes agents of deterioration for paper-based and other objects.

Livingston, Richard A. "Implementing an Environmental Monitoring Program," *Construction Specifier* 43:7 (July 1990), 136–143.
Reviews the elements of an effective environmental monitoring program, including an overall strategy with clear objectives, the variables to be monitored, desired data quality, and clear data interpretation.

Lull, William P. *Conservation Environment: Guidelines for Libraries and Archives.* Albany, NY: New York State Program for the Conservation and Preservation of Library Research Materials, 1991. 88p.
Discusses environmental concerns, assessment, monitoring, and the establishment of practical solutions, both interim and low-cost measures to improve the environment.

Lull, William P. "Selecting Fluorescent Lamps for U.V. Output," *Abbey Newsletter* 16:4 (August 1992), 54–55.
An analysis of UV output of typical fluorescent lights. Chart.

MacLeod, K.J. *Museum Lighting.* Ottawa, ON: Canadian Conservation Institute, 1978. 14p. Eng./Fr. (CCI Technical Bulletin, 2)
A general description of the nature of light, with recommended safe levels for museums.

MacLeod, K. J. *Relative Humidity: Its Importance, Measurement and Control in Museums.* Ottawa: Canadian Conservation Institute, 1978. 14p. Eng./Fr. (CCI Technical Bulletin, 1)
Describes relative humidity (RH) and the part that it plays in conjunction with atmospheric pollutants in the deterioration of objects.

Meckler, Milton. "How Will New Ventilation Standards Affect

Indoor Air Quality? *Strategic Planning and Energy Management* 8:1 (Fall 1988), 57–75.

Describes the standards and how they can be implemented in new and renovated structures. Addresses the problem of "sick building syndrome" and the implications of new technologies on building environment.

Metcalf, Keyes D. *Planning Academic and Research Library Buildings,* 2nd ed. by Philip D. Leighton and David C. Weber. Chicago: American Library Association, 1986. 544p.

An updated version of Metcalf's classic text on the planning, design, and construction of library buildings. The principles of the original are combined with guidelines for accommodating contemporary requirements. The 1965 edition should be consulted for the best information on library lighting, heating and ventilation requirements.

Motylewski, Karen. "A Matter of Control," *Museum News* 69:2 (April 1990), 64–67.

Describes the appropriate climate controls for protection of collections. Emphasizes the need for a stable environment and a monitoring program.

Padfield, Timothy. "Climate Control in Libraries and Archives," *Preservation of Library Materials,* ed. Merrily Smith, vol. 2. Munich: K. G. Saur, 1987, 124–138.

Describes mechanical control systems, needs for collections, and how these can be met. Discusses passive climate control.

Pascoe, M. W. *Impact of Environmental Pollution on the Preservation of Archives and Records.* Paris: UNESCO, 1988. 44p. (RAMP Study)

Considers the nature of pollutants and their influence on the degradation of archival materials. Provides strategies for dealing with pollutants. Bibliography.

Ramer, Brian. "The Development of a Local Humidity Control System," *International Journal of Museum Management and Curatorship* 3:2 (June 1984), 183–191.

Describes a system for exhibition cases using silica gel.

Rhodes, Barbara, ed. *Hold Everything! A Storage and Housing*

Information Sourcebook for Libraries and Archives. New York: METRO, 1990. 63p.
Provides considerable information on storage and housing; list of suppliers and services, including environmental control and monitoring, shelving and other storage furniture, protective enclosures, cleaning and moving collections.

Robertson, Gray. "Ventilation, Health and Energy Conservation—A Workable Compromise," *Strategic Planning and Energy Conservation* 8:4 (Spring 1989), 65–78.
Describes the causes and sources of indoor air pollution, including "off-gassing" from a variety of products, fibers, microbes, and dirt, with solutions presented.

Romer, Grant B. "Can We Afford to Exhibit Our Valued Photographs?" *PictureScope* 32:4 (Winter 1987), 136–137.
Addresses concerns; urges monitoring programs and a change in the philosophy of exhibition.

Rose, Cordelia. *CourierSpeak: A Phrase Book for Couriers of Museum Objects.* Washington, DC: Smithsonian Institution Press, 1993. 271p.
A book of terms in French, German, Spanish, Russian, Japanese, and English relating to all aspects of the transport of art objects, with discussion about the role of the courier.

Severson, Douglas G. "The Effects of Exhibition on Photographs," *PictureScope* 32:4 (Winter 1987), 133–135.
Presents the results of a photographic print monitoring program that demonstrated that photographs change when exhibited "in ways difficult to understand and predict."

Silberman, Richard M. "A Mandate for Change in the Library Environment," *Library Administration and Management* 7:3 (Summer 1993), 145–152.
Discussion of the need for environmental controls for protection of people and materials; notes increased concern with the indoor environment.

Stolow, Nathan. *Conservation and Exhibitions: Packing, Transport, Storage and Environmental Conditions.* London: Butterworths, 1987. 266p. Illus. (Butterworths Series in Conservation and Museology)

A practical and detailed manual covering all aspects of the exhibition of materials. Includes standards, guidelines, and extensive notes.

Thomson, Garry. "Control of the Environment for Monitoring, Good or Ill," *National Gallery Technical Bulletin* 5 (1981), 3–13. Illus.
Discusses the practical considerations and problems involved in the reliable monitoring and control of environmental factors in museums and galleries.

Thomson, Garry. "Impermanence—Some Chemical and Physical Aspects," *Museums Journal,* 64:1 (June 1964), 16–36.
Discusses chemical changes and the movement of water in organic materials; concludes that research on "permanence" needs to be done.

Thomson, Garry. *The Museum Environment.* 2nd ed. London: International Institute for Conservation/Butterworths, 1986. 293p.
An essential text on the environmental control of buildings housing and displaying cultural property.

"Ultraviolet Filters for Fluorescent Lamps," *CCI Notes* (Canadian Conservation Institute) 2:1 (June 1983), 1 leaf.
A brief note on problems and solutions.

U.S. Environmental Protection Agency. *Building Air Quality: a Guide for Building Owners and Facility Managers.* Washington, DC: Environmental Protection Agency, 1991. 228p and appendixes.
Provides clear guidelines for preventing indoor air quality problems and resolving them when they occur.

U.S. National Bureau of Standards. *Air Quality Criteria for Storage of Paper-Based Archival Records.* Washington, DC: Government Printing Office, 1983.
See Baer and Banks for a discussion of the standard.

Weintraub, Steven and Gordon O. Anson. "Natural Light in Museums: An Asset or a Threat?" *Progressive Architecture* 71 (May–August 1990), 49–54.
Discussion of light and its effect on exhibited materials, with emphasis on the distortive attributes of light.

Chapter 6

Allen, Susan M. Theft in Libraries or Archives," *College and Research Libraries News* 51:10 (November 1990), 939–943.
Outlines actions to be followed after a theft is discovered; emphasizes the need for the inclusion of theft in a disaster plan.

American Library Association. Rare Books and Manuscripts Section. Security Committee. "ACRL Guidelines for the Security of Rare Book, Manuscript, and other Special Collections," *College and Research Libraries News* 51:3 (March 1990), 240–244.
Guidelines for factors to be considered in an adequate security program.

Anderson, Hazel and John E. McIntyre. *Planning Manual for Disaster Control in Scottish Libraries.* Edinburgh: National Library of Scotland, 1985. 75p.
A well-organized manual covering prevention, insurance, response, and recovery, with a model disaster plan. Bibliography.

Association of Research Libraries. Office of Management Services. *Collection Security in ARL Libraries.* Washington, DC: Association of Research Libraries, 1984. 94p. (SPEC Kit 100)
Includes two questionnaire forms, ten policies and procedures documents, and two task force reports, plus a selective bibliography.

Association of Research Libraries. Office of Management Services. *Insuring Library Collections and Buildings.* (Washington, DC: Association of Research Libraries, 1991. 149p. (SPEC Kit, 178)
Presents the results of a survey of academic library administrators' planning for insurance needs and examples of insurance policies.

Atkins, Winston and Ellen Belcher. "Coordinating a Bomb Blast Recovery," *Conservation Administration News,* No. 55 (October 1993), 1–2, 24–27.
Case study of recovery of research materials following a campus bombing.

Balon, Brett J. and H. Wayne Gardner. "Disaster Planning for Electric Records," *ARMA Records Management Quarterly* 22:3 (July 1988), 20–22, 24–25, 30.
   Covers the elements of a disaster plan: cost analysis; optional site locations; planning, testing, and maintenance.

Banik, Gerhard. "Freeze Drying at the National Library of Austria," *International Preservation News,* No. 4 (August 1990), 9–12.
   Describes a process using a chamber developed for the mass deacidification and strengthening of newspapers.

Barton, John and Johanna G. Wellheiser, ed. *An Ounce of Prevention: A Handbook on Disaster Contingency Planning for Archives, Libraries and Record Centres.* Toronto: Toronto Area Archivists Group Educational Foundation, 1986. 192p.
   Covers all variety of disasters, prevention, planning, materials, salvage. Bibliography.

Blades, William. *The Enemies of Books,* rev. and enl. London: Eliot Stock, 1886. 196p.
   A classic, still relevant study on the care and preservation of library materials. An abridged text from the 1888 edition was published in *AB Bookman's Yearbook,* pt. 1 (1971), 3–22.

Bozeman, Pat, ed. *Forged Documents: Proceedings of the 1989 Houston Conference.* New Castle, DE: Oak Knoll, 1990. 180p.
   A discussion of the legal and emotional impact of forged documents on library and archive collections.

Bryan, John L. *Automatic Sprinkler and Stand Pipe Systems.* 2nd ed. Boston, MA: National Fire Protection Association, 1990. 568p.
   Current sprinkler system technology and how it has evolved.

Buchanan, Sally A. *Disaster Planning, Preparedness and Recovery: A RAMP Study.* Paris: UNESCO, 1988. 187p.
   A manual with guidelines for planning for disaster and recovery. Appendices include sample forms prepared by the Southeast Library Network (SOLINET) and an extensive bibliography prepared by Toby Murray.

Buchanan, Sally. "The Stanford Library Flood Restoration Pro-

ject," *College and Research Libraries* 40:6 (November 1979), 539–548.
   Describes the restoration project for the 500,000 volumes damaged in their flood, the various tests conducted on how to dry books in a vacuum chamber.

Burgess, Dean. "The Library Has Blown Up!" *Library Journal* 114:16 (October 1, 1989), 59–61.
   Frank post-mortem of an electrical fire, decisions made, and lessons learned.

Butler, Randall. "The Los Angeles Central Library Fire," *Conservation Administration News,* No. 27 (October 1986), 1–2, 23–24; No. 28 (January 1987), 1–2.
   A description of the damage caused by the fires and the library's approach to salvage.

Campbell, Robert P. "Disaster Recovery: A Game Plan," *Security Systems Administration* 12:3 (March 1983), 16–91.
   Emergency planning and disaster recovery for computer facilities.

Canadian Conservation Institute. "Planning for Disaster Management," *CCI Notes,* 14:1–3 (May 1988), 8p.
   Pamphlets cover planning and hazard analysis, with a basic checklist.

Chartrand, Robert Lee. "Libraries in Parlous Times: Responsibilities and Opportunities, an Introduction," *Special Libraries* 78:2 (Spring 1987), 73–85.
   Analysis of the planning necessary for emergency management (EM) and the role that technology can and cannot play. Describes recently developed EM systems.

Corning Museum of Glass. *The Corning Flood: Museum Under Water.* Corning, NY: Corning Museum of Glass, 1977. 60p.
   Case history of the flood and salvage, with analysis of successes and failures.

Currie, Susan et al. "Cornell University Libraries' Security Checklist," *Library and Archival Security* 7:2 (Summer 1985), 3–13.
   A comprehensive list of questions to be addressed in evaluating library security.

De Candido, Robert. "Out of the Question: From the Ridiculous to the Sublimated," *Conservation Administration News,* No. 31 (Winter 1988), 21–22.
Description of the salvage and treatment techniques of vacuum drying, vacuum freeze drying, thermal freeze drying, and freeze drying.

De Candido, Robert. "Out of the Question: Insurance," *Conservation Administration News,* No. 47 (October 1991), 16–17,31.
Discusses insurance coverage and liability for vendors of preservation-related services.

De Pew, John N. *Statewide Disaster Preparedness and Recovery Program for Florida Libraries.* Urbana-Champaign, IL: University of Illinois, Graduate School of Library and Information Science, 1989. 51p. (Occasional Paper, 185)
Report of a program to increase awareness of the threat of disaster, train people to undertake disaster planning and recovery, and to establish a statewide network.

"Disaster—Preparedness and Response," *Ojo: Connoisseurship and Conservation of Photographs,* No. 4 (Summer/July 1992), 1–8; entire issue.
Information for private collectors and small institutions that lack the resources of large institutional collections. Basic steps for disaster prevention and mitigation; how to write a disaster plan; disaster response and salvage; mold; insurance. Bibliography.

Donnelly, Helene. "Disaster Planning: A Wider Approach," *Conservation Administration News,* No. 53 (April 1993), 8–9, 33.
A manager's approach to disaster planning with an emphasis on the human factors that come into play in disaster recovery.

Drewes, Jeanne. "Computers: Planning for Disaster," *Law Library Journal* 81:1 (Winter 1989), 103–116.
Recommendations for the protection of computers and computer data.

England, Claire and Karen Evans. *Disaster Management for*

Libraries: Planning and Coping. Ottawa: Canadian Library Association, 1988. 207p.
Practical information on disaster planning and recovery and the relation to preservation planning and policy. Bibliography.

Eulenberg, Julia Niebuhr. *Handbook for the Recovery of Water Damaged Business Records.* Prairie Village, KS: ARMA International, 1986. 54p.
Covers general principles, application of salvage.

Fennelly, Lawrence. *Museum, Archival and Library Security.* Woburn, MA: Butterworths, 1983. 912p.
Contributions from security professionals at a variety of institutions. Offers practical information covering all aspects of security fundamentals: insurance, security management, fire protection and emergency planning, physical security controls, utilizing the guard force and investigating theft. Extensive bibliography by John E. Hunter.

Fortson, Judith. *Disaster Planning and Recovery: A How-To-Do-It Manual for Librarians and Archivists.* New York: Neal Schuman, 1992. 181p. (How-To-Do-It Manuals for Libraries, 21)
Addresses the issue of disaster preparedness and recovery; the causes of disasters and protective measures; recovery techniques; developing a plan; risk management; insurance. A comprehensive and clearly written basic text. Bibliography; list of vendors/supplies; reprint of NFPA 910–1991.

Fortson-Jones, Judith. "How to Develop a Disaster Plan for Books and Record Repositories," *History News* 38 (May 1983), 30–31.
Basic, practical approach.

Fu, Paul S. "Handling Water Damage in a Law Library," *Law Library Journal* 79:4 (Fall 1987), 667–687.
Step-by-step disaster recovery with emphasis on insurance issues.

Guldbeck, Per E. "Planning Security for Buildings and Collections," *Care of Antiquities and Historical Collections,* 2nd rev. ed. by A. Bruce MacLeish. Nashville, TN: American Association for State and Local History, 1985, 42–50.
Information on built-in security measures for collections.

Hanff, Peter. "Library Theft Protection," *College and Research Libraries News* 45:6 (June 1984), 289–290.
Report on the results of the Rare Books and Manuscripts Section Security Committee's informal survey of collection security precautions among North American libraries.

Hendriks, Klaus B. and Brian Lesser. "Disaster Preparedness and Recovery: Photographic Materials," *American Archivist* 46:1 (Winter 1983), 52–68.
A thorough review of the topic.

Langelier, Gilles and Sandra Wright. "Contingency Planning for Cartographic Archives," *Archivaria* 13 (Winter 1981/82), 47–58.
Discusses emergency planning in general and describes the contingency planning in the National Map Collection, National Archives of Canada.

Lawrence, Patricia O'Reilly. *Before Disaster Strikes: Prevention, Planning, and Recovery; Caring for Your Personal Collections in the Event of Disaster.* New Orleans, LA: Historic New Orleans Collection, 1992. 40p. Illus.
Presents information to the public about the dangers that can befall valuable possessions and describes measures to safeguard such property.

Leighton, Philip D. "The Stanford Flood," *College and Research Libraries* 40:5 (September 1979), 450–459.
Describes the events at the Stanford University Library from the flood to the start of freeze-drying operations.

Lincoln, Alan Jay and Carol Zell Lincoln. *Library Crime and Security: An International Perspective.* New York: Haworth Press, 1987. 162p.; *Library and Archival Security,* 8:1–2 (Summer 1986), 1–162.
An analysis of library crime and disruption and its impact on an institution. Bibliography.

Lincoln, Alan Jay, ed. "Protecting the Library," *Library Trends* 33:1 (Summer 1984). Entire issue.
A series of essays that examine the issues related to the protection of the library, its contents, and its users.

Lindblom, Beth C. and Karen Motylewski. *Disaster Planning for Cultural Institutions.* Nashville, TN: American Association for State and Local History, 1993. 8p. (Technical Leaflet, 183; *History News,* 48:1 (January–February 1993).
Basic instructions for smaller institutions.

McGiffen, Robert F., Jr. *A Current Status Report on Fumigation in Museums and Historical Agencies.* Nashville, TN: American Association for State and Local History, 1985. 15p. (AASLH Technical Report, 4)
Good brief discussion of the problems with fumigants. Bibliography.

Magrath, Lynn L. and Kenneth E. Dowlin. "The Potential for Development of a Clearinghouse for Emergency Information in the Public Library," *Special Libraries* 78:2 (Spring 1987), 131–135.
The role that the public library can play in creating an on-line clearinghouse for emergency information.

Matthews, Fred W. "Dalhousie Fire," *Canadian Library Journal* 43:4 (August 1986), 221–226.
Description of the library's salvage and drying operation, suggesting areas for further research.

Matthews, Fred W. "Sorting a Mountain of Books," *Library Resources and Technical Services* 31:1 (January–March 1987), 8–94.
Description of the system using computers programmed to sort and reassemble the books that were dried following the Dalhousie Law School fire.

Metcalf, Keyes DeWitt. *Planning Academic and Research Library Buildings,* 2nd ed. by Philip Leighton and David C. Weber. Chicago: American Library Association, 1986. 630p.
Contains considerable information, theoretical and practical, about planning buildings for safety, security, and protection against disasters.

Morentz, James W. "Computerizing Libraries for Emergency Planning," *Special Libraries* 78:2 (Spring 1987), 100–104.
Describes inexpensive computer programs that can provide guidelines on emergency planning for library personnel.

Morris, John. "Fire Protection in the Library," *Construction Specifier*, 42:10 (October 1989), 133–141.
Covers the history of fires and policies of fire protection; bookstack construction and its effect upon the spread of fire; types of automatic suppressant systems, and descriptions of buildings where they are installed.

Morris, John. *The Library Disaster Preparedness Handbook*. Chicago: American Library Association, 1986. 142p.
Review of preventive measures and recovery plans for libraries of all sizes. Good coverage of insurance and risk management issues.

Morris, John and Irvin D. Nichols. *Managing the Library Fire Risk*. 2nd ed. Berkeley, CA: University of California, 1979. 147p.
Presents information relating to fire risk for libraries and means of protecting against loss.

Murray, Toby. "Basic Guidelines for Disaster Planning," *Issues for a New Decade: Today's Challenge, Tomorrow's Opportunity*. Boston, MA: G. K. Hall, 1991, 143–167.
An outline to assist in the preparation of a disaster plan and in the organization of salvage procedures.

Murray, Toby. "Don't Get Caught With Your Pants Down," *ARMA International Records Management Quarterly* 21:2 (April 1987), 12–30, 41.
Step-by-step guidance for recovery operations; extensive bibliography.

National Fire Protection Association, *Automatic Sprinkler Systems Handbook*. Quincy, MA: National Fire Protection Association, 1991. 700p.
Provides technical data on standards and installation requirements for sprinkler systems.

National Fire Protection Association. *Protection of Libraries and Library Collections*. Quincy, MA: National Fire Protection Association, 1991. 45p. (NFPA 910).
Recommended practice for the protection of library collections from fire. Updated frequently.

O'Connell, Mildred. "Disaster Planning: Writing and Imple-

menting Plans for Collections-Holding Institutions," *Technology and Conservation* 8:2 (Summer 1983), 18–24.
  Planning for disaster: conservation survey of buildings and collections, salvage, stabilizing the environment.

O'Connell, Mildred. "Disaster Planning for Libraries," *AB Bookman's Weekly* 71:25 (June 20, 1983), 4693–4701.
  General essay on disaster planning with practical tips.

Olson, Nancy B. "Hanging Your Software Up to Dry," *College and Research Libraries News* 47:10 (November 1986), 634–636.
  Describes the salvage of a water-damaged collection, including computer software; technique explained.

Olson, Randy J. and Larry J. Ostler. "Get Tough on Theft: Electronic Theft Detection," *Library and Archival Security* 7:3–4 (Fall/Winter 1985), 67–77.
  Authors note the lack of evidence to document that electronic security systems curtail theft. Suggests that libraries make a serious commitment to theft prevention.

Reinsch, Mary. "Library Disasters and Effective Staff Management," *Conservation Administration News,* No. 55 (October 1993), 4–5, 31–33.
  Discussion of factors and measures to ensure effective recovery minimizing the emotional toll on staff. Bibliography.

Rhodes, Barbara J., comp. *Hell and High Water: A Disaster Information Sourcebook.* New York: Metropolitan Reference and Research Library Agency, 1988. 58p. (METRO Misc. Publ, 35)
  Provides basic information on disaster planning; the resource notebook is comprehensive.

Sable, Martin H. "Warfare and the Library: An International Bibliography," *Library and Archival Security* 7:1 (Spring 1985), 25–97.
  Covers all aspects of the situation of libraries in armed conflict; bibliography arranged chronologically and by country.

Schmidt, J. David. "Freeze Drying of Historic/Cultural Proper-

ties: A Valuable Process in Restoration and Documentation,"
Technology and Conservation 9:1 (Spring 1985), 20–26."
Discusses freeze-drying as a method for preservation and
describes its development as a tool for museum, library, and
archival collections.

Seal, Robert A. "Insurance for Libraries," *Conservation Administration News,* No. 19 (October 1984), 8–9; No. 20 (January
1985), 10–11, 26.
Overview with selective bibliography.

Sheldon, Ted and Gordon O. Hendrickson. "Emergency Management and Academic Library Resources," *Special Libraries*
78:2 (Spring 1987), 93–99.
The role that academic and research librarians can play in
providing information when disaster strikes.

Spawn, Willman. "Disasters: Can We Plan for Them? If Not,
How Can We Proceed?" *A Manual of Archival Techniques,*
rev. ed., Roland M. Baumann. Harrisburg, PA: Pennsylvania
Historical and Museum Commission, 1982, 71–76; *Preserva-
tion of Library Materials,* ed. Joyce R. Russell. New York:
Special Libraries Association, 1980, 24–29.
A basic article with step-by-step advice.

Trelles, O. M. "Protection of Libraries," *Law Library Journal*
66:3 (August 1973), 241–258.
A brief history of the problems and of librarians' traditional
disinterest in the topic. Covers emergency planning and
includes much useful information on insurance.

Trinkaus-Randall, Gregor. "Preserving Special Collections
Through Internal Security," *College and Research Libraries*
50:4 (July 1989), 448–454.
Summary of the methods that librarians use for security in
special collections; based upon a survey of 26 repositories.

Trinkley, Michael. *Can You Stand the Heat? A Fire Safety
Primer for Libraries, Archives, and Museums.* Atlanta, GA:
SOLINET, 1993. 70p.
Introduction to fire safety with explanations of fire detec-
tion and suppression devices.

Trinkley, Michael. *Hurricane! Surviving the Big One: A Primer for Libraries, Museums, and Archives.* Columbia, SC: Chicora Foundation; Atlanta, GA: SOLINET, 1993. 76p.
Covers disaster planning, storm-proofing facilities, recovery, insurance, and sources of assistance.

Vossler, Janet L. "The Human Element of Disaster Recovery," *ARMA International Records Management Quarterly* 21:1 (January 1987), 10–22.
Discussion of human factors in recovery operations.

Wiktor, Christian L., and Louis G. Vagianos. "The Fire at the Dalhousie Law School Library," *Law Libraries in Canada,* J.N. Fraser, ed., Toronto: Carswell, 1988. pps. 171–187.

Wilson, J. Andrew. "Fire Fighters; An Automatic Fire Suppression System is Among Your Museum's Best and Safest Forms of Insurance," *Museum News* 68:6 (November–December 1989), 68–72.
Explains the need for fire suppressant systems and the hazards of Halon gas; sprinkler systems are clearly described.

Wright, Gordon H. "Fire! Anguish! Dumb Luck! or Contingency Planning," *Canadian Library Journal* 36:5 (October 1979), 254–260.
Discusses the need for disaster planning and provides a review of insurance factors.

Wyly, Mary. "Special Collections Security: Problems, Trends, and Consciousness," *Library Trends* 36:1 (Summer 1987), 241–255.
Describes the increasing awareness of rare books librarians of the vulnerability of their collections and the role that the Rare Books and Manuscripts Section of the American Library Association is undertaking to ensure prosecution and stiffer penalties for thieves.

Zeidberg, David S. "'We Have Met the Enemy . . . ' Collection Security in Libraries," *Rare Book and Manuscript Librarianship* 2:1 (Spring 1987), 19–26.
The problem of theft in libraries and the inadequacy in dealing with it. Author suggests that institutions survey their collections, that collections be marked, and that theft be prosecuted when it occurs.

Chapter 7

American Library Association. Library Technology Program. *Development of Performance Standards for Binding Used in Libraries, Phase II.* Chicago: American Library Association, 1966. (LTP Publ., 10)
   Provisional minimal standards for library binding and a history of how testing evolved.

Barles, George. "Alum Tawed Leathers: A Reappraisal," *Bookbinder* 1 (1987), 18–20.
   Alum tawed leathers were among the earliest of leathers, but the treatment died out about 80 years ago. Because these leathers have outlasted other leathers in bookbinding, there is an effort to have its production reintroduced. Describes its manufacture and the problems it presents.

Bendror, Jack. "Can Oversewing Make a Comeback?" *New Library Scene* 11:3 (June 1992), 10–12.
   Discusses the pros and cons of double-fan adhesive binding, which is increasingly replacing oversewing as a binding technique.

Bendror, Jack. *Technology and Testing of Library Bound Books.* Rochester, NY: Graphic Arts Research Center, Rochester Institute of Technology, 1976. 26p.
   An analysis of the problems faced by library binders in developing standards for their work; discussion of testing methods to determine the performance of a binding.

Carter, John. *Publisher's Cloth, An Outline History of Publisher's Binding in England, 1820–1900.* New York: Bowker; London: Constable, 1935.
   Concise, definitive study.

Clarkson, Christopher. "The Conservation of Early Books in Codex Form: A Personal Approach," *Paper Conservator* 3 (1978), 33–50.
   Author reflects upon his work with early books and observes that restoration has destroyed much of the evidence of early bookmaking. Notes that rebuilding and rebinding of texts must take second place to refurbishing and rejuvenation.

Clarkson, Christopher. *Limp Vellum Binding.* Hitchen, Herts.: Red Gull Press, 1982. 23p.
   Reviews the history of this binding technique and provides instructions for its use on modern book structures. Based upon the author's experience recovering books after the Florence flood.

Cockerell, Douglas. *Bookbinding and the Care of Books,* introd. Jane Greenfield. New York: Lyons and Burford, 1991. 334p. Illus.
   A basic text. "The best text on fine binding by an artist/craftsman." (G. M. Cunha) A facsimile of the 1901 edition.

Cockerell, Sydney M. *The Repairing of Books.* London: Sheppard Press, 1958.
   An important manual on book repair by one of England's foremost binders.

Conroy, Tom. "Informal Observations on 'Leather-Burn,' Acidity and Leather Lubricants," *Book and Paper Group Annual* 10 (1991), 43–48.
   Discusses discoloration and deterioration to books caused by binding leathers with acidic contaminants from the tanning process. Extensive notes.

Conroy, Tom. "Teaching Genealogies of American Hand Bookbinders," *Guild of Book Workers Journal* 28:1/2 (Spring/Fall 1990), 64p., charts.
   Author traces the influences on American bookbinders and conservators; identifies "key" teachers.

Council on Library Resources. Committee on Preservation and Access. *Brittle Books.* Washington, DC: Council on Library Resources, 1986. 31p.
   Report focusing on the problem of brittle books with recommendations for action on a national level.

Dean, John F. "The Binding and Preparation of Periodicals; Alternative Structures and Procedures," *Serials Review* 6:3 (July–September 1980), 87–90.
   Describes book structure; reviews current standards and practices for binding periodicals and suggests alternatives. Model specifications.

Dean, John F. "The Role of the Bookbinder in Preservation," *Wilson Library Bulletin* 56:3 (November 1981), 182–186.
Describes the history of binding and its traditional role in the library; cites the Johns Hopkins model (established by the author) and the efforts of the Research Libraries Group to improve understanding and product.

De Candido, Robert. "Dialogue: Between Librarians and a Binding Authority: What Repairs Can Be Done Easily and Economically Within a Library by Library Staff, And What Space and Money Commitment is Required?" *Library Scene* 10:2 (January 1981), 22.
How to set up a small workshop economically.

De Candido, Robert. "Out of the Question: How Are Binding Specifications Developed?" *Conservation Administration News*, No. 27 (October 1986), 9,17.
Discusses how specifications develop, using the Library Binding Institute standards.

Diehl, Edith. *Bookbinding: Its Background and Technique.* 2 vol., New York: Rinehart, 1946; New York: Dover, n.d.
A history of bookbinding and detailed instructions for all hand bookbinding operations. Bibliography and glossary.

Florian, Mary-Lou E. "A Holistic Interpretation of the Deterioration of Vegetable Tanned Leather," *Leather Conservation News* 2:1 (Fall 1985), 1–6.
A review and interpretation of the literature, indicating that the decay of leathers comes as much from inherent vice as from external sources, such as exposure to sulphur dioxide.

Foot, Mirjam M. "The Binding Historian and the Book Conservator," *Paper Conservator* 8 (1984), 7–83.
A binding historian discusses how physical treatment can obliterate or distort historical evidence about a book's production and history; items in very poor condition are especially vulnerable.

Forde, Helen. "Domesday Bound, 1086 to 1986," *Book Collector* 36:2 (Summer 1987), 201–206.
A history of its repair and binding.

Fredericks, Maria. "Recent Trends in Book Conservation and

Library Collections Care," *Journal of the American Institute for Conservation* 31:1 (Spring 1992), 95–101.

Discusses the trend away from full physical treatment unless absolutely necessary and the consequent development of less complex and invasive treatments. Notes increased emphasis on collection management, protective housing, and other preventive measures.

Groban, Betsy and Robert G. Lowe. "Book Binding Considerations," *School Library Journal* 29 (October 1982), 101–104.

Explains the economic factors that enter into a choice of paper and bindings for juvenile books, the types of bindings available, and a glossary of basic binding terms.

Haines, Betty M. "Deterioration in Leather Bookbindings—Our Present State of Knowledge," *British Library Journal* 3 (1977), 59–70.

Describes the results of a 35-year study of leather bookbindings undertaken by the British Leather Manufacturer's Research Association.

Harris, Carolyn. "Brittle Books: A Way of Life," *Catholic Library World* 53:6 (March 1982), 332–335.

A general essay on preservation issues, with a look to the future when access to the book itself may be limited.

Honea, Ted. "Music . . . A Binding Challenge," *New Library Scene* 4:3 (June 1985), 1, 8–10.

Describes the unique problems presented by music scores and some appropriate solutions.

Jacobson, Bruce F. "Librarians and Binders: Toward a Cultural Understanding," *New Library Scene* 4:5 (October 1985), 1, 13.

Notes the need for understanding of the problems and procedures of one another's world and regrets the lack of education in binding techniques in library schools; suggests that librarians tour commercial library binderies.

Kellar, Scott. "Binding Structure and Books of Permanent Research Value," *New Library Scene* 6:6 (December 1987), 1, 5–8.

History of binding practices with emphasis on commercial library binding in the twentieth century. Describes current techniques and suggests that sewing through the fold remains the best binding technique for books of permanent value.

Koda, Paul S. "The Analytical Bibliographer and the Conservator," *Library Journal* 104:15 (September 1, 1979), 1623–1626. (LJ Series on Preservation, 6)
Discusses the tension between the need to preserve the contents of a book and to preserve it as a physical object.

Lazar, Jon H. "Bidding Library Binding," *New Library Scene* 7:5 (October 1988), 1, 5.
Sound advice on the bidding process for library binding and discussion of how the Library Binding Institute standards should be used.

Library Binding Institute. *Standard for Library Binding*, 8th ed. Paul A. Parisi and Jan Merrill-Oldham, eds. Rochester, NY: Library Binding Institute, 1986. 17p.
A flexible standard, allowing a variety of options.

McCrady, Ellen. "How Leather Dressing May Have Originated," *Abbey Newsletter* 14:1 (February 1990), 19–20.
Notes that the practice of oiling bindings in an effort to preserve them is derived from traditional practice rather than twentieth-century research; there is no evidence that leather dressings help preserve books and considerable circumstantial evidence that they may be harmful.

McCrady, Ellen. "Research on the Dressing and Preservation of Leather," *Abbey Newsletter* 5:2 (April 1981), 23–25.
Summary of the author's investigation of the literature on the treatment of leather bookbindings; concludes that, at best, dressing makes little difference in the preservation of a leather binding.

McMurtrie, Douglas C. *The Book: The Story of Printing and Bookmaking*, 3rd ed. New York: Oxford University Press, 1943. 676p.
A basic history of the book, its construction, and production.

Merrill-Oldham, Jan. "Binding for Research Libraries," *New Library Scene* 3:4 (August 1984), 1, 4–6; flow chart, p. 22.

Describes the alternatives available in rebinding materials and the decision-making process that should be in place to make such decisions.

Merrill-Oldham, Jan. "Getting Educated: A Librarian's View," *New Library Scene* 3:3 (June 1984), 1,6,13.
Notes the changes in library binding techniques over the years; what the librarian can do to become familiar with commercial library binding, which consumes a substantial part of a library's budget.

Merrill-Oldham, Jan and Paul Parisi. *Guide to the Library Binding Institute Standard for Library Binding.* Chicago: American Library Association, 1990. 62p.
A supplement and complement to the *LBI Standard;* translates technical terms into language that can be understood by librarians.

Middleton, Bernard C. *A History of English Craft Bookbinding Technique,*" 3rd rev. ed. London: Holland Press, 1988. 307p.
The basic work on the topic.

Middleton, Bernard C. *The Restoration of Leather Bindings,* rev. ed. Chicago: American Library Association, 1984. 201p. Illus. (Library Technology Program, 20)
A manual for librarians describing the techniques for restoring leather bindings. Glossary.

Mielke, Gerald P. "Keeping Book Covers on the Straight and Narrow," *New Library Scene* 2:5 (October 1983), 1,6.
Discusses the causes of cover warp on commercially bound books; determines that it is caused by the "moisture-sensitive substrates" in the cover.

Milkovic, Milan. "The Binding of Periodicals: Basic Concepts and Procedures," *Serials Librarian* 11:2 (October 1986), 93–118.
Outlines methods for managing a serials binding unit, with emphasis on preservation. Bibliography.

Miller, Deborah R. "The Challenge of Binding Music," *Conservation Administration News,* No. 31 (Winter 1988), 8–9.
A review of current methods for binding music scores.

Morrow, Carolyn Clark. "Library Bindings and Conservation," *Illinois Libraries* 64:5 (May 1983), 357–360.
Library binding procedures and options for the library.

Mosher, Paul H. "Book Construction Quality: A Librarian's View, or The Self-Destructing Library," *Library Resources and Technical Services* 28:1 (January–March 1984), 15–19.
Discusses the importance of book production guidelines to ensure permanent and durable books in library collections.

Parisi, Paul A. "Methods of Affixing Leaves: Options and Implications," *New Library Scene* 3:5 (October 1984), 9–12.
Describes methods and when they might be appropriate.

Parisi, Paul A. "New Directions in Library Binding—Life After Class A; Technical Considerations: 1986 LBI Standard," *New Library Scene* 11:3 (June 1992), 6–9.
Discusses the pros and cons of various types of binding construction.

Peacock, P. G. "The Selection of Periodicals for Binding," *ASLIB Proceedings* 33:6 (June 1981), 257–259.
Argument for and against binding, and a methodology for decision-making.

Raphael, Toby. "The Care of Leather and Skin Products: A Curatorial Guide," *Leather Conservation News* 9 (1993), 1–15.
Summarizes current practices for objects made of leather or skin; describes physical nature and agents of deterioration and discusses concervation treatment concerns.

Rebsamen, Werner. "Acid-pHree Binders Board: A Reality," *New Library Scene* 3:6 (December 1984), 13–17.
Describes how binders board is manufactured and why acid-free boards are necessary.

Rebsamen, Werner. "Binders Board—The Only Coverboard Used in Library Binding," *Library Scene* 10:2 (June 1981), 14–17.
Describes binders board and how it is made.

Rebsamen, Werner. "C-1 Book Cloth vs. Grade F Buckram," *New Library Scene* 8:6 (December 1989), 6–9.

Testing demonstrates that the lighter-weight buckram covering is appropriate for smaller volumes.

Rebsamen, Werner. "Cutting and Trimming," *New Library Scene* 7:4 (August 1988), 13–16.
Describes the operations of cutting and trimming in book production and in library binding.

Rebsamen, Werner. "Librarians—Have Questions About Binding? Binding Institute Lab Is Your Answer," *Library Scene* 7:3 (September–December 1978), 18–19.
Describes the LBI Book Testing Laboratory and its services for libraries.

Rebsamen, Werner. "Library Binding Quality . . . Do You Get What You Pay For?" *New Library Scene* 7:2 (April 1988), 13–16.
Discusses the causes of poor quality binding and how the American Library Association and the Library Binding Institute have dealt with the problem. The LBI standards and its Book Testing Laboratory are described.

Rebsamen, Werner. "Oversew or Adhesive Bind?" *New Library Scene* 5:6 (December 1986), 12–15.
Describes the techniques of oversewing and adhesive binding.

Rebsamen, Werner. "Rounding and Backing . . . Fact and Fiction," *New Library Scene* 3:4 (August 1984), 18–21.
Discusses the necessity of this practice in binding.

Rebsamen, Werner. "Sewing Threads Used in Bookbinding," *New Library Scene* 3:3 (June 1984), 15–16.
Describes the strengths and weaknesses of the threads used for binding.

Rebsamen, Werner. "Spine Preparation Techniques Used on Adhesive Bound Books," *New Library Scene* 8:2 (April 1989), 7–13.
Describes the problems and techniques of adhesive binding.

Rhodes, Barbara. "Hell's Own Brew: Home Book Renovation from 19th Century Receipts to Today's Kitchen Chemistry: Its

Legacy for Preservation," *Paper Conservator* 15 (1991), 59–70.

A survey of the type of book care information available in domestic encyclopedias, bibliophilic handbooks, and library manuals, with their implication for preservation. Presents "a broad picture of the treatment to which books and prints may have been subjected." Bibliography.

Roberts, Matt T. "The Library Binder," *Library Trends* 24:4 (April 1976), 749–762.

Reviews the needs of libraries and describes the services that the library binder can provide; recommends testing procedures.

Roberts, Matt. "Oversewing and the Problem of Book Preservation in the Research Library," *College and Research Libraries* 28:1 (January 1967), 17–24.

Discusses the decline in binding standards and the economics that have led to oversewing and perfect binding; notes that these techniques are harmful to research materials that need to be preserved in their original binding.

Roberts, Stephen H. "What the Library Binder Expects from the Librarian," *Library Scene* 7:3 (September–December 1978), 2–4.

A review of library binding operations and how librarians can prepare their work for the binder.

Silverman, Randy. "Pamphlet Binders and Their Use in Research Libraries," *Archival Products News* 1:1 (Spring 1992), 2–3.

Describes the damage caused by a variety of traditional pamphlet binders and offers criteria for durable, non-damaging pamphlet binders.

Swartzell, Ann. "Preservation: Library Binding Information," *Resources and Technical Services Newsletter* 12:1 (Winter 1987), 6–8.

The application of automated serials control and other systems to commercial library binding.

Walker, R. Gay. "Library Binding As a Conservation Measure," *Collection Management* 4:1–2 (Spring-Summer 1982), 55–71.

Examines commercial library binding and what the librarian should look for; reviews the requests that a librarian should make of a binder to ensure appropriate bindings.

Walters Art Gallery, Baltimore. *The History of Bookbinding, 525–1950 A.D.* Baltimore, MD: Walters Art Gallery, 1957. 275p., plates.
A comprehensive, illustrated history.

Chapter 8

Association of Research Libraries Office of Management Studies. *Brittle Books Programs.* Washington, DC: Association of Research Libraries, March 1989. 121p. (SPEC Kit 152)
Policies and guidelines for dealing with books and documents that are so deteriorated that they must be reformatted.

Banks, Joyce N. "Mass Deacidification at the National Library of Canada," *Conservation Administration News,* No. 20 (January 1985), 14–15, 27.
A description of the Wei T'o system in operation.

Barnard, Bob. "The Way Ahead," *Library Conservation News,* No. 26 (January 1990), 1, 7–8.
On the use of acid-free paper by Her Majesty's Stationery Office (HMSO), Great Britain, for publications judged to be of special significance or of permanent value.

Barrow, William J. *Deterioration of Book Stock, Causes and Remedies, Two Studies on the Permanence of Book Paper,* ed. Randolph W. Church. Richmond, VA: Virginia State Library, 1959. 70p. (Virginia State Library Publication, 10)
A summary of Barrow's research.

Barrow, William J. *The Manufacture and Testing of Durable Book Papers,* ed. Randolph W. Church. Richmond, VA: Virginia State Library, 1960. 63p.
Methodology for Barrow's experiments on the permanence and durability of paper.

Barrow, William J. *Manuscripts and Documents, Their Deterioration and Restoration.* Charlottesville, VA: University of Virginia Press, 1955.
Discusses deacidification techniques.

Bittner, Nancy, comp. *A Selected Bibliography on Paper Conservation,* vol. 1: *1954-December 1981,* ed. Patricia Knittel. Rochester, NY: Rochester Institute of Technology Center of Graphic Arts, 1983. 20p.
Annotated bibliography of 84 references.

Browning, B. L. and W. A. Wink. "Studies on the Permanence and Durability of Paper; I: Prediction of Permanence," *TAPPI Journal* (Technical Association of the Pulp and Paper Industry) 51:4 (April 1968), 156–163.
Results of accelerated aging tests at five temperatures.

Burgess, Helen D. "Evaluation and Comparison of Commercial Mass-Deacidification Processes: Part 1: Project Planning and Selection of Materials," *Book and Paper Group Annual* 10 (1991), 22–42.
Describes the testing program developed by the Canadian Conservation Institute to assess three commercial mass deacidification processes to determine the effect of treatment on new and deteriorated paper, binding media, and special paper types.

Burgess, Helen D. "Practical Considerations for Conservation Bleaching," *Journal of the International Institute for Conservation—Canadian Group* 13 (1988), 11–26.
A comprehensive technical review of the testing of bleaches carried out at the Canadian Conservation Institute.

Butler, Randall R. " 'Here Today . . . Gone Tomorrow' . . . A pH Investigation of Brigham Young University's 1987 Library Acquisitions," *College and Research Libraries* 51:6 (November 1990), 539–551.
Results of a study to examine the acidity of current acquisitions in a North American academic library.

Butterfield, Fiona J. "The Potential Long-Term Effects of Gamma Irradiation on Paper," *Studies in Conservation,* 32:4 (November 1987), 181–191.
Results of a study on a variety of papers; results indicate that gamma irradiation causes an unacceptable level of paper deterioration.

Cali, Charles L. "A Hidden Enemy: Acidity in Paper," *Library and Archival Security* 7:3–4 (Fall/Winter 1985), 33–39.

Discussion of paper manufacture and techniques for treating paper, and a review of the Wei T'o and DEZ deacidification treatments.

Clapp, Verner W. " 'Permanent/Durable' Book Papers," American Library Association *Bulletin* 57:9 (October 1963), 847–852.
Summary of William Barrow's research and Clapp's vision of needs for the future of library collections.

Clapp, Verner W. *The Story of Permanent/Durable Paper, 1115–1970.* Copenhagen, 1972. (*Restaurator,* Suppl. 3); *Scholarly Publishing* 2 (January 1971), 107–124; April 1971), 229–245; (July 1971), 353–367.
History of the manufacture of book papers; report on Barrow's work.

Clements, D. W. G., C. E. Butler and C. A. Millington. "Paper Strengthening at the British Library," *Conservation in Archives.* Paris: International Council on Archives, 1988, 45–50.
Report on research at the British Library into the strengthening of paper by impregnating it with polymers. Discusses mass treatment by chemical means as an alternative to reformatting.

Cloonan, Michèle Valerie. "Mass Deacidification in the 1990s," *Rare Books and Manuscript Librarianship* 5:2 (1990), 95–103.
A review of the development of mass treatments for the preservation of paper-based materials, and attendant controversies.

Cote, Wilfred A., ed. *Papermaking Fibers, a Photomicrographic Atlas.* Syracuse, NY: Syracuse University Press, 1980. (Renewable Materials Institute Series, 1)
Illustrated atlas of fibers used in papermaking. Glossary.

Cunha, George Martin. "Mass Deacidification for Libraries," *Library Technology Reports* 23:3 (May–June 1987), 361–472; "1989 Update," 25:1 (January–February 1989), 5–81.
A study of the mass deacidification processes that have been or are being developed, their strengths and weaknesses.

Dean, John F. "The Self-Destructing Book," *Yearbook of Sci-*

ence and the Future, 1989. Chicago: Encyclopaedia Britannica, 1988, 212–225.
Describes the physical nature of paper, causes of its deterioration, and the potential of deacidification treatments.

Eulenberg, Julia Niebuhr. "Ink and Water: the Creation and Dissolution of Records," *ARMA Records Management Quarterly* 16:1 (January 1982), 18–20.
Assesses the effect of water damage on several brands of inks, pens, and other writing media; part of a long-term study to asses the effect of damage on writing media over time.

Frangakis, Evelyn. "Dropping Acid . . . From Paper," *Archival Outlook* (July 1993), 20–21.
Describes causes and effect of acids in paper; reviews history of and standards for the poroduction of permanent/durable paper.

Garcia, Debra A. "Recycling Capacity to Increase at Record Rates as Laws Proliferate," *Pulp and Paper* (May 1990), S1–5; S11–16, S25–28.
Technology, predictions, and problems are reviewed; author concludes that paper permanence will suffer because of high mechanical pulp content in recycled paper.

Gaylord Brothers. *Archival Storage of Paper.* Syracuse, NY: Gaymord Brothers, 1993. 17p. Illus. (Gaylord Preservation Pathfinder, 2)
Provides information for the selection of appropriate storage systems for paper-based records.

Grattan, David. "The Parylene Project: An Update," *CCI Newsletter,* No. 11 (April 1993), 3–4. Eng./Fr.
Reviews research on the application of parylene for preservation of artifacts and paper.

Grove, Lee E. "Paper Deterioration—An Old Story," *College and Research Libraries* 25:5 (September 1964), 365–374.
History of efforts by concerned librarians to deal with the problem of acid paper in books, which led to the research by Barrow.

Hamm, Patricia Dacus. "A History of the Manufacture of Printing Ink from 1500–1900 with Notes for the Conservator," *The*

Institute for Paper Conservation Conference Papers, Manchester 1992. Leigh, Worcs., Institute of Paper Conservation, 1992, 30–35.
Description of a study to identify printing inks and their composition to aid in conservation treatments.

Hey, Margaret. "The Deacidification and Stabilization of Iron-gall Inks," *Restaurator* 5:1–2 (1981–1982), 24–44.
Brief history of the development of inks; testing and deacidification methods are described.

Hey, Margaret. "Foxing: Some Unanswered Questions," *Antiquarian Book Monthly Review* 10:9 (September 1983), 340–343.
Discussion of "foxing," theories about its causes, and the author's conclusions based upon her research.

Hudson, F. Lyth. "Acidity of 17th and 18th Century Books in Two Libraries," *Paper Technology* 8:3 (1967), 189–190, 196.
Comparison of the effects of storage conditions of books in the Portico and Chatsworth Libraries, England. "Results confirm that atmospheric pollution is one of the causes of low pH value, particularly at the edges of the pages."

Hudson, F. Lyth and C. J. Edwards. "Some Direct Observations on the Aging of Paper," *Paper Technology* 7:1 (1966), 27–28; *Abbey Newsletter* 11:7 (October 1987), 109–110.
Report on the condition of a 1909 Everyman volume frozen in the snow in Antarctica, 1912–1959. Demonstrates that cold storage delayed the deterioration of the paper.

Humphrey, Bruce J. "Paper Strengthening With Gas-Phase Parylene Polymers: Practical Considerations," *Restaurator* 11:1 (1990), 48–68.
Describes the parylene process and its effect on materials and tests that have been performed to determine possible limitations of the process.

Hunter, Dard. *Paper Making: The History and Technique of an Ancient Craft,* 2nd ed., rev. and enl. New York: Knopf, 1967; reprint edition, New York: Dover, 1978. 611p.
The basic history of papermaking.

Institute of Paper Science and Technology. *Physical Properties of Library Books Deacidified.* 4 vol. Atlanta, GA: Institute of Paper Science and Technology, June 10, 1991.

The technical reports of the analysis of three deacidification systems: FMC Corporation (Lithco), Akzo Chemicals, Inc. (DEZ), and Wei T'o Associates, Inc., in response to the Library of Congress Request for Proposal (RFP 90–32). Presents the testing procedures and results.

Jackson, Cheryl. "A Short Research Project into the Permanence of Thermal Fax Papers," *AICCM National Newsletter* (June 1989), 10–11; *Abbey Newsletter* 13:8 (December 1989), 134–136.

Results of tests undertaken at the Australian National Archives; results indicate that even under optimum conditions the papers should last only five years.

Jones, Roger. "Barrow Lamination: The North Carolina State Archives Experience," *American Archivist* 50:3 (Summer 1987), 390–396.

After reviewing the documentation on the Barrow laminating process, the archives concluded that the process is sound and appropriate for certain materials.

Kelly, George B., Jr. "Mass Deacidification With Diethyl Zinc," *Library Scene* 9:3 (September 1980), 6–7.

A brief description of the process by its developer.

King, Ed. "British Library Book Preservation Process," *Library Conservation News,* No. 35 (April 1992), 1–2.

Briefly describes the development of the process and the feasibility and testing studies.

King, Ed. "New Hope for Decayed Paper," *Library Conservation News,* No. 12 (July 1986), 102; "An Update," No. 25 (October 1989), 2–3.

Describes the graft copolymerization process to stabilize and strengthen brittle books that is being developed at the University of Surrey for the British Library.

Koob, Stephen P. "The Instability of Cellulose Nitrate Adhesives," *Conservator* (International Institute for Conservation—United Kingdom Group) 6 (November 6, 1982), 31–34.

Instability due to light and its inflammability; not recommended for conservation.

Langwell, W. H. "The Vapor Phase Deacidification of Books and Documents," *Journal of the Society of Archivists* 3:3 (April 1966), 137–138.
Note on his VPD process for interleaving and with powder for deacidification.

Laughton, Louise W. "Paper Industry Moves Into Alkaline Age," *New Library Scene* 8:5 (October 1989), 1, 5.
Reasons for the industry's change to production of alkaline paper, effect on the market and impact on libraries and archives.

Lienardy, Anne. "A Bibliographical Survey of Mass Deacidification Methods," *Restaurator* 12:2 (1990), 75–103.
Summarizes the bibliographic review undertaken prior to the testing of the processes.

Louden, Louise. *Paper Conservation and Restoration.* Appleton, WI: Institute of Paper Chemistry, 1978. (Bibliographic Series, 284)
Annotated bibliography on storage, maintenance, repair, and restoration of paper for librarians and archivists.

Lowell, Howard P. "Permanent Paper for State Government Records," *NAGARA Clearinghouse* (National Association of Government Archives and Records Administrators) 6:2 (Spring 1990), 4–5.
Summarizes national and state legislative activities to foster the use of alkaline paper for archival records.

Luner, Philip, ed. *Paper Preservation: Current Issues and Recent Developments.* Atlanta, GA: TAPPI Press, 1990. 151p.
Papers from the 1988 international seminar address the problem of impermanence; describe mass treatment procedures; and discuss the production of alkaline paper.

McCrady, Ellen. "Deacidification vs. Microfilming," *Abbey Newsletter* 14:6 (October 1990), 112–113.
A lucid discussion of the options.

McCrady, Ellen. "Definitions of Permanence and Durability," *Alkaline Paper Advocate* 2:4 (October 1989), 42–44.
Author quotes standard definitions, noting their difficulties and ambiguities, and discusses them in the context of use.

McCrady, Ellen. "The Nature of Lignin," *Alkaline Paper Advocate* 4:4 (August 1991), 33–34.
A clear description of what lignin is and how it can interact with other materials.

McCrady, Ellen. "Three Deacidification Methods Compared," *Abbey Newsletter* 15:8 (December 1991), 121–122.
A careful analysis of the Institute of Paper Science and Technology (IPST) reports on books deacidified by Akzo Chemicals, FMC Corporation, and Wei T'o (see citation above).

McCrady, Ellen. "Why Collections Deteriorate: Putting Acidic Paper in Perspective," *Alkaline Paper Advocate* 1:4 (October 1988), 31–32.
Discusses contemporary causes of deterioration and increased wear on paper; the solution is permanent and durable paper.

McCrady, Ellen. "Wood Is Good," *Mid-Atlantic Archivist* 13:2 (Spring 1984), 11–12.
The reason for problems with wood pulp paper and developments that have enabled manufacturers to make permanent and durable high-quality paper from wood pulp.

McGee, Ann E. "Evaluating and Comparing Mass Deacidification Benefits: Enhanced and Extended Useful Life," *Restaurator* 12:2 (1991), 104–109.
FMC Corporation, producer of the Lithco deacidification process, suggests that treated and untreated papers be tested both before and after artificial aging to evaluate deacidification processes.

Meynell, G. G. and R. J. Newsom. "Foxing, a Fungal Infestation of Paper," *Nature* 24:3 (August 1978), 466–468.
A biological examination of foxed papers from books published between 1842 and 1910 suggests that fungal spores germinated in areas rich in nutrients. Prevention depends on maintaining a low relative humidity during book production and in libraries.

Mihram, Danielle. "Paper Deacidification: A Bibliographic Survey," *Restaurator* 7:2/3 (1986), 81–98, 99–118.
Bibliographic survey, limited to publications in English through 1982.

Mowery, J. Franklin. "Leafcasting: 'Filling the Holes': The Current State of Leafcasting Technologies," *Conservation in Archives*. Paris: International Council on Archives, 1989, 37–43.
An overview of the leafcasting process for filling losses in paper documents; discussion of equipment needs and effectiveness.

Paris, Jan. *Choosing and Working With a Conservator*. Atlanta, GA: Southeast Library Network, 1990. 24p.
Explores the issues surrounding the selection of a conservator and the nature of conservation treatments.

Parker, A. E. "The Freeze-Drying Process," *Library Conservation News*, No. 23 (April 1989), 4–6, 8.
Explains the general principles of the process and evaluates its usefulness for treating a wide range of library materials.

Pilette, Roberta and Carolyn Harris. "It Takes Two To Tango: A Conservator's View of Curator/Conservator Relations," *Rare Books and Manuscript Librarianship* 4:2 (Fall 1989), 103–111.
Discusses the information necessary for an intelligent discussion about treatment options.

Ritzenthaler, Mary Lynn. *Preserving Archives and Manuscripts*. Chicago: Society of American Archivists, 1994. 225p.
A manual on the physical nature of archival materials; causes of deterioration; storage and housing; conservation treatments. Bibliography.

Roosa, Mark. "U.S. Promotes the Manufacture and Use of Permanent Paper," *International Preservation News*, No. 2 (January 1988), 1–3.
Summary of the actions taken in the United States to foster the use of permanent/durable paper.

Schaefer, Karl R. "The Great Foxing Debate," *Conservation Administration News*, No. 53 (April 1993), 4–5, 31.
Discussion of the "foxing" phenomonon and research into its causes. Bibliography.

Schlosser, Leonard B. "Papermaking and the Industrial Revolution: The Search for a New Fiber," *American Book Collector* 1:6 (November-December 1980), 3–12.

History of the development of the manufacture of paper and the research to find new materials, especially in the 18th century. Bibliography.

Schmude, Karl G. "Can Library Collections Survive? The Problem of Paper Deterioration," *Australian Library Journal* 33:1 (February 1984), 15–22.
Reviews the problem of the physical deterioration of library collections and the efforts to deal with it, with emphasis on U.S. initiatives. Discusses Australia's needs and efforts.

Schrock, Nancy Carlson and Mary Campbell Cooper. *Records in Architectural Offices: Suggestions for the Organization, Storage and Conservation of Architectural Records,* 3rd rev. ed. Cambridge, MA: Massachusetts Committee for the Preservation of Architectural Records (COPAR), June 1992. 31 p., appendices.
An introduction to records management and preservation concerns for architectural firms, with practical guidelines for implementing programs. Bibliography.

Schwerdt, Peter. *Mass Deacidification Procedures for Libraries and Archives: State of Development and Perspectives for Implementation in the Federal Republic of Germany.* Washington, DC: Commission on Preservation and Access, 1989. 9p.
Summarizes the research on deacidification conducted by the Battelle Institute. Translated from German.

Selawy, Adrian C. and John C. Williams, "Alkalinity—The Key to Paper Permanence," *TAPPI Journal* 64:5 (May 1981), 49–50.
Observes that permanent/durable paper can be produced at reasonable cost; library purchasing agents should be educated to ask for it.

Shahani, Chandru J. and William K. Wilson. "Preservation of Libraries and Archives," *American Scientist* 75:3 (May–June 1987), 240–251.
Brief history of papermaking; discussion of the problems of paper and causes of deterioration; conservation treatments. Bibliography.

Smith, Merrily A., Norvell M. M. Jones, Susan L. Page, and

Marian Peck Dirda. "Pressure-Sensitive Tape and Techniques for Its Removal from Paper," *Journal of the American Institute for Conservation* 23:2 (Spring 1984), 101–114.
History of the development of pressure-sensitive tape from its introduction in 1845 to the present. Aging properties of different tapes are described; testing of solvents and methods for removal are discussed.

Smith, Richard D. "Mass Deacidification: the Wei T'o Understanding," *College and Research Libraries News* 48:1 (January 1987), 2–10.
Review of the brittle books problem and its impact on library collections. Discussion of deacidification processes, costs, and funding.

Smith, Richard D. "Mass Deacidification Cost Comparisons," *College and Research Libraries News* 46:3 (March 1985), 122–123.
Comparison of the Wei T'o and Library of Congress diethyl zinc deacidification processes, with some cost data.

Sparks, Peter G. *A Roundtable on Mass Deacidification.* Washington, DC: Association of Research Libraries, 1992. 115p.
Report of a meeting of research librarians held in September 1992 to examine the several different processes, issues of cost, and priorities for treatment.

Sparks, Peter G. *Technical Considerations in Choosing Mass Deacidification Processes.* Washington, DC: Commission on Preservation and Access, 1990. 22p.
Summary of technical and logistical factors to be considered when contemplating a commitment to the mass deacidification of collections.

Thomas, D. L. *Survey on National Standards on Paper and Ink to Be Used by Administration for Records Creation: A RAMP Study with Guidelines.* Paris: UNESCO, 1986. 47p.
Surveys national archives and the paper permanence standards for their countries.

Thompson, Claudia G. *Recycled Papers: The Essential Guide.* Cambridge, MA: MIT Press, 1992. 162p.
A concise overview of issues surrounding the recycling of paper products. Brief history of papermaking and production;

discussion of fibers and inks. Advocates standards for paper production and recycling.

Thompson, Jack C. "Mass Deacidification: Thoughts on the Cunha Report," *Restaurator* 9:3 (1988), 147–162.
A review of George Cunha's review of mass deacidification systems, 1987. Raises a number of provocative questions about the processes and their evaluation.

U.S. Congress. House. Government Operations Committee. *Establishing a National Policy on Permanent Papers.* Washington, DC: Government Printing Office, 1990. 9p.
Text of a report accompanying the joint resolution establishing a national policy on permanent paper.

U.S. Government Printing Office. *Use of Alkaline Paper in Government Printing; Report and Plan Prepared at the Direction of the Committee on Appropriations, House of Representatives.* Washington, DC: Government Printing Office, 1990. 18p.
Cites the role that alkaline papers have played in government printing and use.

Vallas, Philippe. "Mass Deacidification at the Bibliotheque Nationale (Sablé-sur Sarthe Center): Assessment After Two Years of Operation (Late 1992)," *Restaurator* 14:1 (1993), 1–10.
Description of the treatment and a positive assessemnt of its effectiveness.

Van Der Reyden, Dianne. "Recent Scientific Research In Paper Conservation," *Journal of the American Institute for Conservation* 31:1 (Spring 1992), 117–138.
Reviews interest since 1988 in the chemical, physical, and optical properties of paper; aging; and recent findings concerned with washing, bleaching, solvents, enzymes, and sizing.

Verheyen, Peter S. "Basic Paper Treatments for Printed Book Materials," *Guild of Bookworkers Journal* 29:1 (Spring 1991), 1–15.
Reviews the methods of conservator Betsy Palmer Eldridge for dealing with the paper in books. A synopsis of her presentation at the Guild's Standards of Excellence Seminar,

1989; a clear and thorough description of what a conservator can do.

Walkden, Stephen A. "New Momentum for Alkaline Paper-makers," *TAPPI Journal* 72:11 (November 1989), 8.
Describes how alkaline papermaking is meeting the challenge of new printing technologies. Estimates that by 1993 more than fifty percent of the uncoated paper production will be alkaline.

Warren, S. D., Company. *Paper Permanence: Preserving the Word.* Boston: S. D. Warren, 1983. 83p. Illus.
History of paper manufacture; discussion of the production of permanent/durable paper.

Weber, David C. "Brittle Books in Our Nation's Libraries," *College and Research Libraries News* 48:5 (May 1987), 238–244.
A statement before the Subcommittee on Postsecondary Education, Committee on Education and Labor, House of Representatives (March 3, 1987), presenting the national plan for the preservation of library materials and a request for a federal policy of commitment to help resolve the problem of brittle books.

Wedinger, Robert S. "The FMC Mass Preservation System", *Restaurator* 12:1 (1991), 1–17.
Describes the Lithco mass deacidification system, its evaluation, and the results of independent laboratory testing.

Wedinger, Robert S. "The FMC Mass Preservation System: Enhancement and Extension of Useful Life," *Restaurator* 14:2 (1993), 102–122.
Presents modifications in the Lithco mass deacidification system, with test data.

Wedinger, Robert S. "Lithco Develops Deacidifying Strengthening Process," *Alkaline Paper Advocate* 2:4 (October 1989), 39–40.
Brief description of the Lithco process, developed by the Lithium Corporation of America, for deacidifying, buffering, and strengthening paper.

Werner, A. E. "The Lamination of Documents," *Problems of*

Conservation in Museums. Paris: International Council of Museums; London: Allen and Unwin, 1969, 209–224.
Survey of the more important lamination techniques being used, their advantages and disadvantages. Brief discussion of deacidification. Bibliography.

Wessell, Carl J. "Paper," *Deterioration of Materials; Causes and Preventive Techniques,"* ed. Glenn A. Greathouse and Carl J. Wessell, New York: Reinhold, 1954, 355–407.
Composition of paper; biological, physical, and chemical causes of deterioration. Bibliography.

Williams, John C. "Paper Permanence: A Step in Addition to Alkalization," *Restaurator* 3:5 (1979), 81–90.
Research demonstrating the need for an alkaline reserve in paper to neutralize the acids generated by polluted air and oxidation.

Wilson, William K. and E. J. Parks. "An Analysis of the Aging of Paper: Possible Reactions and Their Effects on Measurable Properties," *Restaurator* 3:1–2 (1978/79), 37–61.
Examples of chemical reactions that occur during natural aging due to the composition characteristics of paper are cited; suggestions are made for tests to detect changes in paper and to determine what occurs during aging.

Wilson, William K. and E. J. Parks. "Comparison of Accelerated Aging of Book Papers with 36 Years Natural Aging," *Restaurator* 4:1 (1980), 1–55.
Examination of papers developed for testing at the National Bureau of Standards in 1937 and modern papers, after accelerated aging, in 1973.

Wilson, William K. and Edwin J. Parks. "Historical Survey of Research at the National Bureau of Standards on Materials for Archival Records," *Restaurator* 5:3–4 (1983), 191–241.
Historical survey of the NBS's research on conservation of records. Bibliography.

Zappala, Antonio. "Problems in Standardizing the Quality of Paper for Permanent Records," *Restaurator* 12:3 (1991), 137–146.
Reviews worldwide efforts in the 1980s to develop a standard for permanent papers.

Zimmerman, Carole. *Bibliography on Mass Deacidification.* Washington, DC: Library of Congress Preservation Office, 1991. 32p.

Chapter 9

American Institute for Conservation. Book and Paper Group. *Paper Conservation Catalogue,* Washington, 1984– . Updated frequently.
    An inventory of current conservation treatments for art on paper. Its aim is to record current practices, not to establish definitive procedures.

Applebaum, Barbara. *Guide to Environmental Protection of Collections.* Madison, CT: Sound View Press, 1991. 270p.
    Describes the physical nature of objects in collections and how to assess their needs. The role of the conservator is emphasized.

Banks, Paul N. "The Conservation of Maps and Atlases," *AB Bookman's Yearbook, 1976: Maps and Atlases.* New York: Antiquarian Bookman, 1976, 53–62.
    Covers environmental controls, storage, and physical treatment of maps.

Blomquist, Richard F. *Adhesives—Past, Present and Future.* Philadelphia, PA: American Society for Testing and Materials, 1964. 34p.
    Describes what adhesives are and how they work.

Buchberg, Karl. "Paper, Manuscripts, Documents, Printed Sheets, and Works of Art," *Conservation in the Library,* ed. Susan G. Swartzburg. Westport, CT: Greenwood Press, 1983, 31–54.

Clapp, Anne F. *Curatorial Care of Works of Art on Paper: Basic Procedures for Paper Preservation.* New York: Nick Lyons, 1987. 191p.
    Considers factors that are harmful to paper and outlines treatments. Bibliography. A completely revised edition of her classic text.

Cohen-Strayner and Brigitte Kuppers, ed. *Preserving America's*

Performing Arts. New York: Theater Library Association, 1986. 167p.
Papers cover all aspects of the care and preservation of materials in theater collections.

Cruse, Larry. "Cartography's Photographic Revolution: Microcartography," *Wilson Library Bulletin* 60:2 (October 1985), 17–20.
Brief history of the production of maps, discussion of preservation needs and initiatives.

Cruse, Larry. "Storage of Maps on Paper, Microforms, Optical Disks, Digital Disks and Magnetic Memories," *Science and Technology Libraries* 5:3 (Spring 1985), 45–57.
Describes the characteristics and outlook for newer technologies applied to cartography; advantages and disadvantages.

Cunningham, Veronica Colley. "The Preservation of Newspaper Clippings," *Special Libraries* (Winter 1987), 41–46.
Discusses the problems of preserving newspapers and the option to microfilm.

Ehrenberg, Ralph E. *Archives and Manuscripts: Maps and Architectural Drawings.* Chicago: Society of American Archivists, 1982. 64p. (SAA Basic Archival Series)
Covers all aspects of the care and handling of maps. Bibliography.

Ellis, Margaret Holbin. *The Care of Prints and Drawings,* Nashville, TN: American Association for State and Local History, 1987. 253p.
Reviews the nature of paper and parchment and the media applied to these supports. Offers recommendations for storage and environmental controls for collections.

Ferguson, Ann. *Conservation Framing for the Professional Picture Framer.* Galveston, TX: Windsor Graphics, 1985. 82p.
A basic, clearly illustrated text on picture framing.

Gerber, Gloria S., John W. Ellison, Susan E. Ledder, and Fred Sandner. "Map Storage and Care in Active Collections," Special Libraries Association, Geography and Map Division *Bulletin,* No. 125 (September 1981), 15–18.

Review of recommended storage and care practices in heavily used collections.

Guldbeck, Per E. *The Care of Antiques and Historical Collections,* 2nd rev. ed. by A. Bruce MacLeish. Nashville, TN: American Association for State and Local History, 1985. 245p.
Manual on the care of "historically significant materials," including paper, photographs, leather, metal objects, textiles, ceramics, glass, stone, and bone. Appendix on adhesives. Bibliography.

Harley, R. D. *Artist's Pigments Circa 1600–1835: a Study in English Documentary Sources.* 2nd ed. London: Butterworths, 1982. 236p. (Technical Studies in the Arts, Archaeology and Architecture).
Discusses early manuscript and literary sources, then reviews each pigment.

Johnson, E. Verner and Joanne C. Horgan. *Museum Collection Storage.* Paris: UNESCO, 1979. 56p.
A practical manual; covers planning, records management; security, conservation; storage systems.

Keck, Caroline K. *A Handbook on the Care of Paintings for Historical Agencies and Small Museums.* Nashville, TN: American Association for State and Local History, 1965.
Provides basic information on surveying the collection, setting conservation priorities, and procedures.

Keck, Caroline K. *How To Take Care of Your Paintings: Art Owner's Guide to Preservation and Restoration.* New York: Scribners, 1978. 96p.
Handbook on the care and conservation of paintings.

Kidd, Betty. "Preventive Conservation for Map Collections," *Special Libraries* 71 (December 1980), 529–538.
Preservation methods and guidelines for handling by staff and researchers.

LaHood, Charles G., Jr. "Reproducing Maps in Libraries; the Photographer's Point-of-View," *Special Libraries* 64:1 (January 1973), 25–28.
Discusses problems of size, format, color, and type.

Larsgaard, Mary. *Map Librarianship, an Introduction,* 2nd ed. Littleton, CO: Libraries Unlimited, 1987. 382p.

Information on all aspects of map librarianship, survey of existing practices and guidance in choosing specific procedures. Excellent summary of storage, handling, and preservation issues.

LeGear, Clara Egli. *Maps, their Care, Repair and Preservation in Libraries.* Washington, DC: Library of Congress, 1956.

Detailed instructions in processing, filing, preservation, repair and storage. Bibliography.

Library of Congress. *Polyester Film Encapsulation.* Washington, DC: Library of Congress, 1980. 23p.

Instruction manual.

McAusland, Jane. *Guide to Conservation Mounting and Framing of Works of Art on Paper.* London: Sothebys, 1988. 6p.

Pamphlet prepared by the Institute of Paper Conservation on conservation framing and causes of damage.

Makepeace, Chris E. *Ephemera: A Book on Its Collection, Conservation and Use.* Aldershot, Hants.; Brookfield, VT: Gower, 1985. 247p.

Discusses the storage and preservation of ephemera in library collections.

Maling, D. H. "Some Thoughts about Miniaturisation of Map Library Contents," *Cartographic Journal* 3 (September 1966), 14–15; discussion, 17.

Advocates miniaturization on microfilm but notes the attendant problems.

Mayer, Ralph. *The Artist's Handbook of Materials and Techniques,* 3rd rev. ed. New York: Viking, 1970.

Covers materials used in producing artworks. Chapter 14 deals with the conservation of pictures. Classic text. Bibliography.

Morris, John William. "The Long Term Protection of Private Map Collections," *Map Collector* (March 1985), 16–19.

Practical; covers environment, storage, use, and problems with paper and adhesives.

Nielsen, T. F. "Mounting and Restoration of Cartographic Material," *Archives and Manuscripts* 6:7 (August 1976), 311–312.
A technical note on preparing maps for heavy use.

Nolan, Charles. "Philatelic Conservation," *American Philatelist* 93:3 (March 1979), 242–245.
Covers problems with paper, inks, adhesives, albums, mounts, hinges, and the environment.

Ogden, Sherelyn. "Preservation Options for Scrapbooks and Album Formats," *Book and Paper Annual* 10 (1991), 149–163.
Describes problems, conservation considerations, and treatment options.

O'Loughlin, Elissa and Linda S. Stiber. "A Closer Look at Pressure Sensitive Adhesive Tapes: Update on Conservation Strategies," *Institute of Paper Conservation Conference Papers, Manchester 1992*. Leigh, Worcs.: Institute of Paper Conservation, 1992, 280–287.
A history of pressure-sensitive tapes and their changes in composition over the years, resulting in continuing challenges for conservators.

O'Reilly, Priscilla. *Preservation Guide 3: Paintings.* New Orleans, LA: Historic New Orleans Collection, 1986. 13p.
Covers environment, physical protection, storage, and display. Glossary and bibliography.

Reike, Judith L., Suzanne Gyeszly, and Leslie Steele. "Preservation of Sheet Maps: Lamination or Encapsulation, a Durability Study," *Special Libraries Association, Geography and Map Division Bulletin,* No. 138 (December 1984), 2–10.
Results of a study to determine if preservation methods for archival collections were also effective for heavily used materials; concluded that items in heavily used collections should be encapsulated for protection.

Reiter, Ed. "Numismatics: Little 'PVC' Holders Can Cause Big Problems," *New York Times,* Sunday, January 25, 1981. D35.
Describes the destruction of coins by corrosion caused by polyvinyl chloride coin holders used by collectors.

Rickards, Maurice. *This Is Ephemera; Collecting Printed Throwaways.* Brattleboro, VT: Gossamer Press, 1977.
Collecting ephemera, organizing and preserving collections.

Rickman, Catherine. "Conservation of Philatelic Materials," *Institute of Paper Conservation Conference Papers, Manchester 1992.* Leigh, Worcs.: Institute of Paper Conservation, 1992, 273–279.
A review of British Postal History and the special problems presented to the conservator by philatelic materials.

Schoolly-West, R. F. "Philatelic Conservation," pt. 1: "Historical Background and Nature of the Materials;" pt. 2 "Hazards to Materials: Preservation and Cure," *Library Conservation News,* No. 13 (October 1986), 4–5, 8; No. 14 (January 1986), 4–5, 8.
Describes the different materials and processes used to make stamps and the problems they present to the conservator; discusses physical and atmospheric hazards, chemical effects, and adhesives.

Sherwood, Arlyn. "Map Preservation: an Overview," *Illinois Libraries* 67:8 (October 1985), 705–711.
Covers the care and storage of maps, problems of reproduction, conservation options.

Smith, Merrily A. and Margaret R. Brown. *Matting and Hinging of Works of Art on Paper.* Washington, DC: Library of Congress Preservation Office, 1981. 32p. Illus. (National Preservation Program Publication)
Comprehensive set of instructions for the physical treatment of paper. Glossary; list of suppliers.

Smith, Richard Daniel. "Maps: their Deterioration and Preservation," *Special Libraries* 63:2 (1972), 59–68; *Map Librarianship,* ed. Roman Drazniowsky, Metuchen, NJ: Scarecrow Press, 1975, 395–410.
Historical survey of the problem of deterioration of paper; discussion of the author's analysis of the deacidification treatments on selected U.S. Geological Survey maps.

Stout, George L. *The Care of Pictures.* New York: Columbia University Press, 1948. 125p.

Describes the structure of paintings and the damage and deterioration they can exhibit.

Zigrosser, Carl and Christa M. Gaehde. *A Guide to the Collecting and Care of Original Prints,* New York: Crown, 1965. 120p.
Describes print techniques and curatorial considerations, how to evaluate prints. Chapter 7, by Gaehde, a conservator, deals specifically with the preservation and conservation of fine prints.

Zucker, Barbara. *Preservation of Scrapbooks and Albums.* Washington, DC: National Cooperative Preservation Project, 1991. 4p. (Preservation Basics, Leaflet 1)
Outlines storage and handling of scrapbooks and options for preservation and conservation. Bibliography. Updated version of "Scrapbooks and Albums: their Care and Conservation," *Illinois Libraries* 67:8 (October 1985), 695–699.

Chapter 10

Adelstein, Peter Z. "History and Properties of Film Supports," *Conservation in Archives.* Paris: International Council on Archives, 1989, 89–101.
Describes photographic film supports: paper, cellulose nitrate, cellulose esters, polyester, polycarbonate, and their properties.

Albright, Gary. "Photographs," *Conservation in the Library,* ed. Susan G. Swartzburg. Westport, CT: Greenwood Press, 1983, 79–102.
History of photography, care and storage, causes of deterioration, conservation.

Albright, Gary. "Which Envelope? Selecting Storage Enclosures for Photographs," *PictureScope* 31:4 (Winter 1985), 111–113.
Description, advantages, and disadvantages of available enclosures.

Anderson, Stanton and George Larson. "A Study of Environmental Conditions Associated with Customer Keeping of Photographic Prints," *Journal of Imaging Technology* 13 (1987), 49–54.

Report on a study to better understand the types of environments in which photographic materials are housed; predictions of image stability depend upon an understanding of these conditions.

Anderson, Stanton and Robert Ellison. "Natural Aging of Photographs," *Journal of the American Institute for Conservation* 31:2 (Summer 1992), 213–223.
Describes a program of long-term monitoring of image change through accelerated aging.

Barger, M. Susan. *Bibliography of Photographic Processes in Use Before 1880; their Materials, Processing, and Conservation.* Rochester, NY: Graphic Arts Research Center, Rochester Institute of Technology, 1980. 149p.
1,048 annotated entries, arranged by topic, with keyword index.

Barger, M. Susan. "Characterization of Corrosion Products on Old Protective Glass, Especially Daguerreotype Cover Glasses," *Journal of Materials Science* 24 (1989), 1343–1356.
Study of protective cover glasses on daguerreotypes to determine why such glass causes corrosion and the deterioration of images that it was intended to protect.

Barger, M. Susan, A. P. Giri, William B. White, and Thomas M. Edmondson. "Cleaning Daguerreotypes," *Studies in Conservation* 31:1 (February 1986), 15–28.
A review of silver cleaners, which are harmful; splatter cleaning, which leaves a residue; and electrocleaning, which appears to be the most effective method.

Barger, M. Susan, A. P. Giri, William B. White, William S. Ginell, Frank Preusser. "Protective Surface Coatings for Daguerreotypes," *Journal of the American Institute for Conservation* 24:1 (Fall 1984), 40–52.
Discusses the advantages and disadvantages of protective surface coatings; test results are discussed.

Barger, M. Susan, R. Messier, and William B. White. "Daguerreotype Display," *PictureScope* 31:2 (Summer 1983), 57–58.
How daguerreotypes can best be displayed to curtail damage from light.

Barger, M. Susan, Russell Messier, and William B. White. "Nondestructive Assessment of Daguerreotype Image Quality by Diffuse Reflectance Spectroscopy," *Studies in Conservation* 29:2 (May 1984), 84–86.
    Describes a nondestructive method for monitoring changes in the appearance of daguerreotypes from aging or treatment.

Barger, M. Susan and William B. White. *The Daguerreotype: Nineteenth-Century Technology and Modern Science.* Washington, DC: Smithsonian Institution Press, 1991, 252p. Illus.
    A history of the daguerreotype and the scientific aspects of the process. Traces previous scientific work and examines the problems of conservation and preservation of these images.

Bohem, Hilda. "A Seam-free Envelope for Archival Storage of Photographic Negatives," *American Archivist* 38:3 (July 1975), 403–405.
    Reason for this design explained.

Booth, Larry and Jane. "Duplication of Cellulose Nitrate Negatives," *PictureScope,* 30:1 (Spring 1982), 12–18.
    Describes a copying project, how it was accomplished, and what was learned.

Burgess, Helen D. and Carolyn G. Leckie. "Evaluation of Paper Products With Special Reference to Use with Photographic Materials," *Topics in Photographic Preservation* 4 (1991), 96–105.
    Discusses some aspects of the evaluation and selection of appropriate paper materials for photographic collections; reviews methods of testing papers.

Cribbs, Margaret A. "Photographic Conservation—An Update," *ARMA Records Management Quarterly* 22:3 (July 1988), 17–19.
    How to determine the best environment for storage and use; distinguishes between archival and heavily used research collections.

De Bardeleben, Marian Z. and Carol G. Lunsford. "35mm Slide Storage and Retrieval for the Novice," *Special Libraries* 73:2 (April 1982), 135–141.

A slide storage system simple in concept and design, inexpensive to create and maintain.

Eastman Kodak Company. *Conservation of Photographs.* Rochester, NY: Eastman Kodak, 1985. 156p. illus.
Provides technical information for photographic conservators on the care, treatment, and use of Kodak materials.

Eaton, George T. "Preservation, Deterioration, Restoration of Photographic Images," *Library Quarterly* 40:1 (January 1970), 85–95.
Discusses preservation and restoration.

Gill, Arthur T. *Photographic Processes, a Glossary and a Chart for Recognition.* London: Museums Association, 1978. 12p. (Museums Association Information Sheet, IS 21, 1978)
Brief descriptions of many photographic processes, alphabetically arranged.

Gillet, Martine, Chantel Carnier, and Francoise Flieder. "Glass Plate Negatives: Preservation and Restoration," *Restaurator* 7:2 (1986), 49–80.
Discusses manufacturing processes, surveys preservation literature, and reviews experiments. Extensive bibliography.

Haist, Grant Milford. *Modern Photographic Processing,* 2 vols. New York: Wiley, 1979.
Comprehensive history and study of the physical nature of photographic images.

Haynes, Ric. "A Temporary Method to Stabilize Deteriorating Cellulose Nitrate Still Camera Negatives," *PhotographiConservation* 2:3 (September 1980), 1, 3.
Describes an ingenious method for the storage of this unstable, highly flammable material.

Hendriks, Klaus B. "The Conservation of Photographic Materials," *PictureScope* 30:1 (Spring 1982), 4–11.
Discusses the concerns in photographic conservation, describes photographic processes; case study of the collection in the National Library of Venezuela.

Hendriks, Klaus B. et al. *Fundamentals of Photographic Conservation: A Study Guide.* Toronto: Lugus Publ., 1991. 560p. Illus.

A basic textbook on photographic conservation for use in training of practitioners. Produced by the National Archives of Canada and the Canadian Communications Group.

Hendriks, Klaus B. "The Preservation, Storage and Handling of Black-and-White Photographic Records," *Conserving and Preserving Materials in Nonbook Formats*, ed. Kathryn L. and William T. Henderson. Urbana-Champaign, IL: University of Illinois Graduate School of Library and Information Service, 1991, 91–104. (Allerton Park Institute, 30)
Reviews the factors affecting stability, guidelines for handling and use, and contingency planning for disaster.

Hendriks, Klaus B. "Preserving Photographic Records: Materials, Problems and Methods of Restoration," *Industrial Photography* 27:8 (August 1978), 30–33.
Discusses research in photographic conservation and where information can be found; describes major causes of deterioration and what can be done.

Hendriks, Klaus B. *The Preservation and Restoration of Photographic Materials in Archives and Libraries: a RAMP Study with Guidelines.* Paris: UNESCO, January 1984, 119p. (PGI-84/WS1)
Basic study of the nature and problems associated with photographs; recent research; recommended measures for preservation. Bibliography.

Hendriks, Klaus B. and Anne Whitehurst, comp. *Conservation of Photographic Materials; a Basic Reading List.* Ottawa: National Archives of Canada, 1988. 32p. Eng./Fr.
References on the preservation of still photographic images.

Image Permanence Institute. *Polysulfide Treatment of Microfilm Using IPI Silverlock (TM)—Some Questions and Answers.* Rochester, NY: Image Permanence Institute, 1991. 7p.
Discusses the role of polysulfide toning of silver-gelatin microfilm.

Irvine, Betty Jo. *Slide Librarianship,* 2nd ed. Littleton, CO: Libraries Unlimited, 1979. 321p.
Basic text on slide library management, storage and handling of slides, with a chapter on conservation issues.

Jones, G. William. "Nitrate Film: Dissolving Images of the Past," *Conservation Administration News* 31 (October 1987), 1–3, 12.
Description of the hazards and the deterioration of nitrate film, with options for storage and preservation.

Keefe, Lawrence E., Jr. and Dennis Inch. *The Life of a Photograph: Archival Processing, Matting, Framing, and Storage.* 2nd ed. Boston, London: Focal Press, 1991. 400p.
How to process film, make prints, and store both for maximum life.

Kennedy, Nora and Peter Mustardo. "Current Issues in the Preservation of Photographs," *AB Bookman's Weekly* 83:17 (April 24, 1989), 1773–1783.
Covers problems and issues in photographic preservation, including storage, exhibition, and treatments. The role of the professional organizations and the training of the photographic conservator is discussed.

Kerns, Ruth B. "A Positive Approach to Negatives: Photographic Microfilm Technology," *American Archivis,* 51:1–2 (Winter/Spring 1988), 111–114.
Case study of the conversion of a deteriorating collection of negatives into microfilm.

Limbacher, James. "Beware the Red Menace," *Film Library Quarterly* 8:1 (1975), 31.
Warning about the color fading properties of Eastman Kodak color film.

McCabe, Constance. "Preservation of Nineteenth-Century Negatives in the National Archives," *Journal of the American Institute for Conservation* 30 (1991), 41–43.
Describes a project to preserve over 8,000 glass plate negatives. Discussion of preservation issues asociated with the deterioration of the glass, collodion, and silver image components of the negative.

Munson, Doug. "Duplication of Glass Negatives," *PictureScope* 30:1 (Spring 1982), 19–23.
Describes methods for making prints from glass negatives.

Norris, Debbie Hess. "Platinum Photographs: Deterioration and Preservation," *PhotographiConservation* 7:2 (June 1985), 1.

How to identify platinum images, store them, and recognize deterioration.

Norris, Debbie Hess. "The Proper Storage and Display of a Photographic Collection," *Book and Paper Group Annual* 2 (1983), 66–81.
Describes the photographic materials found in collections and the problems they present; information on proper storage, matting, and mounting for display. Bibliography.

Orraca, Jose. "Developing Treatment Criteria in the Conservation of Photographs," *Topics in Photographic Preservation* 4 (1991), 150–155.
Describes the development of photographic conservation as a specialty, and the connoisseurship required of a conservator.

Orraca, Jose. "Glossary of Terms Used in the Conservation of Photographs," *Ojo,* No. 4 (Spring 1993), 3–7.
General, condition, and treatment terminology.

Paliouras, Eleni and Susan Richards, comp. *Photographic Conservation: a Selected Bibliography,* vol. 2, *1981–1985,* ed. Richard Schmidle. Rochester, NY: Technical and Educational Center, Rochester Institute of Technology, 1986. 18p.
Seventy-eight annotated citations for major articles; also lists monographic publications, without annotations.

Pedzich, Joan. "Balancing Preservation and Research: Some Principles that Help," *PhotographiConservation* 4:2 (June 1982), 6–7.
Precautions that curators can take to protect collections that receive heavy research use.

Polaroid Corporation. *Storing, Handling and Preserving Polaroid Photographs, a Guide.* Norwood, MA: Polaroid, 1984.
Covers storage, handling, and use; information on restoration.

Porro, Jennifer, ed. *Photographic Preservation and the Research Library.* Mountain View, CA: Research Libraries Group, Inc., 1991. 56p.
Papers presented at a symposium, October 1990, to address preservation problems and solutions.

Puglia, Steven P. "Negative Duplication: Evaluating the Reproduction and Preservation Needs of Collections," *Conservation Administration News*, No. 38 (July 1989), 8–9.
Guidelines for evaluating collections and options for duplication.

Ram, Tulsi. "Molecular Sieves: Antidote to Vinegar Syndrome," *AMIA Newsletter*, No. 19 (March 1993), 1.
Describes a technology that will absorb moisture, acidic
acid, and methylene chloride, which should lessen or prevent "Vinegar Syndrome."

Reilly, James M. "Albumen Prints: a Summary of New Research
About their Preservation," *PictureScope* 30:1 (Spring 1982),
34–36.
Summary of a project to investigate the causes and mechanisms of deterioration in albumen prints. Demonstrated that
they are extremely sensitive to moisture and less stable than
modern black-and-white prints.

Reilly, James M. *Care and Identification of Nineteenth Century
Photographic Prints*. Rochester, NY: Eastman Kodak, 1989.
116p.
Analysis of nineteenth century photographic and photomechanical print processes. Discusses causes of deterioration
and offers recommendations for care, storage, and display.

Reilly, James M. "The Image Permanence Institute: a New
Resource for the Photographic Preservation Community,"
PictureScope 32:4 (Winter 1987), 146–147, 156.
Describes the institute, founded in 1986, which undertakes
research and testing on the stability of imaging media; serves
as a source of information; and assists in the training of
professionals in the photographic preservation field.

Reilly, James M., Peter Z. Adelstein, and Douglas W. Nishimura.
Preservation of Safety Film. Rochester, NY: Image Permanence Institute, 1991. 103p.
Discusses the results of a long-term research project investigating the deterioration processes of cellulose acetate film.

Reilly, James M., Douglas W. Nishimura, Luis Pavao, and Peter
Z. Adelstein. "Photographic Enclosures: Research and Specifications," *Restaurator* 10:3/4 (1989), 102–111.

Reviews the potentially harmful effects of storage enclosure materials and adhesives; discusses ANSI Standards; evaluates materials currently available; offers practical advice in choosing photographic enclosures.

Rempel, Siegfried. *The Care of Photographs.* New York: Nick Lyons, 1987. 184p. Illus.
Covers photographic processes; causes of deterioration; storage and handling; repair and treatment. Bibliography.

Rempel, Siegfried. "Cold and Cool Vault Environments for the Storage of Historic Photographic Materials," *Conservation Administration News,* No. 38 (July 1989), 6–7, 9.
Describes the design of the cold storage facility for photographic collections at the Canadian Centre for Architecture.

Ritzenthaler, Mary Lynn, Gerald J. Munoff, and Margery S. Long. *Archives and Manuscripts: Administration of Photographic Collections.* Chicago: Society of American Archivists, 1984. 173p. (SAA Basic Archival Series)
Covers all aspects of managing and preserving historical photographic collections; glossary, source of supplies, bibliography.

Romer, Grant B. "Can We Afford to Exhibit Our Valued Photographs?" *PictureScope* 32:4 (Winter 1987), 136–137.
Urges stringent monitoring programs for photographic exhibition and recommends a change in the philosophy of exhibition.

Romer, Grant B. "Guidelines for the Administration and Care of Daguerreotype Collections," *Conservation Administration News,* No. 38 (July 1989), 4–5.
Emphasizes protective housing and storage.

Saretzky, Gary. "Bibliographies and Databases for Research on the Preservation of Aural and Graphic Records," *PictureScope* 31:4 (Winter 1985), 119–121.
Covers photographs and negatives; motion pictures and videotape; graphic arts; and sound recordings.

Saretzky, Gary D. "Recent Photographic Conservation and Preservation Literature," *PictureScope* 32:4 (Winter 1987), 117–132.

Selective review of the literature, with emphasis on 1982–1984.

Schrock, Nancy Carlson and Christine L. Sundt. "Slides," *Conservation in the Library,* ed. Susan G. Swartzburg. Westport, CT: Greenwood Press, 1983, 103–128.
History of slides and transparencies, causes of deterioration, problems with film stock, storage and handling, preservation.

Schwalberg, Bob. "Color Preservation Update," *Popular Photography* 89:1 (January 1982), 81–85.
Summary of findings on the causes of instability of color prints and slides.

Schwalberg, Bob, Henry Wilhelm, and Carol Brower. "Going, Going, Gone," *Popular Photography* 97:6 (June 1990), 37–49, 60.
Summary of the research undertaken by Henry Wilhelm to identify the problems that cause color film to fade and deteriorate, with a profile of Wilhelm.

Sundt, Christine L. *Conservation Practices for Slide and Photograph Collections.* Austin, TX: Visual Resource Assn., 1989. 78p. (*VRA Special Bulletin, 3, 1989*)
Covers problems, treatment and products. A collection of the author's practical columns on slide and photograph preservation, originally published in the *International Bulletin for Photographic Documentation,* 1979–1987.

Teller, Alan. "How Good Pictures Go Bad," *Journal of American Photography* 1:1 (January 1983), 24–26.
Why photographs deteriorate: improper fixing, improper processing. Tips to photographers to preserve their work.

Time-Life Books. *Caring for Photographs.* New York: Time-Life, 1982. 191p. Illus. (Life Library of Photography)
Covers the restoration of photographs, processing, storage, display, and exhibition. Mentions some questionable practices.

Visual Resources Association. *Slide Buyer's Guide.* 6th ed. by Nadine Cashman. Littleton, CO: Libraries Unlimited, 1990.

Compendium of art slide sources with an evaluation of slide quality.

Wagner, Sarah S. "Some Recent Photographic Preservation Activities at the Library of Congress," *Topics in Photographic Preservation* 4 (1991), 136–149.

Describes the optical disk projects at the library that make photographic images accessible and the physical treatment necessitated by them; describes treatments and techniques at the library.

Weinstein, Robert A. and Larry Booth. *Collection, Use and Care of Historical Photographs.* Nashville, TN: American Association for State and Local History, 1977.

Traces the history of photographs and provides information on their care.

Wilhelm, Henry. "Color Photographs and Color Motion Pictures in the Library: For Preservation or Destruction?" *Conserving and Preserving Materials in Nonbook Format,* ed. Kathryn L. and William T. Henderson. Urbana-Champaign, IL: University of Illinois Graduate School of Library and Information Studies, 1991, 105–111.

Describes the problem of instability of color films; discusses current research; recommends that libraries keep up-to-date information about the characteristics of color films.

Wilhelm, Henry. "Color Print Instability," *Modern Photography* 43:2 (February 1979), 92–93, 118–124, 134–142.

Discusses the problem and its causes; color print materials available and their suitability for use.

Wilhelm, Henry. "Color Print Instability: a Problem for Collectors and Photographers," *Afterimage* 6:3 (October 1978), 11–13.

Analysis of color print processes in use at the time. Notes the need for storage facilities that are dark with low temperature and relative humidity.

Wilhelm, Henry. "Monitoring the Fading and Staining of Color Photographic Prints," *Journal of the American Institute for Conservation* 21:2 (Fall 1982), 49–64.

Describes the visual and physical changes that can occur

with common types of color photographs; discusses methods for the long-term monitoring and storage of collections.

Wilhelm, Henry. "A Tale of Two Discs—More or Less," *Photo Communique* 3 (Fall 1982), 26–31.
Evaluates the disc camera in the context of other photographic technologies; expresses concern for what these innovations mean for the quality of future photographic imagery.

Wilhelm, Henry and Carol Brower. *The Permanence and Care of Color Photographs: Traditional and Digital Color Prints, Color Negatives, Slides and Motion Pictures.* Grinnell, IA: Preservation Publishing Company, 1993. 744p. Illus.
The basic text on the preservation of color photographic images; results of years of testing and research into film stability.

Young, Christine. *Nitrate Films in the Public Institution.* Nashville, TN: American Association for State and Local History, 1989. 8p.; *History News* 44:4 (July–August 1989).
Discusses the problem of nitrate film, its deterioration, detection, and options for dealing with it.

Chapter 11

Abbott, Andrew D., Jr., and Rosemary A. Salesi. "Preserve Your Media Collection Today," *Audiovisual Instruction,* 24:6 (September 1979), 29–31.
Describes the effect of temperature, relative humidity, and dust on nonprint media; how to deal with the heating system. Includes a "Media Storage Checklist."

Allen, John S. "Some New Possibilities in Audio Restoration," *ARSC Journal* (Association of Recorded Sound Collections) 21:1 (Spring 1990), 39–44.
On digital editing of audio signals, problems, and opportunities for rerecording of sound recordings.

Almquist, Sharon A. *Sound Recordings and the Library.* Urbana-Champaign, IL: University of Illinois Graduate School of Library and Information Science, August 1987. 37p. (Occasional Papers, 179)

Brief history of the development of sound recording technologies; their use in libraries.

Anderson, Pauline H. *Library Media Leadership in Academic Schools.* Hamden, CT: Library Professional Publ., 1985. 260p. Overview of multimedia use in secondary schools; includes a reprint of "What an Institution Can Do To Survey Its Collection Needs," by George M. Cunha.

Angus, Robert. "The Premium Videotapes," *High Fidelity* 36:2 (February 1986), 45–48.
Discusses the problem of identifying quality videotape and why they are necessary.

Bartell, Blaine M. "Preservation and Restoration of the Hearst Metrotone News Collection at UCLA Film and Television Archive," *AMIA Newsletter* (Association of Moving Image Archivists), No. 21 (July 1993), 4–5.
Describes a project to make new 35mm copies of endangered film for access on acetate-base film and the restoration of the original film.

Beaubien, Denise M., Bruce Emerton, Erich Kesse, Alice L. Primack, and Colleen Seale. "Patron-use Software in Academic Library Collections," *College and Research Libraries News* 49:10 (November 1988), 661–667.
University of Florida guidelines for purchasing, cataloging, circulating, and preserving software. Preservation guidelines described. Bibliography.

Bertram, H. Neal, Michael K. Stafford, and David R. Mills. "The Print-through Phenomenon," *Journal of the Audio Engineering Society* 28:10 (October 1980), 690–705.
Surveys existing theories of the print-through phenomenon; recommendations for selection, storage, and handling of tapes. Technical.

Blumenthal, Lyn. "Re-Guarding Video Preservation," *AfterImage* 13:7 (February 1986), 11–12.
Discusses problems of video and states that all video must be considered a short-term medium. Stresses the need to distinguish between master and copies and the importance of national cooperation in the preservation effort.

Bolnick, Doreen and Bruce Johnson. "Audiocassette Repair," *Library Journal* 114:19 (November 15, 1989), 43–46.
Simple repairs for circulating cassette collections.

Boston, George, ed. *Guide to the Basic Technical Equipment Required by Audio, Film, and Television Archives,* Paris: UNESCO, 1991. 104p.
Chapters are devoted to film, video and audio archives; physical characteristics of each medium are explained; preservation concerns addressed; includes an introductory section on the need for technical research.

Bowser, Eileen. "Motion Picture Film," *Conservation in the Library,* ed. Susan G. Swartzburg. Westport, CT: Greenwood Press, 1983, 139–153.
History of film, causes of deterioration, and preservation options.

Bowser, Eileen and John Kuiper. *A Handbook for Film Archives.* Brussels: International Federation of Film Archives, 1991. 194p.
Covers the care and preservation of film and other media found in the film archive.

Brennan, Patricia B. M. and Joel S. Silverberg. "Will My Disks Go Floo If I Take Them Through?" *College and Research Libraries News* 46:8 (September 1985), 423–424.
Discusses the effect of a magnetic security system upon magnetic microcomputer storage media. Tests showed that regular use did not affect disks, but exposure to the activator would erase data.

Brock-Nannestad, George. "A Comment and Further Recommendations on 'International Recording Standards,' " *ARSC Journal* 20:2 (Fall 1989), 156–161.
Emphasized that rerecording should keep the sound quality as close as possible to the original.

Brown, K. C. and R. E. Jacobson. "Archival Permanence of Holograms?" *Journal of Photographic Science* 33:5 September–October 1985), 177–182.
Review of the evidence of the permanence of high-resolution images and holograms photographically recorded on silver halide emulsions, and the influence of degradations

of image quality; preliminary recommendations for the storage and display of holograms.

Brownstein, Mark. "One Disc at a Time: Moldy Discs!" *CD-ROM EndUser* (February 1990), 29.
Observes that if a disk is not protected properly, the metallic coating can oxidize, its optical properties will change, and the disk will deteriorate so that it can no longer be read.

Calhoun, John M. "The Preservation of Motion-Picture Film," *American Archivist* 30:3 (July 1967), 517–524.
Cites intrinsic and extrinsic hazards; discusses nitrate, acetate, polyester, and color film with suggestions for archival preservation. Bibliography.

Calmes, Alan. "To Archive and Preserve: a Media Primer," *Inform* 1:5 (May 1987), 14–17, 33.
A brief evaluation of the media for preserving archival information.

Calmes, Alan A. "Relative Longevity of Various Archival Recording Media," *Conservation in Archives*. Paris: International Council on Archives, 1989, 207–221.
Analyzes the longevity of archival recording media, including magnetic media, according to physical properties, storage environment, and frequency of use. Discusses existing media standards and reformatting in response to demand for access.

Carroll, J. F. and John M. Calhoun. "Effect of Nitrogen Oxide Gasses on Processed Acetate Film," *SMPTE Journal* (Society of Motion Picture and Television Engineers) 64 (September 1955; *PhotographiConservation* 5:1–2 (March/June 1983), 9–15.
An important study that led to the conclusion that nitrate film should never be stored with acetate film.

Chickering, F. William. *Preservation of Nonprint Materials in Working Collections: a Basic Bibliography*. Atlanta: Southeast Library Network, 1985. 9p. (SOLINET Preservation Program Leaflet, 3)
Covers general works, film media, magnetic tape, sound recordings. No annotations.

Copeland, Peter. "Sound Recordings on Optical Discs," *Library Conservation News*, No. 38 (January 1993), 7.
Describes a process for the storage and retrieval of sound and image on optical disk; raises serious questions about permanence and retrieval.

Day, Rebecca. "Where's the Rot?" *Stereo Review* 54:4 (April 1989), 23–24.
An analysis of laser rot on compact disk sound recordings.

DeWhitt, Benjamin L. "The Long-Term Preservation of Data on Computer Magnetic Media," *Conservation Administration News*, No. 29 (April 1987), 7, 19, 29; No. 30 (July 1987), 4, 24.
Definition of magnetic tape, problems, and maintenance.

Dollar, Charles M. "Computers, the National Archives, and Researchers," *Prologue* (Journal of the National Archives) 8:1 (Spring 1976), 29–34.
A brief history of the development of computers. Describes the problems in preserving and making available an "overwhelming" amount of machine-readable data, and the effect of changes in computer technology.

Dollar, Charles M. *A National Archives Strategy for the Development and Implementation of Standards for the Creation, Transfer, Access, and Long-Term Storage of Electronic Records of the Federal Government.* Washington, DC: National Archives and Records Administration, 1990. 22p. (Information Paper, TIP 08)
Outlines NARA's position on the preservation of records in electronic format.

Empsucha, Joseph G. "Film/Videotape Fact Sheet," *Conservation Administration News*, No. 22 (July 1985), 6, 21.
Preservation and storage of nitrate and safety film and videotape.

Fothergill, Richard and Ian Butchart. *Non-Book Material in Libraries: a Practical Guide.* 3rd rev. ed. London: Library Association, 1990. 328p.
Covers all media, with emphasis on care and handling. Substantial information on optical storage systems and remote data bases.

Gavrel, Katherine. *Conceptual Problems Posed by Electronic Records: A RAMP Study.* Paris: UNESCO, 1990. 44p.
Cites problems raised by electronic records in relationship to aspects of traditional archival theory and practice.

Geller, Sidney B. *Care and Handling of Computer Magnetic Storage Media.* Washington, DC: National Bureau of Standards, June 1983. (NBS Special Publ. 500–101)
Guidelines for the care, handling, storage, and preservation of computer magnetic storage media. Covers media transit and disaster salvage and recovery.

Gibson, Gerald D. "Preservation and Conservation of Sound Recordings," *Conserving and Preserving Materials in Nonbook Format,* ed. Kathryn L. and William T. Henderson. Urbana-Champaign, IL: University of Illinois Graduate School of Library and Information Service, 1991, 27–44.
Describes materials used in sound recording, care, storage, handling, and preservation.

Goldstein, Charles. "Optical Disc Technology and Information," *Science* 215:4534 (February 12, 1982), 862–868.
Information storage using optical disk technology; discussion of archival storage issues.

Gooes, Roland and Hans-Evert Bloman. "An Inexpensive Method for Preservation and Long-Term Storage of Color Film," *SMPTE Journal* 92 (December 1983), 1314–1316.
Describes the film conditioning apparatus designed by the Swedish Film Institute to save and store all motion picture films produced since the 1930s. The film is conditioned and stabilized, placed in a plastic bag, and stored in a commercial freezer; the film must be reconditioned for use.

Happe, L. Bernard. *Basic Motion Picture Technology.* 2nd ed., rev. New York: Communication Arts Books, Hastings House, 1975.
History of motion pictures and their technology.

Harrison, Helen P. "Conservation and Audiovisual Materials," *Audiovisual Librarian* 13:3 (August 1987), 154–162.
Discussion of guidelines for the preservation and conservation of audiovisual materials to be promulgated by the

International Federation of Library Associations and Institutions (IFLA). Media and appropriate methods of storage described.

Haserot, Karen E. "The Colorization of Film: Technical, Legal, Historical, and Sociocultural Considerations," *Techné: Journal of Technology Studies* 3 (Spring 1989), 45–52.
Discusses the technology of colorization and the legal and moral implications.

Hendley, Tony. *The Archival Storage Potential of Microfilm, Magnetic Media and Optical Discs.* Hatfield, Herts.: National Reprographic Centre for Documentation, January 1983. 77p. (BNB Research Fund Report, 10/NCRd Publ. 19)
Review of archival storage media; discussion of the requirements and benefits of each medium and requirements for its preservation.

Hendley, Tony. *CD-ROM and Optical Publishing Systems.* Westport, CT: Meckler, 1987. 149p.
Assessment of the impact of optical read-only memory systems on the information industry; a comparison between them and paper, microfilm and on-line publishing systems. Describes the systems and technology, standards, organization of information, and implications.

Hendley, Tony. *Videodiscs, Compact Discs and Digital Optical Discs.* Hatfield, Herts.: Cimtech, February 1985. 208p. (Cimtech Publ. 23)
Introduction to the technologies and the systems and their potential for information storage, retrieval, and dissemination.

Herther, Nancy. "The Silver Disk: Between a Rock and a Hard Place: Preservation and Optical Media," *Database* 10:2 (April 1987), 122–124.
The difficulties of coping with new technology are summarized and potential problems identified.

Hodges, Anthony. "78s—Preservation or Disposal?" *Audiovisual Librarian* 14:1 (February 1988), 29–30.
The role regional archives should play in the preservation of 78rpm recordings.

Huber, Ella Mae. "How To Reduce Film Damage," *International Innovator* 26:2 (February 1981), 37–39.
Practical advice for circulating media collections; recommends the creation of a Film Damage Committee to address the problem of damaged materials.

Kalil, Ford, ed. *Magnetic Tape Recording for the Eighties.* Washington, DC: Government Printing Office, April 1982. 170p. (NASA Reference Publ, 1075)
Report on the practical and theoretical aspects of magnetic tape recording and technology. Covers the causes of damage, care and handling, and a variety of preservation issues and concerns. Glossary.

Knight, G. A. *Factors Relating to the Long Term Storage of Magnetic Tape.* EMI Research Laboratories, February 1977. 35p., Plates; reprinted in *Phonographic Bulletin* 18 (1977), 15–45.
Discusses guidelines for storage, problem of fungal attack, packaging, handling, and inspection.

Kuiper, John B. "Preserving Our Moving Image Heritage: A Conspiracy of Facts," *Conservation Administration News,* No. 44 (January 1991), 4–5, 29–30.
Describes the effort to preserve our heritage of film and video; the role of film archives.

Lesk, Michael. *Image Formats for Preservation and Access.* Washington, DC: Commission on Preservation and Access, July 1990. 10p.; *Information Technology and Libraries* 9:4 (December 1990), 300–308.
Examines the feasibility of deacidification, microfilm, digital imagery, and computer technologies as techniques for book preservation. Report of the Technology Advisory Committee to the Commission.

Limbacher, James. "Beware the Red Menace," *Film Library Quarterly* 8:1 (1975), 31.
A warning about the color fading properties of Eastman Kodak color film.

Lister Hill National Center for Biomedical Communications. Communications Engineering Branch. *Document Preserva-*

tion by Electronic Imaging, vol. 1: *Synopsis.* Bethesda, MD: Lister Hill, April 1989.

Synopsis of a program to investigate the application of electronic imaging (EI) to document preservation; brief history, background, list of attributes of EI for document preservation, system description, summary of findings, and conclusions.

Lynn, M. Stuart. *Preservation and Access Technology; the Relationship Between Digital and Other Media Conservation Processes: A Structured Glossary of Technical Terms.* Washington, DC: Commission on Preservation and Access, 1990. 68p.

An attempt at a glossary for understanding technical issues in preservation and access.

McQueen, Judy and Richard W. Boss. *Videodisc and Optical Disk Technologies and their Applications in Libraries, 1986 Update.* Chicago: American Library Association, 1987. 155p. (Library Technology Report)

Describes the disk media that is available, its use, and potential for preservation and access.

McWilliams, Jerry. *The Preservation and Restoration of Sound Recordings.* Nashville, TN: American Association for State and Local History, 1979. 138p.

Detailed information, including a history of the technology, model preservation policy. Bibliography.

Mallinson, John C. "Magnetic Tape Recording: History, Evolution and Practical Considerations," *Conservation in Archives.* Paris: International Council on Archives, 1989, 181–190.

A brief history of audio, video and computer tape recording. Discusses deterioration of software; expresses concern over ability of appropriate hardware.

Mallinson, John C. "On the Preservation of Human and Machine-Readable Records," *Information Technology and Libraries* 7:1 (March 1988), 19–23.

Explains why the National Archives and Records Administration, after exploring available information technologies, established a policy that the majority of holdings be on human-readable microform.

Mason, Robert M. "All About Diskettes," *Library Journal* 109:5 (March 1984), 558–559.
Describes how diskettes are made and how they should be handled.

Mazikana, Peter C. "A Strategy for the Preservation of Audiovisual Materials," *Audiovisual Librarian* 14:1 (February 1988), 24–28.
Addresses the problem of preserving audiovisual material, with emphasis on the particular problems of underdeveloped countries. Seeks a multipronged approach to the problems of storage, servicing and accessibility, and local, national, and international cooperation.

Meigs, James B. "How Long Will Videotape Really Last?" *Video Review* 4 (July 1984), 24–26.
Explains why the medium is unstable and impermanent, with suggestions on how to preserve tapes for as long as possible.

National Archives and Records Administration. *Managing Electronic Records.* Washington, DC: National Archives and Records Administration, 1990. 32p.; appendixes, glossary.
Defines electronic records, focusing on records that are a part of an automated information system. Discusses the management and preservation of these records.

National Research Council. Committee on Preservation of Historical Records. *Preservation of Historical Records.* Washington, DC: National Academy Press, 1986. 107p.
Examined technologies for preserving paper records and determined that newer optical and magnetic media were unsatisfactory because of their impermanence.

Neavill, Gordon B. "Preservation of Computer-Based and Computer-Generated Records," *Conserving and Preserving Materials in Nonbook Formats,* ed. Kathryn L. and William T. Henderson. Urbana-Champaign, IL: University of Illinois Graduate School of Library and Information Science, 1991, 45–60. (Allerton Park Institute, 30)
Sketches the historical context from which computer materials have sprung, describes some of the significant work in the preservation of computer-based materials, and explores

the preservation problems and prospects of a number of data storage media. An important overview of the topic.

New York State Archives and Records Administration. Special Media Records Project. *A Strategic Plan for Managing and Preserving Electronic Records in New York State Government: Final Report.* Albany, NY: New York State Archives and Records Administration, August 1988. 36p.

A strategic plan for improved management and selected preservation of valuable electronic records; provides a framework for integrating computer-generated records into information management programs and to ensure that electronic records with enduring value are preserved.

Noble, Richard. *Archival Preservation of Motion Pictures: a Summary of Current Findings.* Nashville, TN: American Association for State and Local History, April 1980. 7p. (Technical Leaflet, 126); *History News* 35:4 (April 1980).

Describes the nature of nitrate, triacetate, and color film, discusses storage, fire protection, atmospheric conditions, storage, inspection, restoration, and duplication. Bibliography.

Paton, Christopher Ann. "Annotated Bibliography of Works Relating to Sound Recordings and Magnetic and Optical Media," *Midwestern Archivist,* 16:1 (1991), 31–37.

Over eighty annotated citations to literature relating to various audio recording media.

Paton, Christopher Ann. "Preservation of Acetate Disc Sound Recordings at Georgia State University," *Midwestern Archivist* 16:1 (1993), 11–20.

How an archivist learned to properly care for recordings, developed procedures for producing archival preservation copies, and located a laboratory to handle rerecording. Recommends initiatives that should be taken by the archival community.

Paton, Christopher Ann. "Whispers in the Stacks: The Problem of Sound Recordings in Archives," *American Archivist* 53:2 (Spring, 1990), 274–280.

Discusses the status of sound recordings in archives; recommends initiatives to improve their management and to address preservation issues.

Pickett, A. G. and M. M. Lemcoe. *Preservation and Storage of Sound Recordings.* Silver Spring, MD: Association of Recorded Sound Collections, 1991. 74p.
  The basic investigation of the factors that cause deterioration of disks and magnetic tape, with recommendations for storage and handling. Originally published by the Library of Congress in 1959, the report remains timely.

Read, Oliver and Walter L. Welch. *From Tin Foil to Stereo; Evolution of the Phonograph,* 2nd ed. Indianapolis, IN: Howard W. Sams, 1976. 550p.
  Detailed history of sound recording media through the mid-1970s. Bibliography.

Roper, Michael. "Advanced Technical Media: The Conservation and Storage of Audio-Visual and Machine Readable Records," *Journal of the Society of Archivists* 7 (October 1982), 106–112.
  Problems of the preservation and storage motion picture film, microfilm, sound recordings, and machine-readable records.

Roth, Stacey. "The Care and Preservation of Sound Recordings," *Conservation Administration News,* No. 23 (October 1985), 4–5, 24.
  Provides basic information. Bibliography.

Saffady, William. "Stability, Care and Handling of Microforms, Magnetic Media and Optical Disks," *Library Technology Reports* 27:1 (January–February 1991), 5–116.
  Reports on the physical qualities of these media. Bibliographic essay on a wide range of topics.

Saretzky, Gary. "Bibliographies and Databases for Research on the Preservation of Aural and Graphic Records," *PictureScope* 31:4 (Winter 1985), 119–121.
  Covers motion pictures, videotapes, sound recordings; cites general bibliographies, data bases.

Sargent, Ralph N. *Preserving the Moving Image.* Washington, DC: Corporation for Public Broadcasting, 1974. 152p.
  Overview of the problems of film and videotape. Survey of preservation methods and recommendations for further investigation.

Schenck, Thomas. "Magnetic Tape Care, Storage and Error Recovery," *Library Hi Tech,* 2:4 (1984), 51–54.
Covers the technology of magnetic tape and its technical problems.

Scholtz, James C. *Developing and Maintaining Video Collections in Libraries.* Santa Barbara, CA: ABC-Clio, 1989. 196p.
Basic text on the organization and management of video service in the public library. Information on the physical nature of videotapes, care, storage, and handling.

Schueller, Dietrich. "Handling, Storage and Preservation of Sound Recordings Under Tropical and Subtropical Climate Conditions," *Restaurator* 7:1 (1986), 14–21.
Discusses the physical nature of conventional sound recordings, provides recommendations for storage.

Schueller, Dietrich. "Sound Tapes and the 'Vinegar Syndrome'." *Phonographic Bulletin* 54 (July 1989), 29–31.
Describes the syndrome, which afflicts motion picture films on cellulose triacetate base, and may also affect acetate-based audiotapes. Procedures for examining audiotapes, handling damaged tapes, and preventing future damage are recommended.

Silver, Jeremy and Lloyd Stickells. "Preserving Sound Recordings at the British Library National Sound Archive," *Library Conservation News,* No. 13 (October 1986), 1–3.
Describes the technology used for the preservation of sound recordings at the British Library.

Smith, Leslie E. "Factors Governing the Long-Term Stability of Polyester-based Recording Media," *Restaurator* 12:4 (1991), 201–218.
Translates the results of National Archives and National Institute for Science and Technology tests on the longevity of microfilm and magnetic tape into practical terms.

Stielow, Frederick J. *The Management of Oral History Sound Archives.* Westport, CT: Greenwood Press, 1986. 192p.
Chapter 6: "Conservation Management," 109–132, describes the media, environment for its storage, equipment maintenance, security, and disaster planning. Bibliography.

St. Laurent, Gilles. *The Care and Handling of Recorded Sound Materials.* Washington, DC: Commission on Preservation and Access, September 1991. 10p.
  A practical guide for the care and handling of recorded sound materials in collections.

Storm, William. "Audio Equipment Considerations for Sound Archives," *Phonographic Bulletin,* No. 57 (November 1990), 38–46.
  Describes the role and function of the sound archive engineer; discusses equipment needed for accurate sound reformatting. Bibliography.

Swartzburg, Susan G. "Preservation of Sound Recordings," *Encyclopedia of Recorded Sound in the United States,* ed. Guy A. Marco. New York: Garland, 1993, 542–546.
  A short overview of preservation issues and concerns for phonograph records, magnetic recordings, compact disks; some discussion of archival concerns.

Swartzburg, Susan G. and Deirdre Boyle. "Videotape," *Conservation in the Library,* ed. Susan G. Swartzburg. Westport, CT: Greenwood Press, 1983, 156–161.
  History and physical nature of videotape, care and handling, preservation problems.

U.S. Congress. Committee on Government Operations. *Taking a Byte Out of History: the Archives Preservation of Federal Computer Records.* Washington, DC: Government Printing Office, 1990. 30p.
  Highlights the need for standardized formats and compatible equipment capable of reading records stored for future information retrieval.

U.S. General Accounting Office. *Valuable Government-Owned Motion Picture Films Are Rapidly Deteriorating.* Washington, DC: Government Printing Office, 1978. 42p.
  Survey of conditions in government facilities with recommendations for improvement. Report to the Congress by the Comptroller General.

Vogelsang, Peter. "Optical Digital Recording," *Conservation in Archives.* Paris: International Council on Archives, 1989, 223–232.

Reviews optical recording, including principles and issues of information access and system obsolescence. Provides a good comparison between optical and magnetic recording.

Volkmann, Herbert. *Film Preservation: a Report to the Preservation Committee of the International Federation of Film Archives.* London: National Film Archive, 1965. 60p.
Addresses the problem of preserving motion picture film; describes the properties of film and tape, storage issues, restoration of film. An important study.

Wagner, Robert W. "Motion Picture Restoration," *American Archivist* 32:2 (April 1969), 125–132.
History of the techniques for restoring and replacing nitrate film.

Ward, Alan. *A Manual of Sound Archive Administration.* Aldershot, Herts; Brookfield, VT: Gower, 1990. 288p.
Provides detailed information on the development and physical nature of aural media; on storage and handling. Deals with reformatting issues that make preservation difficult, and industry standards.

Waters, Donald J. *Electronic Technologies and Preservation.* Washington, DC: Commission on Preservation and Access, June 1992. 8p.
Briefly describes imaging technology within the context of the life cycles of materials. Presents an agenda for action to explore the potential of digital technologies for preservation and access in research libraries.

Waters, Donald J. *From Microform to Digital Imagery.* Washington, DC: Commission on Preservation and Access, June 1991. 41p.
Explores the feasibility of a project to study the means, costs, and benefits of converting large quantities of preserved library materials from microform to digital images, for enhanced access.

White, Robert M. "Disc Storage Technology," *Scientific American* 243:2 (August 1980), 138–148.
Description of optical disk technology.

White, Susan B. and Allan E. "The Computer: When Tomorrow

Becomes Yesterday," *Conservation in the Library,* ed. Susan G. Swartzburg. Westport, CT: Greenwood Press, 1983, 206–219.
    Examines the technology, preservation of information, and implications for the future preservation of information. Selected bibliography.

Chapter 12

Adelstein, Peter Z. "History and Properties of Film Supports," *Conservation in Archives.* Paris: International Council on Archives, 1989, 89–101.
    Describes film supports and their physical properties.

Adelstein, Peter Z. "Preservation of Microfilm," *Journal of Micrographics* 11:6 (July–August 1978), 333–337.
    Discussion of the types of films available; how they should be cared for, stored. Technical bibliography.

Adelstein, Peter Z. and James M. Reilly. "The Image Permanence Institute: New Preservation Resource," *Inform* 1:10 (October 1987), 37–39.
    Describes the purpose and functions of the center, including research, education and training, and contracted research.

Amodeo, Anthony J. "Photocopying Without (Much) Damage," *College and Research Libraries News* 44:10 (November 1983), 368–370.
    Describes the problems with photocopiers, current research into the development of machines that will not damage books.

Atkinson, Ross. "Preservation and Collection Development: Toward a Political Synthesis," *Journal of Academic Librarianship* 16 (1990), 98–103.
    Considers preservation reformatting and what might best be preserved.

Avedon, Don M. "The More Practical Microfilm—Vesicular," *Library Resources and Technical Services* 24:4 (Fall 1980), 325–328.

Description of the use and purpose of vesicular film; note on its care and storage.

Avedon, Don M. and Ann M. DeVilliers. "Microfilm Permanence and Archival Quality," *ASIS Journal* (American Society for Information Science) 30:2 (March 1979), 100–102.
Requirements for materials, processing, and storage of archival microforms.

Ballou, Hubbard W. "The Micrographic Book Cradle in Retrospect and Replica," *Microform Review* 14:3 (Summer 1985), 174–179.
History of the cradles that have been developed for microfilming, with a model.

Barker, Nicolas. "Publishing and Preservation," *Library Publishing,* ed. David Way. London: British Library, 1985, 57–59.
Explains how the publication of library collections in microformat can preserve original materials.

Bell, Nancy J. "Xerography and Preservation: Problems and Potential," *Library Hi Tech* 1:1 (Summer 1983), 69–73.
Summary of advantages and disadvantages. Bibliography on electrophotography.

Bond, Elayne. "Generic Letter of Agreement for Microfilming," *Abbey Newsletter* 14:4 (July 1990), 70–71.
A sample, fill-in-the-blank letter to initiate communication with a vendor.

Boss, Richard W. and Deborah Raikes. *Developing Microfilm Reading Facilities.* Westport, CT: Microform Review, 1982.
Summary, glossary, and bibliography.

Bourke, Thomas A. "The Microfilming of Newspapers: an Overview," *Microform Review* 15:3 (Summer 1986), 154–157.
History of the filming of newspapers at the New York Public Library; current projects and filming methods.

Bourke, Thomas A. "Research Libraries Reassess Document Preservation Technologies," *Inform* 4:8 (September 1990), 30–34.
Discusses the advantages of microforms over other imaging technologies in the research library setting.

Bibliography

Bourke, Thomas A. "Retrospect and Prospect: Micrographics Evolution in Research Libraries," *Inform* 1:10 (October 1987), 28–33.
History of the use of microfilm and other information technologies in research libraries.

Bourke, Thomas A. "Spaulding and Materazzi Revisited: a Ten Year Retrospect," *Microform Review* 17:3 (August 1988), 130–136.
Review of the debate surrounding questions of archival storage, durability in a working environment, and affordability among proponents of silver halide, diazo, and vesicular films.

Bourke, Thomas A. "To Archive or Not to Archive: Is That Really the Question?" *Library Journal* 114:17 (October 15, 1989), 52–54.
Cogent discussion of the use of the term "archival" when referring to collections, and its relation to preservation of materials in a nonprint format.

Burdick, Amrita. "Library Photocopying: the Margin of Caring," *New Library Scene* 5:3 (June 1986), 17–18.
On the proper ways to photocopy materials from bound volumes.

Byrne, Sherry. "Guidelines for Contracting Microfilming Services," *Microform Review* 15:4 (Fall 1986), 253–264.
Outlines the process for selecting a vendor for preservation microfilming, with sample contract.

Cady, Susan A. "The Electronic Revolution in Libraries: Microfilm Deja Vu?" *College and Research Libraries* 51:4 (July 1990), 374–386.
Traces the history of microfilm in libraries and the assumption of its adoption for research. Outlines reasons for lack of acceptance, noting these are the same given for electronic media. Suggests nonprint media use as an adjunct to printed material, not in lieu of it.

Calmes, Alan. "New Confidence in Microfilm," *Library Journal* 111:15 (September 15, 1986), 38–42.
Reviews the advances in page reproduction technology in the past decade, comparing microfilm with optical disk as a

preservation medium. Reaffirms microfilm as the most practical format.

Chapman, Patricia and Stephanie Kenna. "Substitution Microforms: a Survey of the Policies and Practices in U.K. Libraries," *Library Association Record* 90:5 (May 1988), 282–285.
Report of a survey undertaken by the National Preservation Office, British Library. Concludes that staff and readers need to be educated about the reasons for microtext substitution and its advantages.

Chase, Myron B. "Preservation Microfiche: a Matter of Standards," *Library Resources and Technical Services* 35:2 (April 1991), 186–190.
Discusses the standards necessary to ensure the permanence of reformatted preservation copies; describes standards available for microfiche and those currently being developed.

Child, Margaret S. "The Future of Cooperative Preservation Microfilming," *Library Resources and Technical Services* 29:1 (January–March 1985), 94–101.
Describes cooperative efforts under way and how librarians can approach the task.

Child, Margaret S. "Selection for Microfilming," *American Archivist* 53:2 (Spring 1990), 250–255.
Describes the process and theory behind the national preservation microfilming program and argues that the approach is also suitable for archival materials.

Clapp, Verner W., Francis H. Henshaw, and Donald C. Holmes. "Are Your Microfilms Deteriorating Acceptably?" *Library Journal* 80:6 (March 15, 1955), 589–595.
Problems with microfilm and the need for standards. A review of testing undertaken at the Library of Congress.

Clements, D.W.G. "Preservation Microfilming and Substitution Policy in the British Library," *Microform Review* 17:1 (February 1988), 17–22.
Describes the decision-making process, the role of substitutes, costs, and contracting.

Clements, David W. G. "Problems of Cooperative Microfilm-

ing," *Collection Management* 15:3/4 (1992), 503–507.
    Discusses the need for resource sharing in Europe and the
development of cooperative microfilming projects.

Commission on Preservation and Access. Joint Task Force on
    Text and Image. *Preserving the Illustrated Text.* Washington,
    DC: April 1992. 30p.
    A report examining the quality and reliability of reformat-
ted visual images. Concludes that microfilming remains the
most satisfactory reproductive medium at this time.

Darling, Pamela W. "Developing a Preservation Microfilming
    Program," *Library Journal* 99 (November 1, 1974), 2803–
    2809.
    Methodology and costs. Bibliography.

Darling, Pamela W. "Microforms In Libraries: Preservation and
    Storage," *Microform Review* 5:2 (April 1976), 93–100.
    Discusses the use of microform technology as a tool for
storing and preserving information; outlines methods for
storage and preservation of microforms.

De Candido, Robert. "Considerations in Evaluating Searching
    for Microform Availability," *Microform Review* 19:3 (Sum-
    mer 1990), 116–118.
    Discussion of the factors to be weighed in determining how
much bibliographic searching to undertake in a preservation
microfilming program.

De Candido, Robert. "Out of the Question: I'm Searchin', I'm
    Searchin' Every Whi-i-ich a-Way, Yay, Yay," *Conservation
    Administration News,* No. 40 (January 1990), 20–21.
    A formula for evaluating the cost-effectiveness of searching
before microfilming for preservation.

Diaz, Albert James. *Microforms in Libraries: a Reader.* West-
    port, CT: Microform Review, 1975.
    Collection of the best articles on miroforms published prior
to 1975.

Dodson, Suzanne Cates. "Microfilm—Which Film Type, Which
    Application?" *Microform Review* 14:2 (Spring 1985), 87–98.
    Describes the characteristics of the types of available mi-
crofilm and the problem of selecting the appropriate one.

Dodson, Suzanne Cates. "Microfilm Types: There Really Is a Choice," *Library Resources and Technical Services* 30:1 (January–March 1986), 84–90.

Discusses the characteristics of silver halide, diazo, and vesicular films; advocates that the purchaser's choice of film should be governed by an understanding of its attributes.

Dorfman, Harold H. "The Effect of Fungus on Silver Gelatin, Diazo and Vesicular Film," *Journal of Micrographics* 1:4 (March 1978), 257–260.

Report on testing for fungal contamination; methods of prevention.

Dorfman, Harold H. "Quality Control of Microfilm," *Micrographics and Optical Technology* 8:4 (1990), 217–222.

Discusses the elements of quality microfilm; cites standards.

Dupont, Jerry. "Microform Film Stock: a Hobson's Choice. Are Librarians Getting the Worst of Both Worlds?" *Library Resources and Technical Services* 30:1 (January–March, 1986), 79–83.

Addresses the issue of preservation and access to information in microformat and issues of the preservation of microfilm.

Ehrenberg, Ralph. "Reproducing Maps in Libraries and Archives; the Custodian's Point of View," *Special Libraries* 64:1 (January 1973), 18, 20–24.

Problem of photographic reproduction, accessibility, and handling are discussed.

Elkington, Nancy E., ed. *RLG Preservation Microfilming Handbook.* Mountain View, CA: Research Libraries Group, Inc., 1992. 203p.

A comprehensive guide to preservation microfilming, presenting a clear definition of the process, terms, and guidelines. Essential to the manual are its appendixes, which include practical, often step-by-step, information.

Ferris, Valerie. "Don't Film It If You're Not Recording It!" *Library Conservation News,* No. 22 (January 1989), 3, 8.

Discusses the importance of keeping records of what is

filmed and describes the British Library's Register of Preservation Microforms.

Folcarelli, Ralph J., Arthur C. Tannenbaum, and Ralph C. Ferragamo. *The Microform Connection: a Basic Guide for Librarians.* New York: Bowker, 1982.
Basic text for smaller collections.

Frieder, Richard. "The Microfiche Revolution in Libraries," *Microform Review* 16:3 (Summer 1987), 214–216.
Discusses advantages and disadvantages of microfiche for preservation.

Gertz, Janet E. "Preservation Microfilming for Archives and Manuscripts," *American Archivist* 53:2 (Spring 1990), 224–234.
Discusses the advantages of cooperative microfilming projects; planning an effective microfilming program.

Graham, Crystal. *Guidelines for Bibliographic Records for Preservation Microform Masters.* Washington, DC: Association of Research Libraries, 1990. 15p.; reprinted in *Microform Review* 21–2 (Spring 1992), 67–73.
Prepared for use in cataloging preservation microform masters of books and serial publications.

Gunn, Michael J. *Manual of Document Microphotography.* London; Boston: Focal Press, 1985. 232p.
Covers the history of microphotography, types of microforms, equipment, processing. Glossary and bibliography.

Gunn, Michael J. "'Poly' or 'Cell'," *Microform Review* 16:3 (Summer 1987), 231–232.
Comparison of the advantages and disadvantages of cellulose acetate and polyester silver halide films.

Gwinn, Nancy E., ed. *Preservation Microfilming: a Guide for Librarians and Archivists.* Chicago: American Library Association, 1987. 212p.
Manual covering all aspects of preservation microfilming, from inception to completion of projects. Standards, specifications and guidelines; glossary and bibliography.

Gwinn, Nancy E. "The RTSD Preservation Microfilming Committee: Looking to the 1990s," *Library Resources and Technical Services* 34:1 (January 1990), 88–94.
History of the committee, its accomplishments, and current initiatives.

Gwinn, Nancy E. "The Rise and Fall and Rise of Cooperative Projects," *Library Resources and Technical Services* 29:1 (January-March, 1985), 80–86.
Historical overview of cooperative preservation microfilming projects and a look at present efforts.

Hall, Hal W. and George H. Michaels. "Microform Reader Maintenance," *Microform Review* 14:4 (Winter 1985), 24–34.
Describes how to organize a program and provide guidelines for regular machine maintenance and repair.

Harper, James. "Microfilm Reformatting; Linking Past, Present," *Inform* 1:10 (October 1987), 14–16.
Discussion of the issues of reformatting.

Hazen, Dan C. *The Production and Bibliographic Control of Latin American Preservation Microforms in the United States.* Washington, DC: Commission on Preservation and Access, June 1991. 38p.
Provides information on preservation microfilming projects under way, sources of information about them, and encourages closer cooperation to avoiding duplication in the future.

Holder, Carol. "Protecting Your Image: Microform Storage and Security," *Inform* 1:10 (October 1988), 18–21.
Guidelines for corporate records managers for the storage and handling of microforms.

Horder, Alan. *Guidelines for the Care and Preservation of Microforms in Tropical Countries.* Paris: UNESCO, 1990. 20p. (A RAMP Study)
Reviews the factors affecting the permanence of microforms and technical considerations relating to the purchase, processing, management, protection, and control of a microfilm collection.

Image Permanence Institute. *Polysulfide Treatment of Micro-*

film Using IPI Silverlock (TM)—Some Questions and Answers. Rochester, NY: Image Permanence Institute, 1991. 7p.
Discusses the role of polysulfide toning of silver gelatin microfilm to improve image resistance to fading and red spot formation.

Jones, C. Lee. "Mid-Atlantic Preservation Service (MAPS): New Options for Preservation Microfilming," *Microform Review* 18:3 (Summer 1989), 142–144.
Describes MAPS' mission, operations, and goals for the future.

Kenny, Anne R. "Digital-to-Microfilm Conversion: An Interim Preservation Solution," *Library Resources and Technical Services* 37:4 (October 1993), 380–401; "Erratum" 38:1 (January 1994), 87–95.
Reviews the project at Cornell University to test the feasibility of using digital image technology to preserve and improve access to deteriorating materials.

Kenny, Anne R. and Lynn K. Personius. "Update on Digital Techniques," *Commission on Preservation and Access Newsletter,* No. 40 (November–December 1991), 1–6.
Reports on the joint Cornell University-Xerox Corporation project to digitally capture deteriorated volumes to provide network access to text as well as high-quality paper facsimilies or microfiolm copies.

Library of Congress Photoduplication Service. *Specifications for Microfilming Manuscripts.* Washington, DC: Library of Congres, 1980.
Specifications for manuscript preparation, filming procedures, and film processing.

Library of Congress Photoduplication Service. *Specifications for the Microfilming of Books and Pamphlets in the Library of Congress.* Washington, DC: Library of Congress, 1973.
Recommended procedures for the filming for monographs and pamphlets.

Lockhart, Vickie and Ann Swartzell. "Evaluation of Microfilm Vendors," *Microform Review* 19:3 (Summer 1990), 119–123.
Report of a study to evaluate vendors for preservation microfilming.

Luther, Frederic. *Microfilm: a History, 1839–1900.* Annapolis, MD: National Microfilm Association, 1959. 195p.
A history, tracing the careers of the developers of the medium.

McClung, Patricia A. "Costs Associated With Preservation Microfilming: Results of the Research Libraries Group Study," *Library Resources and Technical Services* 30:4 (October–December 1986), 363–374; *Preservation Microfilming.* Chicago: American Library Association, 1989, 63–74.
The results of a study of the practices at seven institutions; results varied significantly.

McCrady, Ellen. "Deacidification vs. Microfilming," *Abbey Newsletter* 14:6 (October 1990), 112–113.
A lucid discussion of the options for preservation.

McCrady, Ellen. "The History of Microfilm Blemishes," *Restaurator* 6:3–4 (Fall 1984), 191–204.
Describes the results of research to determine the cause of blemishes on negative microfilm.

McDonald, Peter. "Color Microform: New Possibilities," *Microform Review* 17:3 (August 1988), 146–149.
Discussion of the issues surrounding the use of color microfilm; suggests further study.

MacKenzie, George. "Preservation of Electronic Media," *Library Conservation News,* No. 38 (January 1993), 1–3, 7.
Describes the problems and challenges of preserving information in electronic formats. Notes that the greatest long-term problem is accessibility.

McKern, Debra. "Public-Use Copiers in Library Service," *Library Resources and Technical Services* 32:3 (April 1989), 160–163.
Discusses a survey to determine what features libraries consider essential for public service use and implications for preservation.

Montague, Robert. "A Nation's Printed Heritage on Microfiche," *Conservation Administration News,* No. 24 (January 1986), 7, 24.
Describes the microfilming program of the Canadian Insti-

tute for Historical Microreproduction to preserve and make available Canada's printed heritage on microfilm.

National Archives and Records Administration. *Optical Digital Image Storage System.* Washington, DC: National Archives and Records Administration, 1991. 378p. (Technical Information Paper, 10)
Reports on NARA's five year project to evaluate the feasibility, costs, and benefits of digital imaging and optical disk technologies to support archival programs. Includes a useful introduction to these technologies.

National Archives and Records Administration and the National Association of Government Archives and Records Administrators. *Digital Imaging and Optical Media Storage Systems: Guidelines for State and Local Government Agencies.* Albany, NY: NAGARA, 1991. 70p. and appendixes.
Report on a project undertaken by the NARA Research and Evaluation staff to assess the experience of sixty state and local governments with digital imaging and optical media storage systems.

National Research Council. Committee on the Preservation of Historical Records. *Preservation of Historical Records.* Washington, DC: National Academy Press, 1986. 108p.
Report of a study of the methods available for the preservation of the documents housed in the National Archives. Methods of preservation were examined and assessed.

Nicholson, Catherine. "Photocopy Preservation Problems and Hazards," *Society of California Archivists Newsletter* 66 (December 1990), 6.
Electrostatic photocopiers as a preservation tool.

Orr, Gloria J. "Preservation Photocopying of Bound Volumes: An Increasingly Viable Option," *Library Resources and Technical Services* 34:4 (October 1990), 445–454.
Evaluation of photocopying equipment that should be considered in preservation photocopying.

Preservation Microfilming. Chicago: American Library Association, 1989. 72p.
Papers by Wesley Boomgaarden, Margaret Byrnes, Myron

Chase, Carolyn Harris, Patricia McClung, and Gay Walker on important aspects of preservation microfilming.

Reilly, James M., Douglas W. Nishimura, Kaspars M. Cupriks, Peter Z. Adelstein. "Stability of Black and White Photographic Images, with Special Reference to Microfilm," *Conservation in Archives.* Paris: International Council on Archives, 1989, 117–127; reprinted in *Abbey Newsletter* 12:5 (July 1988, 83–88; *Microform Review* 17:5 (December 1988), 270–278.

Discusses intrinsic causes of deterioration and describes the research conducted at the Image Permanence Institute, Rochester Institute of Technology, into protecting microfilm from oxidative attack through sulfiding. Paper originally presented at an International Symposium, Ottawa, Canada, May 1988.

Rider, Fremont. *The Scholar and the Future of the Research Library.* New York: Hadham Press, 1944.

An influential analysis of research libraries and the role that microforms can play.

Saffady, William. *Micrographic Systems,* 3rd ed. Silver Spring, MD: Association for Information and Image Management, 1990. 242p.

Covers technology, processes, equipment, retrieval, the relationship of micrographics to other information systems. Glossary.

Saffady, William. "Stability, Care and Handling of Microforms, Magnetic Media and Optical Disks," *Library Technology Reports* 27:1 (January–February 1991).

Examines the physical nature of microforms and other imaging media; bibliographic essay on materials, systems, uses, and expectations.

Sleep, Esther L. "Rejuvenating an Aging Microfilm Collection," *Serials Review* 16:1 (Spring 1990), 81–84.

Case study of the treatment of a deteriorated collection; cites lack of literature on rejuvenation.

Sturge, John, Vivian Walworth, and Allan Shepp, ed. *Imaging Processes and Materials,* Neblette's 8th ed. New York: Van Nostrand, 1989. 712p.

Textbook on imaging technology; provides an overview of traditional and contemporary imaging, methods of forming images, the technologies, effectiveness, and permanence.

Stewart, Robert W. "Does This Project Deserve the Erasmus Prize? Some Troubling Thoughts About a Large Electronic Imaging Project," *Conservation Administration News,* No. 54 (July 1993), 4–5, 33–35.
A critique of the Seville Project at the Archivo General de Indias, Spain, to capture early records in electronic format for preservation and access. Author questions the appropriateness of the technology for the preservation project.

Subt, Sylvia S.Y. "Xerographic Quality Control," *Inform* 1:7 (July 1987), 10–11, 47.
Discussion of testing undertaken at the National Archives.

Swartzell, Ann. "Preservation Microfilming: In-House Initiated Microforms," *Conservation Administration News,* No. 34 (July 1988), 6–7.
How to organize and implement a preservation microfilming program.

Tanselle, G. Thomas. "Reproduction in Scholarship," *Studies in Bibliography* 42 (1989), 25–54.
A provocative essay, tracing the history of the use of facsimiles in historical research, their acceptance, and attendant problems. Expresses concern that facsimiles are not carefully inspected for errors and that original materials are frequently discarded.

Thomas, Bill. "Archival Quality: the Test for Methylene Blue," *Inform* 1:5 (May 1987), 6–7, 46–47.
Describes the test and the advantages of regular testing.

Turner, Jeffrey H. "The Suitability of Diazo Film for Long-Term Storage," *Microform Review* 17:3 (August 1988), 142–145.
Advantages of diazo film for circulating collections.

Veaner, Allen B. "Incredible Past, Incredible Future," *Library Resources and Technical Services* 26:1 (January–March 1982), 52–56.
History of micropublishing and a review of new technical developments.

Vitiello, Giuseppe. "European Register of Microform Film Masters (EROMM)," *International Preservation News,* No. 4 (August 1990), 3–4.

Describes the initiatives of the European Communities for the preservation of library materials and efforts to create a register.

Waters, Donald J. *From Microform to Digital Imagery.* Washington, DC: Commission on Preservation and Access, 1991. 41p.

Explores the feasibility of a project to study the means, costs, and benefits of converting large quantities of preserved library materials from microform to digital images for enhanced scholarly access.

Weber, Helmut. *Opto-Electronic Storage—An Alternative to Filming?* Washington, DC: Commission on Preservation and Access, February 1993. 6p.

Explores optical disk technology, concluding that it is an access, not a preservation medium.

Welsh, William J. "The Library of Congress: a More-than-Equal Partner," *Library Resources and Technical Services* 29:1 (January–March 1985), 87–93.

Describes the library's contribution to cooperative preservation microfilming efforts.

Wilhelm, Henry. "Color Photographs and Color Motion Pictures in the Library: For Preservation or Destruction?" *Conserving and Preserving Materials in Nonbook Format,* ed. Kathryn L. and William T. Henderson. Urbana-Champaign, IL: University of Illinois Graduate School of Library and Information Science, 1991, 105–111.

Describes the problem of the instability of color films and discusses current research. Urges that librarians considering the use of color microfilm for preservation get information about the characteristics of color microfilm.

Willard, Charles Lewis. "Brittle Books: What Order of Preservation?" *Microform Review* 20:1 (Winter 1991), 24–26.

A critical examination of current practice in the national effort to preserve the documentary heritage; suggested alternative approaches.

Wilman, Hugh. "Copying Without Damage: the British Library Strategy," *Archives* 18:78 (1987), 85–88.
Describes the methods used at the library.

Chapter 13

Allison, Terry L. "Toward a Shared Enterprise: Western European and U.S. Preservation Programs," *Collection Management* 15:3–4 (1992), 517–522.
Review of preservation problems faced by Western European and North American libraries; stresses need for international cooperation to preserve materials and to explore new technologies.

American Association of Museums. Commission on Museums for a New Century. *Museums for a New Century; a Report.* Washington, DC: American Association of Museums, 1984. 144p.
Report addresses the role of museums in society and their obligation to preserve and report our culture. Chapter 2 deals with conservation issues.

American Library Association. *Preservation Policy.* Chicago: American Library Association, 1991. 8p.
Outlines the responsibilities of the library profession for the preservation of library materials of all types.

[Barker, Nicolas]. "Libraries and the National Literary Heritage: Two Views from Europe," *Book Collector* 34:2 (Summer 1985), 145–172.
Reviews initiatives in Germany and France to preserve the national patrimony through national planning.

Battin, Patricia. "Preservation: the Forgotten Problem," *Priorities for Academic Libraries,* ed. Thomas J. Galvin and Beverly P. Lynch. San Francisco: Jossey-Bass, 1983, 61–70. (New Directions for Higher Education, 39)
Statement of the scope of the preservation problem; the need for national and international cooperation to address the problem.

Battin, Patricia. "Introduction: Preservation, The National Perspective," *Issues for a New Decade: Today's Challenge, Tomorrow's Opportunity.* Boston, MA: G. K. Hall, 1991, 1–9.

Describes the scope of the preservation problem and the role that the Commission on Preservation and Access has played to address the brittle book problem and to promote the use of alkaline paper.

Byrne, Sherry and Barbara Van Deventer. "Preserving the Nation's Intellectual Heritage: A Synthesis," *College and Research Libraries News* 53:5 (May 1992), 313–315.

Briefly discusses the factors that led to a national strategy for preservation and the move toward comprehensive collection management programs in the 1990s.

Chapman, Patricia. "The National Preservation Office," *Assistant Librarian* 81:1 (January 1988), 6–8.

The goals and objectives of the National Preservation Office, British Library, which was established upon the recommendation of the Ratcliffe report.

Clements, David W. G. "Policy Planning in the U.K.: From National to Local," *Preserving the Word.* London: Library Association, 1987. 17–25.

Describes the approach to preservation taken in Great Britain, preservation options, and the implications of policies in the library for the preservation of collections.

Clements, D. W. G. *Preservation and Conservation of Library Documents: a UNESCO/IFLA/ICA Enquiry Into the Current State of the World's Patrimony.* Paris: UNESCO, 1987. 32p. (PGI-87/WS/15)

Results of an international study, with emphasis on Third World countries.

Clements, D. W. G. and J. M. Arnoult. "Preservation Planning in Europe," *IFLA Journal* (International Federation of Library Associations and Institutions) 14:4 (1988), 354–360.

Summary of preservation activities in European countries.

Cloonan, Michèle Valerie. "Preservation Education in American Library Schools: Recounting the Ways," *Journal of Education for Library and Information Science* 31:3 (Winter 1991), 187–203.

Descriptions of courses offered in selected library schools.

Coleman, Christopher D.G, comp. *Preservation Education Directory,* Chicago: Association for Library Collections and Technical Services, updated periodically.
   Lists library schools with preservation programs or courses, and others that include preservation in their curriculum.

Conservation Unit (U.K.) *Conservation Sourcebook,* London: HMSO, updated periodically.
   Listing of British organizations concerned with the preservation and conservation of cultural property. Organizations are described, publications are listed.

Conway, Paul. "Archival Preservation: Definitions for Improving Education and Training," *Restaurator* 10:2 (1989), 47–60.
   Traces the emerging recognition of the need for education and training and recommends that leaders in the field cooperate to educate librarians and archivists and to train conservators and technicians.

Conway, Paul. "Archival Preservation Practice in a Nationwide Context," *American Archivist* 53:2 (Spring 1990), 204–222.
   Provides the results of a nationwide survey of archival preservation practices.

Conway, Paul. "Preserving History's Future: Developing a Nationwide Strategy for Archival Preservation," *Advances in Preservation and Access,* vol. 1. Westport, CT: Meckler, 1992, 244–260.
   Examines nationwide preservation strategy based upon the model of the Society of American Archivists.

Cooke, George W. "Preservation Group Reaches Out in Bergen County and Beyond," *New Jersey Libraries* 26:3 (Summer 1993), 14–18.
   Describes the initiatives of the Bergen County, New Jersey, Preservation Committee.

Cunha, George Martin. "Current Trends in Preservation Research," *American Archivist* 53:2 (Spring 1990), 192–202.
   An overview of current research in preservation and conservation, including climate control, mold and pest control, disaster prevention and recovery, mass deacidification, and paper strengthening.

Curtin, Bonnie Rose. "Is Conservation Ready for Artificial Intelligence?" *Abbey Newsletter* 14:1 (February 1990), 1–2.
Description of the computer-driven preservation self-study being developed by the National Association of Government Archives and Record Administrators (NAGARA).

Curtin, Bonnie Rose. "Preservation Planning for Archives: Development and Field Testing of the NAGARA/GRASP," *American Archivist* 53:2 (Spring 1990), 236–243.
Description of design and field testing of the automated archives preservation planning system developed by the National Association of Government Archives and Records Administrators.

Darling, Pamela W. "Planning for the Future," *The Library Preservation Program: Models, Priorities, Possibilities,* ed. Jan Merrill-Oldham and Merrily Smith. Chicago: American Library Association, 1985, 103–110.
Suggests that administrators analyze what is being done, then plan for what should be done. Discusses planning and resource sharing on the national level.

DeBakey, Lois. "Book-Burning In Our Medical Libraries: Prevention or Palliation?" *American Journal of Cardiology* 62 (September 1988), 458–461.
Eloquent argument for the use of permanent paper for medical literature.

Densky-Wolff, Lois R. "CAPES: A Summary of Achievement," *New Jersey Libraries* 26:3 (Summer 1993), 7–10.
Describes the initiatives of the Caucus Archival Project Evaluation Service (CAPES) to evaluate archives repositories to assist in planning and implementing sound collection management and preservation programs.

Enright, Brian, Lotte Hellinga, and Beryl Leigh. *Selection for Survival: a Review of Acquisition and Retention Policies.* London: British Library, 1989. 104p.
Addresses the essential nature and responsibility of research collections and presents a "life cycle" model for library materials. Report of a management team that undertook an internal review of the British Library's acquisition and retention policies.

Field, Jeffrey. "The Goals and Priorities of the NEH Office of Preservation," *Conservation Administration News,* No. 25 (April 1986), 4–5, 23–24.
Describes philosophy, funding, initiatives.

Farr, George F., Jr. "NEH's Program for the Preservation of Brittle Books," *Advances in Preservation and Access,* vol. 1. Westport, CT: Meckler, 1992, 49–60.
Description of the program, how it works, and what has been accomplished.

Fox, Lisa L. "The SOLINET Preservation Program: Building a Preservation Network in the Southeast," *New Library Scene* 7:4 (August 1988), 1, 5–9.
History of the program and a review of its activities and accomplishments.

Geh, Hans-Peter. "Conservation/Preservation: An International Approach," *Library Resources and Technical Services* 30:1 (January–March 1986), 31–35.
Goals and objectives of the IFLA Conservation Section to serve as a focal point for research, international agreements on the transfer and storage of information, and to establish regional conservation centers.

Govan, J. F. "Preservation and Resource Sharing: Conflicting or Complementary?" *IFLA Journal* 12:1 (February 1986), 20–24.
Examines the seemingly conflicting needs of preservation and resource sharing; concludes that reformatting into an easily reproducible medium, sensible interlibrary loan guidelines, and new text transmission policies can eliminate the conflict.

Graham, Peter S. "Electronic Information and Research Library Technical Services," *College and Research Libraries* 51:3 (May 1990), 241–250.
Examines the relation of libraries to electronic information and the issue of preservation of intellectual content in electronic media.

Harris, Carolyn, Carol Mandel, and Robert Wolven. "A Cost Model for Preservation: the Columbia University Libraries' Approach," *Library Resources and Technical Services* 35:1 (January 1991), 33–54.

Comprehensive model for identifying the processes involved in preservation, and associated costs.

Harris, Kenneth E. "Preservation at the Library of Congress in the 1990s: Success Is a Long Journey," *New Library Scene* 9:6 (December 1990), 8–15.
Describes the preservation challenges at the library; its past successes upon which the program for the 1990s will build.

Hazen, Dan C. "Preservation in Poverty and Plenty: Policy Issues for the 1990s," *Journal of Academic Librarianship* 15:6 (January 1990), 344–351.
Examines the underlying assumptions in current preservation activities to consider whether they effectively meet needs. Suggests a national collection-based program and examines its international implications. Questions how little has been published on costs for preservation; proposes a surcharge on interlibrary loan transactions for noncurrent material.

Hedley, Gerry. "Finding a Structure of Collaboration," *CCI Newsletter* (Autumn/Winter 1990), 8–9. Eng./Fr.
Emphasizes the need for collaboration between conservator and scientist.

Henderson, Kathryn L. and William T., eds. *Conserving and Preserving Materials in Nonbook Formats.* Urbana-Champaign, IL: University of Illinois Graduate School of Library and Information Science, 1991. 165 p.
Papers from a conference to address the special needs of nonprint collections.

Information Sources on Scientific Research Related to the Preservation of Books, Paper, and Adhesives: Directory. Washington, DC: Commission on Preservation and Access, 1990. 28p.
Includes laboratories and organizations; indexes, abstracts, and data bases; publications and newsletters. Chandru J. Shahani describes "Preservation Research at the Library of Congress; Recent Progress and Future Trends," 17–28.

Invest in the American Collection, ed. Jane Sennett Long. Washington, DC: National Committee to Save America's Cultural Collections, 1987. 51p.

Papers from a forum to develop a national awareness of the need for the preservation and conservation of cultural property.

Jewitt, Crispin. "Conspectus: a Means to Library Cooperation," *Library Conservation News,* No. 22 (January 1989), 4–6.
Discussion of the conspectus system to describe collections by subject classification and its implication for national and international cooperation.

Kaplan, Hilary A. and Brenda S. Banks. "Archival Preservation: the Teaming of the Crew," *American Archivist* 53:2 (Spring 1990), 266–273.
Reviews the current status of archival preservation.

Kenney, Anne R. "Common Problems, Common Solutions: the Preservation Challenge for Librarians and Archivists," *Building on the First Century.* Chicago, IL: American Library Association, 1989, 303–306.
Suggests that librarians and archivists work together to develop collection-level approaches to preservation; to recognize the problem, commit resources, and develop a plan of action to preserve the documentary heritage.

Kruger, Betsy. "Automating Preservation Information in RLIN," *Library Resources and Technical Services* 32:2 (April 1988), 116–126.
Describes the efforts of the Research Library Group and its bibliographic data base, RLIN, to support cooperative and individual preservation efforts.

Larsen, A. Dean and Randy S. Silverman. "Preservation," *Library Technical Services,* 2nd ed., ed. Irene P. Godden. New York: Academic Press, 1991, 205–269.
An overview of preservation management and the issues of the 1990s. Bibliography.

Leigh, David. "A Focus for Conservation," *Library Conservation News,* No. 22 (January 1989), 1–3.
Describes the activities of the Conservation Unit of the Museums and Galleries Commission (U.K.).

Loughridge, Brendan. "Conservation, Culture, and Curriculum," *International Library Cooperation,* ed. Ahmed H. Helal and Joachim W. Weiss. Essen, Germany: Universitatsbibliothek Essen, 1988, 18–38.

Discusses the role of education for preservation in the library school curriculum, with emphasis on the United Kingdom.

Lowell, Howard P. *Preservation Needs in State Archives*. Albany, NY: National Association of Government Archives and Records Administrators, 1986, 1988. 56p.

Report of a survey to document preservation action and needs in state archives, and to make recommendations for the physical preservation of much of our documentary heritage.

McCrady, Ellen. "History of the Abbey Publications," *Library Resources and Technical Services* 35:1 (January 1991), 104–108.

How the *Abbey Newsletter* developed into a full-time advocacy publication and research program.

McCrady, Ellen. "Progress in Preservation," *Alkaline Paper Advocate* 4 (May 1991), 15–18.

Summarizes conservation and preservation developments in the previous few years.

McIntyre, John E. "Preservation at the National Library of Scotland," *Conservation Administration News*, No. 52 (January 1993), 1–3.

Description of the development, organization, and activities of the Conservation Division.

McKeon, Donald. "Considerations for Libraries and Archives: 1981–2001; Considerations of Future Developments and Personnel," *Restaurator* 6:3–4 (1984), 139–146.

Using the Delphi model, the author predicts that conservation personnel for libraries will be trained as administrators with library or scientific background.

Massachusetts Board of Library Commissioners. Task Force on Preservation and Access. *Preserved to Serve: The Massachusetts Preservation Agenda*. Boston, MA: Massachusetts Board of Library Commissioners, February 1992. 36p.

Presents goals to preserve the state's documentary heritage through cooperative initiatives.

Merrill-Oldham, Jan. "Preservation Comes of Age: an Action Agenda for the '80s and Beyond," *American Libraries,* 16:11 (December 1985), 770–772.
Cites goals of preservation administration, programs in libraries, training in preservation and conservation, reformatting projects, issues in library binding, and environmental controls.

Miller, J. Hillis. *Preserving the Literary Heritage,* Final Report of the Scholarly Advisory Committee on Modern Languages and Literature of the Commission on Preservation and Access. Washington, DC: Commission on Preservation and Access, July 1991. 7p.
A thought-provoking report addressing what should be preserved, and how.

Miller, Sally McIntosh. "North Bennet Street School," *New Library Scene* 7:2 (April 1988), 1, 5–6.
Description of its bookbinding and conservation training program.

Morris, Patricia A. "PALMCAP; a Statewide Preservation Effort in South Carolina," *Conservation Administration News,* No. 40 (January 1990), 10–11, 30.
Describes the statewide preservation effort organized for libraries, archives, public records offices, and museums with paper-based materials.

Naslund, Cheryl Terrass. "Preservation Programs in Small Academic Libraries," *Operations Handbook for the Small Academic Library,* ed. Gerard B. McCabe. Westport, CT: Greenwood Press, 1989, 153–162.
Describes elements of a preservation program and how one can be implemented. Discusses preservation as an inherent library function, to preserve unrecognized rare items and to ensure that all collections last as long as needed.

New York Document Conservation Advisory Council. *Our Memory at Risk: Preserving New York's Unique Research Resources.* Albany, NY: New York State Library, 1988. 56p. Illus.
Provides an overview of the preservation problems in the state's libraries and records repositories and recommends

actions to ensure the survival of the state's documentary heritage.

Oakley, Robert L. *Copyright and Preservation: a Serious Problem in Need of a Thoughtful Solution.* Washington, DC: Commission on Preservation and Access, September 1990. 55p.

Focuses on copyright considerations for published materials when reproduction is required to retain information for preservation purposes.

Ogden, Barclay. *On the Preservation of Books and Documents in Original Form.* Washington, DC: Commission on Preservation and Access, 1989. 5p.; *Abbey Newsletter* 14:4 (July 1990), 62–64.

Provides an intellectual rationale for consideration of the book as an artifact and discusses possible selection strategies.

Reed-Scott, Jutta. *Manual for the North American Inventory of Research Library Collections,* rev. ed. Washington, DC: Association of Research Libraries, 1988. 98p.

Guide for librarians undertaking conspectus-based collection assessment.

Reed-Scott, Jutta, ed. *Preservation Organization and Staffing.* Washington, DC: Association of Research Libraries Office of Management Service, January 1990. 135p. (SPEC Kit 160).

Examines the changes in organization and staffing in ARL libraries since 1985. Presents mission statements, organization charts, and job descriptions from selected members.

Rhoads, James B. "Standardization for Archives," *UNESCO Journal of Information Science, Librarianship and Archives Administration,* 3:3 (July–September 1981), 165–169.

Notes the importance of establishing international standards and guidelines in the archival field and describes the work of UNESCO and the International Council on Archives.

Saretzky, Gary. "The Region V Preservation Committee, 1988–1992," *New Jersey Libraries* 26:3 (Summer 1993), 13–14.

Describes an initiative to promote preservation awareness in libraries.

Schmude, Karl G. "The Politics and Management of Preservation Planning," *IFLA Journal* 16:3 (1990), 332–335.
Discusses reasons why preservation has not been a critical component of library management; outlines goals to heighten the profile of preservation.

Schnare, Robert E. "Library Preservation Activities in Russia, the Ukraine, and Hungary," *Conservation Administration News*, No. 54 (July 1993), 1–3, 9, 13, 29.
Report on a study tour to learn about preservation activities in libraries in Eastern Europe: St. Petersburg, Kiev, and Budapest.

Scholarly Resources in Art History: Issues in Preservation. Washington, DC: Commission on Preservation and Access, 1989. 43p.
Summary of a seminar that addressed the technical innovations for preservation and access to text and image for art historians.

Stam, David H. "Finding Funds to Support Preservation," *The Library Preservation Program: Models, Priorities, Possibilities,* ed. Jan Merrill-Oldham and Merrily Smith. Chicago: American Library Association, 1985, 80–83.
Suggests a spectrum of options from deaccessioning unwanted materials to working with philanthropic agencies.

Steckman, Elizabeth. "Preservation Program Thrives in New Jersey," *Conservation Administration News,* No. 48 (January 1992), 1–2, 26.
A report on the Maintenance and Preservation of Library Collections grant program, administered by the State Library. The program is described and examples of its impact on the state's collections are given.

Swartzburg, Susan G. "Continuing Education in Preservation: Challenge for the '90s," *Continuing Professional Education and IFLA: Past, Present, and a Vision for the Future,* ed. Blanche Woolls. Munich, Saur, 1993, 247–252.
Discusses the renewed interest in courses on collection management and the physical nature of library materials; describes the continuing eduction program in preservation at Rutgers University.

Turner, John R. "Teaching Conservation," *Education for Information* 6:2 (June 1988), 145–151.
Describes an ideal syllabus for instruction in preservation and more realistic approaches.

Vaisey, David. "Archivists, Conservators, and Scientists: the Preservation of the Nation's Heritage," *Archives* 18:79 (April 1988), 131–143. (Maurice Bond Memorial Lecture, 1987)
A reflection on the development of a concern for conservation and preservation and discussion of current issues.

Van Zelst, Lambertus. "Needs and Potential Solutions in Conservation," *Conserving and Preserving Materials in Nonbook Formats*, ed. Kathryn L. and William T. Henderson. Urbana-Champaign, IL: University of Illinois Graduate School of Library and Information Science, 1991, 7–22.
Discusses the current state of conservation: public awareness, information, training, research, analytical services, and professional organizations.

Vincent-Davies, Diana. "Preservation Needs of Law Libraries," *Abbey Newsletter* 14:2 (April 1990), 21–22.
Describes the activities of the American Association of Law Librarians (AALL) Special Committee on the Preservation Needs of Law Libraries. The committee is establishing priorities to ensure the preservation of legal material.

Vitiello, Giuseppe. "European Register of Microform Film Masters (EROMM)," *International Preservation News,* no. 4 (August 1990), 3–4.
Describes the initiatives of the European Communities to create a microform register.

Walch, Victoria Irons. "Checklist of Standards Applicable to the Preservation of Archives and Manuscripts," *American Archivist* 53:2 (Spring 1990), 324–338.
Useful summary of standards and how they are created.

Wayne, John J. "Paper Preservation Update: What the Library Is Doing," *LC Information Bulletin,* April 6, 1992, 135–136.
Discusses the library's "Report on Progress in Implementing National Policy on Acid-Free Paper" (December 1991).

Weinberg, Gerhard L. "The End of Ranke's History?" *Syracuse Scholar* 9:1 (198), 51–60.
A historian addresses the threats to traditional historical research by policies that restrict access to records until they have physically disintegrated; the lack of schedules for their reproduction on microfilm; and the use of computers to produce machine-readable records that cannot be reproduced after a brief period of time.

Weiss, Dudley A. "LBI at 50 . . . Achievements and Principles," *New Library Scene* 4:2 (April 1985), 11–14.
History of the Library Binding Institute and a look at the future of the industry.

Welsh, William J. "International Cooperation in Preservation of Library Materials," *Collection Management* 9:2–3 (Spring-Summer 1987), 119–131.
Outlines prerequisites for international cooperation; proposes the development of a "universal preservation program" for saving the world's information resources.

Wright, Dorothy, Samuel Demas, and Walter Cybulski. "Cooperative Preservation of State-Level Publications: Preserving the Literature of New York State Agriculture and Rural Life," *Library Resources and Technical Services* 37:4 (October 1993), 434–443.
Describes a pilot cooperative project to preserve a state's documentary heritage by identifying a core bibliography and undertaking preservation measures on a priority basis.

Wright, Sandra. "Conservation Program Planning at the National Archives of Canada," *American Archivist* 53:2 (Spring 1990), 314–322.
Describes the development and implementation of policies that integrate preservation with other archival functions.

INDEX

ABOUT THE AUTHOR

Susan Garretson Swartzburg (B.A. Philosophy; M.A. English; MLS), Assistant Librarian for Collection Management, Rutgers University Libraries, established the preservation programs at Yale and Rutgers and developed standard procedures for preservation planning and handling deteriorated library materials. She is active in IFLA, ALA, and the New Jersey Library Association and is a founder of the Princeton Preservation Group. She serves on the Advisory Boards of the Northeast Document Conservation Center and the Wells College Book Arts Center. A prolific author, she served as Associate Editor of *Conservation Administration News* until 1994 and contributes regularly to the library literature. Her most recent book, co-authored by Holly Bussey, with Frank Garretson, was *Libraries and Archives: Design and Renovation with a Preservation Perspective* (Scarecrow Press, 1991).

P9-CQN-420

THE PUPPY DIARIES

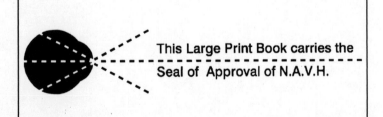

This Large Print Book carries the
Seal of Approval of N.A.V.H.

THE PUPPY DIARIES

RAISING A DOG NAMED SCOUT

JILL ABRAMSON

THORNDIKE PRESS

A part of Gale, Cengage Learning

GALE
CENGAGE Learning™

Detroit • New York • San Francisco • New Haven, Conn • Waterville, Maine • London

Copyright © 2011 by Jill Abramson.

Thorndike Press, a part of Gale, Cengage Learning.

ALL RIGHTS RESERVED

Thorndike Press® Large Print Nonfiction.

The text of this Large Print edition is unabridged.

Other aspects of the book may vary from the original edition.

Set in 16 pt. Plantin.

LIBRARY OF CONGRESS CATALOGING-IN-PUBLICATION DATA

Abramson, Jill, 1954-
  The puppy diaries : raising a dog named Scout / by Jill
Abramson.
    p. cm. — (Thorndike Press large print nonfiction)
  Includes bibliographical references.
  ISBN-13: 978-1-4104-4156-0 (hardcover)
  ISBN-10: 1-4104-4156-3 (hardcover)
  1. Golden retriever — Anecdotes. 2. Human-animal
relationships — Anecdotes. 3. Dog owners — Anecdotes.
4. Abramson, Jill, 1954– I. Title.
  SF429.G63A247 2011b
  636.70092'2—dc23

                                        2011030085

Published in 2011 by arrangement with Henry Holt and Company, LLC.

Printed in the United States of America
1 2 3 4 5 6 7 15 14 13 12 11

To Henry

CHAPTER ONE

The truth about getting a new dog is that it makes you miss the old one.

This reality hit me hard one spring day in 2009 when we arrived at Thistledown Golden Retrievers, near Boston, where my husband, Henry, and I had come to meet Donna Cutler, a breeder of English golden retrievers. Because it was named Thistledown, and because I knew that the golden retriever breed was started by someone actually named Lord Tweedmouth, I was expecting the place to look like a country manor.

Instead, we parked in front of a plain suburban ranch, and the only hint of the litter of the seven-week-old puppies we had been invited to inspect — though we knew it was really us who had to pass muster with the breeder — was a sign on the front door that showed two golden retrievers and said WIPE YOUR PAWS. Why did I suddenly feel like wiping my eyes?

My heart was still hurting over the loss of Buddy, our stone-deaf, feisty-to-the-end West Highland white terrier, who had died in March 2007 at age fourteen. Our two children, Cornelia and Will, who grew up with him but flew the nest years before his demise, often mused that Buddy was my one perfect relationship in life.

Buddy, like me, was a self-sufficient type, and despite his small size he was no lap dog. Like many Westies, he was woefully stubborn and never once came when called. He could be unpredictable and grouchy around small children and once bit my goddaughter's upper lip. He wasn't great with old people, either; years later, he bit the leg of an elderly woman who, for some inexplicable reason, was standing barefoot and dressed in her nightgown in our elevator when the doors opened on our floor. (Happily, that incident triggered an unlikely friendship between Eve, Buddy's victim, and me.) Nonetheless, I was madly in love and forgave Buddy all his sins. I learned a lot from him, too; among other things, he taught me that even in stressful situations dogs have a unique way of steering you in unlikely and interesting directions.

I confess that I spoiled Buddy beyond

Buddy and Jill on the porch in Connecticut

all reason. Houseguests often awoke to the aroma of grilled chicken with a dusting of rosemary, which I liked to give him for breakfast. Henry would sometimes note, without rancor, that when I took business trips and called home, my first question was always "How's Buddy?"

Long after Cornelia and Will began to wriggle out of my embraces and find my made-up games annoying, Buddy was always happy to have me scratch his pink belly and play tug-of-war. While my children filled their lives with school, scouting, and sports — and, later, college, work, and love — Buddy remained my steadfast companion.

When Buddy was a puppy, we lived in Virginia, and together he and I would amble around our neighborhood for miles, discovering new side streets with interesting houses. Someone always stopped to admire him, which is how I met a lot of my neighbors. During our walks I was also able to let go of some of the pressure of my job as an investigative reporter, back then for the *Wall Street Journal*. Sometimes, with my mind wandering free as I pulled the leash this way and that, I would come up with a great story idea or reporting angle on the Washington scandals that were my frequent reporting targets. Buddy, steadfast and true, was my loyal coconspirator.

I once experienced a rare eureka moment while on a walk with Buddy. I had recently left the *Journal* and gone to work in the Washington bureau of the *New York Times*, where I was on the team of reporters covering the Monica Lewinsky scandal. One day in late 1998, as Buddy and I strolled up Second Street South in Arlington, I realized that one of the people I had encountered in a document the previous night was familiar to me; he was a prominent conservative lawyer in New York. Why his name surfaced in my brain during a walk with Buddy the next morning is anyone's guess, but when Buddy and I got home, I took out the documents I had been reviewing and found that this lawyer was mentioned repeatedly. That discovery led to a front-page story about how a cabal of conservative lawyers had secretly worked on the sexual harassment case that triggered impeachment proceedings against President Bill Clinton. Buddy, my silent partner, deserved to share the byline on that story.

Although independent and often fierce, Buddy was always happy to see me. When my children were in their late teens, I couldn't help but notice that he, unlike Cornelia and

Will, was never sullen and didn't ask to borrow the car. And when I became the *Times*'s Washington bureau chief, I noted that unlike the reporters who worked for me, Buddy was unfailingly delighted whenever I came up with what I thought was an inspired idea.

Buddy, you see, was my first dog, and I had fallen hard. Perhaps this new relationship was so intense partly because it wasn't based on words, unlike the rest of my personal and professional life. I spent so much of my day talking, reading, and writing that it was both a relief and a joy to spend time with Buddy. Except for a few simple commands, our conversation consisted entirely of my silly cooings and his appreciative grunts.

My older sister, Jane, has often observed that what she found most surprising about me was my late-in-life transformation into a dog lover. "You were a wonderful parent," she once told me, "but I've never seen you so affectionate or expressive with anyone the way you are with this dog." It was true. At work, where some of my colleagues and sources said they found my tough-girl investigative journalist persona intimidating, I was constantly pulling out the latest snapshots of Buddy and telling everyone my latest dog stories. Buddy was more than my coconspirator; he also seemed to certify me as a nicer person.

It wasn't just Buddy. I also adored Arrow, my sister's Jack Russell mix, who greeted me with ecstasy at her door. Arrow and I formed a special bond when I moved from Washington to New York in 2003 to become the *Times*'s managing editor. Henry — who worked at a Washington, D.C., think tank and was in the process of becoming a consultant in New York — and Buddy weren't able to join me in Manhattan right away, so I lived for a couple of weeks with Jane; her husband, Jim; and Arrow. My love affair with Arrow was kindled during this period by the doggy bags I often brought home from the swanky restaurants where I had business dinners. Arrow, I recall, was especially fond of the grilled liver and bacon from an Italian place called Elio's.

I grew up in an apartment on Manhattan's Upper West Side. Our parents allowed Jane and me to have turtles, fish, parakeets, and even a hamster, who outlived all our other pets. (During the famous blackout of 1965, I spent hours funneling water into a tropical fish tank to provide enough oxygen to save a pregnant fantail guppy and her impending brood.) But my parents drew the line at a dog. "The city is not a good place to raise a puppy," my mother told us. Despite our pleas, and even though we lived across from Central Park, she was unyielding.

Buddy arrived in 1992, when Henry and I were in our late thirties and our kids were nine and seven. That was also the year my father died, so Buddy was especially welcome. Cornelia and Will told the usual children's fib about getting a pet: they assured me that they would faithfully feed and walk this adorable addition to our family. It didn't work out that way, of course, so I took care of Buddy, training him, feeding him, and singing him to sleep in his tiny crate. I didn't mind, though; having new life in our house was a tonic for my grief over the loss of my dad.

Our setup in those days was perfect for an active puppy. We lived in an unfashionable corner of Arlington, Virginia, in a sturdy bungalow ordered out of the 1928 Sears catalog. The house came with a large fenced yard, and since Buddy had a little dog door he could come and go as he pleased. His purpose in life became patrolling our patch of lawn and protecting us from a host of imagined intruders. He also learned to open our mail slot; every day, he would wait inside for the mailman to arrive and then race onto our porch to retrieve the day's post. When it snowed, Buddy would often disappear under the white mounds in our yard and then tunnel and burrow to his heart's content. I especially loved to walk him when the snow was crunchy under my boots — amazingly, Buddy made me look forward to winter.

Buddy was already eleven when we arrived in Manhattan, and I worried that the move might kill him. We sublet a loft downtown, in Tribeca, but happily Buddy loved all the action in his new neighborhood, including the smells of so many other dogs and the fishy sidewalk outside a high-end Japanese restaurant called Nobu.

Once Henry and I settled into our own place in the same neighborhood, I hired a dog walker named Carlos, who took Buddy for a walk each afternoon. Once, when I forgot to bring some papers to work, I returned home to retrieve them and bumped into Carlos on the street walking Buddy in a pack with three other dogs. Buddy hadn't socialized much with other dogs during his yard-patrolling years, but now he seemed perfectly at ease with his cool city friends. When he saw me that day, he regarded me with a dismissive "What are you doing here?" look.

Before going to work, I often took Buddy

to a dog run near the Hudson River where he bonded with a Scottie about his size. They looked like an advertisement for scotch when they romped together, and I enjoyed chatting with the other owners, who sat on benches and loved arguing with me about the theater, movie, and dining reviews in the *Times*. These mornings reminded me of the years when my kids were toddlers and I made a number of good friends while sitting on benches in the playground, talking about everything from biodegradable diapers to our marriages.

One day when I took Buddy for a checkup to the veterinarian in Tribeca, I encountered a woman with two Westies. The woman was wearing a pair of plaid socks emblazoned with Westies. "I have the same pair," I told her. She laughed and then looked at Buddy. "How old is your Westie?" she asked. When I told her Buddy was thirteen, she said, "Oh, we have an eighteen-year-old." Since the two dogs accompanying her were obviously much younger, I asked where the older one was. "He lives in a hospice nearby, and we visit him almost every day," she replied. I was stunned, never having imagined the existence of live-in, end-of-life care for dogs. This encounter marked the beginning of my fascination with the rarefied world of Manhattan dog owners, some of whom seek out dog hospices — not to mention dog massage therapists and dog shrinks who dispense antianxiety medications.

Henry and I were also startled to discover that everything having to do with dogs is so much more expensive in Manhattan than in Arlington. Although we live in an old, unrenovated building that used to be a spice warehouse and has no doorman, Tribeca is one of Manhattan's most expensive neighborhoods, full of Wall Street brokers who earn fat salaries and big bonuses. Signs reading LUXURY LOFTS FOR SALE are everywhere, with *luxury* being code for apartments that sell for two million dollars or more. A rubber ball I purchased at the local "pet boutique" cost six dollars. True, I splurged on a dog walker, but other dog owners in our neighborhood spent even more to send their pups to the Wagging Tail, a doggy day-care center on Greenwich Street.

By the time Buddy turned fourteen, he had lost his hearing, but he was still a hardy boy. In the winter of 2007, though, he developed a persistent cough. "I think it may be his heart," said Cornelia, who was then in her second year of medical school at Columbia. One weekend, he had what seemed like a small stroke: he was temporarily confused but snapped back to his old self pretty quickly. Then, in late February, while Cornelia and I were walking him one evening, he collapsed on the sidewalk. I carried him as we raced to the vet, who told us to take him to an animal hospital on lower Fifth Avenue. After he was given some oxygen, he seemed to stabilize. We were advised to leave him overnight, and I became tearful when we were ushered in to say good night and I saw him lying in a little cage, looking so vulnerable.

At 3 a.m. the telephone rang. It was the vet: Buddy was in full congestive heart failure. "He's having a terrible time breathing and he seems to be in pain," the on-duty vet reported. "I think we should put him down." Cornelia grabbed the phone and said we would be there in just a few minutes.

Henry, Cornelia, and I dashed out of our apartment, almost forgetting our coats in our hurry, and hailed a cab. When we arrived at the animal hospital, Buddy was lying on his side on a gurney, his back heaving up and down, a tiny oxygen mask on his face. We asked a barrage of questions and tried our best to convince ourselves that Buddy could recover, but it was clear there was no hope. As the medical technician prepared the lethal injection, Henry and I couldn't bear to watch, despite the counsel of friends who said that it was comforting to be present when a dog's life came to a peaceful end. Cornelia, in doctor mode, stayed with Buddy to the last.

When we returned to our loft, I felt the silence envelope me. It was heartbreaking; I had become so accustomed to hearing Buddy's metal tags jangle as he walked from room to room. To my ear, that was the music of loyal companionship.

After Buddy died, I was disconsolate. It wasn't simply that I missed the unconditional love or the ecstatic greeting each time I walked in the door, even if I'd been gone for only a few minutes to take the garbage to the basement. I missed everything about our routine, from feeding him grilled chicken to our late-night strolls along the windy riverside. And I assiduously avoided walks that took me anywhere near the dog run.

Most people pushed Henry and me to get another dog right away. But as the weeks passed, I grew accustomed to some aspects of a dogless life. With no dog to walk, I could not only catch up on whatever I hadn't read the previous day in the *Times,* but also scan the *Wall Street Journal,* the *Financial Times,* and a number of Web sites and political blogs — all before work. I got an iPhone and quickly became a master of distracted living, a lifestyle not well suited to the focused playing and training a puppy needs. I filled my digital nest with Facebook friends, including rediscovered distant relatives and former high school classmates. Henry and I often spent weekends in the Connecticut town where he grew up — we had purchased an old farmhouse there in the late 1990s — and now we could go to the beach all day or stay out late without worrying about getting home to let the dog out.

Before long, I had almost convinced myself that my mother was right: the city is probably a bad place for a pup, even one that can live part-time in the country. My days as a dog owner seemed to be over.

Two months after Buddy died, life took another terrible turn. On the morning of May 7, 2007, while walking from my office to a nearby gym, I was struck by a large white truck at West Forty-fourth Street and Seventh Avenue in Times Square. Having grown up in the city, I considered myself an expert navigator of Manhattan's busy streets. Like most New Yorkers, I had had a couple of alarming experiences when a taxi almost clipped me as I stood on a corner or a bicycle messenger whizzed by so close that he touched my jacket. But I walked everywhere in the city and never gave its hazards a second thought.

Now, as I was crossing Seventh Avenue, a huge refrigerated truck making a right turn came barreling straight at me. The truck's right front wheel smashed my right foot and I was dragged to the ground. The truck's rear wheel rolled over my left thigh and snapped the femur. Luckily, other pedestrians stopped to help me. As I lay bleeding in the street, I was conscious but in terrible pain. While some passersby got a policeman to call an ambulance, others chased down and stopped the truck. When the ambulance arrived, paramedics told me I would be taken to Bellevue Hospital, the city's famous trauma center.

I spent the next three weeks in the hospital. Besides my leg and foot injuries, I had broken my pelvis and sustained significant internal injuries. One of the doctors told me that if the truck's rear wheel had struck my left thigh just two inches higher, I would have been killed. After surgeons operated on my leg and inserted a titanium rod, I was told that I would have to spend six weeks in bed and then learn to walk again.

As I began my recovery in Bellevue, I learned to move from bed to wheelchair by using only my arms and upper body. Soon I started an intensive course of physical therapy; working side by side with patients who had sustained terrible head injuries, I realized how lucky I was. The nurses on the front lines of my care were always adroit and warm. I remember that the first time I had to move from my bed to a wheelchair, my nurse Angela told me to clasp my arms tightly around her neck as she carried my entire weight. "Dance with me, baby," she joked, as she supported my limp body.

Once home, a skilled physical therapist named Pearl visited me three times a week. I was like a baby again, but Pearl taught me how to progress from crawling to walking, first by using crutches and then, finally, a cane. Feeling so helpless was very hard for me, and I became easily frustrated when I couldn't do simple tasks, such as putting clean dishes away in the kitchen.

I missed Buddy terribly during this difficult time — it would have been such a comfort to have him by my side. The climb to get back on my feet was hard, and three months after the accident I still walked unsteadily. But the human body, even in middle age, is remarkably resilient, and my years of dog walking and gym workouts helped the bone grow back over the rod in my leg relatively quickly. Slowly, my physical mobility returned.

Just as I was returning to something approximating normal, a depression descended and seemed to smother me like a hot blanket. I had never experienced anything like it and was somewhat reassured when I learned that an episode of depression is fairly common after a traumatic injury. Fortunately, I was able to get some good counseling from a therapist. During one session, my therapist told me that when I talked about Buddy my whole face lit up. "Maybe you should think about getting another dog," she gently suggested.

Henry, the kids, and Jane Mayer — my best friend and fellow dog nut — promptly launched a massive cheer-up campaign. Their collective diagnosis was a severe case of midlife blues: in the past few years I had turned fifty, seen my grown-up children leave our nest, and lost my beloved Buddy. Now, as I struggled to recover from the accident and my depression, they were certain that what I needed above all else was a new dog.

Over the years, Jane and I had enjoyed many capers, both professional and personal. We had cowritten a best-selling book about Supreme Court justice Clarence Thomas, a project that involved some of the most challenging reporting of our careers. This undertaking did have its lighter moments, however; in one instance, our investigation required that we watch X-rated videos featuring a porn star named Bad Mama Jama, and they were so ridiculous and boring that we both fell asleep on my living room couch. A couple of years earlier, we had rescued Jane's lovable yellow Lab, Peaches, from the clutches of a very bad boyfriend who had insisted on keeping Peaches after he and Jane split up. One hot Friday, as I was planning a drive to New England for a summer vacation with the kids and Buddy, Jane enlisted my help in a plot to kidnap Peaches. That afternoon, while the boyfriend was still at work, we pulled up to his house in my creaky green minivan. Jane was so tiny that she had no trouble sneaking into the house through the dog door. In a flash, she emerged through the front door with Peaches, who clambered into the minivan next to Buddy as I stepped on the gas and we sped away.

Now, as part of a relentless campaign to lift my spirits, Jane sent me pictures of a pair of elderly basset hound sisters who needed a home. She suggested that we each take one, but I put her off, arguing that these good old girls should not be torn asunder. Cornelia weighed in by announcing that we should think about names for a new dog, and she regularly e-mailed me with ideas such as Cosmo, Sugar, and Pamplona. Will, not to be outdone, sent me links to impossibly cute pups on Petfinder.com.

But I remained unmoved. No, I said — no new puppy.

In the summer of 2008, Henry decided to take matters into his own hands. Despite my resistance, he was quietly adamant that it was time to get a new dog. And he wanted a bigger dog this time — "while we can still handle it," he explained — but one that would calm down over time. When we took our beach walks in Connecticut after Buddy died, Henry looked longingly at big dogs that fetched and swam. And he preferred a female on the theory that they are easier to manage.

Unbeknownst to me, Henry had fallen in love with a gentle golden retriever who belongs to two close friends of ours in Connecticut, an older couple named Marian and Howard Spiro. Henry particularly admired the perfect manners that the Spiros' dog — named Cyon, after Procyon, the brightest star in the constellation Canis Minor — exhibited in company.

Henry had become smitten during the ritual Sunday morning lawn bowling games when they were hosted by Dr. Spiro. (Most of the competitors were octogenarians, but Henry played to win and often did so.) During the games, Cyon would observe the bowlers placidly, never barking or chasing the ball. That September, at the Spiros' traditional Labor Day party, Cyon never once overtly begged, jumped up to catch a piece of stray cheese, or knocked over a gin and tonic.

Cyon, who is certified as a hospital therapy dog, has a regal stance and is an unusual, almost white color. From the Spiros we learned that she is a special type of golden retriever bred along British standards. Goldens are the second most popular breed in the United States, but until meeting Cyon we hadn't realized that they come in several hues, from deep red to the more common honey color, and finally to Cyon's platinum. By early fall 2008, Henry had become all but fixated on the notion that we should get an English golden retriever puppy, and he then began a gently insistent effort to persuade me to agree to this plan. My heart still ached for Buddy and I still wasn't sure I was ready for a new dog, but finally I consented. After getting a referral from Marian Spiro,

Cyon on the beach in Connecticut

Henry contacted Donna Cutler, a breeder of English golden retrievers near Boston. Donna told him that she expected a new litter the following spring, and in December 2008, with my wary consent, he sent for an application and put down a deposit toward the price of one of the yet-unborn puppies.

I felt guilty. With millions of dogs in shelters across the country waiting to be adopted, and with local animal rescue groups actively looking for new homes for goldens who were given up or mistreated, I was aware that it would make more sense for us to adopt a dog rather than purchase a purebred puppy. Though far fewer dogs are euthanized in shelters than in past decades, about three to four million unwanted dogs are put down each year, according to the ASPCA. How could we justify getting a new puppy?

But Henry had his heart set. A puppy. A female. A blond golden retriever. By the following summer, I would be through with my physical rehabilitation, and Henry wanted a big water dog that we could train, play with at the beach and in the water, and settle down with as we cruised into our sixties. Because goldens need a great deal of exercise, Henry joked that he wanted to train her as a certified therapy dog — for us.

Once we had the application in hand,

Henry suggested that we fill it out together. I still had a lot of concerns, including my big worry that I might never be able to love another dog as much as Buddy. I also worried that goldens have high rates of cancer and hip dysplasia, an inherited condition that sometimes shows up in X-rays of a puppy's parents, but not always. Donna had certifications for any number of health issues regarding all her dogs, although these certifications are never definitive. We also appreciated her insistence we sign a spay/neuter contract, something most reputable breeders require.

Donna was obviously committed to breeding a healthy litter of puppies; meanwhile, we were certain that we did *not* want to buy a puppy from a local pet shop, even if we found one that offered the fairly rare English golden retriever. Most commercial pet stores get their puppies from puppy mills, many of which are located in the Midwest, especially Missouri. The dogs in these mills are kept in cramped cages, lack proper medical care and nutrition, and often develop serious health problems. Millions of puppies are churned out by these notorious mills, and although the Department of Agriculture is supposed to inspect the mills and enforce the Animal Welfare Act, the USDA has few inspectors.

Some of the questions on Donna's application were a bit daunting; I felt almost as if we were applying to college. She asked how we rated ourselves on such things as the number of hours we would be leaving the dog alone during the day and the amount of time we would spend traveling. (In part because Henry works from home as a consultant, we were confident that we would be suitable owners.) We were asked to gauge our family's activity level on a scale of 1 to 10, with 1 being a couch potato and 10 being a triathlete. (Especially since we both love the outdoors, we declared ourselves a solid 7.) Donna's questions were valid because goldens thrive on lots of human company and need a great deal of exercise.

Her application also asked if we were prepared for constant digging and shedding. The digging wouldn't be a problem, but the question about shedding gave me pause, because on dark clothing the white hairs of this breed of retriever stand out, magnificently. After thinking it over, I decided that I was willing to put most of my black work clothes — basically my entire wardrobe — in the back of the closet. Besides, Henry and I are not the fussy *House Beautiful* types; our house and apartment both have dorm-room levels of disarray, perhaps reflecting the fact that we met in college and sometimes think it's still 1976. In the end only one question stumped me. Was our lawn "meticulously kept"? Well, it depended on your definition of *meticulous*.

As we completed Donna's application, I could feel my worries about getting a new dog melting away. English golden retrievers have so many good characteristics: not only are they gorgeous dogs that love the outdoors; they are loyal, smart, and sweet-tempered. I also told myself that after meeting Donna, we could always change our minds. Or at least we could right up to the moment when we actually made contact with a real puppy. One lick on the face and I knew we would instantly be past the point of no return.

Donna accepted our application, but she wanted to interview us in person. So in May 2009, seven weeks after the new litter of English goldens was born, Henry and I drove from our house in Connecticut to Thistledown Golden Retrievers.

During the drive, Henry cruelly informed me that he was replacing me as pack leader because I am neither calm nor assertive, the qualities required by Cesar Millan, the famous dog behavior specialist. (We had watched Millan's television show, *Dog Whisperer,* on the eve of our journey.) There would be no human food prepared for our new dog (good-bye, grilled chicken). This dog, unlike the stubborn Buddy, was going to be well trained. "You are wonderful, but you don't know how to be firm," Henry said as we drove up I-95. "When Buddy would pull the leash so hard that your arm was on the verge of detaching, you'd giggle and say, 'Buddy, no,' and let him keep going."

Henry's assessment was harsh but fair. Although I could be tough and hold the line as a parent and as an editor at the *Times,* I was a pushover with Buddy. In my defense, we had both been so busy with the kids and work that we simply weren't able to devote the time needed to train Buddy properly.

Two hours after setting out, we arrived at Thistledown. We had expected Donna Cutler to look like a Scottish noblewoman, or at least one of those tweedy, stout women who show their dogs at the annual Westminster Dog Show. Instead, the woman who met us at the door was trim, with medium-brown hair, sharp features, and a friendly but down-to-business demeanor. Donna told us that she had just returned from showing one of her dogs in a competition in Canada. She competed in many shows up north, where

the English golden retriever — with its unusual color, chunky head, and thick torso — is much admired.

Donna, who was then in her late forties, was still dressed in the pants suit she'd worn during the competition. We, by contrast, were in shorts and sneakers, hoping to emphasize our vigor and sportiness. As Donna led us to the back of her house — which had big fenced-in pens for the adult dogs and another outside area for puppies — I was nervous and fearing rejection. (Later we learned that Donna had turned down a potential customer only twice. One was a gent who refused to commit to enclosing his yard so the puppy would be safe. The other was a woman in Donna's town who kept brushing the hairs off her coat during the first puppy visit.)

No doubt to put us at ease, Donna told us a bit about herself. She had grown up in Dedham, Massachusetts, where her family had pets of every kind, including wild baby rabbits, stray cats, and a bantam rooster that lived in the house so it wouldn't wake up the neighbors. But the family had only one dog, a pug that belonged to her grandmother. This pug, Donna told us, was simply "not fun." Moreover, pugs are small, and Donna wanted a big dog. For weeks, she and he₁

sister saved up their allowance, and then one day they biked into town and bought a dog collar and a leash. Several times that summer, they rounded up a big dog that had been wandering around town, as dogs did back then. The two girls would drag it home to the garage and remove the collar and leash so as not to give away their gambit. Then they would go into the house and exclaim to their parents that a dog had followed them home. But each time, as soon as the garage door was opened for an inspection, the pooch would bolt out of the yard and beat it back to town.

Donna had been breeding goldens for years, and the puppies' parents, grandparents, uncles, aunts, and great-grandparents still lived on the premises. (This is one of the signs of a reputable breeder, and most experts advise checking out the parents of a puppy for temperament, looks, and health history.) After we'd chatted for a while, she showed us around her yard. On the right, there was an area cordoned off by knee-high portable fences where Tess, the mother of the new litter, was lying down surrounded by her progeny. The nine puppies were not yet completely weaned and were the cutest little fur balls I had ever seen.

Donna explained that the puppies were

Tess and her litter of puppies, with Scout on the side

becoming socialized by romping with one another under their mother's watchful eye. Once in a while, one pup would squeal when a brother or sister nipped an ear too hard. One of the most important things new puppies learn is how to moderate their bites. These pups already had their set of twenty-eight baby teeth, which were like sharp little razors.

There were four females in the litter, and I asked Donna if she had a particular one in mind for us. She said that because our life was split between the country and the city, she thought the smallest female might be best. But her tone when she answered was noncommittal, probably because she hadn't had a chance to observe us with the puppies. No seal of approval yet.

One of Donna's favorites in the litter was a tiny female she called Cindy Lou, named after the smallest denizen of Dr. Seuss's Whoville in *How the Grinch Stole Christmas*. The Seuss character had a yellow streak in her hair, and so did this puppy. We later learned that Donna also saw in this pup the kind of "attitude" that she believed was well suited for life in the big city.

I looked more closely at Cindy Lou. She was tiny, with sleepy eyes, and as some of her brothers and sisters nursed, she hovered

Scout under the green chair

under a green plastic chair. That worried me a little. Was this pup too shy?

"It's okay to pick them up," Donna told us. I cradled the little one in my lap. I was tempted to bring her up to my nose and take in the wonderful smell that all new puppies have; instead, since I knew that very young dogs absorb every new experience primarily through their noses, I let her get a good whiff of me.

Soon all the puppies, including this little one, perked up and wanted to play. Henry jumped into the pen and let them chase his heels. All of the pups had a different color ribbon around their necks so Donna could keep track of who was who.

Tess, the mother, watched all this from a few yards away. She was a blond beauty who when she was younger was a potential champion. But one day, while Donna was in Wyoming on a girls' weekend, a stick had snapped back and sliced Tess's eye, which couldn't be saved by a veterinarian. Still, even with the closed, missing eye, she was a knockout.

Donna took us to the adult dog area to meet the father of the pups, a big boy named Patrick who had won a championship in Austria. Aside from his good looks and fluid movement — a sort of sashay that suggested

Henry and the puppies

powerful legs — Patrick was chosen to be this litter's father for his even temperament, a trait we hoped all the puppies had inherited. Donna also provided us health certificates showing that Tess and Patrick had been checked repeatedly for hip and elbow dysplasia but exhibited no signs of it.

After visiting with Donna and her dogs for two hours, we felt that we were beginning to trespass on our hostess's time. Before we left, Donna put tiny Cindy Lou and one other female pup in an indoor area so we (and, presumably, she) could be sure.

"So have you thought about a name?" Donna asked. (Clearly a hopeful sign!)

Yes, we had. Actually, Henry had been disqualified in the name-the-dog contest, because when I was pregnant the first time he had briefly considered giving Cornelia the name Jemima. Two years later, Will almost became Ichabod. (Henry likes the old-fashioned names from his Puritan family tree. "If we don't use those names, who will?" he would ask, indirectly answering his own question.) But after frantic consultations with Cornelia and Will, we had decided on the name Scout after the spunky little girl in Harper Lee's *To Kill a Mockingbird*.

"Well, Scout can't come home with you for two weeks," Donna said, giving us a date and time to come retrieve our retriever.

We still weren't sure which puppy she meant. But as we walked back to the car, the shock of Donna's last words sank in. We had passed.

On the ride home, I kept thinking about the tiny puppy with the slightly worried expression. And I was slightly worried myself. While watching Donna's litter of puppies, memories of Buddy as a new puppy had flooded my mind. I still wasn't sure whether my heart was ready to replace him.

CHAPTER TWO

In June, when she was nine weeks old, Cindy Lou — aka Scout — was finally ready to join our family.

Remembering how convenient it was to have a backyard for Buddy's early housebreaking, we had decided to have Scout spend her first weeks with us at our home in Connecticut, where we usually spend weekends and part of the summer. An antique colonial — it was built in the 1700s — the house is on a quiet street with an ample lawn. Although both of us usually work in New York City during the week, we had adjusted our schedules so Scout could begin life as a country girl. Manhattan is easily reachable by train, and I planned to spend three days out of every week in Connecticut as often as possible. Meanwhile, Henry could work from Connecticut during the summer and had in any case cleared his schedule of just about everything except puppy training.

While waiting for Scout's homecoming, we had spent a small fortune at Petco, one of the national pet supply chains. We needed a gate to close off our open and now rugless kitchen and family room area. Since Scout would be growing fast, we bought a giant bag of the same kibble that Donna had been feeding her, Purina Pro Plan for dogs with sensitive skin and stomachs. We also purchased a crate where she would sleep.

The aisles of every Petco, a company with an annual revenue of two billion dollars, are jammed with all manner of products, many aimed at humanizing dogs to an almost ridiculous extent, including five different models of puppy strollers, in colors like mango and sage. The sales associates refer to dog owners as "pet parents," which jibes with the times, as do the chain's other policies. Dogs are allowed inside the stores so they can shop with their parents, and Petco also offers a popular pet adoption service. The same Yuppie values that drove the explosive growth of designer products for infants, such as four-hundred-dollar Perego strollers and one-hundred-dollar ergonomic baby carriers, have now been transferred to pets. When Cornelia and Will were young, Henry and I didn't have the money to succumb to the marketing of these upscale baby products. But now we are empty nesters with a lot more disposable income.

Dog food, which used to come in two options, dry or wet, is now a cornucopia of choice, including special formulas for sensitive skin and stomachs and much higher-priced bags bearing "natural" and "organic" labels. Having edited stories about dubious health claims for expensive "organic" food for humans, I was skeptical upon seeing the same marketing techniques used by the seventeen-billion-dollar pet food business.

In Manhattan, I had visited several high-end pet boutiques, including one called Canine Caviar that sells thirty-dollar bags of "holistic" kibble. (There are also vegetarian, vegan, and kosher versions.) A few of our friends feed their dogs only raw food, another new dog food craze. And I also knew that some dog experts insist that it is healthier for dogs to eat only freshly cooked food. How could I possibly navigate this maze of options?

I consulted Marion Nestle, the author of several excellent books on human and pet food politics, including *Feed Your Pet Right*. Dr. Nestle believes that many of these exotic dog food formulas are just plain silly. She said that we should look for products labeled "complete and balanced," which indicate that they meet the nutritional guidelines for cats and dogs listed by the Association of American Feed Control Officials. Dr. Nestle told me that this organization — in conjunction with the Food and Drug Administration, state officials, and the animal feed industry — had developed pretty reliable regulations for pet foods. And she assured me that most of the commercial brands with these labels sold in supermarkets are fine for dogs, since almost all dog foods are made from the by-products of human food production. Paying attention to the basic ingredients is also advisable, she said.

It seems that almost every aspect of dog ownership has fierce, partisan battles lurking just below the surface. Perhaps the most contentious issue is whether a would-be dog owner should get a new dog through pet rescue and adoption or from a breeder. Upon hearing that Henry and I were getting a purebred puppy, several of our friends reacted as if we were buying a Hummer and thus doing something fundamentally bad for society. Cornelia had volunteered at a local animal shelter in Virginia, and we all understood that many dogs needed to be rescued and adopted. The horrified reactions seemed extreme.

Even dog toys provoke raging debates. We

planned to put one of Cornelia's old stuffed animals in the crate to keep Scout company, fearing that she would be lonely once she was separated from her littermates. But nowadays, we were told, these are considered taboo because the synthetic stuffing could harm dogs if swallowed. Petco now offers flat plush toys without stuffing, but they look about as fun and reassuring as paper bags.

I tried to resist both the specious advice and the clever marketing ploys, but I wasn't entirely successful. During our shopping spree at Petco, I discovered that I liked the smell of Halo dog shampoo, which costs eighteen dollars for a sixteen-ounce bottle — a lot more than I pay for my own shampoo. While we stuffed our bags into the car that morning, I was still trying to figure out how our tab had come to four hundred dollars.

As we counted down to the big day, we felt jittery and underprepared, as if we were waiting for the arrival of a new baby. We knew that once tiny Scout was in our car, there would be no turning back.

When the day for pickup finally came, Henry and Will drove up to Thistledown while I stayed behind in Connecticut making final preparations. A little after three o'clock, Henry pulled into our driveway and there she was, a white ball of fluff resting in the backseat of our Subaru on an ancient Superman towel from Will's toddlerhood. Picking her up, I put Scout on the lawn and she padded toward the house. Halfway to the door, she squatted to pee. We clapped in jubilation, and we could scarcely believe our good fortune when she repeated this same routine a few hours later.

Scout seemed to be more than partly housebroken, an unanticipated gift from Donna. It was hilarious watching her trot out the back door onto the lawn; since her back legs were taller than the rest of her, she looked like she might topple over, which she sometimes did. She would scamper a ways and then randomly plop down. Scamper then plop, her legs betraying her as often as they propelled her forward.

Now that Scout was finally home, none of us could stop picking her up to cuddle. I had forgotten how much having a new puppy is like having a new baby. Besides looking for any excuse to inhale that irresistible puppy smell, I felt a reflexive urge to cover the top of Scout's soft head with kisses. It is actually very important for a new puppy to get used to being handled, but I admit that I wasn't kissing and cuddling with her because I knew it was the right thing to do.

Just as I did when our children were little, I made up lullabies with silly lyrics and then sang to her when she cried before sleep. I also felt the unparalleled joy of seeing her tired eyes close, although she would invariably wake again in the middle of the night. Henry, ever the hero, slept next to Scout's crate so that he could hear her stir when she needed to go outside to relieve herself. More than fifteen years had passed since we had performed this routine with Buddy, and we were rusty.

Scout woke every morning at six on the dot. She immediately started crying and whimpering, but she always cheered up the minute she had company. Cornelia, who had a few weeks of summer break from medical school, had come to Connecticut to help, and we traded off the responsibility for taking care of Scout in the early morning. When it was my turn, I didn't mind at all. The soulful brown eyes that greeted me had long lashes that gave Scout a sultry, flirtatious look; she was a canine version of Veronica Lake, down to her blond, silky fur. Although dogs supposedly don't like to be stared at, Scout looked deeply into my reddened, sleep-deprived eyes as if searching for clues. Who was this person? What were all these new smells?

She liked clamping down on my forearm with those needle-sharp teeth. Soon she was chewing on little rawhide bones, and she went through them like jelly beans. We watched carefully while she chewed, hoping we could prevent her from swallowing any of the pieces she worked so hard to detach.

Will's Superman towel now lined the bottom of Scout's crate, and Henry planned to buy a clock to put in the crate with her. He remembered that his mother, Lynne, had told him a story from her childhood about preparing a little bed for her new puppy, Nicky. Nicky slept in a laundry basket filled with soft, clean blankets, into which Lynne tucked an old-fashioned wind-up alarm clock. When Henry had asked her why she put the clock in the basket, Lynne answered, "The ticking reminded Nicky of her mother's heartbeat." This story was especially meaningful to Henry because his mother had died in her sixties of heart trouble.

Scout looked awfully little in her crate, but her big paws were a tip-off that she wasn't going to stay small. While she slept, I loved watching her little back as it rose and fell. Even so, I still sometimes worried that I might not love Scout as much as Buddy, a

Jill and Scout soon after Scout's arrival in Connecticut

fear I kept to myself. I didn't know it then, but this is a very common worry of new dog owners.

It's also not unusual for new dog owners to be reminded of their experiences with infants. In fact, our response to a puppy may be partly hormonal. John Homans, who wrote a perceptive article about dogs and their owners for New York magazine, noted that a recent study showed that a dog's gaze increases oxytocin levels in its owner, and oxytocin is the same hormone that creates such intense bonding between a baby and its mother.

It's long been understood that puppies stir powerful feelings in humans; in fact, over the thousands of years that dogs have been domesticated, breeders have purposely preserved their puppy characteristics, which is one reason why so many older dogs act like perpetual puppies. Temple Grandin, a widely respected animal behaviorist who raised many golden retrievers earlier in her life, was one of several experts I consulted during Scout's early puppyhood. She told me that breeders have also bred dogs to be hypersocialized. "So it's natural," Grandin said, "that some people treat their dogs like children. And the dogs are very attuned to us." Grandin, who is autistic, has written a number of books, and I found one of them, *Animals Make Us Human,* especially useful.

I consulted a number of other books as well. Next to Grandin's book on our shelf was a volume by the monks of New Skete, guide-dog trainers who lived in an Eastern Orthodox monastic community in upstate New York. The monks have written several extremely readable and useful dog-training manuals, including *The Art of Raising a Puppy* and *How to Be Your Dog's Best Friend.* I was amused one day when I realized that Henry and I used these books the same way our parents had turned to Dr. Spock to help raise us.

The monks' general precepts made a lot of sense to us, and their daily regimen for new puppies comported with our idea of how a day with a dog ought to go. Passionate advocates of a rural life, the monks were so persuasive on the subject that Henry decided to stay in Connecticut right through Labor Day, when Scout would be almost five months old. By then she would have had all her shots, which was not a small matter. City pavements can expose puppies to parvo, giardia, and other ailments that can potentially kill them overnight. The green of our backyard seemed a much safer option than the urban wilds of Manhattan.

■ ■ ■ ■

Part of the plan for getting a dog precisely in mid-June was that the weather in Connecticut was likely to be lovely. With any luck, the pestilential heat and humidity of recent summers would hold off until Scout and we got our legs under us. Unfortunately, that's not how it worked out: instead of sweet spring gliding into summer, the weather was almost tropical and there were sudden thunderstorms nearly every day. Happily Scout showed no fear of the storms, but as she got bigger and feistier we all began to go stir-crazy. By the end of June, it was time for Scout to begin socializing with other dogs and with people. And it was time for us to emerge from our puppy bunker, too.

Our friend Marian Spiro came to our rescue. Ever since Scout's homecoming, Marian had been calling us frequently to check in and offer tips. Because her English golden retriever, Cyon, was Henry's inspiration for finding Scout, Henry considered every morsel of advice from Marian extremely valuable. At eighty-four, she had raised many puppies, including goldens, and she knew how to handle almost every challenging situation.

Now Marian invited Henry and Scout to

join her and Cyon at four o'clock every afternoon so Scout could get to know Cyon and begin to learn some social skills. Marian filled an eight-foot-long baby pool in her backyard for the dogs to splash in, and the afternoon pool party soon became the high point of the day. Although Scout was still too little to climb into the pool, Marian gently introduced her to the water and she took to it right away.

A longtime friend of Marian's — an older gentleman named Clyde Campbell who spoke with a honeyed North Carolina drawl — would frequently join the pool party with his dog, Bunny. Another white golden with a rambunctious temperament, Bunny would sometimes splash too energetically in the pool or stomp on Marian's flower beds. "Bunny, no!" Clyde would shout in frustration. Gleefully, Henry called me at the office to tell me that he had new best friends, a couple named Bunny and Clyde.

Dog play can be utterly fascinating, a dance of dominance and submission, engagement and disengagement. At first, the new puppy in their midst interested Cyon and Bunny, but they were accustomed to being a sisterhood of two, and for the most part Scout was happy to watch them from the sidelines while sitting near us. Scout found the two big goldens especially entertaining when they both clamped their teeth on the same tennis ball and held it between them as if in a trance, their bodies in perfect tension for as long as five minutes. Scout knew not to try to get into the middle of that game, but as time went by she began to chase the bigger dogs. When she'd catch their attention, she would quickly lie down on her back in submission, showing her adorable white belly.

Learning to play with other dogs is about much more than having fun; in fact, it's probably the most crucial aspect of puppy development. In *Animals at Play*, Marc Bekoff, a biologist and animal behaviorist, describes the rituals of dog play, including the bow — front legs stretched forward, hips raised — that signals an invitation to play, and the subtle cues that warn another dog that the playing has turned too rough. "Play is how dogs become card-carrying members of their species," Bekoff told me when I called to consult him.

Alexandra Horowitz's *Inside of a Dog: What Dogs See, Smell and Know* includes a wonderful description of a Chihuahua and a wolfhound playing together with total ease, despite their enormous size difference. "These dogs are so incommensurable with each other that they may as well be from different species," she writes. "The wolfhound bit, mouthed and charged at the Chihuahua; yet the little dog responded not with fright but in kind."

Next to full-grown Cyon and Bunny, Scout must have felt like a Chihuahua, but gradually she began to learn how to hold her own. When we walked down our street and let her off the leash in a nearby field, she would cower, tail between her legs, when Bacci, a huge Bernese mountain dog who belonged to a neighbor, approached her to play. Then, when he came up to her, Scout would run for the hills. But after a few minutes, she would return to Bacci and give him a few tentative sniffs. Soon they were playing like the Chihuahua and the wolfhound, just as Horowitz described it.

But it was Marian who remained the touchstone of Scout's early socialization, and they quickly formed a mutual adoration society. Marian has piercing blue eyes and a wonderful laugh, and when Scout was around we heard that laugh often, because Marian seemed to be amused by just about everything Scout did.

We had known Marian and her husband, Howard, casually for many years. Henry and their son, Chip, were roommates in college, and we would often run into Marian and Howard at the beach and around town. But we got to know them much better when I started teaching a course at Yale, where Howard is an emeritus professor of medicine. After a couple of chance meetings on the commuter train, Howard invited us to become associate fellows of one of Yale's colleges, and later he inducted Henry into the Lawn Bowling Association. Marian and Howard have extensive professional networks and a hectic social schedule, but they never let you know it. As a friend of ours remarked upon meeting them over lunch, they possess "not a single drop of pretension between them."

Everyone in the Spiro clan is an avid sailor, and the mix of dogs and the sea comes naturally. One granddaughter wrote for a grade-school class exercise, "I love my Grandma because she has a big dog and a big boat." Howard, who has a deep voice and a penchant for aphorisms, often notes that "there's nothing better for a cut than saltwater and dog saliva."

Unlike many people with goldens, Marian came to the breed later in life. She grew up during the Depression in Fall River, Massachusetts, and her family owned a succession of cocker spaniels. "They ran loose, as all dogs did back then," she recalled. Even before she and Howard had children, they got a mutt. When she brought it back from the dog pound, the puppy was so small that it could fit in her pocket. Over the years, she had a series of pound puppies until one of them mated with a golden, at which point they became smitten with the breed.

The Spiros have owned three goldens, and all three were named after stars or constellations. First came Orion, then Sirius, and now there's Procyon, or Cyon for short. Sirius became famous for accompanying Marian to the science class she taught at a private middle school in New Haven. The dog would rest quietly in his crate during class but then come out so that the kids could pat him while coming and going.

Despite the celestial monikers of her dogs, Marian's dog-raising philosophy is down-to-earth. "Dare I say it's just maternal instinct?" she said to me, reassuringly. Key to her approach is the element of patience, for both dogs and their owners. Very early on in Scout's life, Marian would hold a piece of high-value treat, like a small piece of cheese, mere inches from her snout and say, "Wait . . . wait . . . wait, baby." Only when Scout was calm and sitting still would Marian deliver the goody. Marian repeated this ritual several times a day. Other puppies would practically bite off a finger while trying to get the snack, but Scout learned to hold back and resist temptation, which served us well in our later training work.

At some point we learned that Marian, Clyde, and their dogs are charter members of a dog-walking group that meets at 7:30 a.m. most mornings, even in winter, at a town-owned farm near our house. In mid-July, after Scout received the puppy shots due when she turned thirteen weeks old, Marian and Clyde invited us to join the group. The point of this morning session is to give the dogs exercise by letting them gambol, without leashes, in the acres of lush meadowland owned by our town. The pristine white farmhouse, the ponds filled with flowering yellow water lilies in spring through fall, and the old covered wooden bridge on the property make it look a lot like one of those gorgeous Monet paintings.

On any given morning in July, we saw as many as a dozen dogs walking off-leash with their owners. Besides Cyon and Bunny, the regulars included Olive, a black pug whose smushed face made it hard for her to breathe in the summer heat; Sadie, an older Airedale; and Viggo, a huge, seven-month-old

German shepherd who was being trained by a woman named Lee Gibson to become a seeing-eye dog for the blind. Lee had agreed to give Viggo a loving home and his early puppy training, but when he turned a year old he would be leaving her to begin his formal training in a guide-dog program. Lee also had an extremely shy Japanese chin named Zen, who sometimes walked with us but usually preferred to wait by himself next to Lee's car.

These daily outings taught us far more about how to raise Scout than the monks and our other books did. Lee, for one, knows an enormous amount about dogs and was a fount of training tips. The visits to the farm socialized us, too. Clyde instructed us to guard our knees when the dog pack came running our way. "You could blow out a knee and wind up in the hospital again, Jill," he warned me. He also encouraged me to buy a pair of Muck Boots like his to keep my feet dry in the mornings, when the grass was still covered with dew.

Following the death of the film director John Hughes that summer, we dubbed our little group of early morning dog walkers the Breakfast Club. Especially if Scout had had one of those nights when she needed to be let out a lot, I was often exhausted, but I cherished those morning meetings. Soon I could match the cars to the pet owners, and I would be disappointed if we drove up to the parking area and didn't immediately see any of our friends.

Day by day, Scout became bolder — and bigger. "Scout, you've grown another six inches," Clyde would exclaim nearly every morning, and it almost seemed true. She was eating like crazy, gulping down her kibble with a frosting of yogurt and gaining about half a pound a day. When she arrived in Connecticut in mid-June, Scout had weighed sixteen pounds; by late July she weighed almost thirty pounds. As she grew, Cyon, Bunny, and the rest of the pack sternly enforced what Scout could get away with (joining them in chasing rabbits) and what she couldn't (dashing into the pile of discarded vegetables). Sometimes the other dogs were plainly annoyed by this overeager puppy who followed their every move and tried to steal their balls. Viggo could be particularly grouchy, and sometimes he would turn on Scout and give her a "stay away from me" growl. But though Scout clearly didn't enjoy this sort of rejection, she needed to learn how to interpret social cues.

Marian continued to be amused by Scout's wild and ungainly strides, but her demeanor around all the dogs was relaxed yet firm. If Cyon began to race off into the woods, Marian would immediately call her back. A sharp "Cyon, come!" would result in the prompt reappearance of her dog. If Bunny and Scout had followed Cyon, they would dawdle behind her with mildly guilty expressions. Afterward, Marian would get all three dogs to sit and take out her bag of small treats. "Wait," she'd tell them, wanting to encourage soft mouths and keep them sitting. Only then would she give them each a treat. The Breakfast Club ended each morning with Marian inviting all three white goldens into the back of her car, where she split her last treat three ways.

We copied the Marian technique at home, getting Scout to sit and be patient before bestowing a treat for good behavior. We faithfully spent part of each day training Scout, helping her to learn her name and a few basic commands. Henry also made a point of giving her a ride in the car as often as possible, which at first provoked a lot of howling and braying until Scout finally realized that getting in the car usually meant a trip to Marian's or doing something else fun. And in preparation for Scout's eventual arrival in New York, Henry would take her in the afternoon for rides up and down the

Bunny (left), Cyon (center), and Scout (right) in the back of Marian Spiro's car

elevator at the local commuter train station.

Scout usually spent her downtime in the giant stand of lilacs just beyond our kitchen door, which Henry had enclosed with chicken wire. Aside from providing shade all day, the fenced-in area around the lilacs gave Scout the opportunity to explore her own little forest, bury toys, and chase Henry as he ran around the perimeter. One fine morning Scout was napping in the lilacs and Henry was reading nearby when a UPS delivery-man arrived. "Must be nice," the man remarked as he handed Henry the package. And, indeed, it was very nice.

Because my job as managing editor of the *Times* required that I spend most weekdays in my New York office that summer, I called Henry each afternoon to hear the latest news from his and Scout's farm walk or Marian's pool parties. Finally, in early August, I couldn't stand missing so much of the fun and took a two-week vacation.

I was elated by the prospect of spending an uninterrupted stretch of time with Scout. I was also eagerly awaiting the visit of my friend Mariane Pearl and her seven-year-old son Adam. Mariane was the widow of Danny Pearl, the *Wall Street Journal* reporter who had been my friend and colleague in the

Journal's Washington bureau. Adam was the son Danny had never met, since Danny had been kidnapped and murdered in Pakistan by al-Qaeda while Mariane was pregnant.

Adam loved the beach, superheroes, baseball, and dogs. He was excited to meet our new puppy, and I was anxious for Scout to learn how to behave around a child, since Buddy had sometimes growled at visiting toddlers, which scared them and alarmed me. When the Pearls arrived in Connecticut from New York, Adam brought Scout a Yankees dog shirt as a gift and was determined to teach her how to play left field in Wiffle ball games.

Under Adam's tutelage, Scout became an extremely fast and adept outfielder, but she never got the hang of dropping the ball after she caught it. In my dual role as pitcher and mediator, I would usually have to negotiate a trade, giving her a treat in return for the ball.

It was on this field of dreams that Scout had her first big mishap. One sweltering afternoon, she took her customary position in far left field. As I pitched and Adam endured a long series of balls, hitless swings, and foul tips, sap from a pine tree dripped all over Scout. When Adam saw what had happened, he cried out, "Scoutie looks like a dalmatian!" She was a terrible, sticky mess, and after dragging her into the house I scoured the Internet for remedies. Once I discovered the recommended treatment, I dabbed the spots of tar with olive oil and peanut butter. By the end of this tedious process, Scout was once again blond, but she smelled like a peanut butter sandwich.

Our house wasn't far from Long Island Sound, and during Adam's visit we often took Scout for walks on the beach. She was wary of the surf, but she liked to splash along the shoreline and let the water rise up to her belly. We were all thrilled when Adam threw a stick and Scout dove in, retrieved the stick, and paddled back to shore. Then she wouldn't give up the stick, but we nonetheless celebrated the superb display of her retriever roots. Scout and Adam got along famously, and it warmed my heart to watch the two of them — these two beautiful puppies — cavort in the sand and the sea. By the end of Adam's visit, I was pretty certain that Mariane would be dealing with a major episode of "Can we please get a dog" begging when she and Adam returned to Paris.

The Monday after Mariane and Adam left, my vacation came to an end. That morning, as I dressed in my office clothes, I felt as if

I were assuming another identity, much as I did when I went back to work after maternity leaves. While riding the Metro-North train from New Haven to New York, I began making the transition back to my life at the *Times* by reading the papers and catching up on e-mail.

With the vacation behind me, I plunged back into my job and stayed in the city for two full weeks. This was my first extended separation from Scout, and it was a little depressing to live a solitary life again. As a new puppy owner, I had made so many new friends, both dog and human, and over the summer I had become much calmer and happier. I missed the morning walks with the Breakfast Club, which felt like a much healthier way to start the day than rushing to my computer. Most of all, I missed Scout. Bill Keller, my boss and the paper's executive editor, told me that he noticed a sudden rise in the number of dog stories being pitched for the front page. To curb the trend, he urged me to recuse myself from any discussion about a proposed dog story.

Inevitably, I showed off my latest Scout photos to anyone who betrayed even a hint of interest. Over the years, my office had become a Buddy shrine; many of my friends and colleagues had deluged me with every kind of Westie item, from a needlepoint pillow to a white ceramic pen container. Michiko Kakutani, the *Times*'s chief book critic, was particularly generous: not only had she given me dozens of pairs of socks emblazoned with Westies; she had also given me an antique desk lamp with a bronze terrier perched on its base. It was made in the 1940s, when Scottish terriers were the rage because of President Franklin Delano Roosevelt's beloved dog, Fala.

Even after Buddy died, people who didn't know me especially well kept sending me Westie gifts. Recently, I had tearfully opened a set of Westie coasters and then a white bar of soap in the shape of a Westie. So when I returned to my desk one day and found a package from the columnist Maureen Dowd, I worried that it, too, would contain more Buddy stuff. Instead, the box contained a ceramic plate with a golden retriever puppy painted on it. I displayed Maureen's gift in a place of honor, and now all the white in my office could begin to turn golden.

CHAPTER THREE

Chewing. It was a constant with Scout. Her needlelike baby teeth were being replaced by permanent, bigger ones and the teething was driving her nuts. At fifteen weeks, she had grown bored with our usual cache of rawhide bones and frozen towel bows and was now wild for shoes, preferably Cornelia's fanciest ones. We were vigilant, we thought, but Scout managed to chew and flatten beyond recognition a pair of black satin sandals with sassy bows that our daughter had carelessly flung into the gated family room and kitchen area where Scout slept in her crate, ate her food, and happily chewed. But even sequestered and puppy-proofed, the space offered a thousand temptations, from the cording on the couch upholstery to the wires of our computers. We lived in fear of puppy electrocution.

Partly so we could keep an eye on her, we removed one of the cushions from our couch and encouraged Scout to curl up in the resulting gap. This gave her a cozy place to sit within snuggle distance of us, and it was low enough that she could easily hop on and off. Dogs generally love protected spaces, and the sunken "nest" on the couch quickly became her favorite place to hang out.

One August evening, while we were enjoying a peaceful hour watching *Antiques Roadshow,* Scout climbed down from the couch and went behind it. As we watched the show, we were vaguely aware of what we assumed was the sound of Scout chewing on one of her rawhides, and she was really going at it. Then Henry got up to get a beer and saw, to his horror, that Scout had in fact been chewing on the leg of an old table, which was now completely covered with teeth marks. There was even a scattering of what looked like sawdust around the bottom of the leg.

Clearly drastic action was required, and we began by removing all the nearby wooden chairs and tables. Next we christened the area on top of her crate the Land of No; this became a no-chew zone, and whenever Scout stole a forbidden object we put it there. The roof of the crate soon resembled a clearance sale at Macy's, with layers of outlawed goods stacked up high. Meanwhile, Scout manifested her obsession with chewing outdoors as well. Clumps of grass clippings from the lawn mower, pinecones, and even shells at the beach were all grist for her new set of choppers.

I took some solace from the stories told to me by friends who had made it through the puppy chewing frenzy. Phyllis Goverman, my college roommate, told me that "chewing was almost the end for us." As a young puppy, Lola, her now one-year-old Lab, had shredded Phyllis's most comfortable chair, eating a large helping of the stuffing in the process. Lola had also savaged the linoleum floor in the kitchen, where Phyllis left her during the hours she was teaching. I also consulted with Anna Quindlen, a former *Times* colleague and friend, who had written a book I loved called *Good Dog. Stay*. Anna comforted me by recalling that her queenly Lab, Bea, was fascinated with paper as a puppy — valuable paper. "She once ate a refund check from the State of New York, and $400 in $20 bills," Anna reported in an e-mail meant to reassure me.

By late August, Scout was big enough to launch carefully planned raids on the Land of No. This prompted us to give up her puppy-sized crate and buy one that would suit her when she grew to full size. At four and a half months, she already weighed almost forty pounds and was still gaining weight rapidly. Donna Cutler had estimated that she would ultimately weigh sixty pounds, but by using my powers as a crack investigative reporter, I observed Scout's huge paws and deduced that Donna's estimate would almost certainly prove too conservative.

What to feed Scout, when to feed her, and how to begin more serious training to curb her irrepressible puppy habits — like chewing shoes or jumping up on guests — were sources of growing tension between Henry and me. Since her arrival, we had been feeding Scout the same kibble diet that Donna had started her on. But she was constantly hungry and would have happily eaten twice what we fed her. Meanwhile, Henry had instituted a ban on human food except for the yogurt on the kibble. He was determined that Scout not become the fussy eater and beggar that Buddy was, with his taste for grilled chicken or (I confess) salmon, preferably wild Alaskan sockeye. Our stern pack leader was quick to point out that Buddy had become so spoiled by this richer diet that he utterly spurned unadorned kibble, and it was true.

Henry had been overjoyed to note that during her earliest weeks with us, Scout had been indifferent to our family gatherings at the table, which I attributed to the new, stricter food rules. But one night she began barking excitedly while Henry was eating a bowl of strawberries with whipped cream. Funny, we thought, strawberries don't usually appeal to dogs. Then, as I was scattering cheese on top of a pan of lasagna, Scout went nuts as I shoved the pan into the oven. That night we put two and two together: these white toppings on our food looked like her yogurt.

The fatal connection — between our food and her always-hungry stomach — had been made. And once it was, she was always by our side at the table, pleading at us with those irresistible brown eyes and batting those big lashes. Soon she began barking at us while we were eating. When she wouldn't stop, we had to enforce time-outs and shut her in our laundry room while we downed a meal and listened, all of us miserable, to her pathetic whimpering.

In desperation, I called Jane Mayer, who had trained three Labrador retrievers, including Peaches, yellow and regal, for whom we occasionally dog-sat. Peaches was mellow about everything but food. Once, when I was in the kitchen baking a cake, a stick of butter was softening on the counter. In the instant I turned around to get the eggs out of the fridge, the butter was gone. Peaches had only a slightly guilty expression on her face.

"Food can be your friend," Jane told me. "It is a great reward. She wants to please you, and a treat will help you reinforce her good behavior. Stop focusing so much on what displeases you." Since working together on our book about Clarence Thomas, we often turned to each other for advice when we were covering tough stories or experiencing difficulties in our careers. "Jill, you handled Howell Raines," Jane reminded me, referring to a former *Times* executive editor with whom I had often clashed. "You can handle a puppy."

Henry's strict approach to feeding Scout began to bend when Marian Spiro, whom we considered the ultimate dog authority, agreed with Jane that puppy treats were useful for marking Scout's good behavior. "Use them when you are practicing basic commands like Sit, Stay, and Come," she urged us. Cyon's favorite, Marian told me during a walk at the farm, was Pup-Peroni, especially the "original bacon recipe." (It comes in a bright red package, and thanks to the pet food industry's slick marketing it looks pretty delicious.) When Marian offered my ravenous pup a little taste of the soft beefy treat, Scout's face reminded me of Cornelia's thrilled expression as a toddler when, against my better judgment, I let her have some Cheetos. From then on, whenever Scout saw us drop the red package of Pup-Peroni onto our kitchen counter after one of our regular shopping sprees at Petco, she recognized it immediately and practically toppled over in ecstasy.

As summer drew to a close, a deadline loomed: by Labor Day we had to finish preparing Scout for her introduction to Manhattan. I couldn't wait for her to join me in the city. After my two-week vacation in August, during which I had bonded much more intensely to Scout, I found the weekdays without her almost intolerable.

I knew the transition from Connecticut to New York wouldn't be seamless. For one thing, we couldn't assume that months of housebreaking in the country would carry over. Still, it had been many weeks since Scout had had an accident inside our house, so we were fairly confident that she would quickly learn to wait for an elevator before getting outside our building, though it might prove harder for her to become used to relieving herself on communal pavement instead of the grass on our lawn.

Before she became a part-time city dog, Scout needed to learn how to walk on a leash, and we had already begun practicing. As we moved along our street in Connecticut one day, I thought things were going pretty well until I felt a tug, looked behind me, and saw Scout on her back, her adorable belly exposed, snapping at the leash like a turtle. For her, the leash was simply another object begging for a good chew. More troubling, Scout invariably lunged if a squirrel or chipmunk crossed the road near us. I worried about how she would do crossing the busy, traffic-choked streets of Tribeca.

Sometimes we practiced walking her on a leash at the farm. After one long session during which Henry walked Scout while wearing wet, ill-fitting shoes, he developed painful tendonitis. Now, at least for the time being, I became Scout's sole leash instructor and my left leg — the one with the titanium rod in it — began to ache. Not surprisingly, our temporarily crippled state led me to have some nagging second thoughts about the wisdom of getting such a large puppy who needed so much exercise. The monks, wise though they are, had provided no advice in their books for our situation. There is no Official Puppy Handbook for fifty-somethings.

Despite our infirmities, we couldn't ignore

our 6 a.m. alarm clock, which was the sound of Scout braying to be freed from her crate. Sore and cranky though we were, the sight of her jumping excitedly on her hind legs to greet us each morning brought instant joy. Her favorite game was grabbing a toy in her teeth and prompting me to chase her outside and onto the lawn to play tug-of-war, often in my pajamas. (A new puppy, I quickly came to realize, gave me an unassailable license to be ridiculous in public.) During our morning play, she sometimes forgot about the growing strength of her jaws and drew blood on my hands and forearms.

Right before the summer ended, I had to travel to the *Times*'s Washington bureau for a two-day business trip. I was worried about leaving Henry, who was still disabled, alone with Scout. I also knew I would miss her terribly. But work called, and so off I went.

That evening, when I called Henry to check on how things were going, he delivered an upsetting report. One of his clients was a nonprofit group in Connecticut, and he was racing to complete a proposal for the group in the next week or so. He was so consumed by Scout care that he was already tense about meeting the deadline; then, on top of that, he had made a truly awful discovery. Scout had chewed the frames and broken the lenses of his tortoiseshell glasses, which had slipped out of his pocket and onto the couch. "This is really more than I was prepared to handle," he moaned. Luckily, his optician was able to make a replacement pair and ship the glasses to him overnight. In the meantime, he was wearing prescription sunglasses at his desk in order to get some writing done.

I felt horribly guilty because I was out of town and unable to help. But I also had a deeper concern: Scout's puppy destructiveness seemed to be reaching unacceptable levels. It was time to get professional help.

What happened next was a loopy canine version of O. Henry's famous short story "The Gift of the Magi." On the same day and without telling each other, Henry and I both put in a distress call to the same dog trainer.

I liked Diane Abbott the minute I heard her voice. For every tale of woe I recounted, her reaction was an amused giggle. Diane offered a puppy kindergarten class in a nearby Connecticut town, and in his initial conversation with Diane, Henry had been so favorably impressed that he had booked a home consultation with her for the next Saturday.

I had watched enough Cesar Millan to

know that owners, almost always more than their dogs, are the ones who need training. So in the days leading up to our meeting with Diane, I made a list of all the questions and anxieties about Scout that I wanted to discuss with her.

By then, Henry and I agreed that we had to train Scout more rigorously than we had trained Buddy. It embarrassed me to remember that Buddy had flunked out of dog-training class, in large part because we were not consistent in practicing with him. We had also waited too long: we hadn't signed him up for classes until he was three years old. Diane told us that she liked to begin training with pups as young as three months.

On the morning of Diane's visit, Scout and I waited near our driveway. The woman who emerged from a tan hatchback had blond hair and looked like an athlete; reaching into her backseat, she pulled out a heavy, over-stuffed bag and lugged it over to us. Scout immediately focused on the bag, practically jumping inside. Diane giggled, just as she had on the phone, which put me at ease. "She smells all my goodies," Diane said. Scout happily followed Diane inside.

Diane spent most of the next two hours talking to Henry and me. Scout watched us attentively and was occasionally called upon for a demonstration. During that first consultation, we learned several invaluable lessons.

Diane was particularly insightful about the importance of positive reinforcement. Every time Scout did something we didn't like, we had been using stern voices and telling her "No." Instead, Diane said, we should focus less on correcting her negative behavior and more on rewarding her positive behavior. "Concentrate on what we want," Diane told us. "Don't give attention to what we don't like."

Diane also introduced us to the use of a training clicker. When Scout responded in the way Diane wanted — such as looking at Diane when Diane spoke her name — Diane marked the behavior with a click from a red and yellow plastic clicker. Then she immediately gave Scout a treat from a little pouch that she had attached to her belt. It was filled with bits of chicken, most of them no bigger than a fingernail. Using the clicker and her treats, Diane quickly succeeded in getting Scout to respond to a number of different commands. She offered rewards for every bit of good behavior and suggested that we do the same, even if the treat was just a piece of kibble.

When Scout jumped up on us, Diane urged

Scout gets her first lesson from Diane Abbott

us to turn to the side and look away. Better to ignore Scout for a few seconds rather than scold her, and then get her to sit, followed by a click and a reward. When Scout nipped too hard during play, Diane suggested that we say "Ouch," put our hands up, and stop play. Then, after a few seconds, we should resume playing. Diane explained that this is how puppies play with their littermates. When one gets hurt and squeals, play stops for a bit and then continues.

Diane also said she thought Scout might have become bored with her toys and suggested that we get her a Kong, a cylindrical rubber chew toy that can be smeared with peanut butter or filled with puppy treats and put in the freezer. "It can really keep dogs busy," she said. "It's fun and interesting for them to work at getting what's inside."

At mealtime, Scout had the bad habit of barking loudly as we prepared her bowl. Fortunately, Diane had a cure. She suggested that we ask Scout to sit before we put her bowl down and then reward her patience with a piece of kibble. "Nothing is free anymore," she said. "Always ask for a sit before you feed her. Then give a click and a treat." When we tried this approach the next time we fed her, the barking stopped immediately.

Diane, who believes that small amounts

of human food are good for dogs, gave us a list of approved and forbidden ones. Yogurt, already in Scout's diet, was fine, along with carrot chunks, cheese, and a number of other foods. On the verboten list, because they could poison a dog, were grapes, raisins, macadamia nuts, and, oddly, nutmeg.

This advice, of course, ran contrary to Henry's human food ban. But after hearing more about Diane's commonsense attitude toward food and seeing Scout's eager response to Diane's tiny bits of chicken, Henry declared that Diane had changed his mind. In the wake of Diane's visit, our pack leader's rules underwent a rapid evolution. In no time, they changed from "No Treats Whatsoever" to "Treats at Special Moments" to "Treats Basically All The Time Unless Scout Is Biting You." I was thrilled, of course, and secretly I hoped that one day Henry would let me return to the stove.

Without being pushy, Diane also suggested that we sign up for her next puppy kindergarten class, a package of eight sessions on Tuesday nights during which Scout would learn basic commands and socialize with other pups about her age. At the beginning of the consultation, we had talked with Diane about our plan to introduce Scout to New York, and now she told us that she thought the classes would help us handle Scout in the city. Henry, bless him, declared that he was willing to arrange his schedule around the puppy class. Instead of returning to the city on Sunday, he would work from Connecticut the first two days of the week and then drive to New York with Scout after Diane's class on Tuesday night.

Before she left, Diane gave Scout some hearty farewell pats and the two of us a clicker. Our separate cries for help had been answered.

I didn't want to miss Scout's first day of school, so the following Tuesday I left work early and took the train to Connecticut. Diane had promised that the class would be fun, and it was impossible not to trust someone who signed her e-mails, "Warmest wags, Diane." But it had been eighteen years since our younger child piled onto the school bus for the first day of kindergarten, and I felt the same mixture of anxiety and hopeful pride as we drove with Scout to the town where Diane taught her classes.

What we didn't know then was that by showing us how to use a clicker during her home consultation, Diane had introduced us to a dog-training method known as positive training. Later, I learned of the battle that rages between trainers who favor a more coercive, pack-leader approach and those who prefer a positive reinforcement technique that usually uses a clicker or a familiar sound to mark desired behavior in dogs.

Cesar Millan, whose television show on the National Geographic channel is one of the most popular shows on cable, is the avatar of pack leaders. Another cable personality, Victoria Stilwell, is a persuasive advocate of positive training. Others are also gaining national reputations for their ability to teach positive training; among them is Karen Pryor, the author of several popular dog-training manuals, under whom Diane had studied.

As with child-rearing, dog-training experts sometimes make convincing cases for completely opposing points of view. On the pack leader versus positive training issue, I had no idea which side was right; confusing the matter, the monks' books, which had served as our primary source for puppy advice, combine some of both approaches. When I found time to do a bit of research of my own, one of the experts I consulted was Shawn Stewart, who has worked with all kinds of dogs, including homeland security canine defense units. Stewart told me that the right method depends on individual considerations about the dog, the owner, and the environment. As he put it, "No one out there can say that any one method will fit any dog or any owner." In the face of conflicting advice, this seemed like a very sensible conclusion.

Instinctively, Henry and I leaned toward positive training. Our preferred parenting method had been to use encouragement, not punishment, to teach our children good behavior. And since Scout seemed eager to learn and responsive to instruction, we were happy to try out Diane's clicker training. Besides, if Scout attended all the puppy classes and passed the course, she would earn a basic manners certificate from the American Kennel Club, the organization that sponsors the Westminster Dog Show at Madison Square Garden each year. She would officially be a Good Dog.

It took about twenty minutes to drive to Durham, a town just to the north of us. Diane's class met next to a veterinary clinic in a large commercial garage with high ceilings and roll-up doors. There were six other puppies in the class. At forty pounds, Scout was the largest pupil by far. Diane had the *humans* — she preferred this word to *owners* — and the leashed pups introduce themselves on the lawn outside the classroom.

Because Scout had become well socialized with other dogs at Marian's pool parties and at the farm, she pulled eagerly toward her classmates.

Scout was especially smitten with a tiny Chihuahua named Petunia, who cowered each time Scout approached. Once inside the classroom, which had accident-proof concrete floors and was filled with colorful toys, Diane had to place a puppy fence around Petunia and her owner because the Chihuahua remained so shy and fearful. This only made Scout more besotted, and she expressed her ardor in loud, disruptive barking.

I could feel my face reddening, but Diane remained unfazed by Scout's yelps. "Just relax and have fun," Diane told me. She distracted Scout by inviting her to demonstrate an exercise called "charging the clicker," where the dogs practiced hearing the click, responding to it, and getting a treat. Diane had asked us not to feed the dogs before class so they would remain responsive to the treats.

Diane told us that she had become a devotee of the clicker method after she had attended a puppy class where a coercive trainer had dragged Diane's collie across the floor by her collar, practically choking her. "I wanted

Puppy kindergarten class

to find a different way," she explained. After attending one of Karen Pryor's training conferences, Diane met some other positive trainers in Connecticut and they began perfecting their techniques together. Not long after she gained certification from the Association of Pet Dog Trainers, she quit her job as the vice president of a plaster molding company to become a full-time trainer. "I felt this was my calling," she said.

Diane was a born animal lover, and no situation seemed to fluster her. She had always adored dogs, especially collies, and she enjoyed telling stories about the animals in her life. She had once trained a raccoon, Ziggy, who often palled around town with Diane's beloved collie, Ronnie, and her cat. One day the raccoon had lured Ronnie into the basement of a neighbor who had filled some shelves with jars of homemade raspberry jam. Ziggy climbed up and began smashing the jars on the basement floor. When the neighbor heard the noise and hurried down to the basement, he saw Ronnie's paws and face covered in red jam. Ziggy had slithered away and Ronnie got the blame for the caper. Ziggy eventually returned to the wild, but she came back once with her three babies to show them off to Diane, who almost became teary when she told the story.

Scout was entranced by Diane, as were the other dogs in the class. Happily, the dogs all seemed to get along well. Ella, a black Lab who was about Scout's age, had a sweet disposition and was less barky and jumpy than our pup. A springer spaniel in the class was already remarkably well trained: her owners took turns getting her to sit, stay, and lie down on command, much to the chagrin of the rest of us. A boxer puppy named Oliver was true to its breed and spent most of his time on his hind legs, trying to grab another dog or a human leg with its front paws.

The veterinary clinic itself was located on a large corner lot, and Henry had noticed that most of the owners and dogs showed up a few minutes early in order to get in a little walk. It was obvious that each of us hoped our puppy wouldn't embarrass us by having an accident during class, even though the garage's concrete floor would be easy to clean.

Halfway through the first class, Diane called for playtime and told us we could take our puppies off the leash. Scout's attention turned to Ella, and they were wrestling when I heard a little yelp: Scout had nipped Ella's ear. But I didn't think it was an accident, and I immediately thought of Beverly Cleary's irrepressible heroine Ramona

Quimby, who, in her first days of kindergarten, had a hard time suppressing her urge to pull the "boing-boing" curls of another student. Like Ramona, who loved her patient kindergarten teacher, Scout was crazy about Diane and barked with jealousy when Diane fixed her attention on one of the other dogs in the class. She wanted Diane to belong to her alone.

The biggest lesson Diane imparted in the first class was that dogs are visual creatures who respond to many kinds of cues besides verbal ones. Training, she said, is not effective if an owner uses only verbal communication, and sentences with many words will only confuse a dog. Instead, we needed to learn to employ visual cues, using our faces, bodies, and hands. Diane showed us how to get our pups to sit by moving a hand slightly over and behind the dog's head. Scout wouldn't respond to this signal in class, but after a few days of practice she began sitting in response to the hand motion.

In later classes, Diane taught us how to prepare our puppies for the unexpected. She gave us a sheet with "The Puppy's Rule of Twelve," encouraging us to expose our dogs to twelve different objects, people, and locations in the coming weeks. In one class, she made us put on funny clothes and carry canes and umbrellas. Another time, to help the pups learn to deal with sudden noises, she intentionally let a metal chair fall to the ground and make a loud clang. Henry and I were especially grateful for this phase of the training, since it would help prepare Scout for all the noise and strange people she would soon encounter in the city.

One of the most useful and gratifying exercises involved the command Leave it, which would later prove essential when Scout picked up something truly yucky on the streets of New York. (It still made us anxious to recall Buddy's uncanny ability to scour the city's sidewalks and find chicken bones, which can lodge in a dog's throat.) The premise was simple enough: Diane instructed us to present our puppies with a low-value treat, such as a piece of kibble or a packaged liver treat. When our dog turned her head toward it, we said "Leave it" and presented a far more appealing, high-value treat, like a bit of chicken. Scout responded to this command on the second or third try, and she got better at it within minutes, despite the tumult all around her. Food was a bigger motivator than we had imagined.

Like Buddy, Scout resisted the command Down, which is supposed to prompt a dog to lie on its belly. (We had better luck with

Off, which we used in the early days to break Scout of her habit of jumping up on people.) When she saw that Scout wasn't responding to Down, Diane suggested that Henry sit on the ground and lure Scout under his knees with a treat. At the moment her belly touched the floor, Henry delivered a click and a treat. This exercise was especially valuable because it illustrated the need for creativity and persistence in the face of the challenges dogs always present.

As we learned more about dog training we realized that, although we had started late with Buddy, we had been wrong to give up on him. This time Henry and I vowed to stay the course, and we even set up a few between-classes sessions with Diane. During one such tutorial, Diane spent an hour with me on the road in front of our house teaching me how to pull Scout along on a leash. Though I was an attentive student, Scout was not. She alternated between nipping at the leash and trying to pull ahead of us when she saw something interesting.

As Diane's classes continued, I found myself, once again, immersed in the early education of a family member. Scout made rapid progress, and at some point I admitted to myself that I was hell-bent for my brilliant pup to earn her American Kennel Club basic puppy manners certificate. As part of a generation obsessed with getting our kids into the right schools, I recognized that I was taking these puppy classes a little too seriously. But when Diane told me, "Scout is trying so hard to be a good dog, and I'm sure she'll get her certificate," parents everywhere would have appreciated the mixture of pride and relief I felt. And luckily for Henry and me, after Scout passed kindergarten, we wouldn't have to worry about her getting into college.

CHAPTER FOUR

Now five months old, Scout was completely housebroken, well socialized with all kinds of dogs and people, and the delight of our lives. Our summer of Scout had been full of stresses, but whenever I took a moment to watch her be a puppy in full — paddling in the waves of Long Island Sound or racing for Louis the Lobster (a favorite toy) so that we could play a morning game of chase — I knew we had been right to bring this loopy bundle of energy and love into our lives. When I wasn't with Scout, I missed her. When she was by my side, I felt happy and connected. A walk with Scout was always a good excuse to get outdoors and get outside of myself. And even though she no longer had the floppy ears and irresistible soft fur common to all very young puppies, I couldn't go anywhere with Scout without being stopped by someone who wanted to inquire about her breed or remark on her gorgeousness.

Goldens are known to be great family dogs because of their sweetness and their love of human company. Buddy had been much more independent. He liked to sleep downstairs, near our front door, and he actually preferred being left alone as long as he could patrol our yard and chase critters away. (Westies were originally bred to hunt rats.) But Scout rarely let us out of her sight and liked to curl up at our feet. Lately we had begun allowing her to sleep outside her crate, and sometimes, in the middle of the night, she bounded upstairs to check if we were still there and to give me a lick on my face. "She's a bigger presence than Buddy was," my sister observed one day. "She's needier and more human-focused than Buddy was."

But we were needy, too. After the departure of our children, Buddy's death, and my accident, our home lives had become a little narrow and thin. A new day didn't always bring a fresh store of energy and excitement, nor did we have anyone to baby or spoil. When Scout arrived, she undoubtedly began taking a lot of emotional cues from us, and she eagerly filled the spaces in our lives that used to be dedicated to our kids and, in recent years, had been filled up by work, going to the gym, and other activities that we each did separately.

Thanks to Scout, Henry and I were doing more together as a couple. We took long walks with her and often planned special outings we knew she would delight in, like hiking on the trails near our house in Connecticut. Henry and I had been together for more than thirty years by the time Scout came into our lives. Both caretakers by nature, we had enjoyed having various members of our extended families and friends of our children live with us for lengthy periods at different points during our long marriage. Bringing into our empty nest another living being to make happy and care for helped put our relationship back on its natural axis.

Scout still attended Marian's pool parties almost every afternoon, and as she grew bigger and more confident in the water the hour at Marian's was usually followed by a visit to the beach. She never tired of dashing into the waves to retrieve sticks or balls. When she swam back to shore carrying her prize in her mouth, her very earnest expression always made us laugh.

More than anything else, she loved swimming into deep water with one of us, though we had to teach her not to scratch us with her front paws. She learned that when we said "Turn" she should swim away from us. She absorbed verbal cues quickly, and I taught her to swim laps in the ocean and stay in her own lane. When I said "Race," she would pick up her pace and almost always beat me across an imaginary finish line. This was terrific exercise for both of us.

But now the waters of Long Island Sound were cooler and summer was coming to an end. September often brings a crush of news, which I love. It gives the *Times* a back-to-school atmosphere after the sometimes quieter days of summer. I was a bit worried, though, that Scout-time would eat too much into my work. Somehow Scout seemed to sense this: in the morning, she patiently allowed me to sit at my computer to check the headlines and drink a cup of coffee. But then she would approach with one of her toys and head to the door, indicating that it was time to go outside and play. She was particularly attached to a toy called Crazy Henrietta, an indestructible rubber chicken wearing a purple and white polka-dotted bikini. With Henrietta in her mouth, Scout was pretty much impossible to resist.

September also meant that it was time to introduce Scout to Manhattan. We had always planned to bring her into the city after Labor Day; besides, Henry was working on a big report that was due at the beginning of October, and he needed to be in New York for the final writing and editing. We knew the transition would be difficult for her. Beyond our house and yard, the only places she had known were Marian's backyard, the farm, and the beach.

We planned to drive with Scout to New York right after Labor Day weekend. On the night of our departure, we invited the Spiros over for an early dinner of Italian sausages in a stew with white beans. This was their first visit to our house since Scout's arrival, and Scout was giddy with excitement when Marian walked in. Henry had to sternly insist that Scout not jump on our older friends, but the Spiros seemed little bothered by Scout's exuberance. When everyone was finally seated in our living room, Scout lay down at Marian's feet.

"I love what you have done with this dog," Marian said as I beamed with pride. Since Marian was so good at relating to dogs, her approval meant everything to me. But I knew the biggest test of Scout's newly acquired puppy manners would come when we sat down to eat. I silently prayed that she would not disrupt our meal with begging or barking.

Amazingly, she was perfectly behaved during dinner. Once again, she lay down obediently near Marian. Nothing, not even the tantalizing aroma of the stew, disrupted her tranquil demeanor.

When we had finished the main course, I cleared the table and left the dishes — including a platter with a few leftover sausages — perched on a counter behind Marian's chair. Just then, Scout stirred, and before I could stop her, she hoisted her front paws onto the counter and, with lightning speed, jumped up and snatched a sausage. To my horror, Marian had witnessed the theft.

"Oh, that is very bad," Marian muttered, but then she couldn't help but giggle. "It's really our fault for putting such temptation within reach and not watching Scout carefully." She looked at Scout and said, "You are trying really hard to be good, baby."

After we said good-bye to the Spiros, Henry and I gathered up a few last things. We had already packed Scout's crate, a large bag of dog food, a pile of toys, food bowls, and other basic dog equipment. As the three of us piled into the car, I felt as if we were getting into a moving van. Happily, Scout seemed perfectly at ease. Except for her homecoming to Connecticut in June, Scout had never been on a long car ride, but she slept for most of the two-hour trip to Manhattan.

While Henry unloaded everything in front of our building, I took Scout for a walk. I hoped she would relieve herself, but she alternated between pulling on her leash to chase leaves and stopping dead on the pavement. I had forgotten how few actual patches of grass there are in downtown Manhattan. Moreover, the trees in front of our building are surrounded by two-foot-high wrought-iron fencing to keep dogs off of them.

Once inside our building, Scout sniffed everything nervously. She was reluctant to go inside the elevator, but we pushed her in. On the fourth floor we led her down the hall to our loft apartment; foolishly, we hadn't made the time to do any proper puppy-proofing or cordon off forbidden areas. As soon as we opened the door, Scout bounded straight for our room and did something she never did in Connecticut: she jumped on our bed.

This wasn't just any bed. It was a Swedish Duxiana bed, certainly the most expensive piece of furniture in our apartment. With its customized spring mattress and down topper, the bed had been a lifesaver after my accident, when finding a comfortable position for sleeping with a shattered left leg proved almost impossible. Everyone, including my doctors, encouraged us to buy the Dux, though initially we resisted such a costly luxury. Now, I watched in silent horror as Scout did something else she had never done: she squatted on the bed and peed, a big "I've been holding it for two hours" pee.

Henry and I rushed to the bed, and fortunately we were able to get the topper off before the lower mattress was saturated. After a rigorous washing by hand, the topper was clean again. By the time we all settled down for sleep, we were exhausted. But the street noise outside our windows rattled Scout, and she had a hard time getting to sleep and staying asleep. Like most puppies, she was frightened by the unfamiliar sounds and the barrage of new smells.

The next day, Henry got little work done at home because he was preoccupied with the effort to anticipate when Scout needed to go outside. Understandably, she hadn't yet learned to go to our door and bark, which is what she did in Connecticut. As a result, he was constantly on high alert, watching for any move Scout made that resembled the beginning of a squat, and often mistaking a sit for something more alarming. It was a little like being a new father again, when he would lie awake listening for his newborn's cry to be fed. By the time I came home from the office late that evening, Henry was crabby and anxious about his deadline. "This isn't working," he said, before shutting himself in our bedroom to do some reading, away from Scout.

I put down my things and looked at her. She was happily dozing, having recently eaten her dinner. I remembered Jane Mayer's wise words: "She wants to please you." If we insisted that Scout spend part of her week in Manhattan, I knew she would eventually learn to like it. Besides, she had learned so much during her three months in Connecticut. But I knew it would be hard for her to be a city girl when she had been such a happy country girl.

Taking a cue from all the movies about girls arriving in the big city for the first time, I decided that it would probably help if Scout met a savvy city friend. She could be the canine version of another one of my favorite blondes, Jean Arthur, who in the film *Easy Living* plays a plucky, working-class gal who follows Ray Milland to the fancy penthouses of New York swells and finds true love and good fortune.

The only handsome guy I knew who lived in an almost-penthouse was Charlie, a tiny black and white Havanese who belonged to my pal and neighbor Ellen Pollock. Although it was already 10 p.m., I called Ellen, who had worked with me for years at the

Wall Street Journal, and convinced her that she and Charlie needed to join us on a late night stroll. Since they lived right across the street on the thirty-fifth floor of an apartment building, they joined us on Greenwich Street not five minutes later. Scout joyously began sniffing Charlie, who was a twentieth of her size.

We walked toward the river and soon passed a neighborhood dog run that Ellen and Charlie frequented. The lights were still on and, since it was a hot night, so was a sprinkler. There was also a wading pool, so even if this wasn't Marian's pretty backyard, I hoped that Scout would find the water familiar and fun. Sure enough, the second I unleashed Scout she ran straight to the water.

While Ellen and I caught up on journalism gossip, Scout and Charlie splashed and played in the water. Their huge size difference didn't seem to get in the way of their bonding, which is almost always true with dogs, and it was after eleven o'clock when we called it quits, humans and dogs alike panting and tired. We all felt a little like teenagers out after curfew. And on the way home, the best thing of all happened: Scout peed curbside. I felt like turning a cartwheel.

■ ■ ■ ■

After a fairly peaceful sleep, I woke up the next morning to a horrifying crime scene. Scout had chosen our red velvet living room couch as her sleeping spot. That was bad enough, but as I passed the couch I saw a little pile of broken glass and what looked like a knot of twisted brown plastic on one of the cushions. Upon inspection, I realized that this debris was the remains of Henry's replacement glasses, the ones he had ordered after Scout destroyed the first pair. They were his only pair of glasses; without them he was pretty much blind. The timing of this disaster couldn't have been worse: I knew that Henry was already about to explode under deadline pressure and frustration with Scout.

I walked into the bedroom to deliver the very bad news. I had rarely seen Henry lose his composure, but after he raced to the living room to survey the damage, I saw my fifty-five-year-old husband lying flat on the floor, pounding the wood, sobbing like a three-year-old. "I will never get my report done," Henry wailed. Scout crept into the adjacent room, seemingly ashamed to be the cause of such human misery.

I knew what my husband needed, besides replacement glasses, was a break from Scout. Ellen had told me that she often sent Charlie to spend the day at a day-care center for dogs in our neighborhood called Biscuits and Bath, so I got the phone number from her and immediately called the place. As long as Scout was six months old and we had proof of her vaccinations, she could come in for the day. Her age wasn't a problem, of course, and fortunately we had brought a copy of her health records with us to New York.

I had never thought about putting a dog in day care. In Buddy's time, when Henry and I both had to travel, either my sister or Jane Mayer usually took care of him. After we moved to Tribeca, when Buddy was being stubborn on his walks, I would sometimes tease him by telling him that I was going to leave him at the Wagging Tail, a day-care and dog-boarding place that we often passed on Greenwich Street. It had a plate-glass window that allowed you to watch the dogs, whose tails were rarely wagging. Most of the forlorn faces pressed near the glass looked worried, as if the dogs doubted they would ever be picked up and taken home.

But this was an emergency. Right after breakfast, I walked Scout over to Biscuits and Bath on Franklin Street. The chain —

which combines unleashed (i.e., no cages) day care with various grooming services — has operated in New York City since 1990 and caters to working New Yorkers with unpredictable hours. Its motto is "Fun, Friends, and Freedom." Behind the reception area there are two large rooms, one for small dogs, the other for bigger ones. Both are padded in bright blue foam. Cheerful dog murals adorn the walls. The only problem for me was the fee, a hefty forty dollars a day. But in truth, I would have paid more so that Henry and I could both do our work that day, away from Scout.

Once inside the door, I decided that I might as well check out the fees for the grooming services. Surprisingly (to me anyway), they are not so different from the fees at human spas nearby: it costs twenty dollars to have dog nails clipped — about the cost of a Manhattan manicure — and sixty dollars for a bath and blow-dry. At those prices, I would stick to our home beautification regime of weekly baths, which Scout disliked but tolerated.

Welcome to New York, I thought, where there is a dog version of every kind of human service. At Paw-tisserie, dog owners can drink coffee with their dogs and buy them frosted biscuits. In our neighborhood, there is a retired restaurateur who prepares freeze-dried meals just for dogs. To me, this anthropomorphized dog world is both fascinating and horrifying. I thought about Temple Grandin's descriptions of her dogs during her childhood and how they roamed freely in a pack throughout the day. Manhattan is as far away from that kind of life as one can imagine.

Happily, Fred Holmes, the manager of Biscuits and Bath, seemed like the nicest kind of person. Scout let him pet her right away and, of course, accepted the biscuit he offered. After signing a few papers, providing a copy of Scout's health records, and forking over my forty dollars, I handed Scout's leash to Fred. As I watched, Fred took her into the small dog room, where her friend Charlie and four other dogs were already playing. Feeling a tad apprehensive and guilty — we had never left Scout with strangers before — I headed for the subway to go to the *Times*.

I called Henry in midmorning and was greatly relieved to hear him sounding chipper. And there was good news, too: the replacement for his replacement glasses would be ready the next day. Henry offered to pick Scout up at Biscuits and Bath; later, he actually showed up a few hours early because he missed her.

By the time I arrived home, Scout was sound asleep. "It seemed like she had a great time," Henry said. "She just played and played." Henry had learned that the dog handlers always take their charges out a couple of times a day, and that Scout had relieved herself outside, not inside. He had also discovered that the rates are lower by the month. "I think I'm going to sign her up for the rest of September," Henry said. "It will give me the hours I need to finish the report." During those first few weeks in Manhattan, Biscuits and Bath was a lifesaver. Scout came to like the place so much that she would pull hard toward its front door the second we rounded Franklin Street.

Only later did I learn that we had almost certainly made a big mistake by not exposing Scout to Manhattan in her earliest weeks. When I consulted Dr. Katherine A. Houpt, the James Law Professor of Behavior Medicine at Cornell University College of Veterinary Medicine, she told me that dogs, like children, learn most easily through early exposure to new experiences. Houpt said that it probably would have been less stressful for Scout to acclimate to all the New York sights and smells if she had made visits to our apartment during her first weeks with us. Young puppies, she explained, are open to just about everything, but an older puppy like Scout can find New York City awfully intimidating.

Luckily, though, Tribeca is an unusually dog-friendly neighborhood. True, it's full of trendy restaurants and expensive boutiques, but it is also filled with lots of young families, many of whom seem to own dogs. In our building, which has eight other lofts, there were three dogs for Scout to meet and potentially befriend. I had already spoken to the owner of a pair of dachshunds who lived on the floor above us, and she was excited about introducing Scout to her dogs.

There are also a number of dog runs within easy walking distance of our apartment. Though Scout was kept very busy at day care, Henry and I wanted to be sure that she got plenty of exercise in the mornings and after I returned from work, so we tried out several different dog parks along the river. Each had a slightly different character and clientele. At one near the boat basin at the World Financial Center, the human regulars were a tight group of friends who said "Good morning" to me and Scout but little else. "Is she a golden?" I would sometimes be asked. But it was hard for the two of us to break into this cliquish scene where almost everyone and their dogs already knew each other. Sometimes Scout would succeed in getting a dog to chase her, but within seconds a third dog would run over and lure Scout's newfound friend away. Once again Scout would be pushed out of the play, and soon she would give up trying to get other dogs to play with her.

This dog run is clean and has a beautiful view of the river, so we kept returning to it. Scout's favorite dog at this park was River, a tiny, five-pound Jack Russell terrier that was everyone's second-favorite dog after their own. As in any pack, there was also a cool crowd of bigger dogs; Scout would sometimes try to barge into their play, but she was usually rejected. Occasionally Scout found a big dog eager to wrestle with her, but just as often she would shy away from the other dogs and sit by my feet near the benches. She had learned her social cues from a small pack of country dogs that saw her every day, often in both the morning and afternoon. Now she was discovering that, with the exception of Charlie, making new city friends wasn't easy.

The virtue of dog runs is that they allow city pups to socialize and run around without a leash. But there are dangers, too. Sometimes dogs are unexpectedly aggressive: tails and ears are bitten, and every once in a while an owner will get hurt by a suddenly out-of-control dog. Because my accident left me a bit unsteady on my feet at times, I was particularly anxious about getting in the way of running dogs. Once we entered the dog park, I usually found a bench and took a seat.

I was also turned off by the snobbishness of some owners, which seemed to rub off on their dogs. Although our building is across the street from a middle-class housing development, the artists who once filled our neighborhood are increasingly being crowded out by richer types. When Scout and I entered a dog run, some of the people already gathered there would continue talking on their cell phones and fail to offer even a cursory greeting.

Five minutes from our apartment we found an antiseptically clean, shiny new dog run that bore every mark of urban planning, with tidy landscaping at both entrances. But for me the park had all the charm of a doctor's office, including owners who often stood or sat in stony silence. Because it's long and skinny, the run is excellent for chasing and retrieving balls, which Scout usually loved. But she had no interest in going there, because it was missing the one thing she wanted: friends.

Finally we discovered that a nicer bunch of people and dogs frequented the smelliest and least scenic dog run in Tribeca, about six blocks from our door. Often strewn with garbage, it was more than a little funky, which was why Henry started calling it "the funky run." The run quickly became Scout's favorite; now, whenever we would walk outside, she would pull hard in its direction.

Located on the same block as the local elementary school, the funky run had been there for decades. A plain, flat asphalt rectangle, it offers human visitors little more than some simple wooden shelters and two ancient park benches. Its big attraction for Scout was a large kiddie pool made of rigid plastic; when the weather was warm, she liked to splash around in the water. The other dogs — mainly mutts but also some other goldens — were much more eager to play with her than the dogs at the other parks we'd tried. When the two of us entered the run, a group of dogs almost always barked a welcome and ran over to greet Scout. At last, she had won acceptance in New York.

The owners visiting these dog runs are mainly people in our cohort, aging baby boomers with dogs — or ABBDs, as Henry and I call them and ourselves. We like many of them, but some are a lot more obsessed with their dogs than we are. They will have loud conversations about the quality of their dog's poop (loose stool is a challenging problem in the city) and debate whether tennis balls are safe for play (apparently, dogs can chew the felt covers off of them and choke). I imagine that most of these owners were equally fretful parents, and that they are now as anxious about their dogs as they used to be about their kids. But I tried not to be too hard on them that fall; after all, I sometimes worried that Henry and I were treating Scout more like a human child than a dog, and that we were becoming just as obsessive as the other ABBDs in our neighborhood.

One morning, during a visit to a dog run near the pier where we parked our car, I ran into Julie Salamon, a former colleague of mine at the *Wall Street Journal* who was writing a biography of the playwright Wendy Wasserstein. Once I started talking with Julie and her husband, Bill Abrams, their dog Maggie — a shepherd-chow-ridgeback mix with, as Julie said, "a little Elizabeth Taylor thrown in" — took an interest in Scout. It was almost as if my friendship with her owners certified Scout as a dog worthy of Maggie's attention.

Julie and Bill were in the same boat as Henry and me. Their last child was about to leave for college and, like us, they had decided to fill their empty nest with a new dog.

"You'd think we would both want the freedom," Bill said. "The truth is, I like having Maggie around. I believe that change is one secret to surviving middle age and an empty nest, and for us getting a dog is a really good change."

All four of us are part of the fastest-growing segment of dog owners, over-fifty empty nesters. Curious to learn more about our cohort, I spoke to Kenneth Budd, executive editor of AARP's magazine. Couples who replace children with dogs are a "definite phenomenon," Budd told me. "People who are empty nesters but ten years away from having grandchildren are saying it's time for a fur baby." He added that baby boomers in their fifties have the urge to "fill the void" for a number of reasons. One is the human need to nurture. Another is our generation's compulsion to stay fit, which matches up well with a puppy's need for exercise.

Julie, Bill, and I agreed that watching a group of dogs interact at a dog park and trying to figure out which dogs are "popular" and which are badly socialized or too aggressive is a fascinating way to pass the morning. We also enjoyed the irony that our dogs had helped socialize us, since here we were reconnecting after being out of touch for a number of years. Meanwhile, Bill regaled me with amusing stories about Maggie's first weeks of puppyhood, when he walked her all over downtown Manhattan. "Supermodels at Cipriani SoHo were suddenly interested in talking to me," Bill said, laughing. I knew exactly what he meant. Scout, too, was a magnet for conversations with strangers, and if I had been single and looking to date, she would have been a great ice-breaker.

By the time Henry met his October deadline, Scout was a kindergarten graduate and beginning to feel at ease in the city. We still spent weekends in Connecticut, but we were thrilled to have her with us in Manhattan during the week. And now that Henry had finished his big project, we no longer needed to send her to Biscuits and Bath every day, though she still spent a day or two a week there.

Henry loved having Scout's company while working in our apartment. For my part, the long walks with Scout in the morning and evening bracketed a pressured day, and they provided a much-needed spiritual antidote to

Scout with her kindergarten graduation medal

the worries that come with the job of being responsible for the *Times*'s news report. No longer did I walk alone through the streets of lower Manhattan, second-guessing the choices I had made for the next day's front page or replaying a tense confrontation with someone who had been the focus of a story and called the managing editor to complain. Although I always carried my cell phone in case the *Times*'s news desk needed to reach me, I felt almost total freedom from worry when I was outside walking Scout. But my delight in Scout went beyond the pure pleasure of companionship or the joyous greeting at the door that all dog owners receive. Watching her chase errant leaves in the city or dig at root vegetables in our garden in Connecticut, I noticed the different phases of fall in ways I hadn't the previous year. Even though I don't love winter, I couldn't wait until Scout experienced snow for the first time.

In late October, two months into Scout's city immersion, I found another urban treat for her. Near our loft is an unusual clinic and day-care center for dogs called Water 4 Dogs, which specializes in hydrotherapy for dogs with ailments or postsurgical problems, but also offers fun swims for healthy dogs for thirty dollars.

A trip to Water 4 Dogs would be a luxury for sure. But since it was now too cold for Scout to swim outside in Connecticut, I figured she must be missing the water terribly. When my children were young, I had often taken them swimming in the winter at our neighborhood YMCA, which had an affordable membership fee. Now I would have to pay more for Scout to swim than I ever had back then. But I was curious, so I called and reserved a place for her on a Tuesday evening.

The person I talked to on the phone told me that dogs could swim alone or with their owners, so when Henry, Scout, and I set off for Water 4 Dogs, I took my bathing suit. Knowing that Scout was used to swimming in backyard pools and the Long Island Sound, I anticipated that she might want company at this unfamiliar city pool.

When we arrived, there was only one other dog in the pool. (The manager told me that the maximum number of dogs allowed for the one-hour swims was four or five, a relief to hear since the prospect of swimming with a pool full of dogs seemed about as appetizing as wading into a baby pool full of diaper-free toddlers.) The water, kept at ninety degrees, felt like a warm bath.

I got in first, and Scout quickly followed

me. Henry — who was delighted that I had volunteered to be the designated swimmer — offered to shoot some video. Scout swam in big circles and enjoyed using a ramp that allowed her to get in and out of the water easily. As well, the sides of the pool had rails on which she could climb and rest between laps. We swam for about half an hour and then availed ourselves of the pool's spalike amenities, including fluffy towels, nice shampoo, and hair dryers. There was a shower for me and hoses with hot and cold water for Scout.

While I showered and dried my hair, the staff gave Scout her own professional blow-dry, which she seemed to have mixed feelings about, since I could hear her barking in protest. The fee — about what I paid for guest privileges to swim at a nearby health club — was too high to make this part of our weekly schedule. But it was fun for a special treat.

At the *Times,* where there is a coterie of devoted dog owners, I learned about yet more special dog services in New York. One of the paper's business reporters told me about a palatial farm outside of Manhattan that offers daily or weekly stays for city dogs, along with pick-up and drop-off car service. (The cost is twenty-six dollars a day, but the transportation to and from the place costs a stiff ninety dollars on top of the daily charge.) Scout and I also checked out a hotel for dogs in SoHo, where there are $115-a-night suites, replete with little beds, turn-down service, and flat-screen TVs. Like so much else for the canine set in New York, this hotel is designed to appeal more to humans than to dogs.

Even so, I understand why so many of Manhattan's dog owners are inclined to pamper their pups. A lot of people work in an office and feel guilty about leaving their dogs alone in their apartments for hours on end, and also for depriving them of their natural longing to be outdoors. Understandably, city owners often worry that urban life is simply too confining for dogs.

Experts differ over whether this is true. Temple Grandin told me in an interview that she isn't a fan of raising and keeping dogs in the city, but she also said that pets are usually fine as long as they got enough exercise. "Besides love," she said, "exercise is by far the most important thing for dogs. If a dog gets enough exercise in the city and is loved by its owner, it can have a good life."

Karen Overall, another animal behaviorist, agreed that a dog owner's most important responsibility is spending time with the pet and giving it plenty of exercise. It is true, she said, that dogs who are cooped up for hours in cramped apartments can acquire behavioral problems and are sometimes prone to obesity. But she also said that many city dogs live happy lives. In fact, Dr. Overall — a professor of psychology and behavior in the Psychiatry Department of the School of Medicine at the University of Pennsylvania — splits her year between city and country, and she has owned dogs for years.

Dr. Overall went on to tell me a bit about her current dog, Maggie, an Australian shepherd who was bred to herd cattle but is perfectly happy in her small apartment in Philadelphia. In the summer, Maggie lives at Big Bend National Park in Texas, where Dr. Overall does research. Maggie loves spending part of the year in Texas, but she is basically happy in either place, as long as she is with her owner. "Whether it's swimming in the Rio Grande and flirting with desert foxes and coyotes, or going to class and defending me from muggers, she wants to be with me because we are a team." Companionship trumps location, Dr. Overall concluded.

At the *Times,* one of my younger colleagues, Gabe Dance, tortured himself over whether to bring his dog to New York after deciding to move here in 2005. The dog, named London, had followed Gabe everywhere, from his childhood home in Colorado to graduate school in North Carolina. Because of his responsibilities in the *Times*'s multimedia department, Gabe knew he would rarely be able to get home before 9 p.m. Right before London's designated moving date, Gabe made the decision he calls "the most painful of my life." He decided to leave London with his parents in Colorado, where she could play outside all day with their other two dogs. "I just thought it was the right decision," Gabe explained, but he misses London fiercely and visits her as often as he can.

I appreciated how hard it was for Gabe to be separated from London, in part because Scout sometimes stayed in Connecticut for extra days with Henry, and these separations were hard on me. When Henry didn't have to see clients in New York, he preferred to split the week between New York (Monday night through Thursday) and Connecticut (Thursday night through Monday). This meant Scout could still be part of the farm crowd in Connecticut and then return to the city and reclaim her place at the funky run, where she now had established friends.

By early November, Scout had been visiting Biscuits and Bath regularly for two months, and one day Fred Holmes sent her home with a report card. "She is where she needs to be," Fred wrote. "She is healthy, happy and interacts well with other dogs. That being said, Scout also has a strong personality and sometimes has more love than she knows what to do with and being a puppy this comes out as goofy, mischievous, silly behavior — all of which is encouraged."

She was, I was not surprised to learn from Fred, the class clown.

CHAPTER FIVE

Whether we were in New York or Connecticut, Scout's morning greeting usually came promptly at 6 a.m. when she arrived at our bedside, her big squeaky duck in her mouth. She often carried something in her mouth when she was excited, and in the mornings she brought the duck as an offering, an invitation for immediate play. Even then, two and a half years after the accident in Times Square, my leg was usually quite stiff first thing in the morning, so left to my own druthers I probably would have wanted to sleep a little later. But over the past few months Scout and I had developed a mutually agreeable morning routine.

I would first sit Indian-style on the bedroom floor for a few minutes while Scout walked in circles around me, duck in mouth and braying with happiness. Then I would try to grab the duck, which, of course, I never managed to snatch away. Once I felt limber enough, I would haul myself up and chase her.

But one morning in November, when she was seven months old, Scout failed to appear on cue. It was a weekday morning in the city, and without my trusty alarm clock I overslept. At about eight o'clock, when Scout finally dragged herself into our bedroom, I could see immediately that something was wrong. Her eyes were glazed and she exhibited no trace of her usual morning playfulness.

A few minutes later, I had to pull her out for a walk when usually she was the one who pulled me. She also had no appetite. That afternoon, when she seemed no better, we decided to take her to the veterinarian near our house in Connecticut, where she had gotten her puppy shots.

The vet took an X-ray to make sure she didn't have some sort of intestinal blockage, and we were instructed to take her home and give her some Pepcid from the drugstore. But even after taking several of the acid-controller tablets, she was still out of sorts. I felt helpless and worried; her droopy gaze and listlessness made it apparent that she was ill, but of course she had no way to communicate what was wrong.

As with a sick infant, a dog's illness can be

especially frustrating to diagnose. Whether in my role as a parent or a dog owner, I had never handled these sorts of medical problems very well. We had taken our children to the emergency room a few times with high fevers or after other mishaps; I recall with particular dismay the time Will got one of Cornelia's long crafting needles stuck in his foot. In these situations, I was always a nervous wreck while Henry remained admirably calm and reassuring. And whenever Buddy was ill and had to be taken to the vet, I was similarly agitated.

As soon as we got back to New York, I took Scout to see our vet in Tribeca, where Buddy had received uniformly good care. The vet ordered a blood test and examined a fecal specimen. The results came back with a double whammy of city and country ailments. Scout had giardia, a common parasite in Manhattan that she could have picked up from feces on the sidewalk or at Biscuits and Bath. She also tested positive for anaplasmosis, a tick-borne illness that she might have caught in our yard or at the farm. Our house in Connecticut is near Lyme, the ground zero for Lyme disease, which is also carried by ticks, and although Scout had been vaccinated for Lyme disease, the vaccine didn't protect her from anaplasmosis. Although we routinely checked Scout for ticks and tried to keep her nose off the ground on Manhattan sidewalks, it was impossible to be perfectly vigilant.

Our vet in Tribeca told me that neither of these infections is serious. But it's important, she said, to complete the full course of treatment, a three-week-long regimen of antibiotics. To ensure that Scout would take the medicine, she suggested we use Greenies, a soft dog treat, to envelop the pills.

Scout perked up considerably in the next few days. But because her infections were potentially contagious, we had to keep her away from other dogs while she was taking the antibiotics. Deprived of her dog pals, she was mopey and glum.

It was a relief to see her healthy again, but then one day, just after finishing her drug regimen, Scout was running to greet her friends at the farm when she suddenly let out a piercing yelp. I dashed over to her; she was breathing heavily and obviously in pain. Henry and I called our vet in Connecticut again and were told to take Scout to a twenty-four-hour emergency pet clinic near New Haven.

Upon arrival, we learned that the clinic's X-ray machine was broken, so we were sent to a second clinic. There, the doctors were unable to diagnose the problem, though one of the vets detected sensitivity in her back. After deciding to give Scout a painkiller and inject intravenous fluids to rehydrate her, the vets asked to keep her overnight for observation.

When we went to say good-bye to Scout before leaving, she was lying down in a cage with an IV needle attached to her right front leg, one area of which had been shaved. She looked terribly forlorn and vulnerable.

As we got into the car for the lonely ride home, Henry said, "Please don't assume the worst." He knew exactly what dark corner I was visiting in my mind. I was thinking about our ordeal with Dinah.

In 1995, three years after we got Buddy, Henry and I began thinking about getting a second dog to keep Buddy company. This idea came to us after my then-boss in the Washington bureau of the *Wall Street Journal,* Alan Murray, told me he wanted to get a puppy for his two young daughters. Intrigued by the notion of getting a Westie, Alan asked me for guidance. One thing led to another, and that summer I returned to the same breeder in Maryland from whom we had purchased Buddy and collected two females from a new litter. Carting home those two white puppies in our minivan, I told my children, then twelve and ten, that we would let Alan's girls, who had never had a dog, pick the puppy they wanted.

When we got home, we put the two little puppies in the yard, introduced them to Buddy, and then awaited the arrival of the Murrays. Meanwhile, unbeknownst to me, Will had fallen head over heels for the smaller of the two pups — apparently she had a vulnerable look that claimed his heart. When the Murrays arrived, the two girls couldn't decide which puppy they preferred, so Cornelia, looking out for her little brother, tried to steer them to the bigger pup. Naturally the Murray girls decided they wanted the smaller one, but at the moment of turnover Cornelia handed them the bigger puppy. Unaware of the switch, they accepted it happily. Will was immensely grateful for his sister's intervention, which Henry and I learned about only after the fact.

We named our new puppy Dinah, but we also gave her the nickname Tiny. She didn't grow as quickly as Buddy had, which began to worry me. In September, at about four months, her back legs began to tremble. A passerby watched her one afternoon that fall as she played in our yard. "Look at her back legs," he called over to me. "They wobble.

You should have that checked out."

I called our wonderful vet, Dr. Kay Young, who had given Dinah her puppy shots but hadn't seen her since. Dr. Young looked concerned as she examined Dinah. She ordered tests and did further research. In particular, she wanted to rule out a rare neurological disease called globoid cell leukodystrophy — also known as Krabbe disease — that is specific to Westies and cairn terriers. She sent Dinah's tests to the University of Pennsylvania's School of Veterinary Medicine, one of the best in the country.

A week later, Dr. Young called me with a devastating diagnosis. Dinah did indeed have Krabbe disease. There is no cure, and most afflicted dogs die within a year. This disease also affects humans, and in infants it's often fatal before age two.

When I got home from work that night, I found it almost impossible to believe that the perky little pup licking my face was likely to be gone in a few months. After a flood of tears, I called the breeder and informed her about Dinah's disease — since both parents have to carry the Krabbe gene for it to be transmitted, I knew she would immediately stop breeding Dinah's parents. Happily, the Murrays' puppy, named Furry, did not exhibit any signs of the disease; as well, she had

Tiny Dinah

already been spayed, so there was no danger of her passing on the gene for Krabbe. As heartbreaking as this situation was, I was glad it was our misfortune and not the Murrays', whose little girls were over the moon about their first dog. After all, we were still blessed with healthy, wonderful Buddy.

Not long after receiving Dinah's diagnosis, I got a phone call from Dr. Mark Haskins, a professor at Penn's School of Veterinary Medicine. Dr. Haskins told me that having a dog with Krabbe would be extremely valuable to his research, because while some Westies and cairns carry the Krabbe gene, it's extremely rare for a living dog to have the actual disease. He also hoped we'd donate Dinah to the large animal colony at Penn's veterinary hospital complex and invited me to come for a visit.

The notion of giving Dinah up was even tougher for our family to absorb than the fact that we would soon be caring for a puppy who would suffer seizures, blindness, deafness, and loss of motor control. We wanted to give her our love, not give her away.

Nonetheless, right after the Thanksgiving break I traveled to Philadelphia to meet Dr. Haskins, a kindly man with a gray beard and mustache. The Penn veterinary facilities are impressive indeed. The animal colony has enough room for dogs to roam free, and there are treatment rooms with little gurneys, some with tiny stirrups, just like human ones but in miniature.

Then Dr. Haskins gave me a stack of newsletters to read. They contained accounts written by the parents of children with Krabbe, and most were accompanied by pictures. The stories documented how this disease ravaged families by robbing children of their early motor development and then causing death. Reading the newsletters was emotionally draining, but it also put our own family's plight in perspective. If Dinah could aid the research of this fatal disorder — if she could help researchers take even a tiny step toward finding treatment for these children — how could we say no?

I asked Dr. Haskins if we could strike a compromise: what if we kept Dinah at home but brought her to Penn, as frequently as he wanted, for testing and observation? He agreed and even said he would help with the commute. For the next eight months, we alternated: sometimes we drove Dinah to Penn; sometimes Dr. Haskins's students or aides drove down to Virginia to pick her up. Usually she returned home in a matter of days. Although some of the tests were painful, Dinah showed no overt signs of suffering, and the people at Penn treated her like a medical celebrity. She remained sweet and playful, a great companion to Buddy and to us.

Several months after the diagnosis, Dinah did lose her eyesight, but her quality of life was still pretty good when she marked her first year. Dr. Haskins was surprised by her relatively stable condition. But a few months later, Dinah's limbs began buckling beneath her, and she started having seizures. When the seizures grew frequent, I was forced to accept the sad fact that it was probably time to end her suffering. I called Dr. Haskins and made arrangements to make one last trip to Philadelphia.

Because Dinah's most valuable contribution to Dr. Haskins's research would come from an autopsy, she needed to be put to sleep at Penn's veterinary hospital. I cried while I drove, but I'd composed myself by the time Dinah and I arrived at the hospital. A group of young doctors came to collect Dinah, and Dr. Haskins sat beside me in the waiting room for more than an hour to comfort me after Dinah had received her lethal injection.

Surprisingly, Buddy did not seem particularly traumatized by the loss of his companion. We wondered if he sensed something was wrong with Dinah and whether it had interfered with the normal bonding between dogs. When I asked our vet, Dr. Young, about this, she said she thought that may have been the case. Either way, Buddy seemed to enjoy being the sole focus of our love and attention once again.

One lesson I took away from the experience with Dinah was that it's very important to have a vigilant vet. Another — which we've learned from our own experience and from talking to many friends who have nursed their dogs through cancer and other chronic illnesses — is that a sick dog is often especially loyal and lovable, and can bring the pack, dog and human, closer together.

While Scout was suffering through her season of ill health, I got back in touch with Dr. Haskins. He remembered Dinah well, not least because she was the oldest dog with Krabbe his team had ever seen. He reported that there had been some new developments in research and treatment of the disease, including a requirement in New York State that every newborn be tested and research conducted on cord blood transplantation. Unfortunately, though, there was still no cure. He wished me luck with Scout and tried to reassure me by saying that most dogs make it through puppyhood with no serious illnesses.

During those weeks when Scout was sick, I did my best to keep my misery to myself around most friends and colleagues. Although some people understand immediately how involved a person can be in caring for a dog, a lot of people just don't get it. If I spoke too honestly, some might think I was crazy to be so distraught over Scout's illness.

Partly to work through my anxiety, I consulted Dr. Ann E. Hohenhaus, a specialist in oncology and internal medicine at the Animal Medical Center in New York. "A sick pet is scary just like a sick baby, because neither can communicate their illness verbally, and both rely on the adults in their life to recognize and respond to the illness," Dr. Hohenhaus said. "Kids and dogs are both so darn cute that we can hardly stand it when they feel bad, but people without kids or dogs aren't always sympathetic to our plight."

Dr. Hohenhaus told me that many owners feel distressed when their pets are sick, especially when the diagnosis is unclear. She also suggested that we think seriously about getting pet health insurance. When Henry and I began comparing various plans, we discovered that, as with insurance for humans, pet insurance programs are complex.

Some are expensive, and it's hard to know for certain what kinds of illnesses and conditions will be covered. Most plans offer tiers of coverage, which grow in price depending on the breadth of coverage, the breed of pet, the location of the owner, and other factors. When comparing the cost of the plans offered by two leading companies, I found that monthly premiums ranged from twelve to forty-five dollars.

Fortunately, Henry and I could manage to pay this cost, whereas many pet owners, of course, cannot afford either pet health insurance or veterinary care for complex health problems. But given Dinah's illness and now this scary experience with Scout, we were both concerned about the possibility of incurring another big out-of-pocket puppy health expense. It didn't help that Scout was, in dog-training parlance, extremely food-motivated. While her chewing had abated somewhat, I worried that her occasionally successful sneak attacks on our laundry basket could result in her swallowing a sock or something else that could cause an intestinal blockage. I had a number of friends whose dogs had suffered through the surgeries that resulted from this sort of problem, so I knew how expensive a blockage could be.

I also had several painful memories of Buddy's health crises. When he was a pup, Buddy got into a box of chocolates that one of our children had carelessly left within reach. (Chocolate is potentially poisonous, especially for smaller dogs.) An expensive nighttime visit to the emergency clinic ensued, during which Buddy had to have his stomach pumped. Then, at midlife, Buddy developed terrible skin allergies, requiring tests and even biopsies, before a change in his diet brought the problem under control. In the end, what we spent on Buddy's health care — as well as on Dinah's more serious problems — likely exceeded the cost of insurance.

When Buddy was alive, however, I hadn't even known pet insurance was available. And although it is growing in popularity, only about 2 percent of dog owners buy insurance. About a dozen companies currently offer pet coverage, including VPI Pet Insurance, which has been offering policies since 1982, and Hartville Group, which has a licensing agreement with the ASPCA. With most policies, the dog owner picks the veterinarian, pays the bill for any health problem, and is reimbursed from the insurance company after deductibles are paid.

But like human insurance, pet insurance

can be hard to get. Sometimes preexisting conditions are not covered, and older dogs with congenital ailments may be rejected for coverage altogether. Sarah Kershaw, a colleague of mine at the *Times*, experienced just that sort of difficulty. About a year ago, her dog, a young shih tzu named Sammy, started shaking, panting, and even biting the dog walker. After absorbing medical expenses of about $1,200, Sarah learned that Sammy had liver disease, one that made it impossible for him to metabolize regular dog food. Worse, the vet told Sarah that Sammy might need a $1,500 operation. Sarah didn't have pet insurance and set about trying to get it. Unfortunately, the company she approached rejected Sammy, saying his liver condition made him ineligible for coverage. "It was not a happy ending," Sarah said, "because he will be four in January, and if this liver disease doesn't shorten his life, that's another ten years at least of potential health problems with no insurance."

In the long run, insurance can not only save an owner money, it can also save a dog's life. During my conversation with Dr. Hohenhaus, she cited cases where dogs with insurance were treated successfully for health problems that otherwise might have been too expensive to solve. Recalling her work with several of these owners, Dr. Hohenhaus said, "We were able to make the decisions based on medicine, not on money." Dr. Hohenhaus is such a believer in pet insurance that she gave her two nieces, both dog owners, pet insurance policies for Christmas one year. Later, when one of the dogs needed surgery for bladder stones, Dr. Hohenhaus received an extra thanks for the gift.

After completing my research, I finally decided that we should get insurance for Scout. Henry agreed, and we ultimately purchased it through the American Kennel Club for about thirty dollars a month.

Henry and I were miserable after leaving Scout overnight at the animal hospital in New Haven. Despite the reassurances I'd been given by Dr. Haskins and others, I couldn't stop worrying. It's true that most puppies never get dangerously ill, but it's also true that most people don't get run over by trucks in Times Square. Nonetheless, this had happened to me, and I'd probably been a little paranoid about medical issues ever since. Henry was attuned to this tendency and knew that even though I had been remarkably healthy in recent years, any encounter with doctors made me extra jittery — and that extended to Scout and vets.

We arrived home that night at 2 a.m., exhausted but too upset to sleep. Later, Henry told me he kept thinking about our friend Clyde Campbell, who had gone to heroic lengths to save his golden retriever, Sunny, from cancer, only to lose her after a year of costly treatment.

At nine the next morning, we were hugely relieved when the vet called to say that Scout had had a good night and seemed stronger. He told us we could visit her later that day.

Scout was mad with happiness when the technicians at the animal hospital escorted her into the examination room to see us. We had brought a ball to entice her to play, and she chased after it and covered us in kisses. She still had the IV in her shaved right front leg, and she looked so vulnerable that I almost cried again. But the sensitivity in her back that the vet had detected the previous night was gone. After a consultation with the doctors, during which they admitted that they weren't sure what was wrong with Scout, we decided to take her home. We left the animal hospital with another course of antibiotics and what the doctors called an "open" diagnosis — as well as a bill for $2,000. The enormous relief we felt compensated for the staggering size of the bill.

As soon as Scout got home, she plopped on the dog bed near our couch and went to sleep. She spent the next day or two taking it easy, and then, on her third day home, she appeared in our room on cue at 6 a.m. The squeaking of her toy duck and, better yet, her joyous braying were the sweetest music we had heard in weeks.

CHAPTER SIX

By December, Scout had entered full-blown puppy adolescence. She was now eight months old, and at more than sixty pounds she was large enough to pull me in any direction. And if she stubbornly planted her rear end on the ground, there was no way I could budge her.

In puppy kindergarten, Diane Abbott had warned us that adolescence could set in as early as six months and that it could provoke epic tensions between dogs and their owners, just as it often does for moody teens and their parents. Earlier that fall, I had occasionally bumped into Diane in Connecticut, and more than once I told her about a recent episode of disobedience and then asked, "How will I know when Scout hits adolescence?" Diane, who usually offered expansive answers to my questions, would merely laugh and roll her eyes. "Don't worry," she'd say. "You'll know."

Most animal behaviorists agree that dog adolescence, like human adolescence, is a period of testing and turmoil during which a dog tries out different ways of proving independence from the pack. The first sign of change is often physical. Just as, years ago, I had noticed the pimples that suddenly appeared on Cornelia's forehead or the deepening of Will's voice, I marked the onset of Scout's adolescence from changes in her appearance. By the end of the summer she looked like a somewhat awkward cross between a puppy and an adult dog. Her snout had become longer, and the hair around her neck, just like Cyon's and Bunny's, had turned curly, reminding me of the frilly neck lace favored by Queen Elizabeth. But Scout was much skinnier than her two older friends, and her back legs still looked ungainly and too long for the rest of her. Looking her over one August morning at the farm, Clyde had said, "She's still filling out."

Over the past two or three months, her behavior had changed, too. Although she still shadowed me wherever I went and was always ready to play, in early fall she began showing an independent, even rebellious streak. At the farm, she struck out on forbidden side paths, delighted when other dogs followed her into the brushy woods where

Adolescent Scout playing with her friend Newton

we could not see them. She knew the location of a few hidden swimming holes, and she would often race off to find them while pretending not to hear me calling her back. (I would quickly stop shouting "Come, Scout," because calling a dog that refuses to come is pointless and only reinforces its recalcitrance.) After a cold dip, she'd saunter back to the pack, looking as though she were wearing black boots because her paws had been dirtied by the brackish water. Occasionally during our visits to the farm Henry and I would force her to walk with a leash to prevent her from wandering off, but her misery over losing her freedom and being kept from her friends was usually too much for either of us to bear. Once free, she would run right back into the prohibited zones.

One weekend toward the end of October I decided to take Scout on a long walk around our neighborhood in Connecticut — but this time I would keep her on her leash, and I vowed that I would correct her each time she pulled. An hour later, my forearm aching and my willpower sorely tested, I let her run free on the beach across from Marian and Howard Spiro's house. Scout was thrilled to be off the leash and had a marvelous time retrieving a stick that I kept throwing in the Sound. By then she was a very strong swimmer, and her boundless hunger for physical exercise never failed to amaze me.

As Scout and I played at the water's edge that afternoon, Henry was just a few houses away participating in one of his last Sunday lawn bowling games of the 2009 season. He caught sight of us down the beach and waved. When Scout spotted Henry, she took off like a rocket and moments later plowed right into the game and began chasing the lawn balls. Miraculously, she did not knock over any of the bowlers, most of whom were in their eighties and had been enjoying their usual round of cocktails during the game. Finally, Henry managed to grab Scout as she flew by. He waited for me to arrive with her leash and then helped me drag her to the car. On the way home, we felt as though we were retrieving a rowdy teenager who had badly misbehaved at a friend's house.

Manhattan, meanwhile, seemed to incite Scout to behave in a particularly headstrong manner. One weeknight when I took Scout for a walk by the river, we approached Locanda Verde, a posh Italian restaurant that had opened on our corner a few months earlier. Although it was fall, the weather was still warm, and the restaurant's outdoor tables were filled with customers. Henry and I had tried the restaurant soon after it opened, if only to sample its signature dish, a garlicky roast chicken that we could sometimes smell from our apartment four floors above.

As Scout and I walked past Locanda Verde's sidewalk tables that evening, I wasn't paying close attention to her. Suddenly I felt a wrenching tug on the leash, and in a flash Scout had jumped up on a table where two gentlemen were sharing a dish of the famous chicken. Though she failed to grab any of their entree, she did succeed in knocking over practically everything on their table. Once I regained control of her, I offered the men profuse apologies. In true New York fashion, they took the disruption in stride and even offered to give Scout a piece of chicken, which I politely refused as I led Scout away. She certainly didn't deserve a reward for the chicken lunge, which I suspected she had long been contemplating.

Despite her rebellious behavior, Scout was still intensely human-focused, much more so than Buddy had been. She wanted to be with us at all times and accompany us no matter where we were going. To prevent the possibility of being left behind, she would sprint into the back of our car at even the slightest hint that we were driving off somewhere.

With her keen sense of smell, she always knew where Henry and I were. At Marian Spiro's suggestion, we had played hide-and-seek with Scout when she was a small puppy, which taught her how to locate us whenever we were out of sight. (We never fooled her, no matter where we hid.) Now, even when exploring the deepest woods on the farm, she could always run and find us within a minute or two.

Much to our relief, her wanton puppy destructiveness had abated, but in the meantime she had acquired some less than charming new habits. She now took particular pleasure in digging deep holes in our yard, where she often buried her toys and the marrow bones she loved to chew. When younger, she had learned to retrieve and return balls and Frisbees; now, this harder-headed Scout would dash after a ball but refuse to return it. Instead, she would grab it tightly in her jaws and then run away, trying to trigger a game of chase, her favorite. Even the best treats, such as chicken livers, were often useless in the effort to persuade her to drop something she coveted and wanted to keep, no matter how persistently we bargained. She would simply bat those sultry eyelashes at me, as if to say, "Catch me if you can."

Besides being headstrong, adolescent dogs,

like teenagers, are often obsessed with sex because of hormonal changes. One of my friends at the farm remarked that "female dogs can get quite flirty" after their first heat. Scout had been spayed at six months, which was part of our agreement with Donna Cutler, the breeder. But male dogs, and even some female ones, humped her anyway.

Scout's frequent declarations of independence were easier to handle in Connecticut because we had a yard and could visit the farm or the beach. But in Manhattan she was always on a leash when she was outdoors, and this led to power struggles almost every time we went for a walk. On the streets of Tribeca, she usually knew exactly where she wanted to go and showed little interest in being led in a different direction. When we passed Charlie's apartment building, if someone happened to be holding the front door open, Scout would pull me right in. If I wanted to walk by the river, she would invariably pull me toward the side street that led to a favorite dog run. And when I approached the local pet store where we bought her toys and treats, she would plant herself at the entrance and refuse to move, even if it was after closing time and the store was shuttered and dark.

By late fall, leashed walks had become

an ordeal. Besides the annoyance and occasional aching shoulder, I worried that Scout's relentless pulling might somehow cause me to reinjure my leg, especially now that the sidewalks near the Hudson River were sometimes icy at night. My biggest fear, though, was that one night she might pull free of her leash altogether, race into the heavy traffic near the river, and get hit by a car.

Sometimes it seemed as if Scout had forgotten just about everything she learned in puppy manners class. My patience running out, I called Diane, who once again confirmed that Scout was simply displaying all the classic symptoms of puppy adolescence. "It can seem as if they never learned simple commands like Come or Sit," Diane said. But just as she had told me that I would know puppy adolescence when I saw it, Diane now reassured me that Scout would eventually outgrow these behaviors and that we would somehow survive.

Because adolescent dogs can forget what they learned as puppies, Diane urged us to go back to the basics of clicker training and once again reinforce Scout's positive behavior by clicking and then rewarding her. She also encouraged us to try one of several

Scout on a leash in New York City (James Estrin)

leashes that are designed to keep dogs under tighter control. At her suggestion, we bought a head harness called the Gentle Leader, which wrapped around Scout's snout and made it almost impossible for her to lunge ahead while we were walking. But Henry and I didn't like it, partly because it looked so much like a muzzle, but mainly because Scout seemed utterly miserable and resistant every time we attached it.

My frustration growing, I wondered if we had dismissed Cesar Millan's stricter training methods too quickly. Maybe we had made a mistake by not teaching Scout to view either Henry or me as the all-powerful alpha pack leader in our family unit. Maybe she would behave if I, like Cesar, demanded more dog obedience. Still, I hesitated to embrace Millan's tactics, because I knew that dogs could be damaged by the command-and-control approach. Even some of Millan's more gentle precepts, such as withholding affection until a dog is calm, seemed both harsh and hard to follow. Every time I saw Scout at the end of a stressful day, I wanted to greet her as enthusiastically as she did me, even if that meant that she sometimes jumped up on me and showered me with her kisses.

When Cornelia and Will were misbehaving adolescents, Henry and I had kept our cool and been relatively permissive. Our house in Virginia became a place for our children and their friends to hang out, and it remained so well into their teen years. This required that Henry and I be extremely vigilant about prohibiting alcohol, and we sometimes confiscated car keys and insisted that one or more of our kids' friends sleep over. Our approach during these years was straightforward: we tried to make our children and their friends feel safely supervised in a house where we applied fair and consistent rules.

But now, with adolescent Scout, we had fallen down on the job. When we were in a hurry to go outside, we would occasionally forget to bring the clicker or the treats that were Scout's rewards for behaving well. When she pulled on the leash, we wouldn't always correct her right away and pull her back to a stance parallel to ours before allowing her to resume walking forward. We knew that, especially during a dog's adolescence, consistency is vital to successful training. But it was easier to let her pull us forward, and too often we allowed her to have her way.

Just before Christmas, Henry and I decided that enough was enough: it was time to become more serious about mastering Diane's training methods. Taking bold action,

Henry volunteered to fly out to California and serve as my eyes and ears at ClickerExpo, a series of well-attended clicker-training sessions led by Karen Pryor, the trainer who had introduced Diane to the positive reinforcement approach. Henry thought about bringing Scout with him — Pryor allowed dogs to attend the sessions with their owners — but that would have been too much of a production. So Scout and I stayed in New York, eagerly awaiting the fruits of Henry's education.

Despite our exposure to Diane's remarkable skills and her endless enthusiasm for clicker training, we hadn't quite grasped the depth of zeal within what Henry came to call Clicker Culture. Its truest adherents regard the clicker method not only as an enlightened way to train dogs but also as a means to a better life. That's a lot to claim for the average dog owner, who just wants to achieve a reliable Sit and Stay and, occasionally, an obedient Come. But having observed a pattern of interaction between Diane and dogs that seemed almost magical, we were eager to know more.

The ClickerExpo took place at the Hyatt Regency hotel in Newport Beach, usually a place to play golf and sit in the sun, not train dogs. Over four hundred people attended, almost all of them pet professionals of one kind or another. Surprisingly, women outnumbered men by a ratio of about 20 to 1, which was consistent with a dramatic demographic shift in the animal-training world since the 1980s.

In California, you can tell a lot about a crowd by the cars in the parking lot. Henry noted that a sturdy gray SUV with personalized plates claiming DOG WIZ stood just a few spaces down from RUFF FUN. Next to LABRADOR was PAWWFCT, while GOODDOGU was parked not far from a stray equestrian, HOSNRDR.

The training sessions and workshops were due to be held in a number of plush conference rooms inside the hotel. A good number of the participants, Henry discovered, had attended a ClickerExpo before. At any given moment, between twenty and forty dogs were present, most of them from midsized breeds and all of them alert and well behaved. A few tiny dogs were rolled about in canine strollers, which were just catching on in Tribeca and rare in Connecticut.

Whether human or canine, all of the attendees were there because of Karen Pryor. A petite woman with sandy hair and an open, kindly face, Pryor had been a scientist and dolphin trainer in Hawaii earlier in life. She developed her theories about the use of positive reinforcement while working with dolphins; as she explained to those attending the expo, a dolphin can't be leashed, whacked, yelled at, or threatened. Since such behavior would cause a dolphin simply to swim away, a trainer has to use rewards to persuade it to deliver a desired performance.

In the 1930s, the pioneering behaviorist B. F. Skinner demonstrated that what he called *operant conditioning* could train a rat to get a food pellet by pressing a lever when a light came on in its cage, and to ignore the lever otherwise. Later, dolphin trainers discovered that captured dolphins were astonishingly quick to learn that certain actions earned a reward. So the underlying principles of clicker training had been established years before — in fact, they could be traced back to Pavlov's use of dinner bells to prompt dogs to salivate even before food was presented to them.

Pryor first made waves in the pet-training world in the mid-1980s when she published *Don't Shoot the Dog!: The New Art of Teaching and Training,* a book that popularized positive reinforcement as an antidote to the coercive, aversion-based training. In the bad old days, training too often relied on yelling at dogs, yanking their leashes and collars, and whacking them with rolled-up newspaper — not to mention using a range of dubious housebreaking practices. Pryor's approach was revolutionary, but for all its scientific underpinnings, her method appealed to many pet lovers because it was humane.

At the heart of Pryor's method is the consistent use of a clicker, which she employs as a tool for communicating a positive response to a particular behavior by a dog. As Pryor explained in her books and at the expo, a clicker's effectiveness goes well beyond the impact of spoken commands or praise. In her view, the technique — which she calls a technology — establishes new neural pathways in a dog's brain. She argues that clickers can prompt long chains of canine behavior that require split-second changes, such as those required in agility tests and other forms of competition.

During the expo's opening session, Pryor decried the popularity of Cesar Millan, asserting that he "legitimized the use of heavy punishment." But she also conceded that Millan's approach had recently become less coercive, and she seemed reluctant to appear too critical of his controversial methods.

Then, after providing brief outlines of the expo's planned workshops, Pryor told the packed Hyatt ballroom, "We are changing civilization, starting in this room."

If that claim seemed overly ambitious, the expo did demonstrate that the clicker method had come a long way over the past couple of decades. In one workshop, a trainer of world-class female gymnasts showed how clickers — or sounds known as TAGs, for Teaching with Acoustical Guidance — helped teach young gymnasts how to land their heels precisely on the balance beam after executing a back flip. In that same session, several special education teachers discussed the use of TAGs to help autistic kids learn to socialize. And clickers were also catching on in zoos, where trainers taught large animals to lie down at the sound of a click. One zookeeper even trained a rhinoceros to recline for routine shots and nail trimming, thus avoiding the need for anesthetic darts.

Pryor's featured speaker at the expo was Victoria Stilwell, the star of Animal Planet's hit TV show *It's Me or the Dog*. Like her program, Stilwell's presentation was upbeat and amusing, and she incorporated a lot of entertaining video from the show. As well, she delivered her talk in an accent perfectly suited for the London stage, which is where she got her start.

As the name of her show suggests, Stilwell, like Millan, often parachutes into fairly desperate family situations. But unlike the pack leader, she never wrestles a dog in order to establish who's boss. The look in her eye, the tone of her voice, and the consistent lessons she teaches families and their dogs are what make her so effective — along with clickers and an avalanche of treats, of course. Perhaps the most revealing moment of her presentation came when she said that 80 percent of dog training depends on the owners and only 20 percent on the dogs; a hundred heads nodded as one.

Scout pined for Henry while he was away in California, and I often found her lying in her bed with one of his socks. When he arrived home, she was overjoyed. Once she calmed down, Henry presented me with some gifts from his trip, including books by Pryor and Stilwell and a new plastic clicker. Over dinner, Henry told me all about the trip, and it was immediately apparent that he had returned from California, as had many others before him, filled with the zeal of the newly converted. His eyes alight, his voice firm with conviction, he made a vow that very evening. "We are going back to Diane's basics," Henry said.

■ ■ ■ ■

Soon after Henry's trip, I had the good fortune to meet Temple Grandin, the subject of a biographical film produced by HBO. I had asked to interview her before a screening of the film in Manhattan, though I worried that conversing with her might prove difficult because of her autism. But within minutes, Grandin put me at ease, and I was soon telling her tales about Scout's sudden transformation from gentle puppy to headstrong adolescent. For Grandin, whose autism gives her remarkable insights into how animals think and react, my story was familiar. But my talk with her meant something special to me in part because she had grown up with golden retrievers, including her beloved Andy, one of the dogs she wrote about in the book *Animals Make Us Human*.

Despite her flamboyant, bright blue satin shirt — which featured an embroidered image of cowboys riding horses — Grandin was understated, plainspoken, and authoritative. Because I thought highly of her books, including her autobiography, *Thinking in Pictures: And Other Reports from My Life with Autism,* I was predisposed to believe her theories about canine behavior and dog training. She, too, rejects many of Cesar

Millan's methods as too punitive. But she does approve of some aspects of his approach to training, and she agrees with Millan that owners need to provide dogs with the equivalent of firm parenting, most especially by placing limits on their behavior.

When I told Grandin about my accident and the injury to my leg, she was quick to say that it was vital that we teach Scout to heel while walking on a leash. She also told me that even with the clicker and abundant treats, teaching a dog to walk on a loose leash is difficult. "What you have to understand is that walking on a leash is not their preferred state," she said. "Dogs need time to roam unleashed, either with humans or, better yet, with other dogs they know." I described our walks with Scout at the farm in Connecticut, which she thought sounded ideal. She told me she is not a fan of urban dog parks, although she conceded that taking a dog to a park is at least preferable to keeping it shut away by itself in an apartment all day.

I asked Grandin about the role that dogs played in her New England childhood, and she described how Andy would spend the day patrolling her neighborhood, exploring the nearby fields and woods, and participating in all the goings-on in town with the

many other dogs who lived in her neighborhood. "That's not how we live anymore
— dogs don't roam around unleashed," she
said. "But the dogs preferred it that way."

She didn't view Scout's rebellious behavior as a serious problem. "It sounds like she
is getting lots of love and exercise, which
are the most important things. I think you
should relax and just enjoy her." It was
simple, commonsense advice, but because
it came from Grandin I felt more resolved
than ever to stick with Scout's training. I
also felt new hope, because talking with her
about goldens and seeing her light up at the
memory of Andy reminded me of how much
fun, love, and happiness Scout had brought
into my life.

With winter came snow, and in Connecticut
great drifts of it now stood right outside our
doorstep. Just as I hoped she would, Scout
adored playing in the snow almost as much
as she liked splashing about in the water.
But when she bounded outside I sometimes
worried that her whiteness would make it
difficult for me to keep her in sight. Years
ago, after a very deep snowfall in Virginia, I
became convinced that Buddy had become
trapped under the snow. I called and called
for him but saw no sign of his frisky little

self. Soon I became frantic, certain that he would be smothered by the piles of snow. I ran to find Henry, who was taking a shower, and begged him to mount a search. Dutifully, Henry donned waterproof waders and boots and began trekking through the more than two feet of snow in our yard in search of Buddy — who, it turned out, had found a dry place in our greenhouse and was taking a peaceful nap. "You always think that Buddy is lost or in danger, and he never is," Henry complained afterward, with some justification. My tendency to blow up ordinary anxieties into life-threatening, worst-case scenarios annoyed Henry, and he often cited the Buddy Smothered in the Snow story to remind me how ridiculous I could be.

By now, though, Scout was too big to become lost in the snow, so I had little reason to worry. On snowy weekends, Scout and I usually met my friend Barbara Pearce and her Lab, Xena, at the farm. Xena was two weeks younger than Scout and about the same size, but she was much wilder. (Barbara used to take Xena running with her, but she had stopped because Xena pulled too much.) While Barbara and I chatted, Scout would lead Xena down the paths into the woods where we could no longer see them. Then, suddenly, they would dart back into our view, snow flying off their coats.

When they were small puppies, Xena was dominant; during their play, Xena would usually end up on top, sometimes with Scout's throat, or at least an ear, in her teeth. But now Scout gave as good as she got, and sometimes she pinned Xena to the ground. The shy puppy of a few months earlier was gone.

Also gone was the omnivorous eater. One cold morning, we put Scout's bowl of kibble and yogurt frosting down for her as usual. She wouldn't take a single bite. At dinner, she repeated the performance.

"Don't worry," Henry reassured me, "she won't starve."

Once again I was reminded of my children. As a teenager, Will had become a fussy eater. He would reject whatever dinner I made and cook a hot dog for himself. I worried that he would get nitrate poisoning, but like many adolescents he seemed to remain healthy and fit no matter what went into his stomach.

Reflecting on Scout's sudden disdain for the food she'd been eating all her life, I decided that she had become bored with the same bland diet. I could understand her reaction: being fed kibble with yogurt day in and day out might get a little tedious. I still yearned, of course, to return to my epicurean days of cooking a plat du jour for Buddy. But Henry was still insisting that we refrain from giving Scout human food at mealtimes, using it only for high-value treats.

Unwilling to allow Scout to go without food, I went to our local pet shop with the notion of purchasing several "natural" brands of kibble to try out on her. They were far more expensive than the Pro Plan we usually bought at Petco, but I thought these so-called better brands might be worth a try. The store generously gave me several samples, so Henry and I decided to conduct a taste test. We put the samples in different bowls, labeled them, and then watched as Scout happily scarfed down all of them. To our discerning eyes, though, she seemed to favor one called California Natural, which claims to be grain-free and thus better for dogs with sensitivities to wheat or corn.

These "natural" kibbles had recently become all the rage, and even Petco planned to unveil a new premium line of "natural" kibble. At the very least, these brands make sense from a marketing point of view, since they can be priced more aggressively and appeal to upscale consumers who themselves prefer eating "natural" or "organic" foods. But some animal nutritionists I respected had expressed doubts about whether they offer real nutritional advantages.

Meanwhile, a number of dog owners had moved beyond the arguments about which purchased foods are best. They passionately espoused cooking for their pups using some of the same foods — such as chicken, fish, sweet potatoes, and green vegetables — that humans eat. (For these owners, there are cookbooks full of dog-friendly recipes.) Scout even had a puppy friend named Newton, also a golden, who was fed only raw food. Henry and I were intrigued enough by the raw diet to give it a try with Scout, but when we purchased the recommended product — a tube of frozen brown matter that included beef lung in the list of ingredients — neither she nor we liked the looks of it.

In the end, the concoction that Scout found tastiest was one I designed myself, a special mixture of Pro Plan and California Natural, laced with a bit of meat and vegetables from our previous night's dinner. Soon Scout was eating again, I was cooking again, and Henry wasn't raising any objections. Everyone was happy.

Right after the new year, I had to go on a business trip to China, and Henry — who wanted to seize the opportunity to see the country for the first time — decided to come with me. This would be our first planned separation from Scout, and since we'd be away for a full week, we were nervous about leaving her. Fortunately, Will and his girlfriend, Lindsey, offered to dog-sit for Scout, in part because they were yearning to get a puppy of their own. I wondered whether they were really up to handling a puppy in full-bore adolescence, and naturally I worried that there might be some terrible mishap while we were away. During the workday, Will would be dropping Scout off at Biscuits and Bath; would he forget to pick her up in the evening? And if Lindsey, who was even smaller than I was, took Scout out for a walk, would Scout drag her into the gutter? I didn't share my fears with Henry, knowing that he would immediately roll out the Buddy Smothered in the Snow story.

The trip went off without a hitch, and while we were in Asia Will sent us several e-mails saying that Scout was fine. I didn't quite trust his cheery reports, though; I expected that upon our return we would hear a few horror stories. But after we walked in the door and basked in a deluge of kisses from Scout, Will and Lindsey assured me that Scout really had behaved extremely well.

The unexpected benefit of our time away

was that it opened Will and Lindsey's eyes to the considerable responsibilities of owning a dog. "Cold reality set in the first morning," Will admitted. He worked in the music industry and was accustomed to staying up late at night and sleeping late in the morning. Lindsey, meanwhile, left for work by 8:30 a.m. and didn't have time to take Scout for a walk before heading out the door. But Scout had her habits and demands too, and at 6:00 each morning there she was, up and ready to play. During that long week with Scout, Will and Lindsey realized that at this point in their lives, their schedules were incompatible with dog ownership. "We don't want a dog less," Will told us, "but we better understand the limitations it puts on your life." Henry and I were glad he and Lindsey learned this lesson now, since too many people buy or adopt a dog on impulse, only to find out later that they can't care for their pet.

As for Scout, she seemed to have enjoyed her time with Will and Lindsey. While Henry and I unpacked, Lindsey proudly urged Scout to demonstrate some new tricks she had taught her, including how to stay in a down position and how to roll over. With Lindsey clicking away, Scout seemed thrilled to show off her newly acquired routines. No longer was she a wide-eyed new pup, but she was still wonderfully teachable and eager for new experiences.

Seeing our beautiful girl again after a week's absence gave Henry and me new confidence that we would indeed get through Scout's adolescence. We had survived Will's adolescence, after all, and now he was a loving and responsible adult. In the weeks and months ahead, we needed to reclaim the patience and grit that had made it possible for us to navigate our children's adolescent years and help them reach their full potential. We owed that to ourselves — and, more important, we owed it to Scout.

CHAPTER SEVEN

Now nine months old, Scout was the whitest golden retriever we had ever encountered — as Henry's sister put it, she was the color of a polar bear. Except for one precious soft spot on the top of her head, her coat was wiry. She was a bit stocky, too, with powerful legs and a solid middle. And her brown eyes and long lashes were still irresistible.

When Henry and I weighed her in January 2010, we were amazed to see that Scout tipped the scales at seventy pounds, ten pounds heavier than Donna Cutler had originally guessed she would weigh. She was close to her adult size, and when we took her for a winter outing to the farm in Connecticut or to the funky run in Manhattan, it was hard to believe that she had once been so tiny that Donna's nickname for her, Cindy Lou, invoked the smallest creature in Dr. Seuss's Whoville.

But though Scout looked all grown up, she

was still in the early stages of adolescence, and suddenly she was gripped by a fear that wouldn't let go. She was scared of German shepherds — all German shepherds, even friends like Viggo.

Viggo, a large, one-year-old shepherd, belonged to our friend Lee Gibson, a warm woman with red hair who had become a big dog lover in her thirties. We often saw Lee and Viggo during our walks at the farm, and when Scout was a young pup she had happily played with Viggo. Now Scout responded very differently. On those winter mornings when Viggo didn't make an appearance at the farm, Scout jumped out of our car and ran ahead of me to greet the other dogs in the Breakfast Club, throwing snow off her fur as she galloped. But if Lee and Viggo were there, Scout stuck by my side, almost cowering. Since Scout was nearly as big as Viggo, I could not figure out why she was suddenly afraid of him.

It wasn't just Viggo. If a German shepherd entered the funky dog run in Tribeca, Scout would instantly become wary; instead of continuing to wrestle with her friends, she would lie underneath the bench where I was sitting. When I tossed a ball for her to retrieve, she would not run after it if a shepherd was nearby. Given the popular-

Scout at nine months (JAMES ESTRIN)

ity of the breed — German shepherds are sturdy working dogs, famous for their work with police forces and as guide dogs for the blind — we ran into them pretty frequently. They were beautiful, intelligent, extremely loyal dogs.

I vividly remembered our first encounter with Lee and Viggo at the farm the previous summer. On a beautiful Sunday morning, I saw Lee working alone with Viggo in a field, teaching him how to retrieve and then relinquish his ball. Since I was trying to get Scout to master the same skill, Scout and I watched them for a while. Lee — who was clearly an expert trainer — used a clicker to mark those times when Viggo brought the ball back and dropped it at her feet.

After about half an hour, Lee introduced herself and suggested that we let the dogs play together. As Viggo and Scout happily chased each other around the field, Lee explained that Viggo would not always be hers. He had been placed with her when he was just eight weeks old, she told me, and for the first year of Viggo's life she would be training him to be a guide dog for the blind. In early 2009, she had volunteered at a non-profit organization called Fidelco, which had matched her with Viggo. The organization, based in Bloomfield, Connecticut, has been training guide dogs for the blind since the 1960s, and at the time Lee volunteered, Fidelco had more than a hundred dogs in foster homes around Connecticut.

There were ten puppies in Viggo's Fidelco litter, all of whom were given names that began with *V*. Fidelco's standards are extremely demanding: not all of the puppies who begin the program ultimately graduate and are matched with a blind person. If Viggo got through the first stage of training, which would end soon after he was fifteen months old, he would return to Fidelco for intensive training. Then, if he passed the final hurdles, he would be placed with a blind person. If Viggo flunked out at any stage of his training, Lee would be given the option to keep him.

Fidelco's rules are strict and Lee added some of her own. She gave Viggo several hours of exercise a day, fed him a special raw diet, and kept him in a crate most of the time he was inside her house. Once a week, Lee and Viggo were required to attend a group class with the other pups in the *V* class. Besides exercise, the most important thing for Viggo to learn was proper socialization with people and other dogs. The farm, with its pack of playful dogs, was a perfect testing ground.

Not long after Lee and I first met, Lee noticed that Viggo would occasionally bully Scout. Lee knew Viggo's every move; she also knew that German shepherds as a breed are protective. Early on she had perceived that Viggo was *dog reactive,* a term she used to describe his intense reaction to unfamiliar dogs. If Viggo saw a dog he didn't know in the distance, his hackles (the hair on the back of his neck) would rise and his ears would prick up. As Lee knew well, these are signs of watchfulness and possible aggression — or, as she put it, "a display to create a barrier."

Viggo's response to strange dogs — Scout included — was hardly unusual, especially for an adolescent male. But Scout was too young to read Viggo's body language, and she did not always respect his barrier. She treated Viggo like everyone else, dog and human, rushing to greet him too impulsively. When she did, Viggo would indicate his displeasure by thrusting himself into Scout's physical space and staring her down. This hostile behavior wasn't at all difficult for Scout to interpret, and long before I did, Lee saw that Viggo's bullying scared Scout quite badly.

Lee worried about Viggo's aggressiveness because he had to be consistently calm and focused in order to be accepted into formal guide-dog training. Viggo could not pull on his leash, as Scout routinely did, whenever anything of interest — a squirrel or a blowing leaf — appeared in his field of vision. After all, a sudden pull could potentially be calamitous for a blind person. Viggo also couldn't act up around new people or around new dogs. Lee knew that, by nature, Viggo was both protective and sweet-tempered, which is why she worried when he suddenly became uncharacteristically aggressive.

Lee was especially bothered, she told me later, by an incident at the farm that had happened before we met her. Viggo had run over to a gentle Lab, stolen the stick in its mouth, and then nipped the Lab. That experience made Lee particularly vigilant when Viggo encountered other dogs. Often, she preferred to walk him alone, on the leash, at a state park a few miles away. But Viggo needed to be almost perfectly socialized if he was going to succeed as a guide dog, so Lee continued to bring him to the farm and monitor his behavior around Scout and the other dogs.

I didn't understand that Viggo was bullying Scout until weeks after their first antagonistic encounters first began occurring. Even then, it took me a while longer to associate

Scout's discomfort around all German shepherds with Viggo. I, like Scout, was only just beginning to learn the skill of interpreting dogs' social cues. Because Buddy had spent most of his time alone, patrolling our yard, I had missed out on the chance to learn about dog manners and socialization. Now, raising Scout and witnessing her behavior in various social situations — including Marian's backyard, the farm, Biscuits and Bath, and the funky dog run — I was learning a lot about how dogs interact.

Meanwhile, Scout's fear of German shepherds continued to grow. In the city, she insisted on performing a thorough inspection of a dog park before entering it. She would stand for a minute or two at the fence enclosing the run, casing the joint to make sure that no shepherds lurked inside. If one appeared with its owner while we were inside the run, she would stop playing and come lie down under my legs. On the outside, she was Scout, a beautiful, nearly full-grown dog. On the inside, though, she was sometimes still Cindy Lou, a born worrier and the littlest resident of Whoville.

All dogs live with some measure of fear, and because puppies are inexperienced in the ways of the canine world, they tend to be especially susceptible to a range of anxieties. In this way, too, they are not unlike children.

Anxiety, whether in dogs or humans, is complicated and interesting, and perhaps because I grew up among a collection of lovable neurotics in New York City, I have long been fascinated by my family's various phobias. My sister Jane, for instance, developed a deep-seated fear of the Babar books when she was a little girl. Where previously the books had been her favorite read-aloud stories, Jane suddenly became fearful of the illustrations of a minor character, the wizened and white-haired Old Lady. Although our mother explained that the Old Lady was a good character who often came to Babar's rescue, my sister was nonetheless petrified of her prune face and long black coat. But since she couldn't bear the thought of putting the books away altogether, Jane instructed Mom to continue reading about Babar's adventures but skip the pages involving the Old Lady. Not only did this on-the-fly editing prove to be a successful work-around; it also may have planted the seed of a future career, since Jane ultimately became a successful children's book author and editor.

But Jane was hardly alone, and I had my own battles with fear when I was a girl. In the third grade, I was mercilessly bullied by a clique of alpha girls in my class. Although only nine years old, they hatched a sophisticated plan for torturing me. Pretending to be twice their age, they called Saks Fifth Avenue and an expensive butcher shop in Manhattan with instructions to deliver a number of items — including fancy clothing and several pounds of extremely costly cuts of meat — to my family's apartment. When my mother started receiving packages addressed to me that she hadn't ordered, she knew something was wrong. And when a succession of little girls phoned our house, asked for me, and then collapsed into giggles before hanging up, she quickly figured out that some of my classmates were playing a mean practical joke at my expense.

It didn't help that the miscreants were ultimately identified, because suddenly I did not want to go to school. I also developed an irrational fear that I was going to be "left back," or not promoted to the next grade, which had happened to a classmate the year before. The mean girls were making me feel like a loser, both socially and intellectually, and though they soon moved to another target, I couldn't keep my eyes off them during recess and lunch, terrified that they might strike again.

Years later, my own children battled phobias of their own. When Will was in first grade, he had trouble adjusting to a new school in Virginia. Though Will and I were close, he wasn't able to admit to me that he was very anxious about this change. Each morning, when I walked Cornelia and Will to the bus stop, Will seemed eager to go to school. But once there he refused to take off his jean jacket. While the other pupils removed their coats and put them in their cubbies, Will insisted on wearing his jacket throughout the day. His teacher Mrs. Larson knew a lot about children and wisely interpreted this as a sign that Will wasn't happy and wanted to be prepared in case he decided to make a sudden getaway.

That September, when I came to her classroom for the ritual parent-teacher meeting, Mrs. Larson mentioned her concern about Will's refusal to take off his jacket. This did not sound like my boy, who had always been so easygoing. After several nights of casual chatting right before he would nod off in bed, I gently broached the topic of his jacket. Out tumbled all his worries: Did the kids in his new class like him? Would he ever have friends to eat with in the lunchroom? Were his sneakers cool enough? I reassured Will that it was normal to feel scared in a new school and that he would make lots of friends, just as he always had. (I also silently reassured myself that when winter arrived his heavier parka would be too warm to wear inside.) Sure enough, Will's fears gradually eased, and a few weeks later Mrs. Larson gave me a call to say that his jacket had come off and his troubles seemed to be over.

In all of these cases, time and a little cleverness were the best antidotes, and so it was with Scout's shepherd phobia. At the funky run, plenty of dogs of other breeds raced to greet Scout when she appeared in the morning. Often she was so busy running or wrestling with one dog or another that she didn't notice when a German shepherd visited the park.

One day, a ten-year-old shepherd named Daisy entered the funky run and soon joined the fray. A few minutes later, she bowed before Scout, inviting her to play. I expected Scout to run in my direction and try to hide, but this time she didn't. The two dogs wrestled, and when Daisy pinned Scout to the ground, Scout made her mock-ferocious wolfie face. They continued playing happily for the next ten minutes, until it was time for us to go.

As we left the run, I took Daisy's owner aside and asked if she would be willing to coordinate her visits to the funky run with ours for a week or two. She graciously agreed, and the next few times Scout encountered Daisy she was always happy to play with her.

Scout's acceptance of Daisy as a playmate proved to be a breakthrough. At the farm, she was no longer intimidated by Viggo. Though they didn't engage each other in play, Viggo stopped bullying her, and Scout stopped cowering at my side whenever he was around. Now, she would rush to her friends even if he was present.

Then, suddenly, Viggo was gone. In late January, a month before Lee was due to deliver Viggo to Fidelco for his final training, Lee's partner, Deb, badly broke her ankle. Lee — who also had a full-time job — could not possibly take care of Deb, give Viggo his two hours of exercise, and go to work every day. Fortunately, Fidelco allowed her to return Viggo a bit early.

Before driving Viggo to Bloomfield, Lee took him on one last walk at the farm. The day was cold, and the only other dogs there were two rambunctious golden-doodles, Ikey and Kaboo. Lee watched as Viggo played with the two dogs in a light, easy way, even sharing his beloved Chuckit ball with them. "I was so proud of him," Lee told me later. It was a testament to her patient training that Viggo had turned out to be a good, social boy after all.

Months after Lee said good-bye to Viggo, I asked her about that last day, but she still had trouble talking about it. At first, she brushed past the subject, but then she admitted that it had been very painful. She wanted Viggo to have his toys with him, but packing them up had been terribly hard. Their parting had been upsetting, too, in part because after arriving at Fidelco she had helped lure Viggo into a crate, one that she thought was too small. And the drive home was simply awful. A couple of hours after our conversation, she sent me an e-mail in which she confessed, "I was too embarrassed to admit that I sobbed on the ride back from Fidelco. Now you are the third person who knows that — the other two are my mom and Deb."

Reflecting on how attached I was to Scout, I found it inconceivable that anyone could give up a dog after pouring so much love and effort into training him or her. But dogs, like people, are happiest when they have a job to do, and Lee was very invested in helping Viggo achieve his purpose in life, which was to be a superb guide dog. However difficult it was to let him go, she was comforted by

Viggo just before returning to Fidelco (LEE GIBSON)

the knowledge that Viggo might soon be providing essential aid to a blind person.

Now that our pup's former nemesis had a serious job, I found myself wondering about Scout's purpose in life. Her current work — to get fully trained and stop pulling on her leash — seemed so trivial compared to what Viggo was doing. But Scout's job, I realized, was hard in its own way. She was struggling to grow up, to make the transition from a wantonly destructive, overenthusiastic puppy to a law-abiding, loyal, and happy dog. Like all major transitions, it wasn't easy.

Part of growing up involved learning new skills. In the front hall of our apartment in New York, which we called "Scout's school," we practiced all of her commands — Sit, Stay, Lie down, and the rest — but we also taught her new tricks like shaking hands with her paw and finding some of her toys by name, like Ball. We used the clicker to compliment her when these moves were well done, and we augmented the clicks with plenty of hugs and pats. She lapped up our attention and practically glowed with pride. Equally important, she craved to learn more.

But Scout was still a puppy, and sometimes she was destructive or just plain naughty. At the farm, she would forget herself and lead other dogs down forbidden paths. More worrisome, she continued to pull on her leash despite our best efforts to train her not to. By February she weighed seventy-five pounds, and now she could pull me right into the gutter, which she too often did if she spied a discarded McDonald's bag or some other irresistible temptation. In fact, just before Henry and I had left on our trip to China, Scout pulled me down and dragged me a few feet along the icy walk by the Hudson River. My lower back hurt enough that I was sure the long plane ride to Beijing would be ruinous; I was so concerned, in fact, that I even kept the news of this disaster from Henry. To my relief, my back was sore but not injured, but the experience delivered a sobering message. Scout was now so strong that she was capable of causing me serious physical harm. And given the residual effects of my accident, I couldn't help but worry about the damage that might occur the next time she pulled me to the pavement.

Far more often, though, I took pleasure in watching Scout behave like a typical adolescent. At my sister's house one day, Scout found a closet full of children's paraphernalia, most of it related to a series of books my sister had written about a character called Fancy Nancy. Among other things stowed in the closet was a little white stuffed dog named Frenchie. One afternoon, Scout broke in and stole her. My sister took the toy and returned it to the closet. On our very next visit, Scout stuck her head in my sister's fireplace and was instantly covered in black soot. Then she made a beeline for the closet and stole Frenchie again. When my sister saw that Frenchie, after being covered with Scout kisses, had become a little gray stuffed dog, she gave up and told Scout she could keep Frenchie for good. Laughing, she said, "I guess you want a baby now that you're big." Scout, seeming to understand that she had won her coveted toy, wagged her tail and kept her sooty jaws firmly clamped on Frenchie's hindquarters.

CHAPTER EIGHT

Not long after Henry and I returned from our trip to China, we decided that we had to do something about Scout's pulling. Even when I carried a sack of her favorite treats and gave her constant rewards for walking parallel to me on a loose leash, she frequently darted sideways or lunged forward at unpredictable moments. Now I had a phobia of my own: I worried that every walk to the funky dog run could end in calamity, with me sprawled on the icy sidewalk or, worse, with both of us lying in the street facing oncoming traffic.

In our use of positive reinforcement to train Scout on her leash, we employed a range of tools and techniques. We continued to use our clicker, which often but not always proved effective. We regularly dipped into the ever-present treat bag, which was stocked with enough meaty, moist, and delectable tidbits to provision a small expedition down the Amazon. We also tried attaching Scout's leash to a harness instead of to her collar, but although this relieved some of the strain on her neck, it did nothing to diminish her power to pull either of us along. Too often it felt like Scout was walking us, not the other way around.

Henry and I were convinced that in the right setting and with enough time and patience, the positive approach to loose-leash training could be highly effective. Neither of us had forgotten Diane Abbott's instruction to reward Scout every time she appeared at our sides in the heel position, and we did our best to be consistent about doing so. But when I was trying to hurry across a busy avenue in front of a flotilla of racing cabs, I could spare little time to entice Scout to forge on or follow my lead.

Scout did her best as well. She learned to sit at red lights when instructed, and then, on the command Let's go, to quickly cross the street. But though she was reasonably well behaved in traffic, whenever we approached the block leading to the funky dog run, she could not control herself. Every morning, the two of us presented the same absurd spectacle: as we approached the run, there was Scout running in front and me trailing behind, holding on for dear life. I felt like I was waterskiing — or, on snowy days, ice-skiing — behind a big golden boat.

Of particular concern was Scout's habit of pulling my arms from their very sockets at the sight of another dog. And there were dogs everywhere: in our building, on the street, walking along the river. Scout was curious about each dog we encountered, whether known to us or not, but if she saw a dog with whom she was especially friendly she would pull to kingdom come. One day that February I realized that Scout, at ten months old, weighed only forty pounds less than I did. No wonder her pulling frightened me so much.

I called Diane Abbott yet again, and she urged us to give the Gentle Leader one more try. But Scout simply wouldn't walk with it on; instead, she would plop down on the narrow and very busy sidewalk in front of our building. Since we live only a few paces from a gigantic apartment building and the downtown offices of Citigroup, our sidewalk is a human highway day and night, so lying down on it is not advised.

After I told Diane that the Gentle Leader wasn't working, she had another idea. Whenever Scout pulled, Diane said, I should stand without moving on the sidewalk. Then I was to divert Scout with a noise, either the clicker or another sound, and pull her back toward me. When she returned to my side, I was to turn and walk with her in the opposite direction for a few paces. Then I should command her to sit and give her a treat, after which I was to turn again and resume walking in the desired direction. At first I was optimistic about this strategy, but I quickly realized that following it required that I budget at least an hour to get anywhere because of Scout's persistent pulling.

More frustrated than ever, I spoke to Lee Gibson, who through Scout's first winter became almost as invested in Scout's training as I was. Lee loaned me a training manual called *My Dog Pulls: What Do I Do?* which was written by Turid Rugaas, a well-known dog trainer from Norway. Rugaas's book, replete with diagrams illustrating the preferred method of correcting a dog that pulls, confirmed Diane's basic principles of stopping, changing direction, and offering a treat before proceeding. But the approach described in the book only underscored how laborious a process this antipulling regimen could be.

As much as I would have liked to follow their advice, both Diane Abbott and Turid Rugaas assumed unlimited time for dog walks and a relatively calm environment in

193

which to take them. But the realities of my life in Manhattan called for other means and methods. I needed time in the morning to read the full *Times* news report, master what the competition had published, and then take the subway to work. All this came on top of making sure that Scout had her walk as well as enough exercise and playtime. If I dutifully followed the Rugaas regimen and was constantly stopping to correct Scout's pulling, I would be hopelessly off schedule. And, frankly, dog owners like Diane Abbott and Lee Gibson were a lot more patient than I was. After weeks and weeks of working to get Scout to stop pulling, I began longing for a surefire cure.

The day of reckoning came when Scout encountered the two dachshunds that lived in our building. They and their owner were standing on a corner across Greenwich Street; when we arrived at the opposite corner, our light for crossing was red. As usual, I commanded Scout to sit while we waited for the light to change. But when the two dachshunds saw Scout and began barking at her, Scout bolted into the street, pulling me behind her. We were both nearly hit by a taxi, which screeched to a halt.

Our close call left me shaken and miserable: Scout could have been killed and I could have been run over again. This time, I didn't keep the incident secret from Henry, and when I told him about it he immediately agreed that we had to take more drastic measures.

That evening I happened to be having dinner with Sam Sifton, the *Times* restaurant critic. One of the perks of my job is occasionally accompanying Sam on visits to a restaurant he plans to review. That night we ate at Maialino, a new Roman-style trattoria that had recently been opened by Danny Meyer, one of the city's best restaurateurs.

Sam, a fellow dog lover, often asked about Scout, and he had particularly enjoyed the story of Scout's petty thievery at Locanda Verde. (After hearing my tale of woe, Sam commented, "At least she has good taste. That chicken is sensational.") Mere minutes after arriving at Maialino, I told him about my harrowing experience on Greenwich Street earlier in the day.

Sam immediately understood the seriousness of my problem. "You need to call in the heavy artillery, pal," he told me sternly. "You need CujoCop." He then handed me a business card for a dog trainer and New York City police officer who had trained bomb-sniffing dogs after 9/11.

Noting that CujoCop's card had an image of a German shepherd on it, I told Sam about Scout's aversion to the breed. "It doesn't matter," Sam said. "Cujo can train any dog and any breed. I know, because Joe — our huge and very ill-behaved mutt — became the perfect dog after an hour with Cujo."

Sam then told me the story of how Cujo had come to the rescue not long after Sam and his wife, Tina, adopted Joe from an animal shelter in Linden, New Jersey. Claire, their younger daughter, "found" him on Petfinder .com, and though the director of the shelter told Sam that Joe was already spoken for, the Siftons decided to drive out to the shelter just to meet him. Joe — who was then two years old and weighed seventy-five pounds — was gentle and calm, and he sniffed at the two girls affectionately. Claire's instinct that he would be a sweetheart seemed correct.

Barely an hour after the Siftons returned to their home in Brooklyn, they got a call from the shelter. Joe was suddenly available again. "It didn't work out," a worker at the shelter told Sam. The man who had the first claim on Joe owned another dog, and when the two dogs were introduced tempers had flared. That same day, the Siftons drove back to New Jersey to collect Joe.

As advertised, Joe was a big, sweet, Lab-related mutt. But he also displayed some wildness: he had a tendency to nip the kids during play and to run hard at Sam or Tina. Sometimes he would jump up as if to bite them, his paws tearing at a loose pant leg or sleeve. Understandably, everyone in the Sifton family found Joe's occasional bad behavior frightening.

The final straw came when Joe attacked a couple of other dogs in the park and then bit a neighbor whom he perceived as a threat. "It was terrifying," Sam said. "We thought we'd have to get rid of him." Tina called the shelter to ask what to do. Someone at the shelter told her they occasionally worked with a trainer named Chris Velez, whose nickname was CujoCop. He'd know what to do, the person at the shelter said.

As it happened, Chris was stationed in the Siftons' Brooklyn precinct. Sam and Tina immediately arranged for Chris to make a home visit, which would involve a one-hour consultation and training session. When Chris arrived, he greeted Joe and then asked Sam and Tina a number of questions. While they talked, Joe sniffed Chris a few times before lying down at his feet. About half an hour later, Chris suggested taking Joe for a walk.

"Incidentally," Chris said as they made for

the door, "you have a great dog. There is absolutely nothing wrong with him. You may have to change your behavior more than he will. He's a good guy."

Over the next few minutes, Chris taught Sam a completely new way to walk Joe. His approach was definitely pack-leaderish, like Cesar Millan's. "You can give him treats and rewards," Chris told Sam. "But someday you're not going to have treats or rewards in your pocket, and then you're gonna be in trouble."

Chris also stressed the need for Joe to have a job: a walk was about doing his business (defecating and peeing), not taking a leisurely stroll. There was to be no stopping to mark trees or greet other dogs. "We walk — that's the job," Chris instructed Sam. Only when Joe was thoroughly exercised and tired would he be released from his job.

Chris spent most of the session training Sam, not Joe. After Chris's initial visit, the Siftons scheduled a few follow-up consultations, and Sam sometimes called Chris with questions or problems. But from that first hour on, Joe's behavior changed. By following Chris's regimen, Sam said, they had brought out the best in Joe, and there had been no alarming incidents in more than a year. "Joe's a happy member of our household now," Sam reported. "That would never have happened without Chris."

As Sam told me the story of how CujoCop had worked wonders with Joe, including stopping his leash pulling, I became convinced that it was time to bring a tougher brand of trainer into our lives. Scout had learned her basic puppy manners in Diane Abbott's class. She had mastered a number of our commands and for the most part responded well to them. Henry and I, meanwhile, had clicked and treated her beyond all reason. Fundamentally, Scout was a good dog who tried very hard to please — except when she was on her leash. So after months of using positive reinforcement to train her to stop pulling, it was time to take a harder line. I would probably never become the calm, assertive pack leader extolled by Cesar Millan, but maybe Chris Velez could get me closer to that ideal.

I called Chris the next morning and spoke to his wife, Darcie. She was sure Chris would want to help with Scout's pulling, but there was a practical problem: Chris was finishing a tour in Iraq in the Army Reserves and wouldn't be back for several weeks. Darcie promised that Scout would be first on Chris's dance card when he returned.

True to his wife's promise, Chris called shortly after he arrived back in the United States. He could fit in an appointment one morning before he returned to work on the police force. Henry and I both arranged our schedules so that we could be there for his introduction to Scout.

Chris, a muscular, balding man with a wide smile, had been a police officer and detective for twenty years. Since 1995, he has trained search-and-rescue dogs for the New York Police Department. He has also long served as a corporal in the U.S. Army Reserves, and in Iraq he has trained dogs to search for explosives. When he came to our apartment that morning, he brought a brochure about his services that included a list of problems that he could mitigate or correct. When I scanned the list, there it was, just what we were looking for: "pulling on leash."

Like many New York cops, Chris has a genial but business-like manner that suggests both a high degree of competence and a quiet confidence that he has seen it all before. His dog-training equipment consists of a leather leash and metal slip collar, sometimes known as a choke chain or choke collar. After a few minutes of preliminary conversation, he explained how to position the slip collar. "It won't choke or hurt her if you use it correctly," Chris promised, seeing my frown at the notion of putting a chain around my puppy's neck. But I had resolved to get tougher — maybe the slip collar would help, I rationalized. Soon, Chris, Scout, Henry, and I all headed outside to test the Cujo magic on the street.

Dog trainers are close observers of people, too, and Chris seemed to sense our anxiety about Scout's difficulties. Before we left the apartment, he complimented Scout's demeanor and behavior, saying, "She doesn't have an aggressive bone in her body." Once outside, we had walked only a few steps when Chris praised our "step off" from the curb into the crosswalk.

It was clear that Chris had great hopes for us, and by the time we reached the river he was encouraging me to give the leash a firm tug, pulling sharply from the waist, every time Scout got a little too far ahead. Henry tried the same technique, and we could both see that the chain collar was definitely helping. Scout seemed to understand what we were trying to teach her even before we returned to our apartment.

Back at home, Chris gave Henry and me a pep talk, encouraging us to continue with the slip collar and firm correction.

Consistency and repetition would be our watchwords, and the use of the collar would remind Scout that we were serious about controlling her.

Over the next few days, we were pleased to note that Chris's instruction had made a difference. Scout pulled less, and we began to trust her more. It helped that we had seen her walk perfectly and obediently, not only with Chris holding the leash but with me holding it. Now we knew she was capable of walking on the leash without misbehaving.

Even so, I could tell that Henry was brooding about the same issue I was. We were both having real trouble letting go of the positive approach; deep down, we still believed it would work. Besides, Scout's job was not to sniff out bombs. Her purpose in life was simply to get her exercise and be a great companion, to share our adventures, and to keep us moving.

Happily, we eventually came up with a method that worked for us and for Scout. By stopping dead in our tracks every time she pulled, we managed to significantly reduce the problem, even when she was wearing her regular collar. True, she still pulled hard when we approached the dog run, but she did that on the chain collar as well.

The slip collar took its place in the Scout

drawer, along with the harness and Gentle Leader. All served as reminders that when yank came to pull, we could take any one of them out and temporarily keep Scout under stricter control. Sometimes Henry's back would ache after moving furniture, and he would use the slip collar. For my part, I would use it in bad weather, when the sidewalks and street were slick and dangerous.

In the end, the truth seemed to be that no single training approach consistently worked for us. We extracted the parts of Chris Velez's prescriptions that made the most sense to us and blended them with some of Diane Abbott's positive-training rules. We also decided that training was fundamentally an issue of trust: as Scout became an integral part of our lives, we needed to trust her, she needed to trust us, and — perhaps most important — we needed to trust ourselves to know how best to raise her.

As spring approached, I was eager to show Chris that Scout had made real progress. As it happened, I had been invited to a promotional event in Manhattan for Swiffer, a line of cleaning products that, among other things, does a good job of collecting dog hair. The event was a cocktail party, humans and dogs invited, at a midtown hotel, and the guest of honor was Cesar Millan, Swiffer's celebrity sponsor. Since I was hoping to interview Millan and I knew Chris admired him, I called Chris and invited him to join Henry, Scout, and me at the party.

The scene was charmingly chaotic. Scout was very excited to see Chris, as well as the dozen other dogs who were "guests" at the soiree. The party's reception area — which led out to the hotel's roof deck — was adorned with oversized martini glasses that had been placed on the floor. The glasses, which were about the size of large dog water bowls, were filled with home-baked dog biscuits in three different flavors.

Scout was indifferent to the celebrity in our midst, but once she discovered what those martini glasses contained and realized that their rims were level with her snout and mouth, she was in heaven. Every time I tried to lead her away from the biscuits, Scout pulled hard on her leash. Observing this struggle, Chris gently took the leash and led Scout away from the dog biscuits. She followed him happily toward the roof deck, where many of the other owners and dogs had already gathered.

Out on the deck was Millan himself, and I walked up to him. Wearing jeans and a diamond earring, he looked relaxed and very

Californian. He was not surrounded by handlers, as many celebrities are, and I found him friendly and eager to talk.

Dog Whisperer, Millan's Friday night TV show on the National Geographic channel, is now in its seventh season and is still one of the most highly rated cable programs. At forty-one, Millan is an industry unto himself, with popular books and other commercial tie-ins to the show. For someone who was born in Mexico and spoke no English when he arrived in this country illegally twenty years ago, he has come far. Now a superstar dog trainer (and a U.S. citizen), he has helped such famous clients as Oprah Winfrey, Nicolas Cage, and Will Smith.

But at this point in his career, Millan is also a man under fire. A growing chorus of critics has assailed his vision of dog owners as assertive pack leaders and labeled his approach to training as too punitive. Some say his techniques — including the alpha roll, which involves forcing a dog to roll on its side — are dangerous and can be psychologically damaging to dogs. (Indeed, his show warns that viewers should not copy his techniques without consulting a professional.) Some respected animal behaviorists, like Temple Grandin, also claim that Millan misunderstands the behavior of wolves and how it applies to dogs.

I had read a lot of the criticism, including an oft-cited op-ed article in the *Times* called "Pack of Lies." And, of course, Diane Abbott had talked to me about why positive reinforcement trainers believe that Millan's pack-leader approach is completely wrong.

When reading Millan's latest book, *Cesar's Rules,* I was surprised to note that he goes out of his way to document his use of positive reinforcement "in one form or another" in two-thirds of his first 140 TV shows. And in defense of his leadership-focused techniques, he points out that his work is mostly with problem dogs. As he puts it in his book, "What I'm doing isn't dog 'training' but dog rehabilitation."

In the book, Millan also cites the influence of Dr. Ian Dunbar, the guru of lure-reward training. Millan tells the story of a session during which his pit bull Junior learned to respond to voice commands (Millan usually prefers to work in silence) and picked up an entirely new command — Down — in the course of a few minutes thanks to the use of rewards. Clearly, the Dog Whisperer is trying to send the message that he has an open mind about methodology. He is also trying to establish credibility with his critics without compromising the training principles that made his reputation.

As Millan and I chatted on the roof deck, I mentioned a number of the criticisms I'd heard about his methods. He didn't seem in any way defensive or offended. "I don't disagree with anyone disagreeing with me," he said. "All the people who disagree with me have never walked with a pack of dogs," he said. Back in California, Millan said he had sixteen pit bulls living at his training facility; even when off-leash, the dogs followed him obediently when he walked around his property. Millan had also trained rottweilers, another difficult breed known for aggression, to follow him without leashes. "Animals do not follow unstable pack leaders," he told me in his calm but assertive tone.

That comment bothered me, but not because I believed he was wrong. I thought about Scout's problem with pulling — maybe she dragged me this way and that because I was an unstable leader.

I described Scout's problem to Millan. His response was sympathetic but direct. "She loves you, but that doesn't mean she will follow you." Continuing, he said, "Too many people say, 'My dog is my baby, my dog is my soul mate.' But we need to honor that a dog is a dog."

These words made supreme sense to me.

The setting for our conversation was more than a little surreal — I'd been to plenty of Manhattan cocktail parties, but never one quite like this — yet Millan was right. Dogs are not our soul mates. They are their own beings.

A moment later, Chris approached us with Scout, and Millan gave her an admiring pat. Then it was time for him to return to the reception area and demonstrate his training techniques to the crowd of thirty or so humans and their dogs.

The Swiffer people had arranged for a passel of six-week-old puppies to serve as Millan's trainees during the demonstration. When the puppies walked to the front of the room with Millan, Scout could not be contained, so Chris led her to the front row where she could see everything. Spotting her and seeing how much she yearned to be part of the performance, Millan invited Scout to join in, even though she was a lot bigger than the tiny pups. He drew our attention to the way the puppies eagerly sniffed Scout, thereby using their sense of smell to judge the newcomer in their midst.

Scout proudly strutted around the puppies and then bowed in front of one of them, inviting it to play. "That is what dogs should do," Millan told the audience. The audience

Henry, Jill, Cesar Millan, Chris Velez, and Scout at the Swiffer event (KEN TARO)

clapped, and Scout seemed to bask in the attention. Then, her moment in the sun over, she followed Chris to the back of the room, where she resumed her hunt for biscuits.

CHAPTER NINE

It is simply breathtaking how much a puppy learns and changes in the first year. Sure, Scout still pulled, but as a full-grown girl she had also become the best kind of companion: empathetic when I'd had a bad day at work, funny and always ready to play, and a good-natured advocate for the beneficial effects of exercise. Now, as the cold weather at last receded and the first forsythia buds began to show themselves in Connecticut and Manhattan, Scout regularly persuaded me to crawl off the couch and go for a good walk.

So much of my experience of Scout's first twelve months reminded me of the years when I was surrounded by small children, a passage I missed more than I admitted to myself. When I walked into our apartment at night, Scout would invariably be waiting for me with a toy in her mouth — usually Louis the Lobster or Crazy Henrietta —

and I would often think of my kids and how attached they were to their playthings. (I was pretty attached to them, too; in fact, Will once told me he suspected that I loved playing with his action figures more than he did.)

As happened with our children, Scout would sometimes appear at our bedside in the middle of the night or near dawn, lonely and needing our company. She would also occasionally bark or become agitated when she heard strange noises, particularly when she was new to Manhattan. And she was especially mischievous early in the morning. If we didn't give her enough attention after waking, she was liable to steal one of my socks or a glove and chew it to pieces. Or if Henry and I were making our bed, she was sure to pick that moment to jump on the bed and mess the covers. Like Cornelia and Will, Scout loved it when we covered her with our sheets and blankets.

But just as children can sometimes be infuriating, Scout's antics would occasionally drive me just short of crazy. One night I had to stay at the office unusually late, but since I knew that Henry was at home working on a report, I wasn't worried about leaving Scout alone. When I got back to our apartment, however, it was immediately apparent that

Henry had failed to keep an eye on our devious pup. There was Henry, hunched over his computer and completely absorbed in his work — and there was Scout, snoozing in the front hall with the wreckage of my favorite cowboy boots nearby. A pair of brown Luccheses, they had been specially ordered from Texas and had turned a wonderful, warm color with age. The boots were one of the only pairs of good leather shoes I could comfortably wear after my unfortunate encounter with the truck; otherwise, my closet was filled with orthopedic flats. Clearly Scout had broken into my closet, stolen one of the boots, and gnawed off its burnished, pointed toe. She must have spent a good deal of time accomplishing this wicked task. Annoyed, I accused Henry of not paying enough attention. "I thought she was just chewing on her bone," Henry explained sheepishly. From that point on, we slid pens through the closet's door handle so Scout could no longer break in and steal my footwear.

As was also true when our kids were little, much of our social life now revolved around our friendships with people who shared our giddy fascination with the newest members of our families. When we got together with Marian and Howard and others like them, a lot of our talk revolved around our pups. (At least we didn't have to immerse ourselves in endless discussion about which grade school Scout could or should go to.) And when we encountered strangers on the street or in a park who also had dogs, we often struck up animated conversations about issues small and large that we inevitably had in common.

Scout, meanwhile, was growing up so quickly that we could barely keep pace with how much she was changing. She no longer feared German shepherds, and she was now relaxed and happy around her dog friends and confident when meeting unfamiliar dogs. She never once displayed a bit of aggression, even when strange dogs suddenly growled at her in Manhattan. She had now reached her adult weight of eighty pounds — twenty more than originally predicted! — but she was still in love with Charlie, the toy Havanese that lived across the street, and she was very careful not to trample him or step on his tiny paws during play. Charlie still invited Scout to chase him and rough-house with him, and Scout continued to steal Charlie's toys and gobble the small rawhide bones that Charlie, with his Lilliputian teeth, would spend months chewing on.

Although Scout was now completely at ease in the city, her happiest times were still in Connecticut when she met her friends

at the farm and romped in the fields without a leash. On the weekends, Scout and I
frequently met up with my friend Barbara
Pearce and her young Lab, Xena, who was
extremely wild as a pup and remained so.
Scout and Xena would tear around the farm
at top speed, swim in the mucky ponds even
when the water was freezing, and wrestle
happily in the mud. After a playdate with
Xena, Scout was always absurdly filthy. I
would look at her dirty face and suddenly
remember the look on my kids' faces after
they'd spent a spring morning playing in the
mud. Never have I seen a lovelier image of
pure happiness.

That March, I spent an afternoon with Lee
Gibson, who had recently received good
news from Fidelco: Viggo had successfully
completed his final course of training. Lee
showed me several pictures of Viggo participating in his classes, which involved
intensive work with professional trainers
who acted out the roles of blind people. He
looked happy and proud, and as Lee showed
me the photos, she did too. Of the ten dogs
in Viggo's litter, he was one of only three
who ultimately passed.

Soon after that visit, I was honored when
Lee invited me to go with her to watch Viggo

complete one of his final training walks. We drove to Hartford and met a director from Fidelco at a downtown street corner. The director instructed us to stand at the curb as Viggo passed by; she also told us not to distract Viggo or try to establish contact with him in any way. Viggo would be walking with the director of Fidelco's foster program and leading her as he would a blind person. He had been trained to walk around the many obstacles presented by a city sidewalk; he had also been taught to listen to the traffic so he would know when to cross the street.

Lee and I waited for a few minutes, and then suddenly there he was, walking beside a tall female trainer. Viggo wore a heavy harness, and he appeared thinner and older than when I had last seen him. He also looked so calm and responsible that it was nearly impossible to believe that this was the same dog that had once bullied our little pup.

Lee and I watched as Viggo carefully led the trainer around a tree that was almost directly in their path. Then, at the entrance to the old G. Fox department store, Viggo led the trainer through a revolving door, something I couldn't imagine Scout mastering. Only once, when they passed a group of pigeons, did the trainer have to correct Viggo. For a split second, he seemed about to lunge at the birds, but the trainer brought him immediately back into line. Scout, of course, would have ripped out my arm to get to the pigeons.

After the training walk, Lee was allowed to visit with Viggo for an hour. I gave her one of Scout's favorite balls to pass on to Viggo, but Lee was clearly anxious about having to say good-bye to him all over again. Still, we were both amazed to think that the hapless pup that she had begun working with a little more than a year ago was about to become an actual guide dog for the blind. The hundreds of hours that Lee had spent training and socializing Viggo had paid off.

As I drove home that day, I reminded myself that if Viggo could learn so much in a relatively short time, Scout too could eventually learn not to pull and even not to eat cowboy boots. But Henry and I would have to rededicate ourselves to training her, spend many more hours working with her, and give her plenty of attention and love along the way. In the coming months, we would undoubtedly see as much backsliding as progress; we would also, I was sure, experience surprises both bad and good. But if Chris Velez could train dogs to sniff bombs and Lee could train Viggo to work as a guide dog, we could do our part for Scout. We would do it not because Scout would be working in the real world, but because we knew she wanted to learn how to master the job of being a very good dog.

As Scout approached her first birthday, Henry and I were eager to take her back to Thistledown and show her off to Donna Cutler, the breeder. We also wanted Scout to have a reunion with her mother, Tess, and the rest of her relatives. Partly we wanted to see if Scout shared any of her blood family's physical and personality characteristics, but we were also curious to learn whether, as we had read in some books, the mother-puppy bond remained strong even after separation.

We made the necessary arrangements with Donna, but when the day for the reunion came I was unable to go. Disappointed, I insisted that Henry bring back a full report, and when he returned from Thistledown he gave me a detailed description of the visit, which began when he once again followed instructions and carefully wiped his paws before entering Donna's house, with Scout right behind him.

Scout greeted Donna enthusiastically and eagerly accepted her admiring pats, but she

Donna Cutler introducing Scout to her ancestors

did not seem to remember Donna. Henry and Scout followed Donna outside to the wire-fenced dog pen, where more than half a dozen beautiful British goldens were lounging about. At the sight of Donna and Scout, they got to their feet, moved briskly to the gate, and gave off a mighty homecoming howl, making Scout feel wonderfully welcome. But would she know or get along with her relatives, especially her mother?

First Donna brought out Tess, Scout's gorgeous, one-eyed mother. They greeted each other the way two dog acquaintances would; there was no great joy, just a little sniff, and then Scout wanted to play. But Tess declined the invitation and soon displayed more interest in Donna than in her offspring. So much for the theory that female dogs remain attached to their pups!

Such a cool hello from a birth mother might have been devastating to a human, but mother dogs often become somewhat detached from their puppies after weaning. Interestingly, this may be an evolutionary response brought about by millennia of contact with humans, who usually take over the care of puppies when they're still quite young. (That's what a number of scientists suggest, anyway. Given that a new mother has as many as ten pups feeding off her day and night, I think Momma may just need a break!)

Next came Scout's grandmother, who Henry thought actually looked more like Scout than Tess did. The two dogs immediately took off and began running in circles, which delighted Scout. After a few minutes of play, out came great-grandmother, who greeted Scout with just a sniff or two. Then it was time for a group photograph of the maternal line going back four generations. Looking at this remarkable collection of beauties, Henry felt a little sad to think that Scout couldn't continue the line, but that was our choice, and Donna's rule, from the beginning.

Scout's father — a famous Austrian golden named Patrick — no longer lived with Donna; he had moved to New Hampshire. But to end the procession of relatives, Donna brought out Scout's grandfather, who was much larger than any of the females but still a calm fellow and very handsome to boot. As Henry took a few group photos, he and Donna agreed that it was this big guy whom Scout most resembled.

Once the dogs were put back in their pen, Donna remarked that she thought Scout's temperament was excellent. She also said that Scout could be a good candidate for

Scout (left) with her ancestors

advanced training, which might include retrieving ducks from the water. As it happened, Donna had kept the last of Scout's littermates, Johnnie, and he had become a field champion, winning blue ribbons in a competition in Canada. Donna showed Henry the two ducks she kept in her freezer for Johnnie's practice sessions, but in the end he politely declined her offer to allow Scout a little taste of the wild.

As for the physical conformation that set the benchmark for judging the shows in which Donna's dogs often competed, Donna said that Scout was a bit high in the back, and her feet were a little "eastie-westie," or too far turned out. Otherwise, Donna declared that her little Cindy Lou had grown up to be a very pretty girl. She was happy to hear that we had worked so hard to train her, and that we were using a clicker and mostly following the precepts of the positive method.

After saying good-bye to Donna, Henry packed Scout into the car. From what he could tell, this reunion with her blood family had meant no more to Scout than any other visit with a human who owned dogs. She slept most of the way back to our house in Connecticut, which is exactly what she had done during that first trip home as a new pup. But the road we had traveled since then was a lot longer than the 125 miles that separated Donna's house from ours.

Donna's expert assessment of Scout's appearance may have quashed any lingering thoughts about entering Scout in high-powered competitions, but it didn't prevent us from entering her in an annual event in our Connecticut town called the Parade of Pooches. The show takes place on our town green and is a completely unofficial, just-for-fun competition. It only resembles the real Westminster show — held each year at Madison Square Garden and the pinnacle of U.S. dog shows — in that the dogs are judged by breed and given awards. And there is no Best in Show award, the crown jewel of Westminster and the title of the very funny Christopher Guest movie that spoofs the affair.

In February, I had attended the real Westminster Kennel Club Dog Show, which was established in 1877 and is the second-longest continuously held sporting event in the United States. Henry and I have always been fans of the show, which is broadcast on cable television each year. We especially love it when the handlers — who invariably dress in starchy British clothes — look like the dogs they are showing. In the past, we had often watched the show with Buddy wedged between us on our bed. This year, even though I had tickets, Henry preferred to watch the show with Scout from home, so I went with a friend.

To my eye, the show seemed pretty true to the movie (or perhaps vice versa), complete with stressed-out owners madly blow-drying their dog's fur in the so-called benching area off the floor where the judging rings were. To assist the reporters covering the show, the show's organizers provided hourly briefings on the dogs — more than 2,500 of them — who were the stars of the competition. Meanwhile, journalists were invited to sessions with representatives from all of the major pet supply and pet food companies, all of whom were frantically trying to attract media coverage for their latest products. (Pedigree, a major sponsor of the show, tried unsuccessfully to persuade me to attend a tutorial on its latest, supposedly healthier brand of dry food.)

As with most aspects of dog life, the Westminster show has become a combat zone. Not only are the owners fiercely competitive, but in recent years a conflict has broken out between the American Kennel Club — the primary registry of purebred dog pedigrees in the United States and a promoter of the show — and its numerous critics. These critics argue that by putting a premium on dogs' appearances, the AKC encourages unhealthy breeding techniques, such as mating two dogs with champion traits who are too closely related. The critics also claim that other characteristics — a dog's instinct for performing a specific sort of work, for instance — are not prized sufficiently. Recently some owners have gone so far as to boycott the AKC and the Westminster show.

I timed my visit to the show so that I could see the Best in Breed judging of the golden retrievers. (All the competing goldens, of which there were several dozen, were the much deeper, honey color that is the classic standard for the breed.) My first stop was the benching area backstage, where giant poodles in hair curlers and other dogs of just about every breed primped for their moment in the ring. Next I moved up to the stands and took a seat near a number of the owners' families, some of whom had traveled from as far as California and had been competing in dog shows every weekend for the past year.

When it came time for the goldens to compete, I watched the dogs and their handlers with particular interest. The male and female dogs were judged separately, and all were put through their paces briskly and without a lot of obvious grandstanding. I couldn't help but notice that not a single one of the dogs pulled when their handlers strutted before the judges. Inevitably, perhaps, I tried to imagine Scout joining the goldens vying for a prize, but I got no farther than conjuring a vision of Scout wildly pulling me past the judges and right out of the Garden.

I enjoyed my visit to the Westminster show, and it made me look forward to our show in Connecticut. Diane Abbott, who would serve as one of the judges, assured me that it was nothing like the extravaganza in New York; she also convinced me that Scout would enjoy it and that it was impossible to be disgraced. Diane told me that just about every dog won a ribbon, which put me in mind of those long-ago days when Cornelia and Will, like almost every other child, had come home at the end of the school year with some kind of trophy.

The morning of the show, Scout was excited by our vigorous brushing of her fur, and I even brushed her teeth for the occasion. As we approached our town's green, she began pulling with nearly all her strength when she saw the great number of dogs gathering there. And she was ecstatic when she saw

Diane, who promptly gave her a dog biscuit from the registration table.

About a dozen other dogs had been entered in the golden retriever category, but Scout was the only platinum blonde. Scout was thrilled to be measured and assessed by the volunteer judges, and she gave her competitors a good sniff, as if to size them up. When one of the judges passed us, he looked at Scout and said, "Oh, she's a beauty." Helpless with pride, I beamed.

At the real Westminster show, dogs perform for the judges in four separate rings simultaneously. Here, the breeds are judged in sequence as they walk around our makeshift ring. This year, the goldens didn't get their chance until near the end, and soon Scout became restless, barking and pulling. Diane came over to distract her and play, and finally it was our turn to walk in a circle in front of the judges.

I led Scout on the walk. She proudly strutted as we moved around the ring — and to my amazement she didn't pull on her leash. I was absurdly grateful for this reprieve, and the experience brought back vivid memories of watching my children in school musical productions. Listening to them rehearse was often painful, but their performances, even when my heart was in my throat, were usu-

Scout at the Parade of Pooches show

ally splendid.

When the results of the Best in Breed competition were announced, we were thrilled. When judged against her fellow goldens, Scout won a coveted blue ribbon for having "the longest ears" — a category, needless to say, that isn't included at the real Westminster show. I had never noticed that Scout's ears were longer than any other golden's, but we would take victory however it came. When the show was over, we packed Scout and her ribbon into the back of our car; when we got home, we looked for the ribbon but found only a few telltale bits of shiny blue thread. She had eaten it.

Scout's actual birthday was April 9. Henry and I agreed that there was no question about the appropriate venue for our celebration: the farm. Fortunately, the weather that day was perfect, still brisk but brilliantly sunny. In a few weeks, the gardeners would be back at the farm tending their bulbs, vegetables, and herbs, and we would have to make the garden areas off-limits again. But for now, Scout and her pals still had the run of the place.

We had told other Breakfast Club walkers about Scout's big day, and we also called Barbara Pearce and asked her to bring her

Lab, Xena, who was almost exactly Scout's age. Henry, Scout, and I arrived a bit early, and Barbara pulled in a few minutes later. Scout got excited the moment she caught sight of Barbara's car, and when the car came to a stop I let her bound over to greet Xena. They immediately began wrestling and running after each other, and Barbara, Henry, and I laughed as we watched their joyous reunion. We took photographs, too, but Scout and Xena moved so quickly that it was almost impossible to get a decent picture.

Barbara and I marveled over how far both of our dogs had come since first meeting in Marian's backyard as tiny, teething pups. Less than a year ago, they were little bundles of fur falling over their own paws as they chased each other. And it was at Marian's that Scout had first experienced the pleasures of water when she splashed about in a plastic baby pool, one that was now far too small to hold her.

Soon Marian and Clyde arrived with Cyon and Bunny, Scout's truest and most constant companions. Scout was so busy chasing Xena that at first she barely took time out to say hello to her old friends. But I was pleasantly surprised when Scout and Xena responded to my call, stopped run-

Scout, Xena, and the birthday cookie

ning around, and then sat obediently while waiting for me to share a treat with them. To mark Scout's birthday, I had purchased a yogurt-frosted, heart-shaped dog cookie from the local pet store. I split the cookie in half, and in no time the two dogs wolfed it down.

A few minutes later, Lee Gibson pulled into the farm's parking lot. I was eager for Lee to join Scout's birthday celebration because she had been so helpful with Scout's training.

As Lee approached us, I saw something moving at her heel. For a second I thought a rabbit was walking next to her, but then I realized that it was actually a brand-new puppy. It was another German shepherd, but he was so young that he was all ears and paws. Lee told us that his name was Caleb, and that this one was hers to keep.

As I gave Lee a hug and said hello, I saw that she had circles under her eyes. I also noticed that she was a bit wary when Scout and Xena, now such big girls, raced over to sniff Caleb and check out the new kid on the block. This was me a year ago, bone-tired and worrying over every new experience that came Scout's way.

Now, as Scout approached Caleb, she made a gentle bow, her front paws sticking

Caleb the puppy

out in front of her. It was a dog's invitation to play, a universal gesture that is performed countless times each day all over the world. And as Caleb accepted the invitation and cavorted with Scout, the cycle began anew.

EPILOGUE

When I turned fifty, my friend Jane Mayer gave me the perfect gift. Jane works for the *New Yorker,* and in the magazine's archives she found a photograph of one of my favorite writers, E. B. White, taken at his classic Maine farmhouse. White, then almost eighty, was cradling Susy, his beloved Westie, one of the last in a long line of devoted canine companions. Buddy was still very much alive when I received that photo, and it delighted me to know that the Westie breed connected me to the author of *Charlotte's Web* and some of journalism's finest essays. In one of those essays, in fact, White dispensed the wisest comment about raising a puppy I have ever come across: "A really companionable and indispensable dog is an accident of nature. You can't get it by breeding for it, and you can't buy it with money. It just happens along."

When Scout came into my life, an indispensable dog did just happen along. It wasn't the clickers or puppy kindergarten or feeding her the right meals that made her such a fine companion. More than anything else, it was the passage of time, and the inevitable calming process that occurred as Scout aged. Almost as important was the change in Henry and me: we came to understand that everything we do is more fun and interesting when Scout is by our side.

Whether contentedly snoozing while we watch UConn's basketball team snatch a victory from Arizona, or sniffing at some daffodils as they poke out of the hard winter soil near the Hudson River, Scout has become essential to our daily lives. Moreover, what we choose to do with an hour or an afternoon often mirrors what she most enjoys. When she wants to engage in a game of chase or keep-away or go for a brisk walk, so do we. And no matter what we do, Scout's fundamental sweetness and exuberance make the experience joyful. She is almost always in a state of delight, unlike so much of the world that I help capture each day for readers of the *New York Times*.

Which is not to say that Scout doesn't have an occasional bad moment or misbehave. Every once in a while, for instance, her face will appear above the table line with a hopeful expression. And she still pulls on her leash, though not as savagely. But she has long since conquered her fear of German shepherds, and not long ago she picked Caleb as her favorite walking companion. The happy accidents of nature continue.

Looking back on our first year with Scout, I am amazed by how quickly it passed. The experience of bringing this whirlwind of untamed energy into our lives was so intense and involving that I sometimes felt as if the puppy months would kill us. Like most owners, we worried about everything, from Scout's constant chewing to her fussy eating to her sudden illness. Then, in the blink of an eye, she was fully grown and fully attached to us. And just as our love for her grew to be almost boundless, she became unfailingly loyal and perceptive about our needs and desires.

This almost ineffable transference fascinated me from the start, and it was the main reason I decided to chronicle Scout's first year. I knew that Henry and I enjoyed nearly ideal circumstances, with the time, space, and means to dote on a dog. But as one half of a two-career couple in late middle age, I also knew that some of the stresses we were feeling as new puppy owners were universal, as was the humor inherent in the experience. After all, no matter who you are or what you do for a living, it is invariably humbling to try to persuade a puppy to do your bidding.

Even before Scout arrived, I thought it might be fun to share some of my experiences and draw on the response of the *Times*'s readers. I did so by writing a series of columns for the newspaper's Web site. My hope was that those who followed the column would become engaged by our imperfect efforts to raise a puppy and offer copious advice, which they did. I also asked readers to send in photos of their own pups, an invitation that attracted such an avalanche of snapshots that at one point the paper's Web site crashed.

Because I have dedicated much of my career in journalism to editing and writing serious investigative stories, some of my readers — and a few of my friends as well — found it strange that I was publicly sharing my nervousness over Scout's first day of puppy kindergarten or my persistent sadness over the loss of Buddy. But as I continued writing the column and providing updates on Scout's adventures, I found a natural story emerging, one that connected me to plenty of other *Times* readers who, like me, were simply crazy about their dogs.

■■■■

Almost from the beginning, Scout seemed to accept that my demanding job meant she would rarely receive my undivided attention. She learned, for instance, that although weekend mornings were an apparently languid time, they were in fact dedicated to a longer and even closer reading of the *Times,* page by page and section by section. Though this ritual required that she wait until later than usual to go to the farm or the dog run, she was never impatient. Reflecting on this one day, I realized that Scout didn't need me to spend all my time focused on her. Instead, what she most wanted was my unwavering love.

This, I came to understand, was my test. During her first year with us, Scout had passed *her* test: she had learned how to be a good dog and become a loving companion. But as her second year with us began, I was keeping a guilty secret, which was that sometimes I still longed for Buddy. The essential question remained: could I ever give my whole heart to Scout?

A first, partial answer came in the summer of 2010. More than three years had passed since my terrible accident in Times Square, and I had almost fully recovered from my injuries. I felt so confident that I could meet just about any physical challenge — or at least any challenge appropriate for a woman my age — that I decided to take a break from Scout and accompany Henry and his sister, Elisabeth, on a trip to Yellowstone National Park. Elisabeth loved to hike, and I persuaded her to tackle some fairly demanding trails with Henry, a guide, and me.

We enjoyed three days of excellent hiking, but on the last day of our visit, Henry was suffering from altitude sickness and so decided to take it easy. Still game, Elisabeth and I got our guide, Jeff, to take us on a climb to Specimen Ridge, one of the most scenic places in the park. The hike was about seven miles up and back, which would be difficult but not beyond my capacity — or so I thought.

Jeff was a bit worried that we might come across one or more bears, especially since two people had died earlier in the summer after a horrifying encounter with grizzlies. He reassured us by bringing along some bear spray, and the climb up the ridge proved to be no problem. Near the top, we passed a stunningly beautiful family of elks, and when we reached the summit I lay flat on the ground and looked up at the sun. "I can die happy now," I said to Jeff.

Famous last words. About halfway down the mountain, I slipped on scree and tumbled a hundred feet down a steep slope. My head must have hit something in the fall, and I was knocked unconscious. Elisabeth, with bear spray in hand, slid down to me while Jeff ran for help, which arrived in about twenty-five minutes. By then I was conscious, but my face was a mass of cuts and bruises, my left arm was broken in two places, and one of my vertebrae was cracked. I had to be airlifted to a hospital in Bozeman, Montana, where surgeons, once again, reassembled my bones with titanium.

I felt like a total idiot, although my doctors assured me that such falls are fairly common in the park. When they finally cleared me to fly back to New York, Henry and I both worried that our exuberant puppy would jump on me and reinjure my arm and back. But we had both missed Scout terribly on our longer-than-expected trip, and I couldn't wait to see her, whatever the risk.

When Henry opened our front door, Scout didn't bound over to us. She didn't even have a toy in her mouth. Happily and calmly, she came to greet us and then waited for Henry and me to hug and pat her. When I sat down on our living room couch, she immediately lay at my feet. She stayed there for hours and got up only to follow me to the kitchen or bathroom.

For the next week, that was our routine. I was the patient on pain medication, but Scout behaved as if she were on Valium. She was curious about the brace and bandage on my arm, but she never even jostled me. Other than going for walks with Henry, Cornelia, or Will, she spent all her energy protecting and guarding me. Whenever I set myself up on the couch, she would lie down a couple of feet away. When I moved to our bedroom, she would take up a position at the foot of the bed.

During my convalescence, Scout's breathing and the sight of her white back rising and falling made me feel cozy and safe. About ten days after returning home, I was at last well enough to take her out for a walk. This time, there was absolutely no pulling. Scout seemed to know that I needed her to behave, and she rose to the occasion valiantly. I have no doubt that I recovered from these new injuries more quickly because of her.

I had never felt closer to Scout than after my accident in Yellowstone, and that remained true throughout the fall. I won't say that I stopped thinking about Buddy altogether, but Scout proved to be such a loving and generous companion that my attachment to her grew even stronger.

That Christmas we were buried in snow, as one of the hardest winters in history descended on New York and Connecticut. Then Henry left for California on a business trip, leaving Scout and me alone in our apartment. Within a day or two, we developed a bad case of cabin fever and so decided to go on an extended walk.

It was a freezing Sunday — the temperature was below ten degrees — but at least the sun was shining. Since the funky dog run was iced over and grimy, I didn't want to begin our walk by taking Scout there. Instead, I attached her leash and we began walking uptown.

One of Buddy's favorite places in New York City was Washington Square Park, with its famous archway and two dog runs, one reserved for small dogs weighing less than twenty-five pounds and another for larger breeds. At twenty-two pounds, Buddy was the big man on campus in the park's small run, and he loved strutting around the place as if he owned it. But the park was about a mile and a half from our loft, so taking Buddy there required extra time and energy. In fact, when we visited the park near the end of his life, I often had to carry

Buddy part of the way home because he was dragging and wheezing so badly.

For some reason — actually, I knew the reason all too well — I hadn't been back to the Washington Square dog runs since Buddy's death almost four years earlier. But now, on this bitterly cold afternoon, it seemed like just the right moment to go. Though Scout certainly wouldn't be allowed in the small dog run, I thought she might enjoy the larger area.

The trip north through the wintry city was lovely. Several people stopped to admire Scout, including a little girl who asked if she could pet her. "She's so bee—u—tiful," the little girl chimed. But as we approached Washington Square and then passed by the small dog run, I couldn't help but feel melancholy.

Scout entered the big dog run warily. A yellow Lab came over and gave her a half-hearted sniff before moving on to play with other friends. A pack of hounds chased one another, and Scout watched them enviously. Most of the dogs seemed to know each other well and none showed much interest in her. As Scout padded around in the snow and tried to make friends, I sat on a bench and felt sad for her.

Before long, though, a bundled-up man

in a black down parka entered the dog run with a white golden retriever that looked like Scout's identical twin. This dog — named Daisy, as I quickly learned — bounded right over to Scout, who immediately went into her bow position. In an instant, the two were off, jumping up toward each other, wrestling and chasing. Like Scout, Daisy was about a year and a half old. She had been born in Canada and now weighed seventy-five pounds.

Daisy's owner, a gregarious fellow named Jeff, introduced himself and sat down to share my bench. For the next half hour, while the two dogs made friends, Jeff and I had an animated conversation about the remarkable qualities of English golden retrievers. "They really love playing with their own kind," Jeff observed. Before Daisy, he had had two other goldens. The last one had lived to fourteen, a ripe old age for a large, sporting breed. When I told Jeff that we had had a terrier before Scout, he responded, "Well, now you know just how wonderful goldens are."

And I did. I also knew that Henry and I could not have asked for a friendlier, more loving, or more enthusiastic dog. To complete our voyage through the perils of late middle age, we needed a dog exactly like

Scout. No, not a dog *like* her — we needed Scout and only Scout. Sitting in Washington Square Park with freezing toes on one of the coldest afternoons of the year, I suddenly felt warmer than I had in weeks. I had not forgotten Buddy, but he was now the dog that had been my ideal companion for a different, earlier time. Watching Scout play in the snow with her seeming twin, I knew that I had finally passed *my* test: I had completely given my heart to her.

It was time to turn toward home. I had a happy, tired dog, and at the moment I couldn't imagine feeling any more fortunate. Once again I thought of E. B. White, who was not only a superb writer but a truly wise man. He understood that dogs made his life better, and he acknowledged their gift whenever he wrote about the smart collie of his youth, the eccentric dachshunds that meant so much to him during his middle years, and Susy the Westie, who kept him company when he was old and living alone. Even after reaching an age when he knew the next pup he purchased would probably outlive him, there he was with a dog in his arms. I hoped this would be true of my life, too, from irascible Buddy to vulnerable Dinah to loopy Scout — and, perhaps, to the puppies that would come after.

SELECTED BIBLIOGRAPHY

The books listed below, many of which are mentioned in the text, will help puppy owners gain insights into their pets. Collectively they offer a survival guide for the first year.

Dogs (General)

Elder, Janet. *Huck: The Remarkable True Story of How One Lost Puppy Taught a Family — and a Whole Town — About Hope and Happy Endings*. New York: Broadway Books, 2010. A touching story about how the human-canine bonds deepen when a dog is suddenly lost.

Morris, Willie. *My Dog Skip*. New York: Vintage, 1996. The classic coming-of-age story of a boy and his dog in the South. Skip learns amazing tricks, including how to fetch and pay for bologna at the local store.

Quindlen, Anna. *Good Dog. Stay.* New York: Random House, 2007. The end-of-life experiences of Beau — Quindlen's Labrador retriever — offer lessons, humorous and sad, about a painful time for all dogs and their humans.

White, E. B. *Essays of E. B. White*. New York: First Perennial Classics, 1999. The wonderful wisdom of Fred, E. B. White's dachshund, animates some of the best essays written by the author of *Charlotte's Web*.

Dog and Animal Behavior

Bekoff, Marc. *Animals at Play: Rules of the Game*. Philadelphia: Temple University Press, 2008. Play is how animals learn the importance of truth and justice, as well as just about everything in the realm of social behavior.

Grandin, Temple, and Catherine Johnson. *Animals Make Us Human: Creating the Best Life for Animals*. Boston: Houghton Mifflin Harcourt, 2009. The animal scientist and autism advocate offers unique insights into how dogs feel.

Horowitz, Alexandra. *Inside of a Dog: What Dogs See, Smell, and Know*. New York: Scribner, 2009. A psychologist with a Ph.D. in cognitive science, Horowitz tells what the world is like from a dog's point of view.

Thomas, Elizabeth Marshall. *The Hidden*

Life of Dogs. New York: Mariner Books, 2010. An anthropologist with a gift for storytelling, Thomas describes the pack dynamic through her observations of the roamings of her dogs.

Dog Training

Dunbar, Ian. *After You Get Your Puppy*. Berkeley, CA: James & Kenneth Publishers, 2001. Dr. Dunbar is a veterinarian who helped popularize lure-reward-based training. This is one of several books he has written about his training method.

Millan, Cesar, and Melissa Jo Peltier. *Cesar's Rules: Your Way to Train a Well-Behaved Dog*. New York: Crown Archetype, 2010. The Dog Whisperer of television fame has been criticized by some for using overly disciplinary training methods, but this recent book is careful to include some material about positive, reward-based training.

The Monks of New Skete. *The Art of Raising a Puppy*. Boston: Little, Brown, 1991. The best commonsense guide to how a day with a puppy ought to unfold.

Pryor, Karen. *Don't Shoot the Dog!: The New Art of Teaching and Training*. Gloucestershire, England: Ringpress Books Ltd, 2002. The queen of clicker training explains her system.

Rugaas, Turid. *My Dog Pulls: What Do I Do?* Wenatchee, WA: Dogwise Publishing, 2005. A detailed, pictorial guide that should help owners and dogs break a bad habit.

Stilwell, Victoria. *It's Me or the Dog: How to Have the Perfect Pet.* New York: Hyperion, 2007. The positive training techniques embraced by the popular television dog expert.

Dog Food

Hotchner, Tracie. *The Dog Bible: Everything Your Dog Wants You to Know.* New York: Gotham Books, 2005. This volume, which offers basic information on a wide variety of dog issues, has lots of information about what dogs like to eat and why.

Nestle, Marion. *Pet Food Politics: The Chihuahua in the Coal Mine.* Berkeley: University of California Press, 2008. Written in the wake of a pet food contamination scandal, this is an authoritative look inside the multibillion-dollar pet food industry.

———, and Malden C. Nesheiml. *Feed Your Pet Right: The Authoritative Guide to Feeding Your Dog and Cat.* New York: Free Press, 2010. Credible information in this book will help you be smarter about the labeling and contents of dog food.

ACKNOWLEDGMENTS

The original idea for *The Puppy Diaries* came from two *Times* editors, Trish Hall and Erica Goode, who sat down with me a couple of years ago to talk about adding pet coverage to one of our feature sections. All three of us were (and are) longtime dog owners, and we had noticed that when the paper ran interesting animal stories they zoomed up our list of most popular articles.

Our planned agenda that day was figuring out whether there was a *Times*-ian way to do a pets beat. But, instead of tending to the business at hand, I spent the hour regaling Trish and Erica with tales about my brand-new puppy Scout. I prattled on about my sleep-deprived state, jangled nerves, and full-blown puppy lust. Soon I was agreeing to their proposal that I write about the experience of new puppy ownership in an online column for our Home section.

So I want to thank Trish and Erica — who

later took turns editing the column and generously agreed to review this manuscript — for what became a fun and interesting experience for me and, I hope, for readers. Emily Weinstein of the *Times* had great ideas about adding videos and photos to the columns, and many of the photos were taken by Jim Estrin, the brilliant photographer for the paper. Elisabeth Griggs also chronicled Scout's puppy months lovingly and beautifully in her photographs and videos.

Emma Gilbey Keller, an early fan, encouraged me to turn the columns into a book and introduced me to her friend, agent, and fellow dog lover Suzanne Gluck. Suzanne not only inspired me throughout the book-writing process, she also accompanied me to the Westminster Dog Show.

As an editor, John Sterling is a reporter and writer's dream. John edited one of my previous books, *Strange Justice: The Selling of Clarence Thomas,* and I had my heart set on working with him again, even though an account of a puppy's first year is not exactly the kind of project he usually takes on. His encouragement and advice, some of which he dispensed during walks with Scout along the Hudson River, were instrumental. Thanks also to Stephen Rubin, Henry Holt's president and publisher, whose enthusiasm for the book was galvanizing and infectious, and to Paul Golob, editorial director of Times Books, who supported this project from the first.

The two Janes in my life — Jane O'Connor, my sister and writer extraordinaire, and Jane Mayer, my coauthor on *Strange Justice* and coconspirator in many of the things that matter — reviewed the manuscript at various stages and made it better.

Many of the people who helped Scout become a good dog appear in the book and have my immense gratitude for being part of her life. Lee Gibson generously shared Viggo's story, and I especially appreciate her willingness to let me join her on one of Viggo's final training walks, an emotional and memorable experience.

Scout would never have come into my life without my husband, Henry, who persuaded me that we should get her in the first place and has done the lion's share of the real work involved in her care. He provided crucial research during Scout's initial months with us and later did additional reporting to help me complete the story of her first year, allowing me to deepen the stories of some of the people who played formative roles in Scout's early life, including Donna Cutler, the Spiros, and other friends from Connecticut and the city. Henry even went to San Diego to become a master of clicker training, and his is still the only voice that Scout really listens to.

The story in the book unfolds as we experienced it. In a few instances, I've compressed the time frame a bit, and three events recounted in the final chapter — Viggo's training walk, Scout's reunion with her ancestors, and the Parade of Pooches — actually occurred shortly after Scout's first birthday. But they were so important to the story of Scout's early life that without them the narrative would have been incomplete.

I realize now that most of the people who are important in my life, including the folks thanked above, are certified dog nuts. As James Thurber once observed, "Dogs are obsessed with being happy." This, above all else, is why we need them in our lives.

ABOUT THE AUTHOR

Jill Abramson, a best-selling and award-winning author, is the executive editor of *The New York Times*. An unabashed dog lover, she has long been fascinated by the complex relationship between dogs and their owners. She, her husband, and Scout live in New York City and Connecticut.